60 00

45 00

139701

79131

16-02

Countries and Concepts

Fifth Edition

Countries and Concepts

An Introduction to Comparative Politics

Michael G. Roskin
Lycoming College

PRENTICE HALL, Englewood Cliffs, NJ 07632

Library of Congress Cataloging-in-Publication Data

Roskin, Michael [date]
    Countries and concepts : an introduction to comparative politics
MICHAEL G. ROSKIN.—5th ed.
      p.   cm.
    Includes bibliographical references and index.
    1. Comparative government.   I. Title.
JF51.R54   1995
320.3—dc20   94-32876
  ISBN 0-13-176025-4   CIP

Editorial director: Charlyce Jones Owen
Production editor: Barbara Reilly
Interior design: Lisa Dominguez Jones
Cover design: Tom Nery
Buyer: Robert Anderson
Copy editor: Stephen C. Hopkins
Editorial assistant: Nicole Signoretti

© 1995, 1992, 1989, 1986, 1982 by Prentice-Hall, Inc.
A Simon & Schuster Company
Englewood Cliffs, New Jersey 07632

Printed in the United States of America
10 9 8 7 6 5 4 3 2 1

ISBN: 0-13-176025-4

Prentice-Hall International (UK) Limited, *London*
Prentice-Hall of Australia Pty. Limited, *Sydney*
Prentice-Hall Canada Inc., *Toronto*
Prentice-Hall Hispanoamericana, S.A., *Mexico*
Prentice-Hall of India Private Limited, *New Delhi*
Prentice-Hall of Japan, Inc., *Tokyo*
Simon & Schuster Asia Pte. Ltd., *Singapore*
Editora Prentice-Hall do Brasil, Ltda., *Rio de Janeiro*

For my children:
Alexander, Pamela, Constance

Piši kao što govoriš
—Vuk Karadžić

Contents

Chapter 3   BRITAIN: THE KEY INSTITUTIONS   32

Chapter 4   BRITISH POLITICAL ATTITUDES   45

Part II   FRANCE

Chapter 10   FRANCE: PATTERNS OF INTERACTION   123

Chapter 11   WHAT THE FRENCH QUARREL ABOUT   137

A Note to Instructors

A possibly apocryphal early edition of *Pravda*, printed at the height of the Bolshevik Revolution, advised its readers: "No news today. Events moving too fast." At times I felt that way about the fifth edition of *Countries and Concepts*, which was a good deal harder to do than previous new editions. First, in response to the unanimous views of instructors, I added Japan with the same depth (five chapters) that the European systems receive. Japan is simply so important and so interesting that I believe we must incorporate it as one of the "standard" countries in an introduction to comparative politics. I tried to avoid the common traps of either Japan-praising or Japan-bashing. I found that Japan is not so strange or exotic (what I call the Mystique Mistake) as it is sometimes portrayed but that it readily submits to the same analytical approaches we use in other countries. Japan is different, of course, but not totally different.

It was especially challenging to be doing Japan just as the new Hosokawa government was pushing its electoral reforms through the Diet. The fragility of the eight-party coalition led me to warn in the first draft: "The real test of the Hosokawa government will be if it is still in office by the time you read this." I was more prescient than I knew, for the Hosokawa cabinet, alas, fell before that chapter reached copy-editing stage. But the general warning applies: Japanese prime ministers average two and a half years in office. (Hosokawa served eight months.) They change so often that I inserted, tongue in cheek, a box with blanks for students to pencil in the most recent Japanese prime minister.

If Japan is difficult, doing Russia makes one tremble. (And it used to be so easy: just add one or two obituaries.) But now the Soviet Union has collapsed and what is coming out of the wreckage is not clear. Writing in 1994 about the Russian system may leave the Russian chapters out of date by the time students first read them in 1995. South Africa represents a similar problem: change so fast, so profound, and so unpredictable as to turn the boldest of authors into reticent cowards. Why write something that may soon appear laughable?

How to handle political systems in flux? The way I handled Brazil in previous editions gave me a clue. Exasperated about being unable to say anything definite about Brazilian politics—a permanent work-in-progress—I backed away from the details of Brazilian government institutions and policies and accepted change and uncertainty as the Brazilian system. I learned to avoid saying things such as, "And so Brazil returned to civilian, democratic rule," when there was no telling what the politicians, electorate, and generals would do next year. Change *is* the system.

Further, the upheavals in Russia and South Africa give us the opportunity to define and explore system change in general terms. How do we know a system has truly changed? When old elites are swept out? When new and different institutions are established? Suppose—as in Japan—that change is more apparent than real? Defining system change can be tricky and challenging for students and an exciting opportunity for instructors.

Interestingly, reunited Germany really did not undergo system change. It was indeed a momentous event, but the institutions, parties, and economic policies of West Germany simply expanded to encompass East Germany. The Federal Republic of Germany kept its name and its patterns of politics but just got bigger. (The impact of a united Germany on the *European* system is profound, but that is a question of international systems rather than of domestic systems, which is our chief concern in comparative politics.) Neither did China undergo system change, despite its bloody turmoil in June 1989, although the forces for it are building.

The structure and purpose of *Countries and Concepts* continues as before. It analyzes four European nations and Japan at some length and three Third World nations more briefly. It does not attempt to create young scholars out of college sophomores. It sees, rather, comparative politics as an important, but usually neglected, grounding in citizenship that we should be making available to our young people. The author agrees with the late Morris Janowitz (in his 1983 *The Reconstruction of Patriotism: Education for Civic Consciousness)* that civic education has declined in the United States and that this poses dangers for democracy. Our students are often ill-prepared in the historical, political, economic, geographical, and moral aspects of democracy, and to expose such students to professional-level abstractions in political science ignores their civic education and offers them material that is largely meaningless to them. To repeat what I said in the first edition: An undergraduate is not a miniature graduate student.

Accordingly, the fifth edition of *Countries and Concepts* is designed to include a good deal of fundamental vocabulary and concepts, buttressed by many examples. It is readable. Many students don't do assigned readings; with *Countries and Concepts*, they have no excuse that the reading is boring.

Some reviewers noted that *Countries and Concepts* contains values and criticisms. This is part of my purpose. The two go together; if you have no values, you have no basis from which to criticize. Value-free instruction is probably impossible. If successful, it would produce value-free students, and that, I think, should not be the aim of the educational enterprise. If one knows something with the head but not with the heart, one really doesn't know it at all.

Is *Countries and Concepts* too critical? It treats politics as a series of ongoing quarrels for which no very good solutions can be found. It casts a skeptical eye on all political systems and all solutions proposed for political problems. As such, the book is not out to "get" any one country; it merely treats all with equal candor. *Countries and Concepts* tries to act as a corrective to analyses that depict political systems as well-oiled machines or gigantic computers that never break down or make mistakes. Put it this way: If we are critical of the workings of our own country's politics—and many, perhaps most, of us are—why should we abandon the critical spirit in looking at another land?

The fifth edition continues the loose theoretical approach of the previous editions with the simple observation that politics, on the surface at least, is composed of a number of human conflicts or quarrels. These *quarrels*, if observed over time, usually form patterns of some durability beyond the specific issue involved. What I call *patterns of interaction* are the relationships among politically relevant groups and individuals, what they call in Russian *kto-kovo*, who does what to whom? There are two general types of such patterns: (1) between elites and masses, and (2) among and within elites.

Before we can appreciate these patterns, however, we must first study the *political attitudes* (both mass and elite) of a particular country, which leads us to its *political institutions* and ultimately to its *political history*. Thus we have a five-fold division in the study of each country. We could start with a country's contemporary political quarrels and work backwards, but it is probably better to begin with the underlying factors as a foundation from which to understand their impact on modern social conflict. This book goes from *history* to *institutions* to *attitudes* to *patterns of interaction* to *quarrels*; however, this arrangement need not supplant other approaches. I think instructors will have no trouble utilizing this book in connection with their preferred theoretical insights.

Inclusion of the Third World in a first Comparative course is problematic. The Third World is so complex and differentiated that many (myself included) think the concept should be discarded. The semester is only so long. But if students are going to take only one comparative course—all too often the case nowadays—they should get some exposure to three-quarters of humankind. We continue, therefore, with briefer treatment of three non–European systems: China, Brazil, and South Africa. They are not "representative" systems—what Third World countries are?—but are interesting in their three different relationships to revolution: (1) a sweeping revolution in China; (2) an aborted revolution in Brazil; and (3) a revolution-in-progress in South Africa. Students like the stress on revolutions, and these three systems provide a refreshing counterpoise to the more settled systems of Europe.

More than ever, I believe South Africa presents students with an exciting "brain tease" in a course. South Africa is so much in the news these days that most students recognize its importance. With unrest and a new, untried regime, we can ask: "Given what we know about politics and revolutions in other countries, what could South Africa do to avoid chaos?" If an instructor should choose not to include the chapter on this controversial country, the continuity would not be destroyed.

I welcome your suggestions on any area of the book. Some instructors have responded to my invitation for comments, corrections, and criticism. Especially valuable were the comments of Arend Lijphart of the University of California at San Diego; Yury Polsky of West Chester University; Cheryl Brown of the University of

New York Times *Program*

The New York Times and Prentice Hall are sponsoring *Themes of the Times*, a program designed to enhance student access to current information of relevance in the classroom.

Through this program, the core subject matter provided in the text is supplemented by a collection of time-sensitive articles from one of the world's most distinguished newspapers, *The New York Times*. These articles demonstrate the vital, ongoing connection between what is learned in the classroom and what is happening in the world around us.

To enjoy the wealth of information of *The New York Times* daily, a reduced subscription rate is available. For information, call toll-free: 1-800-631-1222.

Prentice Hall and *The New York Times* are proud to co-sponsor *Themes of the Times*. We hope it will make the reading of both textbooks and newspapers a more dynamic, involving process.

North Carolina at Charlotte; Thomas P. Wolf of Indiana University Southeast; Susan Matarese of the University of Louisville; Frank Myers of the State University of New York at Stony Brook; Phung Nguyen of North Carolina A&T State University; Ivo K. Feierabend of San Diego State University; Ronald F. Bunn of the University of Missouri-Columbia; Marianne C. Stewart of Rutgers University on Brazil; and Christian Soe of California State at Long Beach on Germany. Soe edits the *Comparative Politics* annual edition, which serves as a useful supplement to this text. As a visiting professor for three years at the U.S. Army War College, I was able to have some excellent regional specialists comment on various sections. Offering valuable notes and corrections were Dr. Leif Rosenberger on the German and Russian economy; visiting Brazilian LTC Manoel Oliveira and Dr. Gabriel Marcella on Brazil; Walter Clarke of the State Department on South Africa; and Prof. Eugene Brown of Lebanon Valley College, Col. (ret.) Don Booze, and Col. Lynn Stull on Japan. Old Asia-hand William O'Neill continues to enlighten me on the Far East. All errors, of course, are my own. Professional comments and corrections may be sent to me personally at Lycoming College, Williamsport, PA 17701. I am grateful for any suggestions for subsequent editions.

Michael Roskin
Williamsport, PA

Countries and Concepts

CHAPTER 1

What to Look For

Looking for Quarrels

One way to begin the study of a political system is to ask what its people fight about. There is no country without political quarrels. They range from calm, polite discussions over whether to include dental care in nationalized health insurance to angry conflicts over minority language rights. Some controversies become murderous civil wars over who should rule the country. If you were to visit the country in question, you could get a fair idea of its quarrels by talking with its people, reading the local press, attending election rallies, and even noting the messages of posters, handbills, and graffiti.

So far, this is the approach of a good journalist. Political scientists, however, go further. They want to know the whys and wherefores of these controversies, whether they are long-standing issues or short-term problems. Our next step, then, is to observe the quarrels over time. If the basic quarrel lasts a long time—say, several years or even decades—we may conclude we're on to an important topic, that we have found a window through which to watch the country's politics.

Taking our long-term controversies as a starting point, we try to discern which groups are on which side. Who wants what and who opposes them? Here we may find political parties locked in conflict with each other, or interest groups trying to influence civil servants, or demagogues trying to sway the masses, or the army taking over power and then relinquishing it. We look, in short, for patterns.

Next we want to know why these patterns have formed. We might look first to political attitudes. Who thinks what? Are there deeply held conflicting viewpoints on how the country should be run? Are there important cleavages or splits running through the society? Equally important, we want to know something about governing institutions such as the presidency, parliament, and various political parties. These arenas are where many quarrels take place, and they are often the stakes of those quarrels as well (for example, winning the presidency or becoming the dominant party).

Ultimately, we must probe the country's history to understand how things got to be the way they are, how institutions and attitudes were formed. We may find that some patterns of interaction took shape long ago and that some of today's quarrels are the descendants of much older conflicts.

In sum, we could start studying a political system by noting a country's quarrels, observing them over time to see which are durable patterns of interaction, who is on what side in these interactions, how attitudes and institutions helped set up the interactions, and finally how the nation's past helped create the whole political structure.

To approach the problem in this order, however, might be likened to putting the cart before the horse or to reading a detective story from the conclusion backwards. While the quarrels might be the conclusion, the history is the foundation. Our approach here is to make a country's quarrels intelligible by explaining first the underlying factors.

The Structure of This Book

In this book, we take a broad look at the political systems of eight different countries in turn, considering each in a block of five sections, each section focusing on a general subject area. We start with what might be termed the underlying causes of cur-

SOME COMPARISONS

	POPULATION		PER CAPITA GDP			Infant Mortality Per 1,000 Live Births
	In Millions 1993	Average Annual Growth 1980–90	PPP* 1991	Average Annual Growth 1983–92	Work Force In Agriculture	
Britain	58	0.1%	$16,340	2.2%	2%	7
France	58	0.4	18,430	2.2	6	7
Germany	81	–0.1	19,770	2.7	5	7
Russia	149	0.6	6,930	–2.0	18	20
Japan	125	0.6	19,390	4.1	7	5
China	1,180	1.4	1,680	9.4	61	38
Brazil	150	2.2	5,240	1.9	35	58
South Africa	40	2.7	4,800	0.8	30	54
United States	254	0.9	22,130	2.7	3	9

*Purchasing Power Parity, explained in Chapter 26.

Source: *Statistical Abstract of the United States,* World Bank, Planecon, and World Resources Institute. Regard all such tables with skepticism. Figures from non-OECD countries are often nothing more than estimates. Changing currency rates throw off GDP growth comparisons. Russia's population growth is due not to births (which are very low) but to ethnic Russians fleeing Central Asia. Averages deceive: South African figures, for instance, do not show the major gaps between black and white in incomes, population growth, and infant mortality. Even something as standard as the U.S. labor force in agriculture can vary greatly, depending on whether illegal or temporary alien workers are counted.

rent politics. These are the "givens" or "ingredients" of a political system at a certain time. In the first three sections for each country we explore these underlying causes as we consider:

> The Impact of the Past
> The Key Institutions
> Political Attitudes

We study the *past* in order to understand the present. We are not looking for the fascinating details of history but for the major patterns that set up present institutions and attitudes. We study *institutions* to see how power is structured, for that is what institutions are: structures of power. We study *attitudes* to get a feel for the way people look at their social and political system, how deeply they support it, and how political views differ among social groups.

Moving from underlying factors to current politics brings us to the next two of each country's five sections:

> Patterns of Interaction
> What People Quarrel About

Here we get more specific and more current. The previous sections, we might say, are about the traditions, rules, and spirit of the game; the *patterns of interaction* are how the game is actually played. We look here for recurring behavior. The last section, the specific *quarrels*, represents the stuff of politics, the kind of things you might see in a country's newspaper.

The Impact of the Past

Geography is not necessarily destiny, but it does help explain a country's politics. Is a country easy to invade? If so, it has to have a stronger army and probably a different governing mentality than a country that is difficult to invade. The size and regional diversity of a country may make it more difficult to unite. Natural resources are another factor, although they do not necessarily dominate. Often, poorly endowed countries achieve more prosperity and more democracy than richly endowed lands. It is human resources, not natural resources, that are basic to both economics and politics.

Was the country unified early or late? For the most part, countries are artificial, not natural, entities, created when one group or tribe conquers its neighbors and unifies them by the sword. The founding of nations is usually a pretty bloody business, and the longer ago it took place, the better. We look at Sweden and say, "What a nice, peaceful country." We look at Somalia and say, "What a ghastly bloodbath of warring clans." We forget that if we went back far enough, Sweden would resemble Somalia. Sweden simply got most of its violence over with early.

The unification and consolidation of a country usually leaves behind regional resentments of incredible staying power. People whose ancestors were conquered centuries ago may still act out their resentments in political ways, in the voting booth or in civil violence. This is one way history has an impact on the present.

Becoming "modern" is a wrenching experience. Industrialization, urbanization, and the growth of education and communication uproot people from their traditional villages and lifestyles and send them to work in factories, usually in cities. In the process, people become "mobilized," or aware of their condition and willing to do something to change it. They become ready to participate in politics, demanding economic improvement and often that a new party take power. It's a delicate time in the life of nations. If the traditional elites do not devise some way to take account of newly awakened mass demands, the system may be heading toward revolution.

No country has industrialized in a benign manner; it is always a process marked by low wages, bad working conditions, and usually political repression. The longer ago this stage has happened, the more peaceful and stable a country is likely to be. We must look for the *stage* of development a country is in. If a country is in the throes of industrialization, we can expect ample domestic tensions of the sort that were solved earlier in Europe.

Another historical point to look for is the relationship between the king and the nobles in olden days. Feudalism in Europe was a balanced relationship in which kings and nobles needed each other. Britain preserved a rough balance between the two, and this paved the way for the limited government, civil rights, and eventually even mass political participation. In France, the king captured most of the power and created a rigid, overcentralized system incapable of handling demands for participation. The result was the French Revolution and instability ever since. Germany went the other way, falling apart into myriad petty states that unified only much later, with an identity crisis and a period of explosive nationalism.

Religion is a crucial historical question. Does the country have its church-state relationship in order? If not, it's a lingering political sore. Protestant countries had an easier time of it; because their churches by definition were not linked to Rome, the state early on became stronger than the church, and the church stayed out of politics. In Roman Catholic countries, where the church had power in its own right, there was a long church-state struggle called the "clerical-anticlerical split," which is still alive today in Italy. Even in France, the residues of the split still structure politics: conservatives are more religious and liberals and leftists are indifferent or hostile to religion.

Instituting a democracy is a difficult historical test, one that all but three dozen countries have so far flunked. Democracy can actually come too soon. If the people are too poor and ignorant, they are easily manipulated by political bosses. Americans often think elections are cures for all political ills, but elections in backward countries are seldom free and fair. Democracy can also come too late. If the traditional elite waits too long as the masses mobilize, the movement may turn radical and fall into the hands of revolutionary demagogues. What happened in Russia may happen again in South Africa. The slow, gradual expansion of the electoral franchise, as in Britain, is probably best.

The widening of the franchise means the rise of political parties. We ask, on what was a party first based, when was it founded, what were its initial aims, and how has it changed over the years? Was the party strongly ideological? Did it operate openly or was it driven underground? How have its early decades formed its present characteristics?

With political parties competing, we witness the introduction of the welfare issue into politics, the "distribution crisis." Left-wing parties argue that it is govern-

The Five Crises of Nation Building

Political scientists have delineated five "crises" that nations seem to go through in sequence in their political development:

1. **Identity:** People develop a national identity over and above their tribal, regional, or local identities. Bretons come to think of themselves as French and Bavarians as Germans. We see now that Uzbeks and Latvians never thought of themselves as "Soviets," and because of this the Soviet Union collapsed with astonishing speed. Some countries are still caught up in their identity crisis.

2. **Legitimacy:** People develop the feeling that the regime's rule is rightful, that it should be obeyed. A system without legitimacy requires massive amounts of coercion to keep it together and functioning.

3. **Penetration:** As the government's writ expands through the country, starting usually with the capital city, it encounters resistance, for many people dislike paying taxes to, and obeying the laws of, a distant authority. Local rebellions are crushed and police brought in to enforce national authority.

4. **Participation:** Once the other crises are solved, people start wanting to participate in some way in their nation's governance. There is usually a struggle to expand the electoral franchise. Parties are formed and attempt to control parliament. Mass participation in politics is usually granted only grudgingly by traditional elites, but once it's institutionalized the country is usually more stable and peaceful. Withholding participatory rights can lead to a buildup of a revolutionary anger.

5. **Distribution:** The last great crisis—probably a permanent one—is over the division of the nation's economic pie. Once the masses are participating in politics, their parties (for example, Labour in Britain, Social Democrat in Germany) demand that government use its considerable powers to distribute wealth and income in a more equitable fashion. To fund a welfare state, taxes grow. Better-off people generally fight this trend.

Fortunate is the country that has had its crises one at a time, so that its political system was able to grow and adapt with each challenge. If they all come at once—the case in much of the Third World today—they impose intolerable demands on a weak political system. Breakdowns are then frequent, usually leading to military rule.

This "sequential crises" model of political development is controversial. In some countries it seems to fit well; in others, poorly. As with all theories or models in political science, take this one with a grain of salt. See if it really applies—fully, partly, or not at all—to the country you are studying. What happens when one or more stages are bypassed or when the sequence gets jumbled? Are some countries' histories just too complicated to make the model fit at all?

ment's responsibility to provide jobs, housing, medical care, and education. Other parties, on the political center or right, either reject the welfarist ideas, compromise with them, or steal them. Gradually the country becomes a welfare state. We ask what the various parties have proposed in terms of welfare and how much of it they have obtained.

Finally, history establishes political symbols that can awaken powerful emotions. Flags, monarchs, old buildings, national holidays, and national anthems often serve as a cement to hold a country together, giving citizens the feeling that they are part of a common enterprise. To fully know a country, one must know its symbols, their historical genesis, and their current connotation.

The Key Institutions

A political institution is a web of relationships lasting over time, an established structure of power. An institution may or may not be housed in an impressive building. With institutions we are looking for more or less durable sets of human relationships, not architecture.

One way to begin our search is to ask, "Who's got the power?" The nation's constitution—itself an institution—may give us some clues, but it seldom gives the whole picture. It may, for example, specify that a monarch (king or queen) is the "head of state." This sounds impressive until we learn that in most systems the head of state is a symbolic office, a sort of official greeter. In a monarchy, the head of state is a king or queen; in a republic, it's a president. This distinction, not a very important one, is called the *form of state.* Some monarchies are among the world's most democratic countries (Britain, Sweden), while some republics are terribly repressive. Of the eight countries treated in this book, only two are currently monarchies, but all the others were monarchies earlier in their histories.

If the head of state doesn't have the power, who does? To find out, we next must discover if the system is *presidential* or *parliamentary* (see box on page 8). Both systems have parliaments, but a presidential system has a president who is elected

Left, Right, and Center

The way delegates were seated at French assemblies during and after the Revolution gives us our terms

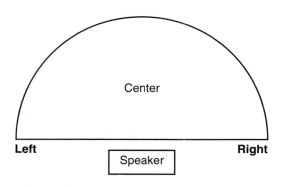

for radical, conservative, and moderate. In a half-circle chamber, the most radical delegates were seated to the left of the speaker's rostrum, the most conservative to the right. This allowed like-minded legislators to caucus and kept apart delegates who might start fistfights.

The precise meanings of left, right, and center have varied through the ages and from country to country. In general, however, the left favors greater equality of incomes, welfare measures, and sometimes nationalization of industry. The right, now that it has shed its aristocratic origins, favors individual achievement and private industry. The center tries to synthesize the moderate elements in both viewpoints. Those just a little to one side or the other are called center-left or center-right.

What about Names and Dates?

"Do you have to learn names and dates and details like that?" moan students of political science. This is not a history course but obviously draws a lot from history. Historians tend to gather lots of evidence on rather narrow topics and are reluctant to generalize. Political scientists, on the other hand, utilize historical findings with an eye for patterns and generalizations rather than for details.

This does not mean we ignore names, dates, and other facts. Instead, for any given detail we ask, "Does it matter for present-day politics?" If, for example, a current institution traces back to the actions of a certain king, it is worth remembering that king's name and century, although his exact dates may not be as important. If a current attitude traces back to early settlers, it is worth learning who they were, what they did, and why they did it. The names and dates included in this book help to explain present institutions, attitudes, and patterns. Learn them.

and serves separately from the legislature; the legislature cannot vote out the president. The United States and Brazil are presidential systems. In parliamentary systems, action focuses on the prime minister, who is usually a member of parliament delegated by it to form a *government* (another word for *cabinet*). The prime minister and his or her cabinet can be ousted by a vote of no-confidence in parliament. Americans used to assume that presidential systems were better and more stable than parliamentary systems. The problems of the last couple of decades (Vietnam, Watergate) might make Americans aware of the advantages of a parliamentary system, which can easily oust a chief executive. Besides, parliamentary systems with the proper refinements, such as Germany's, can be quite stable. It's impossible to say which system is "better"; under various circumstances both have fallen prey to immobilism, instability, and the abuse of power.

Once we have located the center of executive power—a president or a prime minister—we ask, "How powerful is the legislature?" In most cases it is less powerful than the executive and declining. Of course, parliaments do still have the power to pass laws, but for the most part the laws originate with the civil servants and cabinet and are passed according to party wishes. In most legislatures (but not in the U.S. Congress), party discipline is so strong that a member of parliament simply votes the way party whips instruct. Further, legislators must increasingly rely on experts (often from the bureaucracy) for data and ideas in such technical areas as nuclear energy, the environment, regulation of industry, and defense affairs. But parliaments can be important in nonlegislative ways: they represent people, educate the public, structure interests, and most important, oversee and criticize executive-branch activities.

One way of classifying parliaments is by how many chambers they have: *bicameral* (two) or *unicameral* (one). Two chambers are necessary in federal systems to represent the component parts, but they are often extra baggage in unitary systems. Most of the countries studied in this book have bicameral legislatures.

Likewise, national party systems can be classified by how many parties each has. These are usually broken into three categories: one-party systems, such as the ex–Soviet Union and China; two-party systems, such as Britain and the United States; and multiparty systems, such as France, Germany, and Russia. (Actually, both Britain and Germany are more accurately "two-plus" party systems, since they have two large and several small parties.) In looking at party systems it is important to note how the parties compete—by sticking to the center with moderate programs or by moving to the extremes with radical positions. The two modes are called *center-seeking* and *center-fleeing.* The latter may spell dangerous polarization and system breakdown.

The number of parties is partially conditioned by a country's electoral system. Single-member districts, where a simple plurality wins elections, encourage two-party systems for the simple reason that third parties find it hard to capture that large a vote. Multimember districts, where parliamentarians are elected according to the proportion of the vote their party won, permit smaller parties to stay alive. Propor-

Parliamentary versus Presidential Systems

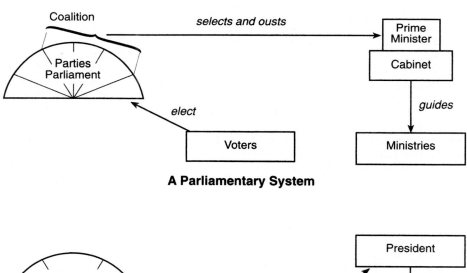

A Parliamentary System

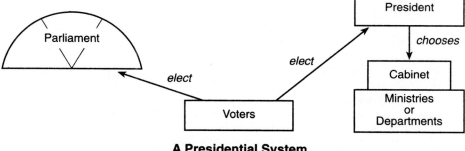

A Presidential System

tional representation, by encouraging multiparty systems, may contribute to cabinet instability as coalition members quarrel.

Political scientists now recognize that a country's permanent civil service—its bureaucracy—is one of its most powerful institutions. The bureaucracy today has eclipsed both cabinet and parliament in expertise, information, outside contacts, and sheer numbers. Some lobbyists no longer bother with the legislature; they go where the action is, to the important decision makers in the bureaucracy. Private industry is sometimes able to "capture" or "colonize" the very government offices that are supposed to be supervising them. One of our questions, then, is: How powerful and autonomous is the bureaucracy?

Political Attitudes

After World War II, political scientists shifted their emphasis from institutions to attitudes. The institutional approach had become suspect. For example, on paper Germany's Weimar constitution was a magnificent achievement, but it didn't work in practice because too few Germans really supported democracy. By the late 1950s, then, a new "political culture" approach to comparative politics became dominant that sought to explain systems in terms of popular attitudes. This is an important ap-

 The Civic Culture Study

In a massive 1959 study, political scientists Gabriel Almond and Sidney Verba led teams that asked approximately one thousand people in each of five countries—the United States, Britain, West Germany, Italy, and Mexico—identical questions on their political attitudes. The Civic Culture study, which was a benchmark in cross-national research, grouped its data in these categories:

COGNITION: How much do people know about politics? Do they feel government has an impact on them?

AFFECT: Are they proud of their political institutions? Do they feel they're fairly treated by the system?

PARTISANSHIP: Why and how intensely do they support political parties? Are they tolerant of other viewpoints?

PARTICIPATION: Do they feel they should participate in politics?

COMPETENCE: Do they feel *able* to participate in politics? Do they feel they can influence government?

SOCIALIZATION: Does the way they were raised influence their political attitudes? Do they feel most people can be trusted?

Almond and Verba discerned three types of political culture: (1) *participant*, in which people feel they should and in which they do participate in politics; (2) *subject*, in which people are aware of politics but cautious about participating; and (3) *parochial*, in which people are not even much aware of politics. They emphasized that each country is a mixture of these types, with perhaps one type dominating: participant in America, subject in West Germany and Italy, parochial in Mexico.

What Is "Ideology"?

Confusion surrounds the term *ideology*. Some use it to mean whatever politicians think, but this is too broad a definition. Political ideologies are belief systems that claim to aim at improving society. Ideologists say: "If we move in this direction, things will be much better. People will be happier, catastrophe will be avoided, society will become perfected." An ideology usually contains four elements:

1. The *perception* that things are going wrong, that society is headed down the wrong path. Fanatic ideologies often insist that total catastrophe is just around the corner.
2. An *evaluation* or analysis of why things are going wrong. This means a criticism of all or part of the existing system.
3. A *prescription* or cure for the problem. Moderate ideologies advocate reforms; extremist ideologies urge revolution and overthrow of the present system.
4. An effort to form a *movement* to carry out the cure. Without a party or movement, the above points are just talk without serious intent.

Seen in this light, Marxism-Leninism is a perfect example of ideology. First, we have Marx's perception that capitalism is unjust and doomed. Second, we have his analysis, that capitalism contains its own internal contradictions, which bring economic depressions. Third, we have a Marxist prescription: Abolish capitalsm in favor of collective ownership of the means of production, in a word, socialism. And fourth, especially with Lenin, we have the determined effort to form a strong Communist party—the "organizational weapon"—to put the cure into effect by overthrowing the capitalist system.

There are some other interesting points about ideologies. They are usually based on a serious thinker, often an important philosopher. Communism traces back to Hegel, classic liberalism to John Locke. But the philosopher's original ideas become popularized, vulgarized, and often distorted at the hands of ideologists who are trying to mass-market them. Deep thoughts are turned into cheap slogans. It often ends up that the original philosopher would reject what's being done in his name. Toward the end of his life, Marx worried about the distortions of his ideas by younger thinkers and sadly commented, "One thing is for sure: I am not a Marxist."

Another point about ideologies is that they are always defective, that is, they can never deliver what they promise: perfect societies full of happy humans. Classic liberalism produced an underclass, while Marxism-Leninism produced a state bureaucracy that stepped on everyone. Still, as long as people can imagine a cure for society's ills, there will be ideologies.

proach, but we must ask not only how attitudes determine government but how government determines attitudes. Attitudes and government are a two-way street; the two continually modify each other. Political culture can change under the impact of events. Americans became much more cynical in the wake of Vietnam and Watergate, while West Germans became more committed democrats as their country achieved economic success and political stability.

The perception of a government's *legitimacy* is one basic political attitude. This is not the same as its being "legal." Originally legitimacy meant that the rightful king was on the throne, not a usurper. Now it means a mass attitude that the government's rule is valid and that it should generally be obeyed. Governments are not automatically legitimate; they have to earn the respect of their citizens. Legitimacy can be created over a long time as a government endures and does a pretty good job of governing. Legitimacy can also erode as unstable and corrupt regimes come and

The Politics of Social Cleavages

Most societies are split along one or more lines. Often these splits, or "cleavages," become the society's fault lines along which political attitudes form. Here are some of the more politically relevant social cleavages.

SOCIAL CLASS

Karl Marx thought social class determined everything, that it was the only important social cleavage. Whether one was bourgeois or proletarian determined most political orientations. Marx held that middle- and upper-class people were conservative; working-class people, progressive or radical. Experience, however, makes it hard for many to swallow such a black-and-white view. Sometimes poor people are extremely conservative while middle-class intellectuals are radical.

Still, social class does matter in structuring attitudes. The working class does tend toward the left, but never 100 percent. Further, the left they tend to is apt to be the moderate left of social democracy rather than the radical left of communism. Such is the case of the German Social Democratic party.

The student of comparative politics has to put class into perspective. By itself, social class is seldom a sufficient explanation for political orientation. Other ingredients are usually present. The question, as Joseph LaPalombara put it, is, "Class plus what?"

GEOGRAPHIC REGION

Most countries have regional differences, and often they are politically important. Once a region gets set in its politics it can stay that way for generations. Often the attitude is a remembrance of past conquests and injustices. Scotland still resents England, and likewise the south of France resents the north. The student should learn to inquire what the regions of a nation and their politics are and how they got to be that way.

RELIGION

We considered how religious struggles were one of the more politically relevant items in a nation's history. In some countries they are still quite important. You can predict with fair accuracy how a French person will vote by knowing how often he or she attends Mass. You can partly predict how a German will vote by knowing if the citizen in question is Protestant or Catholic (and which region he or she lives in). It has been shown that religion accounts for the formation of more political parties than does social class.

URBAN-RURAL

City people are usually different politically from country people. Urban dwellers tend to be more aware of politics, more participatory, and more liberal or leftist. This is especially true in the Third World, where the countryside remains extremely backward while the cities modernize. Even China, despite its revolution, has a significant urban-rural split in terms of living conditions, education, and political orientation.

There are other possible politically relevant social cleavages. In some situations gender matters, especially in Catholic countries where women tend to be more conservative than men. Occupation, as distinct from social class, can also influence political attitudes. A miner and a farmer may make the same amount of money, but chances are the miner will be leftist and the farmer conservative. Age can sometimes be an important political factor. Young people are usually more open to new ideas and more likely to embrace radical and even violent causes than older citizens. Germany's terrorists, China's Red Guards, and South Africa's rioters were all young.

Almost any social cleavage or category can become politically relevant. The student of comparative politics can become sensitive to these categories by asking himself or herself from where they got the political views they hold. Is it your age? Did you get your views from your family? And why, in turn, does your family hold these views? Is it because of their religion? Their ethnic group? Their regional tradition?

Comparative Joke

In the U.S., everything is permitted that's not specif- ited that's not specifically permitted. And in France,
ically prohibited. In Germany, everything is prohib- everything is permitted even when it's prohibited.

go, never winning the people's respect. One quick test of legitimacy is how many police officers a country has. With high legitimacy, it doesn't need many police because
people obey the law voluntarily. With low legitimacy, a country needs lots of coercive
capacity, usually in the form of police.

When we look for signs of legitimacy, we ask: Do people generally obey this
regime? Grudgingly or happily? Are there subgroups that regard the regime as illegitimate? Enough to make an insurrection? Does the regime have to use a lot of coercion? Is the regime taking steps to firm up its legitimacy? Is legitimacy eroding or
increasing?

One way a regime can shore up its legitimacy is by using traditions and symbols. Symbols (especially time-honored ones) are the most effective and economical
way of holding a system together, because one little symbol—say, the flag—can stir
deep emotions. The Communists claimed a revolutionary break with the past, but
they cleverly used old national symbols such as the tsar's Kremlin in Moscow and the
emperor's Forbidden City in Beijing. The Communists in fact worked hard at developing effective symbols, for they knew that people are led more easily by emotion
than by reason. You can learn a lot about a country by understanding its symbols.

One symbol frequently manipulated is ideology. An *ideology* is a grand plan
to save or improve the country (see box, page 10). Typically, leaders at the top of a
system take their ideology with a grain of salt. But for mass consumption, the Soviets and Chinese cranked out reams of ideological propaganda (which, in fact, most
of their people disbelieved).

The other political systems explored in this book are not so ideologically ex-
plicit, but all are committed to various ideologies to greater and lesser degrees: German Social Democrats are committed to the welfare state, British Conservatives to
classic laissez-faire economics, and Chinese Communists to "socialism with Chinese
characteristics." Does every system have some sort of ideology? Probably. A system
run on purely pragmatic grounds—if it works, use it—would be unideological, but
such systems are rare. Even Americans, who pride themselves on being very pragmatic, are usually convinced of the effectiveness of the free market (Republicans) or
moderate government intervention (Democrats). Thus one of our questions: How
ideological or pragmatic is the system and its political parties?

Another point related to attitudes is a country's education system. Almost
universally, education is the main path to political elite status. The way an education
system functions—who gets educated and in what way—helps structure who gets political power and what they do with it. No country has totally equal educational opportunity. Even where schooling is legally open to all, social-, economic-, and even

The Politician as Balancer

One of the most common patterns in political interactions is the one politicians—if they are successful—follow in balancing parties, public opinion, interest groups, and bureaucracies. If a politician can balance these forces, usually making sure everyone gets something but no one gets everything, he or she is apt to be successful and durable.

The more we learn, for example, about so-called dictators, the more we realize they can't just dictate everything but have to play off one interest against another. When the politician loses his or her balancing ability and starts forgetting about the interests of important groups, those groups can become alienated and hostile to the system. Then the system can be headed for breakdown or civil war.

political-screening devices work against some sectors of the population. Typically, the working class is shortchanged and the middle class is overrepresented in colleges and universities. Most countries have elite universities that produce a big share of their political leadership, at times a near monopoly.

The education system leads to a country's elite system. It is usually schooling that gives a person access to elite status. *Elites*—the top or most influential people—are a major determinant of a country's politics. We need to answer some specific questions about them: Where and how were they educated? Did they inherit or achieve their elite status? How do elite attitudes compare to those of the masses? Is the elite system open to all of talent, or is it closed to all but a few? Are the various elites of society (business, labor, government, military, and so on) able to cooperate, or are they locked in conflict? Do elites totally control and manipulate the masses, or is there some mass input into elite deliberations?

With elites we are reminded that politics, even democratic politics, is usually the work of a few. Most people most of the time do not participate in politics, as Joseph LaPalombara has observed. But there are various kinds of elites, some more democratic and dedicated to the common good than others. Later, when considering the "Patterns of Interaction" chapters, be sure to ask yourself: How much of these interactions are an elite game with little or no mass participation?

Patterns of Interaction

Here at last we come to what is conventionally called "politics." In determining *patterns of interaction*, basically we look for who does what to whom. We look for the interactions of parties, interest groups, individuals, and bureaucracies. Do groups come together to compete or strike deals? How do political parties persuade the public to support them? In studying each country, it is the fourth section that will be the crucial one, but the other four are needed too, to fully understand this one.

We look not for one-time events but for things that occur with some regularity. Finding such patterns is the beginning of making generalizations, and generalizing is the beginning of theory. Once we have found a pattern we ask, Why? The

How Important Is the European Union?

Some observers of the European scene argue that it makes less and less sense to consider the nations of West Europe separately, because increasingly it is the European Union (EU)—what until late 1993 was called the European Community and is colloquially still called the Common Market—that determines the politics, laws, and economy of West Europe. They have a point. In standardizing foods and beverages, electronic equipment, and health and safety requirements, it is increasingly the EU staff in Brussels that calls the tune.

But it would be seriously premature to read into these Eurocratic regulations anything like a "union." The Maastricht Treaty, which brought the name EU, is more hope than reality; many nations ignore provisions they dislike. Sovereignty—the ultimate decision-making power—still resides firmly in London, Paris, Berlin, and other national capitals rather than at EU headquarters. The breaking of the European exchange-rate mechanism (ERM) in 1993 illustrates this dramatically. The horror of Bosnia and the EU's inability to do anything about it illustrate the EU's lack of concerted foreign and security policies. Yes, European unity may someday come. And I shall include it just as soon as it does.

answer will be found partly from what we have learned about each country in preceding chapters, and partly in the nature of political life where struggle and competition are normal and universal.

Some interactions are open and public; others are closed and secretive. The interactions of parties and citizenry are mostly open. Every party tries to convince the public that the party is fit to govern. This holds equally true for democratic and authoritarian systems. Do they succeed? Whom do the parties aim for and how do they win them over? By ideology? Promises? Common interests? Or by convincing people the other party is worse?

The parties interact with each other, sometimes cooperatively but more often competitively. How do they denounce and discredit each other? Under what circumstances do they make deals? Is their competition murderous or moderate?

Parties interact with the government. In China, the Party nearly *is* the government. In politically more open countries, parties try to capture and retain governmental power. How do parties form coalitions? Who gets the top cabinet jobs? Once in power, is the party able to move or is it immobilized by contrary political forces? These are some questions to ask.

Politics within the parties is an important point. We ask if a party has factions. Does it have a left wing and a right wing? How do its leaders hold it together? Do they pay off factions with key jobs or merely with lip service? Do factional quarrels paralyze the party? Could it split? Do its more extreme factions frighten away voters?

Parties also interact with interest groups. Some groups enjoy "structured access" to like-minded parties. In Europe, labor unions are often linked formally to political parties. Here we need to know: Does the party co-opt the interest group or vice versa? How powerful are interest-group views in determining party policy?

As mentioned earlier, interest groups often decide it's not worth working on the electoral-legislative side and instead focus their attention on the bureaucratic. One of the key areas of politics is where bureaucracies and businesses interface. Are

The Importance of Being Comparative

"You can't be scientific if you're not comparing," UCLA's late, great James Coleman used to tell his students. Countries are not unique; they are comparable with other countries. When we say, for example, that the parliament of country X has become a rubber stamp for the executive, this is not a very meaningful statement until we note that it is also the tendency in countries Y and Z.

The "uniqueness trap" often catches commentators of the American scene off-guard. We hear statements such as: "The U.S. political system is breaking down." Compared to what? To France in 1958? To China in 1966? Or to the United States itself in 1861? Compared to these other cases, the United States today is in rather good shape. We hear statements like this one: "The trouble with this country is that the labor unions are too powerful." But what percentage of the American labor force is unionized? How does this compare to Britain and Germany? Does U.S. labor have its own political party like some labor movements in other countries?

Our thinking on politics will be greatly clarified if we put ourselves into a comparative mood by frequently asking, "Compared to what?"

---

interest groups controlled by government or vice versa? What kind of relationships do businessmen and bureaucrats establish? Which groups are the most influential? These important interactions are generally out of the public sight. Does money change hands? Or have the two merely established identical viewpoints?

What People Quarrel About

Here we move to current issues, the political struggles of the day. We start with economics, the universal and permanent quarrel over who gets what. (Political scientists should have a grounding in economics; if you haven't already done so, think about taking an economics course.)

First we inquire if the economy of the country in question is growing. If so, is it expanding rapidly or slowly? Why? Are workers lazy or energetic? Are managers stupid or clever? How much of the economy is supervised and planned by government? Is government interference a hindrance on the economy? If the economy is declining, why? Why are some countries economic success stories and others not? How big a role does politics play in economic growth?

Other questions: Are unions reasonable or strike-happy? What political payoffs do unions seek? Are wage settlements in line with productivity, or are they inflationary? Does government try to influence wage increases? Do workers and management cooperate or battle each other? Do workers have any say in running their companies? How much imported labor is there? How much unemployment?

Once we have a realistic picture of the economic pie, we inquire who gets what slice. How equal—or unequal—is the distribution of income and wealth? Does government policy aim at making incomes more equal or at rewarding some people more than others? Does unequal distribution lead to social and political resentment?

Many governments attempt to correct a skewed distribution of income by "redistributing" it. This is what happens when taxation skims off money from better-off people and transfers it to poorer people. Redistribution is another name for a welfare system. To what extent does the system redistribute income? How high and how progressive are taxes? How many and how generous are welfare benefits? Do people want more welfare and higher taxes, or less welfare and lower taxes? Which people? In which direction is the redistribution system heading—more to the economically needy or less?

There are, to be sure, noneconomic quarrels as well. Regionalism is among the nastiest. Even well-integrated Britain has a bloody regional war in Northern Ireland. In France, Corsicans and Bretons set off bombs. In ex-Yugoslavia and the ex–Soviet Union regional problems have turned bloody. Regions want different things; some want outright independence, some merely autonomy, some just a better economic deal or recognition of their language. What are a country's regions? Which of them are discontent? How much? A lot or little? Do they have a political impact? Have extremists turned to violence?

How is the central government reacting to regionalist demands? By crushing them? By setting up regional councils and home rule? Is there a move afoot to decentralize or devolve power to the regions? Or are things going the other way, with a move to centralize more power in the capital?

Some quarrels are unique to a particular country. In recent years, Brazilians have quarreled about whether to hold direct elections, South Africans about transitioning from *apartheid*, and the Chinese about introducing a market economy. The student of comparative politics keeps his or her eyes open for the quarrels that ripple through each system.

Vocabulary Building

affect	distribution	parliamentary	redistribution
anticlerical	electoral system	parochial	regionalism
authoritarian	elites	participant	social cleavages
bicameral	factions	participation	socialization
bureaucracy	form of state	partisanship	subgroup
coercion	franchise	party system	subject
cognition	generalization	pattern	symbol
comparative	identity	penetration	unicameral
competence	industrialization	political culture	unification
cynical	institution	pragmatic	urbanization
democracy	legitimacy	presidential	welfare

Further Reference

ALMOND, GABRIEL, AND SIDNEY VERBA. *The Civic Culture: Political Attitudes and Democracy in Five Nations.* Princeton, NJ: Princeton University Press, 1963.

———, eds. *The Civic Culture Revisited.* Boston: Little, Brown, 1980.

ASHFORD, DOUGLAS E. *The Emergence of the Welfare States.* New York: Basil Blackwell, 1986.

CANTORI, LOUIS J., and ANDREW H. ZIEGLER, JR., eds. *Comparative Politics in the Post-Behavioral Era.* Boulder, CO: Lynne Rienner, 1988.

DOGAN, MATTEI, and DOMINIQUE PELASSY. *How to Compare Nations: Strategies in Comparative Politics.* Chatham, NJ: Chatham House, 1984.

DORFMAN, GERALD A., and PETER J. DUIGNAN, eds. *Politics in Western Europe.* Stanford, CA: Hoover Institution, 1988.

GREW, RAYMOND, ed. *Crises of Political Development in Europe and the United States.* Princeton, NJ: Princeton University Press, 1978.

HEIDENHEIMER, ARNOLD J., HUGH HECLO, and CAROLYN TEICH ADAMS. *Comparative Public Policy: The Politics of Social Choice in Europe and America*, 3rd ed. New York: St. Martin's Press, 1989.

KOLINSKY, EVA, ed. *Opposition in Western Europe*. New York: St. Martin's, 1987.

KRAMER, JANE. *Europeans*. New York: Farrar, Strauss & Giroux, 1988.

LANE, JAN-ERIK, and SVANTE O. ERSSON. *Politics and Society in Western Europe*, 3d ed. Newberry Park, CA: Sage, 1991.

LAPALOMBARA, JOSEPH. *Politics Within Nations*. Englewood Cliffs, NJ: Prentice-Hall, 1974.

LIJPHART, AREND. *Democracies: Patterns of Majoritarian and Consensus Government in Twenty-One Countries*. New Haven, CT: Yale University Press, 1984.

LIPSET, SEYMOUR MARTIN. *Political Man: The Social Bases of Politics*, expanded and updated ed. Baltimore, MD: Johns Hopkins University Press, 1981.

MAIR, PETER, ed. *The West European Party System*. New York: Oxford University Press, 1990.

MÉNY, YVES. *Government and Politics in Western Europe: Britain, France, Italy, West Germany*, 2d ed. New York: Oxford University Press, 1993.

POWELL, G. BINGHAM, JR. *Contemporary Democracies: Participation, Stability, and Violence*. Cambridge, MA: Harvard University Press, 1982.

SMITH, GORDON. *Politics in Western Europe: A Comparative Analysis*, 5th ed. New York: Holmes & Meier, 1988.

TILLY, CHARLES, ed. *The Formation of National States in Western Europe*. Princeton, NJ: Princeton University Press, 1975.

2

Britain: The Impact of the Past

"Island Like England"

A Polish student I once knew at UCLA had to write a paper for her English class on what she most wished for her native land. She thought for a moment and wrote: "I wish that Poland be island like England." She meant that Poland, on a plain between large hostile neighbors (Germany and Russia), has a sad history of invasion and partition. If only Poland had been an island like England, she reasoned, its history would have been much happier. In *Richard II*, Shakespeare said much the same:

> This fortress built by Nature for herself
> Against infection and the hand of war,
> This happy breed of men, this little world,
> This precious stone set in the silver sea,
> Which serves it in the office of a wall,
> Or as a moat defensive to a house,
> Against the envy of less happier lands;
> This blessed plot, this earth, this realm, this England.

The last successful invasion of England was in 1066. The barrier posed by the English Channel has kept Frenchmen, Spaniards, and Germans from conquering Britain. Politically this has meant that England could develop its own institutions without foreign interference, a luxury not enjoyed by most Continental lands. Militarily it has meant that England rarely needed or had a large army, a point of great importance in the seventeenth century when British kings were unable to tame Parliament precisely because the monarch had few soldiers. Britain's insularity also contributed to a seafaring tradition that went hand-in-hand with outward expansion and made Britain both the world's greatest empire and greatest industrial power in the nineteenth century.

Shakespeare was only partly right about the seas serving as England's moat. Centuries earlier, England had been invaded many times. For a millennium and a half, waves of Celts, Romans, Angles and Saxons, Danes, and finally Normans washed upon Britain. One tribe of Celts, the Britons, gave their name to the entire island. Britishers, like most peoples, are not of one stock but of many.

The fierce Germanic tribesmen who rowed across the North Sea during the third to fifth centuries A.D. brought over what we call Old English or *Anglisch*, the language of the Angles, akin to the Frisian of the Dutch and German coast. "England" was simply the land of the Angles. The Angles and Saxons slowly moved across England, destroying towns and massacring inhabitants. The Celts were pushed back to present-day Wales and Scotland, which became a "Celtic fringe" to England. Some fleeing Celts, the Britons (or Bretons), crossed over to France and gave their name to Brittany. Preserving their distinct identity and languages (Cymric in Wales, Gaelic in Scotland), Britain's Celts never quite forgot what the newer arrivals did to them.

Other invaders followed. In the ninth century Danish Vikings held much of eastern England (the Danelaw), but they were eventually absorbed. Another group of Vikings had meanwhile settled in France; these Norsemen (Normans) gave their name to Normandy. In 1066, with the English throne in dispute, William of Normandy put forward his own dubious claim to it and invaded with a force gathered from all over France. He defeated the English King Harold at the famous battle of Hastings, and England changed dramatically.

William the Conqueror replaced the entire Saxon ruling class with Norman nobles, who earned their fiefdoms by military service. Since at first the Norman conquerors spoke only French, vast numbers of French words soon enriched the English language. Backed by brutal military power, administration was better and tighter. William ordered a complete inventory of all lands and population in his new domain; the resulting Domesday Book provided a detailed tool for governance. The Exchequer—the name derived from the French word for a checkered counting table—became the king's powerful treasury minister, a title and office that exist today. Further, since William and his descendants ruled both England and parts of France, England was tied for centuries to the affairs of the Continent.

Magna Carta

The Normans brought to England a political system that had emerged on the Continent, feudalism. The feudal system was a contractual agreement between lords and vassals in which the lords would grant the vassals land (or the use of it) and protection, while the latter would support the former with military service. Feudalism tends to appear naturally when central authority has broken down and a money economy disappears, for then land and fighting ability take on tremendous importance. In Europe, the collapse of the Roman Empire meant that kings could survive and thrive only if they had enough lords and knights to fight for them. The lords and knights in turn got land. Power here was a two-way street: the king needed the nobles and vice versa.

The United Kingdom

The full and official name of Britain is the United Kingdom of Great Britain and Northern Ireland. "Great Britain" refers to the whole island that includes Wales and Scotland as well as England.

The British flag, the "Union Jack," stands for three saints representing different parts of the United Kingdom. The larger red cross is the Cross of St. George of England, the white cross is the Cross of St. Andrew of Scotland, and the thinner, diagonal red cross is that of St. Patrick of Ireland. (This cross is deliberately off center.) The Union Jack is a potent symbol, calculated to evoke both regional pride and national unity.

The mixed monarchy of the Middle Ages was a balance between king and nobles. Its feeling can be summed up in the oath the nobles of Aragon (in the northeast of Spain) swore to a new ruler: "We who are as good as you swear to you, who are no better than we, to accept you as our king and sovereign lord, provided you observe all our statutes and laws; and if not, no."

This oath fitted England better than Aragon, for centuries of English history were dominated by the struggle to make sure the king did not exceed his feudal bounds and become an absolute monarch (which is what happened in most of Europe). This English struggle laid the foundation for limited, representative government, democracy, and civil rights, even though the participants at the time had no such intent.

The Great Charter that the barons forced upon King John at Runnymede in 1215 is nothing so far-reaching or idealistic; it never mentions liberty or democracy. What the barons and top churchmen wanted from John was to stop his encroachment on feudal customs, rights, and laws by which they held sway in their localities. In this sense the Magna Carta, one of the great documents of democracy, was feudal and reactionary. Far more important than its actual content, however, was the principle of limiting the monarch's powers and making sure he stayed within the law.

The Magna Carta meant that the king was in a kind of balance with the nobles and that as long as they balanced, there would be neither despotism nor anarchy, the twin ills of the Continent. In Europe, countries either went to absolutism, a kind of royal dictatorship, as in France, or broke up into small principalities, as in Germany. British and, by extension, American democracy owes a lot to the strength and stubbornness of English barons who stood up for their traditional rights.

Britain's French Legacy

Dating from the Norman Conquest, many English expressions, especially those related to royalty and the courts, are still in ancient Norman French. An English court is called to order with *Oyez! Oyez!* (hear ye). The motto of the elite Order of the Garter, which was founded in 1348 for the best jousters, is *Honi soit qui mal y pense* (evil to him who thinks evil).

Although the king or queen no longer has any real political power, the royal assent is still needed to turn into law an act of Parliament—itself a French word, meaning a place where people *par-*ley (talk). When His Majesty approves a nonfinancial bill, the monarch still writes, *Le Roy le veult* (the king wishes it). For a financial bill, which originally meant that Parliament granted money to the monarch, the formula is appropriately grateful: *Le Roy remercie ses bons sujets, accepte leur benevolence et ainsi le veult* (the king thanks his good subjects, accepts their benevolence, and thus wishes it). The royal veto—used for the last time by Queen Anne in 1707—is a cautious *Le Roy s'avisera* (the king will consider it).

The Rise of Parliament

During the same century as the Magna Carta, English kings started seeing the utility of calling to London, by now the capital, two to four knights from each shire (roughly a county) and a similar number of burghers from the towns to consult with the king on matters of the realm. Kings did this not out of the goodness of their hearts but because they needed to firm up the support of those who had local power and to raise taxes. The fact that English kings also had French holdings meant that England fought wars in France. These were expensive, and the only way to raise revenue to pay for them was by inviting local notables to participate, at least symbolically, in the affairs of state. Little did the kings know that they were founding an institution in the thirteenth century that would overshadow the monarchy by the seventeenth century.

Parliament began as an extension of the king's court, but over the centuries took on a life of its own. Knights and burghers formed what we call a *lower house*, the House of Commons. Those of noble rank, along with the top churchmen, formed what we call an *upper house*, the House of Lords. In time, a leading member of the Commons became its representative to the king; he was called the Speaker. In order that business could be conducted unhampered, parliamentary privileges developed to prevent the arrest of members.

The Commons at this stage was not a "representative" institution, at least not in our sense. It represented only people who were locally wealthy or powerful, not a cross section of the English people. That came much later, in the nineteenth century. But Parliament, especially the Commons, played a role even more important than accurate representation of the nation. It continued the blocking mechanism of the Magna Carta: it diffused power and prevented the king from getting too much. Parliament thus laid one of the foundation stones of democracy without knowing it.

The Common Law

One of England's contributions to civilization is the Common Law, the legal system now also practiced in the United States, Canada, Australia, and other countries once administered by Britain (but not South Africa). Common Law grew out of the customary usage of the Germanic tribal laws of the Angles and Saxons, which stressed the rights of free men. It developed on the basis of precedent set by earlier decisions and thus has been called "judge-made law."

When the Normans conquered England, they decided that the purely local nature of this law was unsuitable to governing the country as a whole, so they set up central courts to systematize the local laws and produce a "common" law for all parts of England—hence the name.

Common Law differs from the Roman Law that is practiced throughout Continental Europe (and in Scotland). Common Law emphasizes precedent while Roman Law stresses formal legal codes. This gave the Common Law flexibility to adapt and change gradually over time.

Henry VIII

Parliament got a major boost during the reign of Henry VIII (1509–47), when Henry declared a partnership with Parliament in his struggle against Rome. On top of underlying tensions between the Vatican and London—the universal Church on the one hand and growing nationalism on the other—Henry wanted the pope to grant him a divorce. His marriage to Catherine of Aragon had failed to produce the male heir that Henry felt he needed to insure stability after him. (Ironically, it was his daughter Elizabeth who went down in history as one of the greatest English monarchs.)

The pope refused—Catherine's Spanish relatives at that time controlled Rome—so Henry summoned a parliament in 1529 and kept it busy for seven years, passing law after law to get England out of the Catholic church and the Catholic church out of England. The new Anglican church, called Episcopalian in America, was at first identical to the Roman Catholic church (it turned Protestant later), but at its head was an Englishman, not the pontiff of Rome. The new church granted Henry his divorce in 1533. He married a total of six wives—and had two of them beheaded. But Henry was not simply eager for young brides; he was desperate for a male heir for dynastic reasons.

Whatever his motives, the impact of Henry's break with Rome was major. England was cut free from papal guidance and direction. Countries that stayed Catholic, such as France, Spain, and Italy, experienced wrenching splits for centuries between pro-church and anticlerical forces. England (and Sweden) avoided this nasty division because the state early on was stronger than the church and controlled it. This meant that in England it was far easier to secularize society and politics than it was in Roman Catholic countries, where the church was still an independent power.

Parliament became more important than ever; Henry needed its support for his momentous break with Rome. In 1543 Henry praised Parliament as an indispensable part of his government: "We be informed by our judges that we at no time stand so highly in our estate royal as in the time of parliament, wherein we as head and you as members are conjoined and knit together into one body politic." A century later Parliament chopped the royal head off one of his successors.

Parliament versus King

In the late fifteenth century several European monarchs were able to expand their powers and undermine the old feudal mixed monarchy. The weakened power of Rome in the sixteenth century gave kings more independence and introduced the notion that kings ruled by divine right, that is, that they got their authority directly from God without the pope as intermediary. Political theorists searched for the seat of *sovereignty,* the highest legal authority in the land, and concluded that it must lie in one person, the monarch. This movement was called *absolutism.* By 1660 absolute monarchs governed most lands of Europe—but not England.

The seventeenth century was one of almost uninterrupted turmoil for England: religious splits, civil war, a royal beheading, and a military dictatorship wracked the country. The net winner, when the dust had settled, was Parliament.

Trouble started when James I came down from Scotland to take over the English throne after the death of Elizabeth in 1603. James united the crowns of Scotland and England, but they remained separate countries until the 1707 Act of Union. James I was intelligent and well educated but imbued with absolutist notions then common throughout Europe. He didn't like to share power and thought existing institutions should simply support the king. This brought him into conflict with Puritanism, an extreme Protestant movement that aimed to reform the "popish" elements out of the Anglican church. James preferred the Anglican church to stay just the way it was, for it was one of the pillars of his regime. James's harassment of Puritans caused some of them to run away to Massachusetts.

By now Parliament had grown to feel coequal with the king and, in the area of raising revenues, his superior. Hard up for cash, James tried to impose taxes without the consent of Parliament, which grew angry over the move. James's son, Charles I, who took over in 1625, fared even worse. He took England into separate wars with Spain and France; both were unsuccessful and increased the king's desperation for money. Charles tried to play the role of a Continental absolute monarch, but the English people and Parliament wouldn't let him.

When the Royalists fought the Parliamentarians in the English Civil War, 1642–48, the latter proved stronger, for the Parliamentarian cause was aided by Puritans and the growing merchant class. The Parliamentarians created a "New Model Army," which trounced the Royalists. (The king, as was mentioned, had no standing army at his disposal.) Charles was captured, tried by Parliament, and beheaded in 1649.

Cromwell's Commonwealth

From 1649 to 1660 England had no king. Who then was to rule? The only organized force left was the army, and it was under Oliver Cromwell. Briefly England became a *republic*—a term that simply means a country not headed by a monarch. It was called

Premature Democrats

Among the antiroyalists were a group of out-and-out republicans called Levellers, who wanted to make men politically more equal. Sergeants and enlisted men in the New Model Army argued that people like themselves—tradesmen, artisans, and farmers—should be allowed to vote. They were influenced in their thinking by Puritanism, which among other things taught that all men were equal before God and therefore needed no spiritual or temporal superiors to guide them. (This Puritan influence also proved to have a powerful impact on American democracy.)

One group of Levellers, meeting in Putney in 1647, even went so far as to advocate one man, one vote. This idea was a good two centuries ahead of its time, and the more conservative forces of England, including Cromwell himself, would stand for no such change. Still, the Putney meeting had introduced the idea of the universal franchise—that is, giving everybody the right to vote.

the Commonwealth, and Cromwell was the leading figure. Problems, however, did not die down; in fact, discord grew worse. To restore order, Cromwell in 1653 was designated Lord Protector, a sort of uncrowned king, and soon imposed a military dictatorship on England. When Cromwell died in 1658, most Englishmen had had enough of turbulent republicanism and longed for stability and order. In 1660, Parliament invited Charles II, son of the beheaded king, to return from Dutch exile and take the throne. The English monarchy was restored, but it was a different kind of monarchy, one in which Parliament was much stronger and had to be treated with respect.

The "Glorious Revolution"

Charles II knew he could not be an absolute monarch; instead, he tried to manipulate Parliament discreetly. A showdown came over religion. Charles was pro-Catholic and secretly ready to return his allegiance to Rome. In 1673 he issued the Declaration of Indulgence, lifting laws against Catholics and non-Anglican Protestants. What we might see as an act of tolerance toward minority religions, Parliament saw as an illegal return to Catholicism, and it blocked the royal move. Anti-Catholic hysteria swept England with fabricated stories of popish plots to take over the country.

When Charles II died in 1685, his openly and proudly Catholic brother, James, took the throne as James II. Again a Declaration of Indulgence was issued, and again Parliament took it as a return to both Catholicism and absolutism. Parliament dumped James II (but let him escape) and invited his Protestant daughter, Mary, and her Dutch husband, William, to be England's queen and king. This was the "Glorious Revolution": a major shift of regime took place with scarcely a shot fired. In 1689 a "Bill of Rights"—unlike its U.S. namesake—spelled out Parliament's relationship to the Crown: no laws or taxes without the former's assent.

The majority of Englishmen approved. If it wasn't clear before then, it was now: Parliament was supreme and had the ability to invite and dismiss monarchs. In

Acton's Dictum

The nineteenth-century British historian and philosopher Lord Acton distilled the lessons of centuries of English political development in his famous remark: "Power tends to corrupt; absolute power corrupts absolutely." Acton feared the tyrannical tendencies of the modern state. Lord Acton's often-quoted dictum is as close as political science can get to a law.

1714, for example, Parliament invited George I from Hanover in Germany to become king; the present royal family is descended from him. Since that time, the English monarch has been increasingly a figurehead, one who reigns but does not rule.

The Rise of the Prime Minister

One of the consequences of bringing over George I in 1714 was that he couldn't really govern if he had wanted to. He spoke no English and preferred Hanover to London. So he turned to an administrative device that had been slowly developing and allowed it to assume top executive power—the *cabinet*, composed of ministers and presided over by a first, or prime, minister. Under Sir Robert Walpole, from 1721 to 1742, the cabinet developed into approximately its present form but lacked two important present-day features: the prime minister could not pick his ministers (that was reserved for the king), and the cabinet was not responsible—meaning, in its original sense, "answerable"—to Parliament.

Royal power had one last gasp. George III managed to pack the Commons with his supporters and to govern with the obedient Lord North. One unforeseen result of this temporary absolutist resurgence was the language of the U.S. Declaration of Independence, which sought to regain the traditional rights of Englishmen against a too-powerful king. Following the British defeat, William Pitt the Younger restored the cabinet and prime ministership to power and made them responsible only to the Commons, not to the King. This began the tradition—it still has no statutory backing—that the "government" consists of the leader of the largest party in the House of Commons plus other people that he or she picks. As party chief, top person in Parliament, and head of government combined, the prime minister became the focus of political power in Britain.

The Democratization of Parliament

Parliament may have been supreme by the late eighteenth century, but it was hardly democratic or even representative. In the country, the right to vote was limited to those who owned land that yielded an income of at least forty shillings a year. In towns, there were often not more than a dozen or two men eligible to vote, although in the cities the franchise was much wider.

In the eighteenth century, parties began to form. At first they were simply parliamentary caucuses, meetings of people from the same area. Only in the next century did they begin to strike roots in the electorate outside of Parliament. The labels "Whig" and "Tory" first appeared under Charles II, connoting his opposition and his supporters respectively. Both were derisive names: the original Whigs were Scottish bandits, and the original Tories were Irish bandits.

During the nineteenth century a two-party system emerged. The Whigs grew into the Liberal party and the Tories into the Conservative party. British Conservatives to this day are nicknamed "Tories." Whatever their party label, parliamentarians were not ordinary people. The House of Lords, of course, was limited to hereditary peers. The House of Commons, despite its name, was the home of gentry, landowners, and better-off people. Elections were often won by bribing the small number of voters.

By the time of the American and French revolutions in the late eighteenth century, however, Parliament noticed that the winds were stirring in favor of expanding the electorate. People began talking about political democracy and the right to vote. Under the impact of the industrial revolution and economic growth, two powerful new social classes arose: the middle class and the working class. Whigs and Tories, both heavily aristocratic in their makeup, at first viewed demands for the mass vote with disdain and even horror; it reminded them of how democracy ran amok during the French Revolution.

Gradually, though, it dawned on the Whigs that the way to head off revolution was to incorporate some of the new social elements into politics and give them a stake in the system. Furthermore, that party which supported broadening the franchise would most likely win the votes of those who were newly enfranchised. After much resistance by Tories in the Commons and by the entire House of Lords, Parliament succeeded in passing the famous Reform Act of 1832.

At the time, the Reform Act hardly looked like a momentous breakthrough. It allowed more of the middle class to vote but still only expanded the electorate by about half: only about 7 percent of adults could then vote. The Reform Act established the principle, though, that the Commons ought to be representative of, and responsive to, the broad mass of citizens, not just the notables. In 1867, it was the Conservatives' turn. Under Prime Minister Disraeli the Second Reform Act doubled the size of electorate, giving about 16 percent of the adult Britons the vote. In 1884, the Third Reform Act added farm workers to the electorate and thus achieved nearly complete male suffrage. Women finally got the vote in 1918.

The interesting point about the growth of the British electorate is that the process was slow. New elements were added to the voting rolls only gradually, giving Parliament time to assimilate the forces of mass politics without going through an upheaval. The gradual tempo also meant that citizens got the vote when they were ready for it. In some countries where the universal franchise—one person, one vote—was instituted early, the result was not democracy but tyranny, as crafty officials rigged the voting of people who didn't understand electoral politics. Spain, for example, got universal suffrage in the 1870s, but election results were set in advance. By the time the British working class got the vote, they were ready to use it intelligently.

With the expansion of the voting franchise, political parties turned from parliamentary clubs into modern parties. They had to win elections involving thousands of voters. This meant organization, programs, promises, and continuity. The growth of the electorate forced parties to become vehicles for democracy.

The Rise of the Welfare State

By the beginning of the twentieth century, with workingmen having the right to vote, British parties had to pay attention to demands for welfare measures—public education, housing, jobs, and medical care—that the upper-crust gentlemen of the Liberal and Conservative parties had earlier been able to minimize. Expansion of the electoral franchise led to the growth of the welfare state.

One force goading Liberals and Conservatives into supporting welfare measures was the new Labour party, founded in 1900. At first, most working-class voters went with the Liberals, but by the end of World War I, the Labour party had won

Conservative Geniuses: Burke and Disraeli

As befits a country that favors tradition, Britain's greatest political thinkers have been conservatives who stressed continuity with the past and respect for traditional symbols.

Edmund Burke was a Whig member of Parliament during the American and French revolutions. He urged Britain to leave the thirteen colonies alone (they were only trying to recover the traditional rights of Englishmen), but he recoiled in horror at the French Revolution, warning well in advance that it would end up a military dictatorship (it did). The French revolutionists had broken the historical continuity and smashed the symbols that make a system work, argued Burke. People need traditions to restrain and guide them, he wrote. Scrap traditional authority—as the French did—and society breaks down only to end under a tyranny. Burke's views on representation in Parliament are also interesting. Burke told his constituents in Bristol that he was not their messenger boy in the Commons; he respected their opinions but voted the way he thought best. The Burkean view of a legislator is a far cry from the extreme constituency orientation of the modern American congressional representative.

Benjamin Disraeli, a Christianized Jew who became prime minister in the 1870s, understood that, to survive, the Tories must offer the workingman the vote and thereby win his support. He led the Conservatives to expand the electorate to encompass most workers. This gave many workingmen a stake in the system. Rather than turning revolutionary like workers in much of Europe, most British workers stayed pragmatic and moderate. Many British working people support the Conservative party to this day. Disraeli's expansion of the electorate was a gamble that paid off: it increased democracy but didn't hurt the Conservatives.

Both Burke and Disraeli understood that to be conservative does not mean to stand pat, never to budge in the face of change. True conservatism, they saw, means constant, but never radical, change. Wrote Burke: "A state without the means of some change is without the means of its conservation." Progress comes not from chucking out the old but from gradually modifying the parts that need changing while preserving the overall structure—in other words, keeping the form but reforming the contents.

COMPARING

The Genesis of Two Welfare States

Both Britain and Sweden are welfare states, Sweden more so than Britain. How did this come to be? In comparing their histories, we get some clues.

• Swedish King Gustav Vasa broke with Rome in the 1520s, a few years earlier than Henry VIII. In setting up churches that were dependent on their respective states—Lutheran in Sweden, Anglican in England—the two countries eliminated religion as a source of opposition to government.

• Because of this, politics in both lands did not get stuck in a clerical-anticlerical dispute over the role of the church, as was the case in France, Italy, and Spain. In Britain and Sweden, the main political split was along class lines, working class versus middle class.

• Britain and Sweden both developed efficient and uncorrupt civil services, an absolute essential for the effective functioning of welfare programs.

• Both countries formed strong—but not Marxist—labor movements, the TUC in Britain and LO in Sweden.

• These two labor movements gave rise to moderate worker-oriented parties, Labour in Britain and the Social Democrats in Sweden, which demanded, and over time got, numerous welfare measures passed. One big difference is that the Social Democrats have been in power in Sweden most of the time since 1932 and have implemented a more thorough—and more expensive—welfare state.

them over and pushed the Liberals into the weak third-party status they have languished in to this day. Unlike many Continental socialists, the British Labourites were never Marxist. Instead, they combined militant trade unionism with intellectual social democracy to produce a pragmatic, gradualist ideology that sought to level class differences in Britain. As one observer put it, the British Labour party "owed more to Methodism than to Marx."

The British labor movement of the late nineteenth century was tough, a quality it retains today. Resentful of being treated like dirt, many workingmen went into politics with a militant snarl that still characterizes many of their heirs in the 1990s. In the 1926 General Strike, the trade unions attempted to bring the entire British economy to a halt to gain their wage demands. They failed.

Briefly and weakly in power under Ramsay MacDonald in the 1920s, Labour won resoundingly in 1945 and implemented an ambitious program of welfare measures. Since at least then, the chief quarrel in British politics has been between people who like the welfare state and people who don't.

Vocabulary Building

absolutism	caucus	Continent	electorate
Anglican Church	Commons	Cymric	English Channel
Bill of Rights	conservatism	divine right	Exchequer

feudalism	Magna Carta	secularization	United Kingdom
Kingdom	mixed monarchy	shilling	vassal
Levellers	notables	sovereignty	welfare state
Lords	Reform Acts	Tory	Whig

Further Reference

BELOFF, MAX. *Wars and Welfare: Britain 1914–1945.* London: Edward Arnold, 1984.

CALLAGHAN, JOHN. *Socialism in Britain since 1884.* Cambridge, MA: Basil Blackwell, 1990.

CHRIMES, S. B. *English Constitutional History.* London: Oxford University Press, 1967.

COLLEY, LINDA. *Britons: Forging the Nation, 1707–1837.* New Haven, CT: Yale University Press, 1992.

GREENLEAF, W. H. *The British Political Tradition,* 3 vols. London: Methuen, 1987.

HIBBERT, CHRISTOPHER. *Cavaliers & Roundheads: The English Civil War, 1642–1649.* New York: Scribner's, 1993.

LLOYD, T. O. *Empire to Welfare State: English History 1906–1976,* 2d ed. New York: Oxford University Press, 1979.

O'BRIEN, CONOR CRUISE. *The Great Melody: A Thematic Biography and Commented Anthology of Edmund Burke.* Chicago: University of Chicago Press, 1992.

ROBBINS, KEITH. *The Eclipse of a Great Power: Modern Britain 1870–1975.* New York: Longman, 1982.

SOMMERVILLE, J. P. *Politics and Ideology in England, 1603–1640.* White Plains, NY: Longman, 1986.

WILLIAMS, GLYN, and JOHN RAMSDEN. *Ruling Britannia: A Political History of Britain, 1688–1988,* 2d ed. New York: Longman, 1990.

CHAPTER 3

Britain: The Key Institutions

An Unwritten Constitution

It is commonly said that Great Britain has no written constitution. This is not completely true, for parts of the British constitution are written. It is more correct to say that the British constitution does not consist of a single document but is rather a centuries-old collection of Common Law, historic charters, acts passed by Parliament, and, most important, just plain custom.

This eclectic quality gives the British constitution flexibility. With no single, written document to refer to, nothing can be declared "unconstitutional." Parliament—specifically the House of Commons—can pass any law it likes. The British political system can therefore grow and change over time without suffering a systemic crisis. Franklin D. Roosevelt's problems with the Supreme Court, which ruled some of his measures unconstitutional, could not have come up in Britain.

The negative side of this, however, is that there is no absolute standard by which to judge acts of Parliament or of the police. In 1991, six men convicted as terrorist bombers for the Irish Republican Army in 1975 were freed with the shameful admission that confessions had been beaten out of them and that the police had rigged evidence. British police and courts essentially monitor their own behavior and do not have nearly the checks and reviews that their U.S. counterparts have. Many Britons began to wish that they did.

The British often speak of "the Crown" but have a devil of a time defining it; often they don't even try. The Crown is an all-encompassing term meaning the powers of government in general. Originally the Crown meant the king, but over the centuries it has broadened to mean everyone helping the king or queen, and this includes Parliament, the cabinet, and civil servants. Let us consider some of these.

The Monarch

In Britain there is a clear distinction between "head of state" and "head of government." In America this distinction is sometimes ignored because the two are merged into one in the presidency. In most of the rest of the world, however, there is a top figure without much power who symbolizes the nation, receives foreign ambassadors, and gives speeches on patriotic occasions. This person—often a figurehead—can be either a hereditary monarch or an elected president, although not a U.S.–style president. Britain, Sweden, Norway, Denmark, the Netherlands, Japan, and Spain are monarchies. This doesn't mean they aren't democratic; it just means that the head of state is a carry-over from the old days.

A hereditary head of state can be quite useful. Above politics, a monarch can serve as psychological cement to hold a country together even without taking an important role in government. Because theoretically the top position in the land—what royalist philosophers used to call the sovereign—is already occupied, there are no political battles over it. The nastiest struggles in the world are precisely over who is to be sovereign; in Britain the issue has long been settled.

The great commentator on the British constitution, Sir Walter Bagehot, divided it into "dignified" and "efficient" parts. The monarch as head of state is a dignified office with lots of symbolic but not real political power. He or she "reigns but does not rule." The king or queen nominally appoints a cabinet of His or Her Majesty's servants (see box on page 35), but otherwise a monarch is more like an official greeter.

The "efficient" office in Britain is that of the head of government, the prime minister, a working politician who fights elections, leads his or her party, and makes

Prince Charles, Britain's future king and head of state, with his wife, Princess Diana, and their children, Prince William, also a futute king, and Prince Henry. Charles and Diana now live apart, but their marital troubles do not affect the succession to the throne. (*Central Office of Information, London*)

COMPARING

The Last Political Monarch

Unlike other European monarchs, King Juan Carlos of Spain retains some crucial political functions. Juan Carlos took over as head of state after Franco's death in 1975 and initiated and backstopped a process that turned Spain from dictatorship to democracy. He named a prime minister who dismantled the Franco structure, carried out Spain's first free elections in forty-one years, and drafted a new constitution—all with the open approval of the king.

Juan Carlos's real test as a defender of democracy came in 1981 when some disgruntled officers tried to carry out a coup; they actually held the entire *Cortes* (Spain's parliament) at gunpoint. In full military uniform, the king addressed the nation on television and ordered the troops back to their barracks. They complied, and democratic Spaniards of all parties thanked God for the king. Democracy and monarchy are not antithetical; one can support the other. *¡Viva el rey!*

political deals. Despite the very significant prestige attached to being prime minister, it does not carry nearly the degree of "dignity" that being the monarch does. Is there an advantage in the way Britain and other countries split the two positions? There is. If the head of government does something foolish or illegal, he or she will catch the public's ire, but the blame will fall on the individual prime minister, and respect will not diminish for the head of state, the "dignified" office. The system retains its legitimacy. Where the two offices are combined, as in the United States, and the president is involved in something like Watergate, the public gets disgusted at both the working politician and the nation's symbolic leader. "The British don't need to love their prime minister," said one diplomat. "They love their queen."

The present queen is highly respected, but royal legitimacy eroded with the marital (and extra-marital) escapades of the younger generation of royals, princes Charles and Andrew, and their one-time wives, "Di" and "Fergie." The public sees them as leading frivolous lives at the taxpayers' expense. Although few would consider exchanging a monarchy for a republic, some Labourites talked about making the monarch pay inheritance taxes and ending the fiction of the monarch choosing the prime minister. Look for a major decision point when Queen Elizabeth dies. Will Charles automatically accede to the throne? Even if he is divorced and remarried? To a commoner? The last time this happened, in 1936, King Edward VIII abdicated, but we need not expect a replay. Britain will likely retain a monarchy, but it may be a monarchy with somewhat altered psychological and political powers.

The Cabinet

The British cabinet is also quite different from the U.S. cabinet. The former consists of members of Parliament (most in the Commons, a few in Lords) who are high up in their parties and important political figures. Most have lots of experience, first as

The Queen Chooses a New Prime Minister

In 1990 an old ritual was repeated. Ostensibly Queen Elizabeth II chose a new prime minister, but of course she really had no choice at all. Events unrolled according to the fiction that the prime minister is still chief advisor to the monarch.

Britain's governing Conservative party saw their voter support erode due to some unpopular policies of Prime Minister Margaret Thatcher. Public opinion polls even showed the Labour party ahead. Fearing the entire party would go down to defeat if Thatcher stayed in power, the 372 Tory members of Parliament gave her only divided support as party chief, and she resigned rather than split the party. The Conservative MPs immediately elected a new chief, John Major. He did not quite have a majority, so the other two contenders withdrew in his favor. Major included both of them in his cabinet. Conservatives do believe in good manners.

No longer leader of her party, Thatcher could not remain prime minister, so the next day she called on the Queen to formally resign as first minister to Her Majesty. (Thatcher later became Lady Thatcher, with the right to sit in the House of Lords.) That same day the Queen called John Major, as leader of the largest party in Commons, to Buckingham Palace and "asked" him to form a new government. He accepted. Compare this British change of head of government with the year-long paralysis of Watergate in the United States. No delay, no agony, and no impeachment: in a few days an unpopular PM was replaced by a new one. Not bad for an "antiquated" political institution!

ordinary "MPs" (members of Parliament), then as junior ministers, and finally as cabinet ministers. The American cabinet often consists of presumed experts from universities, law offices, and businesses, mostly politically unknown and without experience in winning elections or serving in Congress. A British cabinet member is a political being with real clout, someone the prime minister must listen to. The American counterpart can be more safely ignored by the president.

Originally the British cabinet consisted of ministers to the king. Starting in the seventeenth century, however, the cabinet became more and more responsible to Parliament and less and less to the king. A British minister does not necessarily know much about his or her "portfolio" (ministerial job) but is carefully picked by the prime minister for political qualifications. Both major British parties contain several viewpoints and power centers, and prime ministers usually take care to see they are represented in the cabinet. When Prime Minister Thatcher ignored this principle by picking as ministers only Tories loyal to her and her philosophy, she was criticized as dictatorial. Balancing party factions in the cabinet helps keep the party together in Parliament and in power.

Notice that the British cabinet bridges a gap between "executive" and "legislative." British ministers are both; the elaborate American separation of powers (adopted by the Founding Fathers from an earlier misperception of British government by Montesquieu) doesn't hold in Britain. The United Kingdom has a *fusion*, or combining of powers.

The British cabinet practices "collective responsibility," meaning that they all stick together and support the final consensus. Ministers often argue heatedly in the secret, twice-weekly cabinet meetings, but once a policy is agreed upon, they all

British Cabinets and Prime Ministers

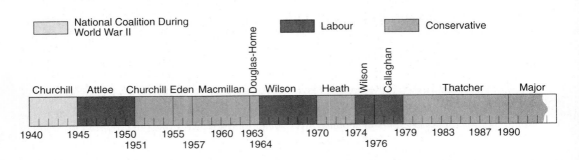

publicly support it. Occasionally, a minister resigns in protest at the cabinet's decision over a major controversy.

In recent years, the cabinet has consisted of more than twenty ministers, although this number and portfolio titles change. The Commons routinely approves the prime minister's requests to add, drop, or combine ministries. In the early 1990s, Prime Minister Major's cabinet consisted of the following "secretaries" or ministers:

> Lord Chancellor (member of Lords, heads judiciary)
> Foreign secretary
> Home secretary (internal governance, including police)
> Chancellor of the Exchequer (treasury)
> Environment secretary
> Defense secretary
> Education secretary
> Transport secretary
> Social Security secretary
> Agriculture secretary
> Employment secretary
> Northern Ireland secretary
> Welsh secretary
> Scottish secretary
> National Heritage secretary (preservation of buildings and monements)
> Citizen's Charter secretary (privatization of public services)

In addition, the leaders of both the House of Commons and House of Lords are in the cabinet, along with a chief secretary for the cabinet as a whole.

Below cabinet rank are more than thirty noncabinet "departmental ministers" and a similar number of "junior ministers" assigned to help cabinet and depart-

The Hierarchy of Britain's Ruling Party

In the cabinet	One prime minister 20 or more cabinet ministers
In the executive but not the cabinet	30 or more departmental ministers 30 or more parliamentary undersecretaries ("junior ministers")
In Parliament only	30–40 parliamentary private secretaries Over 200 other MPs, "backbenchers"

mental ministers. All totaled, at any given time about a hundred MPs are also serving in the executive branch. The hope of being named to one of these positions insures the loyalty and obedience of most younger MPs.

For all intents and purposes, in Britain (and in most parliamentary systems) cabinet equals government; the two terms are used interchangeably. When the "government falls" it simply means that the cabinet has resigned. Britain is often referred to as "cabinet government," although some call it "prime ministerial government."

The Prime Minister

The prime minister, PM for short (don't get it confused with MP, which he or she also is), is the linchpin of the British system. In theory, the PM's powers could be nearly dictatorial. Because the prime minister picks and controls the cabinet and heads the largest party in Parliament, theoretically he or she should be able to get nearly any measure passed. British parliamentarians are well disciplined; party "whips" make sure their MPs turn out for "divisions" (votes) and vote the straight party line. Yet even with the reins of power so tightly held by one person, prime ministers still do not turn into dictators.

The chief reason is that general elections are never more than five years away. Prime ministers are usually cautious about introducing measures that might provoke public ire. When Margaret Thatcher introduced an unpopular "poll tax" (see box in Chapter 6), voter reactions were so negative that she knew she would lose if she "went to the country" with new elections. More typically, prime ministers introduce only piecemeal measures to avoid offending key blocks of voters. The fear of losing the next election keeps most prime ministers cautious.

Further, a prime minister has to be careful of the major currents of opinion within party ranks. As in the United States, the two large British parties contain left, right, and center wings, as well as regional and idiosyncratic viewpoints. As was mentioned earlier, a prime minister usually constructs the cabinet with top MPs representing several views within the majority party. In cabinet meetings the PM tries to fashion a consensus from the several stands. Then the cabinet has to sell the policy to their MPs back in the Commons. Party discipline is good but rarely total. The

John Major: A Kinder, Gentler Thatcher?

After eleven and a half years in office, Prime Minister Margaret Thatcher, the "Iron Lady," was starting to rust. Amidst growing pressure from Tory backbenchers, she resigned in late 1990 but threw her support to a Thatcher loyalist, John Major, as her successor. Major won the support of most of the Conservative MPs and thus became both party chief and prime minister. At 47, Major was the youngest British prime minister of the twentieth century.

Major and Thatcher were both rather similar and also very different. Both came from lower middle-class circumstances, but Major from much lower. Thatcher's father had a grocery shop with an apartment above; Major's father tried many jobs (one was as a circus performer) and their flat had no bathroom. Thatcher, a whiz at school, went to Ox-ford and on to comfortable upper middle-class jobs. Major, a poor student, dropped out of school at 16 and worked at menial jobs; for a while, he was on welfare. He knows first-hand what hardship means. At age 18 Major got a starting position in a bank and worked his way up to respectability and into Conservative party politics. Like Thatcher, he respects the idleness of neither those born to wealth nor those born to poverty. Hard work is the answer both for individuals and for Britain. Thatcher and Major thus both represent a new breed of Conservatives: people of modest origins with a passion for work and success.

As is usual in British politics, Major's party first ran him in a constituency that was safe for the other side. Major lost these two elections to a Labourite, both in 1974, but loyal party work earned him the chance to run in a Tory constituency, in Huntington, and he won in the Thatcher wave of 1979. He has represented Huntington ever since and has bought a home there. As a junior minister (for Social Security) and whip, Major helped enforce Thatcher's policies and earned her attention. In 1987, Thatcher named Major deputy to the Chancellor of the Exchequer (the treasury minister), then briefly foreign minister in 1989. Later in 1989, Thatcher made him Chancellor of the Exchequer, the second most prestigious position in the cabinet, with an official residence at 11 Downing Street, right next door to the prime minister's.

With a record like that, one might think that Major was a perfect Thatcherite, but his attitudes and style were quite different. Both, to be sure, were conservative, but Major was more moderate in his views. Thatcher delighted in being tough and confrontational; Major tried to be pleasant and calm. Thatcher was an ideologue who came to office with a firm plan to kill off "socialism" in Britain and restore competitive capitalism. No one got in her way and kept his or her job. Major was moderate and centrist and seemed to lack direction.

In office, Major did not do nearly as well as Thatcher. He let policies drift and the Conservative party started breaking into factions. Major's standing in the polls set record lows. Thatcherite MPs waited for the right replacement in order to dump him. They felt that if they did not find a stronger leader, the Tories would be voted out.

John Major, Prime Minister. (*British Information Service*)

prime minister, through the chief whip, has a hold on the MPs. One who does not "take the whip" (follow the party line on a vote) risks losing his or her nomination for reelection—in effect, getting fired from Parliament. But this is a two-way street. If a party policy really bothers an MP, the member can threaten to quit and make a stink. In 1979 one Labour MP was so upset by what he saw as left-wing domination of his party that he quit Labour and ran (successfully) as a Conservative, the ultimate slap at party leadership. If a PM fails badly, he or she can even be dumped by MPs. Several times in the past two decades both Labour and Conservative cabinets have had to withdraw or water down legislative proposals for fear of backbenchers' revolt within the ranks of their own party. A backbenchers' revolt helped oust Thatcher in 1990.

The PM does have a potent political weapon: the power to call new elections whenever he or she wishes. By law, Commons can go up to five years without a general election. By-elections to fill vacancies when an MP dies or retires can come any time; they are closely watched as political barometers. A crafty prime minister calls for new general elections when he or she thinks the party will do best. A good economy and sunny weather tend to produce a happy electorate, one that will increase the seats of the incumbent party. In 1974 Britain even had two general elections because Prime Minister Harold Wilson thought he could boost Labour's strength in Commons. (He did.) In 1987 Margaret Thatcher called elections a year early to take advantage of good economic news and disarray in the Labour party; she won handily. Public-opinion polls and by-elections help the prime minister decide when to ask the king or queen to dissolve Parliament and hold new elections.

Commons

One can look at the cabinet as a committee of the House of Commons sent from Westminster (the Parliament building) to nearby Whitehall (the main government

---

 The Deceptive No. 10 Downing Street

Since 1735 British prime ministers have resided in an ordinary brick row house, No. 10 Downing Street. Except for a couple of London bobbies on guard outside, a passer-by might take it for a typical private home. But this is deceptive, for behind the walls, the building on Downing Street is actually the nerve center of Whitehall, the British executive branch.

Upstairs at No. 10, the prime minister has his or her apartment. On the ground floor, in the back, the cabinet meets in a long white room. No. 10 connects to No. 12 Downing Street, the residence of the chief whip, the prime minister's parliamentary enforcer. They can visit without being seen from the street. Also connecting out of sight is No. 11 Downing Street, residence of the important Chancellor of the Exchequer, head of the powerful treasury ministry. Next door is the Foreign Office. At the corner of Downing Street, also with a connecting door to No. 10, is the cabinet secretariat, responsible for communication and coordination among the departments. What looks from the street like an ordinary row house is actually the focal point of British government.

offices) to keep administration under parliamentary control. Another way is to view the Commons as an electoral college that stays in operation even after it has chosen the executive (the cabinet).

The two main parties in the Commons—Conservative and Labour—face each other. The largest party is automatically His or Her Majesty's Government and the other His or Her Majesty's Opposition. The physical structure of the House of Commons explains a lot. It is very small, measuring only 45 by 68 feet (14 by 21 meters) and was originally designed for only about 400 members. How then can it possibly hold the current membership of 651? It doesn't, at least not comfortably. Members have no individual desks, unlike most modern legislators. When there's an important vote, MPs pack in like sardines and sit in the aisles.

By keeping the House of Commons small, the British ensure that members can face each other in debate a few yards apart. The parallel benches go well with the two-party system; the half-circle floor plan of most Continental legislatures facilitates pielike division into multiparty systems. But the main reason for the chamber's small size is that it was always small, ever since 1547 when Henry VIII first gave the Commons the use of the St. Stephen's royal chapel. During World War II when the Commons was damaged by German bombs, Prime Minister Winston Churchill ordered it rebuilt exactly the way it had been.

On each side of the oblong chamber there are five rows of benches. The front row on either side is reserved for the leading team of each major party, the cabinet of the government party and the "shadow cabinet" of the opposition. Behind them sit the "backbenchers," the MP rank and file. A neutral Speaker, elected for life from the MPs, sits in a thronelike chair at one end. The Speaker, who never votes or takes sides, manages the floor debate and preserves order. In 1992, Commons elected its first woman Speaker, Labourite Betty Boothroyd. A table in the center, between the party benches, is where legislation is placed (the origin of the verb "to table" a proposal). The Speaker calls the house to order at 2:30 in the afternoon, and sessions can go on until late in the evening. Unless "the whip is on"—meaning an MP had better be there because an important vote is expected—many MPs are busy elsewhere.

How Commons Works

Each year Parliament opens in November with a Speech from the Throne by the queen, another tradition. The MPs are ritually summoned by Black Rod, the queen's messenger, from the Commons and file into the nearby House of Lords. (Neither monarchs nor lords are allowed to enter the House of Commons.) From a gold-paneled dais in Lords, Her Majesty reads a statement outlining what policies "my government" will pursue. The amusing aspect is that the speech has been written by the prime minister with the queen serving merely as an announcer. A conservative king, George VI, had to read a Labour speech in 1945 promising extensive nationalization of industry. This he did without batting an eye.

Just as the queen takes her cues from the cabinet, so does the Commons. Practically all legislation is introduced by the "government" (that is, the cabinet), and it stands a high chance of passing nearly intact because of the party discipline discussed above. What the cabinet wants, the cabinet usually gets. When a Conservative cabinet introduces bills into the Commons, Conservative MPs—unlike their

American counterparts in Congress—rarely question them. Their job is to support the party, and individual conscience seldom gets in the way.

The task of challenging proposals falls to the opposition, seated on the Speaker's left. From the opposition benches come questions, denunciations, warnings of dire consequences, anything that might make the government look bad. Government MPs, particularly the cabinet and subcabinet ministers on the front bench, are duty-bound to defend the bills. In situations like these, the famous rhetorical ability of MPs produces debates in the House of Commons unmatched in any other legislature.

Although the rhetoric is brilliant and witty, the homework is weak. Because they are expected simply to obey their party, few MPs bother specializing. Traditionally, British parliamentary committees too were unspecialized; they went over the precise wording of bills but called no witnesses and gathered no data. The structure of the committees of legislatures is an important key to their power, and gradually some MPs have seen the need for a more American type of committee system. Since the late 1960s, specialized committees have been set up to scrutinize Whitehall, but compared to their U.S. counterparts the British committees are weak. They have little staff and cannot force ministers to testify.

Neither Tory nor Labour governments have been enthusiastic about specialized committees that can monitor and criticize executive functions. That may be part of the U.S. system of separation of powers, some Britishers have argued, but it has no place in the U.K. system of fusion of powers. In general, the British cabinet

House of Commons in session. Notice how small it is. *(British Information Service)*

What to Do with Lords?

The British Parliament is nominally bicameral. But the House of Lords over the centuries has seen its power erode. Early on, Commons established supremacy in the key area of money, raising revenues and spending them. (The U.S. Constitution provides that money bills originate in the lower chamber, the House of Representatives, an echo of the English tradition.) In Britain, the Civil War and Glorious Revolution of the seventeenth century centered around the power of Commons, and Commons emerged as the winner; Lords gradually took a back seat. By 1867 Bagehot considered Lords a "dignified" part of the constitution.

Since Britain's unwritten constitution does not specify or make permanent the powers of the two chambers, it was legally possible for Commons to push Lords into retirement. Its powers now are severely limited. The 1911 Parliament Act allows Lords to delay legislation not more than thirty days on financial bills and two years (since 1949, one year) on other bills. The Lords can amend legislation and send it back to the Commons, which in turn can (and usually does) delete the changes by a simple majority. Every few years, however, Lords jolts the system with an independence of mind lacking in the House of Commons. In 1984, for example, it embarrassed the Thatcher government and its Commons majority by rejecting a plan to abolish elections to the London regional government.

Lords, then, does play a somewhat larger role than a debating club. It is the only British institution in a position to check the potentially dictatorial powers of a prime minister who has a large and disciplined majority of Commons. It can thus be seen as a weak analog to the U.S. Supreme Court,

a sort of "conscience of the nation." Because the status of the members of Lords as "peers" is untouchable—they can't be voted out—they can consider measures calmly and in depth. In some cases they have been able to point out weaknesses in bills coming from the more-pressured atmosphere of the Commons. They are also able to debate questions that are too hot for elected officials to handle, for example, laws concerning abortion and homosexuality.

There are some twelve hundred Lords and Ladies of the Realm; most of the titles are hereditary, but since 1958, an increasing number have been named just for their lifetime (the title does not pass on to children) for distinguished contributions in science, literature, politics, business, and the arts. Usually less than three hundred turn up in the House of Lords; a quorum is three. A few Lords are named to the cabinet or to other high political or diplomatic positions.

Can anything else be done with Lords? There have been numerous suggestions to revitalize that august body, to give it a greater political role to play. One is to increase the number of "life peers" until Lords is composed mostly of people who have earned distinction rather than inherited it. Another scheme suggested by both parties' leaders in 1968 would create a two-tier chamber with only life peers having the right to vote but hereditary peers having the right to participate in debates. (A backbenchers' revolt shelved the idea.) A radical proposal would turn Lords into a democratically elected body based on proportional representation, unlike the Commons's single-member districts. The Labour party has talked about abolishing the House of Lords.

would like to use Commons to rubber-stamp its decisions. Fortunately, such rubber-stamping is not always the case, as we shall explore later.

The Parties

The House of Commons works as it does because of the British party system. This is a fairly recent development; only since the time of the French Revolution (1789) has it been possible to speak of coherent parties in Britain. Parties are now the cornerstone of British government. If a party elects a majority of the MPs, that party controls Commons and forms the government.

Britain is usually described as a two-party system. This is not completely accurate, for there are small parties that sometimes can make or break a government. In 1979, for example, the withdrawal of support by the eleven Scottish Nationalists in the Commons brought down the Callaghan government in a rare vote of no-confidence. Here we can see how sometimes one of the large parties, in this case Labour, depends on the support in Parliament of a small party. We could more accurately label Britain a "two-plus" party system.

The British electoral system tends to keep two parties big, however, by penalizing smaller parties. Britain, like the United States and Canada, uses "single-member districts" as the basis for elections. This means that each electoral district or constituency sends one person to the legislature, the candidate that gets the most votes even if less than a majority. Single-member districts with plurality victors tend to produce two large political parties. The reason: there is a big premium in such districts to combine small parties into big ones in order to edge out competitors. If one of the two large parties splits, which sometimes happens, the election is thrown to the other party, the one that hangs together. In proportional representation, for instance, in some Continental countries, there is not such a great premium on forming two large parties, and that contributes to party splintering.

British parties are more cohesive and centralized than American parties. It's fair to say there are more differences within the two big American parties than between them; in Britain it would probably be the other way around. The British Labourites, who are sometimes called Socialists—a term most of them don't object to—favor nationalization of industry, more welfare measures, and higher taxes. The Conservatives, nicknamed Tories, urge less government involvement in society and the economy and lower taxes. Internal party differences arise from the *degree* to which party members support these general points of view.

 ## *Two-Party Systems: Variations on a British Theme*

The countries that inherited the British electoral system of single-member constituencies with simple plurality winners tend toward two large parties at the national level, one a bit left, the other a bit right: the U.S. Democrats and Republicans, the Canadian Liberals and Progressive Conservatives. At times, third parties, if they are regionally concentrated, can jump from provincial to national parliaments, as Canada's socialist New Democrats and the separatist *Bloc Québécois* did in 1993.

Until recently, New Zealand used the Anglo-American system, and it too yielded two large parties. It also left many New Zealanders discontent, because other viewpoints got ignored, so in 1993 a new electoral law went into effect, modeled on Germany's hybrid system of half single-member districts and half proportional representation (see Chapter 13). We may expect New Zealand to develop a more complex party system in the future as a result of the new law.

In 1981, the more moderate wing of the Labour party split off to form a centrist Social Democratic party. They argued that Labour had fallen under the control of radicals and had turned sharply leftward. The Social Democrats faced the problem that had long beset Britain's third party, the middle-of-the-road Liberals, namely, that single-member plurality districts severely penalize smaller parties.

The Liberal party illustrates how smaller parties suffer under the British system of electing MPs. In the last century the Liberals were one of the two big parties, but by the 1920s they had been pushed into a weak third place by Labour. Now, although the Liberals are often able to win nearly one vote out of five, they rarely get more than a dozen seats in the Commons. The reason: The Liberal vote is territorially dispersed so that in few constituencies does it top Tories or Labourites.

In 1983 and 1987, the Liberals and the Social Democrats ran jointly as the "Alliance," and in 1988 they merged into the Liberal Democratic party. The Liberal Democrats came in third but, because they were spread rather evenly, won fewer than two dozen seats in Commons. Liberal Democrat leaders voiced support for a proportional representation system that would give them seats in proportion to votes, but it is unlikely the Conservative or Labour parties will give up the built-in advantage that the system of single-member districts with plurality wins confers on the two largest parties.

Scottish and Welsh nationalist parties have shown spurts of growth and decline. Although they are now weakened, their territorial concentration enables them to obtain a few seats in Parliament. We will explore patterns of interaction among the parties and the voters in Chapter 5.

Vocabulary Building

backbencher	constitution	head of state	shadow cabinet
by-election	*Cortes*	junior minister	single-member
cabinet	Crown	minister	district
collective	eclectic	opposition	Westminster
responsibility	head of govern-	portfolio	whip
Common Law	ment	prime minister	Whitehall

Further Reference

ANDERSON, BRUCE. *John Major: The Making of the Prime Minister.* N. Pomfret, VT: Trafalgar Square, 1992.

BIRCH, ANTHONY H. *The British System of Government,* 9th ed. New York: Routledge, 1993.

BRAND, JACK. *British Parliamentary Parties: Policy and Power.* New York: Oxford University Press, 1992.

BUTLER, DAVID. *British General Elections since 1945.* Cambridge, MA: Basil Blackwell, 1989.

DREWRY, GAVIN, ed. *The New Select Committees: A Study of the 1979 Reforms,* 2d ed. New York: Oxford University Press, 1989.

HENNESSEY, PETER. *Whitehall.* New York: Free Press, 1989.

JAMES, SIMON. *British Cabinet Government.* New York: Routledge, 1992.

JOGERST, MICHAEL. *Reform in the House of Commons: The Select Committee System.* Lexington, KY: University Press of Kentucky, 1993.

KING, ANTHONY, ed. *The British Prime Minister,* 2d ed. Durham, NC: Duke University Press, 1985.

MOUNT, FERDINAND. *The British Constitution Now.* London: Heinemann, 1992.

NORTON, PHILIP. *The British Polity,* 3d ed. White Plains, NY: Longman, 1994.

RADICE, LISANNE, ELIZABETH VALLANCE, and VIRGINIA WILLIS. *Member of Parliament: The Job of a Backbencher.* New York: St. Martin's, 1988.

THEAKSTON, KEVIN. *Junior Ministers in British Government.* New York: Basil Blackwell, 1987.

4

British Political Attitudes

A Touch of Class

"England is a snob country," one long-time American resident in London told me. She added: "And I'm a snob, so I like it here." Her candor touched one of the facets of British political life, one that explains a great deal about modern England: the large and often invidious distinctions made between and by social classes.

Social class can be analyzed two ways, objectively and subjectively. The objective approach uses data such as income and neighborhood to put people into categories. The subjective approach asks people to put themselves into categories. There are often discrepancies between the two, as when a self-made businessman, thinking of his humble origins, describes himself as working class, or when a poorly paid schoolteacher, thinking of her university degrees, describes herself as middle class. In Britain and most industrialized democracies the main politically relevant distinction is between working class and middle class.

Objectively, class differences in Britain are not so great; they are basically no greater than in the rest of Western Europe. The time has long passed when Disraeli could write that Britain was not one nation but two, the rich and the poor. Since that time, the British working class has grown richer, the middle class bigger, and the small upper class poorer.

But subjectively or psychologically, class differences remain. Working-class people live, dress, speak, and enjoy themselves in markedly different ways from the middle class. Britons seem to like these differences and try to preserve them.

According to German sociologist Ralf Dahrendorf, the key word in Britain is not class but *solidarity*. While there has been a leveling of objective class differences, Dahrendorf holds, the idea of individual competition and improvement has not caught on in Britain as in other industrial countries. Rather than struggling upward individually, many Britons relish the feeling of solidarity they get by sticking with their old jobs, neighborhoods, and pubs. "Britain is a society in which the values of solidarity are held in higher esteem than those of individual success at the expense of others," Dahrendorf wrote.

Whether one calls it class or solidarity, these divisions influence British politics in many ways. They contribute to the way Britons vote. They color the attitudes of labor unions and of the Labour party. And—very important—they give birth to Britain's elites through the education system.

"Public" Schools

One pillar of the British class system is the "public" school. Actually, these are private boarding schools—whose costs put them well beyond the reach of working-class families—that got their name from their avowed purpose of training boys for public life in the military, civil service, or politics (Conservative). Eton, Harrow, Rugby, St. Paul's, Winchester, and other famous academies have for generations molded the sons of the upper and upper-middle classes into a ruling elite. At present under 7 percent of English children receive a private education.

What they learn from ages 13 to 18 is more than their demanding curriculum. At least as important is the style they pick up: self-confident to the point of arrogance, self-disciplined, bred to rule. Spy novelist John Le Carré recalled with loathing his years in a public school during World War II: "We doubled up with mirth at the sound of lower-class accents." His schoolmates called such people "oiks" and felt nothing but contempt for them. In 1945 Attlee was simply "a Leftie who had seduced the oiks into getting rid of Churchill." In terms of class relations, added Le Carré, "nothing, but absolutely nothing, has changed" since the 1940s.

The English private-school system generates an "old boy" network that assists graduates later in life. The years of floggings, vile food, and bullying by upperclassmen forge bonds among old schoolmates, and they often arrange for each other to get positions in industry and government. A large portion of Britain's elite have gone to private boarding schools, including some two-thirds of Conservative MPs (but few Labour MPs).

    ### *What to Do with "Public" Schools?*

The British Labour party has sought to do away with the country's private boarding schools. Labourites regard them as part of the class system where boys of better-off families learn nothing but privilege. Most Conservative politicians have attended "public" schools, but few Labour politicians have. Conservatives want to maintain the schools, arguing that they train the best people and imbue them with a sense of public service.

In the past, Labour governments essentially let the private boarding schools alone while they tried to upgrade the quality of publicly supported "comprehensive" schools. If anything, the private schools grew stronger as more parents decided they were the only way to insure their children would get into a good university.

While the upper and upper-middle classes send their sons to "public" schools, the middle class send theirs to "grammar" schools, where pupils wear uniforms but do not live in. Until 1944, there was no free high school system in Britain, but since the advent of the first Labour government nearly two hundred grammar schools receive state subsidies to enable them to take in working-class youths; these are called direct-grant schools. Some 80 percent of English schoolchildren, however, especially those of the working class, go to "comprehensive" and technical schools that lead most of them to the workplace. Only 65 percent of British 17-year-olds are still in school (including technical training), the lowest level of any industrial land. (Comparative figures: West Germany, 97 percent; United States, 88 percent; Japan, 83 percent.) In spite of all the efforts of the Labour party since World War II, British education is still strongly divided along class lines.

"Oxbridge"

The real path to position and power in Britain is through the elite universities of Oxford or Cambridge, collectively dubbed "Oxbridge." Nearly half of Conservative MPs are Oxford or Cambridge graduates (usually after attending a public school such as Eton), while a quarter of Labour MPs are Oxbridge products. In the cabinet, these percentages are higher, for the leaders of the two big parties are heavily Oxbridge. And prime ministers are almost always graduates of either Oxford or Cambridge. The only exceptions in recent years have been Labour Prime Minister James Callaghan (1976–79) and John Major. Perhaps in no other industrialized country are the political elite drawn so heavily from just two universities.

As with secondary (high school) education, British university education is also elitist. A far greater proportion of Americans go to a university than do Britishers. British university admission is slanted in favor of better-off families, especially those who send their children to "public" schools. Since World War II, with higher education open to the working and lower-middle classes by direct-grant secondary schools and scholarships for deserving youths, Oxford and Cambridge have become less class-biased in their admissions. In 1993, by the way, an Oxford man became the U.S. president, and he named three other Oxonians to his cabinet. Two U.S. Supreme Court justices are also Oxford men. All the Americans had received Rhodes scholarships.

Only a small percentage of Oxbridge students go into politics, but those who do receive a major boost. In the first place, an Oxford or Cambridge degree—which takes three years to earn—commands respect. Further, the Oxbridge experience hones political skills. One popular major for aspiring politicians is "PPE"—philosophy, politics, and economics—in effect, how to run a country. Debating in the Oxford or Cambridge Union trains students to think on their feet and confound their opponents with rhetorical cleverness, a style that carries over into the House of Commons. Perhaps the main advantage an Oxbridge education confers, however, is the "sense of effortless superiority" that the graduate carries all his or her life.

Class and Voting

Britain used to be offered as a good example of "class voting"—a situation where most of the working class votes for the left party (in this case, Labour), while most

The Establishment

So homogeneous are Britain's ruling elites—in terms of education, dress, speech, mentality, and so on— that critical writers in the 1950s began referring to them as the Establishment, as if they were a sort of exclusive club that only the right kind of people could get into. A typical member of the Establishment went to a private (often boarding) school, then to Oxford or Cambridge, then used connections to get a good position in the civil service or a seat in Parliament. Although a member of the Establishment might prefer Labour, a majority are Tory. Of the ministers in Major's first cabinet, for example, 76 percent had attended "public" schools and 71 percent were Oxbridge graduates.

of the middle class votes for the right (in this case, the Conservatives). Actually, class voting in Sweden is higher than in Britain, but nowhere is it 100 percent. Two shifts dilute class voting in Britain and elsewhere: (1) some working-class people vote Conservative, and (2) some middle-class people vote Labour. Class differences may be part of Britain's political culture, but they do not translate into class voting on a one-to-one basis.

What happens to dilute class voting? Some working-class people are simply convinced that Conservatives do a better job governing than Labourites. Some workers have a sentimental attachment to the country's oldest party. Some issues have little to do with class. The Tories won a large part of the working class in 1992 on the issues of economic growth and keeping taxes down.

Going the other way, many middle-class educated people are intellectually convinced that socialism is the answer to what they see as an establishment-ruled, snobbish class system. Such intellectuals sometimes provide important leadership in the Labour party. The leader of the Labour left is an aristocrat, Anthony Wedgewood Benn, or, as he likes to be known, Tony Benn. Further, some middle-class people grew up in working-class families and have sentimental ties to the way their parents voted.

Class voting changes over time. The British generation that came to political maturity during and after World War II, especially the working class, has been quite loyal to the Labour party, which it swept to power in 1945. Since then, class voting has fallen off in Britain and in many other West European countries. Class is not what it used to be in British voting patterns.

Class, nonetheless, is still a factor. Typically, political scientists find that voting behavior is influenced by social class plus one or more other factors such as region, ethnic group, religion, and urban-rural differences. The 1992 British general election seems to bear this out, as illustrated in the box on page 50. Tories were strongest in England, especially the south of England, and in small towns and rural areas. They were weaker in Scotland and Wales and in the big industrial cities, places with a long-term Labour identification and concern over unemployment. Class by itself explains only a part of British voting patterns. Class plus region explains a good deal more.

The Deferential British?

One image of the British that has been widely promulgated is that they are "deferential," that is, the average Briton defers to the political judgment of elites. According to the deferential model, working- and middle-class Britons recognize the superior leadership qualities of the Oxbridge-educated Establishment and let it take the lead.

The deferential model of British political attitudes has been oversold, for many Britons defer only grudgingly or not at all. Perhaps in earlir decades when class differences were enormous, the working class deferred to its social betters. But while they were tipping their hats, it seems likely they were also building a store of resentment. As noted in Chapter 2, the labor movement came into British politics in the last century with a snarl. In some sectors of the British working class, resentment is as strong as ever and comes out in the militant socialism on the left wing of the Labour party, indifferent work attitudes, and a readiness to go out on strike. The deferential model cannot explain such behavior.

The "working-class Tory" has been explained as a working-class person who defers to the Conservatives and votes for them. But the working-class Tory voter can be explained without the notion of deference. Many such voters think the Conservatives have the right policies, that the Labour party has swung too far left, and that there are too many nonwhite immigrants. Probably no more deference is found in Britain today than anywhere else in Western Europe.

British Civility

Civility here means keeping reasonably good manners in politics and avoiding getting abusive. In Britain, civility is based on a sense of limits: don't let anything go too far, don't let the system come unstuck. Thus while Labourites and Conservatives have serious arguments, neither party, when in power, moves in for the kill. The game is not one of total annihilation, as it has sometimes been in France, Germany, and Russia. Accordingly, British politicians are fairly decent toward each other.

But civility, like deference, has its limits in Britain. In Parliament a cabinet minister presenting a difficult case sometimes faces cries of "Shame!" or "Treason!" from the opposition benches. Margaret Thatcher faced Labourites chanting "Ditch the bitch." It should be pointed out that insults and heckling are a normal part of British debates and are not viewed as out of bounds; some see them as tests of a debater's cool.

Civility is usually the case out in public too—but not always. Amateur orators at the famous Speakers' Corner of Hyde Park in London can have their say on any subject they like, although they too must face heckling. But British politics turned very uncivil on the question of race, which we'll discuss later, and there have been riots and demonstrations that have resulted in deaths. Murder, rather than civility, became the norm for Northern Ireland. British civility has been overstated; Swedes are far more civil.

Pragmatism

The term *pragmatic* has the same root as practical and means using what works without paying much attention to theory or ideology. British attitudes, like American or

The 1992 Elections: Class Plus Region

SCOTLAND

NORTHERN
IRELAND

Industrial
Northeast

Industrial
Liverpool

Industrial
Yorkshire

WALES

ENGLAND

Central
London

The Conservatives won a narrow victory in 1992, but the areas where they scored below average tell a repetitive story: Scotland, Wales, and the industrial areas of London, Liverpool, Yorkshire, and the Northeast. Labour scores well among people who feel disadvantaged: the Scots, Welsh, and the poor. The areas where the Conservatives did above average (the shaded portion) are exclusively in England, especially in rural and suburban parts. In a nearly universal political pattern, large cities tend to vote left.

Where Tories Won Above Average in 1992. (*Source: The Economist,* April 18, 1992, p. 63.)

Swedish ones, are generally pragmatic. The Conservatives used to pride themselves on being the most pragmatic of all British parties. They were willing to adopt the policies of another party if they were vote-catchers. In the last century, Disraeli crowed that he had "dished the Whigs" by stealing their drive to expand the voting franchise. In the 1950s, the returning Conservative government did not throw out Labour's welfare state; instead they boasted that Tories ran it more efficiently. This changed with the laissez-faire economic program of Prime Minister Thatcher. The fixity of her goals contributed to ideological debates within and between the two large and usually pragmatic parties. The Tory tendency to pragmatism returned under Prime Minister Major.

The British Labour party had historically been mostly uninterested in Marxism or any other theory. With the Callaghan government in the 1970s, ideological controversy engulfed Labour. Callaghan was a very moderate, pragmatic Labourite, hard to distinguish from some Conservatives. Many Labour personalities, including the heads of some trade unions, resented Callaghan's centrism and rammed through a clearly socialist party platform. The moderate wing of the Labour party in 1981 split off to form a centrist party, the Social Democrats. We will explore ideology within the two main parties more fully in the next chapter.

There is and always has been a certain amount of ideology in British politics, but it has usually been balanced with a shrewd practical appreciation that ideology neither wins elections nor effectively governs a country. The ideological flare-up of the 1980s in Britain made it perhaps the most polarized land of Western Europe. The British electorate (see box on page 52), like most of Western Europe, tends to cluster in the center, albeit a bit skewed to the conservative side.

One aspect of British pragmatism is their "muddling-through" style of problem solving. The British tend not to thoroughly analyze a problem and come up with detailed options or "game plans" in the American manner. They try to "muddle through somehow," improvising as they go. This often works with small problems, but with a big problem, such as the situation in Northern Ireland, it amounts to a nonsolution.

Traditions and Symbols

As noted earlier, British politics has a good deal of tradition. Things are often done in the old ways, even by left-wing socialists, who, whether they recognize it or not, subscribe to Burke's idea of keeping the forms but changing the contents. As Burke saw, traditions and symbols contribute to society's stability and continuity; people feel disoriented without them.

 ## *Football Hooliganism*

Underscoring the decline in British civility was the rise of "football hooliganism," the violent and vile destruction by British soccer fans. Often drunk at games, some team groupies have been known to charge onto the field in the middle of a game. In 1985, Liverpool fans killed thirty-eight Italian spectators by causing their bleachers to collapse. All over Europe, the English fanatics were feared and sometimes barred from sports events.

What caused the violence? Some blamed unemployment; soccer games offer the jobless one of their few diversions. But most hooligans are employed and some earn good livings. Others see hooliganism as the erosion of civilization itself. "The truth is," said one self-confessed Manchester hooligan, "we just like scrappin'."

The Shape of the British Electorate

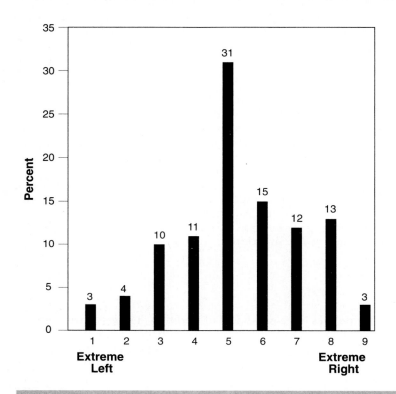

The Self-Placement of British Voters on a Left/Right Ideological Scale.

The British man or woman in the street usually likes traditions and symbols. Although some Britons dislike the tabloid lifestyle of the young generation of "royals," only a small minority would abolish the monarchy in favor of a republic with a president. Parades with golden coaches and horsemen in red tunics are not just for tourists—although they certainly help Britain's economy—they also serve to deepen British feelings about the rightness of the system.

Traditions can also tame political radicals. Once they win seats in the Commons, radicals find themselves having to play according to time-hallowed parliamentary usages. "Well, it simply isn't done, old boy," is the standard lesson taught to newcomers in Parliament. In a few years, the would-be radicals are usually more moderate. In terms of parliamentary behavior, it's hard to distinguish Labour from Tory MPs.

Legitimacy and Authority

One definition of *legitimacy* is a feeling of rightness about the political system. As was pointed out in Chapter 1, originally the word meant that the right king was on the throne, not a usurper. As used by political scientists, it refers to public attitudes that the government's rule in general is rightful. Legitimacy is a feeling among the people; it does not mean "legal."

When a political system enjoys high legitimacy, people generally obey it. They will even do things they don't want to, such as paying their income taxes. When a political system has little legitimacy, it is much harder to govern; instead of voluntary obedience it must rely on coercion. Simply put, societies with high legitimacy need few policemen; those with low legitimacy need many.

Legitimacy is closely related to the idea of authority, obeying duly constituted officials. British legitimacy and authority were long cited as models, but they were exaggerated and oversold. British policemen used to be famous for not carrying guns and for their good relations with people on their beat. Political scientists used to cite such points to illustrate Britain's nonviolent qualities. During the 1970s, however, Britain turned more violent. The Irish Republican Army spread their murderous tactics from Ulster, planting bombs that killed dozens. In 1984, one bomb blew up near Margaret Thatcher. Criminals started using handguns. In Britain's inner cities, relations between police and youths, especially black youths, grew hateful and contributed to urban riots (which nonetheless cost very few lives). A minority of British policemen now carry guns and riot gear, a symbol of the erosion of legitimacy and authority in Britain.

The Ulster Ulcer

While we can say that Britons on the whole still have attitudes of civility, pragmatism, legitimacy, respect for authority, and nonviolence, we must also note that Northern Ireland stands as a massive exception. The case of the six counties of Ireland sometimes called Ulster (although County Donegal, part of the Irish Republic, is geographically Ulster, too) illustrates that a system that works when there is widespread consensus at the grass-roots level fails when underlying consensus is lacking. Unlike the rest of Britain, Ulster is a split society, more like those of Latin Europe—France, Spain, Italy—where part of the population does not see the government as legitimate.

The Ulster problem has its roots in history. For eight centuries England ruled Ireland, at times treating the Irish as subhuman, seizing their land, deporting them, even outlawing the Catholic faith. A low point came with the 1846–54 Potato Famine in which a million Irish starved to death while the English, with plentiful food stocks, watched. (An example of what happens when you make too many babies, admonished English Malthusians.) At that time about a million and a half Irish emigrated, mostly to the United States. The Irish problem was the great issue of nineteenth-century British politics, "the damnable question" of whether to keep it firmly under British control or grant it "home rule."

At Easter time in 1916, while the English were hard-pressed in World War I, the Irish Republican Army (IRA), in what is known as the Easter Rising, rose up with guerrilla-warfare tactics. By 1922, after brutally crushing the rising, the British had

had enough; Ireland became a "free state" of the British Commonwealth. In 1949, the bulk of Ireland ended this status and became a totally independent republic, Eire.

But this did not solve the Ulster problem; 57 percent of the 1.5 million people in these six northern counties are Protestant (descended from seventeenth-century Scottish immigrants), and they are determined to remain part of Britain. Fiercely Protestant, for years these "Orangemen" (after the Protestant King William of Orange) treated Ulster Catholics as a different race and feared "popish" plots to bring Ulster into the Catholic-dominated Irish Republic to the south. The Protestant majority systematically shortchanged the Catholic minority in jobs, housing, and political power. For many years, most Catholics didn't even have the right to vote for the local legislature.

In 1968 Catholic protests started, modeled on U.S. civil rights marches. But peaceful demonstrations turned violent. A "provisional" wing of the IRA emerged to enroll Catholic fanatics in a program of murder. Protestant counterparts, such as the Ulster Defense Association, reciprocated in kind. Assassination became nearly random. Over 3,100 people have been killed—including MPs, Earl Mountbatten, British soldiers in Germany, and Australian tourists in Holland. Thatcher herself had a close call in a hotel bombing. Still patrolled by the British army, Northern Ireland saw its first flicker of hope in 1994 when the IRA, on the defensive, proclaimed a cease-fire, and its above-ground branch, *Sinn Fein*, started negotiating with London.

A Changing Political Culture

We are trying to put British political attitudes into perspective. Britons are neither angels nor devils. Political scientists used to present Britain as a model of stability, moderation, calm, justice, and just plain niceness. In contrast, France was often presented as a model of instability and immoderate political attitudes. The contrast was overdrawn; neither the British nor the French are as good or as bad as sometimes portrayed.

 ## *The IRA: Ballots and Bullets*

The Irish Republican Army is illegal in both Eire and Ulster, but its political arm, Sinn Fein (pronounced *shin fain*) is not. Many Northern Irish Catholics vote for Sinn Fein and in 1983 and 1987 elected IRA apologist Gerry Adams to Parliament from West Belfast. Adams, who as an act of protest never took his seat in Westminster, denies belonging to the IRA but does not condemn its violence: "I honestly see no other way by which the British can be forced to withdraw from this country, except by a mixture of struggle which involves properly controlled, interactive armed struggle." Some people, he says, should be shot. He lost his seat in 1992.

Electing IRA people is not new for Ulster's Catholics. In 1981 they elected Bobby Sands, an imprisoned IRA gunman, who starved himself to death in a hunger strike. The fact that so many men and women of Ulster are willing to vote for an extremist party indicates the depth of hatred and difficulty of compromise.

Observations of a country's political culture can err in two ways. First, if you are favorably disposed toward a country—and Americans are great Anglophiles—you may tend to overlook some of the nasty things lurking under the surface or dismiss them as aberrations. For years American textbooks on British politics managed to ignore or play down the violence in Northern Ireland. Such "incivility" seemed so un-British that no one wanted to mention it. Riots in poor British inner cities caught many observers by surprise.

Second, we may forget that studies of political culture are carried out at certain times, and that things change. The data for one famous book, Almond and Verba's *Civic Culture*, were collected a generation ago. The authors' composite portrait of Britain as a "deferential civic culture" is no longer valid. Since the late 1950s, Britain has undergone some trying times, especially in the area of economics. Difficult times did not erase British attitudes wholesale; they simply made manifest what had been latent. Political attitudes change; they can get nastier.

Vocabulary Building

Anglophile	muddling through
civility	Oxbridge
class voting	potato famine
deferential	PPE
Easter Rising	pragmatism
equalitarian	public school
Establishment	social class
legitimacy	working-class Tory

Further Reference

ALFORD, ROBERT R. *Party and Society: The Anglo-American Democracies.* Chicago: Rand McNally, 1963.

BARDON, JONATHAN. *A History of Ulster.* Chester Springs, PA: Dufour Editions, 1993.

BUFORD, BILL. *Among the Thugs.* New York: W. W. Norton, 1992.

DAHRENDORF, RALF. *On Britain.* Chicago: University of Chicago Press, 1982.

FRANKLIN, MARK N. *The Decline of Class Voting in Britain: Changes in Basis of Electoral Choice, 1964–1983.* New York: Oxford University Press, 1985.

KAVANAGH, DENNIS. "Political Culture in Great Britain: The Decline of the Civic Culture," in *The Civic Culture Revisited*, eds. Gabriel A. Almond and Sidney Verba. Boston: Little, Brown, 1980.

MADGWICK, PETER, and RICHARD ROSE, eds. *The Territorial Dimension in United Kingdom Politics.* Atlantic Highlands, NJ: Humanities Press, 1982.

MARWICK, ARTHUR. *Class: Image and Reality in Britain, France, and the USA since 1930.* New York: Oxford University Press, 1980.

NORDLINGER, ERIC A. *The Working-Class Tories: Authority, Deference and Stable Democracy.* Berkeley: University of California Press, 1967.

PARRY, GERAINT, GEORGE MOYSER, and NEIL DAY. *Political Participation and Democracy in Britain.* New York: Cambridge University Press, 1991.

ROBERTSON, DAVID. *Class and the British Electorate.* New York: Basil Blackwell, 1985.

ROSE, RICHARD. *Politics in England: Change and Persistence*, 5th ed. Glenview, IL: Scott, Foresman, 1989.

———, and IAN MCALLISTER. *The Loyalties of Voters: A Lifetime Learning Model.* Newbury Park, CA: Sage, 1990.

TOWNSHEND, CHARLES. *Making the Peace.* New York: Oxford University Press, 1993.

WALD, KENNETH D. *Crosses on the Ballot: Patterns of British Voter Alignment Since 1885.* Princeton, NJ: Princeton University Press, 1983.

WILSON, TOM. *Ulster: Conflict and Consent.* Cambridge, MA: Basil Blackwell, 1989.

5

Britain: Patterns of Interaction

People and Parties

In Britain, as in most democratic countries, the relationship between people and political parties is complex, a two-way street in which both influence the other. The parties project something called "party image," what people think of the party's policies, leaders, and ideology. Most voters, on the other hand, carry in their heads a "party identification," a long-term tendency to think of themselves as "Tory" or "Democrat" or whatever. The strategy of intelligent party leadership is to project a party image that will win the loyalty of large numbers of voters and get them to identify permanently with that party. If they can do this, the party becomes powerful and enjoys many electoral successes.

Both party image and party identification are reasonably clear in Britain: most Britons recognize what the three main parties stand for in general terms, and a large portion of British voters identify with a party. The situation is never static, however, for the parties constantly change the images they project, while some voters lose their party identification and shift their votes.

In every country, parents contribute heavily—but never totally—to the party identification of their children. In Britain, if both parents are of the same party, their children almost always first identify with that party, although this later erodes as young people develop their own perspectives. By the same token, party images are rather clear, and most Britons are able to see differences between their two largest parties: Labour aiming at helping working people through welfare measures and sometimes nationalization of industry, and Conservatives aiming at economic growth through hard work without state intervention.

For deeply confirmed Labour or Conservative voters—those whose party identification closely matches the image of their preferred party—there is little doubt about whom to vote for. Until recently, most British voters were reliably Labour or Conservative. The element that changes from one election to another—because either their party identification is not strong or their perceptions of the parties' images shifts, or both—is called the "swing" vote. A swing of a few percentage points can determine who will form the next government, for if each constituency shifts a little one way, say, toward Labour, the Labour candidate will be the winner in many constituencies. Single-member districts often exaggerate percentage trends and turn them into large majorities of seats. A "swing" of only one percentage point nationwide usually translates into a dozen or more parliamentary seats changing hands, sometimes changing the majority in Commons (see box).

The game of British electoral politics consists of the parties trying to mobilize all of their party identifiers—that is, making sure their people bother to vote—plus winning over the uncommitted swing vote. Mobilization is the key. In 1970 the Labour government of Harold Wilson suffered a surprise defeat by the Conservatives under Edward Heath. It wasn't that Labour identifiers suddenly switched sides—they didn't—but rather that some were unhappy with Wilson's policies and simply stayed away from the voting booth. Bright party leaders learn to recognize that the prize is in the center of the political spectrum (see box on page 52) and to tailor their campaigns to win the center.

 ## 1992: Tories Win Again

In April 1992, for the fourth general election in a row, Britain's Conservatives won. Although their overall national percentage remained essentially unchanged from the 1983 and 1987 elections, the way it was distributed meant the loss of forty Tory seats in Parliament, but they still had 336 out of 650, enough to govern. As is usual in Britain, this election did not give the Conservatives a *majority* of the votes cast; it gave them only a *plurality* of 42.8 percent, but in single-member districts this yields over-representation.

Labour did better—up 4.4 percent to 35.2 percent of the vote—largely at the expense of the Alliance, which dropped 4.3 percent to 18.3 percent of the votes. But Labour, with its geographical concentration in Scotland, Wales, and the industrial areas, collected 42 percent of the seats, while the poor Alliance, territorially dispersed, got only 3.1 percent of the seats.

For many British voters, John Major and the Tories were the only alternative. Labour's Neil Kinnock was a nice man, but Labour was still way too far left, and the Alliance had trouble defining itself. Unless Labour's new leader, Tony Blair, is able to move his party back to the center of the political spectrum—something its noisy leftists do not wish to happen—the Tories could make it five in a row next time.

	PERCENT OF VOTES		SEATS	
	1987	1992	1987	1992
Conservative	42.3%	42.8%	376 (58%)	336 (52%)
Labour	30.8	35.2	229 (35%)	271 (42%)
Alliance	22.6	18.3	22 (3.4%)	20 (3.1%)

National and Local Party

Political scientists used to describe the British national party—Conservative or Labour—as nearly all-powerful, able to dictate to local party organizations whom to nominate for Parliament. As usual, though, when you look more closely you find that things are more complicated.

The name of the game for parliamentary candidates is the "safe seat" and getting adopted by the local constituency organization to run for it. A safe seat is one in a district with a known, dependable majority for your party. Party leaders are normally assigned very safe seats, for it is highly embarrassing if one of them loses his or her seat in the Commons. About 450 (of 650) seats are usually considered safe. There is a bargaining relationship between the parties' London headquarters and the local constituency party. The local party often requests lists of possible candidates from headquarters, settles on one, and then gets it approved by the central headquarters. Unlike the U.S. system, there is both national and local input into British candidate selection, with a veto on both sides.

Some constituency organizations insist that a candidate actually live in the district. Americans expect all candidates to reside in the district they represent; those who don't are called "carpetbaggers" and have an uphill battle. Most countries, however, including Britain, impose no such requirements, although being a local person can help. Some British constituencies like their people to establish a residence there once they've won. But many constituencies couldn't care less if their MP actually lives there; after all, the MP's job is mainly in London, and periodic visits are sufficient for him or her to hear complaints and maintain ties with electors. Besides, in Britain, party is more important than personality. In any given House of Commons, probably a minority of MPs are natives of the constituency they represent.

What about the unsafe seats, those where the other party usually wins? These are the testing grounds for energetic newcomers to politics. The Conservative or Labour central offices in London may send a promising beginner to a constituency organization that knows it doesn't have much hope of winning. Again, the local unit must approve the candidate. Even if the candidate loses, his or her energy and ability are carefully watched—by measuring how much better the candidate did than the previous one—and promising comers are marked. For the next election, the London headquarters may offer the candidate a safer constituency, one where he or she stands a better chance. Finally, the candidate either wins an election in a contested constituency, is adopted by a "safe" constituency, or bows out of politics. Many of Britain's top politicians, including several prime ministers, lost their first races and were transferred to other constituencies. There's no stigma attached; it's normal, part of the training and testing of a British politician.

Politics within the Parties

British political parties, like British cabinets, are balancing acts. A party leader must neither pay too much attention to his or her party's factions nor totally ignore them. In constructing their policies, leaders usually try to give various factions a say but keep the whole thing under moderate control with an eye to winning the next election.

Party leaders must balance a pretty fine line between sometimes extremist party militants and a generally moderate voting public. If a party takes too firm an ideological stand—too left in the case of Labour or too right in the Conservative case—it can cost the party votes. Thus party leaders tend to hedge and moderate their positions, trying to please both the true believers within their party and the general electorate. If they slip in this balancing act, they can lose either party members or voters, or both. When Labour veered left in the 1980s and the Conservatives followed their hard-right Thatcher course, the centrist Alliance won a quarter of the 1983 vote, a warning to both major parties.

Although long described as ideologically moderate, both the British Labour and Conservative parties have important ideological viewpoints within their ranks. The Labour party is divided into "left" and "right" wings. The Labour left, springing from a tradition of militant trade unionism and intellectual radicalism, wants more nationalization of industry, the dismantling of "public" schools, higher taxes on the rich, to quit the Common Market, and no nuclear weapons, British or U.S. Some Marxists and Trotskyists have won Labour offices. The Labour right, on the other hand, is moderate and gradualist. It favors the welfarist approach of some Continental social-democratic parties such as the German SPD and shies away from government takeovers of industry. It is pro-NATO, pro–Common Market, and pro-American in foreign policy. The rightists in Labour argue that the left wing's ideas are extremist and cost the party votes.

As an amorphous party proud of its pragmatism, Conservatives were long thought immune to ideological controversy or factional viewpoints. This is not completely true, for the Tories comprise two broad streams of thought, which we might label as "classic" and "neoconservative" tendencies. The classic Tory is not a U.S.–style conservative, advocating a totally free economy with no government intervention. Instead, the old-fashioned Tory wants a party that takes everybody's interests into account, plus traditional ways of doing things, under the guidance of people born and bred to lead.

The neoconservative wing (which intellectually traces back to nineteenth-century *liberalism*) is like the American conservatives: They want to roll back government and free the economy. After World War II this view crept into the Conservative party and, with the 1975 election of Margaret Thatcher as party chief, moved to the forefront. Under Thatcher, the classic Tories were dubbed "wets," the militant Thatcherites "dries." (The terms were taken from boarding-school slang: "Wets" are frightened little boys who wet their pants; "dries" are strong and brave lads who do not.)

The trouble here is that some old-style British Conservatives find total capitalism almost as threatening as socialism. As industries went bankrupt in record number, Thatcher faced a revolt of Tory "wets" against her "dry" policies. After Major took over, Thatcherite MPs sought to dump him. Attitudes toward European unity also split the Tories. Thatcher and her followers favored the Common Market but opposed turning it into a European Union. Major and his followers were enthusiastically pro-Europe, including the Maastricht Treaty, which took European unity a big step forward. In short, the Conservatives have as many and as deep rifts as Labour.

Parties and Interest Groups

What politicians say and what they deliver are two different things. Politicians speak to different audiences. To party rank and file they affirm party gospel (championing

The Struggle of the Liberal Democrats

Public-opinion polls sometimes suggest the new Liberal Democratic party could edge out Labour to become Britain's second-largest party. But what Britons tell pollsters and how they vote are two different things; they speak more radically than they vote. Still, widespread disillusionment with the two large parties in the 1990s could give the Liberal Democrats a chance for major-party status.

The Liberal Democrats were born of the 1988 merger of the old Liberal party and the small, new Social Democratic party that in 1981 broke away from Labour. The two strands do not see eye-to-eye. On many questions—especially on the economy and defense matters—the Social Democrats were more conservative than the Liberals. The Liberals tended to be ultra-liberal on questions of gay rights and open immigration. They wanted Britain out of NATO and nuclear weapons—both U.S. and British—out of Britain. True to their origins in the right wing of the Labour party, the Social Democrats

were not unilateral disarmers and felt that lifestyle questions cost the party votes. The new party is a parallel to the many and incoherent viewpoints of the U.S. Democratic party.

The British electoral system—single-member districts with plurality win—is brutal on third parties (just as it is in the United States), especially those like the Liberal Democrats that are territorially dispersed. This discourages potential voters, who don't want to waste their votes on a party they fear will never win many seats. The Liberal Democrats' ray of hope came from its leader, Paddy Ashdown, a former Royal Marine and Labourite who is more appealing on television than John Major or Tony Blair. Many Britons, tired of the rigidity of Labour, liked the idea of a slightly left-centrist party, and in the 1990s were winning many by-elections. The only thing that can really help the Liberal Democrats, though, is the self-destruction of the two large parties, which increasingly they seemed bent on doing.

---

either the welfare state or free enterprise, as the case may be). To the electorate as a whole they usually tone down their ideological statements and offer vague slogans, such as "You've never had it so good," or "Time for a change." But quietly, usually behind the scenes, politicians are also striking important deals with influential organizations representing industry, commerce, professions, and labor. These are known as interest groups, and about half of the British electorate belong to at least one of them.

Some 40 percent of the British workforce, for example, is unionized, a much higher percentage than in the United States or France (but not as high as in Sweden). Labor unions are constituent members of the Labour party, controlling a majority of votes at Labour's annual conference, contributing most of the party's budgets and campaign funds, and providing grass-roots manpower and organization. Especially important are the views of the head of the ten million-member labor federation known as the Trades Union Congress (TUC), which is similar to the American AFL-CIO but proportionately bigger and stronger. No Labour party leader can ignore the wishes of Britain's union leaders.

This has opened Labour to charges that it is run by and for the unions, which have earned a reputation as too far left, too powerful, and strike-happy. To counteract this, both Labour party and union leaders deny union dominance. Indeed, one Labour party campaign tactic is to claim that only the Labour party can control the

Can Anyone Save Labour from the Unions?

From its 1983 electoral disaster, the Labour party struggled to recover. Part of its problem was a too-left party image. Another part was its doddering and ineffective leader, Michael Foot. At its annual conference that fall in Brighton, the Labour party tried to repair both areas by overwhelmingly choosing as its new leader Neil Kinnock, a silver-tongued Welshman as charming as Margaret Thatcher was aloof. At 41, Kinnock, son of a coal miner, was the youngest Labour leader ever. Kinnock first had to curb Labour extremists; he got the Trotskyist Militant Tendency faction expelled. (It formed a miniparty.) Kinnock did well, lifting Labour from 27.6 percent of the popular vote in 1983 to 35.2 percent in 1992. But Kinnock came across as too slick and was still hurt by the Tory charge that Labour was dominated by the unions.

Following Labour's fourth defeat in a row in 1992, Kinnock resigned, making way for John Smith, a pragmatic 53-year-old Scottish lawyer, who was making great strides in healing the party when he died of a heart attack in 1994. Replacing him was Tony Blair, who also tried to reorient Labour more

to the middle than the working class. Higher taxes and public ownership were out; discipline in education was in. But Blair had to break the union hold on the Labour party. Many union leaders resisted; they liked being able to cast the proxy votes of millions of union members at Labour's annual conferences. This union domination, often with a strong leftist slant, rendered Labour unacceptable to most British voters. In 1993, Smith had got a partial change in Labour's rules to return the candidate-selection process back to local party organizations. It was a first step.

The real problem is that Labour was founded by and is still heavily based on trade unions, some led by militant socialists who were proud to say they'd rather lose elections than lose their principles. One Labour Manifesto drafted by these people was so off-putting to average voters it was called a "suicide note." If Blair cannot break the too-close connection between Labour and labor, the party seems doomed to permanent opposition, possibly even to third-party status.

unions, rather than the other way around. The close association of labor federation to a social-democratic party is the norm for the industrialized countries of Northern Europe, as we shall see when we study Germany.

Dozens of union members sit as Labour MPs in Parliament; dozens more MPs are beholden to local unions for their election. This union bloc inside the Labour party can force a Labour government to moderate or withdraw measures that might harm unions. At times, however, Labour party chiefs have made union leaders back down, explaining to them that if the unions get too much the Labour party will never win elections. To reiterate, to be a party leader means performing a balancing act among several forces.

MPs known to directly represent special interests—an "interested member"—are not limited to the Labour side. Numerous Tory MPs are interested members for various industries and do not try to hide it.

The conservative mirror image of the TUC is the powerful Confederation of British Industry (CBI), formed by an amalgamation of three smaller groups in 1965. The CBI speaks for most British employers but has no formal links to the Conservative party, even though their views are often parallel. The CBI was delighted at

The "Poll Tax" Issue

A change in the way Britons pay for local government became the biggest single reason for Thatcher's ouster in 1990. As in the United States, much of British local government revenues came from property taxes, what British call "the rates." The Thatcher cabinet found the rates unfair, for they let renters get away untaxed while putting the entire burden on homeowners. In 1990 the Tories installed a new "community charge" to replace the rates. Everyone in a given district now paid the same, whether they rented or owned. It got the name "poll tax" because those who didn't register for it would not be allowed to register to vote.

Howls of protest erupted; some anti-poll taxers rioted. Many Tory-voting Britons found themselves paying more and didn't like it. Public opinion turned sharply anti-Conservative, and Labour ran ahead by a wide margin. In by-elections Labour won even safe Tory seats. The unpopular poll tax seemed to crystalize resentments against Thatcher; she had gone one conservative reform too far. In 1991 the new Tory government of John Major announced that it would end the poll tax and return to property taxes by 1993.

the antinationalization stance of the Conservative party, although British industrialists gulped when they found this meant withdrawal of subsidies to *their* industries. Under Thatcher, the CBI sometimes joined with Tory "wets" to complain about the damage her policies were inflicting on the economy. Thatcher could not totally ignore them, for CBI members and money find their way into Tory circles, and dozens of CBI-affiliated company directors occupy Conservative seats in Commons. The first director-general of CBI, John Davies, became minister for trade and industry in the 1970 Tory cabinet.

The Parties Face Each Other

There are two ways of looking at British elections. The first is to see them as three-week campaigns coming once every few years, each a model of brevity and efficiency. (All candidates in the 1983 British elections spent $10.3 million. In 1984, the two U.S. presidential contenders spent $134 million.) Another, however, is to see them as nearly permanent campaigns that begin the day a new Parliament reconvenes after the latest balloting. The formal campaign may be only three weeks, but long before then the opposition party is thinking of little but ousting the current government.

The chief arena for this is the House of Commons. Unlike the U.S. Congress, British parliamentarians are seldom animated by a spirit of bipartisanship. The duty of the opposition is to oppose, and this they do by accusing the government of everything from incompetence and corruption to sexual scandal. The great weapon here is embarrassment, making a cabinet minister look like a fool. The time is the Question Hour, held Monday through Thursday from 2:30 P.M. (when Commons opens) to 3:30. By tradition, this hour is reserved for MPs to aim written questions

The Profumo Scandal

In the time-honored game of embarrassment played in the House of Commons, the classic play came with the 1963 Profumo affair. The Labour opposition got wind that Tory War Minister (at the departmental, not the cabinet, level) John Profumo was dating a party girl who at the same time was also seeing the Soviet naval attaché, a known spy. Questioned by Labour in the Commons, Profumo swore there had been no impropriety in his relationship with Christine Keeler and threatened to sue anyone who said otherwise. Being a gentleman of impeccable credentials—Harrow, Oxford, army brigadier—Profumo was believed by the Macmillan government. But the scandal refused to die down; it began to appear that security had been breached and that Profumo was being set up for blackmail.

Sensational news stories charged the Conservative government with laxity on national security, covering up for one of its "old boys," and debauchery at the highest levels of the Establishment. There was some truth to the charges, and Profumo resigned in shame. It was not, however, the shame of a married man, 48, caught with a 21-year-old call girl. That was forgivable. What was unforgivable was that a gentleman had lied to Parliament. The Tory government mishandled the incident; Conservative MPs lost confidence in Prime Minister Macmillan, and voters lost confidence in the Conservative party, which was voted out the following year.

at the various cabinet ministers who are in attendance on the front bench. Each written question can be followed up by supplementary oral questions. The opposition tries to push a minister into an awkward position where he or she has to tell a lie, fluff an answer, or break into anger. Then the opposition, in effect, smirks, "You see, they're not fit to govern."

The Cabinet and the Civil Servants

As we discussed earlier, British cabinet ministers are generalists, not specialists, and are chosen more for political reasons than for any special ability to run their departments. Who then does run them? The nominal head of each British department is the minister; he or she represents that ministry in cabinet discussions and defends it in the Commons. But the minister doesn't run the department; civil servants do.

Ministers come and go every few years; the highest civil servants, known as "permanent secretaries" are there much longer. The permanent secretary often has an edge on his or her minister in social and economic terms as well. Most permanent secretaries are knighted while few ministers are. Although knighthood is now purely honorific in Britain, it still conveys a certain social superiority. Permanent secretaries earn more than ministers, in some cases nearly twice as much. A minister finds it nearly impossible to fire or transfer a permanent secretary. Further, permanent secretaries have a say in determining who will replace them when they retire or leave for lush positions in private industry; they tend to be a self-selecting elite. Permanent secretaries always play the role of humble, obedient servants, but some ministers come to wonder just who's boss around their departments.

The permanent secretary is assisted by several deputy secretaries who in turn are supported by undersecretaries and assistant secretaries. These names look like those of an American department, but there's a major catch: In most U.S. departments all or most of these people are political appointees, serving at the pleasure of the president and resigning when a new president takes office. In Britain, only the ministers assisted by some junior ministers—about a hundred persons in all—change with the political winds. What in America are temporary political appointees are permanent officials in Britain.

This gives them a lot of power. They are not amateurs but know their department: its personnel, problems, interests, and desires. Knowledge is power, and over time top civil servants come to quietly exercise a lot of it. While a permanent secretary or his or her assistants never—well, hardly ever—go public with their viewpoints, they make them felt through the kinds of ideas, programs, bills, and budgets they submit to the minister, their nominal boss. The minister theoretically can command them, but in practice he or she simply doesn't know enough about the workings of the ministry. Instead, the minister relies on them. Accordingly, while most bills and budget proposals *pass through* the cabinet, they do not *originate* there. The permanent civil servants do the jobs that are the stuff of governance.

This brings us to a fine irony. In centuries of British political evolution we have seen how Britons marched toward democracy by first limiting the power of the monarch and then expanding participation. If we look closely, though, we notice that much important decision making is only partly democratically controlled. Civil servants make a great deal of policy without democratic input. Many political scien-

---

 ## The Utility of Dignity

Another seemingly quaint British holdover from the past is the queen's bestowal of honors such as knighthood. But more than just a quaint practice, it's a clever payoff system that serves a number of purposes. The granting of titles is a reward and an encouragement to retire, solving the problem of senility and deadwood at the top. A person looking forward to a knighthood (Sir) or a peerage (Lord) is more likely to go quietly. Getting one of these honors also has a civilizing effect on the recipients; even the most militant union leaders and rapacious businessmen start talking philosophically about the common good once they have a title in front of their name.

Although the queen awards these and other distinctions, she does so only on the advice of the prime minister. A small staff keeps track of meritorious civil servants, business people, unionists, soldiers, politicians, scholars, artists, and writers, and recommends who should get what. In addition to becoming knights and peers, distinguished Britons may be named to the Order of the British Empire, Order of the Garter, Order of Merit, Order of the Bath, the Royal Victorian Order, and many others. The granting of honors is a part of British politics, a way of bolstering loyalty to, and cooperation with, the system.

tists stress the importance of interest groups in determining policies, but we must add that one of the most powerful interest groups is the civil service bureaucrats.

Does this mean there is no real democracy in Britain? No, it means we must understand that no country exercises perfect control over its bureaucracy and that parties and elections are only *attempts* to do so.

The Civil Service and Interest Groups

We mentioned the relationship of interest groups and political parties earlier. But this is only one way interest groups make their voices heard; it is often not the most important way. Much of the impact of interest groups is in their quiet, behind-the-scenes contact with the bureaucracy. Indeed, with Parliament's role curtailed as a result of powerful prime ministers and cabinets, and the cabinet ministers themselves dependent on the permanent civil servants, many interest groups ask themselves, "Why bother with Parliament? Why not go straight to where the action is, the bureaucracy?"

This approach is especially true of business and industry; the major effort of the unions is still focused on the Labour party. The reason for this is partly in the nature of what trade unions want as opposed to what business groups want. Unions want *general* policies on employment, wages, welfare, and so on, that apply to tens of millions of people. Industry usually wants *specific*, narrow rulings on taxes, subsidies, regulations, and the like that apply to a few firms. Thus unions tend to battle in the

Treasury: The Real Power

Among the many British ministries, one holds all the others in awe: the Treasury. Sometimes called the "department of departments," Treasury has the last word on who gets what among the ministries and, since a lot of the British economy is government linked, a major say in the island's economic life. Anyone with a bright idea in British government—a new minister or an innovative civil servant—soon comes up against the stone wall of Treasury, the ministry that says "no."

Britain's treasury minister goes by the old name of Chancellor of the Exchequer—originally the king's checker of taxes—and is now the second most powerful figure in any cabinet, just after the prime minister. Many Chancellors of the Exchequer later become prime ministers, so the person in that office is watched closely.

Under the Chancellor are the usual secretaries and civil servants, but they are a breed unto themselves, smarter and more powerful than other bureaucrats. Operating on a team-spirit basis, Treasury chaps trust only other Treasury chaps, for only Treasury can see the whole picture of the British government and economy and how the many parts interrelate. The other departments see only their corner, hence, in Treasury's view, they should not be heeded. The attitude gives Treasury and its people an image of cold, callous remoteness, "government by mandarins," but no one has been about to replace them.

more open environment of party policy, while business groups often prefer to quietly take a government official to lunch.

In working closely with a branch of Britain's economic life, a given department comes to see itself not as an impartial administrator but as a concerned and attentive helper. After all, if that industry falters, it reflects on the government agency assigned to supervise it. In this manner civil servants come to see leaders of economic interest groups as their "clients" and to reflect their clients' views. When this happens—and it happens in every country—the industry can be said to have "captured" or "colonized" the executive department.

Reinforcing this pattern is the interchange between civil service and private industry. A permanent secretary can make much more money in a corporation than in Whitehall; every now and then one of them leaves government service for greener pastures. (We will also see this pattern in France.) By the same token, business executives are sometimes brought into high administrative positions on the theory that if they can run a company well, they can do the same for government. The point is that fairly cozy relationships develop between civil servants and private business.

What about Democracy?

Most of the interactions we have talked about are not under any form of popular control. Ideological infighting, the influence of interest groups on parties and the bureaucracy, the relationship of top civil servants with ministers, the granting of knighthood—these and other interactions are removed from democratic control. The people do not even choose whom they get to vote for; that is a matter for party influentials. All the people get to do is vote every few years, and the choice is limited.

Again, does this mean there is no democracy in Britain? No, not at all. Some people have an exaggerated vision of democracy as a system in which everyone gets to decide on everything. Such a system never existed at the national level, nor could it. The most we can ask of a democracy is that the members of the leading team—in Britain, the prime minister and cabinet—are held accountable periodically in elections. This keeps them on their toes and anxious to pay attention to the public good, holds down special favors and corruption, and makes sure the bureaucracy functions. It is in the *anticipation* of electoral punishment that Britain, or any other country, qualifies as a democracy. What the great Carl J. Friedrich called the "rule of anticipated reactions" keeps the governors attentive. We will learn not to expect much more of political systems.

Vocabulary Building

central office	knighthood	permanent secretary
classic conservatism	laissez faire	Question Hour
classic liberalism	mobilization	safe seat
Confederation of British Industry	neoconservative	subsity
constituency	party identification	swing
ideology	party image	Trades Union Congress
interested member	peerage	Treasury

Further Reference

BUTLER, DAVID, and DENNIS KAVANAGH. *The British General Election of 1992.* New York: St. Martin's, 1992.

CAMPBELL, COLIN. *Governments Under Stress: Political Executives and Key Bureaucrats in Washington, London, and Ottawa.* Toronto: University of Toronto Press, 1983.

DUNLEAVY, PATRICK, and CHRISTOPHER T. HUSBANDS. *British Democracy at the Crossroads: Voting and Party Competition in the 1980s.* Winchester, MA: Allen & Unwin, 1985.

GRAY, ANDREW, and WILLIAM I. JENKINS. *Administrative Politics in British Government.* New York: St. Martin's, 1985.

HEATH, ANTHONY. *Understanding Political Change: The British Voter 1964–1987.* New York: Pergamon, 1991.

INGLE, STEPHEN. *The British Party System,* 2d ed. New York: Basil Blackwell, 1989.

JONES, BILL, and DENNIS KAVANAGH. *British Politics Today,* 5th ed. New York: St. Martin's, 1993.

JORDAN, A. G., and J. J. RICHARDSON. *Government and Pressure Groups in Britain.* New York: Oxford University Press, 1987.

KAVANAGH, DENNIS A. *Thatcherism and British Politics: The End of Consensus?* New York: Oxford University Press, 1987.

———, and PETER MORRIS. *Consensus Politics from Attlee to Thatcher.* Cambridge, MA: Basil Blackwell, 1989.

KING, ANTHONY, ed. *Britain at the Polls, 1992.* Chatham, NJ: Chatham House, 1992.

NORPOTH, HELMUT. *Confidence Regained: Economics, Mrs. Thatcher, and the British Voter.* Ann Arbor, MI: University of Michigan Press, 1992.

ROSE, RICHARD. *Ministers and Ministries: A Functional Analysis.* New York: Oxford University Press, 1987.

SEARING, DONALD. *Westminstger's World: Understanding Political Roles.* Cambridge, MA: Harvard University Press, 1994.

SEYD, PATRICK, and PAUL WHITELEY. *Labour's Grass Roots: The Politics of Party Membership.* New York: Oxford University Press, 1992.

TIVEY, LEONARD, and ANTHONY WRIGHT, eds. *Party Ideology in Britain.* New York: Routledge, 1989.

WILLIAMS, GEOFFREY LEE, and ALAN LEE WILLIAMS. *Labour's Decline and the Social Democrats' Fall.* New York: St. Martin's, 1989.

WATKINS, ALAN. *A Conservative Coup.* London: Duckworth, 1991.

CHAPTER 6

What Britons Quarrel About

The "British Disease"

Britain has been in economic decline for decades. At first it was only relative decline as the economies of West Europe and Japan grew more rapidly than that of the British. By the 1970s, however, Britain was suffering absolute decline that left people with lower living standards as inflation outstripped their wage increases. The first industrial nation was embarrassed to see Italy overtake it in per capita GDP in the 1980s. In Britain, deindustrialization seemed to be taking place; in some years the British GDP shrank. They called it the "British disease," and some Americans feared it was contagious.

Why did Britain decline? There are two basic approaches to such a complex problem. One begins with what happens in people's attitudes—a psycho-cultural approach. The other begins with what happens in the physical world—a politico-economic approach. The two are not mutually exclusive but have a chicken-egg relationship to each other: one feeds into the other.

Some writers put their emphasis on British nonwork attitudes as the root of the problem. The old feudal aristocracy, which disdained hard work as tawdry moneymaking, was never thoroughly displaced in Britain. Rather, the rising entrepreneurs tried to ape the old elite and become gentlemen of leisure and culture. In public schools and Oxbridge, young Britons learn to despise commercial and technical skills in favor of the humanities. The emphasis was on having wealth rather than creating it. Accordingly, Britain tended to lack daring and innovative capitalists. Many Britons prefer more leisure time to more money.

The British class system makes matters worse. British managers—mostly middle class—are snobbish toward workers; they do not mix with them or roll up their sleeves and get their hands dirty. British workers react by showing solidarity with their "mates" and more loyalty to their union than to their company. If the psycho-cultural approach is correct, the only way to save Britain is to change British attitudes. But deep-seated attitudes resist change.

The other approach, the politico-economic, argues that the bad attitudes are a reflection of faulty governmental policy. Change the policy so as to provide a new context, and attitudes will change. The Thatcherites are among the chief proponents of this view. The problem, they argue, is the growth of government, especially since Labour won with its socialistic program in 1945. The welfare state lets many consume without producing and subsidizes inefficient industries. Unions, given free rein by previous governments, raised wages and lowered productivity. The growing costs of the welfare state drain away funds that should be used for investment. Insufficient investment means insufficient production, which means stagnating living standards. Cut both welfare benefits and industry subsidies and you will force—with some pain—a change in attitudes.

The Thatcher Cure

The Thatcher cure for Britain's economic problems is still hotly debated in Britain. Thatcherites argue that her policies were not implemented thoroughly and long enough. Anti-Thatcherites in all the parties argue that the policies had been brutal and ineffective. The way Thatcherites see it, the permissive policies of both Labour and previous Conservative governments had expanded welfare programs beyond the country's ability to pay for them. Unions won wage increases that were entirely out

---

 "Pluralistic Stagnation"

Harvard political scientist Samuel Beer advanced a provocative thesis on the cause of Britain's decline: too many interest groups making too many demands on parties who are too willing to promise everyone everything. The result is "pluralistic stagnation" as British groups scramble for welfare benefits, pay hikes, and subsidies for industry. The two main parties bid against each other with promises of more benefits to more groups. In the late 1960s, a strong "counterculture" emerged in Britain, which wrecked traditional attitudes of civility and deference and made groups' demands more strident. With every group demanding and getting more, no one saw any reason for self-restraint that would leave them behind. It was as if everyone was looking jealously over

his shoulder to see what the other fellow was getting from the system. Government benefits fed union wage demands, which fed inflation, which fed government benefits. . . .

The interesting point about the Beer thesis is that it blames precisely what political scientists have long celebrated: pluralism, the autonomous interaction of society's many groups on themselves and on government. In U.S. political science especially, this is supposed to be a good thing, the foundation of freedom and democracy. Beer demonstrated, though, that it can run amok; groups block each other and government, leading to what Beer called the "paralysis of public choice." Any comparison with your system?

of line with productivity. Nationalized and subsidized industries were money-losers. The result: hefty inflation and falling production that were making Britain the sick man of Europe. The cure, in part, came from the "monetarist" theory of American economist (and Nobel Prize winner) Milton Friedman, who sees too-rapid growth of the money supply as the cause of inflation. Thatcher cut government bureaucracy, the growth of welfare, and subsidies to industry in an effort to control Britain's money supply and restore health to its economy.

Some Britons wondered if the cure wasn't worse than the disease. Unemployment at one point reached 14 percent of the work force, thousands of firms went bankrupt, and Britain's GDP growth was still anemic. Even moderate Conservatives pleaded for her to relent, but Thatcher wasn't called the Iron Lady for nothing. "The lady's not for turning," she intoned. She saw the economic difficulties as a purge Britain had to experience to get well. One of her economists said: "I don't shed tears when I see inefficient factories shut down. I rejoice." Thatcher and her supporters repeated endlessly, "You can't consume until you produce."

Gradually the argument began to take hold. Many Britons had to admit that they had been consuming more than they were producing, that subsidized factories and mines were a drain on the economy, and that bitter medicine was necessary to correct matters. It was almost as if Britons had become guilty at their free rides and knew they now had to pay up. Typically, now more working-class Britons vote Tory than vote Labour.

But did Thatchernomics work? By the time Thatcher left office in 1990 the picture was mixed. During the mid-1980s, inflation had been down and economic growth up. State-owned British Steel, British Leyland (motor vehicles), and other industries that had been nationalized since the war to prevent unemployment trimmed their bloated, inefficient work forces and raised productivity. Many state-owned plants were sold off, a process called "privatization." Renters of public housing got the chance to buy their homes at low cost, a move that made some of them Conservatives. Unions eased their wage and other demands, and total union membership dropped by three million, down to 35 percent of the work force. Many weak firms went under, but thousands of new small and middle-sized firms sprang up. Capital and labor were channeled away from losing industries and into winners, which is ex-

The Flip Side of the Welfare State

The other side of the welfare state is how expensive it is. In 1993, taxes took these percentages of GDP:

Denmark	50%	Germany	40%
France	44%	Canada	36%
Italy	43%	Britain	34%
		Japan	30%
		United States	30%

Source: OECD.

COMPARING

 The Productivity Race

No production, no goodies. Production is what gets turned out. Productivity is how efficiently it gets turned out. You can have a lot of production with low productivity, the Soviet problem that brought down the Communist regime. Among the major economies, Britain's productivity was weak. In 1991, French and West German manufacturing productivity was about 40 percent higher than British, Japanese about 50 percent higher, and U.S. about 70 percent higher. Small wonder Britain was poorer.

	1960–68	1968–73	1973–79	1979–90
Japan	9.0%	10.4%	5.0%	4.6%
France	6.8	5.8	3.9	2.4
Italy	7.2	5.6	2.9	1.6
West Germany	4.7	4.5	3.1	1.1
Belgium	4.9	8.2	5.0	4.7
Britain	3.4	3.9	0.6	4.3
United States	3.2	3.5	0.9	3.5

Source: OECD

The growth of productivity—the additional amount a worker cranks out per hour from one year to the next—is the measure of future prosperity. Rapid growth in productivity means quickly rising standards of living; low means stagnation or even decline. Taking an annual average during four time periods, we see some interesting changes in productivity in manufacturing.

Most of these countries had slower productivity growth in the last period as opposed to the first two. Some of this falloff is natural. Relatively-backward economies can, with only simple innovations, show big productivity gains. By the 1980s, though, most of the obvious productivity-boosting innovations had been introduced. But the two bottom countries in the 1960s, Britain and the United States, moved into the middle ranks of productivity growth in the 1980s. Many things happened to induce this turnaround; some were Thatcher's and Reagan's economic policies.

actly what a good economic system should do. A California-like computer industry produced a "silicon glen" in Scotland and a "software valley" around Cambridge University.

Part of the impact of Thatchernomics came from making workers genuinely worried about their jobs. Some were so scared they actually got to work. When the government's National Coal Board decided to close hundreds of unprofitable pits and eliminate twenty thousand jobs, miners staged a long and violent strike in 1984, which was supported by some other unionists. Thatcher would not back down; after a year, the miners did. New legislation was introduced, limiting union chiefs' abilities to call strikes, and most of the public—fed up with strike-happy union bosses—approved.

But the number of British families below the poverty line increased under Thatcher. High youth unemployment led to urban riots. Major regional disparities appeared between a rich, resurgent South of England, with new high-tech industries, and a decaying, abandoned North, where unemployment hit hardest. Thatcher never did get a handle on government spending, much of which, like U.S. "entitlements," must by law be paid. British welfare benefits actually climbed sharply during the Thatcher (and Major) years despite their best efforts to cut them. Cutting the welfare state is tempting but rarely successful; too many people have come to depend on its benefits. Furthermore, in the late 1980s, a credit and spending boom kicked inflation back up to over 10 percent, and the economy slumped into recession again. Competitively, British productivity was low and its wages high, so Britain continued to lose manufacturing jobs to other countries.

Thatcher's main legacy is that she changed the terms of Britain's political debate. In 1945, Labour had shifted the debate to the welfare state, and Tories had to compete with them on their own terms, never seriously challenging the underlying premise that welfare is good. Thatcher changed this all around and made the debate one about productivity and economic growth, and now Labour had to compete on *her* terms. It was a historic shift, and one that influenced the political debate in other lands, including the United States.

John Major inherited Thatcher's second recession, a lingering one that shot unemployment to over 10 percent. With welfare costs rising and his budget going

COMPARING

 ## *Thatchernomics and Reaganomics*

On two sides of the Atlantic, conservative chief executives implemented similar economic programs at about the same time. The main difference was that U.S. problems were not nearly as acute as Britain's, so President Reagan's policies didn't have to be as drastic and painful as Prime Minister Thatcher's. Further, Reagan won on personality, Thatcher on program, but the U.S.–British policy parallels are remarkable:

- Both attempted to cut the number of civilian government bureaucrats to save money and "deregulate" the economy. Neither succeeded.

- Both said they would follow Friedman's monetarist approach and tried to restrain growth of the money supply. The United States was more successful in this, under the stern eye of Federal Reserve Chairman Paul Volcker.

- During their first couple of years in office, both witnessed recession, heightened unemployment, and continued inflation; their policies seemed to have failed. But by 1983, both economies were showing improvement, with inflation down and productivity up.

- Both said they would cut welfare expenditures, but neither succeeded; welfare programs are too firmly entrenched in both lands. British welfare outlays actually climbed due to increased unemployment.

- Both met strong union resistance—Reagan faced air traffic controllers and postal workers, Thatcher coal miners—and both refused to back down. Their respective showdowns helped persuade unions to lower their demands, and this contributed to curbing inflation. Both were accused of "union busting," and union membership declined.

- Both said they would cut taxes. Reagan did, and this both stimulated economic recovery and brought massive deficits. In Britain, with its higher welfare costs, the tax burden actually grew during the Thatcher years.

- In both America and Britain, the poor got poorer and the rich got richer during the 1980s.

- Both deregulated banking too much. In the late 1980s, this led to speculative frenzies that produced the U.S. savings-and-loan fiasco and Britain's longest recession since the 1930s.

- Both changed the terms of political debate in their respective countries, putting welfare-minded Democrats and Labourites on the defensive and making people think about production instead of consumption. This was their greatest impact.

deeper into deficit, Major explored ways to shrink the welfare state. This will be difficult, as many middle-class Britons benefit from one program or another. Thatcher, when all was said and done, had largely left welfare benefits be. Fortunately for Major, the 1992 devaluation of the pound (which he had fought) made British products more competitive, and by 1993 Britain had the fastest growing economy in West Europe, the rest of which was still stuck in a nasty recession. Both inflation and unemployment were down, too. Major's chances of staying in office depend primarily on how well and quickly the economy recovers. As one former minister put it: "Never underestimate what economic recovery can do for an ailing leader."

Scottish and Welsh Nationalism

The United Kingdom has problems with its unity. In addition to the low-level civil war in Northern Ireland, Scotland and Wales present problems of regionalism. Wales has been a part of England since the Middle Ages; the thrones of England and Scotland were united in 1603, and in 1707 both countries agreed to a single Parliament in London. But old resentments never quite died. Wales and Scotland were always poorer than England, provoking the feeling among Welsh and Scots that they were economically exploited.

In the twentieth century the political beneficiary of these feelings has been the Labour party, which holds sway in Wales and Scotland. But in the 1960s the small Plaid Cymru (pronounced *plyde kum-REE*, meaning "Party of Wales") and the Scottish Nationalist party began to grow, and in the 1974 election the Welsh Nationalists won three Commons seats and the Scottish Nationalists eleven.

Local nationalism grew in many countries during the 1970s: Corsican and Breton in France, Quebecker in Canada, Basque and Catalan in Spain. It was hard to pinpoint the cause for this upsurge in local separatism. Economics plays a role; local nationalists usually claim their regions are shortchanged by their central governments. Nationalists often emphasize their regions' distinct languages and cultures and demand that they be taught in schools. Some of the impulse behind local nationalism is the bigness and remoteness of the modern state, the feeling that important decisions are out of local control, made by faraway bureaucrats. And often smoldering under the surface are historical resentments of a region that once was conquered, occupied, and deprived of its own identity. Whatever the mixture, local nationalism sometimes turns its adherents into fanatics willing to wreck the entire country to get their way. Happily, this did not happen in Britain. The Scots and Welsh never became as extreme as Basques in Spain or Corsicans in France.

In Scotland, the economic factor played a large part. When oil was discovered in the North Sea off Scotland in the 1960s, some Scots didn't want to share the petroleum revenues with the United Kingdom as a whole. "It's Scotland's oil!" cried the Scottish Nationalists whose electoral fortunes rose with the offshore discoveries. Oil offered Scotland the possibility of economic independence and self-government, of becoming something more than a poor, northerly part of Britain.

Wales had no oil (just coal), but it also felt economically exploited. Most important for Welsh nationalists, however, was language, the ancient Celtic tongue of Cymric (pronounced *kim-rick*). About one Welsh person in five still speaks Cymric, but most are elderly. In recent years, however, there has been an upsurge of people learning Welsh, and the language is now officially coequal with English within Wales. There is even a Welsh TV channel.

The Trouble with National Health

The centerpiece of Britain's extensive welfare state is the National Health Service, which went into operation in 1948 as part of Labour's longstanding commitment to improving the lot of working Britons. Before the war, British medical care was spotty. When millions were examined for military service during the war, many were scrawny and unhealthy. Conservatives and the British Medical Association fought the NHS, but the tide was against them.

Did the NHS work? The answer is both yes and no. The British population is much healthier than it used to be. Infant mortality, one key measure of overall health standards, dropped from 64 out of 1,000 live births in 1931 to 7.4 in 1991. The British working class has especially benefited.

But NHS has some negative aspects. Costs skyrocketed. The British population has become more elderly, and old people consume several times as much medical care as younger people. Technical advances in medicine work wonders, but they are terribly expensive. The system requires many bureaucrats. With a staff of one million, the NHS is the largest employer in West Europe, but personnel and facilities have not kept pace with demand. If surgery isn't an emergency, patients may wait years. Tens of thousands of Britons are on waiting lists for medical treatment.

The upshot is that private medical care quietly returned to Britain. Some three million families are willing to pay for speedy, personal, private medical insurance. Britain actually has a dual health system, one national, funded by taxes, and another private, funded by direct payment or private insurance. Labour's great effort to provide medical treatment for all has succeeded, but its efforts to eliminate class differences in medical treatment has failed.

The strategy of the Labour government of the 1970s was to offer home rule or autonomy to Scotland and Wales. This was called "devolution," the granting of certain governing powers by the center to the periphery. In 1977 Commons passed the Scotland and Wales Bills, which would have set up Scottish and Welsh assemblies and executives. These were to have powers over local affairs in much the same way that American states have, although it would be an exaggeration to equate devolution with American-style federalism.

The catch was that the devolution plans had to be approved in a referendum by 40 percent of all eligible Scottish and Welsh voters, a harder task than getting a simple majority. The Welsh plan was rejected by four Welsh voters out of five, and only 33 percent of Scots voted for their plan, short of the required 40 percent. Many Scottish and Welsh voters thought local nationalism was a nice romantic idea but impractical. Some feared it would just add another layer of bureaucracy. In the parliamentary elections of 1992, the Scot Nats won three seats and Plaid Cymru won four as Scotland and Wales stayed overwhelmingly Labour. Voting Labour in Scotland and Wales, in fact, has become a form of local nationalism, a way of repudiating rule by England, which goes almost totally Conservative. Devolution as a political plan was dead, but Scottish and Welsh resentments remain.

British Racism

British intellectuals, especially those on the left, used to criticize the United States for racism. Then the British left took to denouncing South Africa. That sort of thing,

Britishers used to say, could never happen in tolerant, civilized Britain. At least since the 1958 Notting Hill race riot in London, the English have had to face the fact that they, too, have a race problem and that there are no easy solutions to it.

The race problem in Britain is a legacy of empire. Britain in 1948 legally made the natives of its many colonies British "subjects," entitled to live and work in the United Kingdom. Although the colonies were granted independence in the 1950s and 1960s as members of the British Commonwealth—a loose organization of countries that call the queen their nominal sovereign—their people were still entitled to immigrate to Britain. In the 1950s, West Indians arrived from the Caribbean, then Indians and Pakistanis. Immigrants were willing to take the lowliest jobs that many Englishmen didn't want. Then they would send for their wives, children, fiancées, and cousins. Britain's immigrant population is now about 5 percent of Britain's total.

White resentment soon grew, especially among the working class, who believed the recent immigrants wanted their housing, jobs, wallets, and daughters. Britons began to discover they were racists, sometimes violent racists. In 1967 an openly racist National Front party formed, advocating the expulsion of all "coloreds" back to their native lands. Some National Front leaders had earlier been members of Britain's tiny Fascist party. Young toughs, some supporting the Front or the rival National party, went in for murderous "Paki bashing." With slogans such as "Rights for Whites," votes for the two small parties grew, although neither won a seat in Parliament. Meanwhile, the minute Trotskyist Socialist Workers party attacked racist rallies, and hundreds of police had to hold the two sides apart.

The British race question is not confined to the fringes of politics. Many ordinary Britons view the nonwhites as a social problem and would like them to return to their native lands, although by now many are born in Britain. Some of the swing to the Conservatives was attributed to Margaret Thatcher's call for a "clear end to immigration" before it "swamped" British culture.

In point of fact, immigration to Britain has been successively tightened by both parties since 1962 and has now become quite restrictive. Demographers say there is no chance the immigrants will swamp anything. But the question poses serious ethical dilemmas. The British gloried in their empire for more than a century; now they have responsibility for what they created. Particularly poignant was the situation of "Asians" (Indians and Pakistanis) in East Africa. Brought to Kenya and Uganda by the British decades ago as laborers, Asians soon became small business people and monopolized commercial life. Native Africans bitterly resented the Asians and applauded government policies to "Africanize" commerce—meaning kicking out the Indians and Pakistanis. The Asians pleaded to be let into Britain. With Hong Kong set to revert to Communist China in 1997, many residents of that British crown colony likewise plead to be let into Britain.

Britain and Europe

The British have never thought of themselves as Europeans. Indeed, most English people look down upon anyone from across the English Channel—even if their income is higher and their products better. Rather than working toward a united Europe after World War II, as the main Continental countries did, Britain emphasized its Commonwealth ties and its "special relationship" to the United States. London faced westward, across the Atlantic, rather than eastward, across the Channel.

What to Do with Ulster?

Northern Ireland is a major problem for Britain—Ulster's heavily subsidized economy and security costs Britain some £4 billion ($6 billion) a year—but not yet a major quarrel, for no one has yet offered a solution acceptable to all sides. Fewer than one Briton in three wants to keep Ulster, but none know how to get rid of the problem gracefully. A 1973 act of Parliament guarantees that Northern Ireland will never "cease to be part of the United Kingdom without the consent of the majority." This guarantee is one of the stumbling blocks to any solution, for a majority of Ulster voters—especially Protestants—will not easily consent to a sweeping change.

In 1993, at about the same time Israel began to talk with the Palestine Liberation Organization, the two main antagonists in Northern Ireland, along with the London and Dublin governments, began to talk with each other. Horrifyingly, the mere fact that they began to talk increased the number of random killings by both sides. (The same thing happened in Israel.) The four sides in the Ulster question—the IRA, the Protestant Ulster Unionists, and the British and Irish governments—discussed their very limited number of options:

- **Reunification** with Eire, possibly under a federal setup that would leave Ulster with local autonomy. Unification is exactly what Irish nationalists have been demanding for decades, but Orangemen won't hear of it, and they have veto power.
- **Independence** for Ulster, making it a separate country. Protestant extremists have suggested this as a last-ditch option to prevent unification,

but Catholics would balk, and full-scale civil war might break out.

- **Devolution**, or home rule, as was proposed for Scotland and Wales. Let them manage their own affairs, says this option. But Ulster already had home rule, and it made things worse. From 1921 to 1972 Ulster had its own parliament at Stormont, but its Protestant majority disenfranchised and ignored Catholics. In 1972 the Stormont parliament was suspended and London began "direct rule."
- **Integration** with Britain. Ulster has an anomalous "provincial" status within the United Kingdom. Why not make it the same as Yorkshire? But Ulster Catholics don't like the idea as it would give Protestants power, and Protestants don't like it because they would lose their local autonomy.
- **Consultation** between London and Dublin on Ulster. A 1985 agreement gave the Irish government a small say in Northern Ireland's internal problems. Eire's role was consultative and largely symbolic, but Ulster Protestants raged that this was the first step of selling them out.

Could it be that there is no more a solution for Northern Ireland than there is for Bosnia? A majority of Ulstermen want peace, but it takes only a few militant, armed extremists on both sides to stir up hatred and block any peace. The IRA's 1994 move to talk instead of shoot led many Britons to hope that a settlement was possible.

Rather than signing the 1957 Treaty of Rome, which set up the European Community (EC), Britain in 1960 built a much looser grouping known as the European Free Trade Association (EFTA). While the EC Six (France, West Germany, Italy, Belgium, Netherlands, Luxembourg) surged ahead economically, the EFTA Outer Seven (Britain, Austria, Denmark, Finland, Iceland, Norway, Portugal, Sweden, and Switzerland) found themselves slowly cut off from the main European market. In 1963, Britain applied to get into the Common Market. French President Charles de Gaulle vetoed British entry, charging that Britain was still too tied to the Commonwealth and the United States to be a good European. He was right.

By the time de Gaulle resigned in 1969, Britain was again ready to join the EC, but there were domestic political complications. Not all Britons liked the idea. For old Conservatives it meant giving up a little bit of British sovereignty to the EC headquarters in Brussels and even treating Europeans as equals. For everyone it meant higher food prices. For manufacturers it meant British products would have to compete with possibly better and cheaper Continental imports that would come in tariff-free. For fishermen it meant British fishing areas would be open to all Common Market fishermen. For workers it meant possible unemployment. In short, many Britons were frightened of change and competition.

The arguments in favor of joining stressed that Britain needed change and competition, the very forces that had invigorated European industries. Further, geographically, strategically, economically, even spiritually, Britain really was a part of Europe and should start acting like it. Britain was no longer a great empire and could not stand on its own; the "special relationship" with the United States was unreliable and made Britain into a U.S. dependency.

The Common Market debate cut across party lines, sometimes producing a strange coalition of right-wing Tories and left-wing Labourites, each opposing EC entry for their own reasons. In general, however, Conservatives were pro-Market; Labour, anti-Market. In 1971, under a Tory government, the Commons voted 356 to 244 to join; 69 Labour MPs defied their party whip to vote in favor while 39 Conservatives, freed from party discipline, voted "no" along with Labour. The vote graphically demonstrated that British party discipline is not perfect. On January 1, 1973, Britain, along with Denmark and Ireland, made the Common Market Six, the Nine.

When Labour returned to power, Prime Minister Harold Wilson offered the British public a first—a referendum. Referendums—mass votes on issues rather than on candidates—are quite common in France, but Britain, with its tradition of parliamentary supremacy, had never held one before. The 1975 British referendum on the Common Market found that most Britons wanted to stay in Europe, but one-third voted no.

Thatcher, a British nationalist and "Euro-sceptic," took a tough line on the EC. A common market was fine, she argued, but not turning it into a supranational entity that would infringe on Britain's sovereignty. Her sticking point came with the introduction of the European Monetary System (EMS) that attempted to link currencies and eventually produce a single currency, the European Currency Unit, the *ecu*. That would indeed take away an important part of sovereignty, the ability of each country to control its currency, and give it to the EC authorities in Brussels. Thatcher (and some other Europeans) feared that Europe's strongest economy, Germany's, would dominate the EMS and that policy on money supply and interest rates would be set by the Bundesbank. Actually, this is exactly what happened, but some of Thatcher's own Tories disliked her anti-EC stance and helped dump her because of it. The Conservatives are still bitterly divided over Europe.

Symbolically, at almost the same time Major took over, British and French crews broke through to link Britain to the Continent through their tunnel under the English Channel. This was fitting, for John Major was more pro-European than Thatcher. Major therefore suffered humiliation when he had to devalue the pound in 1992 in the midst of speculation against the pound and in favor of the D-mark, exactly what Thatcher warned about. Next year Major led the divided Tories to ratify the controversial Maastricht agreement to move the EC to a higher stage, that of the European Union (EU). Plainly, Britain is now part of Europe. The question now becomes, "How deeply should Britain submerge itself into Europe?" This quarrel cuts across all three leading parties, although it is probably safe to say that most Britons are on the Euro-sceptical side.

Great Britain or Little England?

This sums up the dilemma of modern Britain: the problem of scaling down its vision of itself. Britain in the course of a century has clearly declined, both internationally and domestically. When Britain was a mighty empire and the most industrialized country in the world, it had power, wealth, and a sense of mission. This in turn fostered order, discipline, and deference among the British people. Losing its empire and slipping down to become one of the weaker economies of West Europe, decay, violence, and resentment appeared.

Britain offers a refutation to the idea that progress is unilinear—onward ever, backward never. On the contrary, in the case of Britain we see that what goes up can eventually come down. But this process is never static. Now that Britain is adjusting to its new reality—as one European country among many—regeneration has begun. To see how another country has turned around, how a society and economy can change from static to dynamic, let us now consider France.

Britain's Education Dilemma

One limit to sustained British economic growth is poor educational levels. Britain's "human capital" does not compare favorably with Europe or America. In the United States, Japan, and West Germany, the number of 18-year-olds in full-time education is over 80 percent, in France nearly 70 percent, but in Britain less than 35 percent. In a comparative science test of 14-year-olds, Britain (and the United States) came in near the bottom. (The winners: Hungary and Japan.) Like many Americans, millions of adult Britons have trouble reading and doing basic math. The Nissan car factory in Britain found that seven out of ten job applicants could not pass its verbal-reasoning test.

The problem stems from Britain's overconcentration on its top students and neglect of everyone else. Britain's brainiest test their way to fine univerisities, where they get very good and nearly free educations. The others in secondary school, who fear they will not pass the demanding college-prep exams (the A-levels) might as well

drop out. And they do: close to two out of three young Britons (including young John Major) leave school as soon as they can. There are few German-style apprentice programs or U.S.–type community colleges to impart job skills to British school-leavers. The result is a serious shortage of skilled technicians and foremen. This takes its toll on productivity. Using the exact same automated equipment, British workers produce 40 percent less than Japanese workers.

Thatcher, with her emphasis on excellence, largely neglected the problem of the school-leavers. A variety of public-private and school-business partnerships have been tried to teach them job skills; none has been very successful (except in Scotland). The result has been the growth of a U.S.–style underclass of seemingly permanently disadvantaged people. One solution being offered: City Technology Colleges in inner cities. The real problem with British education traces back to a snobbish, class-ridden society, and it will be awfully hard to change that.

Vocabulary Building

absolute decline	National Health Service
British disease	periphery
devolution	privatization
EC	productivity
ecu	referendum
EFTA	relative decline
EMS	unilinear
monetarism	

Further Reference

BARNETT, CORRELLI. *The Pride and the Fall: The Dream and Illusion of Britain as a Great Nation.* New York: Free Press, 1987.

BEER, SAMUEL H. *Britain Against Itself: The Political Contradictions of Collectivism.* New York: W. W. Norton, 1982.

EDWARDS, BRIAN. *The National Health Service: A Manager's Tale.* London: Nuffield Provincial Hospitals Trust, 1993.

GAMBLE, ANDREW. *Britain in Decline: Economic Policy, Political Strategy and the British State,* 3d ed. New York: St. Martin's, 1990.

GEELHOED, E. BRUCE. *Margaret Thatcher: In Victory and Downfall, 1987 and 1990.* Westport, CT: Praeger, 1992.

GRAY, JOHN. *Beyond the New Right.* New York: Routledge, 1993.

JENKINS, PETER. *Mrs. Thatcher's Revolution: The Ending of the Socialist Era.* Cambridge, MA: Harvard University Press, 1988.

KRIEGER, JOEL. *Reagan, Thatcher, and the Politics of Decline.* New York: Oxford University Press, 1987.

LEYS, COLIN. *Politics in Britain: From Labourism to Thatcherism.* New York: Verso, 1989.

McGARRY, JOHN, and BRENDAN O'LEARY, eds. *The Future of Northern Ireland.* New York: Oxford University Press, 1991.

RIDDELL, PETER. *The Thatcher Decade: How Britain Has Changed During the 1980s.* Cambridge, MA: Basil Blackwell, 1989.

RUBINSTEIN, W. D. *Capitalism, Culture and Decline in Britain: 1750–1990.* New York: Routledge, 1993.

SOLOMOS, JOHN. *Race and Racism in Contemporary Britain.* New York: Macmillan, 1989.

THATCHER, MARGARET. *The Downing Street Years.* New York: HarperCollins, 1993.

YOUNG, JOHN W. *Britain and European Unity, 1945–1992.* New York: St. Martin's, 1993.

7

France: The Impact of the Past

The Split Hexagon

"France has everything," the French like to boast. They are nearly right. Roughly the shape of a hexagon, with three sides on seas and three on land, France is simultaneously an Atlantic country, a Mediterranean country, and an alpine country. It has lush farmland, navigable rivers, many minerals, and a moderate climate. It does not, however, have the safety of England's moat. France is vulnerable to land attack from the north and east. While England historically did well without standing armies, France needed large armies, a point that helps explain the rise of French absolutism. French kings had their troops to rely on.

Internally, France is divided into a North and a South. Culturally and temperamentally the two regions are rather different and until the late Middle Ages even spoke different languages. The Germanic northerners spoke *langue d'oïl*, "the tongue of *oïl*," their word for yes, which grew into the modern French *oui*. The Mediterranean southerners spoke *langue d'oc*, after their word for yes, *oc*. It declined after the Paris kings conquered the South in the thirteenth century. To this day, southerners may speak with a different accent and resent the region's subjugation to Paris.

The Roman Influence

Like most peoples, the French are a mixture of ethnic stocks. In the centuries before Christ, tribes of Celts pushed into France and merged with the native Ligurians. The Romans conquered the area and called it Gallia (Gaul). The Roman influence in France was longer and deeper than in England. The Anglo-Saxons obliterated England's Roman influence, but the Germanic tribes that moved into Gaul became Romanized themselves. Thus English is a Germanic language and France a Romance language.

By the time the Roman Empire collapsed, one Germanic tribe had managed to take over most of present-day France; these were the Franks. Their chief, Clovis—from whom came the name Louis—was baptized in 496, and France has been mostly Catholic ever since, the "eldest daughter of the Church." The Franks under Charles Martel turned back the invading Moors in 732, possibly saving Christianity in Europe. Charles Martel's grandson, Charlemagne, carved out a gigantic kingdom—the Holy Roman Empire—that encompassed what someday would amount to most of the six original Common Market countries. Although the empire soon disintegrated, Charlemagne had planted the idea of European unity.

The Rise of French Absolutism

In the confusion that followed Charlemagne, France was reduced to several petty kingdoms and dukedoms, as was Germany. While Germany stayed divided until the nineteenth century, French kings pursued unification and centralization of their power with single-minded determination. Pushing outward from the Paris area, the *Ile de France* (Island of France), the Capetian kings added territory while retaining control in Paris.

Feudalism in France began to give way to absolutism with Louis (pronounced *Lwie*) XI, who ruled from 1461 to 1483. The crafty Louis XI doubled the size of France until it was nearly its present shape, weakened the power of the feudal nobles, ignored the Estates-General (the parliament), and developed a royal bureaucracy to increase taxation. It was a pattern that was to be strengthened for at least three centuries, leaving the France of today still highly centralized. Louis XI also cultivated relations with Rome. There was never an English-style break with the Vatican; instead the Catholic church became a pillar of the French monarchy.

Under Louis XIII, Cardinal Richelieu became chief minister and virtual ruler from 1624 to 1642. Obsessed with French power and glory, Richelieu further weakened the nobles, recruited only middle-class bureaucrats, and sent out *intendants* to control the provinces for Paris. Richelieu was an organizational genius who put his bureaucratic stamp on France for all time.

The French nobles did try to fight back, but they lost. In 1648 and again in 1650 some French aristocrats staged an uncoordinated revolt called the *Fronde.* Recall that at this time English nobles and their commoner allies beheaded a king who tried to act like an absolute monarch. In France, the nobles were quickly broken and lost the autonomy enjoyed by English lords.

Louis XIV: The High Point of Absolutism

By the time Louis XIV became king in 1661, French absolutism was already well developed; he brought it to a high point. Louis's emblem was the sun, around which

Great French Expressions: "Paris Is Worth a Mass"

During the Reformation, French Protestants, called Huguenots, were controlled, massacred, and driven into exile. In 1589, however, the royal line of succession fell to a Huguenot, Henry of Navarre. The French Roman Catholic church, horrified at the thought of a non-Catholic king, offered the throne to Henry only if he would convert to Catholicism. In what has become a model of opportunism, Henry shrugged and said, "Paris is worth a Mass." The new convert became Henry IV, an excellent king and founder of the Bourbon dynasty (which still reigns in Spain).

all things revolved. The "Sun King" further increased centralization and bureaucratization, all aimed at augmenting his own and France's power. Louis used his large army in almost continual warfare. He acted as his own prime minister and handled much administration personally. He never bothered convening the Estates-General. He constructed the gigantic Versailles palace and made thousands of nobles live there, diverting them from power seeking to game playing—games of intrigue, love, and flattery. While English lords ruled as small kings on their estates, French nobles were reduced to courtiers.

Louis's policies of "war and magnificence" were terrible financial drains. To harness the French economy to serve the state, Louis's minister, Colbert, practiced "mercantilism," the theory that a nation was as wealthy as the amount of gold it possessed and that the way to amass gold was for the government to supervise the economy with plans, subsidies, monopolies, and tariffs. This helped set a pattern found in most European countries and in Japan: Instead of purely free-market economics, the government is expected to play a helping role.

Louis XIV was an able monarch who impressed all of Europe. Other kings tried to imitate him, and French cuisine, architecture, dress, and language dominated the Continent. From the outside, the France of Louis XIV looked more impressive than England. Without "checks and balances" to get in the way, the centralized monarchy of France was able to accomplish great things. But the English, by slowly developing political participation, had actually devised a more stable system.

Why the French Revolution?

For all its external splendor, France in the eighteenth century was in difficulties. Its treasury was often near bankruptcy. Especially costly was French support for the American colonists against Britain; the French did it more for revenge than for love of liberty. The bureaucracy was corrupt and inefficient. Recognizing too late that mercantilism was bad economics, the regime tried to move to a free market, but by then French industry and agriculture had become used to state protection and objected. Also important was the spread of new ideas on "liberty," "consent of the governed," and "the general will." Ideas can be dynamite, and great thinkers expounded ideas that undermined the *ancien régime* (old regime).

As Alexis de Tocqueville pointed out, revolutions seldom start when things are bad but, rather, when they are getting better. The French people enjoyed improving economic conditions for most of the eighteenth century, but that increased expectations and awakened jealousies toward people who were getting richer faster. As we saw in Iran under the shah, economic growth can be highly destabilizing. Further, Louis XVI had decided to reform the political system and provide for some kind of representation. But as we shall see in Russia and South Africa, the reforming of an unjust and unpopular system is extraordinarily difficult, a bit like taking the lid off a pressure cooker under full steam.

In the spring of 1789, Louis XVI convened the Estates-General for the first time since 1614. Its three estates—the clergy, nobility, and commoners—were elected by nearly universal suffrage. The Third Estate, commoners, demanded that all three houses meet together, meaning that the more numerous Third Estate could override the conservative First and Second Estates. The Third Estate argued that it represented the popular will, but Louis resisted. By the time he gave in, many parliamentarians were angry and radicalized and voted themselves into a National Assembly, which is the name for the present legislature.

Shortly afterward, the common people of Paris, who hated the haughty queen and were furious over rising bread prices, stormed the Bastille, an old and nearly unused jail, on July 14, 1789. Bastille Day became the French national day. Upon hearing of the Bastille the king exclaimed, "*C'est une révolte,*" meaning something that could be put down. A duke corrected him: "*Non, Sire, c'est une révolution.*" It was the first modern usage of the word *revolution*.

From Freedom to Tyranny

In 1791 the National Assembly constructed a constitutional monarchy, and if things had stopped there, the French Revolution might have resembled the English Revolution of a century earlier. But the French constitutional monarchy was undermined

Great French Expressions: "L'état, c'est moi"

"The state—that's me," Louis XIV is often quoted as saying. While there is no record that he actually uttered these exact words, there is ample evidence that he lived them.

Great French Expressions: "Let Them Eat Cake"

One reason that the French monarchy of Louis XVI was unpopular with the common people was the frivolous and extravagant Austrian-born queen, Marie Antoinette. She was said to have once inquired why there had been riots and was told it was because the people had no bread. "No bread?" she tittered. "Then let them eat cake." Marie Antoinette may have never said these words—they were written earlier by Rousseau—but the masses hated her for her arrogant, uncaring attitude. She was guillotined in 1793 a few months after the execution of her husband, Louis XVI.

from two sides, from the king and some aristocrats who wanted to restore absolute power and from a militant faction known as the Jacobins, who wanted a thorough revolution. The king was found to be conspiring with foreign monarchs to invade France and restore him to full power. And the attempted invasion of 1792 helped the Jacobins take over. With a makeshift but enthusiastic citizen army—"the nation in arms"—they repelled the invaders at Valmy.

Power fell into the hands of the misnamed Committee of Public Safety under Maximilien Robespierre, a provincial lawyer and fanatic follower of Rousseau who was determined to "force men to be free." Instituting the Reign of Terror, Robespierre and his followers guillotined more than twenty thousand people, starting with the king, queen, and nobles but soon spreading to anyone who doubted Robespierre. Finally, in 1794, Robespierre's comrades, afraid they might be next, guillotined *him*, and the Terror came to an end.

During all this turmoil, the army became more important, and especially one young artillery officer, the Corsican Napoleon Bonaparte, who had won fame leading French armies in Italy and Egypt. In 1799 a *coup d'état* overthrew the weak civilian Directory and set up a Consulate with Bonaparte as First Consul. Brilliant in both battle and civil reform, Napoleon crowned himself emperor in 1804.

Above all, Napoleon loved war. As Henry Kissinger pointed out, a revolutionary power like France in the midst of hostile conservative monarchies can feel secure only by conquering all its neighbors. Napoleon made France master of all Europe, using dashing tactics and an enthusiastic army to crush one foe after another until at last they went too far. Facing a British-led coalition, harassed by guerrilla warfare in Spain, and frozen in the Russian winter, Napoleon was defeated and exiled to the Mediterranean island of Elba in 1814. The next year he tried a comeback and thousands of his old soldiers rallied around him to fight at Waterloo and lose.

Napoleon left an ambiguous legacy. While he claimed to be consolidating the Revolution, he actually set up a tyrannical police state. Trying to embody Rousseau's elusive general will, Napoleon held several plebiscites, which he always won. Napoleon was not just a historic accident, though, for we shall see similar figures emerging in French politics. When a society is badly split, as France was over

Three French Geniuses: Voltaire, Montesquieu, Rousseau

Each in his own way, these three eighteenth-century thinkers helped persuade a good portion of Frenchmen—especially middle-class intellectuals—that the *ancien régime* was rotten and that it was possible to construct a better system. Their common weapon was reason—abstract, Cartesian, logical—in contrast to English thinkers, who relied more on empirical reality. The French dislike reality for failing to live up to their logical constructs, an approach that lends itself to radicalism.

Voltaire (1694–1778) was the epitome of the Enlightenment, doubting and ridiculing everything stupid he saw around him, of which there was plenty. His number one target: the Catholic church, which he saw as intolerant, irrational, and hypocritical. Voltaire's phrase, *"Ecrasez l'infáme"* (*"crush the infamous thing"*—meaning the Catholic church), became a rallying cry for anticlericalists—people opposed to Roman Catholic influence in society and politics—and spread through most of the Catholic countries of Europe.

The Baron de Montesquieu (1689–1755) traveled all over Europe to gather material for one of the first books of comparative politics, *The Spirit of the Laws*. Montesquieu, like Voltaire, was especially impressed with English liberties, which he thought resulted from the "checks and balances" of the different parts of their government. Montesquieu was actually describing an idealized model of an English system that had already passed into history, but the

American Founding Fathers read him literally. Montesquieu's book suggested that countries could more or less rationally choose their governmental institutions. The French have been choosing and discarding them ever since.

Jean-Jacques Rousseau (1712–78), who was born in Geneva but lived mostly in France, was the most complex and some say the most dangerous of these thinkers. Rousseau hypothesized man in his original "state of nature" as free, happy, and morally good. What ruined him? Society was the culprit, corrupting man with private property, which leads to inequality and jealousy. Rousseau, in a famous phrase at the beginning of his book *The Social Contract*, said: "Man is born free but everywhere he is in chains." How can man be saved? Rousseau further hypothesized that beneath all the individual, petty viewpoints in society there is a "general will" for the common good. This general will could be discovered and implemented even though some people might object; they would be "forced to be free." Critics of Rousseau charge that he laid the intellectual basis for both Nazism and communism in his theory of the general will because it provided dictators with the rationale that they "really know" what the people want and need.

The French political thinkers tended to call for major, sweeping change; English thinkers, for slow, cautious change. The French thinkers fundamentally hated their government; the English didn't.

the Revolution, power tends to gravitate into the hands of a savior, and democracy doesn't have a chance.

The Bourbon Restoration

Europe breathed a sigh of relief once Napoleon was packed off to a remote island in the South Atlantic and the brother of Louis XVI was restored to the French throne as Louis XVIII. In what was called the Bourbon Restoration, exiles from all over Europe returned to France to try to claim their old rights.

A Tale of Two Flags

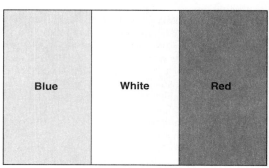

| Blue | White | Red |

The Bourbon flag (left) had been blue and white with a fleur-de-lis (iris) in the center. The Revolution introduced the tricolor of blue, white, and red (right).

The post-Napoleon restoration, in turn, brought back the old flag, for the tricolor symbolized everything the Bourbons hated. In 1830, the Orleanist monarchy, to mollify revolutionary sentiment, resurrected the tricolor, which has been France's flag ever since.

The France they found was badly split. Most aristocrats hated the Revolution, while most commoners supported at least a version of it. The Catholic church was reactionary, for the Revolution had confiscated church lands and ended its fiscal privileges. French Catholics for generations hated the anticlericalist republicans and democrats, who in turn mistrusted the church. Remnants of the clerical-anticlerical split persist to this day. But France had also changed quite a lot in the quarter-century since the Revolution. Parliaments now counted for something; kings could no longer rule without them. The civil reforms of Napoleon were preserved. People insisted on equality before the law.

At first the French, tired from constant upheaval and warfare, accepted the Bourbons. But by 1830 the Bourbons proved to be as pig-headed as ever, and rioting broke out. In a semilegal switch, the liberal Duc d'Orleans, Louis-Phillipe, replaced the last Bourbon ruler, Charles X. He, too, proved inept, and a small uprising in that revolutionary year of 1848 brought in the Second Republic. This didn't last long either.

The French have historically tended to turn from tumultuous democracy to authoritarian rule. In 1848 they overwhelmingly elected Napoleon's self-proclaimed nephew, Louis Napoleon, as president. Using plebiscites, in 1852 he turned the Second Republic into the Second Empire with himself as Emperor Napoleon III. This brought two decades of peace and progress until Louis Napoleon allowed himself to be goaded into war with Prussia in 1870. Bursting with overconfidence, the French were quickly trounced. The Germans sur-

The Original Chauvinist

The original chauvinist was Nicolas Chauvin (pronounced *show-VAN*), a possibly fictitious Napoleonic soldier, who was so rabidly nationalistic his name became synonymous with blind patriotic fervor. The French Revolution and Napoleonic wars unleashed the concept of nationalism all over Europe.

rounded Paris and shelled it daily, but there was no French government that could surrender. In Paris itself, a revolutionary takeover by workers brought the short-lived Paris Commune, which conservative French troops crushed, killing some twenty thousand Parisians. Karl Marx mistakenly saw the Commune as the first proletarian uprising, and among leftists the Commune grew into a legend of worker power.

The Third Republic

Amidst near anarchy, the Third Republic was born. It was a republic not because its founders were enthusiastic republicans—they were mostly monarchists—but because they couldn't agree on a monarch. Their first task was a humiliating peace with Germany that cost France the province of Alsace (which has many German-speaking people) plus a billion dollars in gold. The enraged French ached for revenge and transferred their traditional hatred of Britain to Germany.

Curiously, the accidental Third Republic turned out to be the longest-lasting French regime since the *ancien régime*. The Third Republic was basically fairly conservative and bourgeois. France was not healed during its long tenure; indeed, social tensions mounted. A reactionary Catholic right dreamed of an authoritarian system, while the left organized Socialist and later Communist parties. Economic and population growth was slow, and France slipped further behind the rapidly growing Germany.

Still, the Third Republic staggered through the ordeal of World War I. At first the French were delighted with a chance for revenge against Germany, but soon the appalling losses—a million and a half French lives—turned France bitter and defeatist even though they were on the winning side. France regained Alsace but had no stomach to fight again.

The defeatism played right into the hands of Nazi Germany, which swept easily through France in May–June 1940. Only one French unit fought well, a tank column commanded by an obscure colonel named de Gaulle, who had been warning for years of the need to develop a better French armored force. The French thought they could prevent a repetition of the World War I bloodshed by hiding behind the Maginot Line, a supposedly invulnerable network of tunnels facing Germany. But fixed defenses can't move; the Germans simply went around them on the north.

A Theory of Revolution

The great Harvard historian Crane Brinton in 1938 published *The Anatomy of Revolution*, which argued that all revolutions pass through similar stages. He compared several revolutions, but his main model was the French. Brinton's stages:

- The old regime loses its governing effectiveness and legitimacy. It becomes inept and indecisive. Intellectuals especially become alienated from it. An improving economy provokes discontent and jealousy.
- The first stage of revolution comes with the growth of antiregime groups. Triggering the revolution is a political problem—such as whether the three estates should meet separately or together—that the old regime can't handle. Rioting breaks out, but troops sent to crush it desert to the rioters. The antiregime people easily take over power amidst popular rejoicing.
- Moderates initially seize power. They opposed the old regime but as critics rather than as revolutionaries. They want major reform rather than total revolution. Extremists accuse them of being weak and cowardly, and true enough, they are not ruthless enough to crush the extremists.

- Extremists take over because they are more ruthless, purposeful, and organized than the moderates. In what Brinton likened to a high fever during an illness, the extremists whip up revolution to a frenzy, throwing out everything old, forcing people to be good, and punishing real or imagined enemies in a reign of terror. In France, this stage came with Robespierre; in Iran, with Khomeini.
- A "Thermidor," or calming-down period, ends the reign of terror. Brinton named Thermidor after the French revolutionary month—the revolutionaries even devised a new calendar—in which Robespierre fell. Every revolution has a Thermidor, which Brinton likened to a convalescence after a fever, because human nature can't take the extremists and their revolutionary purity for too long. Power usually then falls into the hands of a dictator, who restores order but not liberty—a Napoleon.

Brinton's theory became a classic and has largely stood the test of time. Revolutions do seem to pass through stages, although their timing cannot be predicted with accuracy. Iran, for example, has followed the Brinton pattern.

Vichy: France Splits Again

The Germans largely let the French run occupied France. Named after the town of Vichy in central France where it was set up, the Vichy government was staffed by the same sort of reactionaries who earlier had reviled Dreyfus, people who hated democracy and admired the authoritarian Germans. The aged Marshal Pétain, hero of World War I, became chief of state, and an opportunistic politician, Pierre Laval, became premier without benefit of elections. Many French thought Vichy was an improvement over the Third Republic which had permitted a left coalition, the Popular Front, to come to power in 1936. "Better the Nazis than the Communists," muttered Vichy supporters. French SS units fought in Russia. French police rounded up Jews for deportation to death camps. French workers volunteered to work in Germany. Although most French people today are loathe to admit it, many collaborated with the Germans and even liked them.

Great French Expressions: "They Learned Nothing and They Forgot Nothing"

Frenchmen who favored the Revolution considered the Bourbons arrogant fools. When the Bourbons and their aristocratic helpers returned with the Restoration, some Frenchmen said they were as bad as ever, that they had learned nothing from the revolutionary upheaval and had forgotten none of their old privileges. A related expression: *Quand Dieu a voulu punir la France, il a fait retirer les Bourbons.* ("When God wanted to punish France, he brought back the Bourbons.")

Other French, however, hated the Germans and Vichy. Some joined the *Résistance*, a loosely knit underground network that sabotaged and spied on the Germans, rescued British and American airmen, and occasionally killed collaborators. Again France split. The Vichy period was, in the words of political scientist Stanley Hoffmann, "a Franco-French war."

The Resistance attracted French people of many political persuasions, but the left predominated. The Communists, who refused to attack Germans until the 1941 invasion of Russia, became the most effective *maquisards* (underground fighters) and emerged from the war with prestige and a good organization. The rallying point of the Resistance was Charles de Gaulle (promoted to general in the last days of the Third Republic), who broadcast from London: "France has lost a battle. But France has not lost the war!" Organizing French-speaking people around the world—France had sizable colonies, and thousands of able-bodied men fled from France—de Gaulle declared a provisional government comprised of "Free French" expatriates. Participating in military action in North Africa, the Normandy landings, and the liberation of Paris in 1944, the Free French Army was of considerable help to the Allies. During the war de Gaulle came to think of himself as the savior of France, a modern Joan of Arc.

The Fourth Republic

From 1944 to early 1946, de Gaulle headed a provisional government. A newly elected constituent assembly, dominated by parties of the left, drafted a constitution for the Fourth Republic that gave great power to the legislative branch. De Gaulle opposed the new constitution and resigned with the warning that the Fourth Republic would have the same institutional weaknesses as the Third. He retired to the small town of Colombey-les-Deux-Eglises, not to return to power until the people called him back to save France again late in the next decade.

He was right about the Fourth Republic resembling the Third: From its inception the Fourth was plagued by a weak executive, a National Assembly paralyzed by small squabbling parties, and frequent changes of cabinet. The result was, as before, *immobilisme*, the inability to solve big problems. Politicians played games with each other; they were good at wrecking but not at building.

The Dreyfus Affair

Nothing better illustrates the deep division of French society in the late nineteenth century than the trial of Captain Alfred Dreyfus, a Jewish officer on the French general staff. In 1894, accused of selling secrets to the Germans, Dreyfus was given a rigged military trial with fake evidence and sent to the infamous penal colony of Devil's Island for life. It soon became clear that Dreyfus could not possibly have been the culprit; he had been chosen by the bigoted military simply because he was a Jew, a handy scapegoat.

France split in two. Those defending Dreyfus—the *Dreyfusards*—felt they were defending the republican traditions of equality. These tended to be people on the left. Novelist Emile Zola published his famous letter *J'accuse!* (I accuse!), charging the government with covering up for the military. The *Antidreyfusards*—reactionary aristocrats, army officers, fanatic Catholics, and anti-Semites—grew equally passionate in defense of their prerevolutionary values. Virtually all French people took one side or the other; there was even street fighting.

Finally, in 1906, Dreyfus was exonerated. But his trial had left deep scars. It showed how underneath the beautiful, civilized veneer of *belle époque* France lurked the primitive passions of reaction and anti-Semitism. The lesson was not lost on one Viennese journalist covering the trial. Theodore Herzl was so shocked by the anti-Semitism he had seen in France that he immediately organized a world Zionist movement to save Jews from what he feared would be other, similar outbursts.

Still, like the Third Republic, the Fourth might have endured had it not been for the terrible problems of decolonization, problems the fractious parliamentarians could not solve. The first problem was Indochina, a French colony for nearly a century that was occupied by the Japanese in World War II and then reclaimed by France. War with the Communist-led Viet Minh broke out in 1946 and dragged on until the fall of the French fortress of Dienbienphu in 1954. (The United States came close to jumping into the Vietnam conflict that year but backed off.)

The Indochina War was bad for France, but Algeria was worse. The French had been there since 1830, at first to vanquish pirates but later to settle. Close to a million Europeans dominated Algerian economic, social, and political life; Algeria was even declared a part of France. The revolt of Algerian nationalists started in 1956 with urban terrorism. This time the French army was determined to win. They hunted down nationalists and tortured them. When the civilian politicians in Paris started opposing the Algerian War, the French army in Algeria began a *coup d'état* in 1958. Paratroopers were ready to drop on their own country; France tottered on the brink of civil war. At the last minute both sides agreed to call back General de Gaulle. The army assumed he would keep Algeria French. (He didn't.) De Gaulle, acting as if he had known all along that history would recall him to lead France, demanded as his price a totally new constitution, one that would cure the ills of the Fourth Republic. He got it. In the next chapter, we will explore the institutions of France's Fifth Republic.

Vocabulary Building

ancien régime	chauvinist	Huguenots	Reign of Terror
anticlericalism	collaborator	*immobilisme*	Resistance
authoritarian	Commune	*intendants*	Restoration
Bastille	*coup d'état*	Jacobins	Sun King
belle époque	decolonization	*maquisards*	Thermidor
Bourbon	Dreyfus Affair	mercantilism	Third Estate
bourgeois	Estates-General	paternalism	Third Republic
Cartesian	Free French	plebiscite	Versailles
Charlemagne	general will	Popular Front	Vichy

Further Reference

ARENDT, HANNAH. *On Revolution.* New York: Viking, 1963.

BERNIER, OLIVIER. *Louis XIV: A Royal Life.* New York: Doubleday, 1987.

———. *Fireworks at Dusk: Paris in the Thirties.* Boston: Litte, Brown, 1993.

BRINTON, CRANE. *The Anatomy of Revolution.* New York: Vintage Books, 1965.

BURNS, MICHAEL. *Dreyfus: A Family Affair, 1789–1945.* New York: HarperCollins, 1992.

GILES, FRANK. *The Locust Years: The Story of the Fourth French Republic, 1946–1958.* New York: Carroll & Graf, 1994.

KOHN, HANS. *Making of the Modern French Mind.* New York: Van Nostrand Reinhold, 1955.

LACOUTURE, JEAN. *De Gaulle: The Rebel, 1890–1944.* New York: W. W. Norton, 1990.

———. *De Gaulle: The Ruler, 1945–1970.* New York: W. W. Norton, 1992.

MCMILLAN, JAMES F. *Dreyfus to De Gaulle: Politics and Society in France, 1898–1969.* New York: Edward Arnold, 1985.

PRICE, ROGER. *A Social History of Nineteenth Century France.* New York: Holmes & Meier, 1988.

ROUSSO, HENRY. *The Vichy Syndrome: History and Memory in France since 1944.* Cambridge, MA: Harvard University Press, 1991.

SCHAMA, SIMON. *Citizens: A Chronicle of the French Revolution.* New York: Knopf, 1989.

TILLY, CHARLES. *The Contentious French.* Cambridge, MA: Harvard University Press, 1986.

TOCQUEVILLE, ALEXIS DE. *The Old Regime and the French Revolution.* New York: Doubleday, 1955.

WEBSTER, PAUL. *Pétain's Crime.* New York: Macmillan, 1990.

ZUCCOTTI, SUSAN. *The Holocaust, the French, and the Jews.* New York: Basic Books, 1993.

8
France: The Key Institutions

Fifteen Constitutions

The English constitution grew piecemeal and has never been formalized into one document. French constitutions—and there have been fifteen of them since the Revolution—are always spelled out with logic and clarity. Whereas the Americans regard their Constitution with an almost religious awe, not to be touched in its basic provisions, the French, and most other European countries, have seen constitutions come and go and are not averse to rewriting the basic rules of their political game every few decades.

By 1958, many French citizens agreed that the Fourth Republic was inherently flawed and unable to settle the ghastly Algerian War. The chief problem, as defined by de Gaulle, lay in the weakness of the executive, the premier. The president was simply a figurehead, typical of European republics. The premier (or prime minister) depended on unstable coalitions; faced with controversial issues, one or more coalition parties would usually drop out, vote against the government in a "vote of no-confidence," and thereby bring it down. In all, there were twenty cabinets, or "governments," in less than twelve years. Personal jealousies sometimes played a role; if a premier was too effective, other politicians sometimes voted against him out of resentment. Pierre Mendès-France, for example, settled the Indochina War in 1954, but that made him too popular and effective, and the National Assembly voted him out a few months later.

The Fourth Republic embodied all the weaknesses of the multiparty parliamentary system that still plagues Italy. Such a system can work well and with stability, as in Sweden, but it depends on the *party* system and the national political style.

Given French parties and political style, however, it is doubtful that a pure parliamentary system could ever work well.

A Semipresidential System

De Gaulle hated the executive weakness of the Fourth Republic, but neither did he like the American-style presidential system with its checks and balances that might hamper his style. So he devised what has been called a "semipresidential" system, a

Parliamentary versus Presidential Systems

Most West European governments are parliamentary; that is, they depend on votes in parliament to put a cabinet into executive power and keep it there. The cabinet is usually composed of members of parliament and can be seen as a sort of parliamentary steering committee that also guides the ministries or departments. If no party in parliament has a majority, a coalition of parties is necessary, and this may be unstable. In policy splits, a "vote of no-confidence" ousts the cabinet. Where a single party dominates the parliament—which is mostly the case in Britain—the system can be very stable.

A presidential system, such as exists in the United States, does not depend on parliamentary support, for here the chief executive is elected more or less directly for a fixed term. The parliament can

do what it wants, but it cannot oust the president in a vote of no-confidence. (In the United States, of course, Congress can impeach the president.) The advantage of a presidential system is its stability and certainty: there will always be a president to lead. The disadvantage is that the president and the legislature may deadlock, producing the same *immobilisme* that plagues parliamentary systems.

The French system has been called "semipresidential," for the cabinet still has a certain parliamentary connection. The premier is named by the president but can be censured and forced to resign by the National Assembly. If that happens—and it has occurred only once, in 1962—the president can dissolve the legislature and order that new elections be held.

The French System

The French System. Compare with the parliamentary and presidential systems as shown on page 8.

The Presidential Election of 1988

In a replay of 1981, France had both presidential and legislative elections back-to-back in 1988, illustrating the two-round French electoral system. In the first round of the presidential election, held every seven years, every party ran its chief on April 24, with the following results:

François Mitterrand (Socialist)	34.1%
Jacques Chirac (Gaullist)	20.0%
Raymond Barre (Union for French Democracy)	16.5%
Jean-Marie Le Pen (National Front)	14.4%
André Lajoinie (Communist)	6.8%

All but the top two were eliminated for the second round two weeks later, on May 8, which the incumbent Mitterrand won:

Mitterrand	54%
Chirac	46%

Mitterrand then used his presidential power to dissolve the National Assembly and hold new elections for it. While the Socialists fell short of a majority of seats, Mitterrand won over some centrists from the UDF to allow him to keep a Socialist premier instead of relying on *cohabitation*.

hybrid with features from both parliamentary and presidential systems (see box on page 95). For over a quarter-century, however, the system didn't work that way. Instead of some kind of balance between the powers of the president and those of the premier, the president held sway by virtue of commanding the largest bloc of votes in the National Assembly. Thus for most of the history of the Fifth Republic, the system functioned as a presidential or even "superpresidential" system. Only with the parliamentary elections of 1986 and 1993—which produced conservative National Assemblies while a Socialist president was still in office—did we get a chance to see semipresidentialism in action.

Let us first examine the "old" system of the Fifth Republic, the one de Gaulle devised and commanded from 1958 to 1969. The general structure of it, of course, continues to this day, but the powers of its components have changed. The French president is elected for seven years and may be reelected without limit. Originally, the president was selected by an electoral college of parliamentarians and local office holders. De Gaulle soon discovered he wanted nothing—certainly no politicians—to stand between him and the people, so in 1962, by means of a referendum, he changed the constitution to provide for direct election of the president, and it has been that way ever since.

The constitution specifies some powers as belonging to the president and some to the premier, but the practice was unclear. On paper, the president picks a premier who then selects his own cabinet. Until 1986, however, the president was so assured of an obedient National Assembly that he hand-picked both premiers and cabinet ministers as mere helpers to carry out the president's program. This gave the president incredible power. Virtually all foreign and defense affairs were in his hands (still mostly the case). The president originated most legislation, often with the advice of ministers, and could even force the National Assembly to vote on executive proposals in a simple yes-or-no manner. De Gaulle saw the role of president in almost mystical terms, as a "guide" and "arbiter" of the nation.

One important—and perhaps overused—power de Gaulle liked is the calling of referendums. You'll recall that such mass votes on issues are alien to British tradition but very much a part of French usage, especially by figures who believe they embody the general will and communicate directly with the people, bypassing the politicians. De Gaulle called five such plebiscites (see Chapter 10) and won each except the last. Feeling repudiated, he resigned, perhaps establishing another constitutional tradition.

Another potentially major power at the disposal of the French president is the prerogative to invoke "emergency powers" in time of danger to the nation. While many democracies have such an emergency provision, there is always the fear that it can be abused, as Hitler used Article 48 of the Weimar constitution to snuff out freedom. Article 16 of the French constitution seems to place no limits on what a president can do during an emergency, a situation that is up to the president to define. During such an emergency the National Assembly must meet, but it has no power to veto presidential decisions. The emergency clause has been invoked only once—in 1961, when the same generals who put de Gaulle into power tried to overthrow him for pulling out of Algeria—and many agreed that it was a genuine emergency.

The presidential paradise came to an end with the National Assembly elections of 1986, which produced, as expected, a legislature dominated by conservative parties. The problem was that President Mitterrand, a Socialist, had two years remaining in his seven-year term. For the first time in the history of the Fifth Republic, a president did not control the National Assembly. No one could predict what was going to happen; the constitution was unclear. Some feared a hostile deadlock and paralysis of government. Others thought Mitterrand would have to resign to make way for the election of a conservative president. Instead, Mitterrand played a waiting game that preserved him as president but reduced the powers of the presidency. Mitterrand thus clarified the French constitution and set a precedent when the same situation occurred in 1993.

Mitterrand in 1986 called upon the leader of the largest conservative party, Jacques Chirac, to become premier and went along with most of Chirac's cabinet choices. Mitterrand also did not block most of Chirac's legislative program, which rolled back many of Mitterrand's socialist experiments in the economy. The two struck an informal bargain, called *cohabitation,* in which Chirac concentrated on domestic affairs and Mitterrand on foreign policy. Mitterrand took a back seat and contented himself with foreign and defense affairs and the symbolic functions of the presidency. During cohabitation, the French presidency lost some of its domestic power, although it was still more powerful than the weak presidency of the Fourth Republic. In 1993, faced with another conservative victory in parliamentary elections, Mitterrand named another neo-Gaullist, Edouard Balladur, as his premier. Cohabitation had become routine; institutions evolve.

If the French want to avoid cohabitation and its uncertainties, they would be well-advised to cut the last link between legislative and executive branches (the "can-censure" arrow) and become a straight presidential system, U.S.–style. They should also shorten the seven-year presidential term so that it matches the five-year term of the National Assembly and thus avoid the two lame-duck years that came at the end of each Mitterrand term. True, the U.S. system often deadlocks between the

A Socialist Romantic for President

For its first twenty-three years, conservatives presided over the Fifth Republic: de Gaulle, Pompidou, and Giscard d'Estaing. But in 1981 France elected a Socialist president, François Mitterrand, and a National Assembly dominated by his Socialist party. But it was a pre-Marxist, very French, sort of socialism, one stressing humane and romantic values rather than economics. Symbolically, the elections of 1981 represented a swing back to the

leftist and revolutionary half of France's longstanding political split. In practice, *hélas*, Mitterrand's program was a disappointment for most French. He promised more than the French economy could possibly deliver.

Mitterrand was born in 1916 in the Cognac region of southwest France, one of eight children of a Catholic and *petit bourgeois* family. As a student in Paris in the 1930s, Mitterrand was drawn to *rightwing* politics. In World War II, Sergeant Mitterrand was wounded and captured but escaped to serve the Vichy regime as a minor official. Like many French, Mitterrand at first saw Vichy as a way to save France. By 1943, however, he was firmly in the Resistance, for whom he supplied forged papers. In the Fourth Republic he was repeatedly elected to parliament as a leader of several small centrist parties and served in eight cabinet posts, including the important position of interior minister under Pierre Mendès-France.

As de Gaulle consolidated his Fifth Republic, Mitterrand—who already hated de Gaulle for his haughty ways during the war—moved to the left. His plan was to strengthen the non-Communist left but to use the Communists when necessary to win elections. Mitterrand made a strong showing against de Gaulle in the 1965 presidential race. In 1971 he simultaneously joined and became the leader of the Socialist party (PS), whose electoral fortunes were at a low ebb. Patiently building the PS, Mitterrand came in a close second to Giscard in 1974. In 1981, after France had had seven years of Gisard's aristocratic arrogance, Mitterrand won the presidency at age 64. He won again in 1988.

For a politician, Mitterrand is almost antipolitical. He prefers literature to politics. A shy intellectual, he has written eleven books, some of them conveying an almost mystical attachment to France and its revolutionary values. Said Mitterrand: "The soul of France lives in me."

François Mitterrand, President of France. *(French Embassy Press and Information Division).*

Great French Expressions: Cohabitation

This tongue-in-cheek journalistic expression was invented for the circumstances of 1986–1988 to describe a French president having to name his opponent as premier. Cohabitation, spelled the same in French and English, connotes a couple forced into a marriage neither wants. The term instantly became part of French political vocabulary and a French political institution.

White House and Capitol Hill, but the president still has plenty of power to govern without permission from Congress.

Premier and Cabinet

Until cohabitation, French ministers, including the prime minister, served as little more than messenger boys for the president. The premier's main function was to push presidential measures through parliament. Under cohabitation, however, Premiers Chirac and Balladur restored much of the power of that office by pursuing their own conservative legislative agendas.

The French president chooses a premier, who in turn picks a cabinet. Ministers do not have to be approved by the National Assembly but usually are. A cabinet not to the liking of parliament could be censured and ousted. Accordingly, Socialist Mitterrand felt he had to name neo-Gaullists Chirac and Balladur, because they had majority support in parliament. This is the way European prime ministers are usually chosen (compare with Britain, p. 35, and Germany, p. 167).

The president can also dismiss a premier. In 1988 Mitterrand named the bright Michel Rocard, but dumped him in 1991 when he became a too-obvious rival for the leadership of the Socialist party. Then Mitterrand named the fiery Edith Cresson, France's first woman premier, a person of strong opinions but shaky leadership qualities; she served ten months until Mitterrand dropped her. In 1992, Mitterrand named Pierre Bérégovoy, a seasoned politician but one who could not stem the Socialist slide to electoral defeat in early 1993; he lasted eleven months in office. (Under suspicion of corruption, Bérégovoy committed suicide a few weeks later.) In short, the French president is strong and durable; the French premier comes and goes.

A French twist found in few other parliamentary democracies: a deputy (French for MP) chosen to be a minister must resign his or her seat. De Gaulle wanted to make sure ministers wouldn't run back to parliament to protest his policies. By the same token, unlike Britain, French ministers do not have to be members of parliament; many are experienced administrators and apolitical technicians who have never been elected to anything. De Gaulle picked as one of his premiers Georges

Pompidou, a man who had absolutely no elected political experience (but who went on to become an effective president in his own right). Balladur picked as minister for social affairs, health, and towns the effective but nonpartisan Simone Veil, who had served in previous center-right cabinets.

Like most European cabinets, the French cabinet can be easily remade to suit the premier. Ministries are not quite the same as U.S. departments, which are firmly fixed by statute and change only after great deliberation. Paris ministries are almost ad hoc combinations of existing French agencies and bureaus, which change according to the policy goals of the executive. The cabinet named by Primier Balladur in 1993 consisted of ministers for:

Economy	Industry, Posts, and Telecommunications
Labor	Budget and government spokesman
Justice	Housing
Agriculture	Transport and Tourism
Defense	Interior (police)
Cooperation (foreign aid)	Youth and Sport
Culture	Universities and Research
Communications	Environment
Economic Development	Education
Foreign Affairs	Social Affairs, Health, and Towns
Foreign Trade	Overseas Departments
Government Service	War Veterans and Victims

No cabinet change is final; these positions will be repeatedly divided, combined, and reshuffled. In general, left-wing governments seek large and specialized cabinets since they propose major changes under government supervision. Conservative governments, on the other hand, usually like smaller cabinets as they do not plan to remake society. Such repeated change sounds chaotic to Americans, but bear in mind the career civil servants in the various bureaus change very little; the changes are at the very top in who is their ultimate boss. The more it changes, the more it stays the same.

The National Assembly

During the Third and Fourth Republics the National Assembly was dominant. Making and unmaking cabinets, the parliament controlled the executive. Some say this sort of parliamentary system has a weak executive and strong legislature. That's not quite accurate. In this case the legislature wasn't strong either. Divided into several quarrelsome parties that were unable to form stable coalitions, the French National Assembly was no more able to govern than were the cabinets. To Americans this sounds like complete chaos. The government "fell" every few months on the average. This is not quite so horrendous as it sounds. When a government in a parliamentary system "falls," it does not mean the entire structure of government collapses; indeed, little changes. It just means there has been a policy quarrel among the parties so that the cabinet coalition no longer commands a majority of the parliament. The cabinet then either resigns, is ousted in a vote of no-confidence, or limps along as a minority government. After several days or even weeks of negotiations, another cabinet is put together that wins majority approval. Often this cabinet is composed of the same ministers in the same jobs as the previous cabinet. Instead of too much change, parliamentary systems often suffer from too little. Premiers have their hands so full just keeping the coalition together they are often unwilling to risk doing anything that might make it come apart. The result is *immobilisme*.

Meeting in the windowless Palais Bourbon, members of parliament, or deputies, prior to 1958 tended to play politics with each other and ignore what was happening outside. In a massive avoidance of responsibility, deputies concentrated on getting into the cabinet or, when unsuccessful, bringing it down. Things changed with the Fifth Republic; the legislators' paradise came to an abrupt end.

The National Assembly no longer makes cabinets; today that power belongs to the premier in consultation with the president. Indeed, the relationship between the cabinet and legislature has been deliberately weakened; as noted earlier, a deputy named to the cabinet must resign his or her seat. One link does remain: the National Assembly can censure a cabinet. When that happens the president can dissolve (send home) the National Assembly for new elections before the end of its normal five-year term. The president is limited to one dissolution a year.

The premier and the president, not the legislature, now hold key powers of legislation. Most bills originate with the government. The government sets the agenda. If the government specifies, its proposals must be considered without amendments on a take-it-or-leave-it basis called a "blocked vote." That is to prevent parliamentary dilution of legislation. The National Assembly no longer has the time or structure to consider legislation closely: its sessions are limited to five and a half months a year; it has only six committees; and a bill cannot be bottled up in committee but must be reported out.

The government is able to pass many laws by simple decree, provided the premier and the president agree (and sometimes they don't). The 1958 constitution specifies the types of laws that must go through parliament; all others presumably don't need to. While most decrees concern details, the power of government decree also extends to the budget. Here the legislature has lost its original, most fundamental power—the power of the purse. Any parliamentary motion to either decrease revenues (for example, a tax cut) or increase spending (for example, a new program) are automatically out of order. And if the parliament can't settle on the budget within seventy days, the government may make it law by simple decree.

Great French Expressions:
"Plus ça change, plus c'est la même chose"

The French, used to seeing cabinets come and go with no substantive change taking place, developed the cynical expression: "The more things change, the more they stay the same." The phrase perfectly sums up the contempt many French citizens felt toward the institutions of the Third and Fourth Republics.

COMPARING

 The Israeli Parliamentary System

Israel is the way France used to be: a weak executive dependent on a shaky coalition of parties elected by proportional representation. De Gaulle ended the Fourth Republic's parliamentary system and founded the Fifth's semipresidential. Israel stays classically parliamentary.

Israel's single house, the 120-member Knesset, is elected by proportional representation, a system that permits any party that wins at least 2 percent of the national vote to have at least a few seats in parliament. (It used to be only 1 percent.) Israel has a dozen or more parties, none of them with a majority in parliament. Thus every Israeli government has been a coalition and prone to breakup when the parties in it quarreled. Israel too has suffered immobilism in the face of major problems.

The Party System

Parties can make or break a political system. Britain's stability and efficiency would diminish if instead of one party with a solid majority in Commons there were half a dozen parties of about equal size. Much of what was wrong with the Third and Fourth Republics was not government institutions but the parties that tried to operate them.

We must avoid evaluating all two-party systems as good and all multiparty systems as bad. Americans especially are disdainful of multiparty systems and often cite Italy and the Fourth Republic as examples of the ills they create. But several multiparty parliamentary democracies with institutions not too different from Italy's and the Fourth Republic's are stable and effective: Sweden, Switzerland, Holland, and Belgium. At least as much depends on the way the parties behave as on how many parties there are.

By the same token, the Fifth French Republic wouldn't have worked the way it did had not the Gaullist party ballooned into the largest of all French parties. Indeed, if the Fourth Republic had been preserved but with Gaullists occupying the largest slice of the National Assembly, the most troublesome problem of that system—*immobilisme*—would have disappeared, for de Gaulle would have had a stable majority at his disposal.

France has at present three large parties and three small ones, plus a sprinkling of oddball groups. The Socialists (PS) occupy the center-left and for most of the 1980s were the largest party. But two parties allied in 1986 and again in 1993—the center-right Republicans (UDF) and the farther-right Gaullists (RPR)—to win a majority of parliament. Flanking the large parties are the Communists on the left and the racist National Front on the right. Fitting in somewhere on the left, the combined Ecology Generation and Greens failed to win any seats in 1993 (for more on parties, see Chapter 10).

French legislative elections come every five years (or sooner in case the president has dissolved parliament), presidential elections every seven years (or sooner if the president resigns or dies). Legislative and presidential elections were intended

A Senate That Fights Back

Most parliaments are composed of two chambers, and most don't know what to do with the upper chamber. Sweden simply abolished its upper house. The greatest value of an upper house is in representing territorial subunits, as the U.S. Senate represents the states. Where the system is unitary (Britain, France, Sweden) rather than federal (the United States, Germany, Brazil) an upper chamber doesn't have much use.

France's main legislative body, comparable to the British House of Commons, is also the lower house, the 577-member National Assembly elected every five years (or sooner in case of dissolution). The upper house, the *Sénat*, has 316 members elected for nine years each—with elections for about a third every three years—by a gigantic electoral college made up of National Assembly deputies plus more than 100,000 regional and municipal councilors. De Gaulle thought that these councilors, because they would disproportionately represent rural and small-town France, would produce a conservative Senate amenable to Gaullist direction.

Rural and small-town France is not necessarily conservative; it looks out for farming. Above all, the *Sénat* represents farmers' viewpoints; it has been called the agricultural chamber. The French Senate has criticized and amended numerous government bills. *Sénateurs* aren't under pressure like lower-house assembly members to pass what the government wants. The French Senate is listened to by the government on farm matters, for when French farmers get mad they can create havoc. Still, when the government wants a measure passed, it can override Senate objections by a simple majority in the National Assembly.

The French Senate, although not equal in power to the National Assembly, cannot be dissolved by the government. Apparently de Gaulle came to regret that he had allowed the Senate an autonomous existence, for in 1969 he tried to dilute its power by means of another plebiscite. The French people, annoyed by de Gaulle, supported their Senate, the last area of French parliamentary freedom, and rejected the referendum.

to be deliberately out of kilter. President Mitterrand solved this problem following his elections in both 1981 and 1988 by immediately dissolving the National Assembly so that his Socialists could increase their number of seats.

The traditional electoral system of the Fifth Republic is actually taken from the Third Republic. Like the English and American systems, the French use single-member districts. But unlike the Anglo-American systems, where a simple plurality is all that's required to win, the French victor needs a majority (more than 50 percent). If the candidate doesn't get it on the first ballot—and that is usually the case—the contest goes to a runoff a week later, this time with candidates that got under 12.5 percent of the district's registered voters eliminated and only a simple plurality needed to win. The second round, then, is the decisive one; the first round is the functional equivalent of U.S. primaries.

For the 1986 parliamentary elections, however, the Mitterrand government, as they had long promised, reverted to proportional representation (PR), which had also been used by the Fourth Republic. Instead of single-member districts with runoffs, the PR system used multimember districts and only one round. Voters cast a ballot for a party, not an individual, and seats were awarded according to the percentage won by each party. In Europe generally, parties of the left favor PR, arguing that it is inherently fairer and gives adequate representation to the parties of the

The Parliamentary Elections of 1993

The Socialists knew they were in trouble in early 1993—the economy was bad, officials had been accused of corruption, and they showed no leadership or new ideas—but it had been five years since the last elections to the National Assembly, so new elections were required by law. But the PS did even worse than expected in the first round, held Sunday, March 21, 1993:

Socialists (and allies)	20.3%
Rally for the Republic (RPR, neo-Gaullist)	20.4%
Union for French Democracy (UDF)	19.1%
National Front	12.4%
Communists	9.2%
Greens and Ecology	7.6%

Some candidates won actual majorities in their districts, and they were declared winners immediately. In most French districts, however, voters had to go to a runoff a week later on March 28. Candidates who had polled less than 12.5 percent in the first round were dropped. In many districts weaker candidates also withdrew and endorsed the candidate who most matched their preferences. For example,

by prearrangement among the two large conservative parties, a UDF candidate might withdraw and urge his supporters in the first round to vote for the neo-Gaullist candidate in the second round. The final results and number of seats:

Socialists (and allies)	28.3%	70
Gaullists	28.3%	247
Union for French Democracy	25.8%	213
National Front	5.7%	0
Communists	4.6%	23
Other rightists	4.0%	25

With the allied center and right parties, the UDF and RPR, virtually owning the National Assembly, Mitterrand, with two years to go in his second presidency, named one of the leaders of the largest party, the Gaullists, the calm and polite Eduard Balladur, as premier, thus beginning another period of cohabitation. Balladur did such a good job and showed such good manners that he was soon being mentioned as the strongest candidate for the next presidential election. With Mitterrand's health uncertain, that election could come before it is due in 1995.

poor and working class. Critics charged Mitterrand with changing the rules to favor his Socialist party, which did somewhat better under PR than single-member districts. They pointed out that PR enabled the extremist National Front to obtain seats in the National Assembly; under single-member districts it would have won few or none. Inadvertently, Socialists aided racists. The 1986 experiment in PR was short-lived, and France returned to single-member districts with runoffs. Presidential elections are played out under similar rules. All but the top two candidates for president are eliminated in the first round; a second round two weeks later decides between the top two (see box on page 96).

The French system permits or encourages several parties to exist; the Anglo-American systems frankly discourage third parties. Unlike proportional representation, the French (like the British) system penalizes small parties. In Germany, for example, a Green vote of 7.6 percent would have won them over 50 seats. Some have suggested that adoption of the English-style single-member districts with plurality winning would help the French reduce the number of their parties by forcing smaller parties to amalgamate with larger ones. But the French party system is rooted in French society, and this is a more complex and fragmented society than the British or American. The French have several parties because they need them, and any attempt to reduce them to two might lead to two big extremist parties rather than two big moderate parties. In any case, the French party system seems to be coalescing into two large blocs, one left and one right. Over the decades, there have been fewer and fewer relevant parties in France. Indeed, simplification of the party system has been a trend in many countries with multiparty systems.

A Decentralized Unitary System

Both Britain and France are unitary systems, concentrating power in the capital. France used to be more strongly unitary than Britain, where cities and counties enjoy a certain autonomy. (Curiously, conservative Margaret Thatcher attempted to *cut* the autonomy of Britain's cities and counties; she saw local councils as bastions of socialism.) Under Mitterrand, France decentralized, rolling back a tradition that started with Louis XI. French monarchs tried to erase regional differences but sometimes only worsened local resentments. Napoleon perfected this centralizing and homogenizing pattern. He abolished the historic provinces and replaced them with smaller, artificial units called *départements*, many named after rivers. The *départements* were administrative conveniences to facilitate control by Paris. Each *département*—

COMPARING

 A French Supreme Court?

In the 1980s, a little-noticed branch of the French government started taking on a life of its own: the Constitutional Council. Although it was part of the 1958 constitution, it came into its own as a buffer between Mitterrand and the conservative-dominated parliament during the cohabitation periods. Some started comparing it to the U.S. Supreme Court. The comparison is shaky:

- Both have nine members, but the French serve for nine years, not life. Three members of the French court are appointed each by the president, the speaker of the National Assembly, and the speaker of the Senate.

- The French Council members are rarely lawyers and see their role as political rather than legal. The U.S. Supreme Court sees its role the other way round.

- The scope of the French Council is much more limited. It can review the constitutionality of laws only after they've been passed by parliament but before they've been signed by the president. It considers cases not from lower courts but on demand by the executive or any sixty members of either house of parliament.

- Rather than establishing legal precedents as the U.S. Supreme Court does, the French Constitutional Council has acted as a brake against hasty and ill-considered legislation. As such, the ruling parties in France tend to dislike its decisions while the opposition parties often like them.

The role and powers of the U.S. Supreme Court are unique. Some French thinkers would like to see their council become more like the U.S. Supreme Court. Only the German Federal Constitutional Court approaches the Supreme Court in importance (see page 173).

there are now ninety-six—was administered by a *prefect*, a lineal descendant of Riche-lieu's old *intendant*, now an official of the interior ministry. It got to be pretty absurd; towns had to ask Paris if they could put in a new traffic light or pave a street. Prefects, very bright and highly trained, monitored laws, funds, and mayors with Olympian detachment.

In 1982, Mitterrand got a law that on paper reduced the domain of pre-fects and increased local autonomy. Elected councils in the *départements* and re-gions (there are twenty-two regions, each comprising two to eight *départements*) won policy-setting and taxation powers in education, urban and regional plan-ning and development, job training, and housing. In short order, French local and regional government became more important, and elections to their coun-cils were hotly contested. Ironically, Mitterrand's conservative opponents won most of these elections. Competition set in as cities, departments, and regions sought to attract new industries. Local taxes increased, but the ways of assessing them became widely divergent and innovative. In sum, the subnational units of French government started acting somewhat like their American counterparts, developing their own strategies for prosperity. France in no sense became a fed-eral system—indeed, its decentralization didn't go as far as Spain's during this same period—but it was Mitterrand's most important and lasting contribution to the French political system.

Vocabulary Building

apolitical	decree	interior ministry	presidential system
blocked vote	*département*	left	runoff
center	deputy	multiparty	Socialist
coalition	emergency powers	parliamentary system	technician
Communist	Gaullist	prefect	unitary

Further Reference

BLONDEL, JEAN. *The Government of France.* New York: Harper & Row, 1974.

COLE, ALISTAIR, and PETER CAMPBELL. *French Electoral Systems,* 3d ed. Brookfield, VT: Gower, 1989.

ELGIE, ROBERT. *The Role of the Prime Minister in France, 1981–91.* New York; St. Martin's, 1994.

HAYWARD, J. E. S. *Governing France: The One and Indivis-ible Republic.* 2d ed. New York: W. W. Norton, 1983.

NORTHCUTT, WAYNE. *Mitterrand: A Political Biography.* New York: Holmes & Meier, 1992.

PÉAN, PIERRE. *Une Jeunesse Française: François Mit-terand, 1934–1947.* Paris: Fayard, 1994.

PIERCE, ROY. *French Politics and Political Institutions,* 2d ed. Lanhan, MD: University Press of America, 1983.

POULARD, JEAN V. "The French Double Executive and the Experience of Cohabitation." *Political Science Quarterly* 105 (Summer 1990) 2.

SAFRAN, WILLIAM. *The French Polity,* 4th ed. White Plains, NY: Longman, 1995.

SCHMIDT, VIVIEN A. *Democratizing France: The Political and Administrative History of Decentralization.* New York: Cambridge University Press, 1991.

STONE, ALEC. *The Birth of Judicial Review in France: The Constitutional Council in Comparative Per-spective.* New York: Oxford University Press, 1992.

WILLIAMS, PHILIP M. *The French Parliament: Politics in the Fifth Republic.* New York: Praeger, 1968.

9
French Political Attitudes

A Tale of Two Families

Two Parisian families I knew during the Bicentennial of the French Revolution in 1989 illustrate the deeply divided nature of French society. One couple, although not university-educated, were bright and hard-working and had turned their small suburban house into a tidy and pleasant home. They read the conservative daily *Figaro* and the Catholic weekly *La Voix*. They did not like the current Socialist government. When they entered a church, they crossed themselves. They showed little interest in celebrating the Bicentennial July 14 and cautioned me about the crowds in Paris. They suggested a picnic in the countryside instead.

The other family were typical Parisian intellectuals, both university-educated, inhabiting a charming, book-strewn older apartment not far from one of Paris's great boulevards. They read the leftish *Le Monde* and were indifferent to religion. They liked the current Socialist government. They urged me to join the street festivities the night before July 14 and then try to catch the spectacular parade. They thought the French Revolution was really something worth celebrating.

There, in miniature, was conservative France and radical France, the former indifferent or even a little hostile to the French Revolution, the latter enthusiastically for it. The split created by the French Revolution continues to this day, although in subdued form. Conservative France no longer battles radical France; rather, the two preserve a chilly distance.

Both families deeply love France, but they love different facets of France. France has a mystique, a kind of strange drawing power that can equally attract conservatives such as de Gaulle and Socialists such as Mitterrand. The conservatives are drawn to French civilization, its Catholic roots, and its *grandeur* (greatness). Liberals and leftists, on the other hand, are drawn to the ideals of the French Revolution—liberty, equality, and fraternity—and see France as the repository of these ideals. Some French envision their land as a person, a princess, or even a Madonna. They have a reverence for their country that few Americans or Britons can match. The dramatic and stirring French national anthem, "*La Marseillaise*" (see box on page 110), gives one a sense of the depth of French patriotism.

French patriotism in the abstract, however, does not carry over into the real, grubby, daily life of French politics. The French are usually far more cynical about politics than Britishers or Americans. France in the abstract is glorious; France in the here and now is shabby. This is why de Gaulle said France needs national greatness, for only with a vision of something great can French people rise above the sordid reality and pursue the mythical ideal.

Mitterrand was elected in part because of his ability to project an idealistic vision of France with a leftist twist. "It is natural for a great nation to have great ambitions," he proclaimed. "In today's world, can there be a loftier duty for our country than to achieve a new alliance between socialism and liberty?" The French liked the sentiment, but once Mitterrand was in power they grew quickly disillusioned with the reality.

Historical Roots of French Attitudes

Where did this French political schizophrenia come from? Part of the problem is historical, traceable to the centralization of French kings, who implanted an omnipotent state, a state that tried to supervise everything. In theory, a centralized system should be excellent, capable of planning and building rationally. In practice, it often falls far short of the goal. The French, trained to expect a powerful government to help them (the ideal), are always disappointed when it doesn't (the real).

French paternalism also stunted the development of a voluntary do-it-ourselves attitude, something that is common in the United States. France simply has no tradition of voluntary groups of neighbors undertaking local governance. When local groups take responsibility and something goes wrong, you can only blame yourselves. In France, with all responsibility until recently in the hands of the central government, the people blame Paris.

Centuries of bureaucratized administration also left the French used to living by uniform, impersonal rules—and lots of them. This creates hatred, the hatred of the little citizen on one side of the counter facing the cold, indifferent bureaucrat on the other.

Centralization and bureaucratization are the products of the "order and reason" approach to governance that has been practiced in France for centuries. Order and reason, unfortunately, are mere ideals. Since they are always deficient in practice, the French become unhappy with a reality that always falls short of ideals.

A Climate of Mistrust

In personal relations French people are sometimes distant and mistrustful to people outside their family. Indeed, attitudes of mistrust are widespread throughout Latin Europe—they are extremely pronounced in Italy—while trustful attitudes are

How to Celebrate a 200-Year-Old Revolution

The French Revolution was still a divisive political issue in 1989. Even choosing the official historian for the Bicentennial was a political decision. Con-

"Liberty, Equality, Fraternity," the great slogan of the French Revolution, is proclaimed here on a provincial city hall on the bicentennial of the Revolution. *(Michael Roskin)*

servative historians called the Revolution a gigantic mistake, subsequently the root of France's troubles. Such viewpoints anger the left and were hardly a way to celebrate the Bicentennial. Radical or leftist historians, on the other hand, read into the Revolution the harbinger of all things good and of the Bolshevik Revolution in Russia. This was hardly acceptable to conservative France.

In François Furet the Mitterrand government found their historian: a former Marxist who had turned away from radicalism to produce a moderate and sober synthesis with something for everyone. Furet finds nothing wrong with the revolutionary ideals of *liberté, egalité, fraternité*, but he argued that with the collapse of the monarchy and takeover of therevolution by extremists, the revolution had to "skid out of control." The French word Furet used for skidding is *dérapage*. It was not just evil or foolish people—many of these people had the best of intentions—that caused the revolution to skid out of control, Furet argues, but the logic of revolutions themselves. Furet's thinking is not far removed from that of Crane Brinton, discussed in Chapter 7.

A change in the current political context enabled Furet and other French intellectuals to accept this rather unhappy analysis of the French Revolution. For decades, many French intellectuals naively celebrated the 1917 Russian Revolution as a continuation of the French Revolution. With the erosion of French leftism and decay of Soviet communism, French intellectuals saw that the Bolshevik Revolution had been a mistake. But if 1917 was the culmination of 1789, then logically the French Revolution itself must have been badly flawed. The new attitude about communism forced the French to reevaluate their own revolution.

"La Marseillaise"

Possibly the world's greatest national anthem is the French "*Marseillaise.*" Dashed off in a single night in 1792 by a 32-year-old army officer, Rouget de Lisle, to accompany volunteers from Marseille headed north to defend the Revolution, the "*Marseillaise*" soon became the Revolution's and then France's anthem.

Extremely stirring and bloodthirsty, it is the perfect song for fighting for a nation. The refrain:

> *Aux armes, citoyens, formez vos bataillons!*
> *Marchons! Marchons!*
> *Qu'un sang impur abreuve nos sillons!*

(To arms, citizens, form your battalions! We march! We march! Until [the enemy's] impure blood overflows our furrows!)

If you've never heard it sung, try to catch the movie *Casablanca* the next time it's on television.

Like the French flag, the "*Marseillaise*" became a controversial political symbol. Part of the Revolution, it was banned by Napoleon and the Bourbons, accepted by the liberal Orleans monarch in 1830, banned again by Napoleon III, and made permanently the national anthem in 1879.

---

more common in Northern Europe. The American scholar Laurence Wylie found villagers in the Vaucluse, in the south of France, constantly suspicious of *les autres*, "the others," those outsiders who talk behind your back, blacken your name, and meddle in your affairs. The best way to live, people there agreed, was not to get involved with other people and to maintain only correct but distant relations with neighbors. With modernization, such extreme mistrust has receded.

Foreigners notice how shut off the French family is. Typical French houses are surrounded by high walls often topped by broken glass set in concrete. Shutters aren't just for decoration; they bang shut as if to tell the world to mind its own business. Traditionally, French people rarely entertained at home—they'd go to a restaurant instead, for inviting outsiders to your table was an invasion of family privacy. This attitude, however, has changed; I have been invited into several French homes for superb meals.

Special mistrust is reserved for the government. In Wylie's village it was taken for granted that all government is bad, a necessary evil at best. The elaborate duties of a good citizen that schoolchildren memorize in their civics course are lovely ideals, but in the real world government is corrupt, intrusive, and ineffective. French children learn to love *la patrie* in the abstract but to disdain politics in the here and now. Politics are also best kept private and personal; discussing politics with others only leads to arguments. Besides, it's none of their business.

The Nasty Split

Catholic countries have a serious problem that Protestant (and Eastern Orthodox) countries don't have to worry about: the role of the church. When Britain and Swe-

Great French Expressions: "L'enfer, c'est les autres"

French philosopher and playwright Jean-Paul Sartre voiced a very French feeling about interpersonal relationships when he wrote, "Hell is other people." He meant, in his play *No Exit*, that having to get along with other people was his idea of hell. But it was a peculiarly French vision of hell, and Sartre could have more accurately said, "Hell is other Frenchmen."

den broke with Rome and established national churches, they also subordinated churchmen to the state. The Anglican church in Britain and the Lutheran church in Sweden depended strictly on London and Stockholm for support; they could not turn to Rome. As a result, in these societies the church no longer played an independent political role.

In Latin European countries—France, Italy, Spain—the Roman Catholic faith retained its political power, supporting conservative regimes and getting special privileges such as control of education, tax exemption for church lands, and a considerable say in government policy. Because of this temporal power, many people in Latin Europe developed antichurch attitudes. Their most brilliant spokesman was Voltaire (see Chapter 7). "Anticlericalism," as it was called, was not necessarily antireligion; it rather sought to get the church out of government, what Americans call the separation of church and state. Anticlericalism spread in Latin Europe, especially among intellectuals, so that after the French Revolution and later Italian uni-

French and American Party Identification

In a famous if somewhat old study, Philip E. Converse and Georges Dupeux compared French and American party identification. What they found was startling. Most Americans were able to quickly identify which party they preferred; most French people could not. Where did this difference come from? Converse and Dupeux also found that 76 percent of Americans could name their *father's* party while only 25 percent of the French could even specify their father's general political tendency (left or right). Many French respondents reported that their fathers had never talked about politics.

The Converse-Dupeux study illustrated that in French families, politics was not a fit topic for conversation. This lack of political guidance from the old generation to the young contributed to political confusion in France; for example, the rather rapid shift in votes between parties and the quick rise and fall of "flash" parties. People who have not been socialized by their family toward one party or another are like ships without anchors, easily moved from one party to another.

COMPARING

The Instability of Split Societies

Unlike the stable and settled countries of Northern Europe, such as Britain and Sweden, the countries of Latin Europe continued to experience political upheavals well into our century. In France, Italy, and Spain, regimes have tended to be personal creations (for example, those of de Gaulle, Mussolini, and Franco) that end or change with the demise of their creator.

The underlying factor in this instability seems to be the split quality of French, Italian, and Spanish political life that is rooted in their histories. Roughly half the population of each country is Catholic and conservative and favors strong executive leadership; the other half is anticlerical and liberal or radical and favors a strong parliament. The center is very small; people in Latin Europe historically tended to identify with either the left or right camp, each severely mistrusting the other. When the right was in power—historically, most of the time—the left denounced the government with shrill Marxist rhetoric as the tool of the capitalists. When the left was in power, the right denounced them as dangerous incompetents, possibly serving Moscow's interests. At any given time, roughly half the country regards the government as illegitimate, and this stunts feelings of legitimacy about government in general. In Latin Europe, few take pride in their nation's governmental institutions.

In the absence of shared values and underlying consensus, political difficulties can lead to violence, coups, and even civil war which in turn leads to authoritarian rule. In the 1930s, Spain split into left and right camps and exploded into a vicious civil war won by the Catholic and conservative forces of General Franco. Disgruntled rightists in the Spanish military attempted a coup as recently as 1981. Portugal had a coup in 1974. In 1958 France very nearly had a military coup. In opposition, François Mitterrand referred to the Gaullist constitution as a "permanent coup." (In office, he found the powers it gave him as president really weren't so bad.)

fication many people wanted a purely secular state, that is, one with no church influence in government. That was easy to do in America, where there was no single established church, but it was hard in France, Italy, and Spain, where church and state were intertwined. To separate them required drastic surgery: sale of church lands, banning of some Catholic orders such as the Jesuits, and state rather than church control of schools. The reaction to this was predictable. Just as the Republic was anticlerical, the church turned anti-Republic. Church sentiment went from conservative to reactionary, and the Roman Catholic faith became a pillar of monarchical restoration because that meant a return of church privileges.

In this way conservative France retained its Catholic viewpoint, while revolutionary France became strongly anticlerical. The battle raged for more than a century. At one point the Vatican instructed faithful Catholics to steer clear of any political involvement with the "Jacobin" Republic. During the Dreyfus affair, French clericalists and anticlericalists lined up neatly on opposing sides. Finally, in 1905 the National Assembly completed the separation of church and state; France no longer had an established church.

The political traditions that grew out of this split were extremely lively. Until this century, to be in favor of the Republic meant to be anticlerical. The great premier during World War I, Georges Clemenceau, *le tigre*, was a passionate republican and supporter of Dreyfus. He recalled how his father used to tell him: "There's only one thing worse than a bad priest—and that's a good one."

Even to this day, the parties of the French left—Socialist and Communist—draw their supporters most heavily from the anticlerical tradition. The parties of the right—Gaullist and Republican—attract mostly people from the prochurch tradition. Indeed, in all of Latin Europe—Italy, Spain, and Portugal as well as France—if you know how often a person goes to Mass you can usually predict his or her vote; strongly Catholic almost automatically means politically conservative.

Some 90 percent of French babies are baptized into the Catholic faith, but less than 15 percent of French people regularly attend Mass. Although the great battles between clericalists and anticlericalists have subsided, some issues are capable of reawakening the old quarrel. The abortion controversy and question of state control of Church schools brought out protest demonstrations in the streets of Paris. Once established, social and political cleavages have tremendous staying power.

School for Grinds

Another contributor to French political attitudes is schooling. The curriculum was set generations ago and is changed only slowly and reluctantly. Heavy on rote memorization, French education tends to produce diligent grinds rather than lively intellects. Even small children lug home briefcases bulging with books. A "good" child is one who puts in long homework hours.

Until recently, everywhere in the country French children learned the same thing, as established by the ministry of education in Paris, with no local input. One legendary story has it that some decades ago an education minister looked at his watch and told an interviewer what Latin verb was being conjugated all over France. Since then, the French school curriculum has become less centralized and less classical.

The curious thing about the standardized, memorized French education, however, is its deeply humanistic and individualistic content. Outwardly, French

---

French Elections: The Persistence of Religion

The first ballot of the 1981 French presidential election provides a graphic illustration of how religion is still part of politics in France. The two leading candidates were Socialist François Mitterrand on the left and Republican Valéry Giscard d'Estaing on the right. A poll showed the more religious were also the more conservative.*

Attend Mass	Percent for Mitterrand	Percent for Giscard d'Estaing
Weekly	8%	48%
2 or 3 times a month	17	34
Less often	20	27
Never	24	16

* IFOP survey reproduced in Howard R. Penniman, ed., France at the Polls, 1981 and 1986: *Three National Elections.* (Durham, NC: AEI/Duke University Press, 1988.), p. 161.

schoolchildren appear to be mechanically digesting the inflexible, unimaginative curriculum; inwardly, they are exposed to ideas that would be banned in many American schools. This tension between outward conformity and inward freedom gives rise to privatistic attitudes and occasional eruptions of rebellion. It encourages young French people to keep their thoughts to themselves. In this way, a set, rigid educational pattern may actually contribute to French individualism.

The French pride themselves on the equality of educational opportunity their system offers. "No English-style private schools for the rich here," they seem to say, "with us, everybody has the same chance." This picture is not quite accurate. While the French school system on paper is open to all, the lofty *content* of French education is tilted toward the children of middle- and upper-class homes. Working-class and peasant children, not exposed at home to correct speech—and the French are maniacs about their language—or abstract, intellectual thoughts, start disadvantaged in the school system and are often discouraged from staying in school beyond age sixteen.

The great gateway to social, economic, and political power in France is the *lycée*, the elite high school. Napoleon developed them with an eye to training army officers. Most *lycées* are state-run. Admission is competitive, and the curriculum is demanding. Not all communities have *lycées*, which are concentrated in cities. A successful student completes the *lycée* with an examination at age 18 and gets a *baccalauréat*, which entitles the student to automatic university admission. Now, as the result of government policy to upgrade French educational levels, more than half of French young people earn the "*bac,*" but they tend to be from middle-class families.

The "Great Schools"

Just as Oxford and Cambridge tower over other English universities, the *grandes écoles* of France are the elite of French higher education. French universities, which stress

---

 ## *How Would You Do on the "Bac"?*

In about twelve hours of nationwide essay exams spread over a week, France's 17- or 18-year old *lycéens* face questions like these, taken from the philosophy section of a recent *baccalauréat* exam. How would you do? Choose one. Spend no more than two hours.

- Why defend the weak?
- Comment on Rousseau's declaration that "one must have societies where inequality is not too

great, where the tyranny of opinion is moderated and where voluptuousness reigns more than vanity."
- What is it to judge?
- Is it reasonable to love?

French students now get their choice of *bac* exams. Some are scientific or technical; the most prestigious is math. The French government is trying to move students from the humanities to technology.

the "impractical" liberal arts, have long been regarded as unimportant. To get into a French university is not hard; indeed, so many have flooded the lecture halls that standards have dropped and graduates have trouble getting jobs. Altogether, some 45 percent of French 20 to 24-year-olds are in full-time education, the highest percentage in Europe and comparable to the United States.

Few, however, make it to one of the Great Schools. Skimming off the brightest and most motivated few by means of rigorous entrance exams, the schools train (rather than "educate") French youths in the practical matters of running a country and then place them in top civil-service and managerial positions. The Great Schools form the people who run France. No other country has anything quite like them. It would be as if West Point produced not army officers but leading administrators instead. Some denounce the *grandes écoles* as elitist and undemocratic, but few suggest abolishing them. Indeed, their stranglehold on French leadership seems to grow stronger.

Although there are several Great Schools, three are considered politically the most important. The *Ecole Polytechnique* was used by Napoleon to train military engineers. Called X for short, *xiens* have their pick of technology and management

French Elections: The Persistence of Region

In 1936 the leftist Popular Front won in the shaded *départements* (map left). In 1981, Socialist François Mitterrand won the presidency with a very similar pattern (map right). Region, as well as social class and religion, often produces distinct and durable voting patterns.

1936: Popular Front vote

1981: Mitterand vote

jobs when they graduate. The *Ecole Normale Supérieure*, founded by Napoleon to create loyal *lycée* instructors, still produces many of France's leading intellectuals—among its graduates have been Jean-Paul Sartre, Raymond Aron, and President Georges Pompidou. The newest Great School, founded just after World War II, is the *Ecole Nationale d'Administration* (ENA), which quickly became the most important. Many of the country's top civil servants are "enarchs," as they call themselves. In keeping with France's new pro-business trend, the hottest Great School is the School of Higher Commercial Studies. One of its graduates: Premier Edith Cresson.

Like all Great Schools, the ENA is extremely selective. Entrance is slanted in favor of the best graduates of the *Institut d'Etudes Politiques* in Paris, a university-level school which itself is hard to get into. This in effect screens out persons of working-class origin who haven't gone to a top *lycée*. Typically fewer than one in ten passes the legendary written and oral exams to join the entering class of less than a hundred. Once in, ENA students get healthy monthly stipends during their program; about half of their 25 months is spent interning in government ministries. Upon graduation, rewards are great. At age 25, the average ENA graduate obtains a high position in government or diplomatic service. About one-third of France's prefects and ambassadors are ENA graduates.

Training in a Great School epitomizes the best and worst of French education. You have to be very smart and hard-working. But you also have to be cold, logical, and removed from ordinary people. Products of the *grandes écoles* may be

The unassuming front of the ENA in the center of Paris conceals its importance in training France's government elite. *(Michael Roskin)*

brilliant, but they often lack common sense and humanity. Some critics call them, pejoratively, "technocrats," people who rule by technical criteria.

The Fear of "Face to Face"

Whatever the educational institution—*lycée*, university, or Great School—the teaching style is similar: cold, distant, uninvolved. Class discussion is discouraged. Questions are from the instructor, not the students. When I taught at the University of Toulouse I was determined to break this pattern; I urged and demanded that my students ask questions and participate in discussion. The result was stony silence; what I requested was totally outside the experience of French students.

By the time they are teenagers, French adolescents have picked up one of the basic characteristics of French culture, what sociologist Michel Crozier called "*l'horreur du face-à-face*." Aside from family and intimate friends, French people feel uncomfortable with warm, cozy, face-to-face relationships. Sometimes tourists say the French are unfriendly to foreigners. They really aren't; they are simply reserved and formal to everyone, including other French people. The French style is opposite that of the American, which places a premium on informality and friendliness. In the United States everyone is supposed to be outgoing, call others by their first names, smile, and say, "Have a nice day." Such behavior—much of it shallow—boggles the French mind.

To avoid face-to-face relationships, the French prefer a highly structured system with clear but very limited areas of competence and set, impersonal rules. That way people know exactly where they stand and nobody butts into another's private domain. British-style pragmatism and "muddling through" are definitely not the French style.

Freedom or Authority?

The points discussed so far—the lack of trust, fear of face-to-face relationships, rigid and rote education—all contribute to a French political personality that can't quite

---

 ## *Rule of the Enarchs*

In 1981 the outgoing conservative cabinet of Valéry Giscard d'Estaing had seven graduates of the elite *Ecole Nationale d'Administration* (ENA), including Giscard himself (class of 1951). The new incoming Socialist cabinet of François Mitterrand had eight ENA graduates.

In 1986 Mitterrand named ENA graduate Jacques Chirac ('59) as prime minister. His cabinet had thirteen *enarques*. In 1988, Michel Rocard ('58) duplicated the pattern. Paris governments may come and go, but the enarchs seem to be always in command.

make up its mind whether it wants freedom or authority. Actually, it wants both, the abstract *liberté* extolled by philosophers and the controlled hierarchies built for centuries by French bureaucrats. What happens is compartmentalization: the private French person loves freedom, while the public French person—in school, on the job, facing the bureaucracy—knows he or she needs reason, order, and formal, impersonal rules. A typical French person has been described as an anarchist who secretly admires the police but could equally be a policeman who secretly admires the anarchists.

The result of this mental split is a continual longing for freedom and a perfect society but an almost equally continual surrender to authority and a highly imperfect society. The balance is unstable; from time to time the quest for liberty bursts out as in 1789, 1830, 1848, the Paris Commune of 1871, and the Events of May of 1968. We will explore this pattern more fully in the next chapter, but it is interesting to note that each of these outbursts ended with a surrender to authority. French political culture has been described as limited authoritarianism accompanied by potential insurrection.

COMPARING

French and American Press Conferences

A French presidential press conference offers a quick insight into French political style. A rare event—maybe once or twice a year—the press conference takes place in an imposing salon of the Elysée Palace, the French White House. The president is seated. On the wall behind him is either a brocade or tapestry. In keeping with the elegant setting, the president is attired in a conservative suit and plain tie.

The journalists sit quietly taking notes. The president expounds abstractly on progress, national greatness, reason, and order, like a professor giving a lecture. He speaks beautiful French, slowly and clearly, with utter confidence and literate, witty phrases, for he is the product of an elite education. Then, if there's time, the president takes a few questions from the reporters. The questions are polite, even timid, for no one dares try to catch or embarrass the president. The president in return treats the journalists like small children who do not understand the logic and clarity of his policies. The president is, in keeping with French political style, magisterial, rational, and aloof.

The American presidential press conference, held more frequently, takes place against a plain blue backdrop. The president stands at a lectern. He is wearing an indifferent suit and striped tie. The president may be nervous and ill-at-ease, for he knows that the newspeople are out to get him, just as they have been out to get every president. As they see it, that's their job. He offers a few opening remarks in an almost defensive tone to explain his recent actions. Then, with a forced smile, he throws the conference open to questions from the floor. The journalists descend like a wolf pack, clawing at the air with their upraised hands, each one demanding attention.

The newsperson called upon—often by name, as the president wants to show he cares about them personally—gives a little lecture setting the background for his or her question. The question itself—on how the president's policies contradict themselves or on his political enemies—is hostile in tone, trying to catch the president in an uncomfortable situation. The president replies in stammering, ungrammatical English, for he is the product of an American college. After a half-hour or so of this ordeal, the dean of the White House press corps lets the victim off the hook with the prearranged. "Thank you, Mr. President." The president, in keeping with the democratic American style, tries to treat the journalists as his equals, but his smile and handshakes as he leaves can scarcely conceal his adversary relationship with the media.

President Mitterrand prepares to instruct journalists at a press conference in the Elysée Palace. *(French Embassy Press and Information Division)*

Legitimacy in France is weaker than in Britain. Rather than a strong feeling of the rightness of institutions and authority, some French accord their system only half-hearted support. A few, on the extreme left and right, hate it.

Social Class

As is Britain, France is a class society. The gap between working and middle class is substantial and—with the educational system slanted in favor of middle-class children—social mobility is not what it could be. In France, as in Britain, if you're born into the working class you'll probably stay there. Distribution of income in France is more unequal than in Britain or even Spain. The rich live superbly in France; the poor scrape by.

Class differences tend to reinforce other cleavages in French society—clerical-anticlerical, urban-rural, radical-conservative, even to a certain extent North-South. That is, these factors tend to line up on one side—never perfectly, of

Great French Expressions: "The Heart Is on the Left, but the Billfold Is on the Right"

Nothing better explains French ambivalence over voting for leftist candidates than the title of this box. Their ideals tell the French to vote left, but self-interest often pulls the other way.

course—but enough to produce a left-right split in French voting. Very broadly, here are the typical characteristics of French voters for the left and the right:

Left Voter	Right Voter
Working class	Middle class
Anticlerical	Prochurch
Urban	Rural or small town

The Great Calming Down

French intellectuals, some of them from the same *grandes écoles* as the governing elite, were for a long generation attracted to Marxism. Observing the huge gap between the ideal of equality and the reality of gross inequality, many highly educated and middle-class French turned to Marxist explanations and sometimes to membership in the Communist party. Philosopher Jean-Paul Sartre backed every leftist cause he could find and urged other intellectuals to become likewise *engagé*. Another *normalien*, his adversary Raymond Aron, disparaged Marxism as "the opium of the intellectuals," a play on Marx's famous statement that "religion is the opium of the masses."

Under Mitterrand, if not before, this changed. French intellectuals became disillusioned with Marxism, communism, and traditional leftist positions. There seem to be several reasons for this major shift, which has long-term implications for French political life. A new group of French intellectuals emerged who scathingly criticized the Soviet Union and communism. In the early 1980s, many West German intellectuals turned anti-American over how to deal with the Soviets and especially over the stationing of new U.S. missiles on German soil. There is no love lost between French and German intellectuals, and the French were happy to repudiate what they regarded as naive German pacifism. French intellectuals became, in contrast, pro-American. The Soviet-supervised takeover of Poland by a Polish general chillingly reminded many French of the takeover of France by Marshal Pétain in the service of Germany during World War II.

But most important, with the election of a Socialist government in 1981, the left was in power. It was one thing to criticize a conservative government but quite another to run a government yourself. French intellectuals and leftists saw how difficult it was to run an economy, assume a role in world affairs, and transform French society. Clever slogans do not translate into effective policy, and many French intel-

The Shape of the French Electorate

The real winner of recent French elections has been neither the left nor the right but the center. Observers referred to the "normalization" of French political life and a healing of the great split in French society. Politicians of the left and right tended to move to the center. Gone are the old ideological visions; moderation and pragmatism are now fashionable.

Underscoring this was a 1992 poll that asked Frenchmen to place themselves on a nine-point ideological scale ranging from extreme left to extreme right. The results are not too different from Britain (see page 52) and Germany (see page 195): Most people are centrist. French politicians are thus on notice: Any party or candidate perceived as too far left or right will lose. This helps explain the miserable showing of the Communists. Once this lesson sinks in, France may turn into a "two-plus"-party system, like many other industrialized democracies.

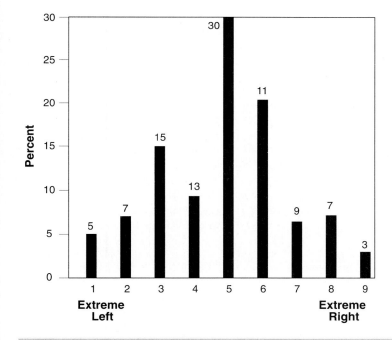

The Self-Placement of French Voters on a Left/Right Ideological Scale.

lectuals became middle-of-the-roaders. Some celebrated free-market capitalism, a strange position for French intellectuals. The Mitterrand presidency contributed a lot by freeing French society from the allure of leftist ideology and guiding it to a middle-of-the-road pragmatism. French politics became centrist, a bit like American politics. With the onset of the Bicentennial, much of the passion that earlier surrounded the French Revolution seemed to go out of it. French politics entered into what might be termed "the great calming down" of de-ideologized pragmatism. As François Furet put it, "The Revolution is over." Most French people seemed to agree.

Vocabulary Building

anticlericalism	*grande école*	*"La Marseillaise"*
baccalauréat	*grandeur*	*normalien*
bureaucratized	inequality	*patrie*
class bias	intellectuals	privatistic
Elysée Palace	*liberté*	schizophrenia
ENA	*lycée*	

Further Reference

BERNSTEIN, RICHARD. *Fragile Glory: A Portrait of France and the French.* New York: Knopf, 1990.

BON, FRÉDÉRIC, and JEAN-PAUL CHEYLAN. *La France qui Vote.* Paris: Hachette, 1988.

CONVERSE, PHILIP E., and GEORGE DUPEUX. "Politicization of the Electorate in France and the United States," *Public Opinion Quarterly (1),* Spring 1962.

CROZIER, MICHEL. *The Bureaucratic Phenomenon.* Chicago: University of Chicago Press, 1964.

EHRMANN, HENRY W., and MARTIN SCHAIN. *Politics in France,* 5th ed. New York: HarperCollins, 1991.

GAFFNEY, JOHN, ed. *The French Presidential Elections of 1988: Ideology and Leadership in Contemporary France.* Brookfield, VT: Dartmouth Publishing Co., 1989.

JUDT, TONY. *Past Imperfect: French Intellecutals, 1944–56.* Berkeley: University of California Press, 1993.

KHILNANI, SUNIL. *Arguing Revolution: The Intellectual Left in Post-War France.* New Haven, CT: Yale University Press, 1994.

READER, KEITH, A. *Intellectuals and the Left in France since 1968.* New York: St. Martin's, 1986.

SINGER, DANIEL. *Is Socialism Doomed? The Meaning of Mitterrand.* New York: Oxford University Press, 1988.

WEBER, EUGEN. *My France: Politics, Culture, Myth.* Cambridge, MA: Harvard University Press, 1991.

WYLIE, LAURENCE. *Village in the Vaucluse.* Cambridge, MA: Harvard University Press, 1957.

10

France: Patterns of Interaction

Parties in Confusion

Party image and voter identification with parties are probably less developed in France than in Britain. We say "probably" because British party ID has been declining whereas French party ID may be stabilizing. Still, many French people do not have long-term party preferences, and French parties have tended to come and go and change their names, blurring the images they have built up. The result is a certain number of voters not firmly attached to one party who shift parties from one election to another. In most of West Europe, elections show only small swings of a few points from the previous contest. In France, new parties sometimes rise and fall within a few years. French parties may gain 10 to 20 percentage points from their previous showing. French voting can be volatile.

Few French parties haven't changed their names at one time or another. Founded in 1905, the Socialists originally called themselves the French Section of the Workers International, or SFIO. In 1969, merging with some smaller left groups, they changed the name to the *Parti Socialiste* (PS). In 1981 the PS under Mitterrand won both the presidency and National Assembly.

The Gaullists seemed to have a new name for each election. From 1947 to 1952 they called themselves the Rally of the French People (RPF). With de Gaulle's coming to power in 1958 it became the Union for the New Republic (UNR), then in 1967 the Democratic Union for the Fifth Republic (UDV^e), in 1968 the Union for the Defense of the Republic (UDR), in 1971 the Union of Democrats for the Republic (with the same initials, UDR), and in 1976 the Rally for the Republic (RPR). Gaullist leader Jacques Chirac was premier from 1986 to 1988. His finance minister at that time, also of the RPR, was Edouard Balladur, who became premier in 1993.

The *Union pour la Democratie Française* (UDF), now one of the three large parties, began as a parliamentary grouping only in 1962 and first ran in elections in 1966 as the Republicans. In 1974 its leader, Valéry Giscard d'Estaing, was elected president and later merged several small centrist parties with the Republicans to form the UDF.

One French party does not play around with name changes—the Communists (PCF)—although they too have trouble with their party's image, plunging from 25 percent of the French vote in 1972 to only 9 percent in 1993. On the other side of the spectrum, the National Front emerged in 1986 as the party of racial hatred. To make things even more confusing, left parties often run jointly as the Union of the Left or Common Program (Socialist and Communist), and right parties as the "Majority" or "Union for France"(Gaullists and UDF).

The Emerging Party System

The French party system is not as complex as it used to be; it is down from ten parties in 1958 to four or five today. Smaller parties have been dropping out, and larger ones are consolidating and forming into two blocs—one left and one right. Schematically it looks like this:

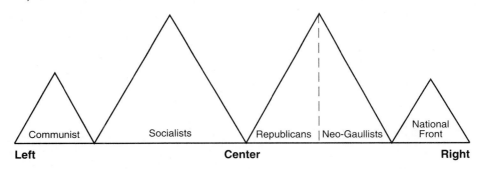

The two blocs are by no means internally harmonious. As we shall see, the Communists are always feuding with the Socialists, and the Republicans constantly striving for the predominance with the Gaullists. If they can help it, none of the other parties wants anything to do with the racist National Front. In terms of voter appeal, however, the two blocs fit into two great French "tendencies" of which we spoke earlier. The left favors ways to make people more equal, by taxing the rich, controlling or nationalizing some industries, and providing more welfare benefits. The right also claims to be for change, but much more cautiously, based on capitalistic economic growth and modest reforms. The National Front wants expulsion of North African immigrants.

The Socialists and the Communists

In most countries, Socialist and Communist parties are natural enemies, partly because they both claim to be ideologically correct. Typically, when one is strong the other is weak. Britain, Sweden, Germany, and Spain all have large socialist-type parties and small Communist parties. In Italy, on the other hand, a large Communist party—now renamed the Democratic Party of the Left—overshadows the Socialists. In France it used to be that way, but during the 1970s and 1980s the Socialists grew and the Communists shrank, so that now the PS is the largest left party in France.

The two parties have common roots. In fact, the PCF is a 1920 offshoot of the Socialists. In a battle that has raged all this century, the Communists claim the Socialists aren't militant enough, that they have abandoned revolutionary Marxism to settle for gradual, pragmatic reformism. Since its founding, the PCF had been faithful to Moscow. For example, the French Communists didn't join in the Resistance until Germany attacked the Soviet Union in 1941. Since Stalin's time, however, the PCF had been gradually becoming more moderate. It denounced the 1968 Soviet invasion of Czechoslovakia and claimed to favor "Eurocommunism," a doctrine developed by the Italian Communists that swore independence from the Kremlin and acceptance of democratic norms. French voters can't trust the Communists, though, for old Stalinist tendencies reappear, as when the party expels a dissenting intellectual, lays down a dogmatic line, or stabs fellow leftists in the back.

The result is an unstable alliance of Socialists and Communists. The two parties hate each other but know they need each other. The second round, or runoff, of a French election places a great premium on combining parties, for in the French runoff a simple plurality wins. If the Communists and Socialists ran separately on the second ballot they would always lose to the combined Gaullists and Republicans. Accordingly, the left parties, the PS, PCF, and sometimes leftist splinter groups, generally support the strongest left candidate, regardless of party, on the second ballot. It is the French electoral system that drives two rivals on the French left together.

Their alliance, or misalliance, seldom lasts, however. The Communists are disciplined and doctrinaire, always citing the "correct" Marxist interpretation of events. The Socialists are loose and sloppy, home to a wide variety of people ranging from Marxists to moderate Social Democrats who care more about capitalism than about welfare. The PS even permits the organization of factions within its ranks, something no Communist party ever allows.

The two parties speak to different electorates. The Communists concentrate on the urban proletariat; some of their greatest strength is in the industrial "Red belt" around Paris. The Socialists typically try to reach the more middle-class civil servants and skilled workers; they have been called "the party of schoolteachers." Indeed, 58 percent of the Socialists elected to the National Assembly in 1981 were teachers or professors. The leadership of the PS is composed almost completely of intellectuals; that of the PCF is heavily working class.

The Gaullists and Republicans

Whereas the French left bloc is unstable, the French right bloc is in somewhat better shape. For the right, doctrine is much less important; they essentially want to keep things the way they are. The Gaullists and Republicans differ little on their main goals. They also tend to speak to much the same electorate. In elections, the Republicans and Gaullists cooperate so closely they often agree on a single candidate on the *first* ballot. Some observers think the two parties have begun to merge, and a majority of French citizens think they should, for there is little difference between them. But merger will be difficult, because on the right—and this is true of many countries—personality becomes a dominant issue.

The French Left: Smother Thy Brother

When François Mitterrand took over the shrunken and demoralized Socialist party in 1971, it was overshadowed on the French left by the Communists, who regularly won a fifth of the vote. Given France's peculiar electoral system—single-member districts with runoff—Mitterrand knew the PS couldn't grow on its own. He also knew that a good third of the Communist vote was not from committed Communists; it was a protest vote that could be won over by an attractive Socialist party. His plan was to embrace the Communists, use them, win away their lukewarm supporters, and then discard them. He did that, and it worked.

In 1972 the PS and PCF worked out their Common Program, spelling out what they would do in power: some nationalization of banks and industry, wage increases, and more welfare funding. They agreed to support each other in the second round of parliamentary and presidential balloting. The Socialist vote grew, in part at the expense of the Communists. Many French on the left didn't trust the Communists but found Mitterrand and the reinvigorated PS attractive. By 1977 the PCF was getting worried and sabotaged the Common Program by making it more radical—something the Socialists refused to go along with. This effectively lost the 1978 National Assembly elections for the left, even though public-opinion polls foresaw them beating the Gaullist and Republican "Majority."

But it was too late for the PCF to dominate the left; the PS was bigger, and the Communists were discredited for wrecking the Common Program and for applauding the Soviet invasion of Afghanistan. In 1981 they went into the first round of the presidential elections denouncing the Socialists but did so poorly—they lost a quarter of their vote—that they meekly supported Mitterrand on the second round. Mitterrand had them where he wanted them: junior partners on whom he depended not at all, for the Socialists held an absolute majority of the National Assembly. Why then did Mitterrand bring the PCF into his cabinet with four rather minor ministries?

The United States was upset with this move that brought Communists into a West European government; Vice President Bush went to Paris to protest. He needn't have worried; Mitterrand knew what he was doing. The Communists in the cabinet (1) kept them from criticizing the government, (2) held down strikes by the largest, Communist-led union, and (3) humiliated the PCF by making it follow Mitterrand's policies, which included a pro-American tilt to build Western defenses against the Soviets. In 1984 a shrunken, demoralized PCF left the cabinet and has done poorly in elections ever since. The crafty Mitterrand had destroyed them.

Here the shadow of de Gaulle still looms large. The French right is torn between those who want to keep his image alive and those who favor more traditional center-right politics. De Gaulle, curiously enough, never aimed at founding a political party. Like Franco, Mussolini, and Latin American military dictators, de Gaulle hated parties, blaming their incessant squabbles for all the troubles of the Third and Fourth Republics. De Gaulle didn't even much care for the Gaullist party; he never formally headed or endorsed it. His attitude seemed to be: "All right, if you must, go ahead and worship me." During his long reign (1958–69), the Gaullist party was simply a tool for his control of the National Assembly. In the legislative elections of 1968, the Gaullists won 46 percent of the popular vote and an outright majority of National Assembly seats. With de Gaulle no longer the party's rallying point, however, Gaullist electoral fortunes declined.

Mitterrand Skunks Chirac

President Mitterrand, losing his Socialist majority in parliament in 1986, amazingly turned the loss to his advantage. He had to name his political archenemy, neo-Gaullist leader Jacques Chirac, as premier. Now all the dirty work fell to Chirac, especially difficult problems of economic growth and unemployment. Mitterrand, by giving up day-to-day political tasks to Chirac, regained popularity while Chirac's popularity plummeted. Mitterrand's old image of the "tranquil force" served him well as the Olympian president above the fray, and after a year he was the most popular political figure in France. All agreed that Mitterrand, simply by staying quiet and dignified, had skunked the energetic but effusive Chirac.

A single charismatic figure leading a national movement is a tough act to follow. A charismatic leader doesn't tolerate other important personalities around him; he prefers obedient servants and yes-men. As a result, when de Gaulle departed in 1969, he left a vacuum that no one in the Gaullist party could really fill. His former premier, Georges Pompidou, won the presidency that year, but by the time Pompidou died in 1974 the Republican candidate, Valéry Giscard d'Estaing, was more attractive than the Gaullist candidate. Because de Gaulle disdained parties, he never bothered institutionalizing his movement into a durable party. The real genius in politics is the one who builds lastingly; de Gaulle didn't.

Trying to fill the vacuum, Jacques Chirac in 1976 reorganized the moribund Gaullists into the Rally for the Republic, commonly called the "neo-Gaullists." A slick performer who alienated many French people by his high-handedness, Chirac alternately quarreled and made up with Giscard and the UDF, whom he needed to sustain his cabinet during his premiership from 1986 to 1988.

The relationship of the two French right parties is similar to that of the two French left parties: they hate each other but need each other. The difference is that the hatred is largely personal, a struggle between two bright, ambitious party leaders who both want to be president, Giscard d'Estaing and Chirac. Just plain jealousy plays a role here. In 1989, Giscard came out strongly in favor of a Republican-Gaullist merger. Over half the general electorate approved, and over three-fourths of right-wing voters supported it. But Chirac, who has long been jealous of and competitive with Giscard, vetoed the merger idea. Nonetheless, the drift of the two large conservative parties toward an unofficial but de facto merger was clear.

The Stalemate Cycle

French politics seems to run in a roughly cyclical pattern. "Normal" politics in France usually means a stalemate in which political groups, constantly feuding among themselves, block major change. This is punctuated every decade or two by an explosion, a crisis the stalemated system can't handle. To get out of the fix, the French people

Balladur Upstages Mitterrand

Premier Edouard Balladur *(French Embassy)*

In an almost reverse play of the first cohabitation period (1986–88), the second cohabitation period (starting in 1993) featured the conservative premier, Edouard Balladur, upstaging and outshining President Mitterrand. Instead of deliberately colliding with the president, as Jacques Chirac had done, Balladur treated Mitterrand with unfailing courtesy and deference. By always conferring with and informing Mitterrand, Balladur won his confidence and gained greater room for personal initiative. Two factors contributed to this new type of cohabitation: Mitterrand, showing his age and health problems, did not wish a terribly active role and clearly would not be running for reelection. Second, Balladur voiced no intrest in running for the presidency; he supported his boss within the RPR, Chirac, for Chirac's third run for the presidency. This made Balladur appear loyal and unthreatening. Ironically, it was qualities such as these that made Balladur France's most popular politician in the early 1990s and the first choice of many for the presidency. The ambitious and energetic Chirac had done it wrong; the calm and polite Balladur did it right, turning his premiership into a gate to the presidency.

have repeatedly turned to a hero, a charismatic figure who hasn't been sullied by "status quo" politics. French politics seems to require a Napoleon from time to time.

After a dozen years of revolutionary turmoil, France welcomed the first Napoleon as a hero who would end chaos. Half a century later, they turned to Louis Napoleon for the same reason. In 1940 the French parliament actually voted dictatorial powers for the aged Marshal Pétain. Pierre Mendès-France was the thinking-person's hero in 1954 when he got France out of Indochina, but he lacked the charisma of the outsider who is above ordinary politics. That figure arrived in 1958 in the person of de Gaulle, who saved France from civil war over Algeria.

De Gaulle believed he had put an end to France's recurrent stalemates and crises by constructing a Fifth Republic with a strong president. But did the Fifth Republic really transcend French history? At first it appeared to. France withdrew from the Algerian debacle, streamlined its party system, and surged ahead economically.

In 1968, however, all hell broke loose (see box) and people began to wonder if the Fifth Republic wasn't suffering from some of the same ills that had plagued predecessors.

Mitterrand also found that the transformation of French politics was not as complete as de Gaulle believed. De Gaulle's personal popularity insured not only his election as president but a large Gaullist party in the National Assembly. This made it easy to govern; any law or budget de Gaulle wanted was rubberstamped in the Palais Bourbon. The Fifth Republic did not depend on the unstable coalitions of the Third and Fourth to govern. But how much did it depend on the same party maintaining control of both the executive and legislative branches?

The Events of May 1968

Just ten years after the near civil war over Algeria that brought de Gaulle into office, his regime suffered another explosion almost as powerful, the "Events of May," as it was euphemistically called. A month of student and worker strikes and battles with the police revealed that under the law-and-order surface of Gaullist France throbbed the old revolutionary tradition. The great split that had plagued France for generations had not completely healed; the cleavage still ran through French society like an earthquake faultline in California—ready to crack open without warning.

Trouble began at the University of Nanterre in a suburb of Paris. Students—fed up with overcrowded facilities, a rigid curriculum, and complete lack of student input—staged a strike. The students' immediate grievances were real and specific. But the strike spread like wildfire because it also appealed to the revolutionary dreams of left-wing students in general. Soon most universities in France were occupied by students playing at revolution. Slogans went up on campus walls: "Be realistic, demand the impossible." "I am a Marxist—of the Groucho tendency." For the students, the Events of May was a cross between the Paris Commune and Woodstock.

It wasn't quite so funny when the student protests spread to workers. With some seven million workers on strike, France virtually shut down. Workers' complaints were more concrete: low wages and long hours. In several occupied factories, workers put up the red flag. *Lycéens* and professional employees joined in the strike. The Communist reaction to all this illustrates how far the party had come from its revolutionary origins. The PCF and its CGT trade union *opposed* the strikes! Fearing a loss of their dominant position on the French left, the Communists denounced the strikers as adventurists who thought they could change society overnight. In some respects the Communists had become a conservative force in French politics, antileft leftists.

The police waded into protesters with tear gas and truncheons. Special riot police, the Republican Security Companies (CRS), seemed to enjoy cracking student skulls. De Gaulle quietly conferred with the French army stationed in Germany, and troops and tanks could be seen around Paris.

But then the revolution—if that's what it was—burned out, like many previous uprisings in French history. De Gaulle went on television with soothing words; he had heard the demand for more participation and would submit himself to the voters' approval in a referendum. De Gaulle changed his mind about a plebiscite and held parliamentary elections instead. The 1968 elections showed, once again, that only part of France was revolutionary, for a majority of the voters supported conservative candidates; Gaullists won an actual majority of seats in the National Assembly.

France found out in 1986. With the election of a National Assembly dominated by the Republicans and Gaullists, Mitterrand named a conservative as premier but stayed on as president. Cohabitation (see Chapter 8) kept the government functioning, but only because Mitterrand consented to letting Premier Chirac pretty much have his way in naming ministers and pursuing conservative policies. Mitterrand played a waiting game, letting Chirac take the blame for unpopular policies. After some time, when Mitterrand's popularity eclipsed Chirac's, Mitterrand began to oppose some of Chirac's policies. A U.S.–style deadlock emerged as neither the president nor the premier could get his way. Chirac controlled parliament, but Mitterrand could block his legislative program and veto bills. If such a deadlock returns to French politics, it could lead to the stalemate cycle starting anew.

Referendum Madness

One technique French leaders revert to is the plebiscite or referendum. This poses major questions directly to the people without going through elected representatives in parliament. The referendum, almost unknown in Britain, has been used eighteen times since 1793 in France. It fits neatly into a very French tradition: Rousseau's idea of the general will. On the surface, nothing could be more democratic than consulting the people directly on their wishes.

In reality, plebiscites can be very tricky, an authoritarian tool that manipulates the masses rather than serving them. The key power in a referendum belongs to the one who writes the question. The question can be posed in such a simplified way that one almost has to vote yes. Furthermore, a referendum often comes after the decision has already been made and the leader just wants popular endorsement.

De Gaulle played the plebiscite game to the hilt. For de Gaulle, the purpose of a referendum was not merely to gain mass approval for a given policy but to reinforce his personal rule. After every plebiscite he could turn to his old enemies, the traditional politicians and say, "You see, the people understand and support me. Who needs you?" In French political theory, again derived from Rousseau, a nation run by a leader who stands in direct communication with the people—without parties, parliaments, politicians, or interest groups getting in the way—is the ideal democracy. Some, however, see in this model the seeds of dictatorship.

De Gaulle attached his personal prestige to each referendum. "If the nation rejects the measure," he in effect told France, "it also rejects me, and I shall resign." This blunt approach worked every time until the last. In 1958 people were glad to see a new constitution. In 1961 and 1962 they were delighted to see Algeria become independent and French troops come home. But de Gaulle's second referendum of 1962 raised some questions. De Gaulle had made a mistake in the 1958 constitution by having the president chosen by a gigantic electoral college composed of local office holders, whom he assumed would be conservative and pro–de Gaulle; they weren't. So in October 1962, bypassing the National Assembly, he asked the voters to amend the constitution to allow direct election of the president. The referendum passed with a 62 percent yes vote, but this represented only 46 percent of the total electorate, far less than de Gaulle expected.

The hint was clear—the French people were happy to get out of Algeria but not so happy about tinkering with the constitution—but de Gaulle ignored it. In 1969, after riding out the 1968 Events of May with resounding electoral success, de

The Five Plebiscites of de Gaulle

YEAR	QUESTION	PERCENT "YES"
1958	New constitution for Fifth Republic	79%
1961	Self-determination for Algeria	75
1962	Approve Algerian independence	91
1962	Direct election of president	62
1969	Reform of Senate and regions	47

Gaulle once again sought to demonstrate that the people were behind him. He picked a rather technical issue that didn't require a plebiscite: the reform (that is, weakening) of the Senate and the setting up of regional subunits. The French people said no, and true to his word, de Gaulle resigned. He went back to Colombey-les-Deux-Eglises, where he died the following year.

Since then, there have been only three referendums. In 1972 Pompidou proposed enlarging the Common Market to include Britain, Ireland, and Denmark. Mitterrand held a referendum in 1988 on granting the Pacific territory of New Caledonia greater independence. It passed, as expected, but only 37 percent of the voters bothered turning out. In 1992, Mitterrand brought the Europe-unifying Maastricht Treaty before the French electorate, who narrowly endorsed it. In none of these cases were referendums really needed to solve a political impasse, and only the last aroused any popular interest. Rather, both presidents tried to use a referendum to bolster mass support and deflect attention away from more serious matters. Voter apathy suggests that France has finally tired of plebiscites.

Fragmented Labor Unions

In Britain we saw how interest groups were well-organized and powerful, especially big labor and big business. This pattern is true of Northern Europe in general, as we shall consider when we come to Germany. In France and in Latin Europe in general there are also plenty of interest groups, but they are usually splintered along party lines.

COMPARING: LATIN EUROPE'S DIVIDED UNIONS

	FRANCE	ITALY	SPAIN
Communist	CGT	CGIL	CO
Socialist	CFDT	—	UGT
Catholic	—	CISL	—
Other	FO (centrist)	UIL (soc. dem.)	CNT (anarchist)

Boring! Boring! No New Faces

Few of France's major political figures has changed in two or even three decades. The major contenders of the 1970s are still the major contenders of the 1990s, and they are all now in their sixties or even seventies. Even Michel Rocard, the bright young kid of the Socialist party (dumped by Mitterrand in 1994), first stood for the presidency in 1969. There is something about the French party system and political culture that does not replace leaders even when they have been unsuccessful. U.S., British, and German parties usually abandon losers.

The thought of a 46-year-old like Bill Clinton becoming president is mind-boggling to the French. Said one French politician, "The French like to have a father figure for their president." Both de Gaulle and Mitterrand served until 78; age was never held against them. A young premier is possible: brainy Laurent Fabius was all of 37 when Mitterrand appointed him in 1984. But, said Mitterrand, "he needs time to suffer and mature."

The trouble with a political system that offers no new faces in twenty years is that it gets boring. French voters, especially young ones, get turned off and turn away from all the major parties. They think no one speaks to their needs. Their discontent then builds until it becomes explosive. Unlike the American system, where state governorship may open the way for the presidency (Carter, Reagan, Clinton), in France, as in most of Europe, people must slowly work their way up through party ranks. You can't "come from out of nowhere" as in America. As we will consider again in Germany, the boredom problem is not a trivial one in European politics.

In Britain (and Germany and Sweden), for example, there is one big labor federation. In France (and Italy and Spain) there are several labor unions—Communist, Socialist, Catholic, and independent unions—competing against each other. The Communist-led CGT *(Confédération Generale du Travail)* is considered powerful in France, but on a comparative basis it isn't very powerful at all. It speaks for perhaps 10 percent of the French work force. Indeed, only about a fifth of French labor is organized into unions. Only U.S. unions are weaker.

French unions also quarrel among themselves. In 1983 when the Talbot car plant wanted to trim its work force, the CGT agreed, but the smaller, Socialist-oriented CFDT *(Confédération Française Democratique du Travail)* refused. Opposing unionists hurled nuts and bolts at each other; fifty-five were injured. Finally, the CFDT called in the riot police. Labor's voice in France is weak and divided. Accordingly, French unions are strong neither in bargaining with management nor in making an impact on government. There are many strikes in France, but they tend to be short because unions lack strike funds.

Part of the problem with French unions is their political slant. Since the largest union, the CGT, is led by Communists, the other parties, especially those who control the government, ignore their demands. French unions engage in political strikes, actions aimed at government policy rather than bread-and-butter demands. In the 1980s French unions often protested closures or layoffs at state-owned industries, much as in Thatcher's Britain. Few French unions take the American view that a union is a device for negotiating better terms with management, not a political tool.

The relative weakness of French unions has an important side effect: it makes them more, rather than less, militant and ideological. Feeling that the government has turned its back on them, French workers are more bitter than the workers of Germany and Sweden, where strong unions have an important voice in government. In those two countries, large and well-organized unions have become moderate and pragmatic.

Business and the Bureaucracy

French business is perhaps less fragmented than labor, for business people rarely dabble in ideology if the present system suits them. The National Council of French Employers (*Counseil National du Patronat Français*) speaks mostly for large firms and generally enjoys good relations with the government, for both are committed to economic growth. Indeed, the state sees its role as guiding and helping industry, a pattern of paternalism going back centuries (and highly developed in Japan). At first, Mitterrand thought he could ignore business interests and pursue a leftist economic program. This worried businesses, and they cut investment in France; some French firms invested in the United States. Mitterrand backed off and tried to make peace with French business. Premier Chirac, borrowing a leaf from Reagan and Thatcher, announced himself to be totally pro-business and proceeded to "privatize" large sections of France's nationalized industries, including a state-owned television network.

The *Patronat* is probably not as influential as the CBI in Britain because of the French tendency toward individualism. A French firm may belong to the *Patronat*, for example, but rely only on its own resources for discreet contacts with the bureaucracy.

The big advantage business has over labor in dealing with government contacts is that the French business executive and civil servant are the same kind of people, often graduates of the same *grande école*, who move back and forth between top jobs in government and industry. Such connections give France's major firms "structured access" to the machinery of administration, something small-business people, farmers, and labor unionists don't enjoy. This builds up bitterness and frustration in the latter groups that explode from time to time in flash parties such as the National Front, in produce dumping by farmers, and in wildcat strikes. The political-bureaucratic systems of Northern Europe, by providing access for all major groups, generally avoid such outbursts.

But neither do French business people dominate government decision making. French political tradition is stacked against it. In the Anglo-American tradition, pluralism is respected, sometimes even celebrated. *Pluralism* is the open and welcome interplay of interest groups with government. When farmers, business people, trade unionists, and ethnic groups lobby in Washington, it is considered perfectly normal. In Britain's Commons, "interested members" make no secret of the fact that they represent certain industries. French political theory, however, still devoted to Rousseau's notion that interest groups are immoral—because they represent partial wills rather than the General Will—tends to view such groups as illegitimate. The French tradition is *étatisme*, "statism," the national government firmly in control, ignoring interest-group demands, and doing what it deems best for French power and prestige. This gives great power to bureaucrats.

The Eternal Bureaucracy

France has been developing its bureaucracy for five centuries. Almost every change of regime has led to growth in the number and functions of French bureaucrats. During the revolving-door cabinets of the Fourth Republic, people used to say that the fall of governments didn't really matter that much because the bureaucracy ran the country anyway.

In France, civil servants oversee a great deal more than do their U.S. counterparts. The closest parallel to the power of French bureaucrats are Japanese bureaucrats, who have a similar frame of mind. France has several nationalized industries—aircraft, automobiles, coal mines, banks, steel, gas, and electricity—in addition to the areas that are state-run throughout Europe, such as the "PTT" (post, telephone, and telegraph) and the railroads. Workers in these industries are not considered civil servants, but top management people are. Every French teacher, for that matter, from kindergarten to university, is a civil servant.

The bureaucrats we are concerned with, however, are the several thousand who staff the Paris ministries, the *Grands Corps,* most of whom are graduates of one of the Great Schools. Even more powerful than their British counterparts, French civil servants of the administrative class (about the top 20 percent) run France. If anything, the bureaucrats' power was enhanced with the coming of the Fifth Republic, for de Gaulle so hamstrung the National Assembly that it could no longer provide a policy counterweight to, or check on, the actions of the top civil servants. Furthermore, under de Gaulle and his successors, including Mitterrand, many of those named ministers were themselves civil servants, often graduates of the ENA or of another *grande école.*

This is not to say that French bureaucrats run things badly; often they do their jobs very well. It's the bureaucratic attitude that alienates their countrymen: aloof, arrogant, cold, logical, and rigid. It's not that they don't meet and interact with other Frenchmen; civil servants sit on some fifteen thousand committees and

---

 "Putting on the Slippers"

The movement of top civil servants to the executive suites of industries is so well known in France that they even have a word for it, *pantouflage,* or "putting on the slippers." This means that a graduate of the *Ecole Polytechnique* or the ENA, after a few years in a Paris ministry, can slip into a cushy, high-paying management job, often in a firm he or she used to deal with as an official. *Pantouflage* is an important connecting link between French business and bureaucracy.

councils all over the country with representatives of business, labor, and farming. The highest of these is the national Social and Economic Council, but even it has a purely advisory capacity, and often advice is ignored as "unobjective." The composition of many of these consultative bodies is increasingly bureaucratic; some 30 percent of the Social and Economic Council is named by the government, for example. The French bureaucratic approach is expressed in their term *tutelle* (tutelage), for they act far more as protectors or guardians than as equals, much less as true "servants" of the public.

Government by Bureaucracy

More than in Britain, the civil service in France constitutes a powerful governing body uncontrolled by elected officials, who sometimes denounce the bureaucracy as an "administrative labyrinth" or even as "administrative totalitarianism." But they can't seem to do much about it.

We should not think France is unique in this regard, for no country has devised a way to keep its bureaucracy under control. France, with a longer history of bureaucratization and the Great Schools' monopoly over the top civil service, merely reveals the pattern more fully. In Japan, it reaches a kind of high point. If you look closely at your own country, you will find much the same thing: government of the bureaucrats, by the bureaucrats, and for the bureaucrats.

In trying to reform, trim, or democratize a bureaucracy we run into a problem underscored by Yale political scientist Joseph LaPalombara: almost any solution we can think of entails *adding* more bureaucrats. In France, for example, Mitterrand once tried a ministry for the reform of administration—still more bureaucracy.

We can see here why the French people, faced with an unresponsive, undemocratic bureaucratic maze, turn frustrated and bitter. Where bureaucracy thrives, democracy shrivels. In trying to fix this, Mitterrand stepped into a contradiction. Socialism needs lots of bureaucracy—to run welfare programs, supervise industry, and

 ## *The Real Power: The Inspection*

Some say that the real elite that runs France is the *Inspection Générale de Finance* (IGF). Selected from among the top ten ENA graduates (see page 116) each year, the superbright *inspecteurs de finances* snoop all around France to see how public funds are spent. Virtually all levels of French government are afraid of them. Few countries have the precise equivalent of the IGF. It would be as if the U.S. General Accounting Office (a branch of Congress) had the enforcement powers of the FBI. *Inspecteurs* of all ranks and ages agree to always see each other. And inspectors who chose to "put on the slippers" (see box on page 134) still have clout, as they continue to offer each other the best public and private jobs. And if they tire of these, that can return to the IGF at a top salary.

plan the economy. But decentralization means loosening bureaucratic controls and returning power to local decision-making bodies. It took Mitterrand about three years to realize he had been working at cross purposes; he turned away from socialism and continued with decentralization.

Vocabulary Building

bloc	Events of May	PCF	RPR
CFDT	factious	plebiscite	stalemate
CGT	fragmented	pluralism	Stalinist
charismatic	Gaullism	PS	*tutelle*
Common Program	Majority	referendum	UDF
étatisme	*pantouflage*	reformism	UDR
Eurocommunism	*Patronat*		

Further Reference

ANDREWS, WILLIAM G., and STANLEY HOFFMANN, eds. *The Fifth Republic at Twenty.* Albany: State University of New York Press, 1981.

BAUMGARTNER, FRANK R. *Conflict and Rhetoric in French Policymaking.* Pittsburgh, PA: University of Pittsburgh Press, 1989.

BELL, DAVID SCOTT, and BRYON CRIDDLE. *The French Socialist Party: The Emergence of a Party of Government,* 2d ed. New York: Oxford University Press, 1988.

CHARLOT, JEAN. *The Gaullist Phenomenon: The Gaullist Movement in the Fifth Republic.* New York: Praeger, 1971.

CHRISTOFFERSON, THOMAS R. *The French Socialists in Power, 1981–1986: From Autogestion to Cohabitation.* Newark, DE: University of Delaware Press, 1991.

CONVERSE, PHILIP E., and ROY PIERCE. *Political Representation in France.* Cambridge, MA: Harvard University Press, 1986.

FREARS, JOHN. *Parties and Voters in France.* New York: St. Martin's, 1991.

FRIEND, JULIUS W. *Seven Years in France: François Mitterrand and the Unintended Revolution, 1981–1988.* Boulder, CO: Westview Press, 1989.

LAPALOMBARA, JOSEPH, "Bureaucratic Pathologies and Prescriptions," chap. 8, in *Politics Within Nations.* Englewood Cliffs, NJ: Prentice-Hall, 1974.

LEVY, DAVID A. L., and HOWARD MACHIN. "How Fabius Lost: The French Elections of 1986," *Government and Opposition* 21 (Summer 1986), 3.

PENNIMAN, HOWARD, R., ed. *France at the Polls, 1981 and 1986: Three National Elections.* Durham, NC: Duke University Press, 1988.

SMITH, W. RAND. *Crisis in the French Labour Movement: A Grassroots' Perspective.* New York: St. Martin's, 1987.

SULEIMAN, EZRA N. *Elites in French Society: The Politics of Survival.* Princeton, NJ: Princeton University Press, 1978.

WILSON, FRANK L. *Interest-Group Politics in France.* New York: Cambridge University Press, 1988.

CHAPTER ***11***

What the French Quarrel About

From Stagnant to Dynamic

In some ways, the state of the French economy has been the opposite of the British. Britain suffered a long-term economic decline, dropping further and further back in the front rank of industrialized countries. France, whose economy grew only slowly in the nineteenth and early twentieth centuries, awoke as if from a slumber after World War II and zoomed ahead economically. With growth rates reaching 6 percent a year—more recently, however, much lower—France became the fourth industrial power in the non-Communist world (after the United States, Japan, and West Germany). The French experience illustrates that decline need not be permanent and that a country, with the right policies and the right spirit, can turn its economy from stagnant to dynamic.

What did the trick? The typical French business firm prior to World War II was a small family affair. Growth was not emphasized; keeping it in the family and earning just enough for a good living was all that mattered. This meant lots of little companies and stores rather than a few big ones. Rather than compete by cutting prices or offering better goods and services, the French, with a *petit bourgeois* mentality, sought to hide behind a protective government that would set prices and keep out foreign competition by high tariffs. It was a cozy arrangement for French business families, but it kept France economically backward.

World War II produced quite a jolt. The French elite, smarting from the German conquest and eager to restore France to world leadership, realized the economy had to change. A Planning Commission issued what were called "indicative plans" to encourage—but not force—French business people to expand in certain sectors and regions. Quite distinct from Communist-style centralized plan-

137

ning, indicative planning in effect said, "Look, everything is favorable for a new widget factory in the southwest. If you build one you'll probably make a lot of money." As we saw in the last chapter, there are warm connections between French bureaucracy and business, and it didn't take business people long to get the hint. The French Planning Commission provided the business community with economic research and gentle nudges to push it along what are deemed desirable paths.

Foreign competition was another jolt. First the European Coal and Steel Community starting in 1952, then the Common Market starting in 1957, dismantled France's protective tariffs. At first French business people were terrified, sure that more aggressive German industry would swamp them. But gradually they learned that French firms could be quite competitive and enjoy the enlarged sales opportunities afforded by the Common Market. French business firms changed, becoming bigger, more modern, and expansion-oriented. But success brought its own problems.

Big Guys versus Little Guys

On a street where I lived in Toulouse, in the space of a few blocks, there were not only pharmacies, dairy shops, bakeries, houseware shops, furniture and vegetable stores, butchers, cafés, and tobacco shops, but at least three of each type of store. Perhaps two miles distant, in a suburb, was a mammoth single-stop shopping center named *Mammouth*. There, under one roof, were a combined supermarket (offering perhaps a hundred different cheeses), discount house (everything from clothes to auto parts), and cafeteria. Not only was the selection bigger at *Mammouth* than among the myriad neighborhood stores, but prices were lower, too.

Such developments have been going on throughout France for years. Some call it the Americanization of France, but it's really just the modernization of an old-fashioned economy. The impact on the small shopkeepers is predictable: they are being squeezed out, screaming all the way. What they regarded as their birthright—the small, family-owned, uncompetitive shop—is being destroyed. As Marx put it: "One capitalist kills many."

A parallel problem hits French farmers; there are also too many small farms. French peasants, for a variety of reasons, became overly attached over the years to their holdings and lifestyle. With few jobs in the cities anyway, almost 40 percent of French people stayed on the family farm through World War II. France remained a nation of peasants for an unusually long time. With postwar industrialization, this changed; now only 6 percent of the labor force works on the land (still a bit high for an advanced country). Since 1950, two-thirds of France's farms, mostly small, have disappeared; they either lie fallow or have been swallowed up by larger, more mechanized farms. France is the world's second largest food exporter (first place: the United States). Still, French agriculture, like its U.S. counterpart, frequently overproduces, and French farmers often dump produce on highways to protest what they regard as inadequate price supports. The Paris government, like most governments, is extremely protective of farmers, and French insistence on subsidizing farm products has been one of the Common Market's main stumbling blocks (and bones of contention with the United States).

The small shopkeepers and farmers who are being squeezed out contribute to France's electoral volatility. They shift allegiances rapidly, to whomever seems to promise their survival. The Gaullists have been a major beneficiary, but the frightened little shopkeepers have also contributed to the French tendency for "flash parties" to suddenly appear on the scene, sparkle for a few years, and then fade to oblivion. There is no nice solution to the problem of too many small shops and farms; they've got to go, and it hurts. Attempts to retain them are hopeless and even reactionary, the stuff demagoguery is made of.

The Nationalization Question

For much of the postwar period, a fourth of French business and industry was state-owned, more than any other West European country. Now, after major privatization programs, about a tenth is still state-owned. Some nationalization of French

---

 ## Nukes, French Style

The French complain and quarrel about many things, but, curiously, nuclear energy isn't one of them. The French mostly accept nuclear energy, and none of the three major parties is against it. The anti-atom Ecology-Greens won no seats in the 1993 legislative elections.

The French, short of other energy sources, have gone all-out for nuclear-generated electricity and have made a success of it. Three-quarters of France's electricity is from nuclear power plants. In comparison, only a little over a fifth of U.S. electricity is nuclear, a level unlikely to rise in the face of astronomical cost overruns in power-plant construction. Some U.S. plants have been scrapped before they were finished. Overall, French nuclear-generated electricity costs less than half America's, and New Hampshire's problem-plagued Seabrook reactor could have been built by the French for one-sixth its cost.

How do the French do what Americans can't? Here we see some of the occasional advantages of centralized, technocratic rule. The state-owned utility, Electricité de France, developed a single type of reactor and stuck with it. Competing U.S. manufacturers proffer a variety of designs, some not well tested. When Paris gives the word to build a reactor, the political, financial, regulatory, and managerial sectors mesh under central direction, and the project gets done on time. In the United States, those sectors quarrel, with no central guidance, and the project takes years longer than it should. Environmentalist groups in France—not very big anyway—have no legal power to block or delay projects. The centralized French system is also better able to train personnel; there have been no Three Mile Islands in France. Nuclear power plants are an important and growing part of France's export trade. The very strengths of the American system—decentralization, competition, light regulation, and pluralist interplay—tripped up the U.S. nuclear industry.

The "other" nuclear question—nuclear weapons—also drew relatively little attention in France. Whereas British and West German peace marchers mightily protested the installation of new U.S. missiles, the French did not. In the first place, no U.S. missiles were put on French soil; de Gaulle had expelled all American bases in 1966. Second, most French, including President Mitterrand, saw the need for a greater West European counterweight to growing Soviet strength. Third, ever since de Gaulle, the French have had an independent nuclear *force de dissuasion* of which they are proud. Accordingly, banning the bomb may have been an issue in Britain and Germany, but it never was in France.

The Poujadists: A Classic Flash Party

In 1953 Pierre Poujade founded the Union for the Defense of Shopkeepers and Artisans (UDCA) to protect small-business people from the bigger, more efficient department stores and supermarkets that were driving many of them out of business. Tinged with reaction and anti-Semitism, *Pou-*
jadism caught fire, and in the parliamentary elections of 1956 won 12 percent of the popular vote; some thought it was the coming party. It fell as quickly as it rose, however; *Poujadism* disappeared in 1958 when de Gaulle took over the French right.

---

industry took place right after World War II. Louis Renault, founder and owner of the auto firm, had collaborated with the Germans, so the Free French seized his empire in 1944. Other industries, such as steel, were taken over by the state because without government subsidies they'd go under, creating unemployment. Still other areas, such as aviation, are prestige industries aimed at boosting France's world standing.

The left in France had traditionally demanded more nationalization, including all big banks and industries. They argued that under state control big industries would pay workers more, hire more workers, and produce what French people really need rather than capitalist luxuries only a few can afford. Traditionally much of the French right also liked state-owned industries, believing that they contributed to national power and greatness and could be best run by brilliant *xiens* and *enarques* (see page 115). De Gaulle and the Gaullists, for example, did not embrace a totally free-market economy but supported a major state sector in heavy industry, what the French call *étatisme* (statism, a pattern we shall see more fully developed in Brazil). Remember, to be conservative in Europe is not the same as being conservative in America. Some center-rightists understood that nationalization guarantees inefficiency, which in turn requires subsidies and tariff protection, a step backward in France's economic history.

Under President Giscard d'Estaing, these free-market conservatives got their chance. His premier, economist Raymond Barre, instituted a "new revolution" that aimed to give France a free economy for the first time. Barre scrapped the government price-control system (consisting of over thirty thousand decrees) that France had used for decades to try to hold down the cost of living. (It didn't work: manufacturers went to their friends in the bureaucracy and got them to raise price ceilings.) Barre understood that a free market in the long run restrains prices better than decrees. In the short run, however, the French economy behaved like the British economy under the first few years of Thatcher's very similar program: inflation and unemployment increased. This contributed to the Socialists' electoral victories of 1981. Good economics is sometimes bad politics.

Within two years, however, Mitterrand discovered that good politics—promising growth and greater equality—can be bad economics. Mitterrand pumped money into the economy by increasing welfare benefits, raising the minimum wage, shortening the work week to thirty-nine hours, and adding a fifth week of paid vacation. In 1982 the Socialists nationalized five giant industrial groups and thirty-nine banks. The governmental deficit led to increased inflation, and the franc slid to ten to a dollar. Increased purchasing power in the hands of the public sucked in a prodigious amount of foreign goods and gave France a gigantic international debt. Unemployment rose. Some of the newly nationalized firms, which the Socialists had naively believed were making profits, turned out to be money-losers that had to be propped up with government funds. By 1983, observers were calling the Socialist economic policy a debacle.

To his credit, Mitterrand backed down. He replaced some of the more *dirigiste* (directing things from above, the longstanding French technocratic style) ministers with moderates who favored private business. Calling for "socialist rigor," he increased taxes and reduced public spending to bring down inflation, which fell from 10 to 2 percent a year. Gone were the Socialist promises to use state power to correct social wrongs. "You don't want more state?" asked Mitterrand. "Me neither." Believers in socialism had received a real slap in the face and abandoned their leftism

The Concorde: A Prestigious Dinosaur

The Concorde supersonic aircraft illustrates what can go wrong with nationalized industries: they can build the wrong product for the wrong reason and cost taxpayers a fortune. The Concorde's development began in 1962 as a joint Anglo-French enterprise to give their lagging aircraft industries a technological jump on the Americans. They thought the graceful bird would be purchased by airlines all over the world.

Things didn't work out that way. Huge overruns boosted development costs to $4.28 billion and the price per plane to $92 million, close to ten times what had been estimated. The Concorde consumed three times the fuel per passenger mile of a Boeing 747. Only British and French airlines purchased Concordes and then only because the nationalized air carriers were required to by law. Because they seldom filled their one hundred seats, the airlines lost money on Concorde runs. Only fourteen Concordes were ever finished before production shut down in 1978.

Why did Britain and France do it? A nationalized industry often has different priorities than a normal commercial venture. In this case "technological nationalism" was a factor, that is, their need to show the world how advanced they were. Employment was another factor; both Britain and France created thousands of jobs with the Concorde. Once the project was underway and the cost overruns mounting, neither country wanted to admit it had made a mistake. Because the aviation companies building the supersonic plane had access to their national treasuries, they did not have to undergo the discipline of raising capital in the marketplace.

This is not to say that nationalized industries always do things wrong. Aerospatiale of France, once it made the decision to drop Concorde and participate in a European consortium to produce the more conventional Airbus in Toulouse (purchased by some U.S. airlines), started doing much better, although it is still subsidized. Nationalized industries can prosper if they are run like private industries, the way Renault is run.

for middle-of-the-road liberalism, a move salutary for the entire French political system. The economy improved, but not enough to prevent the Socialists from losing the 1986 legislative elections to conservatives.

Premier Jacques Chirac began an immediate program of privatization, the selling off of state-owned enterprises to private investors, as Thatcher had already done in Britain. Some sixty-five French industries and banks were thus returned to private hands. Mitterrand mostly went along with the privatization—some had begun earlier, under a Socialist premier—but drew the line on sales to foreigners for reasons of "national independence." Premier Balladur vowed to continue and expand privatization.

Privatization by itself did not solve France's economic problems, for in 1993 France, and indeed the Common Market as a whole, fell into recession. Much of the problem was a spillover from German unification (see Chapter 16), which caused the German central bank to boost interest rates so high that they slowed down economies throughout West Europe. Unemployment shot past 10 percent. As in Britain, much of France's social security costs are mandated by law, so when more people are jobless, they are automatically entitled to fairly generous benefits. As in Britain, France's budget deficit climbed toward 6 percent of GDP—that is, the government is pumping out 6 percent more than it is taking in—a point that is considered dangerously inflationary. (The U.S. deficit was about 3 percent and not considered dangerous.) The result: The franc fell in relation to other currencies, undermining the European Monetary System that France had sworn to uphold.

The Wealth Gap

Income differences in France are among the largest in Europe. This by itself is a political issue. Indeed, a 1976 report on income differences in Europe, showing France

COMPARING

 The Spanish Socialists Do It Better

Just a year after the French Socialists, the Spanish Socialists swept to power in 1982 with a resounding 46 percent of the vote and a majority in parliament. Young, attractive Felipe González became Spain's first Socialist prime minister since the 1930s. Unlike Mitterrand, though, González stayed relatively popular. The secret of his success: Unlike Mitterrand, González had turned his PSOE (*Partido Socialista Obrero Español*) into a moderate, center-left party *before* the election, not after. Mitterrand whipped up leftist phraseology and promised a socialist France with prosperity and equality. González earlier overcame Marxists within PSOE to rededicate the party merely to consolidating democracy—an important enough task in a Spain only recently emerged from Franco's authoritarianism. González promised no quick improvements in the economy and had little interest in nationalizing industry. The result: The Spanish Socialists won reelection in 1986, 1989, and 1993. The moral: Don't promise too much.

more unequal than Spain, confirmed precisely what the Socialists and Communists had been saying. The wealth gap in France—and in most countries—is even wider than the income gap. Wealth and income are not the same: *income* is what you acquire (wages, dividends, and so forth), and *wealth* is what you own or have saved (houses, stocks, and other investments). Wealthy French people often have a chateau in the country as well as a house or apartment in Paris. Giscard d'Estaing, who was raised in a chateau, has at least three country houses. Even Socialist President Mitterrand has a nice country home. At the bottom of the French socioeconomic ladder, an estimated two million French people form a "subproletariat" of unemployed, illiterate, despairing people. Mitterrand promised to make all French citizens more equal; he has made little progress.

It's easy to promise, but the question is how to accomplish this goal. Taxes are supposed to provide one classic way: soak the rich and distribute the revenue to the poor. In few countries has this worked, however, for most taxation systems have loopholes that help the rich stay wealthy. In France, as in America, the tax burden falls most heavily on wage and salary earners, lighter on those with "unearned" income from financial wheeling and dealing. And trying to collect taxes in France is a difficult task. The French, like the Italians, are masters at deceiving tax collectors. Wealthy French put their money in diamonds, gold and paintings (goods that can be hidden out of sight), agricultural or forest land (taxed at only one-fourth its value), and even government bonds, which because they don't list the owners' names are advertised as a "convenient and exceptionally discreet investment."

To make up for its tax shortfall, France—following Common Market policy—has a "value-added tax" (VAT), a large, hidden sales tax that doesn't show on the purchaser's receipt. Like sales taxes generally, the VAT penalizes poorer people more than rich; economists called it a "regressive" tax. But the French government

Is There a VAT in Your Future?

Throughout West Europe, governments raise close to 30 percent of their revenues through hefty (10 to 20 percent) sales taxes called "value-added taxes" (VAT). In contrast, U.S. sales taxes, mostly at the state level (America has no national sales tax), account for some 15 percent of all U.S. taxes (federal, state, and local). But European VATs are invisible; they are calculated at every stage value is added to a product (for example, after pieces of cloth are sewn together to make a shirt), not added to the purchase price at the cash register, as in America. Accordingly, European governments reason that it's not so painful as other kinds of taxes.

VAT makes some economic sense, too. It is a very broad-based tax that everyone has to pay; you cannot cheat on it, as many do on income taxes. By making prices higher, it encourages people to consume less and save more. This helps contain inflation and makes more money available for loans that promote economic expansion and new employment. For these reasons, some U.S. presidents have considered implementing VAT. With big U.S. budget deficits, VAT is an appealing possibility as Congress considers how to raise revenues without increasing income taxes.

relies on it for over 40 percent of its revenue because, since it is hidden, people don't complain too much.

Unequal income and wealth and unfair taxation remain a Communist and left-Socialist battle cry in France. The mainstream Socialists now realize how difficult it is to correct these imbalances.

France's Racial Problem

Even more than Britain and Germany (and the United States), France has a problem with immigrants. There are over 3.6 million foreigners living in France, but if one counts naturalized citizens and second generation, the total is some 9 million, about 16 percent of the French population. France has long assimilated European immigrants. From 1880 to 1960 some 7 million Italians, Spaniards, Portuguese, Poles, and Russians were integrated into French life with little discrimination.

Some 3.5 million Muslims, mostly from former French colonies in black and North Africa, however, have created major racial tensions. From unemployment and misery in Algeria, Morocco, Tunisia, Senegal, and Mali, immigrants come to France to take the hardest, dirtiest, lowest-paid work—tasks French workers won't do anymore. Some immigrants, often illegals, become street peddlers or petty criminals. They live in poor, shabby housing (although nothing nearly as bad as urban U.S. ghettos). When I lived in a suburb north of Paris in 1989, I reckoned that a third of my fellow rail commuters were black or North Africans. One French homeowner in this area, in Aulnay-sous-Bois, ruefully wisecracked that it had become "Aulnay-sous-Cameroun."

In public, few French people will say or do anything hostile to the African immigrants. The French have a tradition of tolerance and personal freedom. In private, though, many indicate their fear and dislike of Africans. Some would like immigrants sent home, a feeling that the National Front feeds on. All of France's main parties are against further immigration. Mitterrand stated that immigration had passed "the threshold of tolerance" and took steps to cut it, so that now immigration is as tight as in Britain.

Meanwhile, what to do with the black and North Africans currently in France? Many wish to become French and work hard at improving their French language and job skills. But France has Europe's largest Islamic community, and Muslims resist assimilating to European cultural norms. Some become defiantly Islamic, as if to underscore their pride in their religion and culture. One point of friction among many is Muslim girls coming to school defiantly wearing head scarves as a sign of their religion. Should they be suspended? Thundered one imam (Muslim cleric): "Allah's law takes precedence over French law." (The French deported him.) Now, as one official observed, "for the first time, we have people born in France who are not French."

The result has been the de facto creation of U.S.–type ghettos, where angry, uneducated youths slide into crime and drugs. The French police harass them, and some Muslim youths have died at police hands in recent years. From time to time, the youths riot. "We have American cities as a warning of what could happen here," said one official. The dislike of French and Muslim communities toward each other has fed the growth of Islamic fundamentalism, which many French regard as a foreign threat. Tense as the Muslim problem is in France, it should be pointed out that there have been no skinhead or neo-Nazi killings of immigrants as in Germany.

The National Front: Another Flash Party?

Somewhat like the Poujadists of the 1950s, the National Front (FN) sprang from out of nowhere to capture over 10 percent of the French vote in the late 1980s. The National Front's leader is Jean-Marie Le Pen, a former French paratrooper in Algeria and Poujadist deputy, who preaches a racist and nationalist line against France's Muslim immigrants and its long-standing Jewish community. Le Pen, a spellbinding orator, knows just how to push French anti-Muslim, anti-black, and anti-Jewish psychological buttons. He denies that he is a racist; he's just pro-French. In 1984 he authored *Les Français d'Abord* (*The French First*).

FN voting strength, although rarely a majority, is concentrated in localities where there are many black and North African immigrants. Some FN supporters were earlier Republican, Gaullist, and even Communist activists. The working class can be quite racist, especially in times of high unemployment.

Will the FN last longer than the Poujadists, the earlier party of resentment? Although winning no seats in the 1993 parliamentary elections, the FN won one vote in eight in the first round. Because the immigrant problem is so large and visible, the FN will probably have a constituency for many years. Notice how Britain and Germany, facing the identical immigrant problem, produced, respectively, the anti-immigrant National Front and National Republican parties.

Most French politicians agree that the immigrants should be better integrated into French economic and cultural life, but they disagree on how to do this. Improving the immigrants' housing, schooling, and jobs all costs money. The tax burden is dumped most heavily on the municipalities where there are the most immigrants. One mayor of a working-class suburb pointed out that Muslim immigrants have prodigious numbers of children "whose schooling our town has to pay for." This is one reason the National Front vote is the strongest where there are more Muslims. The parties on the left, Socialist and Communist, are more willing to spend additional funds. The National Front, of course, is militantly against such expenses. Said one FN activist: "The solution for the immigrants is not integration; it's sending them back to their country."

France's Education Problems

Related to the immigration problems are France's problems with schooling. Basically, the problems grow out of the French effort to rapidly expand educational opportunity in order to give everyone a chance for social mobility and integrate immigrant children into French society. In itself, this effort is praiseworthy, reminiscent of U.S. efforts to solve social problems by increased school integration. And, as in the United States, this leads to new problems.

First, immigrant children tend to live in ghettos. Sending them to schools with each other, with few French children in the classroom, makes it difficult to teach them proper French language and culture. Many cannot speak any French when they first enter school. The threat of having their schools inundated by a wave of immigrant children prompted local French authorities in some cases to prohibit enrolling African and Arab children, a move that was shot down by the national authorities. Leftists put up banners proclaiming "the right to school for all children." Rightists approved of the anti-immigrant stance.

For both French and immigrant children, the government decided that a much larger portion of French young people have to finish high school with the "bac," discussed in Chapter 9. The Socialist government in 1985 announced an ambitious plan to send 80 percent of all young people to *lycées* by the year 2000 and has made good progress toward this goal. The bac has been enlarged to include technical and vocational options. The object is to form a literate and qualified labor force of the sort needed by a modern economy. But even with a major upsurge in education spending, the public *lycée* system became severely overburdened, as evidenced by dilapidated buildings, crowded classrooms (some with over 40 students per teacher), and crime in the hallways and restrooms. Sound familiar? (Middle-class French parents, afraid of school decay, increasingly send their children to private *lycées*.) French student street protests from time to time shake the Paris government, for the protests remind them of the 1968 Events of May.

The Covering Up of Things Past

Almost annually, a new case comes to public attention of Vichy France's collaboration with Nazi Germany. It is a source of continuing embarrassment that many French would like to forget. In 1983 Klaus Barbie, the Gestapo's wartime chief of Lyons, was extradited from Bolivia to France. Barbie had tortured and killed dozens

COMPARING

 How U.S. and French Youth Handle the School Problem

American and French school problems so far sound quite similar, but U.S. and French young people part company in how they handle the problem. In America, young people, especially from disadvantaged groups, simply drop out of school. Dispirited, they act like they are beaten before they start. In France, angry but hopeful students take to the streets in protest. In cities throughout France in 1990, tens of thousands of high school students marched to demand cleaner, newer schools, smaller classes, and more security officers in schools.

Can you imagine such protests from U.S. high schoolers? The difference is that American youth often dislike school, culture, and books, and no longer see education as their ticket to the middle class. French students, including immigrant children, see schooling with some enthusiasm as their way up and out of the ghetto. They accept the basic premise that education is good; they just want more and better education. They also come from a tradition of mass protest to change government policy. In comparison, many American youth seem passive and hopeless. An earlier generation of Americans, especially immigrant children, gladly embraced education as their path to upward social mobility. What has happened in America to change this attitude?

of Resistance members and shipped hundreds of Jews, including small children, to death camps. His 1987 trial pointed out how he could not have done these things without many French helpers. Barbie was sentenced to life and died in prison.

In 1994, a high-ranking officer of the collaborationist French *Milice* (militia), Paul Touvier, then 79, received a life sentence for crimes against humanity. Touvier had hidden forty-four years in some fifty fundamentalist Catholic monasteries. His arrest in 1989 pointed up the connection between the Catholic right and the Vichy regime. Touvier had been tried *in absentia* after the war and sentenced to death, but his church friends sheltered him and his family.

In 1990, the high Vichy police official who rounded up Jews and put them on death trains was ordered to trial before the Special High Court of the Liberation, a court that had not existed for decades. Critics accused the government of stalling until the 81-year-old René Bousquet died, in order to avoid embarrassment. Some accused Mitterrand of not wanting to bring Bousquet to trial. The spritely Paris daily *Libération* asked, "Will the French state continue to protect high French officials accused of crimes against humanity?" A flamboyant eccentric solved the Bousquet problem by plugging him four times with a handgun. The underlying problem remained, however, and that was that France had never adequately come to grips with its past, especially its Vichy past. To see how another land has tried to come to grips with its past, let us turn to Germany.

Vocabulary Building

chateau	nationalization	subsidy
Common Market	*petit bourgeois*	tariff
decontrol	Planning Commission	technocrat
flash party	Poujadism	technological nationalism
income	regressive tax	value-added tax
indicative planning	subproletariat	wealth

Further Reference

ADAMS, WILLIAM JAMES. *Restructuring the French Economy: Government and the Rise of Market Competition since World War II*. Washington, DC.: Brookings, 1989.

AMBLER, JOHN S., ed. *The French Socialist Experiment*. Philadelphia, PA: Institute for the Study of Human Issues, 1985.

ARDAGH, JOHN, *France Today*, rev. ed. New York: Penguin, 1989.

CERNY, PHILIP, and MARTIN SCHAIN, eds. *Socialism, the State and Public Policy in France*. New York: Methuen, 1985.

ESTRIN, SAUL, and PETER HOLMES. *French Planning in Theory and Practice*. Winchester, MA: Allen & Unwin, 1983.

FLOWER, J. E. *France Today*, 6th ed. New York: Methuen, 1987.

FREIBERG, J. W. *The French Press: Class, State, and Ideology*. New York: Praeger, 1981.

GAFFNEY, JOHN, ed. *France and Modernisation*. Brookfield, VT: Avebury, 1988.

GODT, PAUL, ed. *Policy-Making in France: From de Gaulle to Mitterrand*. New York: Pinter, 1989.

HALL, PETER A. *Governing the Economy: The Politics of State Intervention in Britain and France*. New York: Oxford University Press, 1986.

ROSS, GEORGE, STANLEY HOFFMANN, and SYLVIA MALZACHER, eds. *The Mitterrand Experiment: Continuity and Change in Modern France*. New York: Oxford University Press, 1987.

PART III ✳ *Germany*

CHAPTER 12

Germany: The Impact of the Past

Germany's Uncertain Borders

Britain has natural borders. France claims to have natural borders, but one of its six sides (the northeast) has been disputed. Germany, however, has natural borders only on its north and south (the Baltic Sea and Alps), and this fact has contributed to its tumultuous history. Germany has expanded and contracted over the centuries, at times stretching from Alsace (now French) to East Prussia (now Polish and Russian). After World War II its eastern wing was chopped off, and the country was divided into eastern and western occupation zones, which in 1949 became East and West Germany. The Federal Republic of Germany that reunified in 1990 is considerably smaller than the mighty Second Reich at the turn of the century.

Germany's location in the center of Europe and the flat, defenseless North German Plain imposed two unhappy options on the nation. If Germany was divided and militarily weak—its condition through most of history—it was Europe's battle-ground. On the other hand, if Germany was united and militarily strong enough to deter any combination of potential attackers, it was also strong enough to beat all its neighbors one at a time. When Germany unified in the last century, it automatically became a threat to the rest of Europe; it was big, populous, and strategically located. Some Europeans still fear a united Germany. Geography, in making a united Germany a threat, has been unkind to Germany.

Who Are the Germans?

Contrary to Nazi race theory, the Germans are as much an ethnic mixture as any people in Europe. The original Germans identified by the Romans were a collection of several barbarian tribes, some of which became Romanized. The invasion of the Huns in the fourth century set off gigantic migrations throughout Europe as everyone fled from their advance. Many Germans sought refuge in Roman territory, and soon Germanic tribes were roaming through and destroying the Roman Empire, eventually settling in various parts of it.

Since that time Germans have presented one face to the West and another to the East. To the West, to France and Italy, the heirs of Rome, they were awed and respectful of the superior culture, which they tried to copy. To the East, however, they saw barbarians—first Huns, then Slavs—whom they either Germanized, exterminated, or pushed back. Whole Slavic- or Baltic-speaking areas were Germanized, and many of today's Germans are of East European descent. Some Germans hate to admit it, but they are a combination of Celts, Romans, several Germanic tribes, Slavs, Balts, and even Jews. When the Nazis introduced their model of the perfect Nordic specimen, some Germans quietly chuckled, for practically none of the Nazi leaders matched the tall, athletic, blond, blue-eyed image.

The Fragmented Nation

The Germanic tribes were so impressed by Rome—whose empire they were inadvertently destroying—that they pretended to preserve and continue the empire. When in 800 the Frankish king Charlemagne (German: Karl der Grosser) was crowned in Rome, he called his gigantic realm the Holy Roman Empire. Although it soon fell apart, the German wing continued calling itself that until Napoleon ended the farce in 1806.

In England, as we saw, power between king and nobles was kept in balance, resulting in a constitutional monarchy that moved in spurts toward civil liberty, limited government, and rule by Parliament. In France, absolutism upset the equation, and the French kings amassed more and more power leading to a centralized, bureaucratic state. Germany went the other way: the nobles gained more and more power until by the thirteenth century the emperor was a mere figurehead while princes and leading churchmen ran ministates as they saw fit. Germany was not one country but a crazy-quilt of hundreds of independent principalities and cities.

The split between Roman Catholic and Protestant accentuated Germany's fragmentation. Protestant reformer Martin Luther reflected the feeling of much of northern Germany that the Roman church was corrupt and ungodly. The North German princes especially didn't like paying taxes to Rome and found Lutheranism a good excuse to stop. South Germany stayed mostly Catholic. A predominantly Protestant north and Catholic south still characterize modern Germany.

Two wars resulted from the religious question. In the first, the Schmalkaldic War (named after the town of Schmalkaden where Protestant princes formed a coalition) of 1545–55, the Habsburg Emperor Charles V nearly succeeded in crushing Lutheranism, when the Protestants allied with Catholic France to beat Charles. Trying to decide which parts of Germany should be Catholic and which Protestant, the Religious Peace of Augsburg in 1555 came up with the formula *cuius regio eius religio*— "whoever reigns, his religion." Thus the religion of the local prince decided an area's religion, a point that deepened the disunity of Germany and the power of local princes.

The peace proved shaky, though, and in 1618, as the Habsburgs again tried to consolidate their power, a much worse war broke out, the Thirty Years' War. Again, at first the Catholic Habsburgs won. By 1631, help from other countries arrived. Cardinal Richelieu of France saw that the Habsburgs might encircle his country, so he sided Catholic France with the Protestants. In international relations, power and national interests are a lot more important than religious or ideological affinity. A strong Swedish army under Gustavus Adolphus battled in Germany for the Protes-

The Changing Shape of Germany

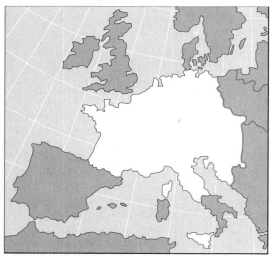

800: Charlemagne's Holy Roman Empire

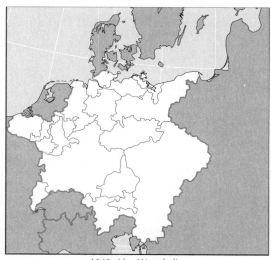

1848: After Westphalia

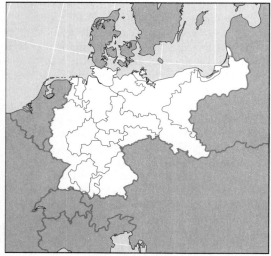

1815: The German Confederation

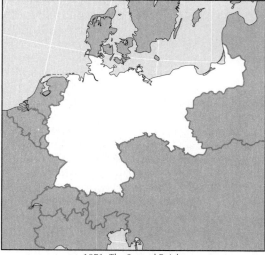

1871: The Second Reich

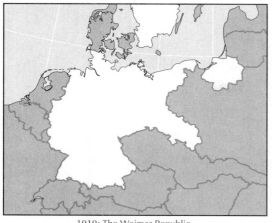

1919: The Weimar Republic

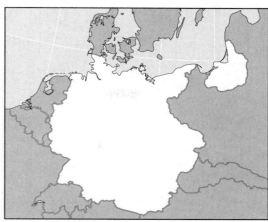

1939: Hitler's Third Reich

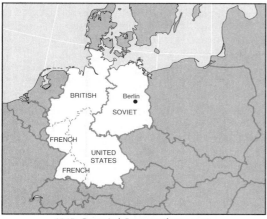

1945: Occupied Germany (four zones)

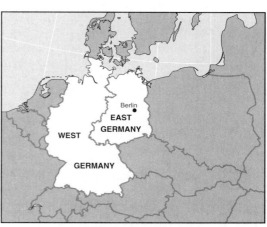

1949: Two Germanies

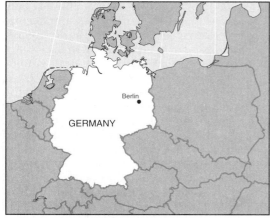

1990: Reunited Germany

Impressive German Words: Obrigkeit

One of the offshoots of the Protestant Reformation and breakup of Germany into ministates was the exaltation of the power and authority of each prince. *Obrigkeit*, "authority," was preached by Luther in defending princely rule against rebellious peasants. While Luther's religious doctrines aimed at making people free, his political doctrines aimed at making them obedient to authority. Blind obedience to authority became a German characteristic, and a German thought of himself or herself as an *Untertan*, a "subject," someone who is under (*unter*) authority.

tants. Germany suffered terribly, losing perhaps 30 percent of its population, many by starvation. Until World War I, the Thirty Years' War was the worst war in human history. The Treaty of Westphalia in 1648 confirmed *cuius regio eius religio* and left Germany atomized into 360 separate political entities.

Consider the political impact of religion on the three countries we have studied so far. In Britain, there was a nearly clean break with Rome; the return of Catholic kings merely confirmed the power of Parliament. In France, the Catholic Church and *ancien régime* stayed loyal to one another while many French turned anticlerical, leading to a division of French society into conservative Catholics and anticlerical radicals. Germany didn't split into clerical and anticlerical factions but into Catholic and Protestant. The result was ghastly: a long and ruinous war, further breakup of an already fragmented country, and centuries of ill will between Germans of different faiths.

The Rise of Prussia

One German state eventually came to dominate the others. Brandenburg, later known as Prussia, situated in North Germany around Berlin, expanded greatly during the eighteenth century, taking over the eastern German conquests of the Middle Ages along the Baltic and adding Silesia and parts of the Rhineland. In the eastern Baltic regions a type of nobility had developed, descended from the old Teutonic knights, that had a major impact on German history. The *Junkers* (from *Junge Herren*, "young gentlemen") held great estates worked by obedient serfs. Unlike the English lords, however, they did not retain their independence and act as a counterweight to the king but became a state nobility, dependent on the government and controlling all the higher civil-service and military positions. Famous for their discipline and attention to detail, the *Junkers* contributed to modern Germany a passion for excellence in both military and civil administration.

Prussian kings, with potential enemies on all sides, became obsessed with military power, leading to the wisecrack that "Prussia is not a country with an army but an army with a country." In the early eighteenth century, King Frederick William acted as drillmaster to his entire people, demanding military obedience and Prussian

Impressive German Words: Machtstaat

Prussia was the prime example of a *Machtstaat*, a state (*Staat*) based on power (*Macht*, a cognate of might). Prussia expanded by means of *Machtpolitik* (power politics), using a strong army and tricky diplomacy. Prussia also grew into a *Soldaten und Beamtenstaat*, a state run by soldiers and bureaucrats. Its characteristics were passed on to a unified Germany in the nineteenth century.

efficiency not only on the parade ground—where he personally marched his hand-picked corps of oversize soldiers—but in civilian life as well.

His son, Frederick the Great, who ruled from 1740 to 1786, like France's Louis XIV, perfected what he inherited. In Frederick's case this inheritance was the Prussian army which he kept in such a high state of readiness that it frightened the monarchs of larger states. Administering his kingdom personally, Frederick became known as the "enlightened despot" who brought art and culture (Voltaire stayed at his court for a while) as well as military triumphs and territorial expansion to Prussia. A brilliant commander and daring strategist, Frederick served as a model for expansion-minded German nationalists. Trying to identify himself with Frederick the Great, Adolf Hitler in 1933 announced the founding of the Third Reich from Frederick's tomb in Berlin.

German Nationalism

At the time of the French Revolution, there were still over three hundred German states. Prussia and Austria were the strongest of them, but they too were pushovers for Napoleon's conquering legions. German liberals, fed up with the backwardness and fragmentation of their country, at first welcomed the French as liberators and modernizers. Napoleon consolidated the many Germany ministates—but not Prussia or Austria—into about thirty, calling them the Confederation of the Rhine, and

Impressive German Words: Volksgeist

A combination of *Volk* (people) and *Geist* (spirit), German nationalist intellectuals of the nineteenth century used "spirit of the people" in a racist sense, meaning that the spirit of the German people was superior to all others. German professors and writers attributed mystical qualities to the German *Volk*, a term that came to mean *race* and was heavily used by the Nazis.

introduced new laws to free the economy and society from the accumulated mire of centuries.

The French brought with them more than liberalism, however; everywhere they went they infected conquered lands with the new idea of nationalism, the exaggerated belief in the greatness and unity of one's country. Nationalism is the most contagious "ism" of all; when one country catches it, the fever soon spreads to neighboring lands. In short order Germans, Russians, and Spaniards were fired with anti-French nationalism. Napoleon, without realizing it, had let an imp out of the bottle; the push he gave to German nationalism indirectly led to three German invasions of France. Great historical events have highly unpredictable aftereffects.

As we saw in the case of France's borrowing English and American notions of freedom, ideas conceived in one country often become warped, exaggerated, or distorted when applied to another. This happened with German nationalism. The French already had a unified country and secure national identity; the Germans didn't. French nationalism was first and foremost a defence of *la patrie*, then a desire to spread liberalism throughout Europe. There was little racist about French nationalism. German nationalism was emotional, hate-filled, racist, and conservative. The French loved reason; the German nationalists were romantics, harkening back

 ## Bismarck's Dubious Legacy

Otto von Bismarck, Germany's chancellor from 1871 to 1890, was a Prussian *Junker* to the bone, and the stamp he put on a unified Germany retarded its democratic development for over half a century. Bismarck and Disraeli knew and liked each other, and many compared them as dynamic conservatives. English and German conservatism, however, are two different things. Disraeli's Tories widened the electorate and welcomed a fair fight in Parliament. Bismarck hated parties, parliaments, and anyone who opposed him. Bismarck left Germany an authoritarian and one-man style of governance that was overcome only by Allied occupation following World War II.

Bismarck's most dangerous legacy to Germany, however, was in his foreign policy. To *Machtpolitik* Bismarck added *Realpolitik*, the politics of realism, and with these he manipulated first his own Prussia and then the rest of Europe to produce a unified Germany. War for Bismarck was just a tool. Cynical amorality was another pattern Bismarck bequeathed to Germany.

Germany's real problem was that Bismarck was a tough act to follow. Bismarck used cynical power politics for very limited ends—the unification of Germany. His successors picked up the amoral *Machtpolitik* but forgot about the limits, the *Realpolitik*. Bismarck, for example, could have easily conquered all of Denmark, Austria, and France, but he didn't because he knew that would bring dangerous consequences. Bismarck used war in a very controlled way, to unify Germany rather than to conquer Europe. Once that was done, Bismarck spent the rest of his career making sure potential enemies would not form a coalition against the Reich.

Bismarck cautioned that a tight alliance with Austria, supporting Austrian ambitions in the Balkans, could eventually lead to war. "The entire Balkans," he said, were "not worth the bones of one Pomeranian grenadier." His fear came true, for that was precisely the way World War I came about. Bismarck's successors, men of far less ability and far greater emotion, let Austria pull them into war over the Balkans. The real tragedy of Bismarck is that he constructed a delicate balance of European power that could not be maintained without himself as the master juggler.

to the primitive tribal passions still lurking in the German soul. Hitler plugged into exactly the same theme.

Germany looked to Prussia for leadership in throwing off the French yoke, and Prussian troops did contribute to Napoleon's downfall. Like France, Germany after Napoleon was not the same. Caught up in nationalism and liberalism—more of the former than the latter—German thinkers wanted a unified and modernized nation. The ultraconservative Austrian Prince Metternich, who hated both nationalism and liberalism, helped create a German Confederation of thirty-nine states, which he thought would contribute to European stability after Napoleon.

In 1848 revolution broke out all over Europe as discontented liberals and nationalists sought to overthrow the Metternichian system. In the midst of urban uprisings German liberals met in Frankfurt to set up a unified, democratic Germany. They sent a delegation to Berlin to offer the king of Prussia leadership of a German constitutional monarchy, but he contemptuously refused it with the remark that he "would not accept a crown from the gutter." The army cleared out the National Assembly in Frankfurt, and German liberals either converted to pure nationalism or emigrated to the United States. The first big tide of German immigrants to America was in 1848–49.

The Second Reich

In contrast to the attempts of liberal nationalists in 1848, German unification came not from the people but from above, from the growth of Prussia. Neither was it the work of liberals but rather of a staunch conservative, Otto von Bismarck, who had seen the liberals in action in 1848 and thought they were fools. Bismarck, who became Prussia's prime minister in 1862, wasn't really a German nationalist; he was first and foremost a loyal Prussian servant of his king who saw German unification under Prussian leadership as the only way to preserve and defend Prussia. As such, Bismarck's goals were quite limited; he had no intention of turning a united Germany into a military, expansionist state.

 ## *Impressive German Words: Kulturkampf*

Bismarck, following Prussian tradition, put the state ahead of any church. There could be nothing higher than *der Staat*, held Bismarck, and Germans should have no other loyalties. The many German Catholics saw things differently, namely, that in questions of faith and morals they should turn to Rome, not Berlin. Bismarck's efforts to break the German Catholic church of this attitude took the name *Kulturkampf*, meaning culture struggle. Between 1871 and 1875 Bismarck had the Jesuits expelled, broke diplomatic relations with the Vatican, made civil marriage compulsory, and did everything he could to harass the church into giving in. It didn't, and Bismarck finally backed down. The *Kulturkampf* left a sense of Catholic differentness within Germany, of resentment of Catholic south against Protestant north, and led to the formation of the Catholic Center party.

For Bismarck, armies and warfare were simply tools. In 1862 when the Prussian parliament was deadlocked over whether to increase the military budget, Bismarck ordered new taxes and spent the money without parliamentary approval. He declared: "Not by speeches and majority decisions will the great questions of the time be decided—that was the fault of 1848 and 1849—but by iron and blood."

Bismarck used his military tools to solve the great question of his day—who was to lead a unified Germany, Prussia, or Austria? In a series of three limited wars—in 1864 against Denmark, in 1866 against Austria, and in 1870 against France—Bismarck first consolidated the many German states behind Prussia, then got rid of Austria, then firmed up German unity. The new Second Reich (Charlemagne's was the first) was actually proclaimed in France, at Versailles Palace, in 1871.

The Second Reich, lasting from 1871 to 1918, was not a democracy. The legislature, the *Reichstag*, had only limited power, namely, to approve or reject the budget. The chancellor (prime minister) was not "responsible" to the parliament—that is, he couldn't be voted out—and hand-picked his own ministers. The German *Kaiser* (from Caesar) was not just a figurehead but a working executive. The individual states that had been enrolled into a united Germany retained their autonomy, a forerunner of the present federal system.

Germany, which had been industrially backward compared to Britain and France, surged ahead, especially in iron and steel. The once-pastoral Ruhr became a smoky workshop. With the growth of industry came a militant and well-organized German labor movement starting in the 1860s. In 1863 Ferdinand Lassalle formed the General German Workers' Association, partly a union and partly a party. In 1875 the group became the *Sozialdemokratische Partei Deutschlands* (SPD), now the oldest and one of the most successful social-democratic parties in the world.

Bismarck so hated the SPD that he suppressed it in 1878 and tried to take the wind out of the Socialists' sails by promoting numerous welfare measures himself in the *Reichstag*. In the 1880s Germany became the first country with medical and accident insurance, a pension plan, and state employment offices. Germany has been a welfare state ever since.

The Catastrophe: World War I

The Second Reich might have evolved into a democracy. Political parties became more important. After Bismarck was fired in 1890, the SPD came into the open to

 ## *Impressive German Words: Dolchstoss*

Surprised by Germany's surrender in 1918, right-wing Germans darkly muttered the word *Dolchstoss* (stab in the back) to explain the Reich's defeat. According to the *Dolchstoss* myth, Germany had not lost militarily but had been betrayed on the home front by democrats, socialists, Bolsheviks, Jews, and anyone else right wingers could think of. The *Dolchstoss* legend contributed to Hitler's rise and to German willingness to march to war again.

The Horrors of Polarized Pluralism

Italian political scientist Giovanni Sartori has described what happens when a multiparty system such as Weimar's or Spain's in the 1930s gets terribly sick. The leading parties in the center face nasty opposition on both their right and left. In competing for votes in a highly ideological atmosphere, extremist parties try to outbid each other by offering radical solutions. Votes flee from the center to the extremes, to parties dedicated to overthrowing the system. Sartori called this syndrome "polarized pluralism," and the last years of Weimar are a good example of it. Compare the percentage of votes parties got in 1928 with what they got in 1933, and the "center-fleeing" tendency is clear:

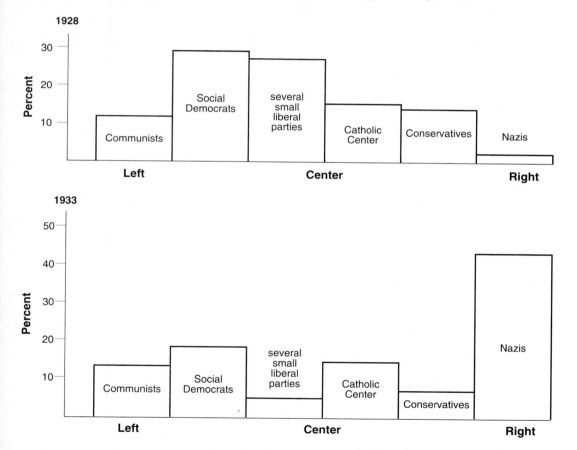

Main extermination camp of the Nazi regime was at Auschwitz-Birkenau in southeast Poland. Here both millions of Jews and inconvenient Christians were gassed and incinerated. *(Michael Roskin)*

Republic without Democrats

Looking back, we can see how the Weimar Republic—which got its name from the town of Weimar, where its federal constitution was drawn up in 1919—started with three strikes against it. In the first place, Germans had no experience with a republic or democracy; yet suddenly the nation became a democratic republic when the Kaiser fled to Holland at the war's end. Second, for many Germans, the Weimar Republic lacked legitimacy; it had been forced upon Germany by the victorious Allies and "back stabbers" who had betrayed the Reich. Third, the Versailles treaty was so punitive and its demands for payment so high that Germany was humiliated and economically hobbled.

It has been estimated that only about one German in four was a wholehearted democrat. Another quarter hated democracy. Other Germans went along with the new republic until the economy got rough and then shifted their sympathies to authoritarian movements of the left or right. Weimar Germany, it has been said, was a republic without republicans and a democracy without democrats.

The German government, in a crisis with France over reparations, printed money without limit. The result was a "hyperinflation" so insane that by 1923 it took a wheelbarrowful of marks to buy a loaf of bread. Especially hard hit were middle-class families who saw their businesses and savings wiped out; many of them became eager recruits for the Nazis. The period left an indelible mark on Germans, and to this day the German government places great emphasis on keeping inflation low. Inflation is a frightening word in Germany.

By the mid-1920s the economy stabilized and things looked better. Cabinets changed frequently: twenty-six in fourteen years. The Social Democrat, Catholic Center, and Conservative parties were the largest; the Nazis were tiny and considered something of a joke. Then the world Depression started in 1929, and German democ-

win a million and a half votes that same year. By 1912 it had won more than four million votes and almost a third of the *Reichstag*'s seats; it was Germany's largest party. Gaining responsibility in elected offices, the German Socialists slowly grew moderate, turning away from their Marxist roots and toward "revisionism," the idea that socialism can come gradually through democratic means rather than by radical revolution. So domesticated had the SPD become that in 1914, when the emergency war budget was placed before the *Reichstag*, SPD deputies forgot about the "international solidarity of all workers" and voted like good Germans—for it.

After Kaiser Wilhelm II dismissed Bismarck in 1890, Germany's foreign policy lost its sense of limits. Wilhelm placed more and more generals in his cabinet and started seeing Germany as competing with Britain. A program of naval armament, begun by Germany in 1889, touched off a race with Britain to build more battleships. Wilhelm supported the Boers against the British in South Africa and the Austrians who were coming into conflict with the Russians over the Balkans. By the time the shots were fired in Sarajevo in 1914, Germany had managed to surround itself with enemies, exactly what Bismarck had worked to prevent.

The Germans, with their quick victories of half a century earlier in mind, marched joyously off to war. In early August of 1914 Kaiser Wilhelm told his troops: "You will be home before the leaves have fallen from the trees." All of Europe thought the war would be short, but it took four years and ten million lives until Germany surrendered.

Many Germans couldn't believe they had lost militarily. They had done so well: in 1914 they'd almost reached Paris, and in 1917 they'd knocked Russia out of the war. Fed nothing but war propaganda, Germans didn't understand that the army and economy had given their utmost and could give no more. The war ended before there was any fighting on German soil, so civilians didn't see for themselves how their troops were beaten. Making matters worse was the Versailles treaty, which unjustly placed total blame for the war on Germany and demanded an impossible $33 billion in reparations. Germany was stripped of its few colonies (in Africa and the South Pacific) and lost a chunk of Prussia to make a "Polish corridor" to the Baltic. Many Germans could think of nothing but revenge. If a treaty is to be judged on what it produces, then Versailles was a supercatastrophe, for it led straight to Hitler and World War II.

Impressive German Words: Gleichschaltung

The Nazi style of running an economy and a country was not to nationalize everything like the Communists but rather to "coordinate" things by placing loyal Nazis in all the key positions in industry, the army, civil service, news media, education, and the justice system. *Gleichschaltung* (coordination) signified leaving the existing institutions pretty much in place but "coordinating" their function so as to serve party ends.

racy went down the drain. Moderate parties declined, and extremist parties—the Nazis and the Communists—grew (see box on page 159). Unemployment was the key: the more people out of work, the higher the Nazi vote.

One combination might have blocked the Nazis' rise to power. If the Social Democrats and Communists had forgotten their differences and had formed a united front, the Weimar system might have been saved. But the German Communists, who split off from the SPD after World War I, reviled the Social Democrats as nonrevolutionaries who had sold out to the capitalists. Under Stalin's orders, the German Communists rejected a joint program with the Socialists on the theory that Hitler would be a passing phenomenon and when Germany collapsed the Communists would take over. This was one of Stalin's greatest blunders, and Communists and Socialists alike paid for it with their lives.

By late 1932, the Nazis had won a third of the German vote, and the aged President Hindenberg, a conservative general, named Hitler as chancellor the following January. The Weimar Republic, Germany's first try at democracy, died after a short life of fourteen years (1919–33).

The Third Reich

Nazi was the German nickname for the National Socialist German Workers party. Nazism, like other forms of fascism, had a pseudosocialist component that promised jobs and welfare measures. Many Germans were delighted to get work on government projects, such as building the new *Autobahnen.* Although the Nazis never won a majority in a fair election, by the late 1930s it is certain a majority of Germans supported Hitler, whom they saw as restoring prosperity.

Since most Germans had not been enthusiastic about democracy, relatively few protested the systematic growth of tyranny. Some Communists and Socialists went underground, to prison, or into exile, and some old-style conservatives disliked Hitler, who, in their eyes, was nothing but an Austrian guttersnipe. But most Germans got along by going along. Centuries of being taught to keep their place and obey authority led them to accept Nazi rule.

For opportunists, membership in the Nazi party offered better jobs and sometimes snappy uniforms. Many ex-Nazis now claim they joined only to further

 Impressive German Words: Lebensraum

In Nazi race theory, the "superior" German Nordics deserved more space in which to live—*Lebensraum,* literally "living space." The natural area for expansion, Nazis argued, was eastward, like the old Teutonic knights had pushed along the Baltic. This *Drang nach Osten* (push to the east) would lead to a gigantic German Reich in which some of the Slavic inhabitants (Poles, Russians, Czechs, and others) would be exterminated and the rest enslaved. Such was Hitler's dream and motivation for his invasion of Poland and Russia.

their careers, and most are probably telling the truth. You don't need true believers to staff a tyranny; opportunists will do just as well. The frightening thing about Nazi Germany was how it could turn normal humans into coldblooded mass murderers.

Among the first and worst to suffer were the Jews. Exploiting widely held racist feelings, Hitler depicted the Jews as a poisonous, foreign element who aimed to enslave Germany in the service of international capitalism, international communism, or both. Logical consistency was never the Nazis' strong point. Jews were deprived, one step at a time, of their civil rights, their jobs, their property, their citizenship, and finally their lives.

Few Germans were aware of it, but Hitler ached for war. At first he seemed to be merely consolidating Germany's boundaries, absorbing the Saar in 1935, Austria and the Sudetenland in 1938, and Bohemia, Moravia, and Memel in 1939. And it was so easy! Germany's enemies from World War I, still war weary, did nothing to stop the growth of German power and territory. Hitler's generals, it is now known, were ready to overthrow him if the British had said no to his demands at Munich in 1938. It looked as though Hitler could amass victories without even fighting, and the German generals suppressed their doubts. Finally, when the Germans invaded Poland in September 1939, Britain and France declared war. France was overrun; Britain was contained beyond the Channel, and by the summer of 1940 Germany or its allies ruled virtually all of Europe.

The following year Hitler ordered that his "final solution" to the Jewish question begin: extermination. Death camps killed some six million Jews and a large number of inconvenient Christians (Poles, gypsies, and others). A new word was added to mankind's vocabulary: genocide, the murder of an entire people. To this day, some Germans claim they didn't know what was going on, but neither did they show any inclination to find out.

Hitler—just a week before he attacked Poland in 1939—had completed a nonaggression pact with Stalin. In the summer of 1941, however, Hitler assembled the biggest army in history and gave the order for "Barbarossa," the conquest and enslavement of the Soviet Union. Here, at last, Hitler's dream totally parted company with reality. The Russian winter and surprising resistance of the Red Army devoured whole German divisions. From late 1942 on it was all downhill for Germany.

Might Have Been: The Plot to Kill Hitler

On July 20, 1944, a group of high-ranking German officers tried to kill Hitler. Had he not stepped away from the map table, the briefcase-bomb under it would have surely succeeded. More than two hundred anti-Nazi Germans were cruelly executed for their part in the plot. They came from all walks of life: generals, diplomats, Weimar politicians, trade unionists, scholars, theologians of both Christian confessions, and students. They were united in their opposition to totalitarianism, mass murder, and the war, which they would have ended as quickly as possible. Although they failed, they left a valuable legacy: the symbol that Germans fought Hitler, a moral statement for present-day Germany.

Another Tale of Two Flags

Like France, Germany's divided loyalties have been symbolized by its flag's colors. The German nationalist movement flag was black, red, and gold, colors of a Prussian regiment that fought against Napoleon. By 1848 it symbolized a democratic, united Germany. Bismarck rejected it. For the Second Reich's flag he chose Prussia's black and white, plus the white and red of the medieval Hansa commercial league.

The Reich's collapse in 1918 and founding of the Weimar Republic brought the democratic black, red, and gold back to the German flag. Hitler, a fanatic on symbols, insisted on the authoritarian black, red, and white colors. Finally the Bonn republic designed the present German flag with the original democratic colors.

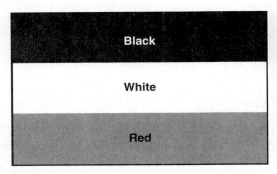

The Occupation

This time there could be no *Dolchstoss* myth; Germans watched Russians, Americans, British, and French fight their way through Germany. German government ceased to exist, and the country was run by foreign occupiers. At Yalta in February 1945 the Allied leaders agreed to divide Germany into four zones for temporary occupation; Berlin, inside the Soviet zone, was similarly divided.

The Cold War grew in large part out of the way the Soviets handled Germany. The Soviets, having lost some twenty million people in the war, were intent on looting the conquered nation. They dismantled whole factories, shipped them home, and flooded the country with inflated military currency. The British and Americans, on the other hand, distressed at the brutal Soviet takeover of East Europe, decided to revive German economic and political life in their zones. The U.S. Marshall Plan and other aid programs pumped $3.5 billion into German recovery. In 1948 the British and Americans introduced a currency reform and a new *Deutschmark*, which effectively cut out the Soviets from further looting the western zones. In retaliation, the Russians blockaded Berlin, which was supplied for nearly a year by an incredible British-American airlift. The Cold War was on, centered in Germany.

In 1949, the Western allies decided to give governing power back to Germans in order to insure West German cooperation against Soviet power. Accordingly, both German regimes were children of the Cold War with the Americans and the Soviets acting as respective godfathers. When the Cold War ended—and its end is conveniently marked by the fall of the Berlin Wall in 1989—prosperous and democratic West Germany swallowed weak and dependent East Germany. To examine how West Germany succeeded, let us turn to Germany's institutions.

Vocabulary Building

Alps	hyperinflation	principality	*Staat*
Baltic	*Junker*	Prussia	Versailles
Barbarossa	*Kaiser*	*Reichstag*	*Volk*
Dolchstoss	Marshall Plan	reparations	Weimar
final solution	Nordic	revisionism	Westphalia
Gleichschaltung	opportunist	Second Reich	Yalta
Habsburg	polarized pluralism		

Further Reference

BESSEL, RICHARD. *Germany after the First World War.* New York: Oxford University Press, 1993.

BRACHER, KARL DIETRICH. *The German Dictatorship: The Origins, Structure, and Effects of National Socialism.* New York: Praeger, 1970.

CARR, WILLIAM. *A History of Germany, 1815–1990,* 4th ed. New York: Routledge, 1992.

CRAIG, GORDON A. *Germany, 1866–1945.* New York: Oxford University Press, 1978.

FELDMAN, GERALD D. *The Great Disorder: Politics, Economics, and Society in the German Inflation, 1914–1924.* New York: Oxford University Press, 1993.

FLOOD, CHARLES BRACELEN. *Hitler: The Path to Power.* Boston: Houghton Mifflin, 1989.

MAIER, CHARLES S. *The Unmasterable Past: History, Holocaust, and German National Identity.* Cambridge, MA: Harvard University Press, 1989.

MARSHALL, BARBARA. *The Origins of Post-War German Politics.* New York: Croom Helm, 1988.

MARTELL, GORDON. *Modern Germany Reconsidered, 1870–1945.* New York: Routledge, 1992.

MERKL, PETER H. *The Origin of the West German Republic.* New York: Oxford University Press, 1963.

PEUKERT, DETLEV J. K. *The Weimar Republic: The Crisis of Classical Modernity.* New York: Hill & Wang, 1992.

PFLANZE, OTTO. *Bismarck and the Development of Germany,* 3 vols. Princeton, NJ: Princeton University Press, 1990.

SARTORI, GIOVANNI. *Parties and Party Systems: A Framework for Analysis.* New York: Cambridge University Press, 1976.

STERN, FRITZ. *Dreams and Delusions: The Drama of German History.* New York: Knopf, 1987.

13
Germany: The Key Institutions

A True Federation

After World War II, West Germany revived an old pattern in German history: giving its component parts plenty of local autonomy, true federalism. Germany's *Länder* (states) have at least as much power as American states, maybe more. Education, medical care, police, and many other functions are the province of the *Land* government. Part of the reason for this strong federalism was to repudiate the centralization of the Nazi period and to make sure that such power could never again become so concentrated.

Berlin was a strange situation. Located 110 miles (180 kilometers) inside East Germany, Berlin was nominally governed by the four occupying powers. The Soviet sector, however, was turned into the capital of East Germany, and the American, British, and French sectors became to all intents and purposes a part of West Germany. Bonn counted West Berlin as its eleventh *Land*, but the wartime Allies did not recognize it as such. So officially West Berlin was not part of the Federal Republic, but in practice it was. West German currency, laws, and passports applied in West Berlin, but the city sent only nonvoting representatives to the Bonn parliament. The anomaly was solved in 1990 with the unification of the two Germanys. With the Berlin Wall down, Greater Berlin became a *Land* and in 1991 the nominal capital of united Germany, although many government offices, including the federal parliament, remained in Bonn for some years.

East Germany, after it was set up by the Communists in 1949, continued the Nazi pattern of centralized rule with fourteen administrative districts, each named after its leading city, without autonomy. Unification in 1990 brought back to life East

Germany's five *Länder*, so now the Federal Republic has sixteen *Länder*, ten from West Germany, five from East Germany, plus Greater Berlin.

The President

Germany's federal president (*Bundespräsident*) is the classic type of European president, a figurehead with few political but many symbolic duties. Like the monarchs of Britain and Scandinavia, the German president is an official greeter and ambassador of good will rather than a working executive. The French president of the Third and Fourth Republics and the Italian president today are other examples of forgettable presidencies. De Gaulle, of course, greatly strengthened the French presidency.

The president is the "head of state" rather than "head of government" (for the distinction, see Chapter 3), and as such receives new foreign ambassadors who present their credentials to him rather than to the people they will actually be working with, the chancellor and foreign minister. In addition, the president proclaims laws (after they've been passed by parliament), dissolves the *Bundestag* (upon the chancellor's request), and appoints and dismisses the chancellor (after the leading party has told him to). In short, the German president is, to use Bagehot's terms, a "dignified" rather than "efficient" part of government.

The president is elected by a special Federal Assembly composed of all *Bundestag* members plus an equal number from state legislatures. The president serves five years and may be reelected once. The dead-end job is usually given as a reward to distinguished politicians about to retire. In 1994, CDU candidate Roman Herzog the 60-year-old chief justice of the Federal Constitutional Court (see pages 173–174), was elected president with the support of FDP deputies.

 ## *Impressive German Words: Bundesrepublik*

In Germany today almost everything associated with the federal government bears the prefix *Bundes-*, meaning "federal." Thus:

- *Bundesrepublik Deutschland* is the Federal Republic of German, FRG.
- *Bundestag* is the lower house of the federal parliament.
- *Bundesrat* is the upper house.
- *Bundeskanzler* is the federal chancellor (prime minister).

- *Bundeswehr* is the federal army.
- *Bundesbank* is the federal national bank.
- *Bundesministerium* is a federal ministry.
- *Bundesregierung* is the federal government.

The prefix *Bundes-* is new, stemming only from the founding of West Germany in 1949, and has a modern, democratic ring to it. The old prefix to many of the same words, *Reichs-* ("imperial"), has a slightly sinister, discarded connotation. In Germany, "federal" has become synonymous with "democratic."

Impressive German Words: Grundgesetz

In 1949, the founders of West Germany were hopeful that the east and west sections of their country would be reunified. Accordingly, they called their founding document the Basic Law (*Grundgesetz*) rather than constitution (*Verfassung*), which was to come only when Germany reunified. They meant to indicate that the Federal Republic was temporary and operating under temporary rules. By now the name is a legal quibble, for the Basic Law continued as the Federal Republic's permanent constitution and an excellent one at that.

The Chancellor

Germany has a weak president but a strong chancellor, the German term for prime minister. Unlike the changing chancellors of the Weimar Republic, the FRG chancellorship has been a stable and durable office. Part of the reason for this is that the Basic Law makes it impossible to oust the chancellor on a vote of no-confidence unless the *Bundestag* simultaneously votes *in* a new chancellor. This reform ended one of the worst problems of parliamentary (as opposed to presidential) governments, namely, their dependence on an often-fickle legislative majority.

The German reform is called "constructive no-confidence" because parliament has to offer something constructive—a new chancellor—rather than a mere negative majority to get rid of the old one. This has happened only once, in 1982, when the small Free Democratic party abandoned its coalition with the Social Democrats in midterm and voted in a new Christian Democratic chancellor. Constructive no-confidence makes ousting a chancellor a rarity.

Another reason the chancellor is strong stems from the first occupant of that office: Konrad Adenauer, a tough, shrewd politician who helped found the Federal Republic and served as chancellor its first fourteen years (1949–63). First occupants, such as Washington in the American presidency, can put a stamp on the position, defining its powers and setting its style for generations. As may be judged from German history, Germans respond more to strong leadership than to democratic principles. With Adenauer, they got just that. In the Bismarckian tradition, Adenauer made numerous decisions without bothering parliament or his cabinet too much. This is not to say that Adenauer was antidemocratic; rather he understood that to lead Germans, especially in founding a new republic out of the rubble of the past, he had to show strength. Chancellors ever since Adenauer have been measured against him. His successor, for example, the amiable and intelligent Ludwig Erhard, was found wanting precisely because he couldn't exercise firm leadership.

Partly thanks to the style Adenauer set, the German chancellor is approximately as powerful as the British prime minister, which is to say powerful. The chancellor picks his own cabinet—with political considerations in mind, like the British PM. He is responsible for the main lines of government policy and has to defend

Der Alte: Konrad Adenauer

Arrogant, high-handed, crusty, obstinate, authoritarian, and maybe a little senile. All of these complaints were made about Konrad Adenauer (1876–1967), but even his critics admitted that *der Alte* (the Old Man) more than any other German contributed to the founding of democracy in West Germany.

The most amazing thing about Adenauer was that his career really didn't begin until he was 70 years old. Trained in law, Adenauer became mayor of Cologne in 1917 and lasted until the Nazis kicked him out in 1933. Vaguely implicated in the 1944 plot to kill Hitler, Adenauer was arrested and held in jail for two months. A devout Catholic, Adenauer was active in the prewar Center party. After World War II, people like Adenauer decided not to revive a Catholic-only party but to form a larger center-right grouping, the Christian Democrat Union, which welcomed both Catholics and Protestants. In 1946 Adenauer became chairman of the CDU's Rhineland branch and in 1948 president of the parliamentary council in Bonn. Some say the city of Bonn was chosen as West Germany's capital because it was near his home on the banks of the Rhine.

In 1949 the first *Bundestag* elected him chancellor. Adenauer's choice of coalition partners had a major and positive impact on Bonn's democratic stability. Instead of a "grand coalition" with the

Social Democrats, Adenauer formed a small coalition of the CDU and other conservative parties, most of which the CDU eventually absorbed. This polarized politics in a healthy way. The SPD in opposition had to rethink its program and patiently build electoral support before finally entering the cabinet in 1966. The wait did both major parties good and contributed to the long-standing "two-plus" party system in Germany.

In foreign relations, Adenauer pointed the Federal Republic decisively westward. As a Catholic Rhinelander, Adenauer didn't have to think twice about whether to integrate Germany with the West or with Protestant Prussia. In 1952 Stalin hinted that Germany could reunify if it were neutral. Adenauer would have none of it; he cemented Germany into NATO, the European Coal and Steel Community, the Common Market, and a special relationship with France. The price was the decades-long division of Germany.

Some say that Adenauer was never a German nationalist but rather a West European Catholic. It's a good explanation of his foreign policy. A symbolic high point came in 1962 when Adenauer and de Gaulle knelt together in prayer in the ancient French cathedral of Reims, the two old enemy nations united at last in the arms of the church. Bismarck must have turned in his grave: the Catholics had finally won the *Kulturkampf*.

them before the *Bundestag* and the public. As such, he is implicitly held responsible for what his ministers say and do.

The Cabinet

The typical German cabinet is somewhat smaller than its French or British counterpart, but it too changes over the years as specialized ministries are created and other ministries are combined or split apart. In the early 1990s the German cabinet was staffed by the following officials:

Minister of the Chancellery (chief of staff)
Foreign Minister

Interior Minister
Justice Minister
Finance Minister (that is, treasury)
Economics Minister
Minister for Nutrition, Agriculture, and Forestry
Minister for Labor
Defense Minister
Minister for Health
Minister for Family and the Elderly
Minister for Women and Youth
Transport Minister
Minister for Regional Planning and Urban Development
Minister for Research and Technology
Minister for Post and Telecommunications
Minister for Education and Science
Minister for Economic Cooperation (foreign aid and trade)
Minister for Environment, Protection of Nature and Reactor Safety

The German cabinet has some interesting features. There are two ministries concerned with science and research. (The United States has none.) There are at least four ministries dealing with social welfare: labor and social affairs; health; family and the elderly; and women and youth. Even under the conservative CDU, Germany remained very much a welfare state.

As in Britain (but not in France), practically all German cabinet ministers are also working politicians with seats in the *Bundestag*. Like their British counterparts, they are rarely specialists in their assigned portfolio. Most are trained as lawyers and have served in a variety of party and legislative positions. The job of parliamentary state secretary serves as a training ground for potential cabinet ministers. Below cabinet rank, a parliamentary state secretary is assigned to each minister to assist in relations with the *Bundestag*, in effect a bridge between executive and legislative branches, as in Britain.

The *Bundestag*

Konrad Adenauer, the authoritarian democrat, did not place great faith in the lower house of the German parliament, the *Bundestag*. Germany never had a strong parliamentary tradition. Bismarck all but ignored the *Reichstag*. During the Weimar Republic, the *Reichstag*, unprepared for the governing responsibilities thrust upon it, could not exercise power. Then in 1949 came Adenauer who, like most Germans, had never seen an efficient, stable, responsible parliament and so tended to disdain the new one. Since Adenauer's time, the *Bundestag* has been trying to establish itself as a pillar of democracy and as an important branch of government. Success has been gradual and incomplete. Many Germans still do not respect the *Bundestag* very much.

The *Bundestag*'s 656 members (temporarily enlarged to 672 in 1994 due to a special provision in the electoral law) make it the largest democratically elected parliament in the world. Deputies are elected for four years and paid a generous $89,000 a year. Under a parliamentary (as opposed to presidential) system, the leg-

Helmut Kohl: The Underestimated Chancellor

"I make my living by being underestimated," said FRG Chancellor Helmut Kohl. German intellectuals tended to look down on Kohl as a visionless plodder and unsophisticated bumpkin. But by the time he won his fourth straight election in 1994, many observers appreciated that Kohl knew a thing or two about German politics. No one called him a great leader, but his calm pragmatism fit many German voters like an old shoe.

A Catholic Rhinelander—like Adenauer—Kohl was put into uniform at age 15, but the war ended before he faced combat. Kohl never had any liking for the Nazis. While earning his doctorate in law in the 1950s, Kohl worked his way up in the

German Chancellor Helmut Kohl. *(German Information Service)*

Rhineland-Palatinate CDU party organization, becoming its chairman in 1966 and *Land* minister-president (the equivalent of a U.S. governor) in 1969. Like most FRG politicians, Kohl started with extensive experience in state politics. Kohl was elected to the *Bundestag* only in 1976 but immediately headed his party in an unsuccessful bid for the chancellorship in the 1976 election. Kohl, like Mitterrand, knows how to wait, and when the Social Democrat–Free Democrat coalition split in 1982, the *Bundestag* voted him in as chancellor. In 1983, he called a new election ahead of schedule and won resoundingly. He repeated the feat in 1987, 1990, and 1994. Some have compared Kohl to Ronald Reagan. Both were optimistic conservatives who knew how to communicate in simple language to the average citizen. Both emphasized traditional and nationalistic themes and steered away from intellectual complications. From time to time, Kohl got caught in political blunders—such as accepting suspicious money from the giant Flick holding company and bringing Reagan to the Bitburg military cemetary, where some SS soldiers are also buried—but Kohl always recovered politically.

Kohl had at least three things going for him. First, a sunny, upbeat personality. Second, the opposition SPD lurched leftward, much like the British Labour party, scaring some moderate voters. SPD chancellor-candidates tended to be eloquent intellectuals but without Kohl's common touch. Third, and most important, when German unity became possible in 1990, Kohl went for it without delay or doubt. While the SPD criticized the rush to unify, Kohl won major—but not very durable—support among East German voters. Kohl's pragmatism matched that of many Germans: If it works, keep the man in office.

islature can never be a severe critic of the administration in the manner of the U.S. Congress. After all, the *Bundestag*'s majority parties produce the government; they can't very well criticize it too harshly. Neither is the *Bundestag* the tumultuous assembly of the French Third and Fourth Republics; the FRG legislature can unmake a government only when it makes a new one. Nor is the *Bundestag* the docile rubber stamp that de Gaulle made of the French National Assembly. Still less is it the col-

The Grand Coalition: A Dangerous Experiment

From 1966 to 1969 West Germany was ruled by a joint Christian Democrat–Social Democrat government, a so-called "grand coalition" because it included both the large parties and left only the small Free Democrats, who had but 6 percent of the *Bundestag* seats, to oppose and criticize. The advantage of a grand coalition is obvious: it has such an overwhelming majority in parliament that it can't be ousted and can pass any laws it likes.

The negative side became more obvious with time: people came to feel that nobody could criticize the government, that politics was a game rigged by the powerful, and that democracy was a sham. An "extraparliamentary opposition" of leftist bent began to grow and criticize the government in radical terms. Some of West Germany's terrorists first became active in disgust at the wall-to-wall grand coalition. A grand coalition is probably useful only for emergencies; if it stays in office too long it starts undermining faith in democracy. A good democracy requires a lively interaction between "ins" and "outs" rather than collusion between the two.

orful debating chamber of the House of Commons, where brilliant orators try to sway the public for the next election. On balance, the *Bundestag* has less independent power than the U.S. Congress but more than the French National Assembly and possibly even the British House of Commons.

The *Bundestag*'s strong point is its committee work. Here, behind closed doors (most sessions are secret) *Bundestag* deputies, including opposition members, can make their voices heard. German legislative committees are more important and more specialized than their British counterparts. German party discipline is not as tight as the British so that deputies from the ruling party can criticize a government bill while opposition deputies sometimes agree with it. In the give and take of committee work, the opposition is often able to get changes made in legislation. Once back on the *Bundestag* floor—and all bills must be reported out; they can't be killed in committee—voting is on party lines, with occasional defections on matters of conscience.

The approximately twenty standing *Bundestag* committees are almost exactly the same as the cabinet ministries listed earlier in this chapter. The system was designed that way: each cabinet minister can deal directly with a parallel, relevant *Bundestag* committee. The ministers, themselves *Bundestag* members, sometimes come over from their executive offices to explain to committee sessions what the government has in mind with a proposed piece of legislation.

The composition of the *Bundestag* membership is interesting: its membership is heavily composed of civil servants. German law permits bureaucrats to take a leave of absence to run for and serve in the *Bundestag*. Another important category is people from interest groups—business associations and labor unions. Together, these two groups usually form a majority of the *Bundestag* membership. While we can't be sure that this does any harm to German democracy, it does contribute to a public feeling that parliament is a place where the powerful meet to decide matters with little reference to popular wishes.

"To The German People," proclaims the old *Reichstag* building in Berlin, the once and future home of the German parliament. It will undergo extensive reconstruction and expansion before the *Bundestag* officially moves in. Now it is a museum. Note bullet marks in columns. *(Michael Roskin)*

The Constitutional Court

In very few countries is the judiciary equal in power to the legislative or executive branches. The United States and Germany are two; both allow the highest court in the land to review the constitutionality of laws. The Federal Constitutional Court (*Bundesverfassungsgericht*, BVG), located in Karlsruhe, was put into the Basic Law partly on American insistence. The American occupiers reasoned that something like the Supreme Court would help prevent another Hitler, and many Germans agreed with what was for Germany (and indeed all of Europe) a new concept.

The Karlsruhe court is composed of sixteen judges, eight elected by each house of parliament, who serve for nonrenewable twelve-year terms. The BVG operates as two courts or "senates" of eight judges each to speed up the work. Completely independent of other branches of German government, the court decides cases between *Länder*, protects civil liberties, outlaws dangerous political parties, and otherwise makes sure that statutes conform to the Basic Law.

The Constitutional Court's decisions have been important. It has declared illegal both neo-Nazi and radical-left parties, on the grounds that they sought to overthrow the constitutional order. It found that abortion bills collided with the strong right-to-life provisions of the Basic Law and thus ruled them unconstitutional. (In 1993, however, it decided not to prosecute women who had first-trimester abortions.) In 1979 it ruled that "worker codetermination" in the running of factories was constitutional. In 1983 it found that Chancellor Helmut Kohl had acted within the constitution when he arranged to lose a *Bundestag* vote of confidence so he could hold elections early (which he won). In 1992, the court found unconstitutional Germany's public funding of parties (DM 5 for every vote a party receives). Judicial review has worked well in Germany, although the *Bundesverfassungsgericht*, because it operates in the context of the more rigid Roman law, does not have the impact of the U.S. Supreme Court, whose decisions literally *are* law within the U.S. Common Law system.

The Parties

Much of the reason the FRG government works rather well is the party system that has evolved since 1949. The Weimar *Reichstag* was bedeviled by a dozen parties, some of them extremist, that made forming a stable coalition difficult. Germany today, like Britain, has a "two-plus" party system, that is, two big parties and a few small ones. A two-plus party system decreases the difficulty of coalition formation; governments consist typically of one of the large parties plus one of the small parties. A single party has seldom had a majority of the *Bundestag*, and thus "monocolor" (one-party) cabinets have been rare.

Most of the time the largest party has been the Christian Democratic Union (*Christlich Demokratische Union*, CDU) with its Bavarian branch, the Christian Social Union. Sometimes the party is designated CDU/CSU. The original core of the CDU was the old Catholic-related Center party, one of the few parties that held its own against the growth of Nazism in the early 1930s. After World War II, Center politicians like Adenauer decided to go for a broader-based center-right party, one in which Protestants would feel welcome. This was largely successful, and the CDU now draws as many Protestant as Catholic voters. The CDU/CSU has been West Germany's largest party in every election except 1972 (when the SPD edged it out). In 1994 it drew 41.5 percent of the national vote.

The Bundesrat: A Useful Upper House

Neither Britain nor France really needs an upper house because Britain and France are unitary systems. The German federal system has a useful upper house, the *Bundesrat*. Not as powerful as the U.S. Senate—an upper house that powerful is a world rarity—the *Bundesrat* represents the sixteen *Länder* and has equal power with the *Bundestag* on legislation that will affect state affairs. On other issues the *Bundesrat* can veto a bill, but the *Bundestag* can override it.

The *Bundesrat* consists of 69 members. Every German *Land*, no matter how small, is represented by at least three *Bundesrat* delegates. More populous *Länder* get four; the most populous get six. Each *Land* has the right to appoint its delegates, and in practice this has meant delegations of the leading state-level politicians, officials elected to the *Landtag* who become cabinet members in the *Land* government. This often means that members of a state's delegation will all belong to one party. Each *Bundesrat* delegation must vote as a bloc, not as individuals. The theory here is that they represent states, rather than political parties or their own individual viewpoints.

The Social Democrat party (*Sozialdemokratische Partei Deutschlands*, SPD) is the grand old party of socialism and the only party in Germany that antedated the founding of the Federal Republic. Originally Marxist, the SPD gradually became more and more "revisionist" until, in 1959, it dropped Marxism altogether. It was then that its electoral fortunes grew as it expanded beyond its traditional working-class base and into the middle class, especially middle-class intellectuals. Now a center-left party, the SPD's socialism amounts basically to support for welfare measures plus opposition to the use of military force. It won 36.4 percent of the national vote in 1994.

The small Free Democratic party (*Freie Demokratische Partei*, FDP) is a descendant of the classic liberal parties that tried to stick to a center ground between socialists and conservatives. The FDP had trouble defining itself and at times dropped to under 10 percent of the vote. In 1994 it won 36.9 percent. Like Britain's Liberals, the FDP offers a middle way to voters mistrustful of the two big parties.

In 1983, a new ecology-pacifist party, the Greens, made it into the *Bundestag*, and in 1994 they won 7.3 percent and again made it into parliament. Several small leftist and rightist parties, including Communists and neo-Nazis, win a few seats in local elections but have won no seats in the *Bundestag*.

When East Germany held its first free, competitive elections in 1990 (before unification), West Germany's parties simply moved in and took over. The small, new parties that had spearheaded the ouster of the Communists were elbowed aside by the CDU and SPD, who had the money and organizational skills. The prime minister of the short-lived East German government was CDU leader Lothar de Maizière. The West German party system expanded to include East Germany.

A Split Electoral System

Both Britain and the United States use single-member districts in their parliamentary elections. The advantage with this system is that it anchors a deputy to a district, giving the representative an abiding interest in his or her constituents. The disad-

Impressive German Words: Regierungsfähig

Meaning "able to form a government," the term *regierungsfähig* has both a numerical and psychological connotation for Germans. It means not only that a party has enough parliamentary seats to build a cabinet but that it is mature enough to carry out the responsibilities of governing. Before 1959, when the Social Democrats were still rigid and somewhat Marxist, they were not considered *regierungsfähig*.

When the SPD shifted toward the center in the 1960s, they came to be seen as more and more *regierungsfähig*, a serious party capable of ruling. Invited into a grand coalition in 1966, they proved they were responsible people and went on, in 1969, to govern Germany quite well in coalition with the small FDP. *Regierungsfähig*, in other words, means that a party has graduated to adult tasks.

vantage is that the system does not accurately reflect votes for parties nationwide; seats are not proportional to votes. The alternative, proportional representation (PR), makes the party's percentage of seats nearly proportional to its votes. Weimar Germany had a PR system, and it was part of its undoing. PR systems are theoretically the fairest but in practice often lead to difficulties. They permit many small parties in parliament, including antidemocratic extremist parties. They make coalitions hard to form and unstable because usually several parties must combine. Italy (see box) suffered these consequences of pure proportional representation.

The German system combines both approaches, single-member districts and proportional representation. The voter has two votes, one for a single representative in one of 328 districts, the other for a party. The party vote is the crucial one, for it determines the total number of seats a party gets in a given *Land*. Some of these seats are occupied by the party's district winners; additional seats are taken from the party's *Landesliste* to reach the percentage won on the second ballot. This *Landesliste* (the right-hand column on the sample ballot, in the box on page 177) is a list of persons who will become deputies, starting with the names at the top of the list. The "party list" is the standard technique for a PR system. Leading party figures are assigned high positions on the list to insure that they get elected; people at the bottom of the party list don't have a chance.

The German system works like proportional representation—percentage of votes equals percentage of *Bundestag* seats—but with the advantage of single-member districts. As in Britain and the United States, voters get a district representative. More than in straight PR systems, personality counts in German elections; a politician can't be just a good party worker but has to go out and talk with voters to earn their confidence on a personal basis. It is a matter of considerable pride among FRG

COMPARING

 ### *Germany's Electoral System: An Export Product*

Germany's hybrid electoral system was much talked-about for decades. Then, in the early 1990s, several countries paid Germany the highest compliment by adopting similar systems, albeit with national variations. The aim in all cases was to combine the simplicity of single-member districts with some of the theoretical fairness of PR. Some of the German-inspired hybrids:

- The Russian elections of 1993 filled half of the 450-seat lower house by single-member districts and half by PR with a 5 percent threshold.
- In 1993, Italy voted to drop its traditional PR system to one in which 75 percent of the seats

of both chambers are filled from single-member districts and 25 percent by PR.

- In 1994, Japan turned from its unique electoral system of multimember districts with plurality victors to a system in which more than half the members of each house are elected from single-member districts while the remainder are elected by PR at the national level. (See pages 300–302.)
- New Zealand in 1993 turned from straight Anglo-American single-member districts to a new system for its unicameral legislature of 60 such districts plus 60 elected by PR at the national level with a 5 percent threshold.

"You Have Two Votes": A German Ballot

Stimmzettel
für die Wahl zum Deutschen Bunderstag im Wahlkreis 130 Lahn-Dill
am 5. October 1980

hier 1 Stimme
für die Wahl
eines Wahlkreisabgeordneten
(Erststimme)

hier 1 Stimme
für die Wahl
einer Landesliste (Partei)
(Zweitstimme)

	Erststimme			Zweitstimme	
1	**Daubertshäuser, Klaus** Oberregiernungsrat a D Wilhelm- **SPD** Sozialdemo- str 48 kratische Partei 6349 Dnedort Deutschlands	◯	◯	**SPD** Sozialdemokratische Partei Deutschlands Leber, Maithöler, Jahn Frau Dr. Timm, Zander	1
2	**Lenzer, Christian** Oberstudenrat a D Am Turm- **CDU** Christlich chen 1 Demokratische 6348 Herborn-Burg Union Deutschlands	◯	◯	**CDU** Christlich Demo- kratische Union Deutschlands Dr. Dregger, Zink, Dr. Schwarz Schilling, Frau Geier. Haase	2
3	**Dette, Wolfram** Junst Rosenegger- **F.D.P.** Free str 6 Demokratische 6330 Wetzlar Partei	◯	◯	**F.D.P.** Freie Demokratische Partei Mischick, von Schoeler, Hoffie, Wurbs, Dr. Prinz zu Sima-Hohensolms-Lich	3
4	**Ulm, Hermann Philipp** Forstbeamter Am Plent- **DKP** Deutsche ter 16 Kommunistische 6330 Wetzlar-Garbenheim Partei	◯	◯	**DKP** Deutsche kommunistische Partei Mayer, Knopf, Frau Dr. Weber, Funk, Fray Schuster	4
5	**Kirchschläger, Peter** Forstbeamter Jäger- **GRÜNE** DIE str 3 GRÜNEN 6344 Dietzhölztal-Ewersbach	◯	◯	**GRÜNE** DIE GRÜNEN Frau Ibbeken, Hecker, Hora- cek, Kerschgens, Kuhnert	5
			◯	**EAP** Europälsche Arbeiterpartei Frau Liebig, Haßmann, Stalleicher, Frau Kastner, Stalla	6
7	**Lang, Bernd** Werkzeugmacher Hermann- **KBW** Kommunistischer steiner Str 29 Bund West- 6330 Wetlar deutschlands	◯	◯	**KBW** Kommunistischer Bund Westdeutschland Schmierer, Frau Nönich, frau Eckardt, Dresler, Lang	7
			◯	**NPD** Nationaldemokratische Partei Deutschlands Phillipp, Brandt, Stürtz, Lauck, Bauer	8
			◯	**V** VOLKSFRONT Götz, Taufertshöfer, König, Riebe, Frau Weißert	9

1994: A Modified PR System in Action

The October 1994 German elections gave Chancellor Helmut Kohl his fourth victory in a row, although it was a narrow one. In the new *Bundestag*, Kohl's Christian Democrats, in coalition with their long-standing partners the Free Democrats, have a slim ten-seat lead over their leftist opponents (341 to 331). This was a big reduction from the previous *Bundestag*, where the CDU-FDP coalition had enjoyed a mammoth 134-seat lead.

But Kohl's narrow majority in parliament is enough to govern. "A majority is a majority," said Kohl, trying to put a positive spin on his party's loss of votes from 43.8 percent in 1990 to 41.5 in 1994. Social Democrat leader Rudolf Scharping, whose party enjoyed a 3 percentage point increase over 1990, predicted the Kohl government would soon be in difficulty and might not last.

The 1994 elections, the second for the newly unified nation, operated under the long-established FRG rules that are based on PR but add single-member districts. First, notice how close the percent of vote (on the right-hand, PR ballot) is to the percent of *Bundestag* seats, as shown in the table.

	PERCENT OF VOTE	SEATS
Christian Democrats	41.5	294 (44%)
Social Democrats	36.4	252 (38%)
Free Democrats	6.9	47 (7%)
Greens	7.3	49 (7%)
Democratic Socialists (ex-Communists)	4.4	30 (4%)
Republicans	1.9	0

But notice also the discrepancies: Most parties got more seats than their percentage of the votes might indicate. This is partly because some small parties (the neo-Nazi Republicans, for example) won less than 5 percent and got no seats. Further, ticket splitting—voting, for example, for the CDU candidate on the left-hand half of the ballot but for the FDP on the right-hand side—won the two big parties more seats than did the percentage of their party votes. The FDP, in fact, wins seats only on the second ballot, the party list; almost nowhere are they big enough to win a single-member district.

Those who win in a single-member district (the left half of the ballot) keep the seat even if it exceeds the percentage their party is entitled to from the PR (right half of the ballot) vote. For this reason, the *Bundestag* often expands beyond its nominal size to accommodate these *Uberhangmandate* (literally, "overhang" seats). The new all-German *Bundestag*, designed for 656 seats, had to expand to 672 to accommodate sixteen *Uberhangmandate* following the 1994 elections

The Party of Democratic Socialism, which fell below the 5 percent threshold in 1994, still won seats due to a little-used provision of the electoral law: Any party that wins a plurality in at least three single-member districts (the left-hand side of the ballot) gets into the *Bundestag* with whatever percent it won nationwide. The PDS, led by ex-Communists, won four districts in former East Germany and so collected 30 seats. It is unlikely, however, that the PDS will ever be included in a governing coalition. It is a party for East Germans unhappy with their economic situation.

East Germany, in general, went left in the 1994 elections. Every East German *Land* except Saxony gave a majority of its vote to the three leftist parties, the SPD, the Greens, and the PDS. This is a measure of *Ossi* disgruntlement with the CDU for not delivering prosperity fast enough. In 1990, East Germany had gone heavily CDU in gratitude for Kohl's speedy unification.

Is the German electoral system now clear to you? Don't worry. Even many Germans don't fully understand it. Basically, all you have to remember is that it's a split system: roughly half single-member districts and half PR.

politicians to be elected from a single member district with a higher percentage of votes than their party won on the second ballot. It means that voters split their tickets because they liked the candidate better than his or her party.

Just as the British and American systems tend to be two-party, the partially single-member German system has slowly cut down the number of parties from Weimar days until it is two-plus. Small parties seldom have a chance in the single-member districts; their best hope is for a showing on the second (PR) ballots of over 5 percent. This is another electoral innovation of the Federal Republic: A party must win at least 5 percent nationwide or three single-member seats to gain admittance into the *Bundestag*. (In 1990, the Constitutional Court ruled that this was unfair to small parties just getting organized in East Germany, so a one-time exception allowed parties to reach 5 percent in either East or West Germany. The Greens fell short of this in West Germany with 4.7 percent but squeaked through in East Germany with 5.9 percent.) The "threshold clause" is designed to keep out splinter and extremist parties. The German hybrid electoral system was adopted in whole or in part by several countries (see box on page 176).

Vocabulary Building

Basic Law	constructive	party list
Bundes-	no-confidence	proportional
Bundesrat	extraparliamentary	representation
Bundestag	opposition	*regierungsfähig*
CDU	FDP	Rhineland
center left	federation	SPD
center-right	grand coalition	threshold clause
chancellor	*Land*	

Further Reference

CARR, JONATHAN. *Helmut Schmidt: Helmsman of Germany.* New York: St. Martin's, 1985.

CERNY, KARL H., ed. *Germany at the Polls: The Bundestag Elections of the 1980s.* Durham, NC: Duke University Press, 1990.

CONRADT, DAVID P. *The German Polity,* 5th ed. White Plains, NY: Longman, 1993.

JOHNSON, NEVIL. *State and Government in the Federal Republic of Germany: The Executive at Work,* 2d ed. New York: Pergamon Press, 1983.

LOEWENBERG, GERHARD. *Parliament in the German Political System.* Ithaca, NY: Cornell University Press, 1967.

NORPOTH, HELMUT. "The German Federal Republic: Coalition Government at the Brink of Majority Rule," in *Government Coalitions in Western Democracies,* ed. by Eric C. Browne and John Dreijmanis. New York: Longman, 1982.

PINNEY, EDWARD L. *Federalism, Bureaucracy, and Party Politics in Western Germany: The Role of the Bundesrat.* Chapel Hill: University of North Carolina Press, 1963.

SCHWEITZER, CARL-CHRISTOPH, et al., eds. *Politics and Government in the Federal Republic of Germany: Basic Documents.* New York: St. Martin's Press, 1984.

THAYSEN, UWE, ROGER H. DAVIDSON, and ROBERT GERALD LIVINGSTON, eds. *The U.S. Congress and the West German Bundestag: Comparisons of Democratic Processes.* Boulder, CO: Westview, 1990.

CHAPTER *14*
German Political Attitudes

Achtung! You Vill Be Demokratic!

A German woman once recounted to the author how the Americans, in the last days of World War II, had bombed her hometown, a charming North Bavarian place with a splendid church and no military value. The town was a mess: bodies lay unburied, water and electricity were out, food supplies were unmoved. What did the people of the town do to meet this emergency? "Oh, nothing," she shrugged. "We waited for the Americans to come and tell us what to do."

Such were the beginnings of democracy in West Germany: a foreign implant grafted onto a people who were used to being told what to do. Can democracy be transplanted? Has it in fact taken in Germany? This is the really bothersome question. The institutions are fine; in some ways the Federal Republic's Basic Law is better than the U.S. Constitution. But, as we saw with Weimar, good institutions aren't worth much if people don't support them. Are liberal-democratic values sufficiently strong and deep in Germany to withstand economic and political hard times?

Historically, there has long been a liberal tradition in Germany, an outgrowth of the Enlightenment, as in France. In Britain, liberalism gradually triumphed. In France, liberalism and reaction seesawed back and forth, finally reaching an uneasy balance. In Germany, on the other hand, liberalism was overwhelmed by authoritarian forces. In 1848 the German liberals were driven out of the Frankfurt cathedral. In Bismarck's Second Reich they were treated with contempt. In the Weimar Republic they were in a distinct minority position, a pushover for authoritarians. Until the Bonn Republic, the liberal strand in German politics was a losing tradition.

East Germany attempted to develop attitudes of "people's democracy" (communism) rather than liberal democracy in the Western sense. Although communism and fascism are supposed to be opposites, some have noted that both aimed to make individuals obedient and powerless. This left many East Germans confused and skeptical at the onrush of democracy from West Germany in 1990; they had known nothing but authoritarian rule since 1933. It will take years and intensive education for East German democratic attitudes to reach the levels of West Germany.

The Moral Vacuum

In addition to a lack of democratic tradition, Germany faced a more subtle problem after World War II. A liberal democracy requires certain moral foundations. If you are entrusting ultimate authority to the people through their representatives, you have to believe that they are generally moral, perhaps even a bit idealistic. When this belief vanishes, a democracy loses some of its legitimacy. People may go along with it, but without deep faith.

The Nazi period left a kind of moral vacuum in Germany, and filling it has been a long, slow process, one still not complete. One problem that hindered the development of West German democracy was the persistence of ex-Nazis in high places. Every time one was discovered it undermined the moral authority of the regime. People, especially young people, thought, "Why should we respect democracy if there are still the same old Nazis running it?"

Immediately after the war, the Allied occupiers tried to "denazify" their zones. Party members, especially officials and the Gestapo (secret police), lost their jobs and sometimes went to prison. Henry Kissinger, then a U.S. Army sergeant, had a neat trick for rounding up Gestapo agents in the town he was running. He just put an ad in the newspaper for experienced policemen; when they showed up he slapped them in the klink. Still, aside from the 177 war criminals tried at Nuremberg (25 sentenced to death), denazification was spotty, and many Nazis got away, to Latin America or to new lives within Germany. Many Nazis made themselves useful to the occupation authorities and worked their way into business, politics, the civil service, and even the judicial system.

It is this last-mentioned group that kept Nazi mass murderers from coming to trial. There are laws on the books against such people, but curiously, Nazi criminals were rarely brought to trial until the 1960s. By then younger people had worked their way up the judicial ladder and were willing to prosecute cases their elders preferred to let pass. This helps explain why Nazi criminals were still being tried in the 1990s.

Two presidents of the Federal Republic, Walter Scheel of the FDP and Karl Carstens of the CDU, and one chancellor, Kurt Kiesinger of the CDU, were once Nazi party members. All pointed out that they were nominal rather than active members, "just opportunists" out to further their careers during a time when the Nazis controlled many paths to success. While none were charged with any crime, what kind of moral authority did "just an opportunist" lend to the highest offices of a country trying to become a democracy?

Impressive German Words: Gehorsamkeit

Obedience is the counterpart of authority. Germans have been *gehorsam* (obedient) for centuries, an attitude not conducive to democracy. A working democracy requires a certain amount of speaking up, of criticizing, of participation, and until after World War II these qualities were generally lacking among Germans. In one possibly apocryphal incident, Marxist revolutionaries rushing government buildings in 1918 Berlin still wouldn't step on the grass: there was a sign forbidding it. Lenin is said to have wondered, "How are you going to make a revolution with people who won't even step on the grass?"

Forgetting the Past

Can a society experience collective guilt? Was it realistic to expect Germans as a whole to feel remorse for what the Nazis did? The West German response was mostly to flush the Nazi era down the memory hole, to say in effect, "Past, go away!" German fathers were reluctant to say much about what they had done. German history textbooks stopped at 1933 and picked up again in 1945. The result has been appalling ignorance among young Germans about Hitler, the Nazis, and what they did. In survey after survey, some German high schoolers identify Hitler as a CDU politician, the leader of Germany in World War I, or as "the man who built the *Autobahnen*" (express highways). This attempt to forget the past was not merely an oversight; it reflected the inability of the German elite—including education officials—to come to grips with the past and with themselves.

Can a society simply forget its past, blot it out? West Germans tried. Climbing out of the ruins of World War II, Germans threw themselves with single-minded devotion into work, making money, and spending it conspicuously. The results were spectacular; the economy soared, and many Germans became affluent. The West German archetype became the *Wunderkind* (wonder child), the businessman who rose from rubble to riches in the postwar boom with a fat body, a fat cigar, and a fat Mercedes.

But material prosperity could not fill the moral and historical void. Many young Germans were profoundly dissatisfied with the emphasis on materialism that seemed to be a sort of cover-up for a lack of deeper values. Some of them turned to far-left and later "green" politics.

This factor probably contributed to the growth of radical and sometimes violent politics among young Germans in the 1970s and 1980s. Certainly it wasn't because they were poor; their society was prosperous, and often they were from wealthy families. Prosperity and materialism, in fact, rubbed them the wrong way. Said one rich girl: "I'm sick of all this caviar gobbling." Then she joined the terrorists and helped murder an old family friend, a banker. (She and other gang members were arrested in 1990 in East Germany, where they had been protected by the secret po-

Impressive German Words: *Vergangenheitsbewältigung*

Literally, "mastery of the past," *Vergangenheitsbewältigung* means coming to grips with Germany's Nazi past, facing it squarely, and admitting a certain degree of collective guilt. Many German intellectuals take *Vergangenheitsbewältigung* as the necessary foundation of German democracy. If Germans can't come to grips with their own past, if they try to cover it up, German democracy could again be taken over by mindless nationalists. Urgings to look clearly at the past have come from CDU politicians such as former President Richard von Weizsäcker, leftist writer and SPD supporter Günter Grass, and Catholic writer Heinrich Böll, who coined the term. There is, however, greater commitment to learning the lessons of the past on the left, among the SPD and Greens, than on the right. The Bavarian CSU generally shuns the notion that Germany's past needs examining.

lice, the Stasi.) The Baader-Meinhof gang committed murder and bank robbery in the name of revolution, and some young Germans sympathized with them. The terrorists, in their warped, sick way, put their finger on the German malaise: German society, avoiding its past, had developed a moral void with nothing to believe in but "caviar gobbling." The past, it seems, doesn't stay buried; it comes back to haunt the society trying to forget it. In the words of American philosopher George Santayana, "Those who cannot remember the past are condemned to repeat it."

Under Communist rule, the East Germans used a different approach to avoid coming to grips with the past: Deny it was their past. "We weren't Nazis," taught the Communist regime, "We fought the Nazis. So we have nothing to be ashamed of or to regret. The Nazis are over there in West Germany." East Germany avoided moral responsibility by trying to portray the Nazis as a foreign power, rather like Austria has done. In this area, as in many others, East German attitudes lagged behind West German attitudes.

The Generation Gap

As a guest in a German home once, I saw how the family reacted when one of the daughters found, in the back of a china closet, an old poem, *"Die Hitlerblume"* (the Hitler flower), comparing the *Führer* to a lovely blossom. The three college-age children howled with laughter and derision. "Daddy, how could you go along with this kind of garbage?" they asked. The father, an old-fashioned authoritarian type, grew red in the face and stammered, "You don't know what it was like. They had everybody whipped up. The times were different." He was quite embarrassed.

The incident underscores the very real generation gap in German political attitudes; simply put, the younger the generation, the more democratic it is; the older, the more authoritarian. It is the younger Germans who are more willing to

The Rise of "Postmaterialism"

One of the trends among rich nations—especially pronounced in West Germany—is the feeling of some young people that modern society is too focused on material goods. Starting in the late 1960s, "countercultures" sprang up in every advanced country. Young people rejected the work-and-buy ethic of their parents and turned instead to beards, blue jeans, and "quality of life" questions. This caught on strongly in the Federal Republic as young Germans sought to repudiate the supermaterialism of their parents.

Postmaterialism underlies the Federal Re-

public's Marxist, antinuclear, ecology, and pacifist movements, much of which came together in the Greens. Postmaterialism also plugged into German romanticism and nationalism.

Will postmaterialism last or will it decline in a united Germany of the 1990's? One of its causes was the prosperity of the 1960s and 1970s. By the 1980s, the FRG was experiencing economic difficulties; unemployment was at a postwar high. The East German scramble for material goods may persuade the upcoming generation that materialism isn't so bad after all.

come to grips with the past—partly because they were not personally involved—and to give unqualified allegiance to democracy.

The younger generation has also freed up German society a great deal. No longer are German women confined to *Kinder, Küche, Kirche* (children, kitchen, and church); many work outside the home and even participate in politics. German youngsters are not as obedient as they once were, and German fathers no longer beat them as in the old days. If democracy starts in the home, Germany now has a much better foundation for democracy.

The typical German of today is far more democratic in attitudes than the typical German of 1949 when the Federal Republic was founded. Those who would support another Hitler, trade civil rights for "security," or think a one-party system is best have steadily dwindled, while those who think democracy and civil rights are worthwhile values in their own right have steadily increased. West German attitudes are now at least as democratic as any of their European neighbors. The East Germans will need a little work.

Is the change permanent? Political scientist Sidney Verba drew a distinction between "output affect" and "system affect" in his discussion of German political culture. The former means liking the system for what it produces (jobs, security, and material goods), the latter, liking the system for its own sake. Verba thought Germans showed more of the first than the second; that is, they liked the system while the going was good—they were "fair-weather democrats"—but had not yet become "rain-or-shine democrats" the way Britons or Americans are. Verba's point was made in the early 1960s. Since then, system affect among Germans has increased as the younger generation has come of age. Some East Germans, however, are still caught up in the output affect, judging democracy by the cars and refrigerators they can now obtain.

Germans' Declining Religiosity

Germans are growing less religious, a 1992 survey for the newsweekly *Der Spiegel* found. While over 80 percent of West Germans belong to one of the two big churches—about half are Catholic and half are Lutheran—fewer feel personally committed to their religion:

- In 1967, 68 percent of West Germans said they believed in God; in 1992, only 56 percent said they did.

- In 1967, 25 percent of West Germans reported going to church nearly every Sunday; in 1992, only 10 percent did.

- The percentage of declared atheists has increased from 10 to 25 percent.

- East Germans are far less religious; 62 percent belong to no church, 30 percent identified themselves as Protestant, and 5 percent as Catholic.

The government has a lot to do with religious affiliation. In West Germany, newborns are automatically enrolled in their parents' church; not the case in Communist East Germany. Furthermore, German churches are "established," meaning funded by taxes. A certain percentage of an individual German's income tax automatically goes to the denomination he or she has designated. Increasingly, this irritates many Germans, who can save on taxes by declaring that they belong to no religion. Thus a device intended to support religion gives an incentive for religious indifference.

A New German Democracy

In a sense, democratic attitudes have taken root too well in Germany. Now one of the FRG's big problems is that young people, schooled in freedom and democracy, want to see more of it applied in practice. They want to be able to criticize and participate without their elders or the Americans telling them to hush up. The younger generation brings with them new concerns about war and the environment that the older generation didn't worry about and didn't like being reminded of.

A certain distance developed between many young Germans and the mainstream political parties. In the German party system, newcomers must slowly work their way up party ranks, starting at the local and state levels, before they can have a say at the national level. By the time they can, they are no longer young. In the meantime, they are expected to obey party dictates and not have much input. Some youth organizations of both the Social Democrats and Free Democrats became so rambunctious that they had to be disowned by their parent parties. For many young Germans, the Christian Democrats and Social Democrats who alternated in power looked a lot alike, staid and elderly, and neither was responsive to young people.

Belatedly, some German politicians recognized the problem. Former President Richard von Weizsäcker worried openly about "the failure of my generation to bring younger people into politics." Young Germans, he noted, "do not admire the moral substance of the older generation. Our economic achievement went along with a very materialistic and very selfish view of all problems."

Young Germans also developed resentment of the United States. In the 1950s and 1960s, young Germans nearly worshiped the United States; it was their model in politics, lifestyles, and values. Then things happened that shook this. The assassination of President Kennedy—who had recently proclaimed "Ich bin ein Berliner" at the Berlin Wall—horrified Germans and made them wonder about the United States. The Vietnam War was worse; some young Germans compared it with Hitler's war of aggression. Finally, rising tensions between East and West and the warlike posture of President Reagan convinced many young Germans that the United States would be willing to incinerate Germany. A minority began to see Washington rather than Moscow as the source of tension. Some wanted the Americans out of Germany. It was ironic that the United States—which had tutored Germans to repudiate militarism—found itself the object of West German antiwar feeling.

The preceding attitudes fed the Green party. In elections, the Greens do much better among young voters than among the total population. These attitudes also contributed to a new German nationalism that no longer liked following in America's footsteps. Instead of automatically looking west, some young Germans looked to a reunified Germany with neither Americans nor Russians encamped on their soil. Some young Germans turned anti–U.S. and anti-NATO. The entirely new situation created by German unification, the end of the Cold War, and Soviet pullout from Eastern Europe is rapidly changing German attitudes, especially those of young people. We can no longer count on Germans to automatically look to the West or to the United States for guidance or solidarity.

The Disorienting Unification

When the Wall came down in late 1989, it seemed like a dream come true. There was much celebration and good will. *Wessis* (as the West Germans were nicknamed) were generous to the *Ossis* (East Germans), but soon the relationship soured. The *Ossis* kept demanding the bounties of the prosperous West as a right; after all, they were all Germans and the *Wessis* had so much. The *Wessis* didn't see things that way. "We've worked hard for more than forty years for this," they argued, "Now you *Ossis* must do the same." With newly acquired D-marks, courtesy of West German taxpayers, *Ossis* snatched up modern products while their own economy collapsed. West Germans quickly developed negative stereotypes of East Germans living well at *Wessi* expense—like poor relatives who had come to sponge off them.

By the time of official unification, on October 2, 1990, the mood was subdued. The celebration was tinged with fear and skepticism. As the costs of bringing East Germany up to West German levels started to sink in, some Germans grew angry. The East German economy was found to be in far worse shape than foreseen, and it needed a gigantic bailout. Much industry would simply have to be closed. Unemployment shot up. West German business executives talked down to their East German counterparts as if they were children. *Wessis* thought *Ossis* were ignorant; *Ossis* thought *Wessis* were arrogant. Both were probably right.

Making matters worse, a serious recession hit West Germany in the early 1990s (see Chapter 16), making many West Germans frightened of unemployment and resentful at the massive transfer of funds to the east. Some Germans wondered if unification had been worthwhile. The clear, simple split of Europe and of Germany by the Cold War had vanished. The Iron Curtain may have been brutal, but you knew where you stood. Now disoriented Germans ask which way for unified Germany in a vastly different Europe. Some left-wing intellectuals warned of the return of an aggressive, expansionist Germany. Some neo-Nazi youths lent weight to the warnings by murdering resident Turks. Predicting a clearly democratic future for a united Germany is more difficult than was predicting it for West Germany alone.

The End of Shell Shock

Many Germans, especially the older generation who had gone along with the Nazis, felt so damaged by political involvement that they swore never to take an active part in politics again. To appreciate how an older German might feel shell-shocked and cautious about politics, imagine a German born at the turn of the century who was raised under a conservative monarchy and taught to obey authority. All of a sudden a republic comes that expects its citizens to be good democrats (they weren't). Then comes a dictatorship that demands the enthusiastic, unquestioning complicity of all Germans. After that come Allied occupiers telling the bewildered citizenry that they have been very wicked and must now become democratic. No wonder that in the first decades of the Federal Republic many Germans said *ohne mich* (without me) to politics. Many East Germans still feel this way.

In their famous book, *The Civic Culture*, Almond and Verba described the German attitude of 1959 as one of detachment. Germans were often well informed

Why Young Neo-Nazis?

One of the frightening things about unified Germany was the rather sudden appearance of young skinheads and neo-Nazis, some of whom attacked foreign workers and their families, murdering several in arson attacks. Federal German police estimate there are about 42,000 Germans, mostly young, in extremist groups. In 1993, 1,609 crimes were committed against foreigners.

Who are these young Germans? They defy simple categorization. They can be east or west, employed or jobless. The only thing they seem to have in common is their racist hatred of foreigners, either those who have been in Germany for years as "guest workers," or those who are recent political and economic refugees. All frustrations and fears, of unemployment, of strange languages and cultures, and of the disorientation that has come with the end of the Cold War and German unification are rolled into one target: the foreigner.

Furthermore, the young neo-Nazis give voice to many attitudes that adults are too polite to express publicly. The youngsters also find companionship and meaning in the neo-Nazi organizations and ideologies that demagogues offer them. Could Nazism return to Germany? Probably only on a small scale. First, the young neo-Nazis have no deep or abiding ideology; they could just as easily become militant leftists. Second, there are several would-be Hitlers, and their movements and parties are divided, making it hard for any one of them to cross the 5 percent threshold. If they ever get together, though, they could make it into the *Bundestag*.

Willy Brandt: A German Mr. Clean

One of the more optimistic signs that democracy had taken root in Germany was the 1969 election that made Willy Brandt chancellor of the Federal Republic. It would not have been possible even a few years earlier, for Brandt represented a repudiation of German history and society that few Germans could have then tolerated. First, Brandt was an illegitimate child, and in a society as stuffy as Germany's that was a black mark. Adenauer, in fact, had used it against Brandt in election campaigns. Second, Brandt was a Socialist, and in his youth in the North German seaport of Lübeck had been pretty far left (although never Communist). No Socialist had been in power in Germany for decades; the CDU kept smearing the SPD as a dangerous party, and many Germans believed it. Third, and most damaging to Brandt, was the fact that he had fled to Norway in

1933 and become a Norwegian citizen and hadn't reclaimed his German nationality until 1947. Some even unjustly accused him of fighting Germans as a Norwegian soldier.

With a record like that, it seemed Brandt was starting into German politics with three strikes against him. But Brandt also had appeal for many Germans, especially younger ones. He was "Mr. Clean," a German who had battled the Nazis—literally, in Lübeck street fights—and who had never been "just an opportunist" who survived by going along. Brandt seemed to represent a newer, better Germany as opposed to the conservative, traditional values of Adenauer and the CDU.

As mayor of West Berlin from 1957 to 1966, Brandt showed how tough he was by standing up to Soviet and East German efforts at encroachment; he also demonstrated to the West German public that he was anti-Communist. A leading figure in the SPD, Brandt supported the 1959 move away from Marxism. In 1964 he became the SPD's chairman, and this lent a boost to the party's electoral fortunes.

In 1966 the SPD was invited into the cabinet in a grand coalition with the CDU. As is usual in coalition governments, the head of the second largest party is given the position of foreign minister. Here Brandt showed himself to be a forceful statesman. Under his leadership, the foreign ministry began its efforts to improve relations with East Europe (*Ostpolitik*). By 1969 the SPD had enough *Bundestag* seats to form a small coalition with the FDP, and Willy Brandt became the Federal Republic's first Socialist chancellor. The event was a symbolic breakthrough: Germany looked more democratic under an anti-Nazi than an ex-Nazi (Brandt's predecessor, Kiesinger).

The story, however, does not have a happy ending. In 1974 it was discovered that one of Brandt's closest assistants was an East German spy. (West Germany was riddled with East German spies.) Brandt, regretting his security slip, resigned the chancellorship to become the grand old man of not only German but also West European social democracy. He did live to see the fruits of his *Ostpolitik* and died in 1992.

Willy Brandt, FRG Chancellor 1969-1974. (*Michael Roskin*)

about politics but didn't want to participate in much more than voting. They were pragmatic and sometimes cynical about politics. If the system worked it was okay, but there was no point in getting personally involved. Germans showed low levels of social trust or of willingness to discuss politics with others. In the decades since, however, this attitude receded, making West Germans among the most democratic and participatory in the world. Every decade there were fewer and fewer of the skeptical generation and more and more of the postwar generation. But now Germany, with unification, has entered the post–Cold War period, and it is becoming a time of testing.

The German Political Elite

German elite recruitment is quite mixed, more like that of the United States than Britain or France. There is no German equivalent of Oxbridge or the Great Schools. The three German political collapses of this century left a relatively clean slate for bright talent to achieve political office. Some (such as Brandt) were not even university graduates, although practically all politicians now are. There is no single university or institute in Germany that serves as a training ground for a political elite; many universities are considered good.

As in America, the typical German politician has studied law, although in Germany this is done at the undergraduate rather than the postgraduate level. German (and other European) legal systems produce different attitudes than the Anglo-American Common Law system. Continental law is Roman law—often in the updated form of the Napoleonic Code—and it emphasizes rather rigid adherence to fixed rules. The Common Law, on the other hand, is judge-made law that focuses on precedent and persuasion; it is more flexible. The former system produces lawyers who tend to go by the book, the latter, lawyers who negotiate and make deals. Consequently, German politicians with their legal background are heavily law-oriented rather than people-oriented.

Much of the work of the *Bundestag*, for example, is devoted to the precise wording of bills, making that house a rather dull, inward-looking chamber that has failed to win a great deal of admiration from the German public. Likewise cabinet ministers conceive of their role heavily in terms of carrying out laws. Half of Kohl's cabinet were lawyers.

 Impressive German Words: Politikverdrossenheit

"Fed-uppedness with politics" is perhaps the best translation for the new compound word that appeared on the German scene in the 1990s. Especially common among young Germans, it indicates falling interest in parties, politicians, or even voting.

Some of the contributing factors: high youth unemployment and no charismatic political figures. If it becomes a major trend, it could contribute to the rise of extremist parties, which try to exploit youthful discontent.

The German political elite is not all lawyers. A smaller group has had a disproportionate role in German politics: economists. In few other countries have professional economists achieved the stature they have in the FRG. One German chancellor had a Ph.D. in economics: Ludwig Erhard. Under Adenauer, the rotund, jolly Erhard (nicknamed *der Gummilöwe*, the rubber lion), as economics minister, charted Germany's rise to prosperity; later he became chancellor. Helmut Schmidt, an economics graduate, succeeded Brandt as SPD chancellor and managed to keep both inflation and unemployment low in Germany while much of the world went through a major recession. In Germany, economists are not just advisers but often become important politicians themselves.

The German Split Personality

The French, as we discussed, often seem split between demanding impersonal authority and rebelling against it. The Germans have a sort of split personality, too, but it's between romanticism and realism.

Most of the time Germans are workaday realists: hard working, thrifty, clean, orderly, cooperative, family-oriented. But a persistent romantic streak exists in German history that comes out every now and then: the nineteenth-century intellectuals (such as composer Richard Wagner) who reveled in the *Volksgeist*, the Nazi youth who really believed they were building a "thousand-year Reich," and recently the far-left terrorists who thought they could build utopia by means of assassination and kidnapping. The latest German romantics are the Greens, who long for an imaginary pastoral idyll free of atoms and industry.

German romanticism manifests itself in other way too, in the continual striving for perfection, for example. This leads Germans to undertake vast projects they may not have the resources to complete. Hitler's plan to conquer all of Europe, including Russia, is an infamous example. But this drive for perfection also operates on more mundane levels. As an American ski enthusiast remarked: "If you're at an international ski resort where in one day four people break a leg, three of them will be Germans. It's because even on skis they're trying too hard, pushing themselves beyond their limits."

Impressive German Words: Sehnsucht and Streben

Sehnsucht and *Streben*, or "longing" and "effort," are twin characteristics of German romanticism and appear widely in German literature and poetry. *Sehnsucht* implies a deep yearning for something impossible to attain, such as a lofty ideal (or, in Goethe's *Sorrows of Young Werther*, the protagonist's love for Charlotte). And *Streben* means applying utmost effort to try to get it. The twin forces lend a dynamic impulse to German life and work, but they can also lead to despair if frustrated. When Goethe's Werther didn't get Charlotte (who was married), he blew his brains out.

Germans set high store by achievement. To work harder, produce more, and proudly let others know about it seems to be an ingrained cultural trait. This helps explain Germany's rise after the war to Europe's number-one economic power. Both East Germany's leader Walter Ulbricht and West Germany's Helmut Schmidt toured their respective camps giving unsolicited advice on how other countries should copy the German economic miracle. East Germany's, although not as spectacular as the Federal Republic's, nonetheless made it the economic leader of the East bloc. I once told an anti-Communist West Berliner that East Berlin also looked pretty prosperous. He didn't dispute me but nodded and said, "Of course. They're Germans too."

Perhaps the archetypal German figure is Goethe's Faust, the driven person who can never rest or be content with what is already his. This quality can produce both great good and evil. Former Chancellor Helmut Schmidt, himself a stereotype of the German realist strain, once said, "Germans have an enormous capacity for idealism and the perversion of it."

Vocabulary Building

Achilles heel	detachment	Roman law
archetype	materialism	romanticism
authoritarian	opportunist	system affect
Autobahn	output affect	terrorism
Common Law	postmaterialism	*Wunderkind*
denazification	provincialism	

Further Reference

ARDAGH, JOHN. *Germany and the Germans: An Anatomy of Society Today.* New York: Harper & Row, 1987.

BAKER, KENDALL L., RUSSELL J. DALTON, and KAI HILDEBRANDT. *Germany Transformed: Political Culture and the New Politics.* Cambridge, MA: Harvard University Press, 1981.

BALFOUR, MICHAEL. *Germany: The Tides of Power.* New York: Routledge, 1992.

BORNEMAN, JOHN. *After the Wall: East Meets West in the New Berlin.* New York: Basic Books, 1991.

BRAUNTHAL, GERARD. "Willy Brandt: Politician and Statesman," in *Governments and Leaders: An Approach to Comparative Politics,* ed. by Edward Feit. Boston: Houghton Mifflin, 1978.

CONRADT, DAVID P. "Changing German Political Culture," in *The Civic Culture Revisited,* ed. by Gabriel A. Almond and Sidney Verba. Boston: Little, Brown, 1980.

CRAIG, GORDON A. *The Germans.* New York: Putnam's, 1982.

DALTON, RUSSEL J. *Politics in Germany,* 2d ed. New York: HarperCollins, 1993.

EDINGER, LEWIS J. *West German Politics.* New York: Columbia University Press, 1986.

GRASS, GÜNTER. *Two States—One Nation?* San Diego, CA: Harcourt Brace Jovanovich, 1990.

SICHROVSKY, PETER. *Born Guilty: Children of Nazi Families.* New York: Basic Books, 1988.

SZABO, STEPHEN F. "The New Generation: Protest and Postmaterialism," in *The Federal Republic of Germany in the 1980s,* ed. by Robert Gerald Livingston. New York: German Information Center, 1983.

VERBA, SIDNEY. "Germany: The Remaking of Political Culture," in *Political Culture and Political Development,* ed. by L. Pye and S. Verba. Princeton, NJ: Princeton University Press, 1965.

15

Germany: Patterns of Interaction

More Complex, Less Stable

We saw how the Weimar Republic collapsed with the shrinking of the moderate parties and growth of extremist parties—"polarized pluralism" in action. Could this happen in the Federal Republic? For most of the history of West Germany, the answer was "no." With only two-plus parties, they, for good political reasons, stuck close to the center of the political spectrum. Political competition in West Germany tended to be center seeking; that is, the parties struggled to win the big vote in the center and neglect the relatively few votes on the extremes. Voters had their choice of three moderate parties (there were several tiny parties on the ballot, but they were largely ignored), and these three parties could combine in only three different coalitions (CDU and FDP, CDU and SPD, SPD and FDP). This made West German politics stable compared to more tumultuous multiparty systems.

With unification—and even a little before—German politics became less stable and more complex. The party system is still "two-plus," but now the "plus" includes not just one small party, but two or three. The two large parties lost some of their votes to smaller parties. This makes coalition formation more difficult, for now a German coalition may require three partners instead of the previous two. Now there are at least five possible coalition combinations (see box). This in turn makes German government less stable and predictable.

Parties and the Electorate

Social scientists have found that political opinion in most modern democracies resembles more or less a bell-shaped curve: a lot of people are in the center, with fewer

Germany's Possible Coalitions

With at least four parties in the *Bundestag* in the 1990s, coalition building is more complex, especially if either of the two large parties (CDU and SPD) get less than 45 percent of the vote (and therefore of *Bundestag* seats). Why 45 percent? Simple: one of the small parties, to get any seats at all, by definition must have won 5 percent of the vote. Accordingly, two parties, one with 45 percent and the other with 5 percent, would be able to form a coalition with a (bare) majority of the *Bundestag*. By the same token, if one of the small parties won, say, 10 percent, it could form a winning coalition with a large party that won 40 percent. This relatively happy situation gives rise to three possibilities, all of which have already occurred:

1. **Christian-Liberal Coalition.** The CDU/CSU wins 40 percent and the FDP wins 10 percent, allowing for the same coalition that had sustained Kohl and earlier cabinets in power.

2. **Social-Liberal Coalition.** The SPD edges out the CDU with 40 percent and turns to the FDP with, say, 10 percent to rebuild the coalition that had supported Brandt and Schmidt in the 1970s.

3. **Grand Coalition.** Neither the CDU nor SPD do well in elections; say, each wins less than 40 percent. Rather than one of them attempting a coalition with two small parties, they make a coalition with each other, as occurred in the late 1960s with not-so-happy results (see page 172).

Now for two possibilities without earlier examples at the national level:

4. **Red-Green Coalition.** If the SPD (red, as it used to be called in the old days) gets 40 percent and the Greens get 10 percent, they could put together a social-ecological coalition of the sort that has appeared in some *Länder*. Such governments have tended to be unstable as the idealistic Greens often dislike the daily grind of governing.

5. **"Traffic Light"** *(Ampel)* **Coalition.** Red, green, and yellow (for the FDP). If the SPD won under 40 percent, it might need two small coalition partners, each with 6–10 percent, to build a majority. Constructed once at the state level (Bremen), the *Ampel* is a difficult coalition to sustain, as the Greens and Liberals seriously dislike each other.

One other theoretical possibility—a "government of national unity" that would add the CDU to the traffic light—might be useful for an emergency situation such as war, but not for much else. According to the theory of coalitions, you stop adding partners once you have topped 50 percent; there's no point to adding more. And an all-party coalition would not stay together for long.

A Christian-Green coalition would be out of the question; the two are from opposite sides of the political spectrum. If the neo-Nazi Republicans should cross the 5 percent barrier they would be fit coalition partners for no one. If the neo-Communist Party of Democratic Socialism should hold a few seats in eastern Germany, it could contribute to an all-left coalition with the SPD and Greens. The recent fragmentation of the German party system makes one long for the relatively simple "two-plus" system in which the alternatives were, with one brief exception, points 1 or 2 above.

and fewer as one moves to the left or right. If you want to sound more scientific you call this a "unimodal" distribution of opinion. Routinely, citizens of the European Union are asked to place themselves on a one-to-nine ideological scale, one for the most left and nine for the most right. In 1992, Germany came out, like most Common Market countries, as a bell-shaped curve (see box on page 195), which indeed had been its shape for some decades.

How does this affect political parties? When party leaders come to understand the shape of the electorate, either through modern polling techniques or by losing elections, they usually try to modify their party image so that it appeals to the middle of the opinion spectrum. If the Social Democrats position themselves too far left—say, at two on the nine-point scale—by advocating nationalizing private industry and dropping out of NATO, they may please some of the left-wing ideologues in the party but do poorly in elections. In 1992 fewer than 3 percent of Germans placed themselves at the two position on the left. So the Social Democrats tone down their socialism and emphasize their commitment to democracy plus welfare measures, moving to the three or four position. Now they do much better in elections, but the left wing of the party is unhappy with the dilution of socialist gospel. Finally, sniffing the possibility of becoming Germany's governing party, the SPD virtually throws out socialism and tells the electorate that they will do a better job running the capitalist, market economy. At this point they are in roughly the four to five position. The party's left wingers are angry, accusing the SPD leadership of selling out socialist ideals and turning into apologists for capitalism; some left-wing socialists even quit the party. But electorally, the SPD is doing well. By emphasizing democracy and minimizing socialism, they win the support of many centrists.

The preceding, in a nutshell, was the history of the SPD to their electoral high point of 45.8 percent in 1972. In the last century the Social Democrats started to shed their Marxism, in practice if not yet in theory. In the 1950s, seeing the CDU triumphantly win the center, they decided to break out of their left-wing stronghold. Meeting in Bad Godesberg (just outside Bonn) in 1959, they drew up a Basic Program so moderate one can hardly find any socialism in it. Marxism was *kaput*; the SPD proclaimed itself "rooted in Christian ethics, humanism and classical philosophy."

Now, while the Social Democrats moved toward the right, the Christian Democrats moved toward the left, or perhaps more accurately, since they already carved out for themselves a broad swath of the ideological spectrum, they claimed to stand for everything, a party of all Germans, just as the British Conservatives claim to represent all Britons. The CDU downplayed its conservatism, for it too understood that if the party image were too rightist it would lose the big prize in the center. The result, at least until recently, was two large parties that generally tried to be moderate but in so doing rubbed their respective left and right wings the wrong way (see boxes).

The game is never finished, though. While they had transformed themselves into a center-left party, the SPD allowed the area on their left to be taken over by a newer, more radical party, the Greens. (Interestingly, in a 1984 study Green voters placed themselves at 3.4 on the scale.) Partly to try to win over these leftist voters, partly in response to *Juso* (see box on page 196) influence within the SPD, and partly out of irritation at the hawkishness of the Reagan administration, the SPD moved leftwards in the late 1980s, much like the British Labour party had done earlier. The SPD came out against both U.S. nuclear missiles in Germany and nuclear power plants, two key Green demands. But the shift hurt the SPD electorally; they dropped from 42.9 percent of the vote in 1980 to 33.5 in 1990, their poorest showing since 1957.

The Chancellor and the Electorate

Two factors especially hurt the SPD in the 1990s. The CDU's embrace of rapid unification made the SPD look narrow and carping in its warnings about the expense

The Shape of the German Electorate

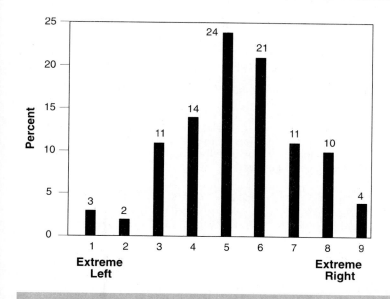

The Self-Placement of German Voters on a Left/Right Ideological Scale.

and economic impact of quick merger. Go slow and think it through, was the SPD message, not a popular one in 1990, although their "I told you so" won them some votes in 1994. SPD chancellor-candidate Oskar Lafontaine in 1990 was also part of the problem. He was too brainy and radical for many German voters and stepped aside after the election. Unfortunately, the SPD's next candidate, the bearded young intellectual Rudolf Scharping came across in 1994 much the same way.

In Germany, as in most advanced countries, personality has become more important than ideology in the minds of many voters. With the decline of *Weltanschauung* parties (see box on page 198) and the move of most large parties to the center of the political spectrum, the personality of candidates is often what persuades voters. This has long been the case in the United States and is now becoming the European norm as well. Some call it the Americanization of European politics, but it is less a matter of copying than it is of reflecting the rise of catchall parties. Throughout Europe, election posters now feature the picture of the top party leader, the person who would become prime minister. Although voting may be by party list, citizens know that in choosing a party they are actually electing a prime minister.

German campaigns, for example, are conducted almost as if they were for the direct election of a president—as in the United States and France. Officially there

Unhappy on the Left: The Jusos

The youth branch of the SPD—the *Jungsozialisten,* or *Jusos* for short—has been a continual thorn in the left side of the party. Limited to people under 35, the *Jusos* attract some young zealots ablaze with Marxist notions of socialism. Impatient and idealistic, many *Jusos* find the mainstream SPD too moderate and gradualist.

Periodically, the SPD has to disown its offspring. If it doesn't, it costs the party votes. In areas where *Jusos* gained control of the party machinery—in Munich and Frankfurt, for example—the SPD lost several seats that it had held for years.

What the *Jusos* can't understand is that Germans as a whole are moderate in their political views and there is little support for pulling out of NATO, nationalization of industry, "cultural revolution," and massive taxes on the rich. When the *Jusos* helped move the SPD toward such positions in the early 1980s, the party lost all three national elections during that decade. Some *Jusos* defected to the Greens. The SPD as a whole was faced with the question of whether to try to retain young radicals by moving leftward, or to win elections by staying centrist.

is no "candidate for the chancellorship," but in practice the leading figures of the two big parties are clearly identified as such—in the press and in the public mind—so that much of the campaign revolves around the personalities of the two leading candidates.

A German candidate for chancellor must project strength and levelheadedness. In a country obsessed with fear of inflation, the candidate's economic background plays a bigger role than in most nations. Two of Germany's postwar chancellors have been economists. The candidate's adherence to democratic rules also plays a role, and Franz Josef Strauss's authoritarian streak contributed to his defeat in the 1980 race.

Personality contributed to the results of the 1994 election, too. The CDU/CSU had the steady, optimistic image of Helmut Kohl. The SPD's candidates of the early 1990s came across as radical intellectuals. Much of postwar German politics can be described as parties groping for the right leader to bring them to power in the *Bundestag* and chancellor's office. When they find the right one—Adenauer and Kohl of the CDU—they stick with him.

German Dealignment?

For many years political scientists have worried that U.S. political parties were showing an increasing "dealignment" with the U.S. electorate. That is, some decades ago, U.S. parties used to present a fairly clear "party image" and most voters carried around in their heads a fairly clear "party ID." Where the two connected (for example, U.S. Democrats and blue-collar workers), you had a semi-stable "alignment" of party with voter. These could change, to be sure, in what were called "realignments."

Thunder on the Right: CSU

Bavaria is the Texas of Germany, a land with a raucous brand of politics all its own. On principle, the Christian Social Union (CSU) never let itself be absorbed into the CDU; instead it calls itself an allied party and sometimes threatens to burst out of Bavaria and set itself up in nationwide competition with the CDU. The CSU is generally to the right of the CDU, demanding a tougher anti-immigrant stance, a firmer crackdown on radicals, and a rollback of welfare.

The guiding force behind the CSU was beefy Franz Josef Strauss, prime minister of the state of Bavaria where they called him "der Franzl" (Little Franz). The Bavarian equivalent of Jesse Helms, Strauss was Germany's right-wing tough guy. Although he was never a Nazi, Strauss used to tell Germans that they should not be ashamed of their past and that Germany was not entirely to blame for World War II. An authoritarian, Strauss had two news-magazine editors jailed in 1962 for publishing alleged military secrets when he was defense minister in Bonn. In the public uproar at his abuse of power, Strauss resigned.

But Strauss was also extremely intelligent, and when he won the joint CDU/CSU nomination for the chancellorship for the 1980 election, he immediately switched to a moderate line. It didn't work. Strauss's image—a major part of the SPD campaign—worked to the CDU/CSU's detriment. He did not run for chancellor again, nor was he invited into the Kohl cabinets of the 1980s. When he died in 1988, many democratic Germans breathed a sigh of relief.

But increasingly, U.S. voters were showing a dealignment: their preferences, often unfocused, connected with no party on a long-term basis. Their votes easily shift from one party to another in response to candidate personality and clever advertising.

Is electoral dealignment catching? Are West Europeans catching it? One sees evidence of it in Britain and France, but in Germany it seems to be most developed. Increasingly, Germans dislike both major parties and doubt that either major party in office would do any better than the other. German turnout in elections is falling, from a high of 91 percent in 1972 to 78 percent in 1990 and 79 percent in 1994. More citizens now scatter their votes among a variety of small parties all over the political spectrum, from left to right. One center-right group that enjoyed a sudden upsurge called itself the *Statt* (instead of) party.

Where does dealignment come from? It is not a sinister plot (although it can have some negative repercussions) but the normal and natural maturation process that many advanced democracies go through. One step in this process, I suspect, is the catchall party (see box on page 199). If two catchall parties face each other, as in the United States and Germany, their positions become so moderate and similar that they become boring. Neither offers much in the way of exciting, new choices or programs.

Meanwhile, the society is being hit by problems scarcely anyone could imagine a generation ago: immigration, environmental degradation, the movement of jobs to low-wage countries, and crushing tax and debt burdens. None of the catchall parties has any convincing solution; all waffle in some vague middle ground. Also,

Impressive German Words: Weltanschauung

In prewar Europe, many political parties used to try to imbue their supporters with a "view of the world" (or *Weltanschauung*) corresponding to the party's ideology and philosophy. This was especially true of parties on the left, particularly in Weimar Germany. Today this insistence on a particular world view implies ideological narrowness and intolerance. After World War II most of the *Weltanschauung* parties disappeared as they broadened their appeal or merged into bigger parties. The Communist parties of West Europe preserve some of the old *Weltanschauung* style—party newspapers, a tight organization, a rather firm set of beliefs—but even they have toned down and diluted their ideology.

suddenly gone is the cement that helped hold the system together: the Soviet threat and the Cold War that came with it. It is a disorienting time, and none of the great catchall parties provides much in the way of guidance. The public response is lower voter turnouts and small and less-stable shares of the vote for the catchall parties, in a word, dealignment.

The *Bundestag* and the Citizen

One reason German elections have turned into almsot presidential-type elections for chancellor is the murky status of the *Bundestag* in the mind of many voters. They know what the chancellor does but aren't too clear on what the *Bundestag* does. Part of the blame for this is the concept *Bundestag* deputies have of their role. As noted in the previous chapter, the *Bundestag* tradition is focused on laws. The *Bundestag*, staffed heavily by lawyers and civil servants, has become a law factory.

But isn't a legislature supposed to legislate? Not entirely. By confining their activities to law books and committee meetings, *Bundestag* deputies have failed to grasp the less obvious but still very important function of a legislature. Actually, the most important role of a legislature is probably in overseeing the activities of the national government, catching corruption and inefficiency, uncovering scandals, threatening budget cuts, and otherwise keeping bureaucrats on their toes. The harsh glare of publicity is often the best medicine for governmental wrongdoing. The overly cozy client relationships between bureaucracy and business thrive only in the dark. It is in this area that the *Bundestag* has been weak. Although there are commissions of inquiry and a question hour, the former are not pursued as thoroughly as on Washington's Capitol Hill—where televised committee hearings are a major preoccupation—and the latter is not carried out with as much polish as in the House of Commons. (*Bundestag* deputies can be quite insulting, but it comes across as crude rather than clever.) In functioning as little but lawmakers, German legislators have contributed to the boredom problem.

The "Catchall" Party

Noting the demise of the prewar *Weltanschauung* parties, German political scientist Otto Kirchheimer coined the term "catchall party" to describe what was taking their place: big, loose, pluralist parties that have diluted their ideologies so they can accommodate many diverse groups of supporters. His model of a catchall party was the CDU, a veritable political vacuum cleaner that draws in all manner of groups: farmers, business people, labor, women, Catholics, Protestants, white-collar workers, blue collar, you name it.

For a while, under crusty Kurt Schumacher, the SPD tried to stay a *Weltanschauung* party, defining itself in rigid and ideological terms that turned away many middle-of-the-road voters. Since 1959, the SPD too has become a catchall party, appealing to Germans of all classes and backgrounds.

Indeed, by now the catchall party is the norm in modern democracies. Almost axiomatically, any large party is bound to be a catchall party, for example, the Italian Christian Democrats, Canadian Conservatives, Spanish Socialists, Japanese Liberal Democrats, and of course both major U.S. parties.

One function the *Bundestag* has failed to develop is that of education. The way a legislature operates, the arguments that are presented, the manner in which members of parliament conduct themselves, these are great teachers of democracy. Instead, *Bundestag* activity seems calculated to make a weak impression. The *Bundestag* doesn't generate good press because it's a dull story. Capitol Hill and Westminster attract much more public interest because they do interesting things.

Another function an effective parliament must perform is to represent people in a way that they feel someone speaking for them really understands their point of view. In this the *Bundestag* suffers from a problem common to all elected legislatures: it isn't representative of the voters. The average *Bundestag* deputy is close to 50 years old, male, trained as a lawyer, and employed as a civil servant, party leader, or interest-group official. Fewer than 10 percent are women, and they are elected only because the party places them on *Land* election lists; only a handful have ever won in a single-member district.

The strong German party system means that people must slowly work their way up in party ranks before they will be put on a ballot. Accordingly, candidates tend to be older, seasoned, party loyalists rather than bright, fresh, new faces. Unlike the American system, a German candidate usually cannot "come from out of nowhere" and win an election on his or her own. You're either a piece of the party machine or you're nothing. The result is unrepresentative representatives. As one German newspaper put it: "This gap between electorate and elected has become too wide." Many Germans do not feel represented; they feel that the *Bundestag* is the arena where the powerful interests of society work out deals with little reference to the common citizen, the little guy. Such feelings contributed to the Green vote.

Movable Mayors

As in Britain, German political figures are not anchored to one spot. They move around as their party places them in higher and higher positions. Hans-Jochen Vogel, for example, the SPD's chancellor candidate in 1983, was born in Göttingen, in the north, but climbed through the ranks in Munich, in the south. He was elected mayor of Munich in 1960 and then to the *Bundestag* in 1972. The SPD government made him minister of planning and urban development, then minister of justice. In 1981 they moved him to Berlin to become mayor. To be the mayor of two different cities is unthinkable in the United States, but it's quite normal in Germany where party counts for more than local roots. The German parties use municipal and state offices as training grounds for national office.

The Union-Party Linkup

One characteristic of North European political systems—and here we include Britain and Sweden along with Germany—is the close relationship between labor union and political party, specifically the social-democratic parties. In these countries unions are large and cohesive; most blue-collar workers are organized, and their unions in turn form a single, large labor federation. Such federations support the social-democratic parties with money, manpower, and influence with the rank and file. Often union leaders actually run for office on the party ticket.

Compare this pattern with the Latin European systems. Labor is not as well organized and is fragmented into several federations. The biggest labor unions are Communist-led and encourage members to vote Communist (with imperfect success). Socialist and Christian unions, supporting other parties, have difficulty cooperating with the large Communist-led unions. The fragmentation reduces the effectiveness of a working-class voice. American unions face a similar problem. They too are fragmented into several federations and historically have not tied themselves to one party. U.S. labor does not have the same kind of political input as North European labor.

In Britain, TUC unions are actual constituent members of the Labour Party. In Sweden, the gigantic LO is so close to the Social Democrats that some of their top personnel are the same. The German Basic Law forbids a formal union-party tie, but here too everyone knows that labor support is an important pillar of SPD strength.

In the United States only a sixth of the labor force is unionized; in Germany and Britain about one-third is (in Sweden, some 80 percent). There are sixteen German unions—the biggest is the metalworkers (*IG Metall*)—but they are federated into a "peak" or "roof" organization, the *Deutscher Gewerkschaftsbund*, DGB for short. With 11 million members, the DGB's voice is heeded by the Social Democrats; its leaders are regularly consulted by SPD chiefs. Although they don't dictate party policy, unions get a good deal of what they want: an elaborate welfare system, support for a shorter work week, and even directors' seats on the boards of large companies

Impressive German Words: Spitzenverband

Spitzenverband (literally, "peak association") is the German term for a federation of like-minded special-interest groups. For example, most labor unions are organized into one *Spitzenverband* (the DGB), and all big businesses into another (the BDI). The interactions of *Spitzenverbände* (the plural) among themselves and with government bespeaks the high degree of interest-group organization in Germany.

(more on this in the next chapter). About one-third of the SPD's *Bundestag* deputies have union ties.

But the catchall nature of the SPD prevents its being dominated by any one group. The more the SPD seeks votes in the center of the political spectrum, the more it has to turn away from one-on-one cooperation with the DGB. The British Labourites face the same problem with the TUC; if they let the union component dominate they lose votes. Accordingly, in the 1970s the SPD and DGB found differences developing between them, something that had never happened before. Helmut Schmidt, representing the SPD right, was a better democrat and economist than he was a socialist. DGB relations with the SPD grew a little cool. Still, the DGB is locked into supporting the Social Democrats for the simple reason that no other party will treat them as well.

On the management side, there is a similar but weaker pattern. The powerful *Bundesverband der Deutschen Industrie* (Federation of German Industries, BDI) has warm connections with the CDU, but not as close as those of the DGB with the SPD. When the Social Democrats came to power, the BDI found it could get along with them quite well too. As in Britain and France, big business doesn't need to get closely involved with one party; it's to their interests to be able to work with all parties. The major focus of business is the bureaucracy, not the parties. Providing information to the relevant ministry, explaining to civil servants why a given regulation should be modified, going along with government economic plans—in these and other ways business quietly cements ties with government.

VARIATIONS ON A THEME: UNION PARTY LINKS IN THREE COUNTRIES

Country	Union	Party Linkage
Britain	TUC	Labour
Sweden	LO	Social Democrat
Germany	DGB	SPD

The Länder and Berlin

Britain and France are unitary systems that have attempted devolution and decentralization. Germany is a federal system that some people would like to make a little

Boring! Boring! Politics without Passion

Germany in many ways is an incredible success story: a prosperous, just society that arose from the ashes of World War II to achieve political stability and peaceful reunification. What then is eating the Germans? The usual explanation is the costs, strains, and resentments that have come with unification. This is, I think, part of the answer. The other part is that German politics is just plain boring. Chancellor Kohl was in office as long as Mitterrand. The German welfare state has been generous, perhaps too generous. The two big German parties, with their similar policies, offer nothing in terms of vision or political passion. This, I think, helps explain the growth of smaller parties. The Greens, the far-right Republicans, and the ex-Communists (Party of Democratic Socialism) are, in their very different ways, not boring. The trouble is that these parties make coalition formation difficult and unstable, and could, in bad economic circumstances, lead to center-fleeing behavior as happened in Weimar. That, of course, would solve the boredom problem.

more centralized. The interesting thing here is that in both unitary and federal systems there are pressures to move toward a middle ground. Centralization in France was rigid, inefficient, and time-consuming and ignored local wishes and regional pride. Federalism in Germany is often uncoordinated, powerless, and deadlocked, and encourages federal-state squabbles. In some ways the distinctions between unitary and federal systems are overdrawn; if you look closely, you see elements of centralization in federations and elements of federalism in unitary states.

West Germany was founded as a federal republic for at least two reasons: (1) Germany has a long history of particularism and regional pride; (2) the occupying powers, fearful of a resurgence of German might in a centralized state, wanted it that way. The French in particular would have been delighted to see Germany broken up into several independent states that could never again threaten France. Postwar German politicians themselves, aware of the abuses of power of Hitler's centralized Reich, were mostly committed to a federal structure.

Germany is probably more federal than the United States; that is, its *Länder* run more of their own affairs and get a bigger portion of taxes than do American states. For example, individual and corporate income taxes are split between Berlin and the *Länder* in equal 40 percent shares; the cities get 20 percent. The *Länder* also get 44 percent of the value-added tax, the large but hidden sales tax used throughout Europe. The result is that, while some additional funds are transferred from Berlin to the *Länder* and cities, the *Länder* do not have to go begging the way American states and cities do in their repeated pleas to Washington for bail-out money.

Germany's federalism has some drawbacks. For example, there's really no nationwide police force (aside from the Border Police), so law enforcement is a *Land* affair. Terrorists who committed their crimes in one *Land* could flee to another, counting on communication and coordination foul-ups to delay police. The cleaning of the seriously polluted Rhine River still lacks a central authority because such matters are controlled by the states, and each state sees its environmental responsibilities differently. Only in 1986 did the *Bundestag* set up a federal ministry, but it could not override *Land* environment ministries. The decentralized nature of education has made it impossible for federal authorities to insist on the nationwide study of the Nazis and their crimes in schools.

Many Germans would like Berlin to have a little more control over things. But the German *Länder*, like American states, stoutly resist moves that would erode the powers of *Land* officials, and they have the perfect weapon to do so: the *Bundesrat*. Not directly elected, *Bundesrat* delegations are designated by *Land* governments, which usually means the state's political chiefs also sit in Bonn (which stayed as the *Bundesrat*'s home). The *Bundesrat* must concur on any move that would alter the balance of powers between federation and state.

As to the preferability of unitary versus federal systems, there is no simple answer. If you have one system, you usually want a little of the other. On balance, the German federation works pretty well. Further, in founding a new democracy it was probably wise to give people a smaller unit to focus on, to serve as a building block for developing nationwide democratic loyalties.

German Voting Patterns

In Britain, as we saw, the vote is structured at least in part along lines of social class and region. That is, Labour usually wins much of the working class, plus Scotland, Wales, and large industrial cities. French voting is similar, with the added factor of religious attitude—clerical or anticlerical. West German voting patterns also tended to follow class, region, and religion, but the addition of East Germany in 1990 muddied some of these generalizations. The general dealignment of the period muddied them further.

In West Germany religion meant Catholic or Protestant. West German Catholics were more likely to vote CDU, so heavily Catholic *Länder* such as Baden-Wurttemberg generally went CDU. The CSU has long had Bavaria sewn up. Further north, in the largely Protestant *Länder*, the SPD tended to do better. In large cities voters tended to go left, a universal pattern. In West Germany as elsewhere, the rural and small-town vote went conservative. West German workers, especially those belonging to a labor union, were generally more loyal to the SPD than British workers were to the Labour party. Accordingly, an ideal-typical SPD voter in West Germany was a Protestant worker in a large northern city. His CDU counterpart was a middle-class Catholic in a small southern town. The Free Democrats appealed to some of the Protestant middle class, and the Greens attracted the young (two-thirds of their voters were under 30), mostly at the expense of the SPD.

East Germany, however, although almost completely Protestant and with a pre-1933 SPD voting tradition, went heavily Christian Democrat in 1990. As the costs and disappointments of unification sank in, some East Germans moved to the SPD in 1994, confirming the SPD as a party more attractive to Protestants and to urban workers. But a good number of *Ossis* lent their votes to the Greens (who had merged with the East German Alternative/90 in early 1993) and to the ex-Communist Party of Democratic Socialism.

Vocabulary Building

authoritarian
Bavaria
BDI
catchall party
DGB

LO
representative
Spitzenverband
unimodal
Weltanschauung

Further Reference

BRAUNTHAL, GERARD. *The West German Social Democrats, 1969–1982: Profile of a Party in Power.* Boulder, CO: Westview Press, 1983.

DALTON, RUSSELL J., ed. *The New Germany Votes: Reunification and the Creation of a German Party System.* Providence, RI: Berg, 1993.

DOWNS, ANTHONY. *An Economic Theory of Democracy.* New York: Harper & Row, 1957.

FRANKLAND, E. GENE, and DONALD SCHOONMAKER. *Between Protest and Power: The Green Party in Germany.* Boulder, CO: Westview Press, 1992.

HANCOCK, M. DONALD. *West Germany: The Politics of Democratic Corporatism.* Chatham, NJ: Chatham House, 1989.

HUELSHOFF, MICHAEL G., ANDREI MARKOVITS, and SIMON REICH, eds. *From Bundesrepublic to Deutschland: German Politics after Unification.* Ann Arbor, MI: University of Michigan Press, 1993.

JESSE, ECKHARD. *Elections: The Federal Republic of Germany in Comparison.* New York: St. Martin's, 1990.

KIRCHHEIMER, OTTO. "Germany: The Vanishing Opposition," in *Political Oppositions in Western Democracies,* ed. by Robert A. Dahl. New Haven, CT: Yale University Press, 1966.

KOLINSKY, EVA, ed. *The Federal Republic of Germany: Innovation and Continuity at the Threshold of the 1990s.* Providence, RI: Berg, 1991.

MARKOVITS, ANDREI S., and PHILIP S. GORSKI. *The German Left: Red, Green and Beyond.* New York: Oxford University Press, 1993.

PADGETT, STEPHEN. *Parties and Party Systems in the New Germany.* Brookfield, VT: 1993.

16

What Germans Quarrel About

The End of the Miracle

Nothing produces economic miracles, it has been said, like losing a war. This would surely be the case in West Germany and Japan following World War II. There was simply nothing to do but work. Some German factories were destroyed by Allied bombing. Many machine tools were ripped out and shipped back to Russia by the vengeful Soviets. Whereas the British and Americans patched up their old industries, Germans were forced to rebuild theirs with new and more efficient equipment.

The aftermath of war had some psychological benefits. Almost everybody was poor; food and fuel were barely sufficient for survival. This brought a kind of rough equality among Germans; income distribution was more equitable in Germany (and Japan) than in the victorious countries. Consequently the bitter class antagonisms found in Britain and France did not develop in Germany. Everyone started from a similar low level, and most West Germans felt that everyone got a share of economic growth. Further, defeat in the war and empty stomachs following it left Germans with more modest expectations than Britons or Americans (who expected to be handed some kind of postwar paradise). For West Germans after Hitler, hard work to foster economic growth was about their only outlet for national pride.

Under the conservative leadership of the CDU and Economics Minister (later Chancellor) Ludwig Erhard, Bonn pursued a largely laissez-faire policy. While Britain turned to Labour's welfare state and France to *planification* after World War II, West Germany relied mainly on market forces. By the 1970s, the West German economy had become a model that others wished to duplicate.

By the time of unification in 1990, however, the German model was showing some limits, and they were not just from the heavy burdens of unification. As in

Impressive German Words: Wirtschaftswunder

"Economic miracle," or *Wirtschaftswunder,* is how West Germans proudly described the rapid transformation of their country in the 1950s. Germans labored like dogs to turn their hills of rubble into the modern, spanking new cities of the Federal Republic. Soon German production and living standards had exceeded prewar levels.

most of West Europe, the miracle had worn off for long-term underlying economic reasons that were made suddenly clear and much worse by the rapid unification.

Basically, rapid economic growth comes from wages that lag behind productivity. That is, where you have skilled workers producing desired goods at prices that beat most others, you will gain many sales and carve out a large piece of the world market. Germany (and Japan, after a couple years' time lag) fit this pattern. German workers' skills were still high, and much of Germany's infrastructure was intact. German labor unions practiced "wage restraint"; they did not demand all they were due but let capital grow until it provided jobs and good wages for all. This was the period of Germany's rapid growth from the 1950s through the 1970s. In contrast, British and U.S. productivity lagged behind wage increases, meaning they could sell less and less to the world.

By the 1980s, however, German wages more or less equaled U.S. wages, and German productivity was no longer growing quickly. But Germany bore an added burden: the costs of the welfare state. In the meantime, the United States was getting more and more competitive; wages had been essentially stagnant (by the time you account for inflation) since the early 1970s but productivity grew. The U.S. welfare state, always much smaller than the German, was less of a tax burden. Result: by the 1990s, with U.S. labor averaging $15 an hour (including fringes and taxes) while West German labor cost $24, and with U.S. productivity some 20 percent higher than German, it cost about half as much to make something in the United States as in Germany. (See box on page 208.) German products became too expensive and sales fell while U.S. products improved in quality to become good buys; sales rose. East Germany was not in the running in these calculations; its labor costs were lower than West Germany's, but its productivity was much lower than West Germany's.

For a while, with *Mitbestimmung* and an elaborate welfare state, it looked like Germany had found the perfect combination of labor harmony: growing productivity and prosperity, short workweeks (36 hours), long vacations (a month), the world's highest pay, and almost no strikes. With the downturn of the 1990s, though, German workers received the news that they had overshot the mark. Management told them they were too expensive for what they produced. Germany was losing sales to the United States, Japan, and other producers who had lower costs.

In 1994 Germany's largest union, *IG Metall,* almost went out on strike against Germany's biggest employers' federation, *Gesamtmetall,* over wages, hours, and job

Impressive German Words: Sozialmarkt

Ludwig Erhard's phrase for his economic policies, "social market," describes what he was trying to do in laying the basis for the *Wirtschaftswunder*. The German economy should be that of a free market, he urged, with individuals and firms deciding for themselves what to produce, invest in, and spend on. But the whole thing should be aimed to socially useful ends—cleaning up the ruined cities, settling refugees, providing a welfare floor, and insuring full employment. You might call Erhard's *Sozialmarkt*, "capitalism with a conscience." Tax breaks and government control over investment banking pointed the German market economy toward filling in the gaps left by the war (for example, apartment-house construction). When the Social Democrats took power in 1969, their economic policies were basically the same.

guarantees. In Germany, these two giants negotiate directly—not firm-by-firm, as in the United States—to reach contracts binding on the entire metal-working industry. German unions settled for little because they knew that amid high unemployment there would be many willing strikebreakers. One creative union proposal was accepted: In slack periods, management could cut the workweek and wages to 30 hours for all workers in a given plant in return for their guaranteed jobs. Better to make sure everyone has a job than getting top individual pay, reckoned many German workers. This attitude, known as "solidarity," is little-found in the United States.

How to Merge Two Economies

The sudden merging of two very different economies added to Germany's economic difficulties. Over 45 years, the largely free-market West German economy had become a world giant, in some years exporting more (in dollar value) than the United States. The centrally controlled and planned East German economy, although it was the envy of the East bloc, had a per capita GDP of little more than half that of West Germany. *Wessis* were roughly twice as rich as *Ossis*. West German products were desired throughout the world; East German products were sold mostly to the Soviet bloc plus some Third World lands too poor to afford better. The two economies could exist side-by-side only with a wall between them to prevent direct competition.

In 1990, the physical and political barriers between the two Germanys suddenly disappeared. West German currency and products flooded into East Germany, and the East German economy collapsed with a speed and thoroughness no one had foreseen. It was thought to have been a working economy that just needed modernization. Many supposed that West German firms would bring their capital and know-how into East German enterprises and quickly lift them up to West German levels. This scenario was much too rosy. East Germans simply ceased buying East German products as soon as they could buy nicer West German goods. As gigantic state subsidies ended, East German factory and farm production plummeted. East German unemployment shot from essentially zero into the millions, and both East and

COMPARING

Who Wins the Manufacturing Race?

Not necessarily those with the lowest wages. What you need to win in the global manufacturing race is lower wages combined with higher productivity. Here's how the situation looked among our five industrialized democracies in the early 1990s:

	TOTAL HOURLY LABOR COSTS	RELATIVE PRODUCTIVITY	UNIT LABOR COSTS
Britain	$13	100	100
United States	15	160	70
France	16	125	90
Japan	18	135	100
Germany (West)	24	135	135

Source: *The Economist*

Total hourly labor costs, here for 1991, include fringe benefits, social security, and other government-mandated taxes, which in Germany and France are quite high. (They are low in the United States and Japan.) Productivity here uses Britain in 1989 as the standard "100" for comparative purposes. Economists Bart van Ark and Dirk Pilat of the University of Groningen then calculated from these two figures unit labor costs, what it would cost to manufacture the same product in each country, using Britain in 1991 as the standard "100" mark. Well, who wins? Who combines lower costs with higher productivity? A word of caution: these relationships change constantly, and winners seldom stay winners for long.

West Germans turned angry. It was estimated that only one-fourth of East Germany's enterprises will ultimately survive the transition to a market economy.

What saved the East German economy? Money, tons of it, far more than anticipated, from the federal government. Ultimately, of course, the money had to come from West Germans, both in the form of higher taxes and inflation. Thus the first great quarrel of united Germany grew out of how to merge the two economies and who was going to pay for it. Chancellor Kohl said the bailout of the East German economy could be done without higher taxes. The opposition Social Democrats scoffed—Lafontaine chided, "read my lips" (in English) in the 1990 election—and sure enough, the Kohl government raised taxes next year. Kohl's popularity plunged.

The issue of German taxes wreaked havoc with Germany's Common Market neighbors. Because FRG taxes were not nearly enough to soak up the heavy spending on East Germany, the *Bundesbank* (Germany's powerful central bank, the equivalent to the U.S. Federal Reserve Board) boosted interest rates sky-high in order to beat back inflation, still a terrible thing in Germany. It was only partly successful, as inflation hit 6 percent in 1993. The real impact was on the European countries that had attempted to link currencies and build the European Monetary Union (EMU). High German interest rates simply sucked funds out of partner countries until Britain and Italy could take it no more; they dropped out of the system after losing billions, and they blamed Germany. Interesting, is it not, how seemingly domestic concerns, taxes and interest rates, in the modern age can have instantaneous and dangerous repercussions in other countries? Nothing is purely domestic anymore.

Can West Germany's earlier economic miracle apply to the East German economy? The desperate postwar feelings that made West Germans work so hard are

Impressive German Words: Mitbestimmung

Sometimes known by its longer name, *Arbeiter-mitbestimmung* (worker codetermination), labor participation in basic management decisions has been part of the coal and steel industry since 1951. It was expanded in 1976 after decades of discussion. Basically it means that large firms—those with over 2,000 employees—must have a supervisory board with half the directors chosen by labor and half by shareholders. The chairperson, elected only by the shareholders, can cast the deciding vote in case of a tie. Smaller firms have less stringent codetermination rules, and companies with less than five employees have none.

How does *Mitbestimmung* work in prac-tice? When a Ruhr steelworks wanted to cut its 7,200-person work force by 300 jobs, it had to negotiate and compromise with worker representatives on the supervisory board. Early retirement, job retraining, and income guarantees cushioned the impact of the cuts. Worker councils throughout the factory discussed the proposals and agreed to them before the labor representatives voted yes. No strikes, no anger, no feeling of powerlessness. Codetermination doesn't mean that the unions run everything. But it does mean that on the general thrust of company policy—the decisions that affect the livelihood of employees—labor has a say that is nearly equal to management's.

not found in post-Wall East Germany. Under the Communists' centrally planned economic system, East Germans did not develop attitudes of hard work and entrepreneurial risk taking. They got used to a vast welfare system that offered security for all but few incentives for individual exertion. *Ossis* say, "It's not our fault that the Communists saddled us with an inferior economic system. Besides, you *Wessis* got billions of dollars in U.S. Marshall Plan aid; we got ripped off by the Soviets. So it's only fair that you boost us up to your standard of living, and quickly."

Many West Germans are appalled at such attitudes, which seem like excuses to avoid work. Why set up factories in East Germany when you can get good productivity out of Poles and Czechs, whose wages are a fraction of the German level? Resentment flared in each half of Germany against the other half. From this resentment, especially in the East, grew some of the extremist groups that targeted foreign workers.

How Much Welfare?

As we considered with Britain, European countries are welfare states, some more than others. One-third of Germany's GDP goes for social spending, a heavy tax burden on Germany's manufacturing competitiveness. Germany's welfare system is Europe's oldest, tracing back to Bismarck's innovations in the late nineteenth century. Since then, it has grown and become accepted by just about everyone, even conservatives. The CDU, for example, has a tradition of Catholic trade-unionism.

But now one of the great questions of European politics has become, "How much welfare can we afford?" Even previously committed social democrats are starting to worry that their generous welfare provisions are pricing them out of the mar-

Could Unification Have Come Gradually?

No. The real problem behind the difficulties and costs of merging the two German economies is the speed with which it occurred. The Social Democrats and some top economists urged taking it easy and merging only gradually, over the course of several years. But that really couldn't happen, for once the ball started rolling, it could not be slowed. Events took on a fast-paced life of their own:

1. **The hard-line Honecker regime in East Berlin** refuses all thought of reform for most of 1989. But East Germans, seeing reforms taking place elsewhere in the Soviet bloc, become more restless.

2. **Hungary lets East Germans exit into Austria.** The Communist regime in Budapest had pledged not to let East German tourists flee to the West, but in the summer of 1989 they stop enforcing this pledge. Why? My hunch is that debt-burdened Hungary, by then under reform-minded Communists, got some nice financing from Bonn. Economic carrots had long been part of West German policy in Eastern Europe. At an accelerating rate, thousands of East Germans "vacation" in Hungary but proceed to West Germany. East Berlin screams in protest, and Budapest shrugs. By September, more than 18,000 East Germans have fled via Hungary, another 17,000 via Czechoslovakia. East Germany closes its border with Czechoslovakia to staunch the flow.

3. **Massive demonstrations break out in East Germany** in September, centered in Leipzig. In October Gorbachev visits to urge reform and warn Honecker, "Life punishes those who delay." Clearly, Gorbachev wishes to be rid of the problems and expenses of maintaining a Soviet empire in Eastern Europe. By now some 100,000 protesters are marching in Leipzig chanting "Gorby, Gorby!"

4. **Honecker orders a "Chinese solution"** and tells his police to get ready to fire on the Leipzig demonstrators. Egon Krenz, in charge of security but sensing catastrophe, countermands the order. On October 18, Honecker is out and Krenz becomes party chief and president. By now a million East Germans, led by a group of intellectuals in the New Forum movement, are protesting for democracy.

5. **On November 9, 1989, Krenz orders the Berlin Wall opened** to gain some good will and time for reform. Tens of thousands pour into the West with no intention of returning. At this point, the days of a separate East Germany are numbered. Krenz resigns; much has happened because he countermanded the order to fire on protesters. Liberal and reform-minded Communists take over the party and government and pledge free elections.

6. **Too many East Germans pour into the West** because they are not sure that their own system is really going to change. They want the good life of West Germany, and they want it now. Some half million come across in the four months after the Wall opens, overburdening West Germany's job and apartment market, financial resources, and patience. Stay home, Chancellor Kohl urges; we'll merge and rescue you soon enough.

7. **Free East German elections in March 1990** put Christian Democrats into power. They see things Kohl's way and also want speedy unification; this is why East Germans voted for them. Impatiently, East Germans want to get in on West German economic prosperity.

8. **Bonn gives East Germans a favorable exchange rate.** East German marks aren't worth much, but East Germans argue that they have worked for and saved *Ostmarks* for decades. They demand a one-to-one exchange. Bonn argues that *Ostmarks* are essentially funny money and should be exchanged at a much lower rate. They compromise on one-to-one for each *Ossi's* first 2,000 marks (about $1,300) and one *Westmark* for two east above 2,000. It is a generous deal for East Germans, but if Bonn hadn't agreed to it, *Ossis* would have continued to pour into West Germany. In a sense, the one-to-one is a bribe to get them to stay put. On July 2, 1990, the *Westmark* becomes the official currency for both Germanys.

9. **East Germans buy everything Western, nothing Eastern.** With *Westmarks* in their pockets and Western products on store shelves, they turn their backs on their own products, now seen as junk. Suddenly competing in a free market with the West, the East German economy collapses; it never had a chance to adjust.

Could anything have been done to prevent or slow the preceding sequence? We would have to go back to step one and get the Honecker regime committed to reforms that would gradually turn the East German economy into a market system that could compete with Western products. Then the two economies could merge without one of them collapsing. But Honecker was a devoted Communist. To marketize means abandoning communism, something he would not budge on. And once East Germans started pouring across, what could Bonn do? Rebuild the border fence between the two Germanys to make East Germans wait at home? The critics of too-rapid unification are right: It would have been better if it had been slower. But that was not in the cards.

November 1989: The Wall opens. (*German Information Service*)

Impressive German Words: Finanzausgleich

Some German *Länder* are rich and populous, others not. To equalize burdens, financially strong states are required to transfer tax revenues to poorer states through a complicated mechanism called the *Finanzausgleich*, "financial equalization," another German sore spot. Rich states, such as booming Baden-Württemberg, complain that they must pay too much. Hamburg, a small city-state, demands more revenue because many commuters live in neighboring *Länder* and don't pay Hamburg taxes. The biggest problem now, though, is that the ex-GDR states are poor and require a major and long-term transfer of revenues through the *Finanzausgleich*. These five new *Länder*, with very small populations, receive close to one-quarter of Germany's federal budget expenditures.

ket. In 1994, for example, with unemployment nearing 12 percent, the CDU/FDP government proposed cutting unemployment benefits from 58 percent to 55 percent of gross pay for married workers and ending the benefits after two to four years, depending on circumstances. This is still very generous unemployment compensation. The SPD, whose vote was needed in the *Bundesrat*, agreed to the small percent reduction but not to the time limit.

German pensions are also generous, but to pay for them German workers must contribute 20 percent of their wages, and this will soon rise to an impossible 30 percent if present trends continue. A complex of supplementary benefits means that essentially no Germans live in poverty, but this too is very expensive. Some German thinkers argue that it's time to move away from the "cradle to grave" concept of a welfare system that covers everyone for everything and to a "social safety net" limited to the truly needy. Some Greens have returned to the old idea of a "negative income tax" that would cut through all the paperwork and just guarantee all a minimum living, never mind if you're unemployed, elderly, or just plain poor. If your income were too low, the government would send you a check instead of the other way around. Both major parties professed interest in the idea. The fear is that if nothing is done to reform the German welfare system, the younger generation, which is having to bear the burdens, will revolt (see box).

The Flood of Foreigners

Like Britain and France, Germany too finds that foreigners from poor countries are attracted to its better jobs and higher pay. But in Germany the numbers—and the problems—are bigger. There are some 6 million foreigners in Germany, mostly from Mediterranean nations (Turkey, Yugoslavia, Greece, Italy, Spain). About 2 million are workers; the rest are spouses and children. All together, they comprise 7.3 percent of the population of the Federal Republic.

The trend started in 1955 when the "economic miracle" had absorbed all working Germans and was still short of labor. Italians and later Spaniards were in-

Impressive German Words: Treuhandanstalt

Germany's Trustee (literally, "true-hand") Institution is a giant state-supervised holding company that has overseen the conversion of some 12,000 state-owned East German firms into money-making capitalist enterprises. It can reorganize East German firms, sell them, or simply fold them. It's an extremely difficult task that requires inflicting much pain. Some 2 million jobs were lost (but an equal number were retained). Communist bookkeeping had been so chaotic it was often impossible to tell just how much money firms had been losing. Some West German firms thought they could take over East German enterprises cheaply or even free, but the Trustee Institution wouldn't let them. After a while, many Germans, both East and West, became angry at the *Treuhandanstalt*. Nonetheless, it did a great job and by 1995 had privatized most of East German industry.

vited to West Germany, and they came, eager for the plentiful jobs. Soon Germans began abandoning dirty, dangerous, and unskilled lines of work for better positions, leaving their old jobs to foreigners. At first the impact seemed temporary: the migrant workers were supposed to stay three years and rotate back home. But the "guest workers," faced with unemployment at home, often decided to remain and to send for their families. Large numbers began arriving from Turkey, where unemployment is especially high. There are now some 1.8 million Turks in the Federal Republic;

Turkish women in the Kreuzberg district of Berlin, a center for Turkish immigrants, of whom there are 1.8 million in Germany. (*German Information Center*)

COMPARING

Running Out of Germans

On average, a German woman now bears only 1.28 children, one of the world's lowest "fertility rates" (which is not the same as the "birthrate," a different measure). In comparison, an average French woman bears 1.83, an American 1.81, a British 1.8, and a Japanese 1.57. Replacement level is 2.1, the rate at which a population will hold steady, and it is found in few advanced industrialized countries. Large families are not prized, and women have increased educational and career options. These rates take no account of immigration and are one reason why all of these countries might wish to have some immigrants. Why? Because without immigrants, who is going to do the work that supports the increasing portion of the population that is retired?

By 2025, an estimated 24 percent of Germans and Japanese will be 65 or over; some 20 percent of Britons, French, and Americans will be in that age bracket. All of these countries face the problem of soon having too few people in the work force supporting too many people in retirement. Germany already has the heaviest burden, with three working persons supporting one retiree, one reason German taxes are so high. By 2025, the ratio will become an impossible 2:1. One very likely way out: countries will lift mandatory retirement and encourage people to keep working past age 65. Another way: get more women into the work force and at higher levels. Of course, if more women work, fewer will have babies.

whole neighborhoods have turned into Turkish ghettos. The "guests" had come to stay.

By the 1980s, poor people worldwide had discovered Germany's very liberal asylum law. Simply upon arriving in Germany, a poor foreigner had only to claim that he or she was politically persecuted back home. Although more often the person was economically motivated, the legal tangles could let the asylum-seeker stay in Germany for years, all the while on welfare. As in Britain and France, antiforeign feeling grew among all social classes. Germans perceived foreigners as crime prone, lecherous, and disorderly. A new racism appeared in Germany, exaggerated by FRG law: a person of German descent arriving from Russia or Romania, whose ancestors had immigrated there centuries ago, gets instant FRG citizenship; a Turk born and raised in Germany cannot, without great difficulty, become a German citizen.

With unification, all manner of people flocked to the Federal Republic from East Europe and even Asia, fleeing collapsing economies. Polish black marketeers and Romanian gypsies were not appreciated. Said a popular T-shirt: "I want my Wall back." The Federal Republic, along with Austria, strengthened border controls and expelled many undocumented visitors. Amid great political controversy (with the SPD fighting it), the asylum law was tightened to exclude most claimants.

The really serious problem the *Gastarbeiter* presented was their families, especially the Turks. Originally it was thought only single workers would come, and no provision was made for educating children. But the Turkish families generally have about three times as many babies as do Germans. The result is a growing mass of underprivileged youth in Germany with inadequate schooling—most drop out before finishing—inadequate command of German, no job skills, and no work permits even if they could find a job. The situation has been called a social time bomb: hundreds

Impressive German Words: Gastarbeiter

Gastarbeiter, or "guest worker," was initially meant to have a nice ring to it, meaning that the many Turks, Yugoslavs, and others who came to work in the Federal Republic were welcome guests. In time, though, *Gastarbeiter* came to mean the foreigners who were taking the lowest jobs available. In effect, the *Gastarbeiter* (same spelling in the plural) had turned into a subproletariat that lived within, but was not part of, German society, nor wanted by it. In German cities appeared the graffito *Turkenraus* (Turks out).

of thousands of foreign children, many of them candidates for juvenile delinquency and drugs. Germany became Europe's number-one drug country; pure heroin from Turkey's poppy fields flowed in with Turkish *Gastarbeiter*.

Now, what to do with the immigrant workers and their families? Many German politicians, especially the more conservative ones, have tried to pretend it isn't Germany's problem: if the foreigners aren't happy in the Federal Republic, they should leave. They see no reason to hire foreign-language teachers and social workers to help immigrant youngsters. In fact, many Germans do not wish to make the *Gastarbeiter* feel at home or to integrate them into German society; they are just temporary guests. (South Africa's *apartheid* system was based on the same fiction, which also could not endure.)

Liberal and leftist Germans, on the other hand, recognize that the immigrants aren't just temporary and that the problem will be helped only by integrating them into German society. They recommend that fees for kindergarten be abolished, that foreign children receive remedial German instruction in school, and that they have the option of assuming German nationality at age 18. All this would cost money, but they point out that *Gastarbeiter* have been paying taxes and social security for years.

Acting out of personal insecurities, limited job possibilities, and a hatred of foreigners, some young Germans became skinheads or neo-Nazis and attacked foreigners. Several Turks, members of families that had been working in Germany for

 ## Impressive German Words: Waldsterben

In the 1980s Germans learned that by the turn of the century all of their forests could be dead or dying. A new word was coined to capture the immensity of the problem, *Waldsterben*, literally "forest death" but more accurately connoting a sort of genocide of entire forests. Pollution of the air by industry and automobiles was believed to be the cause. The specter of irreversible environmental degradation fed the Green party.

Against racism—Although media attention focused on the crimes of a few against foreign workers in Germany, large crowds, such as this one at Cologne's Opera Square, turned out to protest anti-foreigner sentiments as a type of racism. *(German Information Center)*

many years, were murdered in firebomb attacks. In some cases the police and neighbors did nothing to stop the violence. Even members of the U.S. Olympic luge team were beaten by young toughs as they trained in Germany. On the other side, hundreds of thousands of young Germans attended rallies and protests against xenophobia and violence, heeding the call of then-President Richard von Weizsäcker:

We must never forget how the first German republic [Weimar] failed: not because there were too many Nazis too early, but because there were too few democrats for too long. It must never again come to that . . . We are called upon to act.

A Fourth Reich?

Does all the tension in present-day Germany have the makings of a major neo-Nazi movement? It is possible, but I rather doubt it. There are, to be sure, neo-Nazis in Germany (much of their literature is printed in the United States), and Germany

The Stasi Stain

Hatred of East Germany's *Staatssicherheitspolizei* (State Security Police, *Stasi* for short) was one of the motivations of the mass uprising against the GDR. One graffito of the time: *Stasi = Nazi*. The *Stasi* ran a vast network of spies in West Germany, helped terrorists carry out bombings, and then shielded them with new lives and identities in East Germany. Like its Soviet counterpart KGB, the *Stasi* had tentacles throughout society. Some 100,000 *Stasi* agents maintained surveillance and files on just about everyone. They used an estimated 150,000 informants. To further one's career in East Germany, one had to cooperate with the *Stasi* at least a little by describing the activities of friends, colleagues, and even spouses. Even East Germans who protested the regime and struggled for civil rights were thus often stained with a *Stasi* connection. When some of these cases came to light, it was sad and embarrassing and led to many resignations, including some by West German officials.

What to do with *Stasi* files—some 6 million of them—thus became a German political issue. Many argued that they should be opened for public scrutiny. People have a right to see who informed on them, and informants should have their record known. Others wondered if that wouldn't name people who had been involved unwittingly or against their will. Since most East Germans had some contact with the *Stasi*, would all be disqualified from public life in the unified FRG? Could there be violent acts of revenge? The question parallels that of Germany's Nazi past: Should a nation confront or forget its past?

will always bear watching in this regard. But extreme rightists and neo-Nazis are only a few percent and divided into several groups, making it difficult to reach the 5 percent threshold. Many are simply confused and disoriented young people.

By most measures the Federal Republic of Germany is an unqualified success story. Its constitution, leading parties, and economy deserve to be studied by other countries. But some observers have wondered if, under the glittering surface, democracy has taken firm root. Could the present democracy go the way of Weimar's?

All survey data have said no. Decade by decade, West Germans have grown more democratic in their values. By the 1980s, they were at least as committed to a pluralist, free, democratic society as the British and French. They weathered the terrorism of the 1970s and the economic downturn of the early 1980s as well as any of their democratic neighbors. Now, even East Germans are turning into free-market democrats, albeit with much pain and complaint.

We should be aware of the international context of German democracy, however. Both Germanys were children of the Cold War. At times, a third of a million U.S. soldiers were camped in West Germany, while over half a million Soviet soldiers were camped in East Germany. This situation was tense but stable. Both halves of Germany knew where they stood. The FRG was firmly anchored to NATO and the European Community, the GDR to the Warsaw Pact and Comecon. Suddenly the international context changed. The Cold War is over. Germany is unified. Both Soviet and U.S. troops are leaving. Will the new Germany stay cemented to Western ideals and institutions, or could it someday go off on its own, with a nationalistic and expansionist foreign policy?

It is highly improbable that Germany could become a "Fourth Reich," as critics (including some Germans) fear. West German democracy is solid and is rapidly being absorbed by the East Germans. The new institutions of a uniting Europe will likely make Germans good Europeans, and most FRG parties are committed to precisely that. The German army is small and has no ABC (atomic, biological, or chemical) weapons. Three of Germany's European neighbors have nuclear weapons, which by itself means that Germany is unlikely to go on the warpath. Few Germans have any taste for militarism, for they have seen what it can lead to. Germany has accomplished so much more by peaceful economic means than it could ever obtain by warlike means.

The Weimar analogy is misplaced on present-day Germany. For a gigantic country that may be on a Weimar-like brink of an abyss, let us now turn to Russia.

Vocabulary Building

environmentalism
Finanzausgleich
Gastarbeiter
Greens
income distribution
Mitbestimmung
Ostpolitik

Sozialmarkt
Wirtschaftswunder
Waldsterben
Stasi
Treuhandanstalt
unification

Further Reference

Brubaker, Rogers. *Citizenship and Nationhood in France and Germany*. Cambridge, MA: Harvard University Press, 1992.

Garton Ash, Timothy. *In Europe's Name: Germany and the Divided Continent*. New York: Random House, 1993.

James, Harold, and Marla Stone, eds. *When the Wall Came Down: Reactions to German Unification*. New York: Routledge, 1992.

Jarausch, Konrad H. *The Rush to German Unity*. New York: Oxford University Press, 1994.

Keithly, David M. *The Collapse of East German Communism: The Year the Wall Came Down, 1989*. Westport, CT: Praeger, 1992.

Kolinsky, Eva, ed. *The Greens in West Germany: Organisation and Policy Making*. New York: Berg, 1989.

Leaman, Jeremy. *The Political Economy of West Germany, 1945–85: An Introduction*. New York: St. Martin's, 1988.

Livingston, Robert Gerald, and Volkmar Sanders, eds. *The Future of German Democracy*. New York: Continuum, 1993.

Merkl, Peter H. *German Unification in the European Context*. State College, PA: Pennsylvania State University Press, 1993.

Schmidt, Michael. *The New Reich: Violent Extremism in Unified Germany and Beyond*. New York: Pantheon, 1993.

Sinn, Gerlinde, and Hans-Werner Sinn. *Jumpstart: The Economic Unification of Germany*. Cambridge, MA: MIT Press, 1993.

Szabo, Stephen F. *The Diplomacy of German Unification*. New York: St. Martin's, 1992.

Wallach, H. G. Peter, and Ronald A. Francisco. *United Germany: The Past, Politics, Prospects*. Westport, CT: Praeger, 1992.

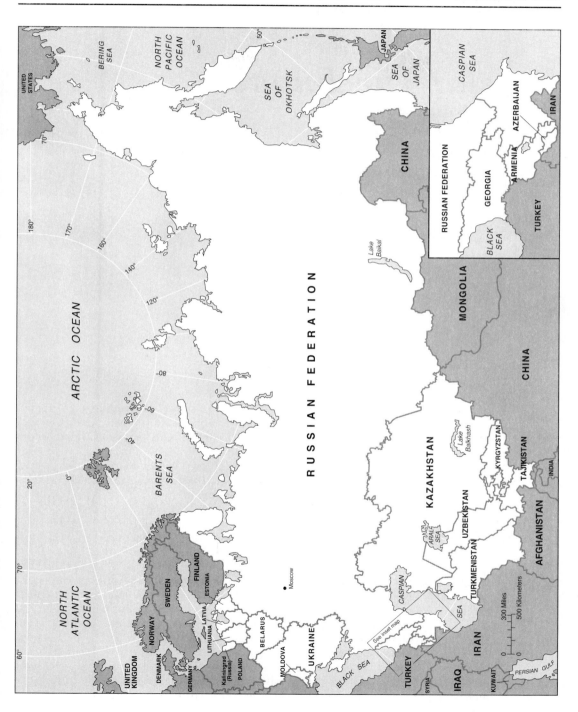

CHAPTER 17

Russia: The Impact of the Past

The Biggest Country in the World

Russia is immense, stretching eleven time zones across the northern half of Asia to the Pacific. Looking at a map of Russia, you notice that only a small part of it is in Europe. (Look at a globe and you'll notice that Europe itself is only a small peninsula of Asia.) Although Russia has few natural boundaries, its very size and harsh winters make it difficult to conquer. Charles XII of Sweden, Napoleon, and Hitler discovered to their horror that Russia's size and fierce winters could swallow whole armies. These same winters give Russia a rather short growing season. Sometimes Russia has the right temperature and rainfall to produce good crops, but agriculture is a chancy business, with crops failing on an average of one year in three. Geography has not been as kind to Russia's agriculture as it has been to the United States'.

The vast territory Siberia adds to Russia's size is problematic; its weather is hostile to settlement, and its mineral and forest wealth is hard to extract. Most of the Russian population continues to live in the "European" part, that is, west of the Ural Mountains. Plans to settle in and develop Siberia, some of them going back to tsarist days, tend to fall short of expectations. Industrial projects tend to be one-shot efforts by temporary labor. The promises of Siberia remain largely unfulfilled.

Another geographic problem has been the difficulty of reaching the open sea. The first Russian states were totally landlocked; only under Peter the Great at the beginning of the eighteenth century did Russians overcome the Swedes to reach the Baltic and the Turks to reach the Black Sea. The Northern Russian ports ice over in winter, and the Black Sea is controlled by the Turkish Straits, still leaving European Russia without year-round, secure ports. One of the great dreams of tsarists and Communists alike was for warm-water ports under exclusive Russian control.

220

Memorable Russian Slogans: "Moscow Is the Third Rome"

After Constantinople fell to the Turks in 1453, Russia felt itself to be the last and only center of true Christianity. Rome and Constantinople had both failed; now Moscow would safeguard the faith. Ivan the Terrible and other Russians have intoned: "Moscow is the third Rome; a fourth is not to be." After the Bolshevik Revolution, Russia's new rulers felt the same way about world communism, namely, that Moscow was its capital and there could be no other.

St. Basil's cathedral recalls Moscow's former role as a center of Christianity. *(Michael Roskin)*

The Slavic People

Occupying most of East Europe, the Slavic peoples are the most numerous in Europe. Russians, Ukrainians, Poles, Czechs, Slovaks, Serbs, Croats, Bulgarians, and others speak languages that are closer to each other than are the Romance languages (Italian, Spanish, French) of West Europe. It is said that a Slovak peasant can converse with any other Slavic peasant—so similar are their vocabularies and syntax.

The way the Slavic languages are written, though, has differentiated them. The Western Slavs (Poles, Czechs, and others) were Christianized from Rome; hence their alphabet is Latin. The Eastern Slavs (Russians, Ukrainians, and others) were converted by Eastern Orthodox monks from Constantinople, and their languages are written in a variation of the Greek alphabet called cyrillic, after St. Cyril, one of the proselytizing monks.

Their Orthodox Christianity (as opposed to Roman Catholicism) and cyrillic writing have contributed to the Russians' isolation from the rest of Europe. In addition to being at the geographical fringe of Europe, Russia was beyond its cultural fringe for centuries. The important ideas that helped modernize Catholic and Protestant Europe penetrated Russia only much later. Rome was a lively fountainhead of thought in West Europe, but the headquarters of the Orthodox faith, Constantinople, under the Turks ceased to provide intellectual guidance for its followers. At the same time that West Europe was experiencing the invigoration of the Renaissance, which rippled outward from Catholic Italy, Russia stayed isolated and asleep. It missed the Enlightenment altogether.

A more important factor in explaining Russia's isolation and backwardness was its conquest in the thirteenth century by the Mongols, also known as the Tatars. The Mongol khans crushed the first Russian state, centered at Kiev in the present-day Ukraine, and enslaved much of the population. For two centuries, while Western Europe moved ahead, Russian culture under the barbaric Mongols declined. Some historians believe that even after the Tatar yoke was lifted, it still took five centuries for Russia to catch up with the West.

Russian Autocracy

Under the Mongol khans, the duchy of Moscow came to be the most powerful Russian state, first as a tax collector for the khans, then as their triumphant enemy. It was Moscovy's Ivan the Terrible (1530–84) who had himself crowned *tsar* (from "caesar"). Ivan was both murderous and successful; his brutal use of force set a standard for later Russian rulers. To this day, many Russians think national greatness can be achieved only by the ruthless actions of a strong leader. Under Ivan, Russian territory expanded greatly, down the Volga to the Caspian Sea and into Siberia.

When the Russian nobles (*boyars*) came into conflict with Ivan, he had them arrested, exiled, or executed. Since that time, the Russian nobility never played an autonomous role in political life. It was as if the absolutism of France was applied early and completely to a culturally backward country. The result was *autocracy*, the rule of one person in a centralized state. Unlike the countries of West Europe, Russia never experienced the mixed monarchy of nobles, church, commoners, and king held in some kind of balance. Accordingly, Russians had no experience with limited government, checks and balances, or pluralism. As Ivan grew older he became madder. Able to trust no one, he murdered those around him—even his own son—at the least suspicion. By the time he died he had carved out the modern Russian state, but his subjects suffered in fear.

Absolutism or Anarchy

One of the reasons Russians put up with autocracy—and sometimes admired it—was because they felt that without a firm hand at the top the system would degenerate into anarchy. This had happened in the early seventeenth century. Lacking a strong tsar, unrest, banditry, civil war, and a Polish invasion plagued the land; it was known as the Time of Troubles. Russians accepted the idea that they had to serve a powerful state under a strong tsar. The Russian Orthodox church transferred its loyalty from the now-defunct Byzantine Empire and became a pillar of the monarchy, teaching the faithful to worship the tsar as the "little father" who protected all Russians. Russia has been called a "service state" in which all walks of life, from nobles to peasants to priests, served the autocrat. Western concepts such as liberty and individual rights did not take root in Russia.

In one crucial area, Russia actually moved backwards in the fifteenth and sixteenth centuries. Previously free peasants became tied to the land, to labor for aristocrats who in turn served the tsar. By the seventeenth century Russia's peasants had become serfs, to be used and discarded by their masters like cattle. While the rest of Europe outgrew serfdom, Russia found itself trapped in backwardness, the vast majority of its population poor and ignorant farm laborers.

From time to time these wretched people revolted. Some ran off and joined the Cossacks, bands of mounted freebooters. One Cossack leader, Stenka Razin, immortalized in ballad, led a peasant revolt that seized much of the Ukraine. In time, the Cossacks turned into semimilitary federations, which the tsars enrolled as effective and ruthless cavalry.

Forced Modernization

By the time Peter I became tsar in 1682, Russia was far behind the rest of Europe. Peter, an enormous man who stood six feet nine inches (206 cm), was determined to modernize Russia and make it a major power. He didn't care about his people's wishes or their welfare; he would force them to become modern. Gifted with enormous energy, some of it dissipated on women and alcohol, Peter personally handled Russia's legislation, diplomacy, and technical innovation. He was the first tsar to travel in West Europe. Admiring its industries, he ordered them duplicated in Russia. Nearly continually at war, Peter pushed the Swedes back to give Russia an outlet on the Baltic. There he ordered built a magnificent new capital, St. Petersburg (later Leningrad), to serve as Russia's window to the West.

 Russia's First Secret Police

Ivan the Terrible started the Russian tradition of a feared and powerful secret police. His *Oprichnina* rooted out suspected treason with ferocity. The *oprichniki*, marked by their black horses adorned with black dogs' heads, in time became a new aristocracy on land confiscated from the old nobles (*boyars*) whom Ivan destroyed. The force was disbanded in 1572.

Copying the excellent Swedish administrative system, Peter divided Russia into provinces, counties, and districts, which were supervised by bureaucrats drawn from the nobility. All male nobles had to serve the tsar from age 15 until death, either as bureaucrats or military officers. Even the bureaucrats were organized on military lines, complete with ranks and uniforms. With Peter, the Russian government apparatus penetrated deep into society. A census determined the number of males available for military conscription, and each community had a quota. Draftees served for life. Taxation squeezed everybody as Peter ordered his officials to "collect money, as much as possible, for money is the artery of war."

When Peter died in 1725, he left behind a more modern and Westernized Russia, but one that still lagged far behind the advanced countries. Peter the Great contributed a pattern of forced modernization from the top, pushing a gigantic, backward country forward despite itself. Russia paid dearly. The mass of peasants, heavily taxed, were worse off than ever. The Westernized nobility—forced, for instance, to shave for the first time—was cut off from the hopes and feelings of the peasantry. The pattern was to continue for a long time.

Westernizers and Slavophiles

After Napoleon's invasion of Russia and capture of Moscow in 1812, Russian intellectuals were painfully aware of the backwardness of their land. Many sought to bring in Western politics and institutions, including a constitutional monarchy that would limit the autocratic powers of the tsar.

Not all Russian intellectuals were Westernizers. An important minority disliked the West; they saw it as spiritually shallow and materialistic. The answer to Russia's problems, they argued, was to dig into their own Slavic roots and develop institutions and styles different from and superior to the West's. "Russia will teach the world," was their view. These Slavophiles (literally, "lovers of the Slavs"), who stressed the spiritual depth and warm humanity of Russian peasants, were romantic nationalists who deplored all aspects of West European culture. In our day this pattern continues, as many Third World countries claim they wish to reject Western materialism in favor of traditional spiritual values.

State Plus Church: "Caesaropapism"

Historically, in European countries the leaders of the state and of the church were almost always two different people, although sometimes the king had a say in naming the church father. But in old Russia, the two offices were one; the tsar was also the head of the Russian Orthodox church, a combined function called "caesaropapism." Russians rendered not just to their Caesar but to their pope—he was one and the same.

For most of the nineteenth century, Westernizers argued with Slavophiles. In many ways the later Communist party of Russia was a synthesis of the two views, favoring Western technology, but using it to build what they claimed would be a superior system.

From Frustration to Revolution

Despite calls for far-reaching changes in Russia, reform during the nineteenth century was largely neglected. No tsar was prepared to give up any autocratic power in favor of a parliament. Even Alexander II, the "tsar-liberator," permitted only limited reforms. In 1861 he issued his famous Edict of Emancipation, freeing all serfs from legal bondage. Most of them remained in economic bondage, however. He set up district and provincial assemblies called *zemstvos*, but gave them only marginal local power.

The reforms were meant both to modernize Russia and to improve the living conditions of the masses. Under certain conditions, however, reforms may actually make revolution more likely rather than less. Alexander's reforms, which he saw as extensive and generous, were regarded by an increasingly critical *intelligentsia* (the educated class) as not going nearly far enough. Whatever he granted, they wanted more. The reforms merely whetted the critics' appetites. Many intellectuals became bitter and frustrated.

Some tried action at the grass-roots level. In the 1870s thousands of idealistic students put on peasant clothes and tried "going to the people" in the villages to rouse them toward revolution. These *Narodniki* (from the word for "people," *narod*) made absolutely no progress; the suspicious peasants either ignored them or turned them over to the police. Others tried assassination, believing that killing the right official constituted "propaganda of the deed," a way to arouse the inert masses. One group of committed terrorists, *Narodnaya Volya* (People's Will), made the tsar their special target and, after seven attempts, killed him with a bomb thrown into his carriage in 1881.

Actually, Russia did make considerable progress in the nineteenth century. Archaic usages were swept away, industry started with an infusion of British, French, and German capital, railroads were built, and intellectual life flourished. But in the crucial area of political reform—parliaments, parties, elections, and the sharing of power—Russia essentially stood still. Political reforms do not make themselves, and in many ways they are more basic to the peaceful evolution of society than social, cultural, or economic reforms. A ruler who modernizes his economy but not his political system is asking for trouble.

Marxism Comes to Russia

According to Marx's theory, backward Russia was far from ready for proletarian revolution. There simply wasn't much of a proletariat (class of industrial workers) in the still overwhelmingly agricultural land, where industrialization was just beginning in the late nineteenth century. Marx believed revolution would come first in the most industrially advanced countries, such as Britain and Germany. Curiously, though,

Premature Democrats: The Decembrists

After Tsar Alexander I died in 1825, there was a period of uncertainty over who was going to be the new tsar. Some army officers, impatient with tsarist autocracy, attempted a *coup d'état* in December. They favored a constitutional monarchy that would bring some democratic concepts to Russia for the first time. Easily crushed and their leaders executed, the Decembrists were ahead of their time, for Russia was too backward, and few Russians wished to change.

Marxism caught on more strongly in Russia than elsewhere. Marx's works were eagerly seized upon by frustrated Russian intellectuals who badly wanted change but didn't have a theoretical framework for it. Here at last they believed they had found a reason and a means to carry out a revolution.

There were several schools of Marxism in Russia. The "Legal Marxists," noting Russia's economic backwardness, thought the country would first have to go through capitalism before it could start on socialism. Marx had a very deterministic view of history and saw it developing in clear stages based on the level of economic development. Loyal to Marx's historical analysis, the Legal Marxists believed they would have a long wait for revolution and must first work to promote capitalism.

Another school of Russian Marxism was called "Economism." Stressing bread-and-butter gains (better wages and working conditions) through labor unions, the Economists thought that the immediate economic improvement of the working class was the essence of Marxism. In this they resembled the course taken by West European social democrats, whose Marxism mellowed into welfarism.

Opposing these two gradualist schools were impassioned intellectuals who wanted first and foremost to make a revolution. They argued that they could "give history a shove" by starting a revolution with only a small proletariat, gaining power, and then using the state to move directly into socialism. Lenin made some theoretical changes in Marxism so that it fit Russian conditions (see box on page 228). Ever since then, the doctrine of Russian communism has been known as Marxism-Leninism.

In 1898, after several small groups had discussed Marxist approaches to Russia, the Russian Social Democratic Labor party was formed. Immediately penetrated and harassed by the *Okhrana*, many of its leaders went into exile in West Europe. Its newspaper, *Iskra* (the *Spark*), was published in Zurich, Switzerland, and smuggled into Russia. One of its editors was Lenin.

In 1903 the small party split over a crucial question: organization. Some of its leaders wanted a normal party along the lines of the German SPD, with open but committed membership that tried to enroll the bulk of the Russian working class. Lenin scoffed at this kind of organization, arguing that the tsarist secret police would make mincemeat out of an open party. Instead, he urged a small, tightly knit un-

Tsarist Repression: The Okhrana

Russia's political police, the *Okhrana*, were instituted by the reactionary Tsar Nicholas I after the Decembrist Revolt. *Okhrana* agents, working under the interior ministry, kept tabs on everyone whom they thought to be suspicious. Once detected, revolutionaries suffered deportation to Siberia or worse. Because the *Okhrana* was so powerful, Lenin argued in favor of keeping the revolutionary movement small and underground in order to resist secret-police penetration.

derground party of professional revolutionaries, more a conspiracy than a conventional party.

Lenin got his way. At the 1903 party congress in Brussels, Belgium (it couldn't be held in Russia), he controlled thirty-three of the fifty-one votes. Although probably unrepresentative of total party membership, Lenin proclaimed his faction *bolshevik* (majority), and the name stuck. The *menshevik* (minority) faction at the congress continued to exist, advocating a more moderate line.

Curtain Raiser: The 1905 Revolution

At the beginning of the twentieth century two expanding powers, Russia and Japan, collided. The Russians were pushing eastward, consolidating their position on the Pacific by building the Trans-Siberian Railway, the last leg of which ran through Manchuria. Japan was meanwhile pushing westward, having taken Taiwan and Korea in 1895, then coveting Manchuria, which was nominally a part of China. The tsar's cabinet, certain that they could defeat any Asian army (and hoping to shift the focus from domestic unrest), thought war with Japan might be a good idea. Said the interior minister: "We need a little victorious war to stem the tide of revolution." It was not to be. The Japanese fleet launched a surprise attack against the Russians at Port Arthur, then beat the Russians on both land and sea.

The Russo-Japanese War revealed the tsarist regime as unprepared, inept, and stupid. Moral: weak regimes shouldn't count on a "little victorious war" to paper over domestic unrest; wars make troubles worse. In Russia, rioting and then revolution broke out. Some naval units mutinied. (See Eisenstein's film classic *Battleship Potemkin*.) Workers briefly seized factories at St. Petersburg. It looked like a dream-come-true for the socialist underground.

Tsar Nicholas II, although none too bright, gave way and decreed potentially important reforms: freedom of speech, press, and assembly, and the democratic election of a parliament called the *Duma*. Briefly, this 1905 October Manifesto by the tsar looked as if it would turn autocracy into constitutional monarchy. The tsar and his reactionary advisors backed down on their promises, however. Nicholas, like his predecessors, refused to yield any of his autocratic powers. Four *Dumas* were

A Russian Genius: Vladimir Ilyich Lenin

It has been said—although no one can prove it—that the dominant passion in Lenin's life was revenge against the tsarist system for hanging his older brother, Alexander; in 1887 Lenin's brother was executed for his part in a bomb plot against the tsar. It is clear that Lenin was dominated by a cold, contained fury channeled toward one goal: revolution in Russia.

Born in 1870 as Vladimir Ilyich Ulyanov, son of a provincial education official, Lenin was from the intellectual middle class rather than from the proletariat in whose name he struggled—a pattern typical of revolutionary socialist leaders. Expelled from university for alleged subversive activity after his first three months, Lenin was sent into rural exile. Nonetheless, with the incredible self-discipline that became his hallmark, Lenin taught himself all he needed to know to breeze through law exams with the highest marks.

In the early 1890s Lenin, like many who hated tsarism, converted passionately to Marxism, devoured everything Marx wrote (some in the original German, which Lenin had taught himself), and wrote Marxist analyses of the rapidly growing Russian economy. Recognized as a leading Marxist thinker, Lenin quickly rose to prominence in underground revolutionary circles.

In December 1895, while editing an illegal socialist newspaper, Lenin was arrested and sent to prison for a year, followed by three years' exile in Siberia. He didn't much mind it. The solitary hours gave him time to read, learn foreign languages, and write. Again, the monumental self-discipline showed. Released in 1900, Lenin soon made his way to Switzerland where he spent most of the next seventeen years. In Zurich you can still sip tea in the Café Odeon, as Lenin used to. He would nurse a cup for hours to read the newspapers for free.

At times during his long exile Lenin despaired that there would ever be a revolution in Russia. The working class was moving more in the direction of Economism, concentrating on higher wages rather than revolution. The Russian Social Democratic Labor party was small; there were only a few thousand members in Russia and in exile.

Lenin was determined to transform this small party into an effective underground force. Size was not important; organization was everything. In his 1902 pamphlet *What Is to Be Done?* Lenin demanded a tightly disciplined party of professional revolutionaries, not a conventional European social-democratic party open to everybody. Ever since, Communist parties the world over were fanatics on organization and discipline. Under Lenin the early Communists forged the "organizational weapon": the Party.

But how could a proletarian revolution happen in backward Russia? This was the great theoretical problem Lenin faced. In solving it, he greatly changed Marxism. First, Marx theorized revolution should come in the most advanced countries, where the proletariat was biggest. Lenin said not necessarily; revolution could come where capitalism is weakest, where it is just starting. Imperialism had changed capitalism, Lenin argued, giving it a new lease on life. By exploiting backward countries, the big imperialist powers were able to bribe their own working class with higher wages and thus keep them quiet. Where capitalism was beginning—as in Russia with heavy foreign investment—was where it could be overthrown. The newly developing countries, such as Russia and Spain, were "capitalism's weakest link," said Lenin.

Secondly, Lenin disagreed with Marx's insistence that the peasantry could never play a revolutionary role—Marx wrote that peasants wallowed in "rural idiocy." Under certain conditions, Lenin believed, they could become highly revolutionary and, throwing their weight in with the small working class, provide a massive revolutionary army. (Three decades later, Mao Zedong would pick up and elaborate on these two themes to argue that backward China, a victim of imperialism, could have a socialist revolution based entirely on the peasantry. Mao simply completed the train of thought Lenin started.)

Lenin showed himself to be not a great theoretician—you can find many inconsistencies and contradictions in his works—but a brilliant opportunist, switching doctrine this way and that way to take advantage of the existing political situation. Lenin was less concerned with preserving a pure Marxism than in using a variation of Marxism to overthrow the system he hated. And in this he succeeded, largely by the sheer force of his brilliant, disciplined, calculating personality.

One City, Three Names

Peter the Great founded St. Petersburg early in the eighteenth century. When war with Germany broke out in 1914, the Russian government felt their capital should have a Russian (rather than Dutch) name, so they Russified it to Petrograd. After Lenin died in 1924 the regime changed it to Leningrad. In 1991, Leningraders voted to change it back to St. Petersburg.

subsequently elected; each was dissolved when it proved too critical and turned into an undemocratic debating society without power. The *Duma* was Russia's last hope for a peaceful transition to democracy. People in modern times need to feel they participate at least in a small way in the affairs of government. Parties, elections, and parliaments may be highly imperfect ways to channel participation, but they are better than violent revolution. Since the Decembrist revolt of 1825, Russian intellectuals had been trying to tell the tsar this simple truth, but he refused to listen.

World War I and Collapse

Communists liked to speak of the Russian Revolution as inevitable, the playing out of historical forces that *had* to lead to the collapse of imperialism and capitalism. There was nothing inevitable about the October Revolution. Indeed, without World War I, there might have been no revolution in Russia at all, let alone a Bolshevik revolution. Lenin himself, in early 1917, stated he doubted he'd live to see a revolution in Russia.

Memorable Russian Slogans: "Bread, Land, Peace"

When Lenin got off the train in Petrograd's Finland Station in April 1917, he knew that the Bolsheviks were only a small minority of the revolutionary forces seething in Russia. He also recognized—in what became an uncanny Communist skill—that the right slogan could galvanize the masses of discontented people into action on the Communist side. Accordingly, Lenin picked out exactly the right three words, the three things that war-weary Russians wanted most desperately: bread for the worker, land for the peasant, and peace for the soldier. The three words had little in fact to do with Marxist theory, but the slogan was tactically brilliant and helped the Bolsheviks grow from a small party to the dominant force of the revolution. Sloganeering became a Communist art form.

Joseph Stalin: "One Death Is a Tragedy; A Million Is a Statistic"

The Soviet system was not so much Lenin's as Stalin's. Lenin was 54 when he died in 1924, before giving definitive pattern to the system. Although capable of great ruthlessness, it is doubtful that he would have been like Stalin. Exactly who is to blame for the horrors that developed—Lenin or Stalin—is still a matter of great controversy both within and outside Russia. Some argue that if Lenin had lived, his intelligence and sophistication would have set the country on the path to "true socialism." Others say the structure Lenin created—concentrating power first in the party, then in the Central Committee, and finally in his own person—made the misuse of power inevitable.

Stalin aptly illustrates Acton's dictum that "power corrupts." Stalin lived in order to amass political power, and he was very good at it. Born Yosif Vissarionovich Djugashvili in 1879, son of a poor shoemaker, Stalin lacked Lenin's intellectual family background and education. Some of Stalin's behavior can be traced back to his family home in Georgia, part of the Caucasus, a mountainous land with a warm climate and fiery people given to personal hatred and blood-feuds. In Georgia, "Soso" (his Georgian nickname) was long praised as a local boy who made good.

The young Djugashvili entered an Orthodox seminary to study for the priesthood but soon became more interested in revolution. Expelled from the seminary, he joined the Georgian Marxist underground as an agitator and strike organizer. Repeatedly arrested, jailed, and exiled to Siberia, he always managed to escape. Going underground, he took the name Stalin, from the Russian for "man of steel."

Never a great theoretician, Stalin attracted Lenin's attention as a non-Russian who could write the Bolsheviks' position on the nationalities question. Playing only a moderate role in the October Revolution, Stalin was named commissar for nationalities in 1918 and then, in what may have been Lenin's worst mistake, picked as the party's first general secretary in 1922. People thought the new office would be a routine job with little real power. Lenin and Stalin were never particularly close—although Stalin's historians tried to make it look that way—and toward the end of his life Lenin had an inkling of what Stalin was like. In one of his last messages Lenin urged the party to reject Stalin as "too rude."

It was too late, however. Using his position as general secretary, Stalin organized the party to his advantage by promoting to key posts only those personally loyal to him. It was this organizational spadework that gave Stalin the edge over his rival, Leon Trotsky, organizer of the Red Army and a far more intelligent Marxist. Stalin beat him in party infighting and had him expelled from Russia in 1929 and murdered in Mexico City in 1940. Reviled as a deviationist traitor, Trotsky did try to organize an anti-Stalin opposition within the CPSU, a point that fed Stalin's natural paranoia and contributed to his ruthlessness in exterminating officials on the slightest suspicion of disloyalty.

Stalin, an uncanny manipulator, played one faction against another until, by the late 1920s, he was the Kremlin's undisputed master. Like Peter the Great, Stalin was determined to modernize regardless of human cost. In 1928, he instituted the first Five-Year Plan, beginning the forced industrialization of Russia. Farmers, very much against their will, were herded into collectives and forced to produce for the state, sometimes at gunpoint. Better-off farmers, the so-called *kulaks*, were "liquidated as a class," a euphemism for killed. Economic development was defined in terms of heavy industry, and steel production became the chief goal of the man of steel.

In 1934, during the second Five-Year Plan, Stalin became obsessed with "Trotskyite" disloyalty in party ranks. Thus began the Great Purge: Up to one million party comrades were killed, some after confessing to be British spies or Trotskyite "wreckers." Perhaps another ten million ordinary citizens also perished, many in Siberian forced-labor camps. *Paranoia* means unreasonable suspicion of other people, not simply fear, and Stalin was a classic paranoid. Much of the population, especially people in positions of prominence, trembled with fear that they might be next. Stalin even had all his experienced generals murdered, a blunder that left him open for the 1941 German attack. In total, Stalin's orders led to the death of some fifteen million people during collectivization and the Great Purge.

Was Stalin mad? It's hard to say. There was some Trotskyite opposition to him, but he exaggerated it. It was Plato who first observed that any tyrant, even one who starts out sane, must eventually lose his mind in office because he can't trust anybody. More than a question of personality, Stalin shows what happens when one person assumes total power. The Communists didn't like to admit it, but it was their *system* that was at fault more than any particular *individual*.

During his lifetime Stalin was deified as history's greatest linguist, art critic, Marxist theoretician, engineer, agronomist—you name it. By the time he died in 1953—while preparing yet another purge—Stalin had turned the Soviet Union into *his* system, and, in basic outlines, it never did change much. When Mikhail Gorbachev attempted to seriously reform it, the system collapsed.

All died in 1935, the victims of Stalin's purges. Here three graves in a St. Petersburg cemetery, ironically shared with Russian Orthodox priests and monks, convey some of the horror of Stalin's "cleansing" of people he supposed were unreliable. The family of the victim on the right, by erecting a life-size statue of the man in Bolshevik Young Guard uniform, meant to show he was a faithful Communist all along. *(Michael Roskin)*

Things were not so terrible in Russia before the war. The *Duma* struggled to make itself effective and in time might have been able to erode tsarist autocracy. Industry grew rapidly. Peasants, freed from old restrictions on land ownership, were turning into prosperous and productive small farmers.

The war changed everything. Repeating their overconfidence of 1904, the tsarist military marched happily to war against Germany in 1914, and this doomed the system. It was a large army, but badly equipped and poorly led. Major offensives ground to a halt before the more effective German forces. The Russian economy started to fall apart. Troop morale disintegrated and desertion was widespread. Peas-

Alexander Kerensky: Nice Guys Lose

In the late 1950s at UCLA the author had an eerie experience: seeing and hearing Alexander Kerensky speak. History lives. Still fit and articulate in his seventies, Kerensky recalled his brief stint (July to November of 1917) as head of the Provisional Government in Russia. One man in the audience, a Russian emigré, asked angrily why Kerensky didn't use his power to have Lenin killed. Kerensky reflected a moment and said, "Sometimes when you have power it's hard to use it."

That was Kerensky's problem. A decent man, he wouldn't have a political opponent murdered. The Western Allies begged him to keep Russia in the war, and he didn't have the heart to betray them.

What Kerensky lacked in political ruthlessness he may have gained in longevity. Living in New York City, he spent his years justifying his brief rule and denouncing both the Bolsheviks and Russian rightists who tried to bring him down. He died in 1970 at the ripe old age of 89.

ants started seizing their landlord's grounds. The government was paralyzed, but the tsar refused to change anything. By 1917 the situation was desperate. In March of that year a group of democratic moderates seized power and deposed the tsar. Resembling Western liberals, the people of the Provisional Government hoped to modernize and democratize Russia. The Western powers, including the United States, welcomed the move, thinking it would rally Russians to continue the war. The Provisional Government, which by July was headed by nominal socialist Alexander Kerensky, tried to stay in the war, and that was its undoing. If Kerensky had betrayed the Western Allies and made a separate peace with Germany, the moderates might have been able to retain power.

Meanwhile, the German General Staff, looking for a way to knock Russia out of the war, thought it would be clever to send the agitator Lenin into Russia to create havoc. In April 1917 Lenin and his colleagues traveled in a famous "sealed train"—so the Bolshevik "bacillus" wouldn't infect Germany, where revolutionary discontent was also growing—across Germany, Sweden, and Finland to Petrograd. Without German help and funds, Lenin might never have made it back to Russia.

In Petrograd, Lenin found a "dual authority" trying to rule the land. The Provisional Government controlled the army and foreign policy. But in the most important city, Petrograd, a council (*soviet* in Russian) of workers, soldiers, sailors, and revolutionaries ran things. Soon these councils appeared in many Russian cities. The composition of these soviets was mixed, with the Bolsheviks a small minority. Lenin pursued a double strategy: make the soviets the only effective governing power and make the Bolsheviks the dominant power in the soviets.

The Revolution and Civil War

The actual seizure of power in October (see box) was amazingly easy. In a scene exaggerated by Soviet historians, soldiers and sailors loyal to the Petrograd soviet

Why the October Revolution Was in November

Every November 7 Russia used to celebrate the anniversary of the Great October Revolution. If this sounds curious, it's because Russia in 1917 was still using the old Julian calendar, which lagged thirteen days behind the Western Gregorian calendar (which introduced leap years), in use in Catholic countries since 1582. The Bolsheviks switched to the Gregorian but in so doing had to recalculate the October Revolution into the following month.

charged across a big square into the Winter Palace to oust the Provisional Government. But control of Petrograd and Moscow was one thing, control of all gigantic Russia was something else.

The tight organization and discipline of Lenin's Bolsheviks paid off. In a situation of almost total chaos, the best organized win. By a series of shrewd moves, the Bolsheviks were able to dominate the soviets and win many converts from deserting soldiers and sailors. Lenin headed the new government and immediately took Russia out of the war, accepting a punitive peace treaty from the Germans at Brest-Litovsk in March 1918. It was a dictated treaty (*Diktat* in German) that enabled the Germans to seize large areas of Russia and redeploy nearly a million troops to the western front.

Feeling betrayed and concerned that allied military supplies would fall into German hands, the Western Allies sent small expeditionary forces into Russia. American troops actually fought the Bolsheviks in north Russia and Siberia in 1918–19. This was the beginning of the Soviet view that the capitalist powers tried to strangle the infant Bolshevik regime in its cradle.

From 1918 to 1920 civil war raged. The White Army, led by reactionary Russian generals and admirals and supplied by the Western Allies, tried to crush the Communists' Red Army. Both sides displayed incredible ruthlessness in what was for them a life-or-death struggle. Millions of Russians perished from starvation. Expecting

Memorable Russian Slogans: "All Power to the Soviets"

With councils of workers and soldiers springing up all over Russia to oppose the Provisional Government, Lenin and the Bolsheviks argued that only the soviets should have power. Gradually, as the Kerensky government weakened, that is what happened.

Not only did the soviets take power—giving the name Soviet Union, a union of worker councils—but within the soviets the Bolsheviks took power. This is what Lenin had in mind with the slogan but did not state openly.

their revolution to spread, the Red Army invaded Poland in 1920 hoping to trigger a Europe-wide socialist upheaval. Instead, the Poles threw back the Red Army and seized Russian territory. Lenin and his colleagues saw there would be no world revolution and so settled down to build the world's first socialist country.

War Communism and NEP

During the civil war, the Bolsheviks tried to plunge directly into their utopian system by running the ruined economy by executive fiat. This "war communism," as it was euphemistically called, was due as much to the demands of a desperate civil war as to visionary schemes. In either case, it was a flop; starvation broke out and only the charity of American grain shipments (supervised by Herbert Hoover) held deaths to a few million.

Lenin saw that Russia was far from ready for pure socialism, so he conducted a planned retreat of state control to the "commanding heights" of heavy industry and let most of the rest of the economy revert to private hands. This period of Lenin's New Economic Policy (NEP), from 1921 to 1928, brought relative prosperity; farmers worked their own land, "nepmen" behaved like small private entrepreneurs, and life in general relaxed. There was one catch: the NEP wasn't moving the Soviet Union, as it was now called, any closer to socialism, and industry grew only slowly. It is likely that Lenin meant the NEP only as temporary rest before moving on to socialist construction.

That changed when Stalin gained power in the late 1920s. In 1928 began the first of the government-enforced Five-Year Plans that accelerated collectivization and industrialization (see box on page 230). Peasants resisted giving up their fields, farm production dropped, and millions (especially Ukrainians) were deliberately starved to death. In new factories, workers toiled with primitive implements to boost production of capital goods. Consumer goods were deliberately neglected, and the standard of living declined. While many admit that the forced industrialization of the 1930s was brutal, some point out that it alone gave the Soviet Union the industrial base to arm against the German invasion in 1941.

As it was, the German invasion caused over twenty million Soviet deaths. The Nazis cared nothing for Slavic lives; starvation was their standard treatment for Russian prisoners of war. Still, it was a time when the Soviet Union pulled together. Stalin,

---

Memorable Russian Slogans: "He Who Does Not Work, Neither Shall He Eat"

In trying to motivate the population during the lean years of "war communism" (1918–20), Lenin laid down this slogan as policy; it later appeared in the 1936 constitution. Draconic as it sounds, we might remember that Lenin borrowed it from the Bible (2 Thessalonians 3:10). The expression was also used in the Jamestown colony of old Virginia, which had similar motivational problems.

Yet Another Tale of Two Flags

In 1991 the familiar communist red flag (with gold hammer and sickle) came down as the Soviet Union dissolved. Red had been the color of socialist movements (taken from the red shirts of Italian unifier Garibaldi) since the nineteenth century; the Bolsheviks made it the national flag in late 1917. The old tsarist flag was developed by Peter the Great, who brought the Netherlands tricolor back with him from his stay in Dutch shipyards in 1699, but changed the stripes from the original Dutch (from the top: red-white-blue) to white-blue-red, sometimes with an imperial double-headed eagle on it. The Provisional Government removed the eagle in 1917; this is what the Russian Federation revived as its flag in 1991.

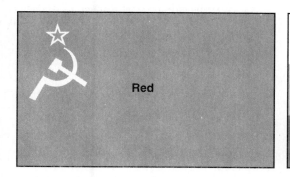

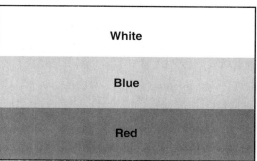

like Lenin, recognized the force of Russian nationalism beneath the Communist surface. Reviewing troops marching from Moscow to the front, Stalin mused: "They aren't fighting for communism or for Stalin; they're fighting for Mother Russia." In Russia today, World War II is known as the Great Patriotic War. By the time he died in 1953, Stalin had transformed a backward country into a gigantic empire and major industrial power. He had also founded a political system, the dismantling of which still preoccupies Russia.

Vocabulary Building

autocracy	*Duma*	Menshevik	Slavic
Bolshevik	Economism	*Narodniki*	Slavophiles
boyars	Five-Year Plans	NEP	soviet
Brest-Litovsk	Georgia	October Revolution	Tatars
caesaropapism	Great Purge	*Okhrana*	Time of Troubles
Cossacks	*intelligentsia*	paranoid	War Communism
cyrillic	*kulaks*	Petrograd	Westernizers
Decembrists	Legal Marxism	Provisional	Whites
deified	Marxism-Leninism	Government	*zemstvo*
Diktat			

Further Reference

BATER, JAMES H. *The Russian Scene: A Geographical Perspective.* New York: Edward Arnold, 1989.

BOBRICK, BENSON. *Fearful Majesty: The Life and Reign of Ivan the Terrible.* New York: Putnam's, 1987.

CONQUEST, ROBERT. *The Great Terror: A Reassessment.* New York: Oxford University Press, 1990.

KORT, MICHAEL. *The Soviet Colossus: The Rise and Fall of the USSR,* 3d ed. Armonk, NY: M.E. Sharpe, 1993.

LINCOLN, W. BRUCE. *The Conquest of a Continent: Siberia and the Russians.* New York: Random House, 1994.

LOURIE, RICHARD. *Russia Speaks: A History Told by the People.* New York: HarperCollins, 1991.

MALIA, MARTIN. *The Soviet Tragedy: A History of Socialism in Russia, 1917–1991.* New York: The Free Press, 1994.

PIPES, RICHARD. *Russia under the Bolshevik Regime.* New York: Knopf, 1994.

RADZINSKY, EDVARD. *The Last Tsar: The Life and Death of Nicholas II.* New York: Doubleday, 1992.

SERVICE, ROBERT. *Lenin: A Political Life.* Vol. 1. *The Strengths of Contradiction.* Bloomington, IN: Indiana University Press, 1985.

SUMNER, B. H. *Peter the Great and the Emergence of Russia.* New York: Collier Books, 1962.

TUCKER, ROBERT C. *Stalin in Power: The Revolution from Above, 1928–1941.* New York: W. W. Norton, 1990.

ULAM, ADAM B. *Ideologies and Illusion: Revolutionary Thought from Herzen to Solzhenitsyn.* Cambridge, MA: Harvard University Press, 1976.

———. *In the Name of the People: Prophets and Conspirators in Prerevolutionary Russia.* New York: Viking, 1977.

WOLFE, BERTRAM D. *Three Who Made a Revolution.* New York: Delta, 1964.

CHAPTER **18**
Russia: The Key Institutions

The Russian political system is changing before our eyes. It is impossible to tell how it will end up. One year the forces for reform seem to be in command; next year conservative forces attempt to turn back the clock to the old system. The best we can do in this chapter is describe two models of the Russian system, the old Soviet system formed under Stalin and a post-Communist system that is struggling to find stability. If the conservative forces entrenched in positions of power have their way, we will see a return to the old system with some cosmetic changes, not enough to warrant the name "system change." If the reformers win, the old institutions and usages will be junked or gutted. That would be system change.

The Stalin System

The Soviet system started by Lenin but perfected by Stalin lasted into Gorbachev's tenure. The system changed over time, but not much. Its main structural features were:

1. Communist Party in Command. The Communist Party of the Soviet Union (CPSU) was constitutionally defined as "the leading and guiding force of Soviet society." No other parties were permitted, and no factions were allowed inside the Party. The Party did not run things directly, however. It served as a nervous system and central brain that transmitted policy lines, kept tabs on the economy, reported discontent, and selected, promoted, and supervised the system's personnel. There was much overlap between Party and state system, so that at the top, most government ministers were also on the Party's Central Committee.

Party membership was tightly controlled. Less than 7 percent of the Soviet population (at one point, about 19 million out of 285 million) were Party members,

What Is "System Change"?

How can you tell when a country has undergone "system change" or "systemic change"? All political systems are constantly changing, but we seldom describe it as system change. If a system changes only gradually and incrementally, we usually describe it as evolutionary change. The slow shift of the British monarch from working executive to figurehead is change of this type. A revolution, on the other hand, is almost by definition system change: old institutions, elites, and patterns are suddenly swept out. The Bolsheviks, for example, clearly changed the Russian system. System change need not require a revolution, however. De Gaulle effectively changed the French system by means of a new constitution.

Has Russia undergone system change? Clearly, it has not undergone a revolution; too many of the old elites and patterns are still in place. But it probably has undergone a system change. One test is to pick up any of a number of books that describe the Soviet system before Gorbachev came to power in 1985. Do they still adequately describe Russian structures and practices today? If the descriptions no longer match present reality, we've had system change. If what was described prior to 1985, however, is still fairly valid today, then we have not had system change. Applying this test to Russia and South Africa, we see system change in recent years, but probably not in the case of Germany and Japan.

selected on the basis of good records as workers, students, or youth leaders. The aim of the CPSU was to skim off the best of Soviet society. The Party was organized like a gigantic pyramid, with primary Party organizations at the bottom; district, province, and republic Party conferences in between; and an all-union Party conference at the top. Presiding over each conference was a committee. Each level "elected" delegates to the next highest level (actually, they were handpicked from above) in what was called "democratic centralism." Full-time Party workers, *apparatchiki* ("men of the apparatus") were the cement that held the thing together.

The All-Union Party Congress of some 5,000 delegates would meet for a few days every few years, ostensibly to elect the Central Committee of about 300 full and 150 candidate members. The Central Committee would meet twice a year, usually just before the meeting of its government counterpart, the Supreme Soviet, for the membership of the two bodies overlapped.

Above the Central Committee and really running things was the Politburo (political bureau), a full-time decision-making body with about a dozen full and six candidate members. Politburo decisions were automatically approved by the Central Committee, whose decisions were approved by the Party Congress, and so on down the line. Running the Politburo was a general secretary (*gensek*), usually called in the West the "party chief." This person in practice usually became supreme boss of both Party and state and could assume dictatorial powers. In most Communist systems, the party chief is the most powerful figure, for he controls the *apparat* and selects *apparatchiki* who are personally loyal to him.

2. A Less Important State Structure. Outside observers agreed that the gigantic Supreme Soviet, with 1,500 members, could not serve as a real parliament. It met only a few days a year to rubber-stamp laws drafted by the top echelons of the Party. Nominally bicameral, the Supreme Soviet would "elect" a governing Presidium

Memorable Russian Slogans: "The Communist Party Is Not a Party Like Other Parties"

Lenin used these words when the Bolsheviks were still a small underground party, most of whose leaders were in exile. In his fight with the Mensheviks, Lenin made it clear that the Bolsheviks were not going to play the normal political games of ordinary parties. After coming to power, Lenin again made it clear that the Communists were not to revert to a normal party role but were to stay firmly in command to guide Soviet society.

of twenty members that overlapped with the Politburo. The Presidium could decree whatever it liked, and its decrees had force of law. The Presidium also served as a collective presidency, and its chairman was often referred to as the "president" of the Soviet Union. Since Brezhnev, the Party general secretary had also had himself named president, so as to make clear that he headed both state and Party.

The Supreme Soviet also "elected" a sort of cabinet, the mammoth Council of Ministers, with some eighty-five highly specialized ministries, mostly concentrated on branches of the economy (for example, the Ministry of Machine Building for Animal Husbandry and Fodder Production). The Council of Ministers rarely met for collective deliberation. Typically, the following ministries were reserved for Politburo members: prime minister, state security (KGB), interior (police), defense, and foreign affairs.

3. A Centralized Federal System. The classic Soviet pattern was a federation—like the United States, Canada, and Germany—but one long dominated by the "center." What the Politburo in Moscow laid down was generally implemented throughout the country by the Party. The Soviet Union had some two dozen major nationalities and many more minor ones—104 in all. The fifteen largest got their own Soviet Socialist Republic (for example, the Uzbek SSR), which together made the USSR (Union of Soviet Socialist Republics). The nationalities, however, are somewhat dispersed; there are ethnic Russians in every republic—a third of the populations of Latvia and Kazakhstan are Russian—and this sharpened a dangerous nationalities question.

The Russian Federative Republic was by far the biggest and is still today a federation of numerous autonomous regions for the bewildering variety of ethnic groups within it. The underlying intention of Soviet federalism was preservation of language rights. Stalin, who developed Soviet nationality policy, recognized that language and culture are potential political dynamite, and that it was best to let each nationality feel culturally autonomous while in fact they were politically subordinate. This, as it turned out, was an unstable solution.

4. A Gigantic Bureaucracy. Karl Marx argued that after socialism eliminated class differences, the state would "wither away." German sociologist Max Weber argued the opposite: that socialism required much more state power and a much larger bureaucracy. Marx was wrong; Weber was right. The Soviet bureaucracy became monstrous, with some eighteen million persons administering every facet of Soviet life. This bureaucracy spelled the ruination of the Soviet Union: slow, marginally competent, inflexible, indifferent to efficiency, corrupt, and immune to criticism except from high Party officials.

Government in a Fortress

The Kremlin (from the Russian *kreml,* "fortress") is a walled city dating back centuries. (The present walls were built in 1492.) Triangular in shape and a mile and a half (2.4 kilometers) around, the ancient Kremlin houses both government buildings and cathedrals (now public museums). Right next to the Kremlin wall is Lenin's tomb, used as a reviewing stand by the Politburo for parades in Red Square on May 1 (International Workers' Day) and November 7 (the anniversary of the Revolution). Also facing Red Square: the colorful onion-shaped domes of St. Basil's Cathedral.

The Party, in fact, interpenetrated and guided the bureaucracy, what the Party called its *kontrol* function. The Party appointed and supervised all important officials, and this kept them on their toes. If they fouled up or were egregiously crooked, they could get demoted or transferred to a remote area. This tended to make officials extremely cautious and go strictly by the book. On the other hand, if officials were effective and successful, the Party could recommend them for higher positions.

WHO WAS WHEN?

Party Chief	Ruled	Main Accomplishments
Vladimir I. Lenin	1917–24	Led Revolution; instituted War Communism, then NEP.
Josef Stalin	1927–53	Five-Year Plans of forced collectivization and industrialization; purges; self-deification.
Nikita Khrushchev	1955–64	Destalinized; experimented with economic and cultural reform; promised utopia soon; ousted.
Leonid Brezhnev	1964–82	Partially restalinized; refrained from shaking up system; let corruption grow and economy slow.
Yuri Andropov	1982–84	Cracked down on corruption and alcoholism; suggested major reforms, but soon died.
Konstantin Chernenko	1984–85	*Nichevo.*
Mikhail Gorbachev	1985-91	Initiated sweeping change, unwittingly ended Soviet system.

The key tool in this was the *nomenklatura,* a list of some 600,000 important positions and another list of reliable people eligible to fill them. Most *nomenklatura* posts went to Party members, and once "nomenklatured," officials generally stayed on the list until retirement. The *nomenklatura* was unmentioned in Soviet law but was an open secret, and the term was often another way of saying "Soviet elite."

5. Central Economic Planning. The State Planning Committee, *Gosplan,* was the nerve center of the Soviet economic system, attempting to establish how much of what should be produced each year and setting longer-term targets for some 350,000 enterprises. Central planning produced both impressive results and massive dislocations. Under Stalin, it enabled the Soviet Union to industrialize quickly, albeit at terrible human cost. But it also meant chronic shortages of items the *Gosplan*

Mikhail Gorbachev: "Life Punishes Those Who Delay"

These words were uttered by the Soviet president in 1989 as he urged the East German Communist regime to reform before it was too late. The East Berlin regime ignored Gorbachev and collapsed. What Mikhail Sergeyevich Gorbachev (sounds like "garbage OFF") didn't grasp at the time was that he too was engaging in delayed and halfway reforms that collapsed the Soviet regime and led to his own ouster from power.

Amidst great hopes, Gorbachev assumed the top Soviet political position—Party general secretary—in 1985. The Soviet Union had been gradually running down. Under Brezhnev's eighteen-year reign, growth rates slumped, while cynicism, alcoholism, and corruption grew. Two elderly temporaries, Andropov and Chernenko, followed, as the Soviet system began to atrophy. Gorbachev—age 54, a mere kid in Politburo terms—announced wide-ranging reforms that would shake up the Soviet system.

Born into a peasant family in the North Caucasus in 1931, Gorbachev graduated from Moscow University's law school in 1955 but immediately returned to his home area for Party work. As Party chief of Stavropol province in 1970, he made a good impression on Brezhnev, who summoned him to Moscow in 1978 to become a Party secretary with responsibility for overseeing agriculture. (Gorbachev had taken another degree, in agronomy, by correspondence.)

Gorbachev by now was under the wing of Andropov, head of the KGB, and Mikhail Suslov, a Politburo kingmaker also from Stavropol. Gorbachev was elected to the Party's Central Committee in 1971, to candidate member of the Politburo in 1979, and to full member in 1980. When Andropov took over in 1982, Gorbachev assisted him closely and implemented his tough anticorruption policies.

Gorbachev began his reforms with great fanfare. He looked like the liberalizing hero who would turn the Soviet Union into a modern, possibly democratic, system. He announced "new thinking" in foreign policy that led to arms control agreements with the United States and to the freeing of Eastern Europe from the Communist regimes that had been imposed by Stalin after World War II. With these steps, the Cold War ended.

Gorbachev ordered *glasnost* (openness) in the Soviet media, which became more pluralist, honest, and critical. Corrupt big shots were fired. Gorbachev also urged *demokratizatzia*; competitive elections were introduced, and a partially elected parliament convened.

As to the economy, Gorbachev at first tried to fix the old system by the old remedies: verbal exhortations, anti-alcohol campaigns, "acceleration," and the importation of more foreign technology. Then, after having hesitated too long, he ordered *perestroika* (economic restructuring) that slowly and gingerly began to decentralize and liberalize the Soviet economy. Farms and factories made more of their own decisions and kept more of their own profits. Private business, called "cooperatives," were founded and grew. But it was too little too late. By 1989 economic disaster loomed on the horizon. Huge dislocations lowered Soviet living and dietary standards and angered everyone.

With a freer press, the many nationalities (including even Russians) demanded greater autonomy or even independence. Violence between ethnic groups flared. The *apparat* and *nomenklatura* sabotaged economic reforms by hoarding food and raw materials. The army and KGB indicated they wouldn't stand for the growing chaos, which was leading to the dismemberment of the Soviet Union, so Gorbachev pulled back from reforms and tightened up in late 1990. In early 1991, Gorbachev appeared to favor reform again. In opposition, conservative hardliners in his own cabinet—every one handpicked by Gorbachev—attempted a coup against him in August 1991. The coup failed due to splits in the Soviet armed forces and the stubbornness of Russian President Boris Yeltsin, who took the initiative in pushing a badly weakened Gorbachev from office and in breaking up the Soviet Union into its component republics.

In some part, Gorbachev had himself to blame for the Soviet collapse. He had dawdled too long and changed sides too many times. He had sought to preserve the Party and "socialism." He never did adopt an economic reform plan. Life indeed punished him who delayed.

forgot about or deemed unimportant. It appears that one year no toothbrushes were produced in the entire Soviet Union, a *Gosplan* oversight.

The Soviets were convinced that a planned and centrally directed economy is more rational than a Western market economy. Actual results disputed that, but bureaucrats were (and still are) reluctant to surrender central planning, long an article of faith of "scientific socialism." In *Gosplan*, the hopes, aims, fears, and sometimes caprices of the Soviet system converged and struggled. *Gosplan*, itself quite sensitive to the wishes of the Politburo, determined who got what in the Soviet Union, whether steel grew at *x* percent this year and plastics at *y* percent next. Heavily computerized, *Gosplan* may be described as the steering wheel of the Soviet economy.

1991: The Coup That Failed

In August 1991, as Gorbachev was on vacation in the Crimea, most of his cabinet tried to overthrow him. An eight-man junta (Russians used the Spanish loan word) of conservatives, calling themselves the "Emergency Committee," said Gorbachev had taken ill and declared his vice-president, Gennadi Yanayev, acting president.

Some Western experts had been predicting a coup for three years. Gorbachev's reforms, cautious as they might be, were threatening the Soviet system and the jobs and comforts of the Soviet ruling elite. Gorbachev had been warned repeatedly of their anger. In December 1990 Foreign Minister Eduard Shevardnadze resigned in public protest at what he said was a coming dictatorship.

Guarding his right, Gorbachev shelved his more ambitious reforms and appointed a cabinet of hardliners. Disillusioned, his liberal advisers deserted him and his popularity plummeted. Veering back to the left, in 1991 Gorbachev indicated he was again ready for major reform, and with the leaders of nine of the Soviet republics (the "nine plus one" meeting) drafted a new union treaty that would give the republics great autonomy within a market economy. This was the last straw for the conservatives. The day before the treaty was to be signed they staged their coup.

For three days the world held its breath. Would the coup by not very bright Kremlin *apparatchiks* succeed? They seemingly held the upper hand. Among them were the head of the military, the KGB, and the interior ministry. These are some of the reasons it failed:

- **Few Soviets supported the coup.** Tens of thousands of citizens favoring democracy publicly opposed the coup. Gorbachev was not very popular, but the junta was much worse.
- **Boris Yeltsin stood firm.** About a mile and a half from the Kremlin is the parliament of the Russian Republic, the "White House," then presided over by strongly reformist Yeltsin. Yeltsin and his helpers holed up in the building and declared the junta's decrees illegal. A tank column sent to take the White House instead sided with Yeltsin and defended it. Thousands of Muscovites came to stand guard and protest the coup. Yeltsin's toughness galvanized opposition.
- **The Soviet armed forces started to split.** Many commanders either stood on the sidelines or opposed the junta. The possibility of a bloody civil war loomed, and the junta lost its nerve.
- **International pressure opposed the coup.** All major foreign powers made it clear that the Soviet economy, desperate for foreign help, would get none if the coup succeeded. Foreign broadcasts (heard by Gorbachev himself) heartened the anti-junta forces.

A haggard Gorbachev returned to Moscow vowing further reform. The junta was arrested (one committed suicide). The coup attempt actually hastened the end of the Soviet Union. After it, Gorbachev was revealed as an indecisive failure. Yeltsin bumped him out of power and proclaimed an independent Russia.

Russian Parliament, the "White House" some distance from the Kremlin, was the scene of two dramatic showdowns. In 1991 Boris Yeltsin stood here and faced down the junta that attempted to oust Gorbachev. But in 1993 it was Yeltsin who ordered the building shelled to break a coup attempt by conservative parliamentarians. The White House was quickly restored and now houses Russia's State Duma. *(Michael Roskin)*

The New System

In the months after the failed coup of August 1991, the old Soviet system collapsed, and from the rubble emerged a new system, one that has not yet taken final form, but with these outlines:

1. No More Soviet Union. All of the fifteen Soviet republics took advantage of the turmoil of late 1991 to declare their independence. The Baltic republics especially—Lithuania, Latvia, and Estonia—led the way to full, immediate independence. They expelled Soviet police, issued their own passports and visas, and took control of their borders. Many European countries soon granted them formal diplomatic recognition. (The United States had never unrecognized the Baltics even after Stalin had brutally seized them in 1940.)

The other republics soon followed and now all are independent. But some are more independent than others. Ukrainians voted overwhelmingly for independence. Although Ukraine had been part of tsarist Russia for centuries and was the breadbasket of the Soviet Union, many Ukrainians resented being ruled by Moscow, especially after they got a chance to hear and read of what Stalin's farm collectivization had done to them—deliberately starved to death six million.

But Belarus (formerly Belarussia, the area between Russia and Poland), which had never been an independent country or harbored much separatist feeling, voted for independence too. But Belarus still uses the Russian ruble as currency and gets sweetheart trade deals with Russia. Its army is closely linked to the Russian army. Belarusian independence is not nearly as strong and clear as Ukrainian independence.

The KGB

Terror was called "the linchpin of the Soviet system," the key element that held it together. During Stalin's time there was a lot of truth to this, but since then, terror—the fear of being arbitrarily arrested, imprisoned, sent to Siberia, or shot—largely disappeared as a means of political control. The political police, later called the Committee on State Security, or KGB, were active until the end (and maybe still are), but their methods were more refined and subtle than the *Cheka* of Lenin's tenure or the NKVD of Stalin's.

Some three-quarters of a million KGB agents were everywhere: guarding the borders; in factories, hotels, universities, keeping tabs on anyone who contacted foreign tourists, handled classi-fied materials, or dissented against the Soviet system. Millions of Soviet citizens had KGB dossiers, and some found out to their surprise the KGB was able to recite even trivial incidents that happened years earlier. Part-time informers, called *stukachi* (squealers), were everywhere.

While the political police lost the power to actually try most cases—which went to a regular court—they still had the power to frighten by selectively intimidating dissidents. Citizens could lose jobs, get sent to psychiatric clinics, be denied university entrance, have their rooms bugged, lose the right to live in a city, and generally be made uncomfortable by a word from the KGB.

The scariest problem was the ethnic tension that came out in the republics. Minorities that had lived in peace for generations (because the KGB was watching) became the target of nationalist resentment. In the Caucasus, blood flowed. Many politicians at the republic level played the nationalist card, and this easily turned into chauvinism. Their messages were simple and effective: Georgia for the Georgians, Uzbekistan for the Uzbeks, Armenia for the Armenians, even Russia for the Russians.

2. A Commonwealth of Independent States. Is anything left of the old Soviet Union? As it officially ceased to exist at the end of 1991, most of its component republics agreed to form a "Commonwealth of Independent States" (CIS), with headquarters in Minsk, Belarus. Conspicuously missing were the three Baltic republics and Georgia. Georgia was later forced to sign the CIS treaty. No one quite knows what the powers of the CIS are. Is it a pretend organization, a working trade bloc, or a Moscow plan to regain control over the other republics?

There are reasons for some republics wishing to retain ties with giant Russia. First, eight of the twelve CIS member republics are landlocked. A hostile relationship with Russia would mean difficulty in exporting their goods. Industrially, all are tied to the Russian economy for manufactured goods and petroleum. Financially, over the decades many of these republics benefited from major Soviet efforts to upgrade them.

3. A New Constitution. Along with voting for a new parliament, in late 1993 Russians also approved a new and completely different constitution, one with Western-type institutions, such as:

- A **strong presidency**, borrowed from France. The Russian president sets basic policy, names the prime minister and other top officials, and can veto bills and dissolve parliament. In many areas the president can simply rule by decree. The president can be

Boris Yeltsin: Another Weak Reformer?

Gorbachev was the first *prezident* (they use the loan word) of the Soviet Union. Boris Yeltsin was the first *prezident* of the Russian Federation. As with Gorbachev, both Russians and the world initially hailed Boris Yeltsin as the great reformer who would make a prosperous and peaceful Russia. Both disappointed, and within a few years, many observers wondered how much longer Yeltsin would be in office. In addition to his weakening political position, Yeltsin has health and drinking problems.

Born in 1931 (as was Gorbachev) near Sverdlovsk (now Yekaterinburg) in the southern Urals of a poor peasant family, Yeltsin studied engineering and worked in the housing industry in his home town. Joining the Party in 1961 at age 30, Yeltsin was promoted to the Central Committee in 1976. Yeltsin drew attention as an energetic manager and reformer, and Gorbachev elevated him to head the Moscow Party organization in 1985 and made him a candidate member of the Politburo. A natural populist, Yeltsin, unlike other Soviet leaders, mingled with the people and denounced the privileges of the *nomenklatura*. The common people rallied to him.

Then came a bizarre series of events which, if the Soviet system had not been collapsing, would have led to Yeltsin's permanent banishment if not imprisonment. In a 1987 speech to the Central Committee celebrating the Bolshevik Revolution, Yeltsin attacked Party conservatives by name for dragging their feet on reform. For that, he was relieved of his Party posts and demoted to a mid-level government job.

But he bounced back. In the first partly competitive election in 1989, he ran on his populist credentials and easily won election to parliament. Increasingly, Yeltsin criticized Gorbachev for dawdling on reforms. Shifting his attention to the Russian (as opposed to the *Soviet*) government, Yeltsin won election to the Russian parliament in 1990. Yeltsin sensed that the Soviet Union was doomed but that Russia would survive. In July 1990 Yeltsin pulled another surprise by resigning from the Party. Now he was free to be as critical as he wished. As a non-Communist, he won fair elections to become president of the Russian Federation in 1991. This gave him another edge on Gorbachev, who, Yeltsin pointed out, had never been popularly elected to anything.

In the attempted coup of 1991, Yeltsin turned himself into a hero, standing firm on a tank in front of the Russian parliament. Mocking Gorbachev as an indecisive weakling, Yeltsin pulled the Russian Federation out of the Soviet Union in late 1991, thus collapsing the entire structure. Conservatives think it was a terrible mistake to let the non-Russian republics go.

The trouble is, as Yeltsin found out, it's hard to reform something as big and obdurate as Russia. Economic plans don't work out, people panic at the thought of unemployment, officials sabotage reforms, and parliaments turn nasty and oppositionist. Like Gorbachev, he felt he had to compromise with the conservative forces who opposed him. This limited the pace and thoroughness of his reform effort.

elected for a maximum of two four-year terms. For various reasons, however, Yeltsin's power was offset by that of an antireformist parliament, and a great deal of responsibility devolved upon Yeltsin's prime minister, Viktor Chernomyrdin, who was cautious about reforms. It was rather like Yeltsin set up a Gaullist presidency but, before he could use it, stumbled into a "cohabitation" situation that diluted his presidential power.

- A **bicameral parliament**, like the U.S. or German. The lower house, the State Duma (reviving the old tsarist name), consists of 450 deputies elected for up to four years. (Because Yeltsin was first elected president in 1991, new presidential elections are due in 1995. They are thus out of kilter with parliamentary elections, which sometimes creates problems.) The Duma passes bills and approves the budget and confirms the president's nominees for top jobs. It can both impeach a president and

1993: The Second Coup That Failed

The 1991 attempted coup was carried out by members of Gorbachev's own executive branch and was stopped by members of the Russian (not Soviet) parliament in its White House some distance from the Kremlin. The October 1993 coup attempt was by conservative antidemocrats, only this time they occupied the White House and were crushed by armed forces under President Yeltsin, who was now in the Kremlin.

What triggered the 1993 attempt was Yeltsin's order to dissolve the Russian parliament and hold new elections. (The old *Soviet* Congress of Peoples Deputies had disappeared with the USSR at the end of 1991.) The Russian parliament had been elected in 1989 under the old regime when the CPSU still held sway; accordingly, a majority was cautious and conservative about reform. Yeltsin could no longer govern with this parliament, and indeed it was high time for free and fair parliamentary elections. But the old parliament didn't like being put out of business and claimed Yeltsin was turning dictatorial. A majority of deputies declared the dissolution illegal and holed up in the White House, hoping that the country and especially the army would side with it. They did not; instead, tanks shelled the White House until it caught fire.

Yeltsin won but he lost. New elections were held in December 1993, but by then so many Russians were disillusioned with reforms that brought crime, inflation, and unemployment that they voted in a parliament, now called the State Duma, that was heavily anti-reformist and anti-Yeltsin. Yeltsin had to dump his reformist ministers and pick as prime minister a man who represented the anti-reform reflexes of the managers of big state-owned industries. With the president once again at loggerheads with parliament, we may not have seen the last coup attempt in Russia.

vote no-confidence in a cabinet. The Duma, along with the upper house, can also override a presidential veto with a two-thirds majority. The upper house, the Federation Council, consists of two members elected locally from each of the eighty-nine constituent parts of the Russian Federation. Its duties are somewhat different than the Duma's. Only the Federation Council can change internal boundaries and ratify the use of armed forces abroad. It appoints the top judges and national prosecutor-general and can remove them.

- A **split electoral system**, borrowed from Germany. Half of the Duma's 450 seats are elected by proportional representation (with a 5-percent threshold), half by single-member districts with plurality win. This can be an excellent system, but Yeltsin's problem was that Russia's first freely elected bicameral legislature, chosen in late 1993, was anti-Yeltsin. Only a minority of its seats were occupied by pro-reform parties. The rest were either go-slow or go-backwards.

- A **constitutional court**, borrowed chiefly from the United States but with some French and German features. The Russian Constitutional Court has nineteen judges appointed by the president and confirmed by the upper house. These judges are supposed to be independent and cannot be fired. They may both act on citizens' complaints as well as on cases submitted by government agencies. The court makes sure all laws and decrees conform to the constitution. If this court operates as planned (that is, free of political control), it will be a great and essential step for the rule of law in Russia.

4. Many Parties Appear. From one strong Party, Russia has gone to many weak parties. At first Gorbachev wanted to keep the CPSU in its monopolistic position, but by 1990 he relented and competing parties were allowed. Gorbachev, angry at the CPSU leadership that supported the 1991 coup attempt, resigned as general secretary,

The Russian Elections of 1993: A Split System in Action

Of the thirteen parties that ran for the Duma in late 1993, here are the main ones that won seats and approximately where they stood on economic reforms that lead to a free market. The seats do not total 450 because elections in six single-member districts were declared illegal.

The outcome shows some serious problems with the party system. First, the party system is a mess, without one or two really big parties and with the balance of power in the Duma held by tiny parties and independents. Next, the five reformist parties together have only 139 seats and aid their enemies by fragmenting the reformist movement. They must merge; personality should not be allowed to get in the way. Third, Yeltsin portrayed himself as above the political fray and refused to sponsor or endorse a party. If Yeltsin is serious about reform, he must build a strong party. Individuals don't last, parties do.

And fourth, if the reformers don't get their act together, the anti-reformers and extreme nationalists will take over and build an authoritarian and aggressive Russia. The deceptively misnamed Liberal Democrats of Vladimir Zhirinovsky, widely held to be insane and a fascist, scored highest on the proportional-representation lists but poorly in the single-member districts. Some take that as a sign that it was a protest vote by people without firm commitment to any party. With a declining economy and parliament and president on opposite sides of the economic-reform issue, the situation is dangerous.

PARTY	STOOD FOR	%VOTES	PR SEATS	DISTRICT WINS	TOTAL SEATS
Russia's Choice	reform	15.4%	40	30	70
Liberal Democrats	fascism	22.8	59	5	64
Communists	anti-reform	12.4	32	16	48
Agrarian	anti-reform	7.9	21	12	33
Yabloko	reform	7.8	20	3	23
Democrats	undecided	5.5	14	-	14
Civic Union	anti-reform	1.9	-	1	1
Dignity & Charity	anti-reform	0.7	-	2	2
Unity & Accord	mild reform	6.8	18	1	19
Women of Russia	reform	8.1	21	2	23
Mov. for Dem. Ref.	reform	4.1	-	4	4
others & ind.	-	-	-	143	143

disbanded the Central Committee, and turned over the Party's plentiful assets to republic authorities. Lenin's once-mighty "organizational weapon" was crushed low.

But what will take its place? New political parties appeared, but they are weak, divided, poorly organized, and constantly changing. And not all these parties are "democratic" in our sense of the word; many preach chauvinism or a return to communism. Political parties are perhaps the foundation in the modern world of political stability. A system with too many parties, some of them extremist, is likely headed toward violence. A system of two large parties, with only moderate differences between them, can calm and stabilize political life and let citizens get on with rebuilding their lives and their country. More than anything else, the establishment of a moderate party system will be the make-or-break of post-Communist Russia.

The Persistence of Pattern

Once laid down, a country's institutions develop considerable staying power. People get used to them. Elites depend on them for their jobs and perquisites. They may not like the institutions and may recognize that they are defective. But they often fear throwing them out and starting from scratch. That is why great reforms, in Russia and elsewhere, often end up resembling the previous system. Several tsars attempted to reform their system, but they usually ended up as bitter reactionaries when the old system refused to follow their benign designs. Khrushchev attempted to reform the system; instead he was ousted by it. The problem is how to change a seriously defective system without it blowing up, akin to taking the lid off a hot pressure cooker.

As soon as Gorbachev began to liberalize, the lid on the pressure cooker began to blow off. Gorbachev found himself resisting powerful forces for change, forces that he had unleashed. By 1991, most thinking Soviets found Gorbachev irrelevant. He had waffled and hesitated too long on serious economic reform. Yeltsin attempted major economic reform but the system resisted, and Yeltsin soon replaced his reformist ministers. By 1994, most thinking Russians found Yeltsin irrelevant. It has been said that revolution is easy; reform is hard.

Vocabulary Building

apparatchik	*nomenklatura*
Central Committee	Party Congress
Congress of People's Deputies	Politburo
Council of Ministers	Presidium
general secretary	republic
Gosplan	Secretariat
KGB	Supreme Soviet
Kremlin	system change
nationalities question	

Further Reference

ARBATOV, GEORGI. *The System: An Insider's Life in Soviet Politics.* New York: Random House, 1992.

BARRY, DONALD D., and CAROL BARNER-BARRY. *Contemporary Soviet Politics,* 4th ed. Englewood Cliffs, NJ: Prentice Hall, 1991.

DODER, DUSKO, and LOUISE BRANSON. *Gorbachev: Heretic in the Kremlin.* New York: Vintage Books, 1990.

KNIGHT, AMY W. *The KGB: Police and Politics in the Soviet Union.* Winchester, MA: Allen & Unwin, 1988.

LITTLE, D. RICHARD. *Governing the Soviet Union.* White Plains, NY: Longman, 1989.

MCAULEY, MARY. *Soviet Politics, 1917–1991.* New York: Oxford University Press, 1992.

MEDISH, VADIM. *The Soviet Union,* 4th ed. Englewood Cliffs, NJ: Prentice Hall, 1991.

MLYNAR, ZDENEK. *Can Gorbachev Change the Soviet Union? The International Dimensions of Political Reform.* Boulder, CO: Westview, 1990.

SAKWA, RICHARD. *Gorbachev and His Reforms.* Englewood Cliffs, NJ: Prentice Hall, 1991.

SHARLET, ROBERT. *The New Soviet Constitution of 1977: Analysis and Text.* Brunswick, OH: King's Court Communications, 1978.

TOLZ, VERA. *The USSR's Emerging Multiparty System.* Westport, CT: Praeger, 1990.

ZEMTSOV, ILYA, and JOHN FARRAR. *Gorbachev: The Man and the System.* New Brunswick, NJ: Transaction, 1989.

19
Russian Political Attitudes

On my first visit to Russia—then the Soviet Union—in 1973 I met a Moscow student and had several good conversations with him. Russians love conversation and place great store in heart-to-heart (*po dusham*, "speaking with the soul") talks. He confided in me: "You should not want the Communist regime to collapse here." Oh? Why not? "Because just below the surface we have the world's greatest gangsters—they put your mafiosi to shame—and without our tough controls soon our gangsters would take over the country and make more troubles for you than the Communists ever did."

I thought my Russian friend was exaggerating and being facetious. I now realize he was speaking the literal truth. The collapse of the Communist regime has unleashed not stable democracy and free-market prosperity but monumental lawlessness and disorder. Mafia gangs are into everything, possibly even nuclear arms sales. The breakdown demonstrates what some scholars long suspected, that under the law-and-order surface of Soviet rule Russian society was very weak—indeed, it had been made deliberately weak—and could not sustain a free democracy, at least not for some time.

The Russian Difference

In Central Europe, Communist regimes were discarded in 1989, and within five years Poland, the Czech Republic, and Hungary were functioning democracies with growing, mostly private, market economies. At about the same time, the Soviet Union, trying to make the same transition, collapsed both economically and politically and then its largest successor state, the Russian Federation, threatened to do the same. Why the difference?

Huntington's "Civilizational" Divide in Europe

In an influential but controversial article in the Summer 1993 *Foreign Affairs*, Harvard political scientist Samuel P. Huntington argued that with the Cold War over, profound differences of culture were dividing the world into several "civilizations" that have trouble understanding each other. What Huntington called "civilizations" mostly follow religious lines: the West European (with its North American branch), the Slavic/Orthodox, Muslim, Hindu, Confucian, Japanese, and Latin American. In Europe, said Huntington, the key dividing line is still where Eastern Orthodoxy meets Roman Catholicism, roughly a line running south from the Baltic republics along the eastern borders of Poland, Slovakia, Hungary, and Croatia. West European civilization, especially after Protestantism, led the way to the establishment of democracy and capitalism. The Catholic countries of Europe followed, some only in our century. Poland and Hungary, for example, turned quickly to market systems and democracy after ousting their Communist regimes in 1989.

But notice the difficulty experienced by Slavic/Orthodox countries such as Russia, Ukraine, Serbia, and Romania in making this transition. Basic assumptions about individual freedom and choice, private property, personal rights, and the rule of law that are widespread in West Europe are much weaker in Slavic/Orthodox Europe. One key point: Orthodox culture is much less individualistic, and this helps account for economic behavior. Economic "shock therapy" (the sudden introduction of a free market) soon brought rapid growth to Poland. Applied in Russia, it simply collapsed the economy: "shock without therapy." Many observers suggest the differences between Poland and Russia are cultural, that Poland has always faced west and Russia not. Huntington's theory does not mean that other civilizations cannot become free-market democracies, just that it may take some time.

First, there are some very basic cultural differences between the Roman Catholic countries of Central Europe and Eastern Orthodox Russia (see box). Second, the Communists succeeded in capturing Russian nationalism, so that a Russian could take a certain pride in communism. For Central Europeans, communism was put and kept in place by Soviet bayonets and was profoundly at odds with local nationalism. A Polish or Hungarian nationalist is almost automatically an anti-Communist.

Perhaps more basically, communism had been implanted in Central Europe much later (after World War II) than in the Soviet Union; it didn't have as much time to take hold. Russians had nearly three-quarters of a century of Communist rule (1917–91), enough for three generations to know only one system. Further, the previous tsarist system had not been democratic either, and was just in the early stages of capitalist economic development.

The system Russians had gotten used to provided them with jobs (constitutionally guaranteed) and a low but generally predictable standard of living. An apartment, once you got one, was tacky by Western standards but cost only a few dollars a month. Few Russians worked hard; there was little point to it. Now, suddenly, Russians are told their jobs are not guaranteed and that reward is linked to individual achievement.

The result has been psychological disorientation and fear. The economy declines, inflation erodes earnings, unemployment increases, and parents worry over how to feed their children. The old legitimacy of Party and leadership has collapsed, and nothing has taken its place. First Gorbachev and then Yeltsin lost their early credibility; they had indecisively zigged and zagged so long on the economy that few saw them as leaders. Marxism-Leninism, long moribund, is dead.

In the vacuum of belief, cynicism and despair reign. While some Russians have rediscovered their Orthodox Church, many believe in nothing and say everything is going wrong. But people have to believe in something; cynicism cannot sustain a society. Western values of a free society, of morality rooted in religion, of civil rights, and of individual achievement in a market economy, are talked about by some intellectuals but not widely held. Seven decades of Communist rule have stomped them out; they will have to be painfully relearned.

The Mask of Legitimacy

For decades, the CPSU tried to pound into Soviet skulls the feeling that the regime was legitimate—that is, it had the right to rule—and was leading the country through the difficulties of "building socialism" to the working utopia of communism. It is impossible to say how many really believed this. At various times, many did. Foreigners were treated to performances of marchers, youth delegations, and seemingly frank conversations with officials that were designed to show that most Soviets believed in the system. In private, Western journalists were sometimes able to establish contacts who told them otherwise: dissident intellectuals, bitter workers, and even Party members who had come to doubt the worth of the system.

With Gorbachev's experiment with relative freedom of expression in the late 1980s, *glasnost* (media openness), torrents of criticism poured out. Freed from fear of the police, citizens bitterly criticized the bureaucracy, the Party, and the corruption of both. The mask of Soviet legitimacy slipped away to reveal a system that satisfied few. The trouble was that there was no consensus on what should replace it. The broad masses (Russian: *narod*) generally wanted a cleaned-up socialism that guaranteed everyone a good standard of living. They showed little understanding of democracy or a market system. Many of the better-educated, on the other hand, understood that socialism was defective and should be scrapped in favor of free politics and free economics. Those whose jobs depended on the old system saw change as a threat. And many Russians simply didn't know what to think. They had never before been asked for their opinions.

In defensive fear, some Russians retreat into Russian nationalism, a powerful impulse long manipulated by the Communists. They feel humiliated by the collapse of the mighty Soviet Empire, which, after all, was their empire. They used to count for something; now they count for nothing. They used to be the equals of the Americans; now the arrogant American capitalists sneer at Russia. Indeed, it was they who craftily engineered the fall of the Soviet Empire and the collapse of the Soviet Union. Now they are getting ready to move in for the kill: the destruction of Russia. This is all terribly untrue—the Soviet system collapsed from its own (chiefly economic) weaknesses—but many Russians believe it was an American plot. These are the kind of Russians who vote for extremist parties and would gladly support a strong-handed leader.

Alexander Solzhenitsyn: Russian Mysticism

In 1963 a short, grim novel, *One Day in the Life of Ivan Denisovich*, burst on the Soviet literary scene like a bombshell. In detailing the horrors of Siberian forced labor, its author spoke from intimate experience: Alexander Solzhenitsyn had lived in such a camp from 1945 to 1953 and then in Siberian exile for another three years. His crime: as an artillery captain he criticized Stalin in a letter to a friend.

But the nightmare conditions did not break Solzhenitsyn; on the contrary, they made him stronger. Freed during Khrushchev's brief period of liberalization, Solzhenitsyn resolved to tell the whole story of Soviet repression through novels and nonfiction. But *One Day* was about as much of the truth as the regime was prepared to allow—and that was under the unusual circumstances of Khrushchev's destalinization drive—and Solzhenitsyn soon found himself expelled from the official writers' union and unable to publish.

Smuggled to the West, though, his works found a growing audience. Solzhenitsyn has a boundless love for Russia and long believed that communism was a temporary mistake—imported from the West—that could be cured. In the classic mold of the nineteenth-century Slavophiles, Solzhenitsyn wrote a long letter to the Kremlin's rulers urging them to abandon communism, world empire, heavy industry, and domination over non-Slavic nationalities and to return to the Orthodox faith, a simple agricultural life, and the tremendous spiritual roots of old Russia.

In 1973 his monumental *Gulag Archipelago* was released in Paris. A massive compilation of the reports of 227 other camp survivors, *Gulag* (the central prisons administration) showed that capricious terror was part and parcel of the Soviet system, that by the 1940s there were from 12 to 15 million people in the Gulag at any one time, and that most had committed no crime. That was the last straw for Soviet authorities, who bundled Solzhenitsyn onto a plane in 1974 and didn't let him back.

Solzhenitsyn is not merely anti-Communist. He hates anything Western: rationality, technology, materialism, legalism, even personal freedom (which, he holds, has degenerated into license). He was not particularly impressed by the United States and lived as a recluse on a Vermont estate. At the 1978 Harvard commencement he thundered:

> Should someone ask me whether I would indicate the West such as it is today as a model to my country, frankly I would have to answer negatively. Through intense suffering our country [Russia] has now achieved a spiritual development of such intensity that the Western system in its present state of spiritual exhaustion does not look attractive. After the suffering of decades of violence and oppression, the human soul longs for things higher, warmer and purer than those offered by today's mass living habits, introduced by the revolting invasion of publicity, by TV stupor, and by intolerable music.

Although Solzhenitsyn became a U.S. citizen, he never became culturally American. Instead, he returned to Russia in 1994 with his mystical Russian nationalism. I suspect he will not find much "intense spiritual development" there and may decide that Cavendish, Vermont, is not so bad after all.

The Illusion of Ideology

Some textbooks on the Soviet Union used to pay considerable attention to Marxism-Leninism, the ideology of communism. Ideology has counted for little in the Soviet Union for many years; with *glasnost* it disappeared from sight. Much of Soviet "ideology" was little more than Russian national pride masking feelings of inferiority. Marxism, by predicting the collapse of the capitalist West, tried to reassure Russians that they would eventually emerge superior. They were "building socialism," which at a certain point would surpass the United States and turn into a Communist utopia with no social or economic problems. In earlier years some Soviets halfway believed it, but many American academics went way overboard in supposing that ideology was the basis of the Soviet system.

Actually, young people joined the Party out of self-interest: to get into universities, to win job promotion, to become military or civilian officials. Most were cynical and cared nothing for Marxism-Leninism. They were motivated by careers, not ideology.

Marxism is basically a method of analysis, one that stresses social classes and their conflicts. As such, it stayed far livelier in the West, where it faced constant argument and challenge. In the Soviet Union, it atrophied. Applying this tool of analysis to Soviet society was the last thing the *apparat* wanted, as it would have revealed a pampered Party elite lording it over a wretched proletariat. Soviet Marxists thus focused on the West and cranked out the standard clichés, such as the "sharpening of contradictions" and "increasing tempo and magnitude of crises." They were getting ready for the West to collapse at any minute. After some decades, no one believed this drivel. Soviet students shuffled off to required classes on Marxism-Leninism with the enthusiasm of American students going to compulsory chapel.

The constant mouthing of a doctrine no one believed in created a climate of cynicism, hypocrisy, and opportunism. With the collapse of the Soviet system, Marxism-Leninism collapsed like the house of cards it always was. Marxist ideology was always a defective foundation, but what kind of society can they build with no foundation?

The Rediscovery of Civil Society

Some analysts hold that the crux of the Soviet system was the stomping out of society by the state. Nothing was to be autonomous; everything in society was to be under strict state supervision. There were to be no independent enterprises, churches, associations, clubs, educational institutions, or morality. State power, in turn supervised by the Party, ran amok. The Communist system partly succeeded and now that it has collapsed, it has left a kind of vacuum where there should be society. Some thinkers argue Russia must urgently reconstruct the "civil society" that the Soviet state tried to stomp out.

The concept of civil society starts with the notion that state and society are two different things, although they clearly influence each other. Society over time evolves informal manners, usages, and customs that make living together possible. The "civil" (as in civilized) indicates a reasonable level of politeness, public spirit, and willingness to compromise. A civil society through parents, churches, and schools "socializes" its members to right behavior and "rules of the game" that continue even when the state, through its police and bureaucrats, is not watching.

The state, the formal institutional structures that wield power, cannot substitute or replace civil society, although the Communists tried. Attempting such a substitution creates a system where people lack basic civility and see no need to play by informal rules of the game. Politicians attack each other hysterically, immoderately, with no possibility of compromise; they have never learned restraint. Citizens feel little need to obey the law if they can get away with breaking it; legitimacy is terribly weak. Mafia gangs muscle into all sectors of the economy.

HOW TO BUILD A CIVIL SOCIETY

 The Philosophical Gap

One of the key differences between us and the Russians is philosophical; namely, we are the children of John Locke and they are not. Although few Americans study the philosopher who is at the root of much of our thinking, most have assimilated what the seventeenth-century English thinker had to say: people are rational and reasonable; they have a natural right to life, liberty, and property; and government is good if it preserves these rights and bad if it infringes on them. If this sounds like the Declaration of Independence, it is; Jefferson was an ardent Lockean, as were most of the Founding Fathers. Ever since, Americans have taken to Locke like a duck takes to water; we love his common-sense emphasis on small government and individuals working for the good of themselves and their families. To Russians, this is not common sense.

Russian thought comes out almost the opposite of Locke and traces back to the geographical dilemma of living on an defenseless plain: either build a strong state or perish. Plugging into the Russian tradition of a strong state is Jean-Jacques Rousseau (see page 87), the radical eighteenth-century French thinker whose theory of the "general will" rejected Lockean individualism in favor of using state power to "force men to be free." With Locke, people form society, and then society sets up a state, all with an eye to preserving property. With Rousseau, the flow goes the other way: the state, guided by the general will, molds society and then redoes individuals. Marxists added a class-struggle gloss to this; Lenin bought the package and then sold it to the Russian people.

Many Americans thought that once communism was overthrown, the Russians would rapidly become like us: capitalist entrepreneurs and moderate democrats. This neglected the centuries of philosophical argument that we have built up that is utterly lacking in Russia. If there is to be a Peace Corps in Russia, the teaching of the philosophical basis of markets, pluralism, and limited government might be one of its first and most urgent tasks. Without a new philosophical outlook, one taken mostly from the West, the Russians will likely stay trapped in their statist frame of mind. (For more on statism, see chapter 28 on Brazil.)

The West has had centuries to build up its civil societies. Philosophers such as Hobbes and Locke explained rationally why civil society is necessary. Churches, often with threats of eternal damnation, inculcated right behavior. The market system generated usages aimed at keeping dealings fair and predictable. Legal systems enforced this with a system of contracts, both written and unwritten. All of this has been missing in Russia since the 1917 Revolution. Americans failed to notice that civil society is the basis of their system; they thought the sudden imposition of democracy and a market economy in Russia would bring quickly bring the customs of civil society. We now see that without the philosophical, moral, economic, and legal understandings of civil society, Russia could revert to authoritarianism. One key question for Russia, then, is how quickly can a civil society be built.

Natural Egalitarians?

Marxism-Leninism may have vanished in Russia, but many Russians display a sort of crude, inborn tendency toward extreme equality, a natural socialism. Russians resent

HOW TO BUILD A CIVIL SOCIETY

 ## *The Moral Gap*

America has its share of crooks and criminals, but what would America be like if one could go back over three generations and systematically strip out all moral teachings? What if parents, churches, and schools did not attempt to inculcate a sense of innate right and wrong in young people? The result, I suspect, would be rather like Russia today. This is another area we overlooked in thinking that once communism was thrown out, Russians would quickly become like us.

Russians had some ethical training, but it was relativistic, superficial, and based on Marxist theories of social class. That which helps the working class is good, went the litany. The Communist Party helps the working class, so it must be good. The Soviet state is totally devoted to the working class, so it must be very good. The Party and the state must therefore be obeyed, respected, and defended. Anyone who goes against them is insane, a wrecker, or a spy. Crime is something that happens only in capitalist countries, where the poor are forced to steal. Private property is inherently wicked, because it has been stolen from the workers who produced it. Under communism, there were no moral absolutes.

Rhetoric aside, Russians soon learned to treat the system with cynicism. With no individual responsibility, stealing, especially from the state, was okay. After all, it really didn't belong to anyone. Under communism, monstrous rip-offs became standard: everyone stole. When Party and Soviet state collapsed, there were essentially no moral guidelines and little to fill the void. The crime rate shot into outer space. Since Soviets had always been taught that capitalists and *biznesmeny* (long a term of derision, now adopted as a loan word) were crooks and their gains were ill-gotten, many Russians went into business with that image as their norm. Russia's massive protection rackets, backed up by professional killers, were all right because they were just stealing from capitalist thieves.

What escaped both Russians and Americans is that a modern capitalist culture has a considerable moral basis; otherwise it can't work. It draws from religious and ethical teachings, legal enforcement, and most of all from the knowledge that cheating businesses don't get repeat customers. It may take a long time to build up this moral consensus. We made the mistake of thinking it would automatically arrive with the free market, which we take to be generally self-policing. (If you get cheated, you won't come back.) For most Russians, a free market means legal cheating. For capitalism to work right in Russia, the moral gap must be filled.

differences of wealth or income and enviously try to bring the better-off down to their level. Some observers argue that the Russian peasantry, who for centuries tilled the soil in common and shared the harvest, developed highly egalitarian attitudes which they brought with them into Soviet and now post-Soviet life. Perhaps so, but attitudes are not genetic; they are learned and can be unlearned, given the right conditions. Until new attitudes are learned, however, the old ones can trip up the best-laid plans of reformers.

Americans also favor equality, but it's "equality of opportunity": everyone has a chance; the results are up to you. An American who gets ahead is usually applauded for his or her ability and hard work. Most Russians do not understand this kind of equality; they expect "equality of result," with each person collecting the same rewards. Those who get ahead are presumed to have cheated, exploited, or bribed. American attitudes of individual work and achievement lend themselves to capitalism; Russian attitudes generally do not. How to remake Russian attitudes away from envious egalitarianism is a gigantic task.

Russian Racism

With *glasnost*, hate-filled attitudes latent among Soviet nationalities came into the open, attitudes so strong as to be racist. Under Soviet law, every citizen had their nationality stamped in their internal passports, and, contrary to U.S. usage, nationality throughout East Europe and the ex-Soviet Union does not equal citizenship. That is, one can be a Russian citizen of the Komi nationality. This approach is asking for trouble, because it encourages people to demand an independent state. Educated Russians admire the U.S. approach which prohibits the official identification of citizens by race or national origin.

And Russians tend to pigeonhole everyone on the basis of their nationality. Some nationalities are acceptable, others despised. Russians, for example, respect the Baltic peoples as European, civilized, and "cultured." On the other hand, Russians speak scathingly of the Muslim-Turkic peoples of Central Asia as lawless and corrupt mafiosi (the loan word "mafia" is much used in the Soviet Union) who do nothing but make babies. The theme of the differential birthrate comes up often. Russian families nowadays rarely have more than two children; one is the norm. Muslim families have many children, sometimes eight or more. Some Russians fear that their stagnant numbers will be swamped by a rising tide of "inferior" peoples. They do not recognize it as such, but this is a racist attitude.

The non-Russian nationalities feel little affection or affinity for the Russians. In Central Asia, several republics have made their local language the only official language. Educated Uzbeks, for example, know Russian perfectly, but now they speak only Uzbek as a way of making ethnic Russians feel unwelcome. Many Russians are getting the message and leaving Central Asia. Virtually none have fled from the Baltic republics, however, and some Russians there even support independence. They feel they would be treated fairly by the cultured Balts. They fear the Muslims of Central Asia.

The highly charged ethnic tensions have led some to compare the present situation to the Time of Troubles in the early seventeenth century. Others use the

---

 ## *A Genie Grants Three Wishes*

In an old Russian joke, a genie, released from a bottle, grants one wish each to an Englishman, a Frenchman, and a Russian. The Englishman wishes for a cottage by the sea. The Frenchman wishes for a vineyard and a couple of mistresses. The Russian, a peasant, tells the genie: "My neighbor has a goat. I have no goat. Kill my neighbor's goat." With people like that, how are you going to build free-market capitalism?

phrase "Weimar Russia" to suggest a coming fascism. Anti-Semitism, a barometer of societal breakdown, is on the rise. Russian nationalists charge that behind all the troubles are Jews, a sinister international conspiracy called "Zionism." Some Russian nationalists turned fascistic; one group even wears black shirts, just like Mussolini's followers. Jews have received anonymous death threats, stampeding tens of thousands of them to Israel.

Can a Democratic Political Culture Be Learned?

Sure. How else did Germans and Spaniards become democrats? How else did you acquire your democratic culture? (There is an element of tautology here: culture by definition is any learned behavior.) The question for Russia is can it be learned before the system slides back into some sort of authoritarianism? All manner of undemocratic people are itching to take over and "restore order": generals, factory managers, Party *apparatchiki*, fascists, and gangsters. A coalition-from-hell of all of the above is conceivable.

We now realize that in the early 1990s, when Communist rule cracked and then collapsed, we were expecting too much. We paid insufficient attention to crucial factors of political culture and assumed that capitalism and democracy bring their own political culture with them. They do, but it takes a long time, and Russia doesn't have much time. Thrust onto an unprepared population, democracy and capitalism have not yet taken root in Russia, and their chances for success are unclear. The Weimar analogy is appropriate: Germans, especially under conditions of extreme economic distress, were unenthusiastic about democracy.

If Russia returns to authoritarianism, we need not despair. The right authoritarian ruler can lay the groundwork (perhaps unwittingly) for future democ-

HOW TO BUILD A CIVIL SOCIETY

 ## *The Legal Gap*

The rule of law is weak in Russia, in part because Soviet law paid minimal attention to property. Any big property (land, factories) automatically belonged to the state, and stealing state property could be harshly punished as a form of treason. The Lockean notion that property is a natural right of individuals and a basis for human freedom was rejected out of hand. Russians, having been inculcated with the Marxist notion that "all property is theft," have trouble grasping the democratic and capitalist notion that "private property means personal freedom."

Weak or absent in the old Soviet socialist legal code, which Russia inherited, are such basics of the Common Law as ownership, contracts, torts, and bankruptcy. If you set up a business in the United States, Canada, or West Europe, you are reasonably confident your property and earnings will not be taken from you. In Russia, you have no such confidence. Not only are there no laws on the books in these areas, there is no legal culture built up over the years that regards these areas as sacred. One result is that foreigners and Russians alike are reluctant to invest in Russia. The climate is literally lawless, and they may lose everything. Russian law institutes are attempting to import Western legal concepts quickly, for they understand that the present uncertain situation stunts Russian economic growth.

HOW TO BUILD A CIVIL SOCIETY

 The Economics Gap

In addition to the philosophical and moral foundations of a civil society, another basic point has been overlooked in the eager assumption that Russians would quickly become like us: people have to learn capitalism. A market economy may be something that occurs naturally (whenever buyers and sellers meet), but it is not understood naturally. You have to take courses in market economics and read books and articles about it. Soviet universities covered "bourgeois economics" as part of the history of economic thought but gave it short shrift as a doomed system riven with contradictions, unfairness, and depressions. When their system collapsed, only a minority of Russian economists had a decent grasp of what makes market economies work.

Especially missing was any appreciation of how money plays an autonomous role in the economy. In Communist countries, there simply was no theory of money. For example, I have tried the following mental experiment on a seminar of U.S.,

Central European, and Russian colonels, all mature and well-educated. Imagine, I tell them, a miniature country with ten citizens, each of whom works in one hamburger shop. The ten workers make a total of ten hamburgers a day and each is paid $1 a day. Then each buys one hamburger a day with their $1. The government of this country decides to be nice to its citizens, so it raises the pay of each to $2 a day (by printing an extra ten $1 bills). The output of the workers is still ten hamburgers a day. Within a day or two, what is the price of a hamburger?

The Americans respond fast and almost instinctively: $2! The East Europeans and Russians don't get it. "You haven't given us enough data," they say. Well, how would you explain it to them? It's not so simple. Phrases like "supply and demand" by themselves don't explain much. What we accept as basic and self-evident, Russians do not. (By the way, once you can really explain the parable, you've got a rudimentary theory of money.)

racy. Franco in Spain and Pinochet in Chile, by creating conditions for economic prosperity and a large middle class, put their countries on the path to democracy. In time and with economic growth, Russia too may develop democratic attitudes.

Vocabulary Building

Balts	contagion	*Gulag*
coercion	destalinization	ideology
collective	equality of result	secular
communism	genetic	xenophobia
consular convention	*glasnost*	

Further Reference

BENN, DAVID WEDGEWOOD. *Persuasion and Soviet Politics.* Cambridge, MA: Basil Blackwell, 1989.

BILLINGTON, JAMES H. *Russia Transformed: Breakthrough to Hope, Moscow, August 1991.* New York: The Free Press, 1992.

CARLISLE, OLGA ANDREYEV. *Under a New Sky: A Reunion with Russia.* New York: Ticknor & Fields, 1993.

CARTER, STEPHEN K. *Russian Nationalism: Yesterday, Today, Tomorrow.* New York: St. Martin's, 1990.

GERNER, KRISTIAN, and STEFAN HEDLUND. *Ideology and Rationality in the Soviet Model: a Legacy for Gorbachev.* New York: Routledge, 1989.

HELLER, MIKHAIL. *Cogs in the Wheel: The Formation of Soviet Man.* New York: Knopf, 1988.

HOCHSCHILD, ADAM. *The Unquiet Ghost: Russians Remember Stalin.* New York: Viking, 1994.

KOTKIN, STEPHEN. *Steeltown, USSR: Soviet Society in the Gorbachev Era.* Berkeley: University of California Press, 1991.

LANE, DAVID. *Soviet Society under Perestroika.* Winchester, MA: Unwin Hyman, 1990.

MILLER, WILLIAM GREEN, ed. *Toward a More Civil Society?: The USSR under Michail Sergeevich Gorbachev: An Assessment by the American Committee on U.S.–Soviet Relations.* Scranton, PA: Ballinger, 1989.

SMITH, HEDRICK. *The New Russians.* New York: Random House, 1990.

SOLZHENITSYN, ALEXANDER. *One Day in the Life of Ivan Denisovich.* New York: Praeger, 1963.

———. *The Gulag Archipelago,* vols. 1–3. New York: Harper & Row, 1979.

SUNY, RONALD GRIGOR. *The Revenge of the Past: Nationalism, Revolution, and the Collapse of the Soviet Union.* Palo Alto, CA: Stanford University Press, 1994.

TARASULO, ISAAC J., ed. *Gorbachev and Glasnost: Viewpoints from the Soviet Press.* Wilmington, DE: Scholarly Resources, 1989.

THOMPSON, TERRY L. *Ideology and Policy: The Political Uses of Doctrine in the Soviet Union.* Boulder, CO: Westview, 1989.

20

Russia: Patterns of Interaction

It is the thesis of this chapter that post-Communist Russian politics reflects and to some extent continues Soviet and even earlier patterns. What we are watching today is not completely new. It is, rather, a very old pattern—going back to tsarist times—of a system that cries out for reform but contains so many conservative forces that they are able and happy to block reform. A hundred years ago educated Russians could recognize the problem: How to reform the unreformable system? Many have tried; Khrushchev, for example.

Reformers versus Conservatives

The trouble with Russia is that there are few rules or institutions to regulate and moderate political clashes. Without experience in multiparty competition, a free press, voluntary associations, tolerance, and simple politeness, the new forces freed by the ending of Party control started to play a new game without knowing the rules. Their clashes were bound to be tumultuous, and they were made worse by bureaucrats who had every interest to sabotage the reform process. Fearful of losing their power, positions, and comfortable livings, they fought change and tried to reverse it.

Earlier editions of this book argued that under the uniform surface of political life in the old Soviet Union, one could detect a permanent tug-of-war between liberals and conservatives, the former for major change in a generally westward direction, the latter for standing pat with the essentially Stalinist structure. It is here argued that this conflict continues in the post-Soviet era, but now it's out in the open.

The reformers who rallied under Gorbachev and then transferred their loyalties to Yeltsin have largely resigned or been dismissed from high office. In many respects they hearken back to the Russian Westernizers of the nineteenth century, who wanted to import Western ways nearly wholesale: a market economy, free democracy, and individualistic philosophy. This led them to attempt the economic "shock therapy" recommended by Harvard economist Jeffrey Sacks, which earlier worked in Bolivia and Poland. The initial stages of such therapy are terribly painful, and the Russian economy plunged the economy downward. (See next chapter.)

What we are calling here "conservatives" covers a broad swath from moderates to extremists. What they have in common is their opposition to shock therapy or anything like it. Russia may need reforms, some concede, but they must be *our* reforms tailored to *our* conditions. Some old-line Party types would go all or much of the way back to a centralized command economy. Like the old Russophiles of the nineteenth century, they reject Western models and would turn inward, to Russia's roots; accordingly, they are nationalistic, some rabidly so.

With some oversimplification, we could compare their attitudes side-by-side:

Liberals	Conservatives
reform	antireform
market	central controls
anti-inflation	soft on inflation
soft on unemployment	anti-unemployment
anti-subsidies	pro-subsidies
intellectuals	*apparatchiks*
younger	older
pro-Yeltsin	pro-parliament
pro-Western	anti-West nationalists

Appearances can be deceptive, especially when the news media characterizes someone they don't like as a conservative. Some people you might suppose are conservatives turn out to be pretty good reformers; they just go about it with a different style. The reforms initiated in 1992 and 1993 largely continued under the alleged "conservative" Prime Minister Chernomyrdin.

President versus Parliament

For most of the post-Communist period, there has been no clear boundary between the executive and the legislative in Moscow, and their competing claims to power have led to violence. The initial problem, as noted earlier, was the carryover from Soviet times of a Russian parliament elected under the old rules and under the Communists in 1989. Most members of this parliament stood firm with Yeltsin during the abortive coup of 1991, including former Colonel Alexander Rutskoi.

But then Yeltsin began to gather more power into the office of the presidency. The Russian parliament reacted, claiming that Yeltsin was showing dictatorial tendencies. More to the point, they disliked seeing their own power and perquisites diminished. Some deputies who had earlier counted themselves as reformers began to discover the negative side of reforms and to slide into the conservative camp. To make clear who was in charge, in 1993 Yeltsin sponsored and won a referendum that endorsed both reform and the power of the presidency. Later that year, he pushed through a new constitution with seemingly Gaullist presidential pow-

Nikita Khrushchev: The First Reformer

Faced with a Soviet Union that had petrified under Stalin, Nikita Khrushchev attempted to revitalize the system and get it moving down the road to communism again. He was only partly and briefly successful, for wide areas of the Soviet Party and bureaucracy resisted him. We now realize that Khrushchev was far from the undisputed master of the Kremlin, the way Stalin was, and that he in fact had to overcome many conflicting forces. Like Gorbachev, he failed.

Born in 1894 of an ethnic Russian family living in Ukraine, Khrushchev joined the Bolsheviks shortly after the Revolution and worked his way up through Party jobs. A protégé of Stalin, Khrushchev did some of the dictator's dirty work in the 1930s, which earned him a full Politburo membership in 1939. During the war he was made a political general and sent to the Ukrainian front. After the war he organized Party work in Ukraine and then the Moscow region, and carefully packed the Party leadership with his supporters, the key to success in Soviet politics.

Stalin's death in 1953 opened a period of jockeying for power. All the Politburo was aware that Stalin had been a monster; they longed for stability and personal security. Accordingly, one of their first steps was to have the head of the secret police, Lavrenti Beria (like Stalin, a Georgian), arrested and shot. This effectively put the KGB under Party control. At first, the premier was Georgi Malenkov, who advocated relaxing the Stalin system and producing more consumer goods. But Khrushchev was made Party first secretary, a post that was always more powerful.

Khrushchev, who later adopted Malenkov's policies, craftily built a coalition against him. Malenkov was depicted as weak, nothing more than a "clerk," and was deposed in 1955. But it was not a Stalin-Trotsky type of struggle; Khrushchev merely had Malenkov demoted to minister for power stations. The Soviet leadership seems to have agreed that violent death is no way to run a political system; after all, anybody might be the next loser.

To consolidate his power, Khrushchev resorted to perhaps the most dramatic incident in CPSU's history: he denounced Stalin to a Party congress. Khrushchev did this not so much to set the record straight or to clear his conscience but rather to trounce his enemies within the Party. A Party that was still Stalinist was immobile, incapable of reform or innovation. The productive potential of the Soviet Union lay under a blanket of fear and routine. To storm through, Khrushchev chose the direct route: get rid of the symbol of the whole system, Stalin.

At the Twentieth Party Congress in February 1956, Khrushchev delivered a stinging, hours-long tirade against the "crimes of Stalin," who, he said, had murdered thousands of Party comrades and top military officers. Khrushchev neglected to mention his own role in the purges or the *millions* of non-Party people killed. The problem, claimed Khrushchev, was that Stalin had built a "cult of personality," something that must never be allowed again. The supposedly "secret" speech did have dramatic impact but not precisely in the intended way. Communist parties the world over had based themselves on Stalin-worship, and when the speech leaked out, all hell broke loose. A Hungarian uprising was crushed by Soviet tanks; a similar insurrection nearly happened in Poland. In the West, many long-time Communists resigned from the Party. Most ominous of all, in China, Mao Zedong decided he couldn't trust someone who was undermining the Communist camp by denouncing its symbol.

Next, to revitalize the Soviet economy, Khrushchev proposed a sweeping decentralization. Outvoted in the Politburo, Khrushchev called a Central Committee meeting in 1957, packed with his supporters and backed up by the army, which forced his opponents to resign. They were designated the "anti-Party group," but none were persecuted.

Unfortunately for Khrushchev, though, Party leaders increasingly became irritated at his "harebrained schemes" to boost production (especially of consumer goods), eliminate class differences (everyone would have to work before college, even the children of bigshots), and outfox the Americans by placing missiles in Cuba. To the West, at that time, Khrushchev appeared as simply another dictator, the "butcher of Budapest," and the man who banged his shoe on the table at the UN. His opponents in the Kremlin, however, considered him a reckless experimenter and liberalizer. In retrospect, the Khrushchev era brought major changes in both domestic and foreign policy. An entire generation of young Party members—including Gorbachev—came of age wanting and planning economic reform. These people, "Khrushchev's children," later staffed the Gorbachev reform effort.

In October 1964 the hitherto unthinkable happened: the leader of the Soviet Union was *voted* out of office by a majority of the Politburo who disliked his economic and Party "adventurism."

Khrushchev was a flamboyant, can-do character, who promised too much and delivered too little. The first Soviet leader to visit the United States, he saw in the Midwest the wonders of corn production and ordered wide regions of the USSR to convert to corn, even areas not suited to it. In his Virgin Lands program in Kazakhstan, he ordered

ploughing and planting. But rainfall is unreliable there, and after a few good harvests, much of the land turned into a dust bowl. By stressing consumer goods, he downplayed the traditional emphasis on heavy industry, and this infuriated both managers and the military. Culturally, he permitted the publication of anti-Stalin works (including Solzhenitsyn's *One Day in the Life of Ivan Denisovich*), then backed off when he felt things were getting out of hand.

We now see that Khrushchev was thrusting his bold ideas up against the ingrained conservatism of Party *apparatchiki*, sometimes giving way to them and finally defeated by them. Gorbachev, whose reform efforts were reminiscent of Khrushchev's, suffered a similar fate. And so could Yeltsin.

ers. The last straw was Yeltsin's dissolution of parliament in order to hold new elections; that produced the parliamentary coup attempt of 1993.

The elections, which we reviewed in Chapter 18, were a shock. The biggest single vote for a party was for Zhirinovsky's misnamed Liberal Democrats. Other anti-reform parties also did well. Zhirinovsky, although he despises Yeltsin, supported Yeltsin's moves to increase the powers of the presidency, because Zhirinovsky intends to be the next occupant of that office. Otherwise, Zhirinovsky led the parliamentary chorus opposing economic reform and favoring nationalistic positions. Yeltsin backed down, jettisoned his main reformers, and appointed Chernomyrdin prime minister. Sensitive to the prevailing winds, Foreign Minister Andrei Kozyrev switched to a Russian nationalist line.

But isn't this just democracy in action? An executive starts showing dictatorial tendencies and institutes policies that go farther and faster than citizens want, so the citizens, through their elected representatives in parliament, put on the brakes. That is the way the State Duma would like to see itself, but the problem in Russia is trickier. Without major economic reforms, democracy in Russia doesn't stand a chance. But such reforms are seldom initiated by purely democratic means; they can't be, as they inflict too much pain, at least temporarily. Major reforms need strong executive leadership; a fragmented parliament cannot do it. If the executive is blocked, the result will likely not be democracy but chaos, and out of chaos grows dictatorship.

The Mafia

The mafia (Russians use the loan word *mafiya*) is an important interest group in Russia largely in the negative sense that it has Russians horrified and demanding that the government break it. There has long been a criminal underworld, even in the Soviet Union, but now it has emerged unchecked. In Russia, the word mafia covers a multitude of meanings. There are some 5,000 criminal gangs in Russia, ranging from local strongarm rackets (virtually all merchants pay protection money) to the

Totalitarian versus Authoritarian

Since the 1930s, political science has debated the existence and nature of modern dictatorships. Some political scientists developed theories and models of so-called *totalitarian* systems to explain Mussolini's Italy, Hitler's Germany, and Stalin's Soviet Union. Carl. J. Friedrich and Zbigniew Brzezinski, for example, argued that totalitarian dictatorships have these six points in common:

An official ideology
A single, disciplined party
Terroristic police control
Party monopoly of the mass media
Party control of the armed forces
Central direction of the economy

Widely accepted for years, the totalitarian model gradually came under criticism as unrealistic and oversimplified. Far from total, the systems of Mussolini, Hitler, and Stalin were quite messy. Many citizens knew the regimes were frauds; plans were often just improvisations. The dictators like their sys-

tems to *look* total. Totalitarianism was an attempt at total control that always fell short.

Totalitarian fell into disuse, and *authoritarian* became the word used to describe modern dictatorships. It means a system with little mass input but one that does not try to achieve total control. In an authoritarian system, politics is in the hands of a dictator, such as Spain's Franco or Chile's Pinochet, but wide areas of the economy and cultural life are open. Most or all of the above six points are missing.

Political scientist Jeane J. Kirkpatrick argued in 1980 that there are still useful distinctions between the two words. Authoritarian regimes, because they are more loose and open, can change and reform themselves into democracies. This happened throughout Latin America in the 1980s. Totalitarian systems, especially Communist ones, she argued, cannot reform; they are too rigid. In a way, Kirkpatrick was right. The Communist regimes of East Europe and the Soviet Union never did reform; they collapsed.

sophisticated theft of state property with the connivance of factory directors. Some murder elderly people in order to get their scarce apartments. Most "banks" are simply money-laundering operations.

Russian mafiosi flaunt their newly acquired wealth as if they were acting out old U.S. gangster movies. Flashy cars (any make you can name), clothes, lady friends, and parties now adorn the major Russian cities. Increasingly, they have international connections and can deliver drugs or murder at reasonable prices. One member of parliament was shot dead on his doorstep, probably because his newspaper had published the names of 266 mafiosi. On another occasion, a member of parliament whipped out his AK-47 first and cut down a hitman. The mafiosi increasingly murder each other, too, but their bullets and car bombs often kill innocent bystanders.

The average Russian hates the gangsters and how they have degraded Russia, and this hatred feeds support for Zhirinovsky, who promises to rid Russia of them by sidewalk executions. Thus the mafia could help promote an authoritarian takeover. The police claim they are so overwhelmed that they can do little. It may also be true that not-so-ex-apparatchiks promote and shelter gangsters both for their own gain and to sabotage attempts at reform. Many mafiosi have friends in high places.

Russians have long argued that without strict supervision and draconic controls they are the most lawless of peoples. Americans, they say, have internal controls which Russians have not. Historically, freedom in Russia meant chaos and bloody anarchy—some call the current period the new Time of Troubles—and Russians have therefore always welcomed rule by a strong hand, however harsh. The mafia is making this old stereotype come true.

The Army

The new Russian armed forces are smaller (3 million members) than the old Soviet armed forces (some 4 million) but much larger than had been planned in the early 1990s (1.5 million). (In comparison, U.S. armed forces are headed for 1.2 million.) Russian armed forces are absurdly top heavy, with as many officers as enlisted sol-

---

Unexpected Reformer: Prime Minister Chernomyrdin

As President Yeltsin played a smaller role in day-to-day political affairs, the initiative slid to Viktor Chernomyrdin, his prime minister since late 1992. Yeltsin felt he needed Chernomyrdin, a spokesman for state-enterprise directors, to cement relations with parliament, where Chernomyrdin is well connected. Many observers saw this as the rollback of reform and the beginning of conservative authoritarianism.

Chernomyrdin, however, was a centrist and demonstrated that he could carry out effective reforms. True, as former Communist energy minister he started with a tilt toward state-owned businesses and spoke of the need to reform slowly so as not to destroy Russian industry. When he took over, he denounced the "market romanticism" of some of Yeltsin's strongly reformist advisors, most of whom resigned or were pushed out of government.

But Chernomyrdin could not be simply anti-reformist. First, the international pressure was strong. If Russia did not lower its runaway inflation rate, it would get no help from abroad. The International Monetary Fund (IMF) would make sure of that. (See chapter 28 on Brazil for the importance of the IMF). Domestic pressures were also strong. With the ruble becoming worthless and the investment climate dangerous, even potential Russian investors were stashing their capital overseas, a typical Latin American situation.

Privatization of industry had become popular, so Chernomyrdin kept on Anatoly Chubais as minister for privatization, and Chubais continued with his ambitious program at a rapid pace. Most industry is now private and off the government dole. Chernomyrdin had come to appreciate monetary policy, of how subsidies fuel inflation. He told the upper house of parliament: "Either we come to grips with the problem of financial discipline or we will never extricate ourselves from this crisis." He starved the powerful lobbies of the funds they demanded until they learn to raise capital from the private sector. Under his guidance, inflation fell to less than 10 percent a month, much lower than it had been. The IMF granted Russia a $1.5 billion loan.

U.S. media portrayed Chernomyrdin as a grey Party *apparatchik*. He was an older man of conservative instincts, but he understood the necessity of reform. The U.S. media did not much like or mention Chernomyrdin; they had attached themselves too closely to the more-colorful, younger, English-speaking reformers who preceded him. By early 1994, however, polls ranked Chernomyrdin as Russia's most influential politician, ahead of President Yeltsin.

COMPARING

The Timing of Reforms

In addition to the cultural factors we have already discussed, the timing of reforms can make a crucial difference to the successful founding of democracy. The differences in timing between what happened in Central Europe and what happened in Russia are instructive.

First, in Central Europe (Poland, Czechoslovakia, and Hungary) a broad anti-Communist movement formed while the Communists were still in power. By the time liberal Communists held free elections in 1989 or 1990 an aware electorate completely ousted the Communists from power, from the president's and prime minister's offices to the main parties of parliament. It was sort of a new broom sweeping clean. The initial winner was the broad catchall of anti-Communist forces, the leader of which became either the president (Walesa of Poland and Havel of Czechoslovakia) or the prime minister (Antall of Hungary). Later these catchalls all fell apart, but they had done their job: the Communists were thoroughly out, and democracy and market economics were established.

In Russia, there was no new broom and the old one did not sweep clean. There was no nationwide anti-Communist catchall movement like Solidarity or Civic Forum. The Communists never allowed that. Instead, the Communists held semifree elections but did not allow themselves to be neatly ousted from power. Gorbachev, who was never elected anything, stayed in office believing he was supervising major reforms. But Gorbachev still faced major conservative (that is, Party) forces and continually changed course in the face of them. Sensing his weakness, Party conservatives attempted to overthrow him. After their defeat, the Party was finally

ousted from office (late 1991) but still retains important influence in parliament, industry, and the countryside. Yeltsin, with no mass movement behind him, attempted serious reform but was still blocked by conservative forces, some of them remnants of the Party.

If Russia had done it like Central Europe, there would have been parliamentary elections in late 1991 instead of late 1993. At the earlier date, there might have been sufficient enthusiasm to elect a pro-reform majority; by the latter date, the declining economy had produced despair and a backlash. But isn't that what happened in Central Europe? Quite so; in both Poland and Hungary economic hardship gave electoral wins to their Socialist parties (renamed Communists). But by then both democracy and the market economy were established and could not be rolled back. The Socialists had no intention of dismantling an economic system that was showing signs of growth; instead, they made minor adjustments in the "social safety net" of Poland and Hungary.

The key difference between Central Europe and Russia then, was that anti-Communist catchalls took shape while the Communists were still in power, these catchalls then cleanly ousted the Communists in early elections, and proceeded with major reforms with the majority of the citizens behind them and relatively few conservative forces to oppose them. The desirable sequence seems to be: first, form a broad mass movement; second, thoroughly oust the Communists in parliamentary elections; third, institute political and economic reforms. It almost seems that the Russians tried to do it backward.

diers (U.S. ratio: 1:6). Officers, fearful of losing their jobs and starved for decent housing, are angry. They overwhelmingly voted for Zhirinovsky's party, for he promised to lift their living conditions and restore their wounded pride.

Several leading generals either supported the 1991 coup or did not oppose it. Many Soviet higher officers were fired. One, Marshal Sergei Akhromeyev, committed suicide. The Soviet armed forces had been consuming a quarter of the coun-

Remembering the Marshal

New York Times editor Leslie Gelb recalled a private conversation he had in 1983 with the Chief of the Soviet General Staff, Marshal Nikolai Ogarkov, who worried semipublicly that the Soviet military was falling behind technologically. He was later pushed out of high office for his outspokenness. "Modern military power is based upon technology," Gelb recalled him saying, "and technology is based upon computers," an area where the Soviets were well behind the Americans. Then, said Gelb, came his punch line:

We will never be able to catch up with you in modern arms until we have an economic revolution. And the question is whether we can have an economic revolution without a political revolution.

By the early 1980s, at least the high-tech sectors of the Soviet military, fearful of falling behind, favored major reform. The proof, if Ogarkov needed it, came with the quick U.S.-led victory over Soviet-equipped Iraq in 1991.

try's gross national product, a figure that was cut drastically. The army is still the strongest and most stable institution of Russia and may yet play a direct political role. Yeltsin increasingly depended on the army, especially during and after the 1993 parliamentary coup attempt.

Veterans, like these in Moscow, wear war medals on their suits, a Soviet custom. Generally conservative, many veterans oppose reforms leading to capitalism. *(Michael Roskin)*

Red-Brown Coalition? Two Russian Nationalist Politicians

Two political figures attract Russian military support: the fascist Vladimir Zhirinovsky and the Afghan war hero Alexander Rutskoi. Zhirinovsky, who shows signs of insanity, thunders out a nationalist and racist line not too different from Hitler's. He came in a weak third in the 1991 Russian presidential elections, but his misnamed Liberal Democratic party, supported by military ballots, won the highest percentage of PR votes cast in 1994. He knows exactly what psychological buttons to press to arouse Russians and was the only candidate to use television effectively. He declares he is pro-military and would restore the army's former power and glory—and use it for imperial expansion southward, toward the Persian Gulf and Indian Ocean. Eventually, he says, a weak and decaying America would be forced to sell Alaska back to Russia. Some dismiss Zhirinovsky as a joke, but others remember that Hitler was first compared to screen comic Charlie Chaplin.

Rutskoi, who was elected vice-president with Yeltsin but soon turned on him, is a more serious figure. A tough and respected air force colonel, he escaped twice from Afghan guerrillas after being shot down. Rutskoi says he never opposed reforms, but not at the expense of the army or working man. In 1993, Rutskoi was one of the anti-Yeltsin rebels who occupied the Russian parliament building (the White House) until forced out by tank shells. Imprisoned for his role in the attempted coup, Rutskoi was pardoned a few months later to the cheers of many Russians.

The big question is this: Could the army get together with far-right nationalists and not-so-ex-Communists to form a "red-brown" coalition? (The red connotes Communists, the brown fascists.) What are the chances of this happening? Much depends on Russia's economy.

When a political system starts falling apart, whatever groups are best organized amid growing chaos are most likely to seize power. This usually means the army. (See the box "Praetorianism" in chapter 28 on Brazil.) In much of the Third World, military coup is the standard way to change governments. Many now believe the Russian army could play such a role. In 1991 and 1993 it played a decisive role in siding with Yeltsin and crushing attempted coups.

The army must surely be counted as an important pressure group within Kremlin politics. For decades, especially under Brezhnev, the military got a growing defense budget and a leading role in foreign policy. Everything else in the Soviet economy took second place to the defense needs defined by the generals. The Russian military complained that its 1994 budget of $20 billion was completely inadequate and demanded more. Since Yeltsin was saved by the army twice, he supported an increase in defense spending, which the Duma rejected. This tends, for a while at least, to keep the army on Yeltsin's side.

Gorbachev tried to limit the Soviet military. With the 1987 INF (intermediate-range nuclear forces) treaty with President Reagan, Gorbachev dismantled an entire class of weapons. In 1988, Gorbachev admitted that the Soviet invasion of Afghanistan had been a mistake and withdrew Soviet forces. He gave up East Europe in 1989 as a waste of resources, even though the Soviet military defined East Europe as an indispensable defensive shield. The quick 1991 defeat of Iraq, a former client state that was Soviet equipped and trained, humiliated the Soviet military, as it suggested that their equipment and training were not very good. Many high officers are angry at the obvious retreat of Russian power and at their shrinking defense budget and manpower.

Vocabulary Building

authoritarianism	INF
Central Europe	pluralism
Civic Forum	red-brown
cult of personality	Solidarity
IMF	totalitarianism

Further Reference

BURLATSKY, FEDOR. *Khrushchev and the First Russian Spring.* New York: Scribner's, 1992.

COHEN, STEPHEN F., and KATRINA VANDEN HEUVEL. *Voices of Glasnost: Interviews with Gorbachev's Reformers.* New York: W. W. Norton, 1989.

DJILAS, MILOVAN. *The New Class: An Analysis of the Communist System.* New York: Praeger, 1957.

FRIEDRICH, CARL J., and ZBIGNIEW BRZEZINSKI. *Totalitarian Dictatorship and Autocracy.* New York: Praeger, 1961.

HAZEN, BARUCH A. *Gorbachev and His Enemies: The Struggle for Perestroika.* Boulder, CO: Westview, 1990.

KAGARLITSKY, BORIS. *Farewell Perestroika.* New York: Verso, 1990.

KAISER, ROBERT G. *Why Gorbachev Happened: His Triumphs and His Failure.* New York: Simon & Schuster, 1991.

KHRUSHCHEV, SERGEI. *Khrushchev on Khrushchev: An Inside Account of the Man and His Era.* Boston: Little, Brown, 1990.

KLUGMAN, JEFFERY. *The New Soviet Elite: How They Think and What They Want.* Westport, CT: Praeger, 1989.

LIEVEN, ANATOL. *The Baltic Revolution: Estonia, Latvia, Lithuania and the Path to Independence.* New Haven, CT: Yale University Press, 1993.

LINDEN, CARL A. *Khrushchev and the Soviet Leadership: With an Epilogue on Gorbachev,* updated ed. Baltimore, MD: Johns Hopkins University Press, 1991.

MEDVEDEV, ROY, and GIULETTO CHIESA. *Time of Change: An Insider's View of Russia's Transformation.* New York: Pantheon, 1990.

RA'ANAN, URI, KEITH ARMES, and KATE MARTIN, eds. *Russian Pluralism, Now Irreversible?* New York: St. Martin's, 1993.

REMNICK, DAVID. *Lenin's Tomb: The Last Days of the Soviet Empire.* New York: Random House, 1993.

TIMOFEYEV, LEV. *Russia's Secret Rulers.* New York: Knopf, 1992.

YELTSIN, BORIS. *The Struggle for Russia.* New York: Times Books, 1994

CHAPTER 21

What Russians Quarrel About

Why the Soviet Union Collapsed

We are interested in why the Soviet Union collapsed not out of purely historical curiosity but to serve as a warning about what can go wrong again. Whatever happened to the Soviet Union can happen to Russia; the problems and resistance Gorbachev faced Yeltsin still faces. The question is also an important part of current Russian politics. Many Russians, especially strong nationalists, refuse to believe that Russia collapsed largely due to the inherent economic inefficiency of socialism. They prefer to blame sinister forces, especially the Americans. It is the functional equivalent of the "stab in the back" myth that so harmed Weimar Germany.

The real explanation is that socialist economies—meaning state-owned and centrally planned, "Communist," if you prefer—work poorly. They do not collapse overnight but over time slowly run down. Under certain circumstances, to be sure, centrally planned economies can grow very fast, as did the Soviet Union under Stalin's Five-Year Plans in the 1930s. A backward country borrowed capitalist technology and threw all its resources, including labor, into giant projects, chiefly into making steel and then making things from steel. From the 1930s through the 1960s, many observers assumed the Soviet Union would catch up with and eventually overtake the United States in terms of economic production.

But as the Soviet Union tried to catch up, its economy became more complex and harder to control. Input-output tables—a sort of spreadsheet for an entire economy—required hundreds of mathematicians to make the thousands of calculations necessary to set the targets of the Soviet economy on a centralized basis. Products were often of poor quality, as only quantity was calculated and demanded.

Apartment houses are prefabricated and small in Russia but there's a terrible shortage, and flats like these in a Moscow suburb are claimed long in advance, often by factory unions. *(Michael Roskin)*

Designs, often copied from old Western products, were out of date. Efficiency counted for nothing; there was not even a Russian word for *efficiency* (the closest is *effective*). Many factories produced things nobody wanted.

The consumer sector, deliberately shortchanged, offered too few products to motivate Soviet workers, who had to wait years for an apartment or a car. Accordingly, workers refrained from exerting themselves. Chuckled workers: "They pretend to pay us, and we pretend to work." Many simply took afternoons off to shop for scarce goods. Standing in lines took hours each week. All these factors and many others made Soviets angry with the system. By the early 1970s, the Soviet economy was clearly slowing down, especially in comparison to the surging economies of West Europe and the Pacific Rim.

This by itself, however, was not enough to bring down the system, which could have lumbered on for a long time in shabby backwardness. The real killer was technological backwardness, especially as it impinged on the Soviet military. The computer age had dawned, and thinking machines were spreading faster and faster into Western businesses, research labs, and military systems. The Soviets could not nearly keep up in computerization, and especially the Soviet military knew what that meant: getting beat. (See the box on Marshal Ogarkov in the previous chapter.) With U.S. President Ronald Reagan came an even worse technological menace: a "Star Wars" shield in space that would make America invulnerable. An important section

Economic Goods versus Economic Bads

Economists call whatever is produced a "good." It consists of raw materials whose value has been increased by labor into something people want and will pay for. Economists had a tough time naming what many Russian factories turned out: goods of such poor quality they were actually worth less than the raw materials that went into them. Labor did not add value; it subtracted value. The name for such products: "bads." In a market system, such a factory immediately closes. In Russia, propped up by state subsidies, some factories turned out worthless products.

of the Soviet military thus turned to economic and technological reform out of the fear of falling behind.

Many thinking Soviet Party people, especially younger ones, by the 1980s knew economic reforms were necessary and were itching for someone like Gorbachev to lead the way. But by themselves, they could not prevail against the conservative forces of managers and *apparatchiki*, many of whose jobs were at stake. It took, I believe, the high-tech sections of the armed forces to ally themselves with Gorbachev and give the green light to economic reforms in the expectation that these would lead to military technology to equal the Americans.

How to Reform?

At no time did Mikhail Gorbachev adopt a thoroughgoing plan of economic reform. His advisors presented him with several, each bolder than the previous, but he never made them policy. He never wanted capitalism; instead he sought a middle path or "third way" between capitalism and socialism. Gorbachev hesitated and changed his mind more or less annually, one year for economic reform, the next year against. Later, he admitted several mistakes. First, he now says, he should have liberalized agriculture, as the Chinese did under Deng (see Chapter 27). Instead, Gorbachev tried a couple of timid steps he inherited from his mentor, the late Andropov: "intensification" and an anti-alcohol campaign. Both failed.

When it came to real reforms, Gorbachev choked in mid-leap, both out of fear for the consequences and in the face of massive resistance by conservative Soviet forces. Gorbachev finally freed most prices, but he did not privatize industry. The result was far too many rubles chasing too few goods: inflation. Everyone wanted dollars as the ruble dwindled in value. Worried citizens muttered that things could not go on like this. It was against this background that Gorbachev's own cabinet plotted a coup in 1991. Before the year ended, the Soviet Union was dissolved, Gorbachev was a private citizen, and Yeltsin was president of the Russian Federation. At last, reform got serious, but Yeltsin too faced opposition from conservative forces.

Why Did We Fail to Anticipate?

The most stupendous change of the late twentieth century took political scientists by surprise. Why did we fail to anticipate—notice that I'm not asking for prediction—the collapse of the Soviet Union? Only a handful of historians and economists sounded any warnings. Political scientists tended to see more of the same with some reforms.

Why did political scientists do so badly? I can see at least five mental blocks that we built for ourselves, mostly by reading each others' books and articles:

1. Systems theory. Since at least the 1960s political scientists have been trained to see all countries as "political systems" that have varying structures but perform the same functions. Whenever the system is thrown off balance, it always corrects itself, by new governments, parties, or reforms. Systems were thus presumed to be highly durable, possibly immortal. Systems theorists could simply not envision system collapse.

2. Anti-anticommunism. The anti-Communist hysteria of the early Cold War years, especially McCarthyism, was so primitive that it persuaded some thinkers to give Communist systems the benefit of the doubt. Scholars tended to accept Communist systems as givens (much like the systems theorists above) and to conduct detailed microstudies of how the system worked. Anyone who sug-

gested that Communist systems were inherently flawed and doomed was read out of the profession as speculative, right-wing, and unscholarly.

3. Ignoring economics. Few political scientists pay much attention to economics; they assume that politics dominates economics. (Economists assume the opposite.) Few appreciated that a nation's economy can deteriorate only so far before it drags the entire country down with it. Some economists issued such warnings on the USSR years in advance, but political scientists largely ignored them.

4. System reformability. Political scientists supposed that Soviet problems could be fixed with a few reforms. (This too derives from point 1 above.) If the system has an economic problem, it will correct it, was the bland assumption. Eventually, some thought, the Soviet system could reform itself into a sort of social-democratic welfare state. The brittleness of the Soviet system occurred to few.

5. Fixation on personalities. Because reforms are necessary, they will be carried out; they just need the right personality. Ah! Here comes Gorbachev, the man both we and Russian liberals have been waiting for. His reforms will produce a much nicer Soviet Union. In this way, we read into Gorbachev heroic and reformist qualities he never had. Hapless would be more like it.

The Pace and Pain of Economic Reform

You can rapidly reform a socialist economy, but how much pain are you willing to inflict on average people to do it? Poland initiated a "shock therapy" at the beginning of 1991 and within two years had gone through the worst of its inflation and industrial decline to emerge as the fastest growing economy of Europe (not really a fair comparison, as Europe was in a recession at the time).

Yeltsin's first prime minister (until late 1992) and later economy minister, the dynamic reformer Yegor Gaidar, came close to shock therapy as he privatized the large, obsolete industrial enterprises the Communists had built. Terribly ineffi-

The Terminology of Economic Reform

Liberalize   to cut prices free to find their own level. Instead of centrally designated prices, factories may charge whatever they can get on the free market (thus sometimes called "to marketize").

Privatize   to turn state-owned enterprises and land into privately owned properties, by selling them to local investors, foreign investors, their own workers, or the citizenry at large through vouchers. (Each Russian at the end of 1992 got a voucher with which to purchase equity shares; the vouchers rapidly increased in value.)

Shock Therapy   doing both of the above simultaneously and rapidly.

Currency Convertibility   the ending of fake, imposed exchange rates by letting the local currency be exchanged for hard currency (U.S. dollars, German marks, Swiss francs) at whatever rate the market sets. Convertibility makes it impossible to disguise inflation.

Stabilization   controlling the amount of currency in circulation, both by limiting the printing of money and by denying government loans to industry, so as to slow inflation and make currency worth fairly predictable.

Tradeoff   the choice between inflation and unemployment, allowing one to rise in order to keep the other low. Most ex–Soviet-type economies elect to let inflation roar in order to hold down unemployment.

cient and overstaffed, many produced not goods but "bads" (see box on page 272). But they were the wealth and power of the bureaucrats and apparatchiks who ran them and guaranteed employment for those who listlessly worked in them. Accordingly, they were able to pressure Moscow to keep the subsidies flowing. In any rational system, they would have been declared bankrupt immediately. But you can't throw millions of people out of work all at once, protested many Russians.

Gaidar, unfortunately, did not control the central bank, which was led by an autonomous official who answered only to the parliament. As discussed in Chapter 19, Soviet economists never had a theory of money and so did not take the problem of money supply seriously. It grew in two ways: (1) the national mint printed far too much money; and (2) enterprises loaned each other extravagant sums in order to stay in operation. These "interenterprise arrears" or chits amounted to a huge but unofficial increase in the money supply. Much as he opposed it, Gaidar saw the output of money grow until inflation was sometimes 25 percent a month. In early 1994, Gaidar left the government, but he had laid the groundwork for economic reform.

Chernomyrdin, as we discussed in the previous chapter, carried on with reforms in order to meet stringent IMF limits on budget deficits. State industry screamed, but he cut subsidies. Over two years, Gaidar, Chernomyrdin, and privatization minister Chubais achieved a lot. By mid-1994, 70 percent of Russia's state-owned enterprises had been privatized, and inflation was down. Many people and firms were making goods and money but not declaring them to avoid taxes. State-owned industrial production was down, but consumption of goods like refrigerators and television sets was up. Beware of figures that show Russian industrial decline;

Traveling Salesmen. Young Russians find a niche in the economy buying Russian medicines, in the big bags, and selling them in outdoor markets in Sofia, Bulgaria. After a few days, they return home for more. Typical of the new breed of entrepreneurs in Russia, they know how to work a chaotic system. They showed the author how to catch a train from Romania to Bulgaria without a ticket: "Just bribe the conductor," they shrugged, "It's a Russian train." *(Michael Roskin)*

much of this is in military equipment and "bads." Meanwhile, private industry—now the majority of Russian industry—is undercounted and wishes to remain so.

The trouble is, consumption is up, but unevenly. That is, some people are getting rich fast, while many factory workers watch their wages being wiped out by inflation. Having long been taught by the Communists that equality of material living standards is good and just, Russians now witness the explosive growth of inequality. Some *biznesmeny* and mafiosi (the two words are linked in the Russian mind) enjoy new wealth while many people live worse than ever. Many Russians are terribly discontent and may be willing to act politically on that discontent. Therefore, even if some of the economic figures are improving, that does not necessarily translate into political contentment.

Along with the collapse of Soviet power went Moscow's power to collect taxes. The chief Soviet tax was a "turnover tax" levied on enterprises between each stage of production. With factories no longer accurately reporting their turnover and private entrepreneurs reporting no income at all and provincial governments skimming off taxes for local needs before sending the rest to Moscow, the Russian budget developed a large annual deficit. If not trimmed, it could re-ignite inflation.

Recover the Lost Republics?

Many Russians still will not admit that the fourteen non-Russian republics that proclaimed their independence are gone. They make no secret of their desire to restore the Russian empire. This feeling is especially prominent in the Russian army, which still has troops in most of the ex-Soviet republics. By hook or by crook, conservative nationalists intend to get back the old Soviet borders. Even the more liberal element envisions a Russian sphere of influence over the old republics.

This will be difficult. Local Communist elites at the republic level had never been happy with subservience to Moscow. They felt that central control limited their power and possibilities of graft and corruption. On purely ethnic grounds, most Soviet nationalities did not like the Russians, whom they saw as a colonial or occupying power. And the Russians returned the favor, with racist attitudes toward Muslim and other Asian peoples.

In many ex-Soviet republics, the "new" leaders were old Party bigshots, and rule by a Party elite continues uninterrupted and intact. Not counting the Baltic republics, Russia had the most progressive and most reform-minded leadership. Other republics lagged behind. A particularly tragic example is Ukraine, potentially rich and European, whose ex-Communist leaders instituted no economic reform program. The result was hyperinflation that headed straight for collapse.

One crucial fact in Russian thinking is the existence of 25 million ethnic Russians who live in what they call the "near abroad," the non-Russian republics of the old Soviet Union. (The term does not refer to the former satellites of East Europe, such as Poland or Hungary.) Some of them are made to feel unwanted and even threatened. Any outright violence against these Russians, however, could provoke the Russian army, which still has units stationed in other republics. Such an army in

How Much Police Power?

In an effort to control the rapid growth of crime and the mafia, in 1994 the Russian government issued new decrees granting the police powers generally not found in a democracy. Police can now make many raids without warrants, can detain suspects for thirty days without charge, and can audit the books of any firm at will. Most Russians agree that tough police measures are necessary.

But some worry that the police now have an invitation to go too far. Most factions of parliament complained that there is little to restrain the police, and they could become the tool of an authoritarian takeover. Zhirinovsky, however, liked the new police powers.

Who Owns Crimea?

Crimea is a lovely Black Sea peninsula that Khrushchev transferred from Russia to Ukraine as a present in 1954 even though a majority of the population is ethnically Russian. At the time, it didn't matter, as it was all the USSR. With Ukrainian independence in 1991, however, Crimean Russians began to agitate to have it returned to Russia. The Ukrainian government in Kiev refuses to consider the idea, arguing that geographically and legally Crimea is part of Ukraine. Tensions grew. Crimea could serve as a pretext for Russian military action. A third group thought Crimea should be theirs: the Crimean Tatars who had lived there for centuries until Stalin expelled them to Central Asia in 1944 as alleged German collaborators.

Moldova shot down hundreds of Romanian-speakers who seemed to be threatening local Russians. No one in Moscow criticized the general in charge. In such situations, the Russian army feels it has a right and duty to come to the rescue. This could someday be used as an excuse to seize all or part of neighboring republics.

Recovery of the lost republics could come about by more subtle means as well: economics. As the Russian economy began to stabilize, the economies of many other republics kept plunging downward, the fault of the old Communists in charge. Desperate for help, some of them turn to Moscow. Under the banner of the Commonwealth of Independent States, Moscow delivers some aid (for example, a good deal on oil and natural gas) but gets in return trade concessions and general obedience. Moscow successfully used this approach on Belarus, which now uses the Russian ruble as currency, and seems to be trying it on Ukraine.

A tricky third way appeared in Georgia, which itself is home to many non-Georgian nationalities. The Abkhazians of western Georgia broke away by force of arms, many of them supplied quietly by the Russian army. Georgia had originally refused to join the CIS in 1991 but, faced with military defeat, did so in 1994. Then the Russians changed sides and began supporting Georgia with arms and troops. They called it "peacekeeping," but it was more like a protection racket.

Should we as Americans criticize Russians for wishing to recover the near abroad? What did President Lincoln immediately do when faced with the breakup of the Union? Americans should have a bias toward holding unions together. If Russians can build a CIS by economic means it should not bother us, provided the trade deals are voluntary. What is West Europe doing, with Germany as the economic powerhouse? If, however, Russian attempts to regain the lost republics by military force, it will mean that a dangerous crowd has taken over in the Kremlin, and that should concern us greatly.

Consider the opposite possibility. Just as the Soviet Union fell apart, so could the Russian Federation. Increasingly, as economic reform inflicts great pain, peoples in the outlying regions see less and less reason to stay part of the federation. Many

COMPARING

Yugoslavia: A Miniature Soviet Union?

The former multiethnic Balkan federal system of Yugoslavia bears many resemblances to the ex Soviet Union. Both countries had a Slavic core nationality: Russians in the Soviet Union and Serbs in Yugoslavia. Serbs and Russians are both of the Eastern Orthodox Christian tradition and use the cyrillic alphabet. Both define themselves as the founders and guarantors of their respective nations. They regard breakaway republics as traitors to the nation.

The other nationalities resent this overbearing attitude. In each country, an advanced northwest (the Baltic republics in the Soviet Union and Slovenia in Yugoslavia) tired of being held back by the technologically backward core nationality, which economically drained the advanced area. Interestingly, the Baltics and Slovenia declared their independence first. The second largest nationality in each country is also Slavic but with a distinctive culture and resentments against being bossed by the center; thus Ukraine and Croatia quickly broke away. In the south, feisty Muslim nationalities demand greater autonomy and fight neighboring Christian nationalities (the Azeris against the Armenians, and the Bosnian Muslims and Albanians against the Serbs). In most of the newly independent republics in both the ex–Soviet Union and ex–Yugoslavia, the "new" leaders had been local Communist bosses prior to independence.

A final touch: Russians and Serbs, respectively, formed the bulk of the officer corps of the old Soviet and Yugoslav armies and now form the core of the Russian and Serbian armies. The top officers are conservative and dedicated to keeping their countries intact. They are not adverse to using force to do so. In 1991, both armies started intervening directly into politics. The key difference so far is that conservative Communists took over in Belgrade, and, with the army's general staff in complete agreement, attempted to hold Yugoslavia together by force. When that quickly failed, they turned to building a "Greater Serbia" by military conquest coupled with "ethnic cleansing." The good news so far is that the ex–Soviet Union has not experienced fighting a fraction so bloody as what has raged in ex-Yugoslavia.

distinct ethnic groups claim sovereign rights of republics; a few have even declared their independence. Since they are landlocked, however, Moscow can ultimately control them. If the Pacific Maritime region of Russia, on the other hand, should decide that its best deal is independence plus massive Japanese investment, Moscow could lose a huge, rich chunk of its territory. The chances of the breakup of the Russian Federation vary inversely with economic recovery.

A Middle Way for Socialism?

Gorbachev's ultimate problem was that he thought there was a middle way between a centrally planned socialist economy and a free-market economy. Reforms, it was argued, could blend a market economy with a socialist economy. They do it in Sweden, don't they? (No, they don't. See box on page 279.) Some Soviets ar-

COMPARING

Scandinavian-Type Socialism for the Soviet Union?

Confusion surrounds the term "socialism." Many Russians and East Europeans now tell you they no longer know what the word means. Some call the welfare states of Scandinavia "socialist" because freely elected Social Democratic governments have gradually introduced elaborate medical, unemployment, educational, housing, and other schemes designed to lift up the lower rungs of society: "cradle-to-grave welfare." These Social Democratic parties started out Marxist but all of them eventually shed Marxism. They are all based on large labor-union federations. The aim of these parties is to wipe out poverty without resorting to coercion or state control.

And here's where Scandinavian "welfarism" differs sharply from Communist-style social-

ism. The Scandinavian lands have little nationalized industry, and it was nationalized for nonideological reasons (for example, to hold down unemployment). The bulk of the economy is private and capitalist. Swedish managers, especially, developed a ferocious reputation for efficient, money-making plant operation. Taxes, to be sure, are high, but the economy is otherwise free.

In sum, Scandinavia is not socialist; it's a variation on capitalism called "welfarism." If you wish to call it "socialism," of course, you may. But please note that it was developed after and on top of Scandinavia's capitalist industrial base. First came capitalism, then came welfare. It is doubtful if the order can be reversed or if they can be built simultaneously.

gued that they could reserve the "commanding heights" of heavy industry for the state while permitting small enterprises to return to the free market. This is what Lenin did under the NEP in the early 1920s, and the NEP was frequently mentioned as a model by Gorbachevites. But the NEP was inherently flawed and was running down in the late 1920s when Stalin dropped it in favor of forced industrialization.

No one has yet found a way to combine capitalism and socialism on a long-term, stable basis. For a while, such a combination sometimes seems to work. Then the private sector starts bumping into the restricted, slow-moving state sector. The private sector needs raw materials, labor, infrastructure, and transportation on a flexible, ever-changing basis. The state sector, still run by a central plan, can't possibly deliver and has no incentive to. If you cut state enterprises free to enter the private-sector market, you are gradually desocializing the economy. It gets more efficient but less socialist. Eventually, you come to a point where you must either bury the socialist sector as a bad experiment or curb and recontrol the private sector. The mix won't hold steady; you must go one way or the other. China is caught up in this dilemma.

Some Russians still think they can find a middle way that is uniquely Russian. These tend to be conservatives, nationalists, and anti-reformers. Experience suggests that if they try to build one, they will create an unstable, declining system with high inflation.

Which Way Russia?

Can Russians govern themselves in a moderate, democratic fashion? I think they can. There is nothing genetically authoritarian about Russians. Earlier in the twentieth century Germans and Spaniards were deemed unfit for responsible self-government, but now they're practicing democracy as well as any Europeans. There is extremist nationalism in Russia, to be sure, but many who voted for Zhirinovsky's party did so out of pure protest and may not do so again. Many Russians now comprehend both the advantages and difficulties of the market economy and are fully prepared to go all the way to a free market.

If we take "democracy" and "free market" as two key variables, we can come up with roughly four scenarios for Russia's future:

1. **Both** are put into place. This may yet happen; there are encouraging signs of economic turnaround and repudiation of extremism in Russia. Granted, it will take some years, but we may eventually have Russia as a fit member of the democracies.

The Horror of Russian Health

Russian health standards also illustrate why economic growth is imperative. The infant mortality rate (number of live newborn who die in their first year, per thousand) is taken as a standard measure of a nation's health. The official Russian rate of 25 was widely doubted; some thought it was closer to 33. Either figure is much worse than West Europe.

Expectant mothers are poorly nourished and so are their babies, 60 percent of whom suffer protein deficiency. There have been isolated reports of children starving to death. Health care is supposed to be free, but medical personnel must be bribed to deliver services. Under such circumstances, it is easy to understand why most Russian families have only one child. In 1989, Russian women bore 2.17 children, a little above the replacement rate; by 1994 it was down to 1.4, well below replacement. In a parallel with Germany, the number of Russians started declining in 1991.

Meanwhile the Russian death rate climbs; the mean life expectancy of adults dropped to 60 years, lower than in much of the Third World. One of the causes: prodigious alcohol consumption (some of it poisonous homebrew) leading to industrial accidents. Women's life expectancy, however, was stable at 72 years, a large gap.

Russian environmental poisoning, both chemical and nuclear, is among the world's worst, and environmentally caused diseases are common. (Russia's closest rival: East Europe.) Even the air in industrial cities is dangerous." To live longer," said one official, "we should breathe less." Many factories just dumped toxic and nuclear wastes in shallow landfills. Even once-pristine Lake Baikal, long revered as a symbol of Mother Russia, is getting polluted. The declining health situation feeds extreme nationalist politics.

2. **Democracy without a free market** would produce a highly politicized system in which everyone expects the government to deliver prosperity and then blames it when it doesn't. Such a system would encourage political extremists to constantly outbid each other with impossible promises, leading to tumult and breakdown. Russia has already tasted some of this combination.

3. **A free market without democracy** has been touted as at least a temporary answer to Russia's ills. Sometimes called the "Pinochet model" after the Chilean dictator who successfully installed capitalism at the point of a bayonet, it has a certain appeal. Many political scientists think there must be a social and economic base before democracy can work (a large, educated middle class, for example). Build this basis by dictatorial means, and democracy will evolve on its own. Unfortunately, there is no known Pinochet in the Russian army.

4. **Neither** happens in Russia. Instead, a red-brown coalition takes over, possibly by means of a coup. Such a regime would attempt to recontrol the economy, crush the mafias, regain the "near abroad," and stop criticism. In short, Russia would be back where it started, an authoritarian dictatorship.

U.S. news media and experts are inclined to the last alternative. Their articles and reports are strongly pessimistic and have made the failure of democracy and the free market in Russia the conventional wisdom. The trouble with the conventional wisdom is that it's often wrong. Newspersons and academics who mostly read each other's analyses can get caught in a closed loop and largely reinforce each other.

I am prepared to believe that Russia is going to make it, that the first alternative is possible, although there may be one or more reversals on the road to democracy and a market economy. Why do I take a moderately optimistic view of this apparently desperate situation? People do have the ability to learn. Many Russians now see that socialism was inherently defective and don't want to go back to it. They notice that privatized farms and factories produce more and better goods, and they work in them with newfound enthusiasm. From a competitive perspective, Russian wages average only $100 a month, and Russia has incredible natural resources. Russian assets, now cheap, are attracting foreign investment. With stability, economic growth could be rapid.

To suppose that Russians can never become democrats betrays a kind of racism. Let us not write off the Russians quite yet. I remember hearing as a boy how the Japanese were nothing but (racist epithet deleted) who would always be poor and passive. What the Japanese have done the Russians can do. Let us now turn to this country of amazing growth.

Vocabulary Building

conventional wisdom
infant mortality
landlocked
marketization
personalize
privatization
Third World
welfarism

Further Reference

ASLUND, ANDERS. *Gorbachev's Struggle for Economic Reform.* Ithaca, NY: Cornell University Press, 1991.

BREMMER, IAN, and RAY TARAS, eds. *Nation and Politics in the Soviet Successor States.* New York: Cambridge University Press, 1993.

BRZEZINSKI, ZBIGNIEW. *The Grand Failure: The Birth and Death of Communism in the Twentieth Century.* New York: Scribner's, 1989.

CARRÉRE D'ENCAUSSE, HÉLÈNE. *The End of the Soviet Empire: The Triumph of the Nations.* New York: Basic Books, 1993.

COOK, LINDA J. *The Soviet Social Contract and Why It Failed: Welfare Policy and Worker's Politics from Brezhnev to Yeltsin.* Cambridge, MA: Harvard University Press, 1994.

DUNLOP, JOHN B. *The Rise of Russia and the Fall of the Soviet Empire.* Princeton, NJ: Princeton University Press, 1993.

GOLDMAN, MARSHALL I. *Lost Opportunity: Why Economic Reforms in Russia Have Not Worked.* New York: W. W. Norton, 1994.

MEDVEDEV, GRIGORI. *No Breathing Room: The Aftermath of Chernobyl.* New York: Basic Books, 1993.

MILLER, JOHN. *Mikhail Gorbachev and the End of Soviet Power.* New York: St. Martin's, 1993.

MOSKOFF, WILLIAM. *Hard Times: Impoverishment and Protest in the Perestroika Years: The Soviet Union 1985–1991.* M. E. Sharpe, 1993.

MOTYL, ALEXANDER J., ed. *The Post-Soviet Nations: Perspectives on the Demise of the USSR.* New York: Columbia University Press, 1992.

ROEDER, PHILIP G. *Red Sunset: The Failure of Soviet Politics.* Princeton, NJ: Princeton University Press, 1993.

TICKTIN, HILLEL. *Origins of the Crisis in the USSR: Essays on the Political Economy of a Disintegrating System.* Armonk, NY: M. E. Sharpe, 1992.

TWINING, DAVID T. *The New Eurasia: A Guide to the Republics of the Former Soviet Union.* Westport, CT: Praeger, 1993.

YERGIN, DANIEL, and THANE GUSTAFSON. *Russia 2010: And What It Means for the World.* New York: Random House, 1993.

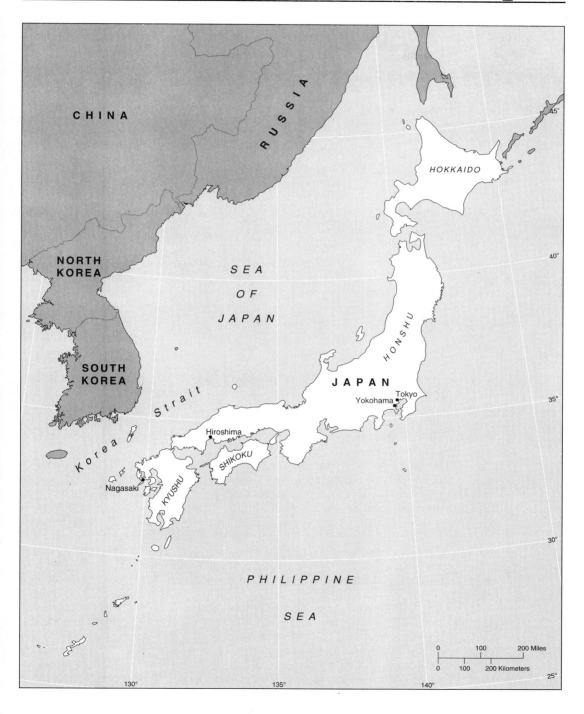

CHAPTER **22**

Japan: Impact of the Past

Close but Different

As with other countries, geography helps explain Japanese history, politics, and culture. Japan was close enough to China to be heavily influenced by Chinese culture, but far enough to resist Chinese conquest. The rough mountainous terrain and division into four main islands and hundreds of small islands made Japan hard to unify. Japan has little arable land, much of it historically devoted to rice, a crop so important it took on religious significance over the centuries.

The Japanese like to see themselves as a pureblooded single tribe, but they are the descendants of immigrants from various parts of the Pacific rim, including the Korean peninsula. The Japanese language has the same grammatical patterns as Korean, and some scholars even suggest that the imperial family may be of Korean origin. This finding is hotly controversial, as Japanese look down on Koreans as racial inferiors. In truth, both Japan and Korea drew a great deal from classic China, a civilization so magnificent it held most of Asia in awe. One can see the clear Chinese influence today in the pictographic writing of Japan and Korea, the architecture, ancient weapons of war, and the philosophical influence of Confucianism and Buddhism.

The Japanese were largely undisturbed on their islands for many centuries, and this allowed their culture and social structure to evolve away from the Chinese model. What came in from China was often accepted, but bent and trimmed to suit Japanese needs. Buddhism and Confucianism arrived in Japan in the sixth century from China along with Chinese writing, but all soon took on Japanese characteristics. This pattern of borrowing ideas and usages but changing them reappeared more recently in Japan's history.

The name Japanese gave to their land, *Nihon* ("sun origin") reflects their mythology that all Japanese are descended from the Sun Goddess. An alternative and more elegant pronunciation of the characters "sun" and "origin" is *Nippon.* Marco Polo seems to have recorded the Mongol name Zipangu, which, among Westerners, gradually turned into "Japan."

In 1274 and 1281, Japan trembled when the Mongol emperor of China, Kublai Khan, who had conquered much of Asia and Europe, sent invasion fleets against Japan. Japanese warriors fought the Mongols to a standstill and both times the invasion fleets were hit by typhoons and withdrew. The Japanese thus claim a "divine wind" (*kamikaze*) plus the fighting ability of their samurai saved Japan. The Japanese nobility treasured and celebrated an image of themselves as a superior warrior race until 1945.

Japanese Feudalism

One of the strongest patterns of Japanese history is its long domination by clans and their leaders. According to Japanese tradition (and still practiced in the Shinto faith), Jimmu, a descendant of the Sun Goddess, founded the Land of the Rising Sun in 660 B.C. More prosaically, a kingly court appeared in Yamato in the third century A.D. and by the seventh century had largely unified central Japan on the Chinese imperial model, complete with a *tenno* (emperor). The form of Chinese centralized rule took hold but the substance did not. Under the surface, the clans continued to exercise their control. The kings' powers were soon usurped by power-

COMPARING

The Uniqueness Trap

The key question for Japan is whether it is a country like other countries or something unique. Can it be compared to other political systems or has its historical experience made it so mysterious and different that foreigners cannot comprehend it? Is Japan strange or not so strange?

Many Japanese and some foreign observers would like outsiders to believe that the Japanese are a race and society like no other, sort of a tribe or large family. Indeed, during World War II, Japanese propagandists cultivated this image for domestic consumption. More recently, some use this image to explain Japan's economic successes.

It is the view of this book—and indeed probably the basis of comparative politics—that descriptions of a country as totally unique are unwarranted. Sometimes called "exceptionalism," it has been applied to Russia, Spain, the United States, and many other countries. When you look more closely, though, you discover that any country's political patterns are intelligible in human terms. You find, for example, that Japanese politicians take money from interest groups, just like politicians everywhere. Avoid the uniqueness trap and the related Mystique Mistake, the overly romantic fascination with another country.

ful clan chiefs, who could make or break figurehead emperors and hold them prisoner in the palace.

As we discussed in connection with Britain, feudalism is a pattern that tends to develop spontaneously as central authority breaks down. This happened in Japan from the ninth to the twelfth centuries and led to seven centuries of feudalism, until the nineteenth century. China overcame feudalism early to become a bureaucratic empire. England overcame feudalism slowly and in a way that set up limited, constitutional government. France overcame feudalism by means of absolutism. Japan, it has been argued, was feudal so long and so deeply that feudal characteristics still remain in Japanese political culture.

The essence of feudalism is power diffused and quarreled over among several aristocratic lords, each of whom has many warrior-helpers, who become the noble or knightly class. Typically, only these men are allowed to bear arms in normal times. They subscribe to a knightly code—in Japan, *bushidō*, the way of the *bushi* (nobles)—that turns obedience and honor into religious virtues and places knights at a high social level. The sure sign of feudalism is castles, as each lord needs a secure base from which to rule his locality and resist the infringements both of other lords and of the king or emperor. To guard his autonomy, the lord had to be ready to go to war at any time. War and feudalism tend to go together. Medieval Europe—with its trinity of king, lords, and knights—corresponds fairly closely with medieval Japan, where they respectively were the *shōgun* (generalissimo who ruled in the name of the emperor), *daimyo* (regional lords), and *samurai* ("those who serve"). Japan was different from Europe, but not totally. Europe started growing out of feudalism in the

COMPARING

 ## *Japan and Britain*

There are interesting geographical similarities between Japan and Britain. Both are offshore islands that have derived much of their culture from the nearby continent. Why then are they so different? England very early became a great industrial seapower, exploring, trading with, and colonizing much of the world. Aside from the short-lived invasion of Korea in the 1590s, Japan stayed home and did not develop industry beyond the craft level. England evolved from feudalism to democracy. Japan stayed feudal.

One possible clue to this puzzle is the power each faced on their respective nearby continents. Europe was fragmented into many competitive states and was rarely a threat to England. Indeed, England played power-balancer on the Continent by injecting its armies at the right time and place into Europe's wars.

Japan faced a unified China that was a nearly permanent threat. Japan early decided that isolation was the safest course. In the ninth century Japan cut most of its contacts with and borrowings from China and turned inward. In Asia, monarchs did not engage in competitive expansion, so Japan had no incentive to discover new lands. (Imagine if Japan had crossed the Pacific about the same time England crossed the Atlantic.)

fifteenth century or earlier, as modernizing monarchs crushed their aristocractic competitors to found the "strong state" of centralized power and sovereignty. Japan lagged far behind this pattern.

The European Jolt

The first Europeans to reach Japan were daring Portuguese navigators in their little caravels in 1543, followed by the Spanish in 1587 and Dutch in 1609. The Japanese could not keep them out, and soon Portuguese traders and Catholic missionaries made great inroads. St. Francis Xavier founded the Jesuits to convert Asia. Dedicated Jesuit priests learned Japanese and made as many as 150,000 converts (2 percent of Japan's population) by 1582. Instinctively, though, Japan's rulers feared foreign takeover and proscribed Christianity in 1597. Gradually, over the next few decades, missionaries were excluded and Japanese Catholics slaughtered. In 1635, Japanese were forbidden to travel abroad.

During this period, the Tokugawa clan managed to defeat the others and establish a powerful shogunate in 1600. (The 1978 TV miniseries "Shogun" is a fictionalized portrayal of this period. Some scholars argue the U.S.–Japanese coproduction is inaccurate.) The Tokugawa shogunate brought Japan two centuries of peace, prosperity, isolation, and stagnation. Aside from one small Portuguese trading post allowed on an island in Nagasaki harbor, Japan effectively shut the door to foreign contact. It was too threatening to Japanese stability.

The shogun's headquarters at Edo (modern Tokyo), however, kept discreet track of happenings in the outside world, through Chinese couriers. The Japanese people were kept deliberately ignorant of the outside world, which was portrayed as barbaric and threatening. Actually, considering what the Europeans, led by Britain, were doing in and to China, the description was not totally false. The Europeans penetrated China by trade, military power, missionaries, and education, slowly deranging and collapsing a great civilization. The Japanese, by keeping the foreigners at bay, preserved their civilization and territorial integrity until they were ready to accept the West on Japanese terms in the mid-nineteenth century.

The Forced Entry

By the middle of the nineteenth century Japan was an unusual country. It had enjoyed internal peace for two centuries. Male literacy (in the very difficult Japanese writing system) was nearly universal. Although lacking industry and trade with the outside world, Japanese were reasonably prosperous. If it were up to the Japanese, they might have preferred to have been left alone forever. But the West would not leave Japan alone.

The United States did a great deal of business on the China coast, which, by the 1840s, was carved up into "spheres of influence." The Americans, proud of not being colonialists, had no such sphere but tagged along after the British, concentrated in Shanghai. Shipwrecks in the East China Sea sometimes washed Western sailors onto Japanese shores. (Even then, Japan controlled the Ryukyu Islands, chief of which is Okinawa, which rim this sea on the east.) There was no way to get these sailors back. Furthermore, Japan looked like a tempting target for commercial expansion.

Traditional Japanese house features extreme simplicity. Shoes are removed to walk on rice mats. Diners at low table sit or kneel on floor. Futon in background is generally rolled aside every morning. Japanese design was modern before we invented the word. *(Michael Roskin)*

In 1846, two U.S. warships called at Edo (later Yokohama) Bay to request relations; they were rebuffed. Then U.S. President Millard Fillmore ordered Commodore Matthew Perry to sail into Edo Bay and force the Japanese to have dealings with us. Perry arrived in 1853 with four ships that combined steam power with sails. The Japanese were greatly frightened by these black, fire-belching sea monsters. Unprepared and confused, they begged Perry to return next year, when they would have a definitive answer to his call for diplomatic relations. How to best deal with the outsiders was a difficult and divisive issue for Edo. Ultimately, the court decided they could keep out the world no longer, and when Perry returned in 1854, a large, splendidly attired Japanese imperial delegation met him and acceded to his demands, not only for diplomatic but also for trade relations. Soon Europeans followed in Perry's wake, and Japan quickly opened. But the Japanese managed to do it their way.

The Meiji Modernization

The Japanese were determined not to go the way of China, to let their islands be overrun and turned into semi-colonies. One of the results of a long period of internal peace in Japan was that it made the samurai castes unemployed and superfluous.

The Meiji Restoration

The tremendous package of Japanese reform and modernization that appeared in 1868 bears the somewhat misleading name "Meiji Restoration." True, in that year a new emperor who took the name Meiji, did accede to the throne. Also true, he issued a number of "imperial rescripts" that ordered the modernization of everything from education and military organization to industry and commerce. But Emperor Meiji was not their author. A group of vig-

orous and farsighted samurai were. They saw what had to be done to save Japan and merely used the emperor, as he had always been used, as a figurehead. Nonetheless, the 1868 Meiji Restoration was a bold turning point in Japan's history, a necessary adjustment to the newly opened outside world. Without the sweeping modernization, Japan would have likely fallen under Western domination.

With the challenge posed by the opening of Japan, a group of these samurai found a new calling: to save Japan by modernizing it quickly, to beat the West at its own game. Taking advantage of the accession of the new Emperor Mutsuhito, whose era took the name Meiji, these modernizing samurai ended the Tokugawa shogunate and had the emperor issue a series of reforms in 1868. The slogan of the Meiji modernizers: "Rich nation, strong army."

Everything changed. Within a generation Japan went from the Middle Ages to the modern age. Various samurai clans were given monopolies on branches of industry and ordered to develop them. These formed the basis of the industrial groupings known as *zaibatsu*. Japanese emissaries were sent out to study and bring back the best the West had to offer: British shipbuilding and naval warfare, French commercial law and bureaucratic organization, and German medical care, steelmaking, and army organization. All was faithfully copied and put into operation. For taxes, the Meiji modernizers unmercifully squeezed the peasants.

The Meiji elite wanted Western technology but not Western attitudes and philosophies on democracy, equality, and individual rights. On questions of governance and social structure, Japanese values were deemed superior. The Western ideas got in anyway and among many Japanese intellectuals were highly influential. The Japanese tried to copy the British political system with a monarch, elected parliament, and parties. The 1889 constitution seemed to put Japan into the ranks of the world's most modern democracies. Underneath, though, patterns of governance were thoroughly Japanese and largely brokered by traditional holders of power.

The results were rapid economic growth. In thirty-four years, from 1885 to 1919, Japan doubled its per capita GDP. Although puny by today's standards, this 2 percent annual growth rate was probably the world's fastest up to that point in time. Japanese products, starting with textiles and simple handicrafts, charged onto the world market, using cheap labor to undercut Western producers. The purpose of Japanese economic growth, however, was less to make individual Japanese more prosperous in the style of Adam Smith than to make Japan more powerful as a nation. Some argue that this impulse never ceased to dominate Japanese thinking.

The Japanese Model of Industrialization?

Notice a couple of points about Japan's impressive, rapid modernization, which is sometimes offered as an example for the Third World to follow. It was not carried out on the basis of purely free-market capitalism; it had a great deal of government guidance and funding. Further, it was not particularly nice or painless; some families, especially those of certain favored samurai, got rich, but many peasants were turned into a downtrodden proletariat. Next, its cen-

tralization set up Japan for takeover by fascistic militarists and later, after World War II, by bureaucrats intent on making Japan a major industrial power no matter what the foreign or domestic costs. It bequeathed present-day Japan the problem of how to turn down a government-led industrializing machine that lumbers on long after it has done its duty. We might wish to think twice before prescribing the Japanese style of modernization for other countries.

The Path to War

As soon as Japan was sufficiently armed in the Western style, it picked a fight with and beat China in 1895, seizing Taiwan as its prize. Then it proceeded to gradually take over Korea—which was even more of a hermit kingdom than Japan had been—finally making Korea a Japanese colony in 1910. If these moves sound wicked, we might pause and ask just what was it that the West had done in Asia over the previous couple of centuries. The West had taken Asia with the sword, so why should not Japan do the same?

In 1904, amid growing diplomatic tensions and military preparations, Japan attacked the Russian fleet at Port Arthur on the Manchurian coast. With a combination of disciplined and enthusiastic soldiers, bright and daring officers, and British naval and German army advisors, the Japanese mopped up the Russians on both land and sea. U.S. public opinion favored the Japanese, partly because tsarist Russia had a terrible, repressive reputation in the United States. President Theodore Roosevelt, in Portsmouth, New Hampshire, personally mediated an end to the war, and won a Nobel Peace Prize for it.

The Japanese officer corps, always a hotbed of fanatic right wing nationalism and emperor-worship, disliked the democracy that began to bloom in the 1920s and moved gradually to bend and subvert it to their wishes. Now established in Korea and southern Manchuria, the army built a state within a state aimed at further conquests. Any civilian politicians in Tokyo who protested the army's expansionist program were assassinated. By the early 1930s, the army was in control of the Tokyo government, although for public purposes many of the official leaders were still civilians. The prime minister from 1937 to 1941, for example, was Fumimaro Konoe, the last head of the powerful Fujiwara house, who liked the fascistic organization of Japan but tried to avoid war.

The ideology of the militarists and their "Japanese spirit" was quite similar to that of the Nazis, then also consolidating their power in Germany. Both defined their peoples as a biologically superior, warrior race, destined to conquer their parts of the world and exterminate or dominate inferior neighboring peoples. Both were convinced they needed new lands for their growing populations. Both built societies structured on military lines into tight, obedient hierarchies. It was no great surprise when Imperial Japan linked up with Nazi Germany in the 1936 Anti-Comintern Pact and in 1940 joined the Axis. The two had little contact during the war and, fortunately for both Russians and Americans, conducted no joint military activity.

The Japanese propaganda line was "Asia for the Asians." The wicked European colonialists were to be kicked out and the nations of the region were to be enrolled in the Greater East Asia Coprosperity Sphere, led, of course, by Japan. Some anti-colonial Asians stepped forward to serve the Japanese (Ne Win of Burma, Sukarno of Indonesia, and Subhas Chandra Bose of India), although the Japanese were worse colonialists and racists than the Europeans had been. The Japanese governed with an iron hand, mostly through the *Kempetai*, their equivalent of the Gestapo.

The Great Pacific War

In 1931, the Japanese army in Manchuria detonated a bomb on some railway tracks at Mukden and claimed the Chinese Nationalist army had done it. Using this as an excuse, the Japanese quickly conquered all of Manchuria and set up a puppet state they called Manchukuo. The civilian prime minister in Tokyo who protested was assassinated. The world did not know what to do. The League of Nations condemned Japan, so Japan simply walked out of the League. Britain and France, with extensive

THE UNITED STATES AND JAPAN

 ## *Collision in the Pacific*

The United States and Japan turned imperialistic at precisely the same time, in the late nineteenth century. Both were relative latecomers to the imperial game, and, with both expanding in the Pacific, it was only a matter of time before they collided. The United States constructed a modern fleet in the 1890s and was eager to use it against Spain in 1898. The cause was supposed to be Cuba, but Washington used the war as an excuse to seize the Philippines from Spain. At the same time, the United States took Hawaii, Midway, Wake, Guam, and Western Samoa. One of the unstated reasons for the U.S. expansion in the Pacific was the fear that if we didn't take the islands, the Japanese would.

Why couldn't America and Japan have lived side-by-side in the Asia/Pacific region? The problem was the U.S. policy of protecting China, a policy that began in 1900 with the Open Door notes. Originally designed to make sure the China trade was open to all, they soon turned into U.S. guarantees for the "territorial and administrative integrity" of China. As the Japanese military began conquering China, starting in Manchuria in 1931, they put themselves on a collision course with the United States.

holdings in the Far East, did not want to antagonize Japan, so they kept silent. The United States, as an avowed "big brother" to China, protested with words but not with military power, which simply made the Japanese militarists more contemptuous than ever.

In 1937, the Japanese army began its ambitious plan to conquer all of China. Sharply opposed but wishing to avoid war, the Americans increasingly applied economic embargoes on Japan. The mercenary Flying Tigers, all U.S. officers on leave, flew to defend China. Starting in 1940, no U.S. scrap steel was shipped to Japan. The Japanese, with no iron ore of their own, had been major buyers on the world scrap metals markets; this was also one of the reasons they needed Manchuria. That same year, the United States, then a major oil exporter, barred shipments to Japan. This convinced the Japanese militarists that they had to conquer the Dutch East Indies (now Indonesia) for their petroleum. Washington thought these moves were important restraints and warnings to the Japanese; Tokyo thought they were steps in an undeclared war the Americans were waging on the cheap. Washington never fully comprehended that these steps were leading to war.

The last straw for Tokyo came in 1941 when Washington froze Japanese assets in American banks, a serious and hostile move. The Japanese immediately began planning the attack on Pearl Harbor, which, as far as they were concerned, was *retaliation* for U.S. economic warfare that had been going on against them for some years. Tokyo never dreamed of physically conquering and occupying the United States. The Japanese hoped that by knocking out the U.S. Pacific Fleet they would persuade Washington to leave the Western Pacific to them. This ignored, however, the crucial if irrational factor of American rage, something the Japanese could not comprehend across the cultural gap. They thought the Americans were cowardly bluffs.

The war itself, probably because of cultural and racial differences, was unusually cruel, even by twentieth-century standards. It was, as one American author put it, "war without mercy." Both Japanese and Americans killed many war prisoners and inflicted tremendous civilian damage. The Japanese fought like fanatics (partly because they thought they'd be killed if they were captured), and this persuaded President Truman to drop the newly developed atomic bomb on Hiroshima and Nagasaki, which finally brought Tokyo to capitulation in August 1945.

Japanese Understatement: "The War Has Not Gone So Well"

The Japanese language is extremely subtle and usually tries to avoid blunt or harsh statements. One example of this occurred in August 1945, when Emperor Hirohito, his army in rags, his country in ruins, and his people starving, went on radio to explain why, after U.S. atomic bombs had destroyed the cities of Hiroshima and Nagasaki, Japan would have to surrender: "Developments in the war have not necessarily gone so well as Japan might have wished."

Up From the Ashes

Japanese cities were seas of grey rubble at the close of World War II. Nothing was running. U.S. bombs had burned much of the crops in the field; starvation loomed. U.S. submarines had sunk a greater percentage of Japanese shipping than German U-boats had sunk of British shipping. In short, the Japanese were desperate, even more desperate than the Germans were.

With not the slightest resistance, Gen. Douglas MacArthur and his staff moved into one of the few buildings in Tokyo still standing, that of the Dai-Ichi bank (now one of the world's largest). Emperor Hirohito called on MacArthur to express his willingness to take the blame for everything Japan had done. MacArthur, speaking as one emperor to another, told him that would not be necessary and that he could keep his throne, but as an ordinary mortal, not as a "living god." (Most Japanese already understood that the emperor was no living god, but some still revered him.)

MacArthur's staff wrote a new constitution, again modeled on the British pattern, that seemed to guarantee freedom, democracy, and peace. The "MacArthur Constitution" has been Japan's basic law since 1947. It does not, however, function precisely as planned, as Japanese power does not flow in neat, Western-type channels. Industry was revived, much of it under the supervision of the old militarists who had run it as part of the Japanese war machine. The old *zaibatsu* industrial families were supposed to be broken up, but they reemerged as new *keiretsu*, industrial conglomerates that served the same purpose and were still sometimes connected by blood ties.

The Japanese economy did revive, and spectaculary, as we shall see in Chapter 26. The economy did not function on a strictly laissez-faire basis, however; much economic growth was supervised and encouraged by government bureaucracies. A democracy also revived, but it did not function on a strictly Western basis either, as we shall explore in the next chapter.

Vocabulary Building

bushido	Meiji
Coprosperity Sphere	mystique
daimyo	Nihon
derivative	samurai
kamikaze	shogun
keiretsu	Tokugawa
Manchukuo	*zaibatsu*

Further Reference

BANNO, JUNJI. *The Establishment of the Japanese Constitutional System.* New York: Routledge, 1992.

BEASLEY, W. G. *The Rise of Modern Japan.* New York: St. Martin's, 1990.

CHITOSHI, YANAGA. *Japan Since Perry.* New York: McGraw-Hill, 1949.

DOWER, JOHN W. *War Without Mercy: Race and Power in the Pacific War.* New York: Pantheon, 1986.

HANE, MIKISO. *Modern Japan: A Historical Survey,* 2d ed. Boulder, CO: Westview, 1992.

HUNTINGTON, SAMUEL P. "The Clash of Civilizations?" *Foreign Affairs* 72 (Summer 1993) 3.

McDougall, Walter A. *Let the Sea Make a Noise . . . : A History of the North Pacific from Magellan to MacArthur.* New York: Basic Books, 1993.

Notehelfer, F. G., ed. *Japan Through American Eyes: The Journal of Francis Hall, Kanagawa and Yokohama, 1859–1866.* Princeton, NJ: Princeton University Press, 1993.

Reischauer, Edwin O. *Japan: The Story of a Nation,* rev. ed. New York: Knopf, 1974.

Sansom, G. B. *Japan: A Short Cultural History,* rev. ed. New York: Appleton-Century-Crofts, 1962.

Storry, Richard. *A History of Modern Japan.* Baltimore, MD: Penguin Books, 1960.

Tiedemann, Arthur E. *An Introduction to Japanese Civilization.* Lexington, MA: D. C. Heath, 1974.

Ward, Robert E. *Political Development in Modern Japan.* Princeton, NJ: Princeton University Press, 1968.

23

Japan: The Key Institutions

If we were to go strictly by appearances and by what many Japanese want us to believe, we would portray Japanese political institutions as variations on the British pattern that was adopted late in the last century. As was the case before, this would be deceptive. Several British-type institutions are present, but none of them function as in Britain.

The Monarchy

The Japanese monarchy, which was constitutionally divine until 1945, still claims it can trace its direct lineage back to 660 B.C. Most of the time, however, the monarch was a figurehead, often a court prisoner of the shogun. For some Japanese, especially older people and conservatives, the monarch still is divine and symbolizes the entire nation in a way that has vanished in Europe. Rightwingers punish critics of the monarchy.

It is not clear if the emperor can influence Japanese politics. The constitution specifies he has no "powers related to government." A prisoner of ritual and ceremony, he goes along with what is expected of him. In 1945, Emperor Hirohito did play a policy role in deciding for peace; with the cabinet deadlocked but many generals willing to keep on fighting, Hirohito threw his weight behind those who were urging surrender, and it tipped the balance. In public speeches nowadays, the monarch is generally vague and idealistic. Some observers believe, however, that the emperor gives a kind of tacit assent; that is, if things are not going badly, he says nothing. This could continue for decades. If during a crisis an emperor should take a clear stand on an issue, however, he would have considerable impact.

COMPARING

 Deference to Monarchs

Both the British and Japanese monarchs are respected figureheads, but the Japanese much more so. Neither has anything but symbolic duties. Much of the British press see nothing divine in the younger generation of "royals." The media snoop on and photograph them and take particular delight in their marital troubles. The Japanese media would never snoop around the imperial household. The *Washington Post* first broke the story of the engagement of Crown Prince Naruhito in 1993, a story the Tokyo press wouldn't have touched until the official announcement. Once the *Post* dared to pierce the "chrysanthemum curtain" around the imperial household, however, the Japanese media began to comment on their royalty, especially on the mood swings of the empress.

Another interesting point of difference: The prince picked a commoner (but one of very good family), Masako Owada, to be the future empress, the second time this has happened in modern Japan. The prince's own mother, Empress Michiko, was herself a commoner (but of a rich family). So far, British royal marriages of those directly in line for the throne have all been with aristocrats. In Britain in 1936, Edward VIII abdicated after less than a year on the throne "to marry the woman I love," an American divorcée. The British press printed nothing on the drama until the formal announcement; Britons in 1936 could read of it only in the American and Continental press.

The Diet

The 1947 constitution, in the best Lockean style, specifies the Diet (legislature) as the "highest organ" of Japanese government. Not strictly true in Europe, it is even less true in Japan. While the bicameral Diet selects the prime minister and can oust him on a vote of no-confidence, much of Japan's real decision-making power lies elsewhere, in the powerful ministries.

Japan's lower house, the House of Representatives, in 1994, had 511 members (the number varied slightly from one election to another), elected from 130 multimember districts for four-year terms, but this is about to change. The House can be disolved earlier for new elections, which happened after a vote of no-confidence in 1993. The new, non-LDP coalition of 1993 immediately redid some of the rules that were widely (if not necessarily accurately) blamed for Japan's endemic political corruption. (See the discussion below on reforming Japan's electoral system.) The new lower house will consist of 500 members, 274 elected from single-member districts and 226 on the basis of proportional representation by parties. The new Japanese system somewhat resembles the German hybrid system.

As is usually the case with parliamentary systems, Japan's lower house has more power than the upper. If the upper chamber rejects a bill from the lower chamber, the latter may override the objection with a two-thirds majority vote.

The upper chamber, the House of Councillors, has 252 members elected for six-year terms; half are elected every three years. Japan's 47 prefectures and dis-

A Woman Speaker for Japan's Diet

In 1993, Japan's House of Representatives elected its first woman speaker, Socialist chairwoman Takako Doi. Curiously, Britain's House of Commons had elected its first woman Speaker, Labourite Betty Boothroyd, the previous year. Doi at first didn't want the politically neutral administrative job but was persuaded to take it as a way to help hold together the new coalition. With a Socialist as speaker, Socialist deputies might be more loyal to the centrist-led cabinet. Symbolically, Doi's election was another small step to political equality for Japanese women.

tricts elect 152 Councillors. A new wrinkle that started in 1982 has another 100 Councillors elected nationwide according to party preference. The upper house cannot be disolved for new elections.

From 1955 to 1993, with the lower house of the Diet (and usually the upper house as well) firmly in the hands of the Liberal Democrats, the Diet served as a sometimes raucous debating society in which the opposition parties, led by the doctrinaire Socialists, attacked the Liberal Democrats, and the Liberal Democratic factions attacked each other, sometimes with fists as well as with words.

Behind the show of parties, elections, and debates, the larger question of any parliament is whether it actually controls the direction of government policy. The career professionals who staffed the Tokyo ministries regarded the members of the Diet as essentially clowns, who put on a show to get reelected but did not have much time, knowledge, or interest to run government. This suited the bureaucrats just fine: Let the parliamentarians play their little games, so long as they leave us alone to run Japan, which they did. Actually, this attitude of civil servants toward elected legislators is found in many governments; it was just stronger in Japan.

Prime Minister

Neither has the prime minister been the real locus of power, as in most European systems. Americans especially mistakenly equated a Japanese prime minister with his English or German counterpart. In trade talks, for example, the Japanese prime minister would make some concessions to the U.S. side, but then nothing would change. The prime minister didn't have nearly the power in the face of major interest groups, and their friends in government ministries, to accomplish much.

A Japanese prime minster, at least until recently, has not been the analog of a European or Canadian prime minister; he was more of a figurehead. No one could name the Japanese equivalent of a Thatcher or Adenauer, tough leaders who really got things done; there had been none in Japan. One question now is whether Japan's reformers have really changed this pattern.

On average, Japanese prime ministers are in office for less than two and a half years, some for just a few months. By far the longest-serving prime minister was Eisaku Satō (1964–72). Ordinary cabinet ministers average about a year in office. The limits to their tenures are not no-confidence votes or the splintering of coalition cabinets in the manner of the French Third or Fourth Republics. Until 1993, the Liberal Democrats had a comfortable majority in the House of Representatives and could brush off no-confidence motions.

The problem, rather, was the fragmented nature of the Liberal Democratic party (LDP), in which the leaders of the several factions made and unmade prime ministers and ministers according to behind-the-scenes deals. The ministers were simply front-men for their factions. Many observers of Japanese politics allege that the LDP faction leaders were considerably more powerful than prime ministers. There are instances when powerful LDP politicians passed up a chance to become prime minister because faction chief was a more important job.

JAPAN'S PRIME MINISTERS

	Dates Served	Months in Office	Party
Yoshida Shigeru	1946–47	12	Liberal
Katayama Tetsu	1948	10	Socialist
Ashida Hitoshi	1948	8	Democratic
Yoshida Shigeru	1948–54	74	Liberal
Hatoyama Ichiro	1954–56	24	Democratic
Ishibashi Tanzan	1956–57	3	Liberal Dem.
Kishi Nobusuke	1957–60	42	Liberal Dem.
Ikeda Hayato	1960–64	53	Liberal Dem.
Sato Eisaku	1964–72	92	Liberal Dem.
Tanaka Kakuei	1972–74	30	Liberal Dem.
Miki Takeo	1974–76	24	Liberal Dem.
Fukuda Takeo	1976–78	24	Liberal Dem.
Ohira Masayoshi	1978–80	18	Liberal Dem.
Ito Masayoshi	1980	1	Liberal Dem.
Suzuki Zenko	1980–82	29	Liberal Dem.
Nakasone Yasuhiro	1982–87	60	Liberal Dem.
Takeshita Noboru	1987–89	19	Liberal Dem.
Uno Sosuke	1989	2	Liberal Dem.
Toshiki Kaifu	1989–91	27	Liberal Dem.
Miyazawa Kiichi	1991–93	20	Liberal Dem.
Hosokawa Morihiro	1993–94	8	Japan New
Hata Tsutomu	1994	2	Japan Renewal

With the eight-party coalition of 1993, short-term Prime Minister Hosokawa had his hands full, as the many parties jockeyed for power within the coalition, just as the LDP factions battled each other. Indeed, many of the members of "new" parties in the Tokyo government of 1993 had recently fled the LDP as its electoral fortunes started to crumble. They brought with them the infighting and power-brokering. The new prime ministers and cabinets are no more stable than the old. As before, the clues will be how long a prime minister stays in office and why he is replaced. The real weakness in the Japanese prime ministership is the parties, either fragmented, as in the case of the LDP, or splintered, as in the case of the newer coalitions.

Fill in the Blanks: A Generic Prime Minister

Because Japan's prime ministers change so quickly there is little point to printing the latest one in a textbook: by the time students read it, there will likely be a new prime minister. To compensate for this loss, students may fill in the name of Japan's latest prime minister (in pencil, please; you may have to erase it) and the other details. The purpose of this exercise is to illustrate that the more things change in Japan, the more they stay the same.

Vowing to change the Japanese system away from "money politics" and rule by bureaucrats, Prime Minister _____ took office in 199__. Although he billed himself as a reformer, _____'s roots go deep into the old system. After graduating _____ university and working briefly as a _____, he worked his way up through the Liberal Democratic party. _____ finally split with the LDP in 1992 to join one of its successor parties, the _____ party.

Reform will be difficult for the _____ government, though, as the [number]-party cabinet is prone to disagreement and breakup. The bureaucrats whose power he intends to curb know how to fight back. And Japan's special interests are as influential as ever. Rumor says _____ received "campaign expenses" from a shady _____ company.

The real question: Is _____ a power in his own right or simply the latest front-man for the genius who put together recent cabinets behind the scenes, former LDP deal-maker Ichiro Ozawa. Accused of corruption in 1993, Ozawa merely offered the incident as proof the system needed reforming. Ozawa himself left the LDP to form the Japan Renewal party, whose composition looks suspiciously like an LDP faction. With so much carryover from the past, it is doubtful that Japan's politicians can or even want to seriously overturn the old system.

Parties

For most of the postwar period, one party, the LDP, was so strong that some jested the Japanese system was a "one-and-a-half party system." This system is now changing. The Liberal Democrats were actually an amalgamation of several existing centrist and conservative parties that had been ruling Japan since 1947. With the growth of the Cold War, however, the United States grew concerned that radical Japanese parties, the Communists and Socialists, might either come to power or make Japan ungovernable. The Americans therefore encouraged (sometimes by CIA cash payments) the mergers that created the LDP. Only one thing mattered: do not let Japan go Communist or turn neutral between East and West.

The Liberal Democrats, although they enjoyed unbroken electoral success and controlled the government until 1993, barely cohered as a party; only the winning of elections and gaining of spoils kept the LDP from breaking up. Some saw it less as a party and more as an electoral alignment of factions grouped around powerful chiefs, much as samurai clans in olden times gathered around *daimyo*. Instead of swords, though, the faction chiefs used money. This feudal arrangement meant that no single faction or chief dominated for long, and no one was interested in or responsible for policy. There were few important ideological divisions within the party, only loyalties to chiefs, some of whom were unsavory holdovers from the World War II militarist government. Asked his political views, one local LDP activist proudly proclaimed, "I am a soldier in the Tanaka faction."

In the early 1990s, the LDP fell into worse disarray. Dozens of leading LDP politicians stalked out of the LDP to form three centrist-reformist parties: Japan Renewal, Japan New Party, and New Party Harbinger. If the newly reformed electoral system (discussed below) works, it is likely that these parties, which worked together in the 1993 coalition, will merge. Meanwhile, the several factions of the LDP quarreled more bitterly than ever.

The "half party" of the system, stuck in permanent minority status, was the Japan Socialist party (JSP), which had actually been born with the warm approval of MacArthur's occupation government because it seemed to repudiate the militaristic regime. (Actually, some Japanese Socialists had cooperated with the old regime.) The JSP hit an electoral high in 1958 with nearly a third of the vote, but declined ever since, because it was extremely doctrinaire and rigid, caught up in the sort of Marxist slogans that Europe's postwar socialist and social-democratic parties soon abandoned. The JSP, for example, proclaimed its neutralism, giving the Soviet Union the benefit of the doubt, while strongly criticizing the United States. Renamed the Social Democrat Party of Japan, it joined and ditched the 1993–94 coalition and then formed a bizarre coalition with its archrival, the LDP. This made a Socialist the prime minister for the first time since 1948. The JSP still voices sympathy for North Korea, whose lunatic regime was building nuclear weapons that could hit Japan. The Japanese Socialists acknowledged Japan's aggression and crimes during World War II. This made them attractive to intellectuals and academics who were aware that the Tokyo government had been covering up the wartime horrors.

Some less-privileged Japanese, who were aware that the LDP was corrupt but who were unattracted to socialism, turned for many years to the strange *Komeito* or Clean Government party. It too was stuck in minority status because it was a 1960s offshoot of the Soka Gakkai religious movement of evangelical-fundamentalist Buddhism, which some Japanese think is fanatic. Komeito's program, aside from clean government, remained vaguely in favor of improved welfare benefits and quality of life.

A small Communist party, rooted in certain sectors of the working class and among radical intellectuals, consistently won a few seats in the lower house. Torn between support for Beijing or for Moscow, the JCP was in a quandry when both headed for capitalism. Surveying Japan's party system, it could be said that no party was really strong, not even the LDP.

Japan's Electoral System

At least part of the blame for the weakness of Japan's parties and party system was placed on its electoral system, which was like no other. Elections for the more-important lower chamber, the House of Representatives, was by 130 districts, 128 of which sent from two to five deputies to the Diet, based roughly on district population. (One small district sent one deputy, and one very large district sent six.) Instead of European-style proportional representation, though, Japanese voters marked their ballots for one candidate rather than for one party, and the winners were simply those with the most votes. If there were seven candidates in a four-person district, the four highest vote-getters were elected. Candidates of the same party

COMPARING

 ## *The LDP and Italy's DC*

Several observers have noted the uncanny resemblance of the Japanese Liberal Democratic party and the Italian Christian Democratic party. Both were founded after World War II with U.S. blessings and dollars by combining preexisting political conservative-to-centrist groups to fight Communist or neutralist takeovers of Japan and Italy. Both parties were successful and dominated their country's political life for most of the postwar decades. The LDP, with an outright majority of parliamentary seats, was able to govern alone; the DC needed a multiparty coalition. Both parties oversaw major economic growth but neither were totally free-market, as both Japan and Italy had major state oversight of the economy (and, in the Italian case, major state-owned industries).

The negative side of the two parties was even more similar. Both were riven by at least half a dozen factions grouped around strong personalities, who mostly hated each other. Corruption was rampant in both parties and scandals were frequent. They stayed in power because not enough voters would switch to the radical parties, the Japanese Socialists or Italian Communists. The LDP and DC were the lesser of two evils in the minds of many voters.

Interestingly, with the Cold War over and the anti-Communist pressure removed, both parties declined in the early 1990s. The DC changed its name to the Popular Party. Voters, who could no longer stomach the crooked ruling parties, scattered their votes among several new, smaller parties. In the same year, 1993, both countries reformed electoral laws in the direction of single-member districts with an eye toward curbing corruption and party factionalism.

actually competed directly against each other in the same constituency, a system that begged for factionalism within the parties and helped explain why the LDP became so terribly faction-ridden and corrupt. The need to spread around campaign money became desperate, and with that the opportunity for corrupt political payoffs by private industry.

The new coalition put into office by the 1993 election blamed the Japanese electoral system for many of the political system's ills and immediately reformed it. First, they divided Japan into 274 single-member districts with roughly the same number of people. This was to solve one problem that cried out for reform: unfairness in the number of voters per elected representative. The 1947 constitution was devised at a time when Japan was still two-thirds rural and used the electoral districts of 1925. Since then, Japan has become over three-quarters urban, but the size of electoral districts changed only a little, some by legislation and some by court order. In 1980, it took up to five times as many urban votes to elect someone to the Diet as rural votes. In the 1993 election, after some reforms, it still took up to three times the urban votes to elect one deputy as it did rural votes. The system greatly magnified the voice of Japan's farmers and gave the LDP an advantage in the countryside, since they promised to keep farm imports either totally out or minimal. This gave Japanese consumers some of the highest food prices in the world and angered foreign food exporters, such as the United States.

Now these 274 districts elect only one member each, and by simple plurality (not necessarily a majority) of the votes. This should do at least two things. It will likely cut down the number of parties in the Diet, as such systems penalize small parties, as we discussed in connection with the British electoral system. This, however, is not absolutely the case, as third and fourth parties that are territorially concentrated have good chances to win in at least a few districts. Next, by ending the old Japanese system of candidates from the same party competing against each other in multimember districts, the reform may help overcome some of the dreadful factionalism within the ranks of the LDP or any other large party.

The remaining 226 members of the lower house will now be elected by nationwide proportional representation based on parties. This too could help heal the factionalism that paralyzes the LDP. In such a system, candidates from the same party would have to run as a team rather than as competitors. This should give Japan's parties overall greater ideological coherence. Note how the new Japanese system borrows from the German model.

Elections for the House of Councillors, in which half the members are up for reelection every three years, are different. Each prefecture has from two to eight Councillors based on population, and here voters also have two ballots, German-style. One goes for an individual candidate, with the top vote-getters winning, as for the lower house. These account for 153 seats. Proportional representation at the national level fills another 100 seats, a 1982 innovation. The electoral system for Japan's upper house thus resembles the system for Germany's lower house, which is roughly half single-member districts and half PR.

The Ministries

Who then does have the power in Japan? First, there is no strongly focused single center of power in Japan as in most other countries; power tends to be diffused among several centers. Many observers, however, point to the 19,000 career bureaucrats who staff the executive levels of the ministries, particularly the Finance Ministry and Ministry of International Trade and Industry, the famous MITI, as the real locus of power in Japan. The Ministry of Construction has clout, too, as it distributes public-works projects to benefit this or that locality or political chief.

The Japanese cabinet, like most European cabinets, can be easily changed from year to year, with ministries combined, renamed, or instituted. In the 1990s, the Japanese cabinet contained the following ministries:

Foreign Affairs	International Trade and Industry (MITI)
Justice	Transport
Finance	Posts and Telecommunications
Education	Labor
Health and Welfare	Construction
Agriculture, Forestry, and Fisheries	Home Affairs

In addition, the cabinet included several specialized agencies:

The 1993 Elections: Is the LDP Down or Out?

In 1993 the Liberal Democrats finally lost the control of Japan's lower house, which they had held since 1955. The LDP, however, was down but not necessarily out. It was still by far the biggest party in the Diet, with more than three times the seats of the perennial runner-up, the Socialists, who in percentage terms lost far more than the LDP. The election, which had the lowest turnout ever (67 percent), was the last one under the old multimember system, and distributed the chamber's 511 seats as follows:

	1993 Elections	1990 Elections
Liberal Democrat	223	275
Socialists	70	136
Japan Renewal	55	—
Komeito	51	45
Japan New Party	35	—
Democratic Socialists	15	14
Communists	15	16
New Party Harbinger	13	—
others	34	25

The three new parties (those not present in 1990) were largely LDP politicians who walked out of the party when it seemed incapable of reforming itself or the system. Ideologically, though, there is no important difference between these three parties and the LDP from which they sprang. The real loser was not the LDP but the JSP, running under its new name of Social Democratic party, which saw its seats cut in half.

The post-LDP cabinets were coalitions of as many as eight parties. Such large coalitions always fall apart, and it is quite possible that one or more of the LDP spinoff parties will return to the LDP, making it again the majority party in the Diet and returning the prime ministership to an LDP leader. The LDP showed it was still alive by forming an improbable coalition with the Socialists in 1994. The next elections, to be held under the reforms discussed here, might favor already large parties such as the LDP. Accordingly, let us wait a bit before we proclaim the demise of the LDP.

Management and Coordination Agency	Self-Defense Agency
Political Reform Agency (newly added)	Economic Planning Agency
Hokkaido and Okinawa Development	Science and Technology Agency
Agencies and National Land Agency	Environment Agency

There are a few interesting points about this cabinet. Notice that Self-Defense is in the cabinet but does not rate the title of ministry. A new agency dedicated to political reform was added in 1993. At least six ministries or agencies deal directly with economic development. The minister of foreign affairs usually doubles as deputy prime minister. In addition to the above, a state minister serves as chief cabinet secretary under the prime minister. The Hosokawa cabinet of 1993 also had three women, the most in Japanese history, a sign of change.

As in Europe, most ministers are elected members of parliament. The ministers are not necessarily experts in their portfolios (ministerial assignments), which are based more on political criteria than on subject-matter competence.

Occasionally respected specialists or academics without party affiliation are named ministers.

As is the case in Europe, every party in the coalition has at least one top leader named minister. The eight-party coalition of 1993, for example, had representatives of eight different parties in the cabinet. Even the small parties got a portfolio, but the coalition-member parties with the most seats got several. Such distributions of ministries are payoffs used to form and hold a cabinet together. The LDP in 1994, for example, gave the premiership to a Socialist in order to win JSP support.

Below the minister, a civil service "vice-minister" generally runs a ministry. The Japanese vice-ministers, who correspond to the British "permanent secretaries," are more powerful than their nominal bosses, also the case in most of Europe. The top appointed officials—and they are appointed internally on the basis of merit as defined by the individual ministry, not on the basis of political connections—have years of experience and knowledge; the minister may last only a few months in office. This gives the top bureaucrats a great deal of power and the feeling that they alone should run Japan.

Japanese Territorial Organization

Japan is a unitary system that looks a bit like a federal system. It has 47 administrative divisions, 43 of them "prefectures," after the French name for the head of a *departement*. The other four are special situations: Tokyo, Osaka, and Kyoto are run as large metropolitan districts, and the thinly populated northernmost island of Hokkaido is one big district.

Each Japanese prefecture has an elected governor and unicameral assembly to decide local matters and raise local taxes. These taxes, though, cover only about 30 percent of prefectural needs, so the prefectural government is always beholden to Tokyo for additional revenues. Japanese call this "30 percent autonomy." The Ministry of Home Affairs in Tokyo still oversees prefectural matters and can override the local governor. The Japanese situation resembles the modern French territorial structure: unitary, but with certain local-democracy features. Many Japanese, who are proud of their local communities, wish they had greater autonomy from Tokyo.

Vocabulary Building

analog	figurehead
assent	LDP
chrysanthemum	Lockean
Councillor	locus
deference	MacArthur Constitution
Diet	MITI
faction	tacit

Further Reference

BUCKLEY, ROGER. *Japan Today*, 2d ed. New York: Cambridge University Press, 1990.

DOLAN, RONALD E., and ROBERT L. WORDEN, eds. *Japan: A Country Study.* Washington, DC: U.S. Government Printing Office, 1992.

HAYES, LOUIS D. *Introduction to Japanese Politics.* New York: Paragon House, 1992.

KATAOKA, TETSUYA. *The Price of a Constitution: The Origin of Japan's Postwar Politics.* Bristol, PA: Taylor & Francis, 1991.

KIM, S. *Japan's Civil Service System: Its Structure, Personnel and Politics.* Westport, CT: Greenwood, 1988.

CHAPTER 24

Japanese Political Attitudes

Poor Little Japan

One thing missing from the U.S. occupation of Japan was the sort of denazification that was practiced, however imperfectly, in Germany. The Western Allies, by means of the Nuremberg War Crimes Tribunal and by virtue of their control of the media and schools, were able to instruct many Germans on the horrors of the Nazis and on the merits of democracy. Little such instruction took place in Japan, partly because there was no Nazi-type party to blame or put on trial (just the army), and partly because MacArthur did not dismantle the Japanese government but used it to run Japan. One result of this indirect occupation is that many Japanese to this day refuse to believe Japan did much evil during the war. The way they see it, the U.S. victors vindictively punished the Japanese losers by hanging some 700 officers who had done their patriotic best. Bayonet practice on Chinese babies? Never. Germ warfare experiments on American prisoners? No way. Korean "comfort ladies"? Not our doing. If you want to see war crimes, say some Japanese, look at Hiroshima and Nagasaki. The Japanese tend to see themselves as poor, downtrodden victims.

Only recently have Japanese officials begun to admit war guilt—or is it shame?—for World War II. In 1991, Emperor Akihito apologized to Koreans for Japan's colonial occupation. In Beijing in 1992, he told Chinese officials that he "deeply deplored" Japan's long (1931–45) war in China. His father, Hirohito, had maintained a discreet silence about World War II. Prime Minister Hosokawa began his term in office in a most unusual way, by describing the Pacific war as Japanese aggression and apologizing for the "pain" Japan inflicted on other countries. In Germany, such addmissions came decades earlier. Many Japanese are still loath to admit the truth. One Japanese countered Hosokawa's atonement by claiming that Japan

COMPARING

 Guilt versus Shame

Some foreign observers of Japan have argued that Japanese, unlike Westerners, are not driven by a sense of guilt but by the more superficial feeling of shame, of not upholding group standards. Guilt is a deeply internalized feeling of personal responsibility and moral failure and is woven into the Judeo-Christian ethos, starting with the Fall and continuing with the Crucifixion. The idea that God gives you moral choices and judges you is an important component of Western civilization and the basis of Western individualism.

Japanese religion—and the Japanese are now probably the most irreligious people in the world—has no such reference points. Shintoism, a form of animism in which one's ancestors play a major role, is basically the worship of Japan. There is no God or code of morality besides serving and obeying. State Shinto was refined into an organized religion by the Meiji modernizers to ensure loyalty during times of tremendous change. Buddhism, which exists side-by-side with Shintoism, is vague on the existence of God; Lord Buddha was merely enlightened, not divine. Either way, from Shinto or from Buddha, few Japanese are on guilt trips.

Instead of guilt, according to this theory, Japanese are strongly motivated by shame. To let down the group is a terrible thing; one would rather die. Never mind if the group's cause is just or unjust. This theory helps explain Japanese anti-individualism and the leitmotif of suicide that runs through the Japanese warrior code, politics, and even personal relationships.

had fought only "for self-defense and the independence of Asian countries," the old Greater East Asia Coprosperity Sphere line. In 1994, a minister resigned after creating an uproar by claiming that the 1937 Japanese "rape of Nanking" was a fiction.

The view of themselves as the permanent disadvantaged underdogs colors many aspects of Japanese life. Japanese point out that all 124 million of them are confined to an archipelago about the size of California, most of it useless for crops, with zero mineral resources. We have to take special steps to ensure our survival, they argue; we cannot afford to be as free and open as big, rich countries. Furthermore, we have just been devastated in a terrible war. Poor little us.

In the immediate postwar years, there was clearly great validity in these attitudes. But after a quarter-century, by 1970, Japan was a sparkling, rich society with no need for special protection for any of its sectors. Psychologically, though, many Japanese, especially older people, act as if they are trapped in the worst years of wartime and postwar poverty and desperation. Thus they "make do" with low wages, outrageous prices, cramped living quarters, and obedience and loyalty to company and bureaucratic authority.

Japanese display the psychological overshoot of insecure, worried people who have had to claw their way out of poverty. Such people work extremely hard and accomplish much, but they are often difficult to deal with, as it is impossible to calm their sense of deprivation. Mercifully, the younger generation, raised in reasonable postwar comfort, is repudiating the old attitudes, and we may expect policies to shift accordingly as more of this generation enters politics. This will take some time, how-

THE UNITED STATES AND JAPAN

 ## Destined to Misunderstand?

Viscount Eiichi Shibuzawa (1840–1931), one of the founders of modern Japanese business and an advocate of strong U.S.–Japanese ties, grew exasperated with the difficulties he encountered. Wrote Shibuzawa: "No other countries exist which are as different from each other as the United States and Japan. These two countries seem to have been destined to misunderstand one another."

ever, as the currently ruling generation of Japan was born before World War II and still has vivid memories of the war and postwar period.

The Cult of the Group

Japanese pride themselves on their group orientation. Almost like a big family, Japanese feel they can communicate with and understand only other Japanese. Foreigners, even among themselves, cannot do this, believe many Japanese, implying that Japanese have evolved to a higher human level. More plausibly, Japanese groupness is the result of centuries of isolation and feudal patterns, which taught that everyone has a place and everyone must keep his or her place. Viewed in a less benign light, Japanese groupness is an expression of Japanese obedience.

And Japanese are rather obedient. The crime rate is low. There are fewer murders in all of Japan in one year than in the District of Columbia most weekends. (There are practically no private handguns in Japan.) Students hit the books with little complaint. Japanese bureaucrats instruct businesspersons on correct strategies, something no American businessman would tolerate for a moment.

There is no mystery where the emphasis on obedience comes from: centuries of feudalism where even the hint of disobedience—such as not bowing low enough—to higher authority could be punished by beheading on the spot. To this day, one can distinguish the social ranking of Japanese by noticing who bows lower. An underling bows very low and from the waist; his superior returns it with a curt, slight bow of the head. The Japanese do not have some special group or obedience gene; they were simply late in getting out of feudalism.

Unlike Western, especially American, individualists, Japanese generally try not to make waves. One should not attract attention to oneself or make a fuss, an attitude called *enryo*, sometimes translated as "non-presumptuousness." Again, the origin is not hard to find: "It is the nail that sticks up that gets pounded down," goes a Japanese folk adage. One should be polite and smile at all times, even in adversarial situations. One should not take legal actions, certainly not take someone to court, but should settle disputes quietly. (Japan has fewer lawyers than U.S. law schools produce in one year.) One should not go to the doctor too much; small maladies will

Nature Tamed. Traditional Japanese gardens feature small trees in enclosed settings, as if nature was something that had to be tamed. Close control is a prominent feature of Japanese life. *(Michael Roskin)*

go away by themselves. (Japanese medical costs are a third of America's, and Japanese have lower infant mortality and live longer.) Wow, maybe we should try a little *enryo*.

There is a negative side to this group-minded obedience: Japanese are severely shortchanged in the civil rights and legal areas Americans take for granted. Some American lawyer-haters celebrate the fact that Japanese almost never go to lawyers; they settle quietly, allegedly for the sake of social harmony. But this almost always leads to settlement in favor of the stronger party, no matter how rightful is the claim of the aggrieved party. In Japan, the rich and powerful company or bureaucracy is always right; the individual is always wrong.

Education for Grinds

The Japanese are strong on education, and this is possibly one of the keys to their success. The Japanese work force is considerably better educated than the American, especially in mathematics, the basis of all high-tech operations. On average, a Japanese high school graduate knows more math than an American college graduate. Children do their homework—often supervised by "education mamas," moth-

THE UNITED STATES AND JAPAN

 Managing Differences

Two business seminars are held in New York City, one for twenty-five Japanese executives in America, the other for twenty-five American executives working for Japanese firms in the United States. The Japanese, all males, arrive in dark suits and keep their coats on even though the room is hot. They take exactly the alotted ten minutes for a coffee break. They ask no questions until they get to know each other over lunch. They politely defer to the speakers.

The American group includes eight women. Many of the men immediately take off their coats in the hot room. Chatting during the coffee break lasts more than twenty minutes. The Americans ask many questions and some contradict the speakers.

These are just a few of the cultural differences between Japanese and American managers. Americans view conflict within the firm as normal; Japanese think harmony is normal. American managers want quick profits; Japanese want bigger market share and greater efficiency, building for the long run. American firms hire people for specific skills, then let them go when these skills are no longer needed. Japanese firms hire for what the person can learn and contribute to improved efficiency and will try to not let the employee go. American managers respond to questions quickly and directly, for that indicates frankness. Japanese managers pause before answering and give discreet replies, for that indicates thoughtfulness. Sometimes one wonders if we are indeed destined to misunderstand each other.

ers intent on their children's academic success—with a determination that puts even French grinds to shame. Of course, if Japanese students do poorly on exams, they may commit suicide out of a sense of shame.

Japanese youngsters run a demanding obstacle course to get into the right schools and universities. As an almost perfect meritocracy, all admissions are based on tests; athletic ability or family connections do not help. Cram courses may help, and many Japanese youngsters attend them after regular school hours. Getting into the right high school or university means "examination hell," a period of several days during which entrance exams are given. Once into college, however, the game is over, and Japanese students relax and do little. It's not what you learn in college that counts; it's the fact that you got into the right college. If you've been admitted to the best, Tokyo University, you've got it made, so there is no reason to work. If you've been admitted to a lesser institution, you already know that the top jobs will be taken by graduates of better schools, so there is no reason to work either. Few Japanese students do graduate study, so few need a high grade-point average.

Under the influence of leftist professors, many Japanese students learn to criticize the system that produced them. Some students go into radical politics and protests, a handful into leftist terrorism. With graduation, though, almost all Japanese students get a haircut and new suit and dutifully become obedient *sararimen* (literally, "salary men," mid-level employees). College in Japan is a brief respite of protest and freedom between the grind of grade school and the grind of work.

The content of Japanese education is heavily slanted to rote learning and multiple-choice exams. Creativity and innovation are not highly prized; going along

Why is Wa?

Some argue that the Japanese word *wa*, roughly translated as "harmony," is the key to Japanese culture. Japanese are trained to seek and cultivate harmonious relations with each other. *Wa* is what gives Japan its cooperative group-mindedness where everyone looks out for everyone else. Critics argue, however, that the concept of *wa* is deliberately hyped to provide a cover story for promoting conformity and obedience. Under the doctrine of harmony, anyone questioning or criticizing the way things are run is considered to be disturbing the domestic peace and tranquility and is therefore labeled a troublemaker. *Wa* can be a device for social control.

with the group is. Debate is normally taught only as part of English-language instruction, as if to imply that only with foreigners does one have disagreements. One interesting difference with U.S. classrooms: in Japan, the fast learners are assigned to help the slow. This is good for the education of both of them and builds groupness.

Americans, and even some Japanese, criticize the rote aspect of Japanese education, arguing that it hampers flexible, new thinking later in life. But problem solving in mathematics does precisely that, and Japanese growth rates and labor productivity indicate that Japanese are plenty innovative. As U.S. classrooms have moved away from rote learning, they have left behind the self-discipline that comes with it. We might actually wish to reintroduce a bit of roteness. Besides, Japanese schooling is changing, producing a more spontaneous, questioning sort of student. Japanese education is losing some of its rigidity.

Death of a *Sarariman*

The typical Japanese *sarariman* would probably like to spend his entire working life with the same company. (We say "he" because, as yet, few Japanese women embark on career tracks, although this is now changing.) The company would like to reciprocate by offering "lifetime employment" to its people. Keep in mind, however, that only about 30 percent of the Japanese workforce are covered by any lifetime commitment from employers, chiefly large manufacturing concerns. Smaller companies are forced to hire and lay off as economic conditions dictate, although for most of the postwar period economic growth has been so consistent that there has been little unemployment.

Still, most Japanese employees feel duty bound to stay with their firm. American-style job-hoping is frowned upon as opportunistic and disloyal. I once assured a Japanese colleague from the Associated Press's Tokyo bureau that it would be perfectly all right for him to leave AP for a much better paying job with the Japanese *Reader's Digest.* It just went against his grain to desert a company. He was finally persuaded, he told me, when he saw me leave AP in New York for a better job, an easy decision for an American.

THE UNITED STATES AND JAPAN

 ## The Minamata Pietà

An environmental catastrophe on Japan's Minamata Bay illustrates the different moral and legal attitudes between the United States and Japan. When children of those who ate mercury-contaminated fish from the bay were born deformed, famed U.S. photographer W. Eugene Smith, a man of great humanistic conscience, felt he had to tell the story. Few Japanese photographers or news media were interested. One of Smith's moving photos, of a Minamata mother bathing her deformed child, won the accolade "Minamata *pietà*," as it reminded viewers of Mary cradling Jesus.

Many Japanese were not moved by the moral or legal challenge of toxic-waste dumping. Chisso Chemical, which had been dumping in the bay for years, was a major employer, and government policy stressed the economy, not ecology. Chisso workers severely beat Smith for daring to impugn their company's honor. Smith had trouble getting his photos displayed until the manager of a big Tokyo department store decided to take the heat for the sake of artistic and ethical truth. He was criticized for disturbing the harmony of Japanese society. The victims finally sued Chisso, but the courts let the case drag on for a third of a century before making Chisso pay a pitiful $30,000 to each victim's family.

In the United States, the media and photographers, many with a strong environmentalist slant, would cover the situation fully. American lawyers would be eager to take the victims' case. U.S. courts generally rule that companies face "strict liability" in such cases; if they caused the damage they must pay for it. Japanese courts make plaintiffs prove "negligence," that the company not only caused the damage but should have known it was doing so. In Japan, judges decide cases, not juries. Lawyers, courts, and lawsuits do have their uses; America may have too many, but Japan has too few.

Japanese work very hard, probably too hard. An 8-hour day is rare for a *sarariman*; 12 hours is common. Some Japanese literally die of overwork, an illness they call *karoshi* (not to be confused with the bar-singing *karaoke*, which is how many *sararimen* relax). Cases keep cropping up of *karoshi* victims working 50 or more days without a day off and of 100 or more hours of overtime a month. Recently, though, some bereaved families have sued the companies that worked the husband into an early grave. The new generation of Japanese does not like to work so hard. They prefer leisure time to overtime and ask, "Why kill yourself for the company?"

One of the great puzzles of postwar Japan is why its people work so hard and produce so much but ask for so little. *Sararimen* are willing to live in rabbit-hutch appartments and commute for hours standing up in a crowded rail car to their urban jobs. The cost of living is outrageous: $6 for a peach, $25 a pound for beef, $4 for a cup of coffee. Europeans and Americans would long since have gone out on strike in such conditions. Japanese unions are weak, many are organized by and for companies, and, if they must strike, do so over lunch hour so as not to disrupt work.

The answer, if there is one, is that Japanese culture really is different—or at least has been different until now. Centuries of obedient, feudal relations have taught

How Would You Do on a Japanese Exam?

This solid-geometry problem is from a recent entrance examination to Japan's elite Tokyo University. It is aimed at young Japanese in their last year of high school:

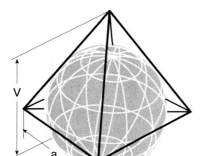

> A regular pyramid with a height of *V* and a square base of width *a* rests on a sphere. The base of the pyramid passes through the center of the sphere, and all eight edges of the pyramid touch the surface of the sphere, as is shown in the illustration. How do you calculate (1) the height of *V* and (2) the volume that the pyramid and sphere share in common?
>
> Well, you say, I'm not a math major and should not be expected to know such advanced stuff. But this question is from the exam for *humanities* applicants!

the Japanese to not ask for a great deal but to work hard for the lord (or company) and take pride in living modestly, even frugally. Japan never had much of a social safety net or social-security system, so Japanese learned to save for hard times and for their retirement. The Japanese are bigger savers than the Germans, and the capital this made available to banks and businesses helps explain much of Japan's magnificent postwar economic growth: plentiful supply of capital. (Americans save very little and suffer shortages of investment capital.)

Political Suicide

Now a minor part of Japanese culture is the willingness to commit suicide under certain circumstances. Originally a component of *bushido*, the nobles' code of honor, *seppuku* (vulgarly known as *hara-kiri*) showed that a samurai was willing to die to avoid shame on himself and his family. Although only a small fraction of the Japanese population is of knightly descent, a greater number pretend to be and admire and affect its styles. As U.S. forces took Saipan in 1944, some 4,000 Japanese women and girls committed suicide by jumping off cliffs. Prince Konoe, grandfather of Prime

The Honor of On

Another remnant of feudalism in Japan is *on*, roughly translated as debt of honor. *On* is social and symbolic rather than legal and monetary and underlies the Japanese sense of obligation. If someone has done you a small favor, he or she has incurred your *on*, and you are expected to remember it and return the courtesy someday. *On* lubricates much Japanese social life. For example, I repeatedly invited an American friend and his Japanese wife to visit me and my family for a weekend, but I was always po-

litely turned down. My American friend explained why. My invitation had come without any basis in *on*, so his Japanese wife felt awkward in accepting. My friend had an idea to overcome the problem. He sent me two lovely books of photos as a gift, thereby incurring my *on*. At that point it was honorable for them to come and visit. The offering of gifts is also a normal and even required part of Japanese political life.

Minister Hosokawa, when ordered to turn himself in for trial as a war criminal by the U.S. occupation, committed suicide in 1945.

In addition to atoning for personal shame, suicide has another use: it induces a sense of shame in others. If I sincerely believe in a cause but am not getting my way, by committing suicide before those I am trying to convince I make them ashamed and thus pressure them to follow my way. By dying, I win. This is still understood if no longer widely followed. In 1993, for example, a right-wing politician went to Japan's leading newspaper, the *Asahi*, to complain about its liberal slant. Af-

Political Suicide: The Mishima Incident

Yukio Mishima at age 45 was internationally acclaimed as Japan's greatest writer. He was also a fanatic right-wing militarist (and homosexual) who sponsored his own private army in an effort to inculcate young men with the old warrior spirit of Japan. Mishima specifically hated the clause of Japan's constitution which forbade it from having an army, even though it does have a hefty "self-defense force." Mishima tried to change this by seizing the old Imperial Army Headquarters in Tokyo with a small group in 1970. When the takeover failed,

Mishima, in a military-type uniform, committed *seppuku* on a balcony at the Headquarters before hundreds of horrified officers. Mishima ritually disemboweled himself with a special knife; then a friend beheaded him with a sword. His aim was to convince the officers to shake off the lethargy of peace and return to the way of the warrior, the true Japanese way. Most Japanese thought he was nuts, but the bizarre incident raised the question, "How many Japanese still think this way?"

Japanese Understatement: Sorry for the "Inconvenience"

Japan's Education Ministry carefully screens textbooks to promote unity and harmony. Truths which could provoke doubt and discord tend to get screened out. How history books handle World War II has long been a touchy subject, as it has been in Germany. One older Japanese textbook said mildly, "We must not forget that Japan caused inconvenience to neighboring Asian countries in the past."

China and Korea protested such a deceptive understatement, and the Education Ministry in 1992 ordered a tougher line substituted: "We must not forget that Japan caused unbearable suffering to neighboring nations in the past." The shift illustrates a couple of points: Japan at long last is starting to admit guilt, and Tokyo's ministries are still very powerful.

ter rambling on before bored editors, he pulled out two guns and shot himself to death with both. Suicide, because it is so traditional, tends to be used by conservatives who harken back to old ways. As such, it occurs less and less frequently.

The "New Human Race"

As you have noticed, the generation gap is big in Japan, the biggest of all the countries we study in this book. Older Japanese are amazed and not completely happy at how much the younger have changed and call the youngsters the "new human race" (*shin jinrui*) because they are so different.

Physically, Japanese 20-year-old males are on average nearly 4 inches taller than those of three decades earlier, females 2.7 inches taller. Japanese youth are now about the same height as European youth and just a shade shorter than their American counterparts. Almost all of the Japanese gain has been in the legs and is believed to be related to a more Western-type diet that is richer in protein than the traditional Japanese rice-based diet. Indeed, rice has been declining in popularity while McDonald's and Kentucky Fried Chicken have become, respectively, Japan's first and second most popular restaurants. With the growth spurt, however, the higher-fat diet has brought some obesity, never before known among Japanese youngsters. Another factor: Japanese no longer kneel in the home and office but sit in chairs; this has eliminated the constant pressure on the knees that stunted the growth of Japanese legs. (Earlier, the children and grandchildren of Japanese immigrants to America showed precisely the same startling increases in size.)

But more importantly, Japanese attitudes are rapidly changing among the young people. Working long hours for the sake of the company is no longer seen as normal and desirable. Desire for leisure time for family, hobbies, and travel makes younger Japanese similar to their European and American counterparts. Holding

COMPARING

Changing Political Cultures of Germany and Japan

West German political culture shared some characteristics with Japan. Both had a history of strong feudal hierarchies and stress on obedience. Both marched eagerly to war under dictators who knew how to manipulate traditional-looking symbols. Neither country took to democracy until it was imposed on them after World War II. After the devastation of World War II and the lean postwar years, Germans too worked hard and did not ask for much. A reliable conservative party, the CDU, delivered growing prosperity, and Germans were not in the mood for experiments. Student radicals could fuss over the U.S. alliance and nuclear weapons, but solid citizens understood they were necessary. The difference is, Germany shed its postwar stablity in about a generation; the Japanese took two generations.

Why was Japan slower? First, Japan's feudalism lasted longer and its obedience patterns were inculcated deeper than Germany's. Second, Japan was more isolated even after World War II and its people traveled less than West Germans. Third, Japan did not go through the reeducation that West Germany did after the war. Fourth, Japan was a poor country, poorer than most of West Europe, until it sprinted forward in the 1960s and 1970s. As Japan gets richer and more open to the world, its political culture becomes less distinctive.

down consumption for the sake of saving is no longer so attractive. Many younger Japanese have traveled or studied in the United States and have sampled the indulgent lifestyle of American youth. American clothing fashions are popular. (One recent craze: the expensive outdoors look of L.L. Bean, imported from Maine and sold exclusively in Bean stores in Japan.) They have learned to want the good life and to want it now.

To a considerable extent, it is the coming of age of the "new human race" that made the political changes of 1993 possible. The older generation, schooled in discipline and deprivation, simply obeyed for most of the postwar period. What the company and government offered was good enough. Younger Japanese have lost some of these characteristics and are more likely to switch their jobs and their votes. Older Japanese could tolerate the corruption and factionalized leadership of the LDP; after all, the party had led Japan to prosperity. Younger Japanese are more likely to say the system needs a thorough housecleaning. Japanese political attitudes are not entirely different from the attitudes of other advanced industrial countries and with time are likely to increasingly resemble them.

Vocabulary Building

enryo	*karoshi*	*sarariman*	*shin jinrui*
"examination hell"	*on*	*seppuku*	State Shinto
guilt	*pietà*	shame	*wa*

Further Reference

BENEDICT, RUTH. *The Chrysanthemum and the Sword: Patterns of Japanese Culture.* Boston: Hougton Mifflin, 1946.

BURUMA, IAN. *The Wages of Guilt: Memories of War in Germany and Japan.* New York: Farrar, Strauss & Giroux, 1994.

CHRISTOPHER, ROBERT C. *The Japanese Mind.* New York: Fawcett Columbine, 1983.

COOK, HARUKO TAYA, and THEODORE F. COOK. *Japan at War: An Oral History.* New York: New Press, 1992.

FALLOWS, JAMES. *Looking at the Sun.* New York: Pantheon, 1994.

FEILER, BRUCE. *Learning to Bow: Inside the Heart of Japan.* New York: Ticknor & Fields, 1992.

MARTIN, CURTIS H. and BRUCE STRONACH. *Politics East and West: A Comparison of Japanese and British Political Culture.* Armonk, NY: M. E. Sharpe, 1992.

MARTINEAU, LISA. *Caught in a Mirror.* New York: Macmillan, 1993.

SMITH, W. EUGENE, and AILEEN M. SMITH. *Minamata.* New York: Holt, Rinehart and Winston, 1975.

CHAPTER **25**

Japan: Patterns of Interaction

The Classic "Iron Triangle"

Prior to the major changes of 1993, Japanese political interactions were clearer and simpler and sometimes described as an "iron triangle," consisting of the Liberal Democratic party, economic interest groups, and the ministries. The new, non-LDP politicians vowed to break the iron triangle. Such triangles, however, are not easily broken.

The classic Japanese pattern formed during the long reign of the LDP (1955–93) worked as follows: The Liberal Democratic politicians would promise various economic interest groups—rice farmers, steelmakers, sporting-goods manufacturers, you name it—to look out for their interests. In return, the groups would deliver plentiful campaign funds, enabling the LDP to greatly outspend rival parties. (Some LDP politicians also put some of the funds in their own pockets.) The LDP, however, rarely translated interest-group demands directly into law and policy; instead, they let the ministries and agencies adjudicate the demands by means of regulations, subsidies, and trade protection. The ministries had been there longer, knew all the right people and how to deal with them, and could generally come up with workable compromises.

The ministries, the commanding corner of the triangle, had their own agenda, and it was not Adam Smith's vision of a free and open market in which competition delivers the best products and the lowest prices. Instead, the Tokyo ministries focused narrowly on their industries and sectors and sought to protect them by controlled markets in which domestic competition was limited, lest it become cutthroat, and foreign competition excluded wherever possible. This setup made the Japanese economy—which superficially looks like a free-market economy—one of

318

the most regulated in the world. Some 11,000 bureaucratic regulations govern every aspect and branch of the Japanese economy. Do not confuse the Japanese economy with a free-market system.

The ministries did not serve the interest groups, the way things often work in the United States. Rather, the interest groups got some of what they wanted from the ministries in return for overall obedience to the ministries' schemes to build regulated markets under the control of bureaucrats. Overall the Japanese arrangement, reminiscent of the controlled, mercantilist system of the French kings, suited practically all Japanese interest groups. Japanese consumers, on the other hand, got robbed by outrageous prices.

Bureaucrats in Command

In emphasizing the political importance of top civil servants, we must understand where Japan's ministries came from. They are not the product of a free-market democracy but of a militaristic system planning for and conducting World War II. Munitions, heavy industry, the development of Manchuria, transportation and communications, and many other sectors of Japan's economy were under state control and supervision. Indeed, the very founding of the modern Japanese economy during the Meiji Restoration was ordered and controlled by the state. Japan has not really known a free-market economy.

 Japan's Major Interest Groups

Japanese interest groups tend to follow the French model; that is, they are usually subordinate to bureaucratic authority, but even more than the French groups, the Japanese are seldom willing to have a showdown with the government. Japanese pluralism is weaker than American pluralism, where interests tend to either capture the relevant agency or, failing that, fight it. That said, here are some top Japanese interest confederations:

Keidanren, Federation of Economic Organizations, the most important business group, speaks for most large corporations and works closely with MITI to promote exports.

Shin Rengo, Japanese Trade Union Confederation, formed from the 1989 merger of smaller union federations, speaks for 8 million members in a moderate and nonideological voice, even though it still has some ties to the Socialist party.

Nisshō, Japan Chamber of Commerce and Industry, with good ties to the LDP, seeks to curb competition, large stores, discounting, and foreign imports.

Nōkyō, Central Union of Agricultural Cooperatives, argues for self-sufficiency in food and the exclusion of farm imports to its close friend, the LDP.

Nikkyōsō, Japan Teachers Union, left-wing and powerful among grade-school teachers; tied to the Socialists.

After the war, precisely the same bureaucrats who ran Japan's war economy were given the job of economic recovery. This they proceeded to do—and do very well—in the same spirit they had displayed during the war: economic development is too important to be left to capitalists. Japan is fighting for its economic life and does not have the luxury of slowly finding its way by means of the inefficient system of supply and demand, went the postwar argument. The attitude of Japan's top bureaucrats was that nothing but Japan's economic growth mattered.

This would not properly be called a "socialist" system, for it kept ownership private and did not attempt to redistribute wealth or income from the rich to the poor. It was not directly aimed at rapid improvement of individual living standards but for the growth of the Japanese economy as a whole. Some call such a system "statist," others fascist, although a fascist system is guided by a single party for party ends, not the case in Japan. A *statist* system, as we have considered in France and will examine again in Brazil, is one where the state is the number-one capitalist and owns major industrial and financial institutions.

Japan has practically no state-owned industry, unlike France or Brazil. The Japanese method of control is to leave industry in private hands but to prod—often over dinner and drinks—the industry to go this way or that by rational persuasion and bank loans. The targets are the likely areas where Japanese advantages could al-

COMPARING

 ### Bureaucratic Elites in France and Japan

The concept of a strong bureaucracy operating on its own, with little guidance or input from elected officials, is nothing new. France had such a system for decades, and it is doubtful if de Gaulle's Fifth Republic or Mitterrand's reforms have made French bureaucrats answerable to the electorate. The Japanese bureaucratic elite is a moderately close analog to the French *grand corps*. Both are very bright and highly educated and placed into the top executive positions with mandates to modernize and upgrade the economies of their respective countries. Both tend to think that they alone can save their countries and that elected politicians are a necessary evil that come and go and are not to be taken seriously.

The French are trained in a Great School, such as the National Administration School or Polytechnical, whereas the brainiest young Japanese gain admission to the prestigious Tokyo University ("Todai"), Japan's only publicly funded university;

all others are private and none are quite as good. Upon graduation, both enter bureaucratic fast tracks for the executive level, but both may retire early into a better-paying job in private industry. The French bureaucratic elite disdains the views of interest groups as un-French and unobjective. The Japanese bureaucrats generally listen earnestly to the views of the interests it is assigned to supervise, but then it gently tries to persuade the interest group to change its views to match those of the ministry.

The difference is that the French bureaucratic elite tend to read from the same sheet of music and to cooperate across ministries. The Japanese are soon inculcated with their ministries' particular point of view and pay little attention to the views of other ministries. There is no grand plan in the Japanese model, and sometimes ministries work at cross purposes.

low them to undercut foreign producers and then go on to secure an overwhelming world-market share. (The strategy with the Japanese camera industry against the German was one such success. See the box on this in the next chapter.) Those industries certified as growth leaders got long-term, low-interest loans from banks which were connected with the important ministries. Those industries not moving down the desired paths did not get big loans. This is a far more subtle way of steering an economy than the outright state control of Soviet-type socialism. The Japanese approach is similar to the French "indicative planning" but stronger and more effective, because it can make the cash flow and takes place in the cooperative Japanese setting where business generally obeys government.

For the most part, the top bureaucrats of Finance and MITI have done a good job. Hand-picked from the brightest graduates, they are promoted rapidly and given major responsibilities while young. Their salaries, however, are not high, and if they wish to move into lucrative positions in private industry in mid-career (what the Japanese call "descent from heaven" and the French call "putting on the slippers"), so much the better. That way the ministry broadens its ties with private industry, and, with it, the breeding grounds for corruption. Japan recovered quickly after World War II and went on to set economic growth records. As we shall explore in the next chapter, however, the bureaucratic guidance may have led to dangerous distortions in the Japanese economy that plunged it into difficulty later.

For some time, defenders of Japan claimed proponents of the overpowerful-bureaucracy theory were engaging in Japan-bashing. Then in 1993 the Hosokawa government publicly agreed that the ministries were too powerful and needed to be curbed and coordinated. Yesterday's Japan-bashing became today's conventional wisdom. It will not be easy; the bureaucrats are used to their power. Fumed one high official of the powerful and conservative Finance Ministry about some of the changes proposed by the new reformist cabinet: "We won't accommodate them, I assure you. They will accommodate us." In an unheard of move, in late 1993 the minister in charge of MITI fired a top career bureaucrat. The cabinet seemed to be telling the bureaucracy, "All right, you want a showdown?"

Corruption Scandals

Another leg of the "iron triangle," connecting the LDP to interest groups, became the fertile ground for corruption, which eventually grew so big that it brought an end to thirty-eight years of uninterrupted LDP governments. It used to be widely accepted, among both foreign and Japanese observers, that a little corruption was normal in Japan—an artifact of the electoral system—and that most Japanese did not especially mind it. "Walking around money" is part of many political systems, and voters expect favors from politicians.

Few books on Japanese politics mentioned corruption except in passing; it did not seem to be an important point. Japanese, according to many area experts, like other Asians, understand and tolerate graft up to a certain level and object to it only when recipients get conspicuously greedy. Maybe this was once the case, but by the early 1990s, something had snapped in Japan. The corruption scandals seemed to get bigger, the previously rather docile Japanese media started going after corrupt politicians, and the Japanese public was less and less tolerant of political corruption.

THE UNITED STATES AND JAPAN

 An American DITI?

If Japan's Ministry of International Trade and Industry helped speed Japan to the upper ranks of the industrialized countries after World War II, could not a U.S. equivalent—a "Department of International Trade and Industry" (DITI)—do the same for the United States? Here we see how hard it can be to transfer institutions from one country to another.

MITI functioned well in a Japanese political culture of cooperation and obedience. MITI bureaucrats, to be sure, did not order businessmen to do things. They persuaded them, often by lengthy wining and dining. Soon enough, businessmen could get the point that what was good for them was also good for Japan. A DITI would have to operate in a far more individualistic American context, one where businessmen are taught to disdain government and go their own way. U.S. antitrust laws might make collaborations between firms illegal, not a problem in Japan. The U.S. government's ability to provide bank loans would mean a whole redo of the U.S. banking system. Actually, the United States is trying government-led techonological development. Sematech brought together five U.S. computer-chip manufacturers, exempt from antitrust laws, to share manufacturing technologies. The results of this small experiment have been positive.

The signs that corruption was a serious problem in Japan had been evident for some time. Everyone knew that public works, such as highways and bridges, rewarded both constituents and contractors, who were expected to kick back a percentage into party or personal coffers. Komeito was founded in the 1950s as the "clean government party," an obvious indication that corruption existed and that a certain fraction of the Japanese electorate wanted to do something about it.

The conventional wisdom has been that corruption is rooted in Japan's "money politics," as the candidates (until the 1993 reforms) did not distinguish themselves by party platform or personality but by size of cash gifts. Under the old electoral system, LDP candidates often ran against other LDP candidates, a system that begged for factionalism and corruption. Prior to 1993, neither the government nor the party provided much funding for candidates or incumbents, who were left to raise funds for themselves.

And running for and holding office in Japan is not cheap. In addition to the usual local offices and constituent services, Japanese politicians by tradition must endear themselves to voters by attending weddings and funerals in their districts and giving nontrivial presents of cash to newlyweds and the bereaved. A typical LDP incumbent in 1987, for example, spent an estimated ¥120 million (then over $1 million) a year but got an allowance of only ¥20 million. The remaining ¥100 million (now about $1 million) had to be raised somewhere, by the donations of friends, supporters, businesses, and even the gangster underworld.

Although supposedly controlled by law, "money politics" led to one scandal after another when the amounts were too big, the conflicts of interest too obvious, the methods of donation were secretive, or the sources too dirty. The new electoral system was designed in part to break this pattern. To further break the "money pol-

The Big Three of Japanese Scandals

Lockheed, 1974. The U.S. aircraft manufacturer was found to be delivering major bribes to Japanese politicians to get them to purchase Lockheed jet fighters for the Japanese air force. Lockheed pleaded that it was just doing business like everyone else in Japan, and that if it hadn't bribed it wouldn't have gotten any contracts. The Japanese politicians said they needed the money for party campaign expenses, but much of it stayed in private pockets. Energetic Prime Minister Kakuei Tanaka (1972–74) was brought down by the scandal and arrested and jailed briefly in 1976.

Recruit, 1988–89. The head of the Recruit Corporation privately sold untraded shares of stock to many LDP and a few opposition politicians at bargain prices. When the shares were publicly traded in 1986, some investors made as much as ¥100 million (over $1 million) overnight. Insider trading laws are not as strict in Japan as in the United States, but the revelation came just as the LDP was considering a major sales tax. The public was enraged, and Prime Minister Noboru Takeshita resigned in shame in 1989. A top aid committed suicide. Former Prime Minister Yasuhiro Nakasone, also implicated in the scandal, resigned from the LDP.

Sagawa, 1992. Sagawa, a parcel express firm, was found to be paying off more than sixty politicians, with the top prize of ¥500 million ($4.2 million) going to LDP faction chief Shin Kanemaru of the old Tanaka faction. During the war rightwinger Kanemaru was an Imperial official in Manchukuo and later became the LDP's main fundraiser. Kanemaru's sources included organized crime. His office safe held $50 million in cash and gold bars, but Kanemaru was fined less than $2,000. Public outrage mounted and carried over into the following year's elections.

itics" system, other new laws allowed corporate contributions only to parties, not to individuals, and offered public subsidies totaling ¥30.9 billion (over $300 million) to parties for campaign expenses.

By the early 1990s, with the Sagawa scandal, the entire LDP was looking dirty, and some LDP politicians, generally younger and with an eye to the future, began bailing out of the party before it tarnished them too and forming new parties. Such is the story of some recent prime ministers. In 1993, voters, many now openly fed up with corruption, deserted not only the LDP but the perennial second party, the Socialists, who were also tarred with scandal. The immediate reason was both parties' failure to devise and lead the reforms necessary to curb corruption, make voting fair, and break out of the rigid patterns of a state-led export economy that was in difficulty.

The increasing clamor related to corruption showed the Japanese voting public was growing more mature and more democratic. What an older generation accepted as normal, a younger generation branded as dirty, dishonorable, and undemocratic. Notice how at this same time Italian and Brazilian politicians were also brought down by the sort of corruption that had been going on for decades. These scandals were good signs, for they showed that people worldwide really do understand that they are ill-served by corrupt governments. A Japanese party that lets itself be drawn into the old patterns now understands that it will suffer electoral punishment.

COMPARING

Can "Money Politics" Be Broken?

One of the questions of interest to political scientists in the Japanese electoral and campaign-funding reforms of 1993 is whether "money politics" is so deeply rooted into Japanese political culture that no amount of legal tinkering can end it. It is an example of a classic question: Which is more important in political systems, structure or psychology? In 1993, the Diet changed the structure. Will the psychology also change as a consequence? Japan's "money politics" will be an interesting test case.

Such reforms do not necessarily work as hoped or planned. The United States has gone through several reforms of campaign financing, only to find that both candidates and contributors come up with new ways to beat the system. The underlying problem is the desperate need for prodigious campaign funds, in America for televised spots and in Japan for soundtrucks and gifts.

The Japanese reformers proposed that changing their electoral system from multimember districts would help eliminate some of this desperate need for campaign money. But will it? The United States, France, and Germany have very different electoral systems, but each have recurring scandals related to fund raising. Why? Because in each system parties and candidates figure out ways to skirt the law. And in each system, some candidates use campaign contributions—both legal and illegal—for personal expenses, which often leads to additional scandals. Notice the underlying similarity: all politicians—American, Japanese, French, and so on—are addicted to money. In the words of California political boss Jesse Unruh, "Money is the mother's milk of politics."

No One In Charge?

One of the most damning accusations of the so-called "Japan-bashers"—chief among them Karel van Wolferen, a Dutch journalist with many years' experience in Japan—was that behind an impressive façade of powerful and orderly government, there was no real locus of decision-making power in Japan, no one in charge. Prime ministers did not lead; they hung on to office for perhaps two years until the LDP faction chiefs dumped them. The faction chiefs did not lead; they simply amassed feudal power with which to battle each other. Parliamentarians did little but collect money from private interests to ensure their reelection. And even the mighty bureaucracies, such as the Finance Ministry and MITI, led only in their narrow subject areas. They promoted their particular vision of the growth of Japanese industry and exports, nothing else. Japanese government, in this light, looks like a computerized, high-tech juggernaut: it rumbles on very efficiently, crushing anything in its path, but no one is steering; it doesn't even have steerable wheels and thus procedes in a straight line.

The "no one in charge" theory—still very controversial—helps explain the maddening difficulty in getting genuine trade commitments from Tokyo. The prime minister might promise very clearly to open up the Japanese market to American products, but Japanese bureaucrats quietly vetoed the idea by failing to implement any policy changes that came from outside their ministry. The ministry was like a feudal fiefdom, answerable to no outside power. Neither did these government agencies have any common purpose or leadership. Each was dedicated to supervising its sector of the economy. The agencies and ministries do not so much respond to the calls of interest groups as direct the various interest groups to go along with bureaucratic plans, few of which are coordinated at the top.

If the "no one in charge" theory is even approximately accurate, it means Japan still suffers from serious institutional underdevelopment. A government that still operates under a basically feudal arrangement is not able to handle the problems of the late twentieth—let alone the twenty-first—century. Most obviously, a monumental and ever-growing trade imbalance puts Japan on a collision course with many other countries.

The Dangers of Multiparty Coalitions

Japan at this time gives us the chance to examine something that is getting rarer in the West European systems we studied earlier: multiparty coalition government. France and Germany, to be sure, have two-party governments (UDF and RPR in France, CDU and FDP in Germany), but they do not capture the complexity and difficulty of coalitions composed of many parties. France under the Third and Fourth Republics and Weimar Germany often had such governments. Nowadays Italy, Sweden, and Israel are examples of extreme multiparty cabinets. Japan has been recently plunged into this situation with no practice; as long as most people can remember, it was governed by a single party that had no need of coalition partners.

Japan's multiparty coalitions tend to bear out the experience of other countries with such governments. The problem, obviously, is getting several parties to agree sufficiently that the coalition hangs together. This often means that bold new policies must be compromised or even abandoned if one or more coalition partner objects and threatens to walk out of the cabinet, thus opening the government to a vote of no-confidence in the Diet. In Japan, this has tended to be the Socialists, the largest party in the coalition but also the one with the least in common with the other parties, which are middle-of-the-road in outlook. When the Social Democrats (SDPJ), as the JSP renamed itself, withdrew their support, the coalition parties longer commanded a majority in parliament. The subsequent LDP-Socialist coalition of 1994 looked like it was made for paralysis.

There are areas in which the Social Democrats have actually become a rather conservative party in the sense that they wish to preserve the status quo rather than reform it. The SDPJ, for example, portraying themselves as defenders of farmers, became the most protectionist of all Japaese parties; they would lock out most foreign farm products. This made cooperation difficult between the Social Democrats and the centrist-reformist parties of the coalition that would open up Japan to more imports.

Hosokawa was very successful in getting the initial electoral reforms of 1993 passed the Diet; his coalition held together because all member parties were committed to those reforms. Many LDP members even voted for the reforms. It is likely, however, that as any reformist cabinet tries economic reforms—namely, upsetting the "iron triangle" described above—one or more of its coalition partners will balk and perhaps drop out of the cabinet. The more members in a coalition, the more likely this is to happen. Then holding the coalition together becomes a full-time job

Plus ça Change . . . Who Is Really in Charge?

Who really organized the new reformist government of 1993 and 1994? It was not Prime Ministers Morihiro Hosokawa of the Japan New Party or Tsutomu Hata of the much larger Japan Renewal Party, but Ichiro Ozawa, the leader of Japan Renewal . Ozawa, himself a former LDP politician, out of public view put together the complex coalitions but took no portfolio for himself. Ozawa, in effect, continued the Japanese pattern of powerful faction chiefs who could make or break cabinets. If this is the case, then we should not evaluate any prime minister as a "strong" or "new type" of prime minister but rather look behind the scenes to see who sets up deals. Hosokawa and Hata lasted precisely as long as Ozawa wanted them to last, which is the way things went during the LDP years.

and major initiatives become impossible. This leads to immobilism—getting stuck over a major issue—which was the fate of Italy's long-ruling *pentapartito* (five-party) cabinets. Poland had a seven-party coalition in 1992–93 and suffered from immobilism on the crucial question of privatization.

Japan's eight-party cabinet—probably a world record—did not function long. If Japanese political reform works, one of its major concerns must be to decrease the number of parties needed to form a coalition. This means a change in the party system toward fewer and bigger parties. This in turn means a change in the electoral system, which Hosokawa already engineered.

The next major step is to consolidate the three LDP-breakaway parties—Japan Renewal, New Party Harbinger, and the Japan New Party—into one, which they tried to do in 1994. There were no ideological differences between them, only personality struggles, just as within the old LDP. These struggles are not trivial, as powerful political personalities do not want to give up their leadership positions. What these three parties and their leaders realized is that under the new, partly single-member system one large party gets a bonus in seats compared to three small parties running separately. In many constituencies, if the three new LDP-spinoff parties insisted on running separately, all three could be beaten by the Social Democrats. Accordingly, the pressure to merge is strong; if they do not succeed, Japan's political reforms won't amount to much.

The Hopes of Reform

If they can pull off a series of reforms, Japan's post-LDP parties will in effect reinvent Japanese government. Reformers are hoping to kill as many as five birds with one stone. Namely, by deregulating the strongly regulated Japanese economy, including its barriers to foreign imports, and pumping lots of money Keynesian-style into public works, they will simultaneously:

Fight recession. The early 1990s found Japan (and West Europe) in the worst recession in living memory. Japan's economy grew not at all, and unemployment topped 3 percent (low for the rest of the world, but bad news in Japan). If the new governments can get Japan out of recession quickly, their popularity and political power will grow. The Finance Ministry was horrified at plans for deficit spending, but the Japanese economy can easily afford a few years of deficit spending with little danger of inflation. Another advantage of this policy is that it will . . .

Raise living standards. As we will discuss in the next chapter, Japanese do not live as well as they should. Consumption has been held down in favor of growth and exports. By encouraging Japanese to consume more—including more imported goods—cabinets could win great support from average citizens. Another advantage of this policy is that it will . . .

Reduce trade surpluses. Japan's gigantic trade surpluses brought little gain and much pain. It helped average Japanese not at all and encouraged foolish (and sometimes lost) investments. Even some business people and MITI began to wonder what Japan was supposed to do with its trade balances. They certainly didn't win Japan many friends worldwide.

Curb the bureaucracy. Japanese from all walks of life, from average consumers to top business executives, say they've had it with regulations and regulators. One big chemicals exec urged the new government to smash the iron triangle with a sledgehammer. The parties in the reformist coalitions agreed that they must cut bureaucratic powers, but it is likely that one or more of these parties have connections to the bureaucracy and will object to anything but cosmetic reform. This will be the showdown point of any reformist cabinet.

Break the LDP stranglehold. This is the big bonus point a reformist coalition will collect if it can carry out its reforms. Once Japanese voters see that another party can do better than the LDP at delivering prosperity, they will break away from the LDP and cast their votes for a new centrist-reformist party that could enjoy many years in office.

Some of these measures will be difficult to carry out. Wide sectors of the bureaucracy, sensing that their power is on the line, will resist and sabotage reforms. Prime ministers will have to be very tough with recalcitrant bureaucrats. Fortunately, they've got a lot of public support on their side. Ultimately, however, if they cannot break the LDP-bureaucracy leg of the iron triangle, it will break them, and the reformist era will be remembered as a short interlude between the usual setup of LDP cabinets and bureaucratic power. What is going on in Japan now is system change that is more subtle but just as important for us as system change in Russia.

Vocabulary Building

analog	juggernaut
assent	"money politics"
deference	multiparty
"descent from heaven"	*pentapartito*
faction	Todai
"iron triangle"	

Further Reference

CAMPBELL, JOHN C. *How Policies Change: The Japanese Government and the Aging Society.* Princeton, NJ: Princeton University Press, 1992.

FLANAGAN, SCOTT, C., JOJI WATANUKI, BRADLEY RICHARDSON, ICHIRO MIYAKE, and SHINSUKE KOHEI. *The Japanese Voter.* New Haven, CT: Yale University Press, 1991.

JOHNSON, CHALMERS. *MITI and the Japanese Miracle.* Stanford, CA: Stanford University Press, 1982.

WOLFEREN, KAREL VAN. *The Enigma of Japanese Power: People and Politics in a Stateless Nation.* New York: Vintage Books, 1990.

ZAHO, QUANSHENG. *Japanese Policymaking: The Politics behind Politics: Informal Mechanisms and the Making of China Policy.* Westport, CT: Praeger, 1993.

CHAPTER 26

What Japanese Quarrel About

The Japanese Economic Miracle

For some years after the war, "made in Japan" suggested a product was junk, probably tin cans recycled from the ashes of Japan's cities. In some cases, the term was justified. All countries that are just starting their economic climb seem to be producing cheap products of dubious quality. Many, however, soon climb out of the junk stage, as Japan did in the 1950s. In 1960, Japan was the richest country in Asia but still had a per capita GDP of only $380, one-eighth the American. By 1990, Japan's per cap was higher than America's. (This is tricky to measure. See the box on "Purchasing Power Parity" on page 334.)

The catalyst was the Korean War that began in June 1950. U.S. forces in the Far East suddenly found themselves underequipped and gave contracts for clothing, footwear, and other items to low-bid Japanese producers. (South Korea's industrial takeoff followed precisely the same pattern in the late 1960s, only now the catalyst was the Vietnam War.) The quality of the Japanese goods was not bad. After the war, many U.S. manufacturers of civilian goods followed the U.S. military lead and gave Japanese similar contracts. The quality got better all the time, and the costs were a fraction of U.S. producer costs. In the 1960s, Japanese cars were looked down on as something of a joke, but by the 1970s they commanded world respect for economy and fine workmanship. A continual pattern has been to underestimate the Japanese product—until it puts you out of business.

As in postwar West Germany, workers in postwar Japan did not ask for too much; they were glad to have a job that put some food on the family's table. In politics they were also cautious and mostly gave their vote to the moderate conservative party with the misleading name Liberal Democrat. This party—more accurately, a

Japan Destroys the German Photo Industry

One of the first indicators of what the Japanese could do in terms of quality came in the photo-optical industry. Photojournalists covering the Korean War tried Japanese-made lenses from Nikon and Canon on their German-made camera bodies and found to their surprise that they were excellent, sometimes better than expensive German lenses. Then they tried the Japanese-made bodies and found they were pretty good, too. The German photo industry should have started running scared, but, like most Westerners, tended to scoff at anything made in Japan.

In addition to lower wages, the Japanese photo industry had something going for it: a compulsion to constantly innovate. The Germans might bring out a new model every decade; the Japanese firms, desperately competing with one another, brought out new models every couple of years. In 1959, Nikon introduced the landmark Nikon F, a top-quality single-lens reflex that allowed the photographer to see exactly what the film saw. Photographers turned from the pricey German Leica rangefinder cameras and embraced the Nikon F, the professional workhorse for more than a decade that was constantly modified and improved. Boasted Nikon ads: "Today, there's almost no other choice." During the 1960s, the Japanese photo industry captured essentially the entire world market as the German photo industry shrank into irrelevance. Change or die.

In this process we see some of the factors that contributed to Japanese manufacturing success in other lines. With low wages (now no longer the case), a skilled and dedicated work force, constantly innovative designs, government encouragement, and farsighted bank loans, Japan went on from cameras to consumer electronics, where it also became the world leader.

collection of political factions—ruled Japan unbroken from the time of its formation in 1955 until 1993 and thus became an important institution and pillar of stability. The Liberal Democrats offered the Japanese growth and jobs. For most Japanese, this was enough. They lived to work and, accustomed to modest living standards and obedience, did not vote for change, at least not until 1993.

By then, several things had changed. Japan's period of extraordinary economic growth finally ended with a major recession that brought unemployment for the first time in a generation. The Tokyo stock market and real-estate market bubble burst, leaving many corporations and banks looking poorer and foolish. The long-ruling LDP started looking incompetent. A younger generation of Japanese were well-educated and well-traveled and saw how people in other industrialized countries did not live in rabbit hutches and pay exhorbitant prices. Many no longer were willing to support the LDP.

The Secret of Japan's Success

Since the 1970s, when the West became aware of how fast the Japanese economy was growing—an incredible average of 7.7 percent a year per capita GDP growth from 1950 to 1990—assorted pundits have tried to explain how they did it. Some of the attempts fall into the Mystique Mistake mentioned earlier. Here are some of the more important nonmystical factors:

Confucianism. As comparativists, we make comparisons to solve puzzles like Japan's rapid economic growth. First, do other countries show similar patterns of rapid growth? Yes, in fact many East Asian countries do. In addition to China (see our later discussion of China's economic growth), the "Four Tigers" of South Korea, Taiwan, Hong Kong, and Singapore have for the last couple of decades also shown remarkable growth. Culturally, all share a Confucian background because all were under the cultural sway of China. Confucianism stresses hard work, stability, and hierarchy. It frowns on high personal consumption; people should save, not spend. Some have argued that a Confucian work ethic gave the Orient the functional equivalent of a Protestant work ethic, a religious or psychological motivation to work hard.

Productivity. Another factor for rapid growth is a level of productivity higher than the level of wages, that is, workers who produce a lot without getting paid a lot. (See the "Productivity" box on page 71.) In Britain, we saw how productivity increases were mediocre while wages and other costs were high, gradually squeezing British products off the world market, something Thatcher attempted to correct. In Germany, we saw how wage restraint coupled with increases in productivity gave German products a competitive edge and a major export market, until recently when wages jumped way out of line with productivity. In Japan, for a long time, productivity raced ahead of wages, giving Japan a marvelous opening to produce much of the world's advanced consumer electronics. Japanese factories could simply put more high-quality labor into a product than other countries.

Education. As we discussed in earlier chapters, productivity is partly the result of new, more efficient machines and partly of increasingly skilled workers and managers who know how to use them. Japan (and the Four Tigers) paid a lot of attention to education, especially at the primary and secondary levels (from elementary through high school). Such education is free, supervised at the national level, and compulsory. This gave Japan a highly skilled labor force, one that can read, follow instructions, and do math computations. (Much of the U.S. labor force can't.) Interestingly, Japan and its high-growth neighbors pay little attention to higher (college and university) education, finding that much of it contributes little to economic growth. Japanese are not encouraged to "find themselves" in college. If young Japanese want a college education, they can pay for it themselves.

Savings. Japanese save a lot, far more than Americans (which may not be a fair comparison, as Americans save little). This has made Japanese banks the world's biggest and made available tremendous capital resources for investment in growth industries. Japanese save for at least two reasons. First, thrift is an old tradition. Second, Japanese pension plans and social security are weak for an advanced country; to have a comfortable old age, Japanese know they must put aside their own money. Some economists think that savings alone is the biggest element in explaining Japanese economic growth.

State Supervision. This is where a discussion of Japanese economic growth gets controversial, although probably more Americans quarrel about it than Japanese. Is state supervision, going back to the Meiji modernizers and continuing with MITI and the Treasury Ministry in our day, the key factor in Japan's rapid growth? Most of the other fast-growth East Asian economies have some degree of Japanese-style state supervision as well. (Hong Kong has none, and China's vigorous free-market sector, based heavily on foreign investment, is essentially unplanned; only China's money-losing state sector is supervised.)

What do we mean by "state supervised"? Does it mean simply getting the macro-economy in order—little public debt, plentiful savings, low inflation, sufficient investment capital—and then standing back and letting the market do its stuff? Some economists call this "the fundamentals"; it fits the postwar German *Sozialmarkt.* Or does it mean government intervention in the microeconomy as well, with state technocrats picking rising and declining industries to, respectively, foster or phase out? This would be the Japanese model.

A classical or neo-classical economist looks at the Japanese economy and says there is no evidence that state supervision boosted Japanese growth rates. Japan got its macroeconomy or "fundamentals" right, which was all that really mattered, and might have done just as well or even better without a MITI. The bureaucrats who persuaded Japanese firms to act according to some government plan were by and large just persuading them to do what they would have done anyway. Supervision may have been superfluous. You hardly need to tell a rapidly growing industry to keep growing. Actually, the only way you could demonstrate that Japanese economic intervention worked is to have two very similar countries operate under different policies, say, one with a MITI and the other without, and see which grows faster. Such controlled experiments are hard to come by in the real world.

From Success to Failure

By the early 1990s, it was occuring to some observers of Japan that government supervisors make mistakes. Under MITI prodding and financing, Japanese electronics firms sunk and lost vast sums in trying to develop the "fifth generation" of computers and high-definition television. Both projects bombed. MITI geniuses pushed Japanese car makers to go for ever-larger world market shares—instead of the usual capitalist goal of profitability—so that during the recession of the early 1990s, the car plants had major excess capacity and only one (Toyota) was making

 Macro and Microeconomics

Economists make a distinction between macroeconomics and microeconomics. *Macro* means the big picture, looking at the country's economy as a whole. Macroeconomics is typically the first course an undergraduate takes in economics. It covers GDP and its growth, aggregate supply and demand, money supply, inflation, public debt, and the like. *Micro* means the little, close-up picture and gets into the running of an industry or firm. It includes product selection, workforce, productivity, financing, and related topics.

Conservative economists tend to argue that getting the macroeconomy right but keeping hands off the microeconomy is all the government needs to do to promote growth. Individual entrepreneurs know better what and how to produce than a committee of bureaucrats. Liberal economists tend to argue that at least some state intervention in the microeconomy is also necessary for really rapid growth and to correct what they call "market failures."

any money. MITI had pushed the car makers to expand until they had overexpanded.

Government supervisors had pushed certain sectors of Japanese industry into high levels of automation, productivity, and efficiency. Other sectors got left behind. Distribution was largely in the hands of neighborhood mom-and-pop stores that were convenient and friendly but did not compete on the basis of price. Until recently, U.S.-style discounting was hated, feared, and denounced in Japan as ruinous of family shops and family values. Gradually, though, as more Japanese traveled and found they could buy Panasonics and Minoltas cheaper in the United States, discount chains started opening in Japan.

Agriculture got left behind. The typical small Japanese farm of a few acres was hopelessly inefficient, but the Agricultural Ministry protected Japanese farmers from cheaper imports. This cost Japanese consumers dearly and angered Japan's trading partners. Many Japanese farmers turned to part-time farming anyway, a pattern typical of industrializing countries. Unprotected, many of these people would soon conclude that they should sell their small holdings, either to larger and more-efficient farmers or to developers, who could build citizens more badly needed apartments. There is protected and tax-exempt farmland in and near major cities that really should be subject to market forces. Its sale would make some "farmers" rich while helping solve Japan's housing deficit.

Japanese were generally well satisfied with their economic growth since World War II. By the early 1990s, however, they were not so satisfied. The shortcomings of their supervised-market system became increasingly clear. The Tokyo stock exchange lost half its value over a few years from the late 1980s to the early 1990s. Real-estate prices plunged as well, and many Japanese banks and corporations were not nearly as rich as they thought they were. Some even went bankrupt, a procedure that the cozy arrangement of banks and bureaucrats had rarely permitted before. But the bankruptcy of an inefficient, money-losing enterprise is not evil; it's good. Keeping it afloat through the standard Japanese pattern of unwise bank loans and government subsidies merely disguises the firm's illness and blocks the market's signals that it's time for this company to fold.

Increasingly, both Japanese and foreign analysts wonder if Japan's economic mechanisms will work in the new age, an age of lower-cost competitors and open markets. Already, Korea and Taiwan have seized the initiative in several areas that

Japanese Understatement: "Japan Has a Trade Surplus"

With the change of government in 1993, many Japanese started admitting what Westerners had long criticized them for. Said one top Japanese corporate executive, "It is a fact that Japan has a trade surplus with the United States, and that Japan's market openings are not sufficient." The trade surplus was gigantic, and many Japanese had at long last come to wonder if it was doing them any good.

used to be Japanese: steelmaking, shipbuilding, and even some consumer electronics. China looms not far behind. If China uses the same approach to economic growth that Japan used, who will be able to compete? Some Japanese are already worried; they fear that their really good days of rapid growth are over. This is no cause for despair; it just means Japan is becoming an ordinary country.

Should Japanese Live Better?

Yes, it would be good for them and good for us, because they would buy more U.S. products, such as foodstuffs and building materials. They have earned it. They lifted their country up from the rubble of World War II to heights few Japanese could have dreamed of. Holding down domestic consumption while accumulating vast capital resources was a great prescription for rapid economic growth. But pursued too long, it overshot the mark and produced serious imbalances. The yen, held too low for too long, shot from over 300 to the dollar to 100 to the dollar. This hurt many Japanese firms that lost foreign sales, for now their products were too costly.

Purchasing Power Parity

Per capita GDP figures can be deceptive, because they do not include the cost of living in each country. Japanese, on average, make more money a year than Americans but live more poorly. To correct this seeming discrepancy, economists have begun calculating "purchasing power parity" (PPP) in addition to the usual per capita GDP that is translated into

	GDP PER CAP AT EXCHANGE RATE	PURCHASING POWER PARITY
Japan	$25,430	$19,390
West Germany	22,320	19,770
United States	22,130	22,130
Canada	20,470	19,120
France	19,490	18,430
Russia	3,220	6,930
Brazil	2,940	5,240
South Africa	2,560	4,800
China	370	1,680

Sources: OECD, World Bank, and UNDP

dollars at the "market exchange rate." Notice how much the two differ.

Which figure is the most valid? In terms of judging a nation's international economic power, the exchange rate is the better indicator; it shows who has the money. In terms of who lives well, the PPP is clearly better. On average, Americans still live best even though several countries have larger per capita GDPs as measured by exchange rate.

What happens when the two measures are seriously out of line? It indicates that the country's currency is overvalued or undervalued, sometimes by market forces and sometimes by deliberate government policy. In the examples given in the table, the four currencies from advanced countries are overvalued in relation to the dollar, but the four currencies from poorer countries are undervalued. For example, Chinese live a lot better than the exchange-rate figure of $370 would indicate. China's real per capita GDP is 8 percent that of America's, not 2 percent.

If the Japanese had simply consumed more—including more imported goods—at an earlier date, they might have avoided the excess liquidity that fueled the stock-market and real-estate bubbles. Too many yen chased investments to the sky; then the bubbles burst, doing great harm to Japan's growth and stability. Ironically, Japanese investors got terribly burned in buying U.S. firms. They overpaid, found the firms were not so profitable, and sometimes had to sell at a loss. Americans for a while were frightened of Japanese investments. They shouldn't have been. The investments are all to our good. If rich people want to overpay for your property, do not discourage them.

But it was foolish for Japan. If more profits had been channeled into pay and dividends, Japanese could have consumed more and lived better. But, curiously, some Japanese don't want to live better, at least not if that means harming the livelihood of other Japanese. For example, Japan, by keeping out foreign rice and subsidizing Japan's small, inefficient rice farms, forced consumers to pay about six times the world price for rice. Many didn't mind, for they understood they were keeping Japanese farmers employed. Thus overpriced Japanese foodstuffs were a sort of indirect welfare transfer to help cousin Kenji on the farm.

More and more young Japanese, however, think this is ridiculous. They notice that cousin Kenji works only part time on his rice patch anyway because he can't earn a living from it; most of the week Kenji works in town. Young Japanese are more likely to have traveled and been amazed at the cheap cost of living abroad. They find the taste of American rice acceptable—California growers now mostly plant short-grain oriental-style rice—and even bring back a bag as tourists. They may have developed a taste for beef and want it at $5 a pound, not $25. Younger Japanese are thus more likely to want a Japan open to two-way world trade than their parents, who prefer the one-way model. Young Japanese also tend to dislike their cumbersome merchandising system—in which everything passes through costly layers of trading companies to small retail outlets—which carries few foreign goods. By law, it was very difficult for foreign firms to break into Japanese retail commerce.

 ## *Silly Excuses to Exclude Foreign Goods*

Over the years, various Japanese officials have offered these excuses to keep out American products and foodstuffs:

- Japanese snow is different from American snow, so U.S.–made skis don't work properly on Japanese ski runs.

- Japanese intestines are different, so Japanese cannot digest U.S. beef, so none should be imported. (Uttered by Tsutomu Hata years ago when he was a member of an LDP cabinet. Hata, who recanted his statement, was prime minister briefly in 1994.)

- American-made aluminum baseball bats do not have Japanese safety-inspection seals on them, so they are unsafe.

- Japanese are used only to their own kind of rice, so American rice tastes terrible to them.

It is this clash of generations which underlays much of recent Japanese politics. Younger voters are more likely to reject the standard postwar parties—the LDP and JSP—and turn to one of the new parties that seem to promise a Japan more open to foreign imports and the lower prices that come with them. This is part of the story of what happened in the 1993 elections. To some degree, they were a vote in favor of a higher standard of living with ballots cast along generation lines.

Should Japan Rearm?

In the aftermath of a devastating war and at the behest of MacArthur's staff, a "no-war clause" was made part of Japan's postwar constitution. In 1947, this seemed like a fine idea, but with North Korea's attack on South Korea in 1950, some Americans and Japanese began to have second thoughts. Would Article 9 mean that Japan would stay defenseless in a rough neighborhood or depend forever on U.S. forces? In the 1950s, Japan began building "Self-Defense Forces." Defense spending has been informally limited to only about 1 percent of GDP, and there is no draft. Nonetheless, given the size of Japan's GDP, its defense budget is now among the world's highest even though its military manpower, at about 238,000, is modest. Japan's Self-Defense Forces are small but well funded and well equipped.

 Poor Man's PPP: The Big Mac Index

Purchasing power parity, described in a previous box, is a more accurate measure of how well people live, but it is hard to calculate. Economists must find a market basket of goods and services that is the same in each country. A quick and cheeky way to approximate PPP was devised by the British newsweekly *The Economist*: compare the price of a

	PRICE IN LOCAL CURRENCY	IN DOLLARS
Brazil	Cr 1,500	$1.58
Britain	£ 1.81	2.65
China	Yuan 9.00	1.03
France	FFr 18.50	3.17
Germany	DM 4.60	2.69
Japan	¥ 391	3.77
Russia	Ruble 2,900	1.66
United States	$ 2.30	—

Big Mac sandwich at the local McDonald's with its U.S. (big-city) price. Since a Big Mac requires the same ingredients, labor, and overhead wherever it is produced, it is actually a mini–market basket that reflects local costs fairly accurately. Some 1994 prices of Big Macs are given in the table. Wherever a Big Mac is more expensive than the U.S. price of $2.30, it implies the local currency is overvalued, the case in West Europe and Japan, where the cost of living is high. Where the Big Mac is cheaper, it implies the local currency is undervalued, as in Russia, Brazil, and China. Notice how the Big Mac Index points the same way (overvalued or undervalued) as the more-complex PPP calculation explained on page 334 but not with the same magnitude. The Big Mac Index is only a rough approximation of PPP because it's too urban and tourist-oriented, and thus often overpriced. Still, it is the handiest test around, something any tourist can do on a stroll.

"No War" for Japan

Article 9 of the Japanese constitution states that the Japanese people "forever renounce war as a sovereign right of the nation and the threat or use of force as a means of settling international disputes" and adds that "land, sea, and air forces, as well as other war potential will never be maintained."

Japanese leftists argue that their Self-Defense Forces are clearly at odds with both the letter and spirit of the constitution, and expanding them would compound the error. Most Japanese think that their forces, which are not supposed to be used outside of Japan, are a prudent and necessary shield; some would be willing to drop Article 9. The United States also thinks Japan should be able to defend itself and take a leadership role in regional security—as Japan has done splendidly in Cambodian peacekeeping—and has encouraged Japan to do more. That is the great question: Should Japan expand its Self-Defense Forces to the point where they can defend Japan on their own and keep the peace regionally? At that point, however, they would also be able to project Japanese military power into neighboring countries, and that is something neighbors fear.

The really explosive question is whether Japan should be willing to acquire nuclear weapons. Before North Korea began its ambitious and dangerous program to build nuclear weapons, the answer to that in Japan was a resounding "no!" But with North Korea already producing bombs—and with North Korean missiles able to reach Japan—more Japanese have begun to think Japan should acquire a few nukes as a deterrence. The United States has not encouraged the idea and has pledged that its armed might protects Japan from North Korean bombs. Like De Gaulle decades earlier, some Japanese have begun to wonder if this U.S. promise is reliable. With the Cold War ended, more and more Japanese do not like to remain de-

Repeal Article 9?

Probably not. The way Japan will likely expand its military power is not by directly repealing Article 9, which would be too controversial. In 1993, for example, Defense Minister Keisuke Nakanishi was forced to resign after he touched off a political furor by suggesting such a constitutional revision. Instead, look for new laws or interpretations permitting the Japanese Self-Defense Forces to participate more fully in UN and other multilateral peacekeeping efforts. The move will be sold to the public as part of Japan's contribution to world and regional peace.

Deficit Spending for Japan?

One of the joys of the Japanese macroeconomy was the absence of public debt. The conservative Finance Ministry had watched government expenditures closely. Then, in the early 1990s, the reformist government of Prime Minsiter Hosokawa proposed major deficit spending to lift Japan out of recession. Many conservatives, including the Finance Ministry, howled in protest. Is deficit spending a danger for Japan?

Probably not, if the size of the deficit and number of years are limited. Unlike the United States and most of West Europe, Japan had run a "public-sector surplus" for some years; that is, all levels of Japanese government (including local) have taken in more in taxes than they have spent. This means Japan now has the wiggle room to do more public spending, even deficit spending. America, with fair-sized deficits (but not, as percent of GDP, nearly the biggest in the world) does not have this option. Increasing U.S. deficit spending now would likely be quite inflationary. Japan doesn't have this problem.

In fact, in the early 1990s Japan was threatened with an extremely rare economic malady: deflation, that is, goods getting cheaper. Although not nearly as dangerous as inflation, it too has some negative consequences. How to combat deflation? Easy, quick, and enjoyable: mildly increase the supply of the yen in circulation to give every Japanese a little added purchasing power. If this brings down the yen a little in relation to the dollar, so much the better, as it will help Japan regain some lost overseas markets. Japan need not worry about inflation. Go ahead, Tokyo, spend and enjoy.

pendent on U.S. protection, and more and more Americans are not enthusiastic about defending distant countries.

Even if the world could persuade or force North Korea to cease its nuclear program, Japan would still face two nuclear powers in Asia: China and Russia. If it faces them alone, it will increasingly debate the need for nuclear weapons. As history's only victims of nuclear war thus far, many Japanese adamantly oppose any nukes on Japanese soil. Even hinting at a nuclear program could set off massive protests. Accordingly, the issue is likely to linger out of public debate for a long time, but it will always be there.

A New Japan?

Japan is difficult to write about now because it is undergoing system change. The certainties of a few years ago—the Liberal Democrats would always lead Japan, corruption doesn't count, the Japanese economy would keep up its rapid growth, and Japan will follow the United States on security matters—have eroded and are not likely to be restored, at least not in their old shape. This is a new and exciting but unpredictable era in Japanese politics.

Will it come out where we want it to come out? Will we have a new, clean democratic partner across the Pacific ready to trade with us on a two-way basis? Or will we face an angry, protectionist Japan where some of the old nationalism links up with an enlarged military?

Neither the Japanese nor ourselves have had time to digest the political implications of Japan's burst economic bubble. If, instead of being a growing economic giant with jobs for all, it becomes one competitor among many lower-cost producers, how will the Japanese people and political parties react? If Japan is at last becoming a "normal" country, one with approximately the same problems as other advanced, industrialized democracies, the changes are all to the good. If not, we may wish we had the old Japan of the LDP and cheap transistors back. How Japan fits into the modern world will determine a great deal for the peace of Asia. To see how another Asian giant has handled the onslaught of modernity, let us now turn to China.

Vocabulary Building

Big Mac Index	"no war" clause
deficit spending	overvalued
exhorbitant	productivity
innovative	Protestant ethic
macroeconomics	purchasing power parity
microeconomics	retail

Further Reference

ANDERSON, STEPHEN J. *Welfare Policy and Politics in Japan: Beyond the Developmental State.* New York: Paragon House, 1993.

ITO, TAKATOSHI. *The Japanese Economy.* Cambridge, MA: MIT Press, 1992.

KOMIYA, RYUTARO. *The Japanese Economy: Trade, Industry, and Government.* Tokyo: University of Tokyo Press, 1990.

OKIMOTO, DANIEL. *Between MITI and the Market: Japanese Industrial Policy for High Technology.* Stanford, CA: Stanford University Press, 1989.

THUROW, LESTER. *Head to Head: The Coming Economic Battle Among Japan, Europe, and America.* New York: Morrow, 1992.

WOOD, CHRISTOPHER. *The Bubble Economy: Japan's Extraordinary Speculative Boom of the 80's and the Dramatic Bust of the 90's.* New York: Atlantic Monthly Press, 1993.

WORLD BANK. *The East Asian Miracle: Economic Growth and Public Policy.* New York: Oxford University Press, 1993.

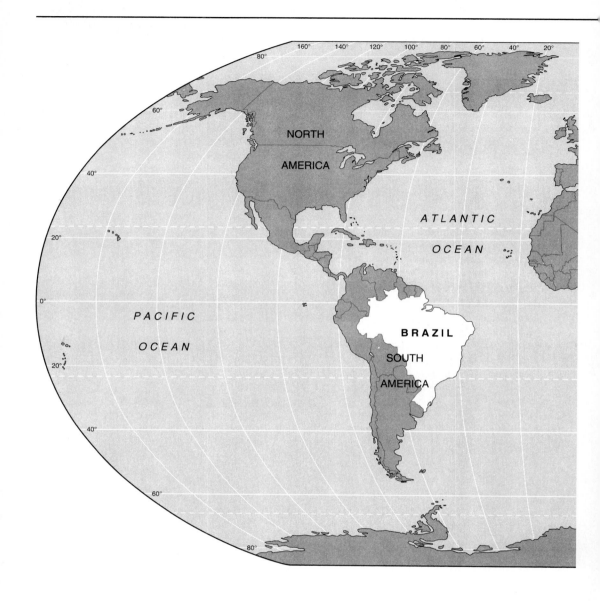

PART VI ❋ *The Third World*

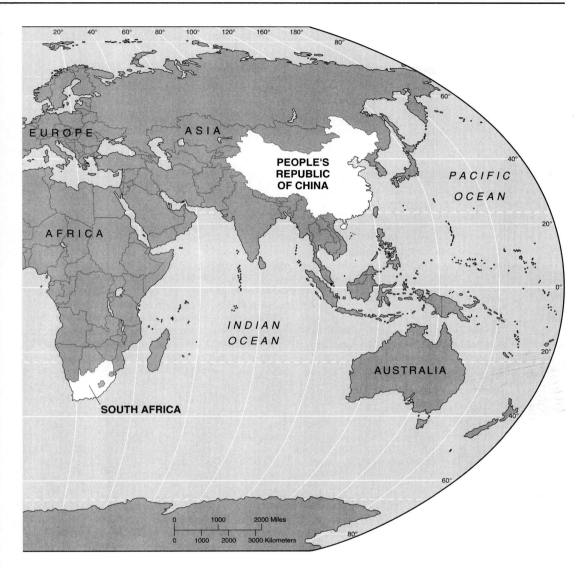

What is the Third World?

Coined by French writers in the 1950's, *le Tiers Monde* (the Third World) indicated the majority of humankind that was in neither the Western capitalist First World nor the Communist Second World. It is an awfully broad-brush term, covering Asia, Africa, and Latin America, that permits few firm generalizations. Now, with the collapse of communism in East Europe and the ex–Soviet Union, the Third World is simply everything that is not "the West," meaning Europe, the United States, Canada, Australia, and now Japan. Some say the only meaningful dividing line is now "the West and the rest." The Third World is mostly poor, but some oil-producing countries are rich, and some of its lands are industrializing so fast that they will soon be affluent. It is mostly nonwhite. Almost all of it, at one time or another, was a colony of a European imperial power. Most of it is hot and closer to the equator than the rich countries, so some writers suggest we call it the Global South.

One generalization stands up fairly well: the Third World, Global South, LDCs (less-developed countries), or what ever else you care to call it, is politically unstable. The political institutions of almost all of its 120-plus countries are weak, and this is their chief difference with the West. Most Third World lands are wracked by political, social, and economic tensions that explode in revolution, coups, and upheavals, and that often end in dictatorship. Few could be classified as stable democracies; all of the West could be. India is an amazing exception—although it went through a bout of authoritarian rule under Indira Gandhi—but Pakistan is a more typical example: unstable elected governments alternating with military rule. We should really come up with some better name than "Third World" to describe the complexity of the lands that are home to three-quarters or more of the human race, but until such a term has established itself, we shall settle for "Third World."

CHAPTER 27

China

The Impact of the Past

A Crowded Land

China's population is 1.2 billion and growing, even though the regime emphatically promotes one-child families. Less than one-third of China's territory is arable (suitable for cultivation)—rice in the well-watered south and wheat in the drier north. China's "man-land ratio"—now only a quarter acre of farmland (and currently shrinking) for each Chinese—long imposed limits on politics, economics, and social thought.

With little new territory to expand into, Chinese society evolved "steady-state" structures that concentrated on preserving stability and making peasants content with what they had rather than encouraging them to pioneer and innovate. Labor-saving devices would render peasants jobless and were therefore not encouraged. China's remarkable achievements in science and technology—which put China far ahead of medieval Europe—remained curiosities instead of contributions to an industrial revolution.

Commercial expansion was also discouraged. Instead of a Western mentality of reinvestment, growth, and risk taking, Chinese merchants sought only a steady-state relationship with peasants and government officials; they depended heavily on government permits and monopolies.

Neither was there much interest in overseas expansion. Once they had their Middle Kingdom perfected, the Chinese saw no use for anything foreign. All outlying countries were inhabited by barbarians who were permitted to *kowtow* (respectfully show homage to) and pay tribute to the emperor. China had all the technology for overseas expansion but simply didn't bother. Expeditions brought back the news that there wasn't anything worthwhile beyond the seas. Thus for centuries China remained a stay-at-home country.

A Traditional Political System

Politically too, China was steady-state. China unified very early. Feudalism was replaced by a centralized empire, complete with impartial civil-service exams to select the best talent. The resulting Mandarin class—schooled in the Confucian classics, which stressed obedience, authority, and hierarchy—was interested in perpetuating the system, not changing it. A gentry class of better-off people served as the literate

The People's Republic of China. Solid black line shows approximate route of 1934–35 Long March.

intermediaries between the Mandarins and the 90 percent of the population that were peasants. The words of one peasant song:

> When the sun rises, I toil;
> When the sun sets, I rest;
> I dig wells for water;
> I till the fields for food;
> What has the Emperor's power to do with me?

Dynasties came and went every few hundred years in what has become known as the "dynastic cycle." As the old dynasty became increasingly incompetent, water systems went unrepaired, famine broke out, wars and banditry appeared, and corruption grew. In the eyes of the people, it looked as if the emperor had lost the "Mandate of Heaven," that is, his legitimate right to rule. A conqueror, either Chinese or foreign (Mongol or Manchu), found it easy to take over a demoralized empire. By the very fact of his victory, the new ruler seemed to have gained the Mandate of Heaven. Under vigorous new emperors, things went well; the breakdowns were fixed. After some generations, though, the new dynasty fell prey to the same ills as the old, and people, especially the literate, began to think the emperor had lost his heavenly mandate. The cycle was ready to start over.

Two millennia of Chinese empire made an indelible mark on the China of today. Not a feudal system—even though the Communists denounced it as feudal— it was, rather, a "bureaucratic empire," with an emperor at the top setting the direction and tone, Mandarins carrying out Beijing's writ, gentry running local affairs, and peasants, the overwhelming majority of the population, toiling in the fields. New dynasties soon found themselves lulled into accepting the system and becoming part of it. Even the Communists have not been able to totally eradicate the classic pattern of Chinese civilization.

Confucianism: Government by Right Thinking

The scholar Confucius (551 to 479 B.C.) advised rulers that the key to good, stable government lay in instilling correct, moral behavior in ruled and rulers alike. Each person must understand his or her role and perform it obediently. Sons were subservient to fathers, wives to husbands, younger brothers to elder brothers, and subjects to rulers. The ruler sets a moral example by purifying his spirit and perfecting his manners. In this way, goodness leads to power.

The Confucian system emphasized that good government starts with thinking good thoughts in utter sincerity. If things go wrong, it indicates rulers have been insincere. Mao Zedong hated everything old China stood for, but he couldn't help picking up the Confucian stress on right thinking. Adding a Marxist twist, Mao taught that one was a proletarian not because of blue-collar origin but because one had revolutionary, pure thoughts. Confucius would have been pleased.

The Long Collapse

For some 2,000 years the Middle Kingdom proved capable of absorbing the changes thrown at it in the form of invasions, famines, and new dynasties. The old pattern always succeeded in reasserting itself. But as the modern epoch impinged on China, at least two new factors arose that the system could not handle: population growth and Western penetration.

In 1741, China's population was 143 million; just a century later, in 1851, it had become an amazing 432 million, the result of new crops (corn and sweet potatoes from the Americas), internal peace under the Manchu dynasty, some new farmland, and just plain harder work on the part of the peasants. Taxation and administration lagged behind the rapid population growth, which hit as the Manchus were going into the typical decline phase of their dynastic cycle in the nineteenth century.

At about the same time the West was penetrating and disorienting China. It was a clash of two cultures—Western dynamism and greed versus Chinese stability—and the Chinese side was no match at all. In roughly a century of collapse, old China went into convulsions and breakdowns, which ended with the triumph of the Communists.

The first Westerners to reach China were daring Portuguese seamen in 1514. Gradually, they and other Europeans gained permission to set up trading stations on the coast. For three centuries the Imperial government disdained the foreigners and their products and tried to keep them at a minimum. In 1793, for example, in response to a British mission to Beijing, the emperor commended King George III for his "respectful spirit of submission" but pointed out that there could be little trade because "our celestial empire possesses all things in prolific abundance."

Still the West, especially the British, pushed on, smelling enormous profits in the China trade. Matters came to a head with the Opium Wars of 1839 to 1842. The British found a product that Chinese would buy, opium from the poppy fields

---

Cyclical versus Secular Change

China offers good illustrations of the two kinds of change that social scientists often deal with. *Cyclical change* is repetitive; certain familiar historical phases follow one another like a pendulum swing. China's dynastic cycles are examples of cyclical change; there is change, to be sure, but the overall pattern is preserved.

Secular change means a long-term shift that does not revert back to the old pattern. China's population growth, for example, was a secular change that helped break the stability of traditional China. One of the problems faced by historians, economists, and political scientists is whether a change they are examining is secular—a long-term, basic shift—or cyclical—something that comes and goes repeatedly.

of British-held India. Opium smoking was illegal in China, and there were few addicts. The British, however, flouted the law and popularized opium smoking. When at last a zealous Imperial official tried to stop the opium trade, Britain went to war to keep the lucrative commerce open. Britain easily won, but the Chinese still refused to admit the foreigners were superior. Moaned one Cantonese: "Except for your ships being solid, your gunfire fierce, and your rockets powerful, what good qualities do you have?" For the Chinese, war technology was not as important as moral quality, a view later adopted by Mao Zedong.

The 1842 Treaty of Nanjing (Nanking) wrested five "treaty ports" from the Chinese. (Britain got Hong Kong outright.) In the treaty ports the foreigners held sway, dominating the commerce and governance of the area. The Westerners enjoyed "extraterritoriality," meaning they were not subject to Chinese law but had their own courts. In the 1860s, nine more such ports were added.

Around the treaty ports grew "spheres of influence," understandings among the foreign powers as to who really ran things there. The British, French, Germans, Russians, and Japanese in effect carved up the China coast with their spheres of influence, in which they dominated trade. The Americans, claiming to be above this sort of dirty business, tagged along after the British. China was reduced to semi-colonial status.

From Empire to Republic

Internally, too, the Empire weakened. Rebellions broke out. From 1851 to 1864, the Taipings—espousing a mixture of Christianity (picked up from missionaries),

Chinese Words in Roman Letters

Chinese—because it is both ideographic (based on symbolic word-pictures) and tonal (the sing-song pattern)—is terribly difficult to transliterate into English. One system, the Wade-Giles, devised in the 1860s by two Cambridge dons, was used for more than a century. Unfortunately, Wade-Giles didn't sound much like the Chinese pronunciation.

In 1958, Peking—sorry, Beijing—introduced a new system, Pinyin, that is much closer to the correct pronunciation. In 1979 China made Pinyin the official form of transliteration. Most English-language publications have since gone along with it. Some of the Pinyin spellings used here may look funny if you are familiar with their Wade-Giles renderings, for example:

Wade-Giles	**Pinyin**
Mao Tse-tung	Mao Zedong
Chou En-lai	Zhou Enlai
Teng Hsiao-ping	Deng Xiaoping
Hua Kuo-feng	Hua Guofeng
Peking	Beijing
Nanking	Nanjing
Chungking	Chongqing
Shanghai	Shanghai (the same!)
Szechwan	Sichuan
Sinkiang	Xinjiang
Yangtze	Changjiang

Confucianism, and primitive communism—baptized millions in South China and nearly overthrew the Qing (Manchu) dynasty. In 1900, with the backing of some reactionary officials and the empress dowager, the antiforeign Boxer movement killed missionaries and besieged Beijing's Legation Quarter for fifty-five days. An international expedition of British, French, German, Russian, American, and Japanese troops broke through and lifted the siege. The foreigners then demanded indemnities and additional concessions from the tottering Imperial government.

Could the Qing dynasty have adapted itself to the new Western pressures? The Japanese had; with the 1868 Meiji Restoration they preserved the form of empire but shifted to modernization and industrialization with spectacular success. (See Chapter 22.) Many young Chinese demanded reforms to strengthen China, especially after their humiliating defeat by Japan in 1895. In 1898 the young Emperor Guangxu (Kuang-hsu) gathered around him reformers and in the famous Hundred Days issued more than forty edicts, modernizing everything from education to the military. Conservative officials and the old empress dowager would have none of it; they carried out a coup, rescinded the changes, and put the emperor under house arrest for the rest of his short life. (He was likely poisoned.)

A system that cannot reform is increasingly ripe for revolution. Younger people, especially army officers, grew fed up with China's weakness and became militant nationalists. Many Chinese studied in the West and were eager to westernize China. Under an idealistic, Western-trained doctor, San Yatsen (Sun Yat-sen), disgruntled provincial officials and military commanders overthrew the Manchus in 1911. It was the end of the last dynasty but not the beginning of stability. In the absence of central authority so-called warlords, local strongmen, in effect brought China into feudalism from 1916 to 1927.

Gradually overcoming the chaos was the Nationalist party or *Guomindang* (in Wade-Giles, *Kuomintang*, KMT). Formed shortly after the Manchu's overthrow, the Nationalists were guided by intellectuals (many of them educated in the United States), army officers, and the modern business element. Their greatest strength was in the South, in Guangzhou (Canton), especially in the coastal cities where there was the most contact with the West. It was no accident that they made Nanjing their capital; the word in fact means "southern capital." (North-South tension exists to this day in China.)

Power gravitated into the hands of General (later Generalissimo) Jiang Jieshi (Chiang Kai-shek), who by 1927 had succeeded in unifying most of China under the Nationalists. While Chiang was hailed as the founder and savior of the new China—Henry Luce, the son of a China missionary, put Chiang ten times on the cover of *Time*—in reality the Nationalist rule was weak. The Western-oriented city people who staffed the Nationalists did not reform or develop the rural areas where most Chinese still lived, usually under the thumb of rapacious landlords. Administration became terribly corrupt. And the Nationalists offered no plausible ideology to rally the Chinese people.

Still, like Kerensky's provisional government in Russia, the Nationalists might have succeeded were it not for war. In 1931 the Japanese seized Manchuria and in 1937 began the conquest of the rest of China. By 1941 they had taken the entire coast, forcing the Nationalists to move their capital far up the Changjiang River from Nanjing to Chongqing. The United States, in accordance with its long support of China, embargoed trade with Japan, a move that eventually led to Pearl Harbor. For the Americans in World War II, however, China was a sideshow. Chiang's forces preferred fighting Communists to Japanese, while waiting for a U.S. victory to return them to power.

The Communist Triumph

One branch of Chinese nationalism, influenced by Marx and by the Bolshevik Revolution, decided that communism was the only effective basis for implementing a nationalist revolution. The Chinese Communists have always been first and foremost nationalists, and from its founding in 1921 the Chinese Communist Party (CCP) worked with the Nationalists until Chiang in 1927 decided to exterminate them as a threat. The fight between the KMT and CCP was a struggle between two versions of Chinese nationalism.

While Stalin advised the Chinese Communists to base themselves on the small proletariat of the coastal cities, Mao Zedong rose to leadership of the Party by developing a rural strategy called the "mass line." Mao concluded that the real revolutionary potential in China, which had little industry and hence few proletarians, was among the long-suffering peasants. It was a major revision of Marx, one in fact that Marx probably would not recognize as Marxism.

In 1934, with KMT forces surrounding them, some 120,000 Chinese Communists began their incredible Long March of more than 6,000 miles (10,000 km) to the relative safety of Yan'an in the north (see map on page 344). It lasted over a year and led across mountain ranges and rivers amidst hostile forces. Fewer than 20,000 survived. The Long March became the epic of Chinese Communist history. Self-reliant

Chairman Mao Zedong proclaims the founding of the People's Republic of China on October 1, 1949. *(Xinhau)*

and isolated from the Soviets, the Chinese Communists had to develop their own strategy for survival, including working with peasants and practicing guerrilla warfare.

While the war against Japan drained and demoralized the Nationalists, it strengthened and encouraged the Communists. Besides stocks of captured Japanese weapons from the Russian takeover of Manchuria in 1945, the Chinese Communists got very little help from the Soviets and felt they never owed them much in return. Mao and his Communists came to power on their own, by perfecting their peasant and guerrilla strategies. This fact laid the groundwork for the later Sino-Soviet split.

After World War II, the Nationalist forces were much larger than the Communists', and they had many U.S. arms. Nationalist strength, however, melted away as hyperinflation destroyed the economy, corrupt officers sold their troops' weapons (often to the Communists), and war weariness paralyzed the population. The Nationalists had always neglected the "rice roots" of political strength: the common peasant. The Communists, by cultivating the peasantry (Mao himself was of peasant origin), won a new Mandate of Heaven. In 1949, the disintegrating Nationalists retreated to the island of Taiwan while the Communists restored Beijing ("northern capital") as the country's capital and proceeded to implement what is probably the world's most sweeping revolution. On that occasion, Mao, reflecting his deeply nationalistic sentiments, said: "Our nation will never again be an insulted nation. We have stood up."

Mao Zedong and Guerrilla War

In what became a model for would-be revolutionaries the world over, the Chinese Communists swept to power in 1949 after a decade and a half of successful guerrilla warfare. During these years, Mao Zedong, often in his Yan'an cave, developed and taught what he called the "mass line." Here are some of his lessons:

1. Take the countryside and surround the cities. While the enemy is stuck in the cities, able to venture out only in strength, you are mobilizing the masses.

2. Work very closely with the peasants, listen to their complaints, help them solve problems (for example, getting rid of a landlord or bringing in the harvest), propagandize them, and recruit them into the army and Party.

3. Don't engage the enemy's main forces but rather probe for his weak spots, harassing him and wearing him out.

4. Don't expect much help from the outside; be self-reliant. For weapons, take the enemy's.

5. Don't worry about the apparent superior numbers and firepower of the enemy and his imperialist allies; their strength is illusory because it is not based on the masses. Willpower and unity with the masses is more important than weaponry.

6. At certain stages guerrilla units come together to form larger units until at last, as the enemy stumbles, your forces become a regular army that can take the entire country.

The Key Institutions

The Soviet Parallel

The institutions of China's government are essentially what the Soviet Union had—interlocking state and Party hierarchies—but China adds a Third World twist: the army is also quite important, at times intervening directly into politics, as happens in other developing countries. China, no less than Brazil (see the next chapter), has experienced upheaval and chaos, which has led to army participation. In this regard, the People's Republic of China (PRC) is still a Third World country.

As in the old Soviet model, each state and Party level ostensibly elects the one above it. In China, production and residential units elect local People's Congresses which then elect county People's Congresses, which in turn choose provincial People's Congresses. China, organized on a unitary rather than federal pattern, has twenty-one provinces. The provincial People's Congresses then elect the National People's Congress (NPC) of some three thousand deputies for a five-year term.

As in the ex–Soviet Union, this parliament is too big to do much at its brief annual sessions. Its recent sessions, however, have featured some lively debate, contested committee elections, and negative votes—possibly indications of eventual democratization. A Standing Committee of about 155 is theoretically supreme, but it too does not have much power in overseeing the executive branch. The chairman of the Standing Committee is considered China's head of state, a largely honorific post currently held by Party Chairman Jiang Zemin.

The top of the executive branch is the State Council, a cabinet of approximately forty ministers (specialized in economic branches) and a dozen vice-premiers led by a premier, China's head of government, the conservative technocrat Li Peng.

The formal structure of the executive does not always correspond to the real distribution of its power. In 1976, after the death of both Party Chairman Mao Zedong and Premier Zhou Enlai, a relative unknown, Hua Guofeng, was installed in both their offices. On paper, Hua appeared to be the most powerful figure in the land.

But an elderly, twice rehabilitated Party veteran, Deng Xiaoping, named to the modest post of senior vice-premier in 1977, was in fact more powerful than his nominal boss, Hua. When Deng toured the United States in 1979, he acted like a head of state. Deng's power grew out of his senior standing in the Party and the army. In 1980, he demoted Hua and assumed power himself, still without taking over the job titles, which he left to others. By 1982, Hua was out of the Politburo and out of sight.

The Party

Like the old Soviet Communist Party, the Chinese Communist Party (CCP) is constitutionally and in practice the leading political element of the country. With 49 million members, the CCP is large, but relative to China's population it is proportionately smaller than the CPSU was. In recent years, as China's economy has decentralized and shifted to markets, the CCP has lost some of its authority. Communist officials use their position for personal gain; corruption has set in.

Tandem Power: Mao and Zhou

For over a quarter of a century, until both died in 1976, power in Beijing was not concentrated in the hands of a single Stalin-like figure but divided between Party Chairman Mao Zedong and Premier Zhou Enlai. This Chinese pattern of tandem power may now be sufficiently deep to continue into the future.

Both men were of rural backgrounds, but Mao was born in 1893 into a better-off peasant family, while Zhou was born in 1898 into a gentry family. As young men, both were drawn to Chinese nationalism and then to its Marxist variation. Neither of them went much further than high school in formal education, although both studied, debated, and wrote in Chinese leftist circles. Zhou was in France from 1920 to 1924, ostensibly to study but actually to do political work among Chinese students in Europe. Mao had no experience outside of China.

As instructed by the Soviets, the young Chinese Communist Party worked closely with the Nationalists. Zhou, for example, was in charge of political education at the Nationalist military academy. In 1927, when Jiang Jieshi (Chiang Kai-shek) turned on the Communists, both Mao and Zhou barely escaped with their lives. Zhou, interestingly enough, was the model militant Chinese revolutionary for French writer André Malraux's novel *Man's Fate*, set in 1927 Shanghai.

The next decade set their relationship. Mao concluded, from his work with peasants, that in them lay the path to China's revolution. Zhou, who briefly remained loyal to Moscow's proletarian line, by 1931 had changed his mind and joined Mao in his Jiangxi redoubt. From there, the two made the arduous Long March to the North. By the time they arrived in Yan'an, Mao was clearly the leader of the CCP, and his "mass line" of basing the revolution on the peasantry prevailed.

Mao dominated mainly by force of intellect. Other CCP leaders respected his ability to theorize in clear, blunt language. Mao became the Party chief and theoretician but did not concern himself with the day-to-day tasks of survival, warfare, and diplomacy. These became in large part Zhou's jobs. Zhou Enlai became the administrator of the revolution. Never bothering to theorize, Zhou was a master at shaping and controlling bureaucracies, smooth diplomacy, and political survival amidst changing lines.

Was there tension between the two? Probably, but Zhou never showed it. Publicly Zhou dedicated himself completely to fulfilling Mao's desires, although at times, in the shambles of the Great Leap Forward (1958–60) and the Cultural Revolution (1966–69), he seemed to be trying to hold things together and limit the damage.

Mao was the abstract thinker while Zhou was the pragmatic doer. Implicitly, this made Mao more radical and Zhou more conservative. Mao could spin out his utopian dreams, but Zhou had to make the bureaucracy, military, and economy function. Different roles require different personalities.

In organization, the CCP parallels the defunct CPSU. Hierarchies of Party congresses at the local, county, provincial, and national levels feed into corresponding Party committees. At the top is the National Party Congress; composed of some 1,900 delegates and supposed to meet at least once in five years, this congress nominally chooses a Central Committee of 175 full members. Since both bodies are too big to run things, however, power ends up in the hands of a Politburo currently of 18 Party chiefs. But this too is not the last level. Within the Politburo is a Standing Committee of five to seven members that has the decisive voice.

The Mouse Catcher: Deng Xiaoping

Deng Xiaoping's return to power in China in the 1970s seemed to outsiders about as likely as Richard Nixon's becoming president again. The diminutive Chinese leader had actually been purged twice before becoming "senior vice-premier" in 1977, a deceptive title. Actually the former protégé of Zhou Enlai—who, like Zhou, was a pragmatic administrator rather than a theorizer—was China's boss.

Deng was born in 1904 into a rural landlord family. Sent to study in France, Deng was recruited by Zhou Enlai and soon joined the Chinese Communists. As a political commissar and organizer of the People's Liberation Army, Deng forged strong military connections. Rising through major posts after 1949, Deng was named to the top of the Party—the Politburo's Standing Committee—in 1956.

Deng was not as adroit as Zhou and kept getting into political trouble. An outspoken pragmatist, Deng said after the Great Leap: "Private farming is all right as long as it raises production, just as it doesn't matter whether a cat is black or white as long as it catches mice." During the Cultural Revolution this utterance was used against Deng to show that he was a "Capitalist Roader." Although not expelled from the Party, Deng dropped out of sight and lost his official position. His son was permanently crippled during the Cultural Revolution.

But the little man—Deng is under five feet (150 cm) tall—bounced back in 1973 when moderates had regained control. In 1975, he seemed to be ready to take over; he spoke with visiting U.S. President Ford as one head of state to another. But just a month later Deng was again in disgrace, denounced by the radicals of the "Gang of Four" as anti-Mao. Again he was stripped of his posts, but an old army buddy offered him sanctuary in an elite military resort.

But the amazingly adaptable Deng bounced back yet again. With the arrest of the Gang of Four in 1976, moderates came back out of the woodwork, among them Deng. In July 1977, he was reappointed to all of his old posts. Many Chinese state, Party, and army leaders, badly shaken by the Cultural Revolution, felt that old comrade Deng was a man they could trust. Deng's roller-coaster ride in and out of power illustrates two facts of Chinese life: (1) politics is alive and well in China; and (2) it pays to have high-ranking friends who see you as a guarantor of pragmatism and stability.

Deng was in no sense a "liberal." He encouraged several economic reforms but pulled back when they weakened Party control and led to calls for democracy. In 1989, Deng brutally crushed a pro-democracy movement in Beijing's Tiananmen Square. Although weak and not taking an active part in governing, Deng at age 90 was still the apex of power in China.

The CCP's structure used to be a bit different from the classic Soviet model. Instead of a general secretary at its head, the CCP had a Party chairman, Mao's title, which he passed on to Hua Guofeng. By then, however, the office was robbed of meaning, and Hua was eclipsed by Senior Vice-Premier Deng Xiaoping, who, to be sure, also held important Party and army positions. In 1982, under Deng's guidance, the Party abolished the chairmanship—part of a repudiation of Mao's legacy—and upgraded the position of general secretary, so that now the CCP structure more closely matches that of the old CPSU. Deng arranged to have his protégé Hu Yaobang named general secretary. Hu, however, proved to be too liberal and a bit unpredictable. He also failed to win approval of the army (see next section) and was dropped in 1987. His place was taken by another Deng protégé, Zhao Ziyang, who in turn was ousted in 1989 for appearing to side with student demonstrators. Replacing him was the hard-lining mayor of Shanghai, Jiang Zemin, who was also named head of state in 1993.

China's nervous system is its Party *cadres*, a French word for "framework," now used by Asian Communists to denote local Party leadership. There are an estimated eighteen million CCP cadres, still important for political control. In 1979, Deng Xiaoping began the ticklish job of easing out both the incompetent old guard—whose only qualification, in many cases, was having been on the Long March—and the extreme leftists who wormed their way into the cadre structure during the tumultuous Cultural Revolution. Quietly, Deng brought in younger, better-educated cadres dedicated to his moderate, pragmatic line.

The Army

Typically the top figures in the Chinese elite hold both high state and high Party offices, as in the old Soviet Union. In China, though, they often also hold high positions atop the military structure, through the important Military Affairs Commission, which interlocks with the CCP's Politburo. Mao, Hua, and Deng were all chairmen of the Military Affairs Commission. Indeed, from the beginning, the People's Liberation Army (PLA), earlier known as the Chinese Red Army, has been so intertwined with the CCP that it's hard to separate them. Deng named an active-duty general to the elite Politburo Standing Committee, and nearly a quarter of the Central Committee is PLA. Fighting the Nationalists and the Japanese for at least a decade and a half, the CCP became a combination of Party and army. The pattern continues to this day. Political scientist Robert Tucker called the Chinese system "military communism."

Mao wrote that "the Party commands the gun, and the gun must never be allowed to command the Party." Where the two are nearly merged, however, it's sometimes hard to tell who's on top. As the Communists took over China in the 1940s, it was the PLA that first set up their power structures. Until recently, China's executive decision makers all had extensive military experience, often as political commissars in PLA units. Said Zhou Enlai: "We are all connected with the army." When the Cultural Revolution broke out in 1966, as we shall discuss shortly, the army first facilitated, then dampened, and finally crushed the Red Guards' rampages. By the time the Cultural Revolution sputtered out, the PLA was in de facto control of most provincial governments and most of the Politburo. In 1980, a third of the Politburo was still occupied by active military men. At various times, during mobilization campaigns, the army is cited as a model for the rest of the country to follow, and heroic individual soldiers are celebrated in the media.

What does PLA influence mean for the governance of China? Armies, as guardians of their countries' security, define whatever is good for them as good for the country. Anyone who undermines their power earns their opposition. During the Cultural Revolution, for example, the army under Defense Minister Lin Biao supported Mao's program to shake up the Party and state bureaucracy. (The army was not touched.) As the chaos spread, however, military commanders worried that it was sapping China's strength and military preparedness. Lin became increasingly isolated within the military. In 1971 Beijing released the amazing story that Lin had attempted a coup and fled to the Soviet Union in a plane that crashed. Outside observers suggest Lin died by other means. His supporters were purged from the military. The PLA thus helped tame Maoist radicalism.

But PLA influence can cut the other way, too. Deng Xiaoping attempted to make Hu Yaobang his successor on the Military Affairs Committee, but the PLA didn't like Hu, a strong proponent of liberalization. They feared that too much freedom would harm morale and too much prosperity would cut off their source of recruits, young peasants, who could make good money on the farm. The top PLA people rejected Hu and apparently had a hand in getting him fired as Party chief. The PLA also did not flinch in mowing down student pro-democracy demonstrators

Tandem Power Continues

When Deng Xiaoping at age 85 gave up his last formal post—as chairman of the powerful Military Affairs Commission—in 1989, he made sure two protégés took over, Party General Secretary Jiang Zemin and Premier Li Peng. They were, respectively, 63 and 61 years old, the younger generation in Chinese politics. Although neither of the two had military experience, Jiang also took Deng's place on the Military Commission. Deng, of course, remained as the behind-the-scenes leader.

Deng's initial pick as Party chief, Zhao Ziyang, was bounced out of office for trying to hold a dialogue with protesting students in 1989. This was a pity, for Zhao had a distinguished record as a rural organizer and reformist governor of Sichuan, where he boosted output by letting farms and factories make many of their own decisions, exactly the course Deng was advocating at the time. Deng brought Zhao to Beijing in 1980, first as deputy premier, then premier, then as Party chief in 1987, only to fire him in 1989 for being too liberal.

Jiang was born in Jiangsu province; little is known of his early years. He joined the Communist Party in 1946 while a student at the Shanghai Technical University. He graduated as an electrical engineer and after the Communist takeover worked in several factories, finally becoming a top engineer at an automobile plant in the northeast of China. In 1980 Jiang arrived in Beijing as an export-import official, and in 1982 he was named minister for the

electronics industry. At this point, if not before, he became well acquainted with Li Peng; both worked in the same general areas. As mayor of Shanghai from 1985 to 1988, Jiang was not well liked and considered by some incompetent. He cracked down on pro-democracy Shanghai intellectuals.

Li Peng, born in Sichuan, was only 2 years old when his revolutionary father was executed. When he was 11, Zhou Enlai's wife sent him for schooling to the Communist headquarters in Yan'an. From 1948 to 1954, Li studied at the Moscow Power Institute and then worked on power projects in China. Deng brought him onto the Politburo in 1985 and got him named education minister. In that position, Li cracked down on student demands for more freedom and democracy, marking him as a conservative figure.

Both Jiang Zemin and Li Peng were, in Chinese Communist terms, centrists, dedicated to keeping firm central control of politics while cautiously moving toward a market economy. Both had experience silencing troublesome intellectuals. Both were graduate engineers, and this gave their rule a technocratic bent. Neither were popular, nor did they seek to please the masses. Neither returned to the philosophy of Mao or to rapid change. With Jiang in charge of Party affairs and Li of the government, the two seem to represent a continuation of the pattern of tandem rule.

in Beijing in 1989. In general, the PLA has been a conservative force in Chinese politics, for almost axiomatically, an army stands for order and sees disorder as a security problem. In China, as will also be seen in Brazil, when chaos threatens, the army moves.

Chinese Political Attitudes

Traditional Attitudes

Mao used to say that his countrymen were "firstly poor, secondly blank," meaning that the Communists could start with a clean slate and create the Chinese citizens they wished. Mao was wrong. Plenty of traditional Chinese attitudes have carried over into the People's Republic. Indeed, even Mao's vision of perfecting human nature by thinking right thoughts is a deeply Confucian notion.

When the Communists restored Beijing as the capital in 1949 they were restoring an old symbol; Beijing had been the capital for centuries until Chiang's Nationalists moved it to Nanjing. Some government offices and elite living quarters now directly adjoin the old Forbidden City of the emperors, just as the Soviets made the Kremlin their home. Tiananmen (Gate of Heavenly Peace) Square is still Beijing's parade and demonstration area, much like Red Square is in Moscow.

In some ways, the Communists' bureaucrats and cadres perform the same function as the old Mandarins and gentry. Reciting Mao instead of Confucius, the new elites strive to place a gigantic population under central control and guidance. Their aim now, to be sure, is growth and modernization rather than conservative stability. But Mao himself recognized the similarity of old and new when he denounced the bureaucrats as the "new Mandarins" during the Cultural Revolution. Like the dynasties of old, the Communists may have been sucked into the old patterns.

To become one of the new Mandarins, Chinese youths must undergo twelve and a half hours of grueling university entrance exams. Out of some three million who take them, only about 300,000 pass each year, meaning that only about 10 percent of China's college-age youths enter institutions of higher education (as opposed

Reverence for Age

Just as in Old China, age seems to confer special qualities of wisdom and leadership in the People's Republic. Mao died at 82 and Zhou at 78, both in office. When he returned to power in 1977, Deng Xiaoping was 73. At age 90 he was still politically influential although weak and deaf. One of the weaknesses of Communist systems is their lack of mechanisms for changing leaders short of their death. This causes the systems to grow dependent on personalities rather than on institutions.

to close to 40 percent in the United States). The three days of exams resemble nothing so much as the Imperial examination system of old China. The new exams, identical and kept secret, are given simultaneously throughout China. They include sections on Chinese literature, math, science, a foreign language, and politics.

Mao argued against the examinations and had them dropped during the Cultural Revolution; they were restored only in 1977. Mao thought the exams were elitist and unrevolutionary, that they created a class of new Mandarin bureaucrats. Mao was quite right, but without the brutally competitive exams, educational standards slid, and incompetent youths got into universities based on their political attitudes. Inferior graduates retarded China's progress in industry and administration, so the post-Mao moderates restored the examinations. It was another example of a long-functional process reasserting itself.

Nationalism

Overlaying traditional Chinese attitudes is the more recent one of the nationalism that has dominated China's intellectual life since the turn of the century. Chinese nationalism, like Third World nationalism generally, is the result of a proud and independent culture suffering penetration, disorientation, and humiliation at the hands of the West. This can induce explosive fury and the feeling that the native culture, although temporarily beaten by foreigners, is still better and more enduring. Russian nationalists still react this way.

In Asia, Chinese and Japanese nationalists vowed to beat the West at its own game, building industry and weaponry but placing them at the service of the traditional culture. The Japanese were able to carry out their designs in the last century; the Chinese are still in the midst of the process. All of the founding generation of Chinese Communist leaders, including Mao and Zhou, began as young patriots urging their countrymen to revitalize China and stand up to the West and to Japan.

As in the old Soviet Union, one prevailing Chinese attitude is the nationalist drive to catch up with the West. During their good economic-growth years—the mid-1950s and 1980s and 1990s—Chinese leaders are proud of their rapid progress. The Great Leap Forward and the Cultural Revolution ruined the economy. A pragmatic moderate such as Zhou or Deng always has a powerful argument against such disruptions: they harm growth and weaken the country. Basically, this is a nationalist argument, and one used by pragmatists today.

Maoism

Maoism, or Mao Zedong Thought, as Beijing calls it, is the latest and weakest layer of Chinese political attitudes. It draws from both traditional and nationalistic values, despite its claim to be totally new and revolutionary. From traditional China, it takes the Confucian emphasis on thinking right thoughts, based on the idea that consciousness determines existence rather than the reverse: Willpower has primacy over weaponry in wars; willpower has primacy over technology in building China. The unleashed forces of the masses, guided by Mao Zedong Thought, can conquer anything. This extreme form of voluntarism—the belief that human will can change the world—is consonant with China's past.

From nationalism, Mao took the emphasis on strengthening and rebuilding China so that it could stand up to its old enemies and become a world power. The trouble is that these two strands are partly at odds with each other. Traditional values call for China to ignore the West and its technology, but nationalistic values call for China to learn and copy from the West. The continuing, unresolved conflict of these two streams of thought spell permanent trouble for China.

Maoism is an outgrowth of Mao Zedong's thoughts on guerrilla warfare. According to Maoist doctrine, what the PLA did to beat the Nationalists, China as a whole must do to advance and become a world leader: work with the masses, be self-reliant, and put willpower on a higher plane than technology to overcome obstacles. Mao can be seen as a theorist of guerrilla warfare who continued to apply his principles to governance.

In the Great Leap Forward from 1958 to 1960, Mao tried guerrilla warfare tactics on the economy, using raw manual labor plus enthusiasm to build earthen dams and backyard blast furnaces. Engineers, experts, and administrators were bypassed. The Soviets warned Mao it wouldn't work and urged him to follow the Soviet model of building the economy by more conventional means. As a matter of fact, the Soviets were right, but Mao refused to follow their lead. In 1960, the Soviets withdrew their substantial numbers of foreign-aid technicians, and the Sino-Soviet split came into the open.

For the Soviet Communists, the revolution was over; the proletariat triumphed in 1917 and moved Russia into the most advanced stage of history. For Mao, the revolution never ends. Mao held that at any stage there are conservative tendencies that block the path to socialism: bureaucratism, elitism, and opportunism. Mao understood perfectly well what Djilas warned against in *The New Class* and resolved to combat these tendencies by means of "permanent revolution," periodic upheavals to let the force of the masses surge past the conservative bureaucrats.

Socialism and bureaucratism are closely connected, but Mao thought he could break the connection. He saw China settling into the bureaucratic patterns he hated and was determined to break them by instituting a permanent revolution before he died. The result was the Great Proletarian Cultural Revolution from 1966 to

 ## Slogans from the Cultural Revolution

"Put destruction first, and in the process you have construction."

"Destroy the four olds—old thought, old culture, old customs, old habits."

"Once all struggle is grasped, miracles are possible."

"Bombard the command post." (Attack established leaders if they are unrevolutionary.)

"So long as it is revolutionary, no action is a crime."

"Sweep the great renegade of the working class onto the garbage heap!" (Dump the moderate chief of state, Liu Shaoqi.)

"Cadres step to the side." (Bypass established authorities.)

"To rebel is justified."

1976, during which young people were encouraged to criticize, harass, and oust almost all figures of authority except army leaders. Administrators, teachers, scientists, musicians, even Party leaders were humiliated and sent to "reeducation" farms for manual labor; thousands committed suicide. Chaos spread through China, and the economy slumped. As we discussed earlier, the army took over. Shortly after Mao's death, power returned to the bureaucrats; they won and Mao failed.

Mao refused to recognize the unhappy truth that if you want socialism you must accept the bureaucratism that comes with it. By trying to leap directly into some kind of guerrilla socialism without bureaucrats, Mao nearly wrecked China. On balance, Mao Zedong Thought is inherently inapplicable, and in post-Mao China, Mao is quoted selectively, if at all.

Concealed Anger

As in Russia, wide sectors of China's population accord their regime less and less legitimacy. The Party, once respected as clean and competent, is increasingly seen as corrupt and irrelevant. Even the peasants, at one time thought to be apathetic or even pleased at their increased incomes from the "responsibility system," turned unhappy as the regime reimposed state controls and high taxes on the semifree farm market. Urban workers, Marx's "proletariat" that was supposed to be the backbone of communism, are trapped between uncertainty and inflation. Many sided with prodemocracy students and founded independent labor unions.

As ever, China's cities are the hotbeds of criticism and reform. Although a small minority, the urban educated classes have often taken the lead in changing China. Student protests in Beijing, for example, go back a century and contributed a great deal to the overthrow of the Empire and the rise of first the Nationalists and then the Communists. The Communists under Mao in the 1930s, to be sure, had a peasant base, but many of the cadres were urban intellectuals. Accordingly, we probably get a better idea of where China is heading by focusing on city attitudes. In most countries, urban intellectuals are the spark plugs of political change.

During the twentieth century, educated Chinese have generally had a cause to believe in. At first it was building a new republic that would not be carved up by foreigners. Then it was in repelling the Japanese invaders. With the Communist takeover, many Chinese idealistically believed that Mao offered them a blueprint for a prosperous, socialist China. After Mao, Deng Xiaoping offered the encouraging image of a prosperous, semicapitalist China gradually moving to democracy. After the June 1989 massacre of pro-democracy students in Tiananmen Square, many Chinese fell into despair. Marx, Mao, and Deng have all been discredited, even among Party officials, although few say so openly. With nothing to believe in, a spiritual vacuum has opened up. What will fill it?

Over the decades, Chinese have become politically numb. They had to mouth slogans and participate in mass campaigns—one year anti–Confucius, the next anti–capitalist roaders, then anti–Gang of Four, then anti–"spiritual pollution," then anti–"bourgeois liberalization"—depending on which campaign was current. Most are awfully fed up with this nonsense and have mentally tuned out.

The great hope for Chinese students is to go abroad. Many study English and dream of joining the 40,000 Chinese students already in the United States. Many, of course, will not return to China. The regime, aware of this brain drain, changed its relatively open policy on sending students abroad and has sharply restricted their

Big Lie and Little Whisper

The Chinese way of handling the government crackdown on freedom and democracy is called *biaotai*, "to express an attitude." Chinese know how to crank out the current line while concealing their true feelings. This leads to what Chinese call *nei jin, wai song*, "tranquility outside, repression within." Everything looks calm, but only because people know they can get in trouble for speaking out. Just below the surface, though, repressed anger waits to erupt.

Some of this shows up in the constant flow of nasty rumors about repression, economic incompetence, and the corruption of high officials. This has been called a struggle between the Big Lie and Little Whisper: The government tries to fool people with big lies, but the people fight back with little whispers. In effect, the Chinese people are practicing psychological guerrilla warfare against the Communist regime.

numbers. Chinese university graduates must first work five years before they can apply for graduate study overseas. Exceptions can be made if relatives abroad send for them. The students must then put up bonds of hundreds of dollars for each year they have studied in China, an impossible sum for most.

The situation is obviously unstable. A considerable fraction of China's population dislikes and distrusts the regime. This feeling is especially prevalent in the South, which has long resented rule by the North. They know that patience is a Chinese virtue, but they are also frustrated that China's progress is blocked by a Party elite that simply wants to cling to its power and good jobs. They know that in the coastal Special Economic Zones (mostly in the South), where capitalism and foreign investment are allowed, the economy is booming. Why then not just expand the Special Zones until they cover all of China? They also know that the Taiwanese per capita income is about 25 times that of mainlanders'. Some Chinese students speak with shame that they didn't have the guts to do what the Romanians did in 1989: stand up to the government's guns and overthrow the regime. In time, Chinese student frustration is certain to boil over again.

In the right situation—for example, a split in Beijing leadership over the personnel and policies after Deng dies—China's peasants, workers, and students could quickly come together and overthrow the regime. Needless to say, the police work hard to prevent a Chinese equivalent of Poland's Solidarity. Political repression, of course, solves nothing; it merely postpones the day of reckoning. What happened in East Europe could happen in China.

Patterns of Interaction

Cycles of Upheaval

Since the Communists came to power in 1949, there have been three major upheavals, plus several smaller ones. Among major upheavals we would count the agrarian reforms (that is, the execution of landlords and redistribution of land) of the early 1950s, the Great Leap Forward from 1958 to 1960, and the Cultural Revolution from 1966 to 1976. Smaller upheavals include the brief Hundred Flowers liberalization of 1956, the antirightist campaigns of 1957 and the early 1970s, the crushing of the Gang of Four and their supporters in the late 1970s, and the repression of the alleged "counterrevolutionary rebellion" of pro-democracy students in 1989.

The big upheavals and most of the smaller ones can be traced to the same underlying problem: Beijing's leaders, having inherited a poor and backward land, intermittently tried to make China rich, advanced, and socialistic. Mao Zedong Thought taught that everything is possible: China can leap into the modern age and even beyond it. But the old, stubborn, traditional China was unyielding; it frustrated the bold plans and tugged the system back toward the previous patterns and problems.

As long as China is not what its leaders wish it to be—modern, powerful, and respected—there is the possibility of another upheaval instituted from the top. Indeed, such upheavals seem to be inherent in the effort to modernize. Similar episodes occurred in the Soviet Union as leaders tried to force their country along: Stalin's industrialization and Khrushchev's experiments. The difference with China is that it is far more backward and hence the remedies preferred tend to be more extreme.

For China's periodic upheavals to cease it will require the abandonment of the Communists' central tenet, namely, that communism delivers rapid progress. To

The Great Leap Forward: "Twenty Years in a Day"

In 1958 Mao Zedong launched one of the strangest efforts in the Third World's struggle to move ahead: the Great Leap Forward. Vowing to progress "twenty years in a day" and "catch up with Great Britain in fifteen years," all of China was urged to "walk on two legs" (use all possible means) to industrialize rapidly. Most peasants—and China has still a largely peasant population—were herded into gigantic communes, some with as many as 100,000 people. Deprived of their private plots, they were ordered to eat in communal dining halls, leave their young in nurseries, and sometimes even sleep in large dormitories.

The communes were ordered to participate in engineering and industrial projects. Relying on "labor-intensive" methods to compensate for lack of capital, millions were turned out to move earth with baskets and carry poles to build dams and irrigation works. Backyard blast furnaces were ordered built so that every commune could produce its own iron.

Within a year the failure was plain for all to see. Even Mao had to admit it; he resigned as president of the PRC but kept his chairmanship of the CCP. The unenthusiastic peasants—as in the Soviet Union—simply failed to produce without private incentives. A serious food deficit developed, and perhaps 40 million Chinese died of malnutrition. The implements produced of locally smelted iron were of miserable quality. The communes were phased out, broken first into "production brigades" and then into "production teams," which were in fact the old villages. Private farming was again permitted. Mao lost; old China won.

The Great Proletarian Cultural Revolution: "Bombard the Command Post"

If the Great Leap Forward was strange, the Great Pro- letarian Cultural Revolution was downright bizarre. In it, an elderly Mao Zedong tried to make his revo- lution permanent by destroying the very structures his new China had created. Of the many slogans from the Cultural Revolution, "bombard the com- mand post" perhaps best summarizes its character. Mao encouraged young people, who hastily grouped themselves into ragtag outfits called the Red Guards, to destroy most authority, even that of the CCP. They did, and Chinese progress was set back years.

The Cultural Revolution began with a 1965 flap over a Shanghai play some radicals claimed crit- icized Mao by allegory. Mao turned what could have been a small literary debate into a mass criti- cism that led to the ouster of several Party officials. First university and then high school students aired their grievances against teachers and school admin- istrators. Behind their discontent was a shortage of the kind of jobs the students thought they deserved upon graduation.

By the fall of 1966, most schools were closed as their students demonstrated, humiliated officials, wrote wall posters, and marched to and fro. China was in chaos. Hundreds of thousands of vic- tims of the Red Guards committed suicide. A much larger number were "sent down" to the countryside to work with the peasants and "learn from the peo- ple." This sometimes included physical abuse and psychological humiliation. Unknown millions were murdered outright. Worried officials set up their own Red Guard groups to protect themselves. Different Red Guard factions fought each other.

Even Mao became concerned and in early 1967 ordered the army to step in. By the end of 1967 the People's Liberation Army pretty much ran the country. To replace the broken governmental struc- tures, the army set up "revolutionary committees" on which sat PLA officers, Red Guard leaders, and "re- pentant" officials who had been duly cleansed by the Cultural Revolution. By 1969, the worst was over, although officially the Cultural Revolution did not end until 1976 when Mao died and the ultra- radical Gang of Four (headed by Mao's wife, Jiang Qing) was arrested.

The effects of the Cultural Revolution were all bad. Industry suffered. Education, when it re- sumed, was without standards, and students were chosen on the basis of political attitudes rather than ability. The more moderate and levelheaded offi- cials, whom the Red Guards sought to destroy, lay low and pretended to go along with the Cultural Rev- olution. When it was over, they reasserted them- selves and made sure one of their own was in high office: Deng Xiaoping.

And what became of the Red Guards? Claiming that their energy was needed on the farm, the army marched more than sixteen million young city people to rural communes for agricultural labor and forebade them to return to their cities. By hook or crook, many of them managed to get back to their homes to try to continue their studies. Some, utterly disillusioned with the way they had been used, turned to petty crime or fled to the British colony of Hong Kong. Some eventually became capitalist mil- lionaires in the burgeoning Special Economic Zones of the South.

admit that China is now making fabulous economic progress—but only by the capi- talist path of foreign investment, markets, and world trade—took a major psycho- logical shift at the top of the CCP. Nothing has been announced publicly, but insiders report that under Deng's leadership China's elite have decided to have a largely cap- italist economy, but to call it "socialism with Chinese characteristics." We have to be careful though. Although the 1990s are characterized by moderation and pragmatism among the Chinese leadership, we might keep a lookout for a new round of revolutionary enthusiasm. Who can tell what will happen after Deng dies? The potential for extremism is still present, and there are no institutional mechanisms— competing parties, free elections, an independent judiciary—to block a new round of extremism. The limiting factors now are the weariness of the Chinese people after all the upheaval and the success of the "capitalist road."

Radicals and Moderates

Outside observers used to label CCP figures as "radicals" or "moderates" according to their willingness to support the kind of upheavals previously described. This is a bit of a simplification, for there are no distinct groups in China bearing these names. And many Party leaders demonstrated how they can play both sides of the fence, depending on where their career advantage lies.

Still, the radical and moderate labels were useful, for they help us understand the kind of struggles that went on within the CCP leadership. The main characteristics are summarized in the box, "Radicals and Moderates in Chinese Politics." Both radicals and moderates, it should be emphasized, wanted China to progress. But the radicals were unwilling to dilute the revolutionary purity of Maoist socialism for the sake of mere economic progress. The moderates, on the other hand, were willing to sacrifice ideology for pragmatic achievements.

China's moderates were and still are those high up in the Party, government, or army. Almost axiomatically, anyone who's part of the establishment will not be a radical. Mao was right: bureaucrats are by nature conservative. China's radicals were drawn largely from those peripheral to power but ambitious for it: students, junior cadres, some provincial leaders.

One of the prime motivations for radicals, especially during the Cultural Revolution, was the scarcity of job openings in Party, state, army, industrial, and other offices. For the most part, positions until recently were staffed by aging Party comrades who go back to the 1949 liberation or even the Long March. They never retire, and their longevity in office breeds impatience and resentment among younger people with ambitions of their own. A further element fueling youthful discontent is the previously mentioned difficulty of getting into a university. Only about 10 percent of university candidates pass the stiff entrance exams. It is no coincidence that one of the educational "reforms" of the Cultural Revolution was the abolition of these exams.

These kinds of tensions underlay the radical outburst of the Cultural Revolution. Those who aspired to power enthusiastically attempted to carry out Mao's designs. Those who held power pretended to go along with it, often by mouthing the correct slogans and self-denunciations. In Mao's words, they "waved the red flag to oppose the red flag." When the campaign burnt itself out, the bureaucrats and cadres took over again, and it appeared that the moderates had won.

Chinese Liberal and Conservative Politics

With the Maoist demon back in the bottle, a new conflict appeared in Chinese politics, a split between liberal and conservative forces, very similar to the what the Soviets went through before their system collapsed. The Chinese moderates who

Radicals and Moderates in Chinese Politics

Radicals	Moderates
celebrate Mao Thought	selectively quote Mao
mass-oriented	elite-oriented
antiauthoritarian	hierarchical
demand purification	demand modernization
want permanent revolution	want stability
want breakthrough growth	want steady economic growth
view politics in command	view economics in command
learn from the people	follow the experts
want wage equality	want wage differentials
expect worker enthusiasm	offer material incentives
emphasize common sense	emphasize science and education
economically self-reliant	import technology
ideological	empirical

opposed the extremism of the Cultural Revolution wanted to essentially go back to the way things were before that upheaval. They earned the nickname the "seventeen-years-before people," because they thought the seventeen years (from 1949 to 1966) before the Cultural Revolution were all right. These tended to be older people, with secure positions in the Party, army, and bureaucracy, very much like Soviet conservatives. They wanted socialism on the Soviet model, with centralized control over the economy, politics, and cultural life.

Facing them were liberalizers, usually younger people, who saw the unfairness and inefficiency of central control. They pointed to the amazing growth in farm output that came with the introduction of the "responsibility system" in agriculture (discussed shortly). With the spread of partially market economics to the cities and special economic zones, industrial growth set world records. "See, the market system works," they said in effect. They also wanted Western-style political democracy and cultural freedoms.

The Chinese conservatives, just like their old Soviet counterparts, feared that such a system would no longer be Communist and, even worse, that their jobs would be scrapped. Fumed one CCP member who supported reforms: "What do the conservatives want? They want to go back to the '50s. Who wants that? Nobody."

It was this split that caused Deng Xaioping such grief. He was prepared to liberalize cautiously, hoping to confine it to the economic sector. But demands came bubbling up to go farther and faster. In the spring of 1989, tens of thousands of Chinese university students staged giant protests and hunger strikes in favor of democracy. Deng fired his hand-picked and liberal-minded successor, Zhao Ziyang, and had the PLA mow down the students in Tiananmen Square. Several hundred died, and some 10,000 were imprisoned. A chill settled over Chinese life. Conservatives also launched anti-Western campaigns (see box). The conservatives had one serious drawback: many were elderly. Time seemed to be on the side of the liberalizers, but not without rear-guard conservative actions.

The Underlying Problem

The earlier radical-moderate and current liberal-conservative struggles have some interesting points in common. First, the old "moderates" are basically today's "conservatives": older cadres who like bureaucratized socialism. They like it because they owe their jobs to it. Further, curious as it sounds, some of yesterday's "radicals"—the Red Guard punks who caused so much destruction in Mao's name—are now ardent "liberalizers" happy to discard Maoism. Both radicals and liberalizers shared the same impulse in trying to break up the bureaucratized socialist system, the former attacking from the left, the latter from the right.

How could they switch from left to right? Some of the switch can be attributed to young people waking up to the fact that they had been cynically used during the Cultural Revolution. Badly burned by the experience, they are now turned off of Mao Thought and open to Western-style reforms and liberalization.

But a more basic factor is that the young people—especially university students and recent graduates—who faced bleak job prospects then, face them still. They have been trained and expect higher-level jobs in the government and economy, but few are available. Why? Because those old conservatives never retire; both Chinese tradition and CCP practice grants lifetime tenure. They stay in office until they die. Making the job situation even worse is the fact that under socialism no new

 ## *Anti-Western Campaigns*

Every few years China is hit with a campaign aimed at making the Chinese pull away from the Western model of economic and political freedom. The work of conservatives within the CCP, these campaigns warned that decadent Western ideas such as free enterprise, open discussion, and a loosening of Party control would mean the end of socialism in China.

In late 1983, the catchword was "spiritual pollution," meaning that Western styles in clothes, music, and thought were ruining China. Deng, fearing the campaign was being used to block his economic liberalization, called it off after only four months.

Somewhat longer lasting, in 1986 a campaign against "bourgeois liberalization" appeared, ruling out any discussion of ending the CCP monopoly on power and replacing it with Western-style liberalism. After the 1989 Tiananmen Square massacre, conservatives charged that it was a "counterrevolutionary rebellion" inspired by Western influences, which had to be curbed. We have likely not seen the last anti-Western campaign.

The Tiananmen Massacre

During the early morning of June 4, 1989, more than 100,000 Chinese troops opened fire on young demonstrators camped out in Beijing's Tiananmen (Gate of Heavenly Peace) Square, killing hundreds and injuring thousands. Much of the killing, including tanks crushing protesters and bicyclists shot at random, took place outside the Square, but the horror went down in history as "Tiananmen."

Tiananmen marked the point at which China's Communist chiefs choked over letting China's 1980s experiment with a partially free market economy spill over into into political democracy. The economic results had been good, but they encouraged people to want democracy, never the intention of Beijing's rulers. The massacre illustrates the danger of halfway reform: it encourages people to want more.

Trouble began with the death of the liberal ex-Party chief Hu Yaobang in April 1989. Students began mourning him and protesting the current CCP leadership. On April 18, thousands began to occupy the Square. While the regime deliberated about how to handle the demonstration, the students organized, gave speeches, and built a Goddess of Democracy statue that resembled New York's Statue of Liberty. Around the country, many sympathized with the demonstrators, and criticism of the regime mounted.

If pro-democracy demonstrations had kept going, the regime would have fallen. The regime knew that and struck back. Zhao Ziyang, who succeeded Hu in 1987, went out to talk with the students. He was conciliatory and appeared to side with them. This gave Politburo hardliners the chance they had been looking for to oust Zhao. Deng Xiaoping, still the real power at age 84, wanted the army to crush the demonstrators. "We do not fear spilling blood," he said.

Troops and tanks poured into Beijing. The soldiers, mostly simple country boys, felt little in common with the urban students. In one memorable videotaped confrontation, a lone protester blocked a tank column; when the tanks tried to go around him, he quickly stepped in front of them again. It seemed to symbolize the individualism of democracy standing up to the coercion of dictatorship. After the bloodbath, thousands were arrested. The top protest figures received sentences of up to 13 years, less for those who "repented." Hundreds were held for years without trial. China's elite decided to keep going with economic change but to keep the lid on political change. Some observers say the ingredients for a 1989-type upheaval are again present.

firms spring up to hire graduates. The result, now as before, is frustration and resentment among young and better-educated Chinese.

Mao tapped this resentment for his Cultural Revolution. The unstated message of the Red Guards who shouted "Destroy the four olds!" was "Get rid of the old guys and give us their jobs!" Now, in a partially market economy, these same people (or their younger brothers and sisters) see their path to success in greater economic decentralization that will let the number of firms multiply and open up new job possibilities. Some of the young Chinese protesting in favor of democracy had little idea what it meant; they just wanted to make sure the old conservatives didn't reimpose their stranglehold. And the old conservatives, fearing for their jobs and status, fought back.

One of the great underlying problems of China is what to do with the younger generation. One solution would be to impose a mandatory retirement age, but this goes against Chinese tradition. Deng Xiaoping ordered many old comrades to retire but hardly set a good example himself. Youthful energy that is badly misdirected, as in the Cultural Revolution, can wreck China. Given productive outlets in a free economy, it could make China the growth wonder of the world.

As we discussed in connection with the old Soviet Union, ideology is often a mask for self-interest. The people who have the cushy jobs warn that democracy and liberalization mean "abandoning socialism." In analyzing Communist (and many other) systems, take ideology with a grain of salt; follow the jobs. (Think the jobs explanation is an exaggeration? What motivates *you*?)

What the Chinese Quarrel About

A Market Economy for China?

In the 1980s, some amazing changes took place in the Chinese economy. China, like all Communist countries, faced the question of how centralized the economy should be and decided on decentralization while retaining centralized political control. This will likely prove to be an unstable combination.

The earliest changes came in the countryside, where most of China's population still live. Collectivized agriculture was reduced and families were permitted to go on the "responsibility system," a euphemism for private enterprise. Peasants lease land from the state—still no private owners—and must deliver a certain quota to the state at set prices. Beyond that, they can sell their produce on the free market for the best price they can get. They can choose their own crops and how to use fertilizer and farm machinery, which they buy at their own expense. When farmers complained that their one- to three-year leases discouraged them from putting in capital improvements, the leases were lengthened to fifteen years, in many cases with right of inheritance. Farm production soared, food stands bulged, and farmers' incomes went up; some even got rich.

By the 1990s, however, things weren't going so well in the countryside. The government held down farm prices and paid peasants IOUs for their grain. Farm incomes declined as inflation soared. In many rural areas, order broke down as peasants rioted and attacked authories. More than 100 million rural Chinese moved to the jobs and riches of the coastal cities, a potentially destabilizing tide the regime cannot control.

The partly free market spread to the cities. Faced with substantial unemployment, the regime let individuals open small shops, restaurants, repair stations, and even manufacturing facilities. It was even permissible to hire workers, something any Marxist would call capitalist exploitation. But it worked. Chinese applied individual hustle to produce and sell more and better products than the indifferent state factories and stores ever could. Hole-in-the-wall "department stores" had customers waiting in line to buy the fashionable clothing and footwear Mao used to scorn. People swarmed to outdoor markets to buy home-produced chairs and sofas.

Starting with the area around Hong Kong, large regions of coastal China were declared "Special Economic Zones," open to private and foreign investors. Capital poured in (much of it from Taiwan and Hong Kong) to take advantage of low Chinese wages, and production soared. These firms (some foreign) compete in a world market to make profits. Because of these firms—which cover only a fraction

The Trouble with Markets

The trouble with a market economy when introduced piecemeal into Communist countries such as Yugoslavia, Hungary, or China is that it tends to run out of control. The country experiences improved economic performance but also develops problems that wreck the socialist system.

- **Unemployment** appears. In most Communist systems unemployment was disguised by the gross labor inefficiency, but once firms have to compete on a market and make profits, they prune unproductive workers. Chinese workers under Mao had an "iron rice bowl"—jobs for life. Deng broke the iron rice bowl and made millions unemployed. China had to permit small-scale private enterprise to soak up some of these unemployed. More than 100 million Chinese, many without permission, left rural inland areas to seek jobs in the cities and coastal Special Economic Zones. More are on their way. Typical of the Third World, this "floating population" lives in shantytowns uncontrolled by authorities.

- **Income Inequalities** develop. With a market system, some Chinese farmers, entrepreneurs, and whole provinces get richer than others. The ones who don't do so well—the inland provinces with poorer soil and fewer natural resources—become jealous and complain to Beijing to redistribute some of the wealth. The richer provinces in the South and along the coast (home of the Special Economic Zones) object, arguing they work harder and produce more. Tensions between regions, especially between North and South, are growing and could lead, some warn, to breakup.

- **Inflation** kicks up. Most of China's food, clothing, and consumer goods are now produced and sold on a free market, and with too many yuan chasing too few goods, inflation passes 25 percent a year. The regime, unable to collect taxes, fuels inflation by printing far too much money, which it needs for its huge bureaucracy and inefficient state sector. (Brazil does exactly the same thing; see the next chapter.) The regime vows to bring down inflation by cooling economic growth, but the fast-growing coastal and southern provinces ignore Beijing.

- **Corruption** increases. Corruption grows at the interface of the private and governmental sectors. Economic liberalization multiplies such interfaces as more and more entrepreneurs need raw materials and permits from government officials. Under-the-table payments become the norm. Party and state officials think, "If everyone else is getting rich, why shouldn't I?" With the growth of corruption, legitimacy erodes.

The problem of an economy that mixes socialism and capitalism is its instability. It tends not to settle in a middle ground but to slide more and more toward full capitalism until blocked by central control. The result is a zigzag every few years as the government alternately tightens and relaxes supervision of the economy, never finding a stable balance. China is caught in this situation.

of the Chinese economy—China's overall GDP grew at an average of around 10 percent a year during the 1980s and into the 1990s—an amazing rate. Imagine if all the Chinese economy shifted to capitalism. By comparison, half the 11,000 state-owned enterprises lose money and have to be propped up by subsidies. Whether to let these industrial dinosaurs go bankrupt (and cause unemployment) is one of the great questions facing Beijing.

While most Chinese liked their taste of the free market, many cadres did not. If you really go to a market system, what do you do with the cadres who make a good living by supervising a controlled economy? They dig in their heels and try to block major change. Deng purged or retired the old guard and replaced them with young technocrats who pursue capitalist-sytle economic growth and call it "socialism with Chinese characteristics."

But market economies produce problems of their own (see box) and awaken resentments and jealousies. Some suggest that the Chinese economy is careening out of control at a time when political authority has weakened. Political reform has been deliberately blocked, for China is still very much a one-party dictatorship. What will happen when the free-market economy gets totally out of kilter with the dictatorial political system?

A Middle Way for the Middle Kingdom?

The basic supposition of Deng Xiaoping and his supporters was that there is a middle way between capitalism and communism, between a controlled and a free-market economy, between the Soviet and American models. They did not, of course, say this openly; for domestic political purposes they reaffirmed that they were Communists and were only "improving socialism." But by bringing in elements of a market economy while retaining a large state sector, they in effect sought a middle way. Is there one? Not really, and many observers now think the Chinese elite has quietly admitted it, at least among themselves.

When a Communist country introduces a bit of market economics—supply and demand, competing producers, profits, family farming, prices finding their own level—the first few years are usually good. Farm output especially grows, and everyone eats well. Consumer goods become far more available, and people live and dress better. Statistically, growth rates shoot up. It looks like they've found the happy balance: a market economy at the "micro" level to provide for consumer needs under the benevolent guidance of a state-run economy at the "macro" level. The farmers, shoemakers, and tailors are mostly private; the steel, chemical, and textile industries, as well as banking and planning systems, are state-owned and under Party control.

But after a few years things start to go wrong. Shortages, distortions, and bottlenecks appear that stall economic growth. The growing private sector keeps bumping into the state sector. Every time it does, there is a "crisis" that can only be resolved by expanding the private sector and shrinking the state sector.

An individual Chinese farmer, for example, may have done well under the "responsibility system" and made many more yuan (a yuan was worth about 12 cents in 1994) than he ever thought possible. Naturally, he wanted to buy things, perhaps a tractor or television. But these came from the big state factories, and they were geared to the state plan, not to consumer wants, so severe shortages of manufactured consumer goods develop. How to fix? Extend the market system to the factories, cutting them free to produce what consumers want and earn profits. But soon these factories run short of materials such as steel, which come from gigantic state industries who produce according to the national plan devised by Party leaders. The solution? Cut the state steel mills free to produce according to supply and demand, to succeed or fail according to their efficiency. Gradually, the capitalist economy subverts the socialist economy.

That may be fine with us—we tend to see it as a natural development that should not be impeded—but it was not fine with conservatives within the ruling Communist Party. They had both ideological and job commitments to keeping the system socialist, and they argued (correctly) that the growth of the market system dooms socialism. Few Communist leaders can resist such arguments, so they pull back from the market system. Result: not enough materials for the factories that produce consumer goods, not enough consumer goods for the farmer, and inflation as too many yuan chase too few goods. In the 1990s Beijing faces serious imbalances as the dynamic private sector bumps against the inefficient state sector.

The Chinese—like the Yugoslavs and Hungarians—found that a little bit of capitalism is like being a little bit pregnant. The choice Communist countries faced was difficult. If they went part of the way with a market economy, they experienced a few years of heady growth followed by dangerous distortions. If they called off the liberal experiment, they returned to the centralized, Stalinist system that was slowly running down, leaving them further and further behind the capitalist world. If they went all the way to a market system, they admitted they had been wrong all these decades.

The box China's Communists got themselves into is how to bring in market economics without appearing to abandon socialism. They can try to redefine "socialism" to mean widespread prosperity rather than state ownership of the means of production. Accordingly, they call capitalism "socialism with Chinese characteristics." This fools no one. But if capitalism comes, can democracy be far behind?

Do Markets Lead to Democracy?

By now most of China's industrial output comes from non-state firms—private, cooperative, or foreign-owned businesses. The inefficient, money-losing, subsidized state sector is declining as the non-state sector grows. China's workers and consumers

---

 ### *How Many Chinese?*

In the early 1980s China carried out a ferocious program to curb births. Urban women were warned to have only one child and could suffer fines and loss of benefits if they had more. Some women had to undergo involuntary abortion. The large excess of boy over girl babies strongly suggests female infanticide. All this was quite painful, for the Chinese love children. The program temporarily brought down China's rate of population increase to about 1 percent a year. Since 1949, however, China has averaged about 1.5 percent a year. Much of the Third World grows at 3 percent; only Europe shows less than 1 percent increase.

The liberalization of the 1980s, however, brought with it higher birthrates, leading to a population of 1.2 billion in 1994, the regime's target for 2000. Now 1.3 billion are expected in 2000. China adds a population as large as Japan's every decade. Part of the reason for the uptick was the fact that an earlier baby boom, from 1962 to 1973, was now having its own babies. But a bigger reason was that Chinese felt more prosperous and freer. Said one woman in a beauty parlor: "I have one child but I want another. And now I have the money to pay the fine."

will not willingly go back to a centralized economy. They are the potential voices of democracy.

Economic liberalization tends to encourage political participation. You can't reform the economy alone, for economic reform generates demands for political reform, namely, democracy. This was the truth Deng Xiaoping discovered late in his life. Amidst economic improvement, Chinese find they have plenty to complain about: rampant corruption, terrible medical care, rising prices, and continued economic controls and restrictions. Immediate and specific grievances turn into general criticism of the entire regime. Student complaints about wretched college conditions—no heat or toilets, incompetent teachers, food fit for hogs, no job prospects—underlay the 1989 student demonstrations, which turned into calls for full-blown democracy.

A market economy generates interest groups. Various businesses, farmers, workers, consumers, and localities discover their grievances and demand that government do something about them. As Party control recedes, pluralism grows, and pluralism is an important building block of democracy. This seems to be the pattern of the fast-growing "Four Tigers" of the Pacific Rim: South Korea, Taiwan, Hong Kong, and Singapore. All began as authoritarian regimes (and still have authoritarian streaks), but with prosperity came groups that wanted a say in government. Many scholars agree with political scientist Peter Burger: "When market economies are successful over a period of time, pressure for democratization inevitably ensues."

That is the favorable scenario. It's also possible that under Chinese conditions—a huge country hard to govern in good times, with economic growth uneven and out of control, central authority weakened, but several provincial governors and military commanders still powerful—that China will break up and revert to the "warlord" pattern of the 1920s. At one time dismissed as impossible, by the early 1990s some observers feared the breakup of China was possible.

Dissent and Democracy

For decades, Communist China had "mass surveillance," meaning the whole community ostracized, observed, and reported on suspected dissidents. For thirty years after liberation and the brutal land reforms, former "rich peasants" (meaning those slightly better off) were systematically discriminated against for their "bad class background." They were verbally abused, couldn't participate in politics, were barred from medical services, and received lower wages. Sometimes even their children were stigmatized.

With the unrest of 1989, things seem to have changed. People no longer respected the Party and the police. Wide sectors of the population sided with the student and intellectual dissidents. Neighborhood snitches kept silent and even aided those evading the police and army. Some of the hunted sneaked out of China; they must have had help.

Those caught suffered brutal imprisonment. The precise numbers are secret, but 10,000 were thought to have been jailed following the 1989 Tiananmen Square massacre alone. Perhaps the most poignant case was that of former Red Guard member Wei Jingsheng. In 1979 Wei, then 29 and editor of an underground newspaper, was sentenced to fifteen years in prison for advocating democracy. What really got Wei into trouble was a wall poster he put up that revealed that Chinese political prisoners are tortured, starved, worked to death, held in solitary confinement,

The Hong Kong Problem

In 1997, the British colony of Hong Kong reverts to China. An important part of Hong Kong actually consists of leased territory on the mainland—the source of the colony's water supplies—and the lease is up in 1997. The British decided to give the whole package back to Beijing. But the prosperous and hardworking Hong Kongese don't want to be part of China. Despite Beijing's treaty guarantees that Hong Kong can keep its economic system for fifty years, Hong Kongese fear that the Communists will take over everything. Many are emigrating.

Hong Kong poses a problem for the Communists, though. Hong Kong is based on 100 percent free-market capitalism, a stinging rebuke to Marxist economics. Beijing faced a dilemma. If they were to communize Hong Kong, they would ruin its marvelous economy. If they were to leave it capitalistic, they would have an island of freedom and prosperity in the middle of an impoverished and repressive China.

In the Special Economic Zones we see Beijing's solution to the dilemma: Surround Hong Kong with controlled areas of capitalist growth, a buffer zone of a partial market economy to insulate the rest of China from Hong Kong. The trouble is, these Zones were so successful the regime let them grow until they covered almost all the Chinese coast. Millions of inland Chinese flocked to them. In trying to insulate against capitalism, Beijing infected the entire country. In a manner of speaking, Hong Kong swallowed China rather than the other way around. Capitalism is contagious.

and not allowed to see relatives. Wei spoke the truth and served almost his whole sentence for it. But when Wei was released in 1993, he was not broken but tougher than ever and immediately resumed his pro-democracy campaign. The regime threw him back in jail.

The United States made a big point about human rights in China and offered Wei as a prominent example. The Beijing regime took American complaints as a slap in the face and told America that dissidents were troublemakers and a purely domestic concern. Washington threatened to end favorable tariffs (so-called "most-favored-nation" treatment) for China if it didn't improve its human rights record. Should the United States make human rights in China its business? This is a delicate time in the life of China. It looks like the Communists are losing their Mandate of Heaven. What will follow? Democracy or chaos? Perhaps a little push from the United States can put China on the path to political as well as economic stability.

Vocabulary Building

arable	Cultural Revolution	Gang of Four	incentives
Boxers	cyclical change	gentry	*kowtow*
cadre	decentralization	Great Leap Forward	Long March
CCP	dynasty	*Guomindang*	Manchus
Confucian	Four Modernizations	Hundred Flowers	Mandarin

Mandate of   Opium Wars   secular change   steady-state
  Heaven   *pinyin*   Special Economic   Taipings
man-land ratio   PLA   Zones   Tiananmen Square
Maoism   PRC   sphere of influence   treaty ports
mass line   Red Guards   Standing Committee   Wade-Giles
National Party   responsibility system State Council   warlords
  Congress

Further Reference

BLACK, GEORGE, and ROBIN MUNRO. *Black Hands of Beijing: Lives of Defiance in China's Democracy Movement.* New York: John Wiley, 1993.

BRUGGER, BILL, and DAVID KELLY. *Chinese Marxism in the Post-Mao Era.* Stanford, CA: Stanford University Press, 1990.

CHENG, CHU-YÜANG. *Behind the Tiananmen Massacre: Social, Political, and Economic Ferment in China.* Boulder, CO: Westview, 1990.

DREYER, JUNE TEUFEL. *China's Political System: Modernization and Tradition.* New York: Paragon House, 1993.

EVANS, RICHARD. *Deng Xiaoping and the Making of Modern China.* New York: Viking, 1994.

FAIRBANK, JOHN KING. *China: A New History.* Cambridge, MA: Harvard University Press, 1994.

FRIEDMAN, EDWARD. *Chinese Village, Socialist State.* New Haven, CT: Yale University Press, 1991.

GOLDMAN, MERLE. *Sowing the Seeds of Democracy in China: Political Reform in the Deng Xaioping Era.* Cambridge, MA: Harvard University Press, 1994.

HAN SUYIN. *Eldest Son: Zhou Enlai and the Making of Modern China, 1898–1976.* New York: Hill & Wang, 1994.

KLEINBERG, ROBERT. *China's Opening to the Outside World: The Experiment with Foreign Capitalism.* Boulder, CO: Westview, 1990.

LEE, HONG YUNG. *From Revolutionary Cadres to Party Technocrats in Socialist China.* Berkeley: University of California Press, 1990.

LINK, PERRY. *Evening Chats in Beijing.* New York: W. W. Norton, 1992.

LIU BINYAN. *A Higher Kind of Loyalty: A Memoir by China's Foremost Journalist.* New York: Pantheon, 1990.

NATHAN, ANDREW J. *China's Crisis: Dilemmas of Reform and Prospects for Democracy.* New York: Columbia University Press, 1990.

OI, JEAN C. *State and Peasant in Contemporary China: The Political Economy of Village Government.* Berkeley: University of California Press, 1989.

OVERHOLT, WILLIAM H. *The Rise of China: How Economic Reform Is Creating a New Superpower.* New York: W. W. Norton, 1993.

RITTENBERG, SIDNEY, and AMANDA BENNET. *The Man Who Stayed Behind.* New York: Simon & Schuster, 1993.

SHIRK, SUSAN L. *The Political Logic of Economic Reform in China.* Berkeley, CA: University of California Press, 1993.

SPENCE, JONATHAN D. *The Search for Modern China.* New York: W. W. Norton, 1990.

TERRILL, ROSS. *China in Our Time: The People of China from the Communist Victory to Tiananmen Square and Beyond.* New York: Simon & Schuster, 1992.

CHAPTER 28

Brazil

The Impact of the Past

The Portuguese Influence

Portugal had a claim to Brazil even before its explorers arrived there. In 1494 the Treaty of Tordesillas gave Portugal lands in the yet-unexplored New World. The treaty drew a line 370 leagues (some 1,100 miles) west of the Cape Verde Islands; land to the east of the line went to Portugal, and land to the west to Spain. This arrangement sliced off the easternmost bulge of present-day Brazil; subsequent Portuguese settlements pushed their control further westward to give Brazil its present borders. The first Portuguese arrived in 1500, when Pedro Alvares Cabral, claiming he was blown off course, took formal possession of the land for the king of Portugal.

Portugal did not administer its new colony in the way Spain did. The Spanish charged quickly into Latin America for "gold, God, and glory." The Portuguese did nothing for thirty years, partly because they were busy with the rich trade route around Africa to India and partly because Brazil seemed to offer little gold. About the only Portuguese interest in the new land was in the red wood that could be used to make dye. From the brazed color of brazilwood came the name Brazil (*Brasil* in Portuguese).

It was when the French started to settle there in 1530, then the Portuguese crown began to take an interest. Ordering the French expelled, Dom João (King John) III parceled out the coastline into fifteen *capitanías* or royal grants, which he gave, in the feudal manner, to wealthy Portuguese willing to finance settlement. The original *capitanías*, like the thirteen English colonies in North America, gave initial

Brazil.

shape to Brazil's present-day states and laid the foundation for its federalism. Growth in the *capitanías*, however, was slow and spotty. Portugal's population at that time was only around one million, and there were not many people eager to become colonists. Compared to the Spanish colonies, there were no quick and easy mineral riches to be found in Brazil.

Economic life centered on sugar, for which Europe had recently acquired a taste. Sugar farming requires lots of labor, however. The Indians of Brazil were relatively few in number and made poor slaves; used to a life of casual hunting, many refused to work. With many trading posts down the African coast, though, the Portuguese found their answer in black slaves. From the 1530s to the 1850s, at least three

In public, all manner of Brazilians—black, white, and all the combinations in between—mingle easily, giving rise to Brazil's image as a "racial paradise." *(Michael Roskin)*

million Africans (perhaps six times the number that were brought to the United States) were brought to Brazil and sold, chiefly to work in the sugar cane fields. Interbreeding among the three population groups—Indians, blacks, and Portuguese—was rife, producing Brazil's complex racial mixture. The Portuguese always prided themselves on being nonracist, and this attitude, in public anyway, carries over into present-day Brazil.

Other Portuguese attitudes distinguish Brazil from the former Spanish colonies of Latin America. Portuguese have been less inclined to violence and bloodshed than Spaniards. As many Portuguese point out: "In a Portuguese bullfight, we don't kill the bull". Flexibility and compromise are more valued in Brazilian politics than in the politics of its Spanish-speaking neighbors.

A Painless Independence

Brazil's independence from Portugal is also in marked contrast to the long struggles waged by the Spanish colonies. Slowly Brazil grew in population and importance. When the Netherlands made Pernambuco (now Recife) a Dutch colony in the mid-seventeenth century, Portuguese, blacks, and Indians together struggled to expel them and in the process began to think of themselves as Brazilians. In the 1690s, gold was discovered in what became the state of Minas Gerais (General Mines). A gold rush and later a diamond rush boosted Brazil's population. Economic activity shifted from the sugar-growing region of the Northeast to the South and stayed there. To this day, the growth area has been in the more temperate climes of the South, while the Northeast, impoverished and drought-stricken, has become a problem area.

By the late eighteenth century, Brazil had become more important economically than Portugal, and thoughts of independence began to flicker in the growing Brazilian consciousness, inspired, as throughout Latin America, by the U.S. and French revolutionary examples. Brazilian independence, curiously, came about partly because of Napoleon.

In trying to seal off the European continent from Britain, Napoleon sent an army to take Portugal in 1807. The royal court in Lisbon—some fifteen thousand people in all—at British prodding, boarded ships and sailed for Brazil. Dom João VI was at first wildly welcomed in Brazil, but the royal court was horrified at conditions in Rio and irritated leading residents by requisitioning their houses. Dom João ordered Rio cleaned, beautified, and turned into a true capital. In 1815, Brazil was raised in rank from colony to kingdom within the Portuguese empire.

In 1821, the British advised Dom João to return to Lisbon to make sure Portuguese liberals didn't get out of hand. He left his son, Dom Pedro, then age 23, as regent in Brazil and gave him some parting advice: If Brazilian independence became inevitable, he should be sure he led it. It was a pragmatic, levelheaded idea, an example of Portuguese flexibility in contrast to Spanish obduracy. In this way the Portuguese royal house served as a bridge between colonial and independent status. In 1822 Dom Pedro proclaimed Brazil independent, and Portugal did not resist.

From Empire to Republic

Monarchy is rare in the Western Hemisphere; it appeared only briefly in Haiti and Mexico (Maximilian). Brazil, however, was a true monarchy from 1822 to 1889, another point of contrast with the rest of Latin America. Dom Pedro I proved an inept ruler, and when the army turned against him he abdicated in 1831 while his Brazilian-born son was still a child. Under a regency—a council that runs affairs until a king comes of age—power was dispersed among the various states; an 1834 act set up states' rights and introduced de facto federalism. Politics became a series of quarrels among the states and the rich landowning families that ran them. The instability was so serious that it led finally to widespread agreement in 1840 to declare Dom Pedro II—only 14 years old—of age.

Dom Pedro II was beloved for his calm, tolerant manner and obvious concern for his nation. He did not, however, do much of anything. Basing his rule on big plantation owners (*fazendeiros*), Pedro was content to let things drift while he exercised the "moderating power" of the liberal 1824 constitution in appointing and dismissing ministers. But the Brazilian economy changed. The large landowners mattered less while vigorous businessmen and bankers gained in importance. The growing modern element came to resent the conservative monarchy and to favor a republic. One big question Dom Pedro II couldn't handle was slavery. Under British pressure, the importation of new slaves ended during the 1850s, but slavery continued, deemed humane and necessary by Pedro's landowning supporters. Various formulas for phasing out slavery were considered, but Pedro let the question drift until his daughter, Princess Isabel, acting as regent while he was in Europe, signed an abolition bill in 1888. Brazil was the last Western country to emancipate its slaves.

By now, wide sectors of the Brazilian population were disgusted with monarchy. Intellectuals, business people, and army officers, imbued with Positivist philosophy (see box), wanted modernization. Deprived of their slaves, even the plantation owners turned against Dom Pedro. In 1889, a military coup ended the monarchy and introduced a republic without firing a shot.

The Old Republic

The relative stability conferred by Brazil's Portuguese heritage, bloodless independence, and nineteenth-century monarchy wore off during the Old Republic (1889–1930), and Brazil came to resemble its Hispanic neighbors. Revolts, rigged elections, and military intervention marked this period.

The 1891 constitution was modeled after the United States', but in practice, power gravitated into the hands of political bosses (*coronéis*, "colonels") and the military. For most of the Old Republic, the presidency simply alternated between the political bosses of two of the most important states, São Paulo and Minas Gerais.

Grumbling increased during the life of the Old Republic. New sectors of the population became aware that their interests were unheeded by the conservative political bosses. Idealistic army officers revolted in 1922 and 1924, believing they could save the republic. The Brazilian army at this time was by no means conservative. Some officers still believed in Positivism and hated conservative politicians, who seemed to

"Order and Progress"

French philosopher Auguste Comte (1798–1857) developed a doctrine known as Positivism. With its slogan of "Order and Progress," this optimistic philosophy held that mankind can and will progress by turning away from theology and abstract speculation and toward the scientific study of nature and of society. By applying the natural-science methods of empirical observation and data gathering, society can be analyzed, predicted, and then perfected, not in a revolutionary way, but gradually and under the supervision of humanitarian spe-

cialists. Said Comte: "Progress is the development of order."

Comte's Positivism launched modern social science (and still holds sway in psychology) and took root especially in Brazil. By the 1880s many Brazilian army officers had been instructed in Positivism by the mathematics professor Benjamin Constant Magalhães, who taught in the national military academy. With the 1889 republic, Positivists put their motto into the Brazilian flag, where it remains to this day: *Ordem e Progresso*.

block progress. To this day, the Brazilian military sees itself as a progressive rather than as a conservative force.

What probably finally destroyed the Old Republic was the worldwide Depression and the collapse of the price of coffee, a crop that Brazil depended upon heavily for export earnings. Further, in 1930 a split developed in the old Paulista-Mineiro combination, and a crafty politician from Rio Grande do Sul—the home of many maverick politicians—took advantage of it to run for the presidency. Getúlio Vargas claimed the election results had been rigged against him (an entirely plausible charge) and, with help from the military and amid great popular acclaim, took over the presidency in Rio in October 1930.

Vargas's "New State"

Latin American populist strongmen (*caudillos* in Spanish, *caudilhos* in Portuguese) are hard to label, for they appear to be both leftist and rightist simultaneously. They expand the economy by statist means (see box). They claim to be for the people and are proud of the many welfare measures they institute. Often they create a labor movement and give it a privileged status that is long remembered among the working class. On the other hand, they are no more democratic than the old political bosses they overthrew and often support the interests of existing elites, such as keeping coffee prices high. And they are very much for "order."

Some call such figures as Vargas of Brazil and Perón of Argentina fascists, but they probably are not. Rather than building a party along ideological lines, these populist dictators mobilized the masses with their personal appeal. During the 1930s

---

The Addiction of Statism

The Old Regime in France started the tradition of "statism," the idea that the government should supervise the economy and own much industry, and it spread throughout much of the world. Regimes intent on rapid change—the Bolsheviks in Russia, Ataturk in Turkey, Perón in Argentina, and Vargas in Brazil—embraced statism as a seemingly logical solution to their problems of backwardness. Statism caught on like an addiction in Latin America: once you had a little state supervision, you soon wanted more. Have a social or economic problem? A new government program, industry, or regulation can solve it.

Statism's basic premises had long been examined and found wanting. Adam Smith, for example, concluded that state intervention merely gets in the way of economic growth. State-owned industries become monopolistic, uncompetitve, graft-ridden, inefficient, and money-losing. Many have to be propped up with state subsidies, money that comes from citizens' pockets. But once established, statist structures defy reform. Politicians, fearful of unemployment and of appearing pro-American or pro-capitalist, do not dare privatize demonstrably inefficient and crooked state enterprises. Once addicted, an economy tends to stay statist. Only in our day have wide areas of Latin America begun to kick the habit and turn to the free market.

and 1940s, however, when fascism in Europe was having its day, they did sometimes throw in fascistic rhetoric.

Vargas, like Perón, looked after the working class. Under Vargas, Brazil instituted an eight-hour day, minimum wages, paid vacations, and collective bargaining. Labor did not fight and win its rights; Vargas handed them over long before there was an organized labor movement to make demands. The result, as in much of Latin America, is a weak labor movement that constantly seeks the protection of a paternalistic state.

Vargas's 1934 constitution brought in a "corporatist" element—one-fifth of the legislature directly represented professional and trade groups—on the pattern of Italy and Portugal. The constitution also limited the president to a single four-year term. By 1937, however, Vargas decided he wanted to stay president and carried out a coup against his own regime (what is called in Latin America an *autogolpe*, "self-coup"). Vargas proclaimed himself president, but this time there was no legislature to limit his powers. Vargas called his regime the *Estado Nôvo*, the New State. His critics called it "fascism with sugar." There was material progress—industry, highways, public health, social welfare—but there was also a loss of freedom. The United States got along well with Vargas, for he did not curb U.S. investments. In 1942, Brazil declared war on the Axis powers (but sent few troops).

Vargas discovered the power of the urban working class and mobilized them to his cause by setting up labor unions and the *Partido Trabalhista Brasileiro* (Brazilian Labor party, PTB for short). The military, however, became alarmed at his populistic dictatorship and forced him to resign in 1945. By then Vargas had become a hero to many Brazilians, who continued to support his PTB. In both Brazil and Argentina, the working masses longed for the return of their respective dictators and reelected them to office, Vargas in 1950 and Perón in 1946 and 1973. Once mobilized by a populistic dictator, the masses may prefer such rulers and their statism to democracy and free markets.

The Rise and Fall of Jango Goulart

The reelected Vargas was a poor president; corruption and inflation soared. Many Brazilians, including top military officers, demanded he resign in 1954. Instead, he committed suicide, blaming reactionary international (that is, U.S.) and domestic forces for blocking his good works. One of Vargas's appointments had particularly angered the military. Vargas named a neighbor from Rio Grande do Sul, the radical João (Jango) Goulart, as labor minister, but the military forced him to resign in 1954.

Goulart, however, continued to head the PTB and in 1955 helped moderate Juscelino Kubitschek win the presidency with Goulart as vice-president. Kubitschek mobilized into his Social Democratic party (PSD) the old political class of state and local elites who had dominated Brazil before Vargas. Kubitschek tried to focus Brazilians' energies on developing the interior; he pushed construction of Brasilia, which became the capital in 1960. Heedless of economic problems, Kubitschek promoted industrialization and allowed inflation to skyrocket.

Brazil's working masses were still responsive to populist appeals. In 1960 a Paulista populist, Jânio Quadros, won the presidency in a landslide with reformist promises; Goulart was vice-president. An unstable alcoholic, Quadros resigned after just seven months, leaving a quixotic note reminiscent of Vargas's. Now Goulart, the very man the military forced out in 1954, was in line for the presidency.

The Brazilian army started talking about a coup, but a compromise was worked out: Goulart could be president but with the powers of that office greatly curtailed. Goulart accepted but played a waiting game. As the economy got worse—inflation climbed to 100 percent a year by 1964—he knew that the Brazilian masses, by now mobilized and seething with demands for radical change, would support him in a leftward course. Goulart's strategy worked: In a January 1963 plebiscite, Brazilians voted five-to-one to restore full powers to the president so he could deal with the economic chaos.

Goulart now veered further left and called for "Basic Reforms": land redistribution, nationalizing the oil industry, enfranchising illiterates, legalizing the Communist party, and turning the legislature, which had blocked his schemes, into a "congress composed of peasants, workers, sergeants, and nationalist officers."

Brazilian society—like France and Germany in earlier decades—split into leftist and conservative wings with very little middle ground. Conservatives, including most middle-class Brazilians, were horrified at Goulart and his appointment of Marxists to high positions. The United States saw Goulart as another Castro, cut off financial aid, and stepped up covert activity to destabilize the Goulart government. Brazil seemed to be on the edge of a revolution.

What finally brought Goulart down was his challenge to the armed forces. Goulart publicly supported some mutinous sailors, which Brazil's generals saw as undermining their military discipline and command structure. On March 31, 1964, with scarcely a shot, the armed forces put an end to Brazil's tumultuous democracy.

The Key Institutions

The Military as Political Institution

As in much of the Third World, Brazil's political institutions are weak. Unlike Europe with its well-established parliaments, parties, and bureaucracies, Brazil's political institutions are incapable of handling the demands of mass politics in an orderly way. In such circumstances, the army is often the only institution capable of governing. Direct military participation ended in 1985, but if things get tumultuous again, we can expect another military takeover.

The Brazilian military had intervened in politics many times before 1964; at the birth and through the life of the Old Republic, at first in support of Vargas and then against him, and at the establishment of reasonably democratic regimes at the end of the two Vargas periods. Prior to 1964, however, the Brazilian military never tried to stay in power. They saw themselves in much the same way as Dom Pedro II had seen his role, that of a "moderating power" to restrain politicians from excesses. Step in when need be, set things right, then step out, was the Brazilian military pattern.

By 1964, both the Brazilian military attitude and the nation's situation had changed. Brazilian officers, partly thanks to U.S. guidance, had redefined their mission from defending Brazil against external enemies to guarding it against internal threats, especially communism. In the Superior War College, the ESG (see box), top officers studied politics, economics, psychology, and counterinsurgency.

Thus the Brazilian military, technically highly trained and newly motivated toward a more active role in their country's politics, was ready to upset a long-held view (especially by Americans) that truly professional military officers do not engage in coups. Looking around, the Brazilian officers found—almost like a case study— that Brazil was sliding rapidly to the left. The Brazilian army chose to intervene, and it did so precisely because it was professionally trained to prevent revolution. This time the officers were determined to stay in power, block the return of divisive politics, and modernize their potentially rich country in an organized, rational manner.

For two decades, Brazil was governed by a succession of generals. The Brazilian military did not rule the country directly, as if it were an army camp. Rather, they structured the political system so that only a military officer or a civilian who worked closely and cooperatively with the military could attain executive office. Once named president, a Brazilian general usually retired from active service and seldom wore his uniform.

Can an army be a political institution? Historically, the evidence is against the military holding power permanently. Armies are clumsy tools to govern with. After some years, military regimes tend to return power to civilians, or turn into civil-

---

Brazil's Powerful Military School

A school facing a luxurious Rio beach would not normally seem a likely spot for a powerful political institution, but in Brazil virtually an entire ruling class emerged from the Superior War College (*Escola Superior da Guerra*, ESG). Founded in 1949 on the model of the U.S. National War College (which trains midcareer officers for higher command), by the 1960s the ESG had shifted its emphasis from external to internal security. Still influenced by the old Positivism—which, in fact, had been spread in the last century through Brazil's military academy—ESG students came to the conclusion that only Brazil's rapid economic development would save it from chaos and communism.

The ESG, it is interesting to note, trained not only the best colonels and generals, but top civilians as well. Government administrators, private industrialists, and leading professional people tended to outnumber ESG's military students. The ESG drew its ninety students a year from key areas of the political and economic power structure: banking, mass communications, education, and industry. ESG's

graduates returned to their branches imbued with the authoritarian developmentalist doctrines they learned at the school. In civilian-ruled Brazil, ESG graduates are not so influential, although many are still in high positions. They still form a cadre of technocrats the military could rely on again should they return to power.

The ESG actually resembles a French *grande école* such as the Polytechnique or ENA, except that ESG students are generally older and already established in careers. In both cases, however, the schools put their stamp on bright, carefully selected people, training them to think and act the same way and to maintain close ties with each other. This is what gave French and Brazilian policy making its cohesion and continuity. "We don't actually make government policy," said a senior Brazilian officer on the ESG staff. "The great contribution of the school has been to establish an elite of people who can think in the same language and who have learned the team approach to planning here." The French couldn't have said it better.

ian regimes themselves, or get overthrown in a new military coup. The first is what happened in Brazil in the early 1980s.

Brazil's military regime was not just military, and that may be why it lasted so long. The Brazilian military had close ties to civilian bankers, educators, industrialists, and governmental administrators, many of whom trained together in the Superior War College in Rio. The weakness of most military regimes is their isolation and lack of contact with civilian elites. Unable to run the complexities of economy, society, and diplomacy without skilled civilians, military regimes frequently blunder so badly they decide to give up power and responsibility.

Brazil's generals mostly avoided this kind of isolation by partially integrating themselves with conservative civilian elites who held views and values close to the military's. Brazil's "military" regime was actually a civilian-military network of authoritarian developmentalists who controlled most of Brazil's economic, political, and military structures. In public, the government looked civilian. Most executive positions were occupied by civilian technocrats. But behind them, making the basic decisions and insuring order, was the military, which still regards itself as the savior of the nation.

The Presidency

The military presidents of Brazil were extremely powerful, their civilian successors less so. When generals ran Brazil—and every president from 1964 to 1984 was a general—the only check that kept them from becoming dictators was the fact that they were part of the military and needed the support of their military colleagues. Brazilian generals, trained in teamwork, disliked the flamboyant, personalistic style of civilian politicians. Consequently, no military president tried to turn himself into a one-man dictator or even to stay in office more than one term.

All but one of Brazil's military presidents were chosen from among its sixteen four-star generals. This meant they were older, around 60, experienced, and well educated, having gone through several highly competitive military schools. All attended the ESG. Additionally, most previously headed the important National In-

The Waltz of the Generals: Brazil's Presidents

1964–67 Gen. Humberto de Alencar Castello Branco
1967–69 Gen. Arthur da Costa e Silva
1969–74 Gen. Emilio Garrastazú Médici
1974–79 Gen. Ernesto Geisel
1979–85 Gen. João Baptista de Figueiredo

1985–90 José Sarney (civilian)
1990-93 Fernando Alfonso Collor de Mello (civilian, impeached)
1993-94 Itamar Franco (civilian, finished Collor's term)

The President Who Never Was

Tancredo Neves was chosen Brazil's first civilian president in twenty-one years, but on the eve on his swearing-in on March 15, 1985, he was hospitalized and died a month later at age 75, never having taken the oath of office. Although not elected by a popular vote, Neves was a popular personality, a grandfatherly figure of moderation and balance.

In his place stepped José Sarney, who had been elected vice-president. This brought political problems for, unlike Neves, Sarney was not an opposition figure but a former president of the pro-military Democratic Social party, who had switched sides only the year before. Sarney turned out to be vain, passive, and ineffectual. Many Brazilians were convinced that things would have gone better with the beloved Tancredo.

telligence Service, which served as a sort of brain center and watchdog for what the generals called their "revolution."

The incumbent president had a large say in selecting his successor but usually did it in consultation with a small circle of fellow generals known as "the system." The choice was simply announced to a government-controlled party which adopted him as its candidate. Then an electoral college composed of legislators of both houses and some from the states—and packed with a pro-government majority—rubber-stamped its approval. They called it an election.

In 1985, Brazil's first civilian president since 1964 was chosen indirectly, by an electoral college of 686 federal and state legislators. Although there was a popular outcry for direct elections, the military was afraid that a radical populist of the Goulart stripe might win. The military thought they had the electoral college stacked in favor of the government party, but it split, and the moderate opposition leader, Tancredo Neves, was elected over the generals' objections. But they had set up the electoral system and could not very well denounce the results. This gave the civilian presidency at least temporary protection from a new military coup. The military indicated they would let the next presidential elections be direct, that is, based on popular vote, which indeed happened in 1989.

A New Democratic Constitution

In late 1988, after a year and a half of debate, a Constituent Assembly approved a new, democratic constitution for Brazil, the country's seventh constitution since independence. The aims and structure of Brazil's new basic law are fine, but so are most Latin American constitutions, and they do not prevent military takeover. Like most modern constitutions, the Brazilian constitution includes numerous social and economic rights—a forty-hour workweek, medical and retirement plans, minimum wages, a 12 percent interest ceiling on loans, the right to strike, Indian rights, and environmental protection. Such details have no place in a constitution. But the writ-

COMPARING

 ## *Spain Turns Democratic*

In 1975, when Franco died, Spain was an authoritarian system with a hand-picked parliament, curbs on the press, and no legal political parties. Just two years later, Spain was a full-fledged democracy with a freely elected parliament, a lively and critical press, and a complete party system. The Franco system had become history. In 1982, the democratically minded Spanish Socialists were elected to power with an absolute majority of seats.

Dictators like to kid themselves that they have built lastingly. Their immediate successors like to think they can give a few tokens of democracy but preserve the authoritarian system. They can't. A little bit of democracy just whets people's appetites for more, and the system tends to slide all the way into full democracy. There are several points of comparison between Spain's rapid shift to democracy and Brazil's, with one important difference. Spain has a mostly middle-class population, and this tends to make for centrist politics. Brazil has a large class of extremely poor people, and this tends to make for unstable politics.

ers of new constitutions, especially in the Third World, are often idealistic and think they can right all wrongs by mandating fixes in the constitution.

The problem with guaranteeing such rights is that they create expectations and demands that cannot possibly be met by a struggling economy. Such details also fail to distinguish between a constitution (the basic rules of the game) and statutes (laws for specific problems). The 1988 Brazilian constitution can never be fulfilled, but it deepens popular discontent. Even worse, it mandates referendums—called "popular vetoes" and "popular initiatives"—to voice these discontents. California, with its myriad initiatives on each ballot, can get away with such hyperdemocratic nonsense; in Brazil it fosters instability. Another potentially disruptive feature of Brazil's constitution: voting age now starts at 16.

In structure, the 1988 Brazilian constitution resembles the U.S. Constitution, with some differences. The Brazilian president is elected for just one five-year term. In 1993, a plebiscite decided to keep the presidential system—Brazil's tradition since 1889 and the pattern throughout Latin America—rather than go to a parliamentary system with a prime minister as chief executive.

Brazil's parliament, the National Congress, is bicameral. The upper house, the Senate, consists of 81 members who are elected for eight-year terms. Each of Brazil's 26 states gets three senators. The lower house, the Chamber of Deputies, has 503 members, each elected for four-year terms on a proportional-representation basis. Each state gets the number of deputies its population warrants.

An Emerging Party System

Under the military, Brazil had essentially fake parties, one a total creature of the regime, the Renovating Alliance (*Aliança Renovadora Nacional*, ARENA), the other a tame opposition, the Brazilian Democratic Movement (*Movimento Democrático*

Collor de Mello: Playboy President

Brazil's first elected civilian president after the military stepped down was young, energetic, smart, rich, and crooked. As such, Fernando Alfonso Collor de Mello was a poor choice to break the Brazilian cycle of unstable civilian governments alternating with military takeovers. He came to office in 1990 with a radical promise to push Brazil from a state-dominated to a market economy, but he did not—perhaps could not—deliver. Caught siphoning off millions of dollars in campaign funds to finance his playboy lifestyle and under impeachment, Collor resigned in 1992.

Collor was born in Rio in 1949 and followed the pampered path typical of the Brazilian elite. His father was a wealthy businessman and politician who gunned down a senator he disliked right on the Senate floor in 1963. (Crimes of "honor" are rather common in Brazil.) The family then moved to Brasília where young Collor cut a custom-tailored figure as an economics student, sports car racer, and karate champ. Collor then took over the family's media business—a newspaper, radio stations, and the local affiliate of Brazil's largest TV network—in the northeast state of Alagoas. Collor married twice; both brides were the teenage daughters of wealthy and prominent families.

Collor got into politics when Brazil's ruling generals named him mayor of the capital city of Alagoas in 1979 when he was just 29. In 1982 he became a congressman from Alagoas, and in 1986 he was elected state governor. Governor Collor, now imbued with the free-market and antistatist views then gaining currency, achieved mass popularity by firing what he called the "maharajahs" (rich and lazy princes) of the overstaffed state bureaucracy.

Using this theme—of liberating the Brazilian economy from government supervision—and his television connections, Collor became a media personality to edge out his socialist opponent Lula by 53 to 47 percent in the December 1989 election. Ironically, Collor ran best among poor and working-class Brazilians, who liked his exuberant, upbeat personality.

Brasileiro, MDB). With the opening up (*abertura*) of the 1980s, the MDB turned itself into the Party of the MDB (PMDB), a moderate center party.

Several Socialist or workers' parties sprang up. The main party of the left, the Workers party (*Partido dos Trabalhadores,* PT), is led by a charismatic union organizer, Luis Inácio da Silva, nicknamed "Lula," who ran for president in 1994. Leonel Brizola, a radical intellectual and Goulart's brother-in-law, set up a center-left Democratic Labor party (*Partido Democrático Trabalhista,* PDT) and won election twice as governor of Rio de Janeiro state. Nationally, though, the PDT party had little strength.

On the conservative side, a deceptively named Social Democratic party (*Partido Democrático Social,* PDS) emerged from the ARENA. In both Brazil and Portugal, "social democratic" connotes center-right, not center-left. The PDS split over a controversial presidential candidate, and out of it came the Liberal Front party (*Partido da Frente Liberal,* PFL), a center-right party led by former President Sarney.

Brazil's parties change like quicksilver. They are founded, merge, and split so fast it's hard to keep up with them. In the early 1990s, Brazil's Congress had nineteen parties. This is the mark of an inchoate party system in which the poorly institutionalized parties are simply personalistic vehicles to get their leaders elected. Few parties articulate a coherent program or implement coherent policies. Rather, once elected, leaders use government resources (jobs, contracts, loans, kickbacks) to keep themselves in power and get rich. President Collor de Mello (see box), for example, created his own National Reconstruction party for the 1989 election, but it soon faded, and he did not care, for he was then able to use the powers of government to enrich himself and his friends. Settling down into a stable, meaningful party system is one of the best things Brazilian democracy could do for itself. But such an evolution will take several elections and patient organizational work, something Brazilians have not been good at.

A Lack of Institutions

Part of the reason Brazil got into its political fix was the lack of sturdy institutions that could handle the influx of newly mobilized sectors of the population and their demands. In the absence of firm, well-established parties and parliaments, demagogic populists aroused both the masses and the military. The military won, and, as we shall see, the masses lost. The trouble was that the Brazilian military did not really found durable institutions either.

The 1994 Election: The Inflation Connection

In the October 1994 presidential election, Brazilians voted massively against inflation by electing Fernando Henrique Cardoso, a former finance minister and author of a plan that stabilized Brazil's currency. Months earlier, fiery Workers Party leader Luis Inácio da Silva, better known as "Lula," had led in the polls. But Cardoso beat Lula 54 to 27 percent.

Cardoso, 63, a formerly radical sociologist from Sao Paulo, ran as candidate of the center-right Social Democratic party. Under the generals, Cardoso had been barred from teaching, was arrested, and forced into exile. Over the years, though, he turned from "dependency" theory to free market theory and pledged to rid Brazil of its state-owned and protected industries. If he does it, Brazil could boom.

Even poor Brazilians preferred Cardoso to Lula. "I'm voting for Fernando Henrique," said one Rio *favelado*, "he invented the Real Plan." He was referring to the economic stabilization plan that was taking hold. On July 1, a new currency, the *real*, began to circulate and to choke off inflation, which dropped from 45 percent in June to 1.5 percent in September. It may not last, but it gave Brazilians hope. Lula, on the other hand, spoke of socialist-type help for the poor. Such programs are inflationary, and most Brazilians saw inflation as their number-one problem.

The 1994 presidential elections paralleled the 1989 contest in which Collor narrowly beat Lula. Brazilians, it seems, despite widespread poverty, tend to vote for moderates.

The centrist parties, the PMDB and Liberal Front, were weak and prone to corruption, factionalism, and breakup. The leftist parties were attempting to play the populist card—arousing the masses, as Vargas and Goulart did—but if they succeeded, the military might step back in. The democratically elected Congress was weak and untried.

The military and its creations proved that they could not become durable institutions either. For a while, they pleased the generals and their technocratic helpers, but they had nothing to say to the vast majority of Brazilians. One of the principal functions of political institutions is winning and channeling mass loyalty to the system. Without such loyalty, mere technical arrangements, even if they work well in promoting economic growth, become more and more isolated from the population they rule. Franco's Spain supervised an economic boom, but there was little positive feeling among Spaniards for the Franco institutions. After his death in 1975, those institutions were dismantled with scarcely a protest.

To their credit, Brazil's ruling generals saw the same situation developing. Wide sectors of the population voiced their displeasure with continued military rule. Workers wouldn't stay cowed; strikes flared. Students again grew rebellious. Even groups of better-off Brazilians—bankers, industrialists, and big farmers—who were earlier supporters of the military regime expressed annoyance over economic intrusion and mistakes on the part of the regime. During the 1970s Brazil's ruling generals came to appreciate how difficult it is to run a country.

But democratization has not guaranteed a happy ending either. The demands on the civilian governments are incredible: growing poverty, joblessness, inflation, crime, and international debt. And all this falling on weak, immature institutions. Can Brazil's infant democracy handle the strain? If it can't, the military will step back in, but that is not a viable solution either. Indeed, by stunting the growth of political institutions, the Brazilian military did great harm to the country. We hold our breath to see if Brazil can escape from its cycle of weak civilian institutions overthrown by clumsy military regimes, which in turn give way to weak civilian administrations again.

Brazilian Political Attitudes

The Easygoing Image

Both Brazilians and resident foreigners tend to describe Brazilians as easygoing people, seldom angry or violent, largely indifferent to politics, and unlikely to rise in revolt. There's a lot of truth to this image. In most of Brazil for most of the year it's too hot to make a revolution. People would rather go to the beach.

Brazilians have better things to do with their energies than take them out in politics. Brazilians are emotional; they laugh, joke, and embrace in public. They love children—possibly, some suggest, because the infant mortality rate is so high—and tend to spoil their offspring, especially the boys. This creates a male-centered society in which the men are expected to indulge themselves but not the women.

Many of the Portuguese who settled Brazil either were minor noblemen or pretended they were. They brought with them antiwork attitudes and looked down on tawdry moneymaking. Until fairly recently this attitude was still present in the Brazilian middle and upper classes, limiting their entrepreneurial energy. Many of

Personalismo and Machismo

Latin American politicians, including Brazilians, frequently rely on personal magnetism—*personalismo*—in politics rather than on clear thinking, party programs, or patient organizing. Most Latin Americans like to be perceived as having a strong personality, the men especially as *macho*. *Macho* simply means male, but *machismo* has taken on the meaning of a strutting, exaggerated masculinity. The typical Latin American politician, civilian or military, combines *personalismo* and *machismo* in varying degrees.

The Brazilian generals, given the way in which they were selected for power, tended to downplay these qualities. With the return of civilian politics, however, *personalismo* and *machismo* reappeared in Brazilian politics. Both Collor de Mello in 1989 and Lula in 1994 exuded *personalismo*.

the more vigorous business and government people have been of non-Portuguese origin (German, Italian, Japanese, and East European). Avoidance of work is common throughout the middle and upper classes in Latin America; people would rather attach themselves to the state bureaucracy than develop private industry. The elements of hustle and vigor are missing from much of Latin American capitalism, a point sometimes offered as an explanation of both backwardness and penetration by U.S. capital.

The image of Brazilians as lazy and laid-back amidst tropical languor, however, may have been overdone. An economy can't expand at several percentage points a year without people working hard. The "tropical languor" theory may have been deliberately cultivated in Brazil, for it serves as a rationalization for keeping the broad mass of Brazilians apolitical while leaving elites free to run the country as they wish. Brazilian elites tell themselves that the poor are content in their ignorance and are apathetic by nature. They, the elites, must shoulder the arduous tasks of running government and the business sector, both of which benefit mostly the elites.

Furthermore, there wasn't anything easygoing about Brazilian attitudes as the country has approached the brink of social collapse. Desperate people, some of them reduced from middle-class jobs to street peddling, turned angry. More than a quarter of Brazilian workers were unemployed, and Brazil has practically no unemployment compensation, welfare benefits, or food stamps. When Brazilians have no more money for food, they are forced to starve or steal.

Brazilian Racism

One area where the easygoing Brazilian attitude has helped to keep society calm and stable is their proclaimed indifference to race. At least one-third of Brazilians have African ancestors, giving Brazil the largest African-descended population outside of Africa. Precise classification is impossible, however, because of both racial mixing and the Latin American tendency to let culture decide race. Throughout the continent, a person with the right education, manners, and money is considered "European" with little regard to skin color. Brazilians have dozens of words to distinguish among the combinations that make up the country's racial spectrum: *branco, alvo,* and *claro* for the lighter skinned, *moreno* and *mulato* for the middle shades, and *negro, preto, cabo verde,* and *escuro* for the darker. In theory and in most public places, there is no discrimination in Brazil. Walking down the street, one Brazilian feels as good as another.

Brazil's dirty little secret, however, is that in fact it is a racist society, one that adheres to the old American song: "If you're white you're all right, and if you're brown stick around, but if you're black get back." Career chances are strongly related to skin color in Brazil. If you're white, your chances of going to a university, entering a profession, making lots of money, and living in a nice house are much, much higher. If you're black, you run a high risk of infant death, malnutrition, rural poverty, and the lowest jobs or unemployment.

The Brazilian economic and political elite is white. This holds true whether the government is civilian or military. A small number of blacks have moved upward, but their way is often blocked by job requirements specifying "good appearance" (that is, white or near-white). Individual blacks can succeed in entertainment and

COMPARING

 ## *Apartheid, Brazilian Style*

South Africa, until recently, classified population groups and then used elaborate laws to discriminate against black and brown. From the Brazilian perspective this was not only unjust but expensive and stupid as well. The Brazilian system, pretending that all are equal, assigns people to social roles on the basis of race as the South African system did, but without the obvious unfairness, the many laws, or the social tension that the *apartheid* system brought. By pretending to be color-blind, Brazilian society dampens the black resentment that could lead to rage and revolt.

Curiously, tacitly racist breakaway movements in Brazil's southernmost provinces, where the population is 85 percent European, parallel South Africa's *apartheid*. People in the clean, prosperous states of Rio Grande do Sul, Santa Catarina, and Parana, upset by the influx of impoverished darker Brazilians from further north, talk about setting up a new country, the Republic of the Pampas. It would be the size of France and have 22 million mostly white citizens. German

and Italian would be coequal languages with Portuguese.

One spokesman for this republic is businessman Irton Marx, the blond son of German immigrants, who argues that Brazil is too big, too statist, and too corrupt. "Our culture and economy are different here in the south. We are part of the First World. We are subsidizing the whole country and getting nothing back." Denying he or his movement is racist, Marx contends his tidy region is threatened by the mass migration of poor northeastern Brazilians, who do not have the local "Teutonic" attitude toward work.

Some municipalities in the south of Brazil already make it difficult for poor nonwhites to settle. They deny them permits or even put them on buses back to where they came from. Chances are, the breakaway movement will get nowhere, but it does illustrate (1) there is racism in Brazil, (2) Brazil is in a declining condition, and (3) the crux of *apartheid*, whether in South Africa, Brazil, or U.S. suburbia, is influx control.

sports, but they are a handful. The world's greatest (and highest-paid) soccer star, Pelé, is black. Even he encountered discrimination early in his career. Intermarriage is perfectly legal but seldom takes place.

Brazil's Poor: Passive or Explosive?

Do poor people turn naturally to social revolution, or are they too busy trying to stay alive to bother with political questions? In Brazil, we have a laboratory to test some of the longstanding debates about why people revolt. The answers depend not just on people being poor—most Brazilians through history have been poor—but on the *context* in which poor people find themselves.

In the dry, overpopulated Northeast, some people starve. Many rural poor, hoping to improve their condition, flood to the *favelas* (shantytowns) surrounding the cities, where some do find work while others eke out a precarious living from peddling or crime. Rich Brazilians, on the other hand, live sumptuously. For most of the military era, there was little open class resentment. First and most important, the Brazilian underclass was deprived of its leadership and organizational alternatives. The radical parties and leaders of the Goulart period were, respectively, outlawed and exiled or had their political rights annulled, *cassado* in Portuguese. Anyone caught trying to form a radical opposition got into bad trouble—"disappeared" to torture or death.

The strong economic growth of the 1970s gave people hope and thus dampened protests, but with the drastic economic downturn of the 1980s hope vanished. "I tell you frankly I'm desperate," said one sidewalk peddler whose pregnant wife stood nearby. "They keep telling us that things will get better, but who can afford to wait? Hunger doesn't wait. Yesterday I sold nothing. Our food is ending. When it ends, what do I do?" The answer for some Brazilians was to raid food stores. Everything from corner grocery shop to supermarket was smashed open by hungry crowds and quickly looted. Brazil's food riots sent chilling warning signs throughout the Third World.

Especially ominous is that this arousal of Brazil's poor from passive to active comes at the time Brazil is democratizing and forming parties, some of them with radical leadership. Even more explosive is the fact that many middle-class Brazilians find themselves getting pushed down into the lower classes, and middle-class people are far more likely to rise in revolt than those who have always been downtrodden. Sectors of the middle class, desperate to hold on to their tenuous positions, could serve as the sparkplug for major unrest.

In sum, the poor are not automatically passive or active but can become either, depending on the situation. If Brazilian radicals attempt once again to mobilize mass discontent, we can expect the military to intervene.

Uneven Democratic Attitudes

While there is a general will to reestablish democracy, not all sectors of the Brazilian population share it equally. Some Brazilians, especially among elites, are convinced democrats. Others, especially poorer and working-class people, are interested in little besides jobs and willing to support whatever will put some food on the table, democratic or not. This is typical of the Third World—and even much of the First.

Marginals in Brazil's Favelas

Brazil's poor are sometimes called "marginals," that is, people on the edge—of society, of the economy, of starvation. Many of them huddle in *favelas*, shantytowns on the edge of cities.

Some *favelados* hold regular jobs, others sell pop on the beach, and some steal. Brazil's crime rates are astronomical. There is no place for the marginals to go, and no one cares about them.

Politically they are on the margin too. Unorganized and too busy just trying to stay alive, they riot only when faced with starvation. Brazilian sociologists point out that however wretched life seems in the *favelas*, it's worse in the countryside. Moving to a *favela* for many is a step up, for there they have access to some education and health services and may even find a job.

Brazil's population growth and its impoverished Northeast indicate that *favelas* will continue to grow as more Brazilians pour in from the countryside. Indeed, the urban shantytown has become a hallmark of the Third World in general. Attempts to clear out urban squatters from illegal settlements inevitably fail; the new arrivals just set up their shacks somewhere else.

As we shall see in the next chapter, the crux of South Africa's notorious *apartheid* system was "influx control," aimed at keeping squatters out of urban areas. With majority rule in South Africa, this too has ended, and we can expect to see the South African equivalent of *favelas*.

"Keep Your Distance," says this Rio roadsign, but it could also serve as a warning about the *favelas* that nestle between Rio's peaks. *(Michael Roskin)*

Commitment to democratic values is stronger among those higher up on the socioeconomic ladder, people who don't have to worry about eating.

Researchers in Brazil and other Third World lands often find that poorer and less-educated people are more interested in law-and-order and bread-and-butter issues than in civil rights and democracy. Many actually prefer an authoritarian populist in command. One survey found that 63 percent of Brazilian illiterates named the dictatorial Vargas as the best president. Those with high school or college education favored Médici, the toughest of Brazil's military presidents. Their reasons? Poor people liked the way Vargas raised wages and looked after the poor; middle-class people pointed to industrialization under Médici.

The strong vote for Cardoso in 1994 was not a vote for democracy; it was a vote for bread on the table. Among better-educated and better-off Brazilians we find interest in democracy for its own sake, and even here it is not overwhelming. And these Brazilian findings are not unique. In many countries—including the United States—commitment to democratic values falls off as one moves down the socioeconomic ladder. The irony here is that democracy—a system that's supposed to favor the broad masses of people—receives its strongest support from elites.

The above doesn't mean that democracy is impossible in Brazil, but it indicates that it's apt to be shaky. Part of the impulse for Brazil's democratization comes from the educated upper middle class, a group that's relatively small but strategically

Latin America's Changing Leftists

During much of the Cold War, Latin American intellectuals subscribed to fashionable leftist views that their region's poverty was the result of exploitation by wicked capitalists, especially by *Norteamericanos*. Some worked this up into a Marxist type of theory called "dependency" that was accepted as an article of faith throughout much of the Western Hemisphere. Only by getting out from the control of U.S. corporations—who dictated what Latin American lands would produce (bananas and coffee) and what they would consume (Chevrolets and Coca Cola)—would Latins find prosperity. Accordingly, revolutionary regimes such as Cuba and Nicaragua were not so bad, because they broke the Yankee connection.

Recently, the Latin left has had to rethink its Marxist and dependency theories. The demise of Communist regimes in the Soviet Union and East Europe made some wonder if "socialism" really worked. The economic success of Chile, where a military dictator enforced capitalism, made many appreciate the vigor of market systems, especially those connected to the world economy. Argentina's restructuring in the early 1990s had a similar impact. And intellectually, many were persuaded by the arguments of Peruvian economist Hernando de Soto that the only effective and dynamic sector of Latin economies is the black market. Why? Every other sector is choked by government controls into stagnation.

The result of this was a rethinking that moved many Latin intellectuals away from their long-term addiction to statism and socialism. Free markets, international trade, and foreign investment no longer looked so bad; maybe they were even good. The new attitude spread unevenly in Latin America, though. It was most pronounced in Mexico, Chile, and Argentina but much weaker in Brazil and Uruguay. (Brazilian President Cardoso years ago had been a dependency theorist.)

positioned to make its voice heard. Brazil makes us aware that democracy—or indeed any kind of political system—is usually the work of the few mobilizing the many.

Patterns of Interaction

An Elite Game

Politics in Brazil has been—and continues to be—largely a game for elites: big landowners, bankers and industrialists, and top bureaucrats and military people. The stakes of the game are political power and the patronage jobs that come with it. The rules of the game are that none of the players gets seriously hurt or threatened and that nobody mobilizes the Brazilian masses in an angry way, for that would destroy the game's fragile balance and hurt them all. Accordingly, Vargas, himself a wealthy rancher, was an acceptable player when he supported coffee prices for the growers, but when he started to mobilize poor Brazilians he had to be ousted. Kubitschek was a good player who looked after his elite friends and deflected potential discontent with his grandiose plans to open Brazil's interior. Goulart, also a wealthy rancher, was a very bad player: he threatened all the elites and mobilized the masses at a furious rate. Lula, an anti-elite labor-union radical, mobilized Brazil's poverty-striken masses in a way that frightened most of Brazil's elites and increased the chances of a coup.

Brazil's entire political history has been the same elite game: Dom Pedro with his *fazendeiro* friends, the Old Republic with its Paulista-Mineiro alternation, and the military technocracy with its industrial and bureaucratic clientele. Since Vargas, however, the political mobilization of the masses has been a recurring threat to the game. Periodically, a politician who doesn't like the elite's fixed rules is tempted to reach out to Brazil's masses, both to secure his own power and to help the downtrodden. Seeing the threat, Brazil's elites, through the military, remove it and try to demobilize the masses. Mobilization and demobilization can be seen as a cycle.

The Mobilization-Demobilization Cycle

Scholars of the Third World in general and Brazil in particular often focus on "political mobilization." Mobilization means the masses waking up, becoming aware, and in some cases becoming angry. Prior to the beginning of mass political mobilization in a country, few participate in politics, and decisions are made by traditional elites, such as Brazil's big landowners and political bosses. Some social stimulus, such as economic growth, however, brings new sectors of the population (in Brazil, the urban working class) to political awareness; they are "mobilized" and start participating in politics with new demands.

The problem with Brazil—and many other Third World countries—is that the existing institutions haven't been able to handle this influx of new participants and their demands. Well-organized, strong political parties can channel, moderate, and calm mass demands in a constructive way. But Brazilian parties are weak, often little more than personalistic vehicles designed to get their chief into power. The chiefs, such as Vargas and Goulart, then use the parties in a demagogic way, whipping up support among the newly mobilized and politically unsophisticated masses by promising them instant reforms and economic improvements.

The more conservative elements in society—the wealthy, who often have close ties to the military—view this process with horror. The military sees it as "leftist chaos" and may end it by a military coup, the story of many Latin American countries. Thus mobilization, which could be the start of democratization, often leads to authoritarian takeovers.

The 1964 military takeover in Brazil ended one phase of what might be termed a mobilization-demobilization cycle. The ruling generals had grown to hate civilian politics, especially political parties and their demagogic leaders. We can to a degree understand their hatred. As guardians of Brazil's unity and security, they witnessed their beloved republic falling into the hands of irresponsible crowd-pleasers.

Typically, the military tries the only solution they know: demobilization. Believing that the solution lies in an end to disruptive political activity, they ban most parties, hand pick political leaders, and permit only rigged elections. Initially, things do calm down. Some people are thankful the army has stepped in to put an end to extremist politics and empty promises. Mass rallies, loud demands, and radical leaders disappear—the latter, sometimes through physical means.

But the problem isn't solved. The demands—although no longer whipped up by politicians—are still there and growing. Indeed, as the economy grows, more people come to live in cities, and the pent-up demands for change increase. To repress such demands, the regime turns to the police-state brutality of arbitrary arrests and torture. Once people are awakened or mobilized they can never by fully demobilized, even by massive doses of coercion.

The Inflation Connection

Inflation is a political problem the world over, especially in Latin America, where regimes may fall over the rate of inflation. Inflation may also be seen as part of the

Political Mobilization, Brazilian Style

The turnouts in Brazilian elections provide a graphic indicator of political mobilization:

1930 and earlier	never more than 0.25 million
1933	1.25 million
1945	6.2 million
1950	7.9 million
1955	8.6 million
1960	11.6 million
1962	14.7 million
1989	63.0 million

Even in 1962, the figure was rather small compared to the total Brazilian population, then about 76 million. But a literacy requirement held down the size of the electorate and eliminated the poorest from voting. Conservative, better-off Brazilians and the military were horrified at the prospect of Goulart's dropping the literacy test and letting lower-class Brazilians into the election booth, with their potentially radical demands. By 1989, there was no literacy requirement and voting was compulsory.

"Praetorianism"

As the Roman Empire ossified and crumbled, the emperor's bodyguard, known as the Praetorian Guard, came to play a powerful role, making and unmaking emperors. Political scientists now use *praetorianism* to indicate a situation where the military feels driven to take over the government.

Praetorianism is not just a problem of a power-hungry army but reflects conflict in the whole society. In praetorian societies, it's not only the army that wants to take power, but many other groups as well: students, labor unions, revolutionaries, and politicians would like to seize the state machinery; institutional constraints and balances have broken down; nobody plays by the rules. In such situations of chaos and breakdown, it is the army among the many power contenders that is best equipped to seize power, so praetorianism usually means military takeover.

mobilization-demobilization cycle. In Brazil, inflation in currency corresponds to the inflation in promises made by politicians seeking mass support.

Controlling inflation is an austere, unhappy task. By restricting credit and cutting the amount of money being printed, a regime can lower the inflation rate, but at a cost of unemployment, slow economic growth, and disappointed hopes. Almost by definition, Latin American inflation cutters tend to be conservatives, usually military men, who can pursue disinflationary measures without regard to mass desires. As in much of Latin America, the Brazilian military in effect say to its citizenry: "We don't care how much it hurts, the sooner inflation ends the better we'll all be. Take the bitter medicine now before inflation wrecks the entire economy."

Encouraging inflation, on the other hand, is easy; regimes can almost do it in a fit of absent-mindedness. Politicians of populist bent, wanting to make everybody happy, just let the national mint's printing presses run to finance government projects. This is the way Kubitschek built Brasilia. Inflation tends to feed on itself and get out of hand, and soon many people are complaining they can't make ends meet. Conservative industrialists and bankers become convinced the politicians have gone insane. The military, whose fixed salaries are eroded by the galloping inflation, seethes in jealous rage and starts planning a coup to save both the republic and their incomes.

When the military does take power, their disinflationary measures correspond to the political demobilization they also try to enforce. In the Brazilian case, this has consisted of controls on wages but not on prices, with the result that lower-class Brazilians have to work like dogs to keep up with food prices while some speculators enjoy an economic boom. Civilian regimes may try to do the opposite, with equally bad results (see box).

Although the Brazilian generals had excellent economic planners, by 1984 the inflation rate reached 223 percent, double what it was in 1964, when the military seized power. This extremely embarrassing fact undermined regime support among the businessmen and bankers who had welcomed the 1964 takeover. One reason Brazil turned democratic was that the military proved as inept as civilians in controlling inflation. And if the military takes over again, it will in large measure be due to the civilian administrations' inability to control inflation, which in the 1990s turned into hyperinflation (more than 50 percent a month).

The Corruption Connection

One of the standard characteristics of the Third World is its massive corruption. Throughout Latin America, officials expect *la mordida* (the bite) to do what they are supposed to do. Some argue that corruption is simply a part of Latin American political culture. Perhaps, but corruption tends to flourish under certain institutional arrangements; namely, it grows at the interface of the public and private sectors. Latin America, with its large state sectors and regulated economies, is thus especially fertile ground for corruption. The solution? Cut the state sector back. Where this was done, in Chile, corruption also diminished.

The interesting thing about Brazil (and some other Latin American countires) is that the public is increasingly fed up with corruption, especially in high places. The presidents of Brazil and Venezuela were hounded from office when the media uncovered the extent of their corruption. Dozens of Brazilian Congresspersons (most in the PMDB) enriched themselves through fake projects (such as pretend help for the poor). The chairman of the budget committee got $51 million richer in five years. (He said he was very lucky in the lottery.)

Brazil's Desperate Struggle Against Inflation

Almost annually, the Brazilian government attempts to end the mad inflation—sometimes running at more than 50 percent a *month*—by freezing wages and prices and taking other drastic steps. "Prices starting tomorrow are halted," said the economy minister in 1991.

Saying is easier than doing. The 1991 effort was the fifth plan to control wages and prices in five years. Five years earlier, Brazilians saw how President Sarney's plan to do the same thing ended in disaster, with prices going up after a short pause and many producers driven out of business. Sarney's popularity plunged lower than ever, unions struck, crowds took to the streets, and the military glowered angrily, as if awaiting their turn to take over. By the time you read this, we will know if Cardoso's 1994 *real* plan has curbed inflation.

The real problem, one about which Col-lor de Mello campaigned, is Brazil's overlarge state sector that has to be propped up with big subsidies, which are provided by simply printing more money. In the early 1990s, Brazil's Central Bank increased the nation's money supply severalfold each year. Result: inflation hit 1,000 percent in 1992 and 2,000 percent in 1993. To turn off the printing presses, though, would mean shutting down a large part of the Brazilian economy, resulting in even more unemployment. Unions warned they wouldn't stand for it. Wage-and-price freezes, experience from many countries shows, simply do not work for more than a few months. They are instituted in desperation when the real cures would hurt too many politically influential groups. Some Brazilians saw Collor and Franco much the same way they saw Sarney: as ineffectual and disgraced failures.

This new public concern is a very good sign, an indication of growing political maturity. Stealing from the starving is no longer acceptable. Brazilian politicians have looted their country long enough; let them now face angry citizens. The danger here is that when Brazilians start to think that democracy equals corruption, the way is open for a coup. Brazil's top general warned Congress to clean up its act: "Beware the anger of the legions," the exact words once used by the Praetorian Guard.

Resurgent Interest Groups

For most of the life of the military regime, the Brazilian government continued the corporatist model that Vargas had borrowed from Italy and Portugal. Under corporatism, interest groups are controlled or coordinated by the government. With the *abertura* of the 1980s, Brazil's interest groups emerged with a life of their own once again.

After the 1964 takeover, the military abolished the big union that had been fostered by Goulart, and placed all labor unions under direct government control. Particularly drastic was the control of rural unions, whose impoverished and militant farm workers threatened the property of the conservative landowning allies of the military government. Union leaders were henceforth handpicked to make sure they would cooperate with the new order and not lead workers in excessive wage demands or strikes.

While this arrangement held down wages, prices rose until workers could stand it no more. New unions and leaders outside government control emerged as a major force. The largest and most radical Brazilian union, the United Confederation of Workers (CUT), is tied to Lula's Workers party. CUT is especially strong in São Paulo and has struck against many big industries there. The military does not like CUT. The tamer General Confederation of Workers (CGT) is tied to the large but corrupt PMBD.

Many businessmen had welcomed the 1964 coup only to find that the military technocrats would sometimes ride roughshod over their interests in the name

The Brazilian Political Cycle

With some oversimplification, Brazilian politics can be seen as a cycle or progression of phases that repeat themselves. If we were to sketch out our discussion of the last few pages, it would look like this:

The cycle could start all over with the mobilized masses falling under the sway of demagogic politicians. That's the way Brazilian politics worked earlier—for example, during the two "Vargas cycles."

Mobilization → Demagoguery → Military Takeover → Demobilization → Liberalization → Democratization
          (*inflation*)   (*disinflation*)

of economic rationality. The "theory of constructive bankruptcy" let weak Brazilian firms go under rather than subsidize them with tariff protection against foreign competition. Now businesses generally want sound money and an end to government economic controls and restrictions. Other groups, such as students and farmers, also voice their discontent. Opposition to the rule of the generals developed across a broad front of conservative and radical Brazilians. The most interesting group, however, was the Catholic church, a force to be reckoned with in the world's largest Catholic country.

The Church as Opposition

Curiously, the Roman Catholic church was the only large Brazilian group that maintained its autonomy and was in a position to criticize the military regime. We say curiously because typically in Catholic countries the church has been conservative and has favored conservative regimes. We saw in France how the long fight between clericalism and anticlericalism split society into two camps. The same thing happened in Spain and Italy.

Brazil never had this kind of split. With the 1891 republican constitution, modeled after the United States', the Brazilian church consented to disestablishment, that is, to losing its special privileges as church and state were separated. Brazil settled this important and divisive issue quickly and early, leaving the church as an independent force.

Still, in social and economic outlook the Brazilian Catholic church was pretty conservative, urging the faithful to save their souls rather than to reform and improve society. With the Second Vatican Council of 1962–65, this conservative attitude changed, and many churchmen, especially younger ones, adopted the "theology of liberation" that put the church on the side of the poor and oppressed. In some Latin American countries, young priests actually became guerrilla fighters trying to overthrow what they regarded as wicked and reactionary regimes.

In the late 1960s, Brazilian church leaders denounced the regime for "Fascist doctrines" and for arresting and torturing priests and nuns accused of harboring political fugitives. During the 1970s, the Brazilian church developed a strong stand for human rights and against the terrible poverty still found throughout the country. When strikes flared in the 1980s, strikers often held meetings and sought refuge from police clubs in churches. As a whole, the Brazilian Catholic church was the most activist in Latin America, usually to the chagrin of the Vatican, which ordered priests out of direct political actions.

In 1980, John Paul II visited Brazil. He was visibly shaken by what he saw in the *favelas.* In one, he removed the ring given him by Pope Paul VI when he became a cardinal and gave it to a local priest as a donation. John Paul seemed to be turning into an activist himself. In a Rio slum he called to Brazil's rich: "Look around a bit. Does it not wound your heart? Do you not feel remorse of conscience because of your riches and abundance?" But he stopped short of endorsing active church involvement in politics. Church people should guide spiritually but not politically. In Brazil, this middle road is hard to tread because concern for the poor tends to radicalize people.

Under the democratic regime, the Brazilian church continued its critical attitudes in support of the poor. Some Brazilian churchmen pretended to not hear

Chico Mendes: Another Death in the Amazon

To Americans the murder of Chico Mendes in 1988 seemed to be part of an environmental outrage concerning the destruction of Brazil's Amazonian rain forest. Less noticed is the murder every year of dozens of leaders of the rural poor in land conflicts with farmers and ranchers intent on keeping their large holdings.

Mendes, who lived in Brazil's westernmost state of Acre, was national leader of rubber tappers who made common cause with environmentalists and Indians in trying to halt the destruction by ranchers and farmers of the lush jungle. The rubber tappers simply use existing trees and have no interest in burning down the forest. The ranchers and farmers, encouraged for decades by Brazil's government to develop the interior, cut and burn tens of millions of acres a year, contributing to global warming and to a shrinking of the earth's capacity to produce oxygen.

Mendes led major protests and legal actions to stop the developers. They in turn detested and frequently threatened him. In 1990, a rancher's son stunned an Acre court by admitting, "I killed Chico Mendes." He probably confessed to protect his father, who was charged with the murder of other peasant leaders. Guns for hire are cheap in the Amazon region, where some 2,000 union leaders, small farmers, lawyers, priests, and nuns have been slain. (The Brazilian Catholic church has taken a leading role in speaking for the rural poor.)

For most Brazilians, poverty is a bigger issue than the environment; people are more important than trees. The question is how and for whom the Amazon region will be developed: for the masses of rural poor or for big ranchers who claim thousands of acres as their cattle pasture?

the Vatican's order to steer clear of radical politics. Their argument is that in order to reach people to save their souls, the church must also help feed them. In poverty-stricken Northeast Brazil, therefore, priests keep reminding the government of its land-reform program while they organize unions and poverty workers. Conservative landlords charge that priests and nuns encourage the poor to illegally occupy private farms. Many are threatened with death.

Especially troublesome were radical French, Dutch, and other West European priests working in land reform. When the Brasilia government tried to keep them out, Brazil's bishops protested. The federal police chief said, "It's necessary to talk to them and pray, to pray above all that priests return to praying."

What Brazilians Quarrel About

The Brazilian Miracle

After the 1964 military takeover, the Brazilian economy improved. From 1968 to 1974 the annual growth rate averaged 10 percent. A series of very bright economic technocrats oversaw what soon became known as the Brazilian miracle, the spectacle of a sleeping giant rousing itself to become a major industrial power. Only Japan enjoyed economic growth like Brazil's.

There were some problems with the miracle, however. For one thing, it was based on foreign capital. There is nothing wrong with this; most developed economies (including the United States) received boosts from overseas investment in their early years. At a certain point, however, a growing economy should be able to generate its own capital for further investment. Brazil hasn't. Brazilian capitalists, instead of reinvesting their money in industrial growth, tend to spend it, speculate with it, or stash it abroad. For new capital investment they get government or foreign loans. This was one of the reasons Brazil accumulated the Third World's largest foreign debt—$100 billion in 1992. This was actually an improvement; it had been $120 billion a few years earlier.

Another reason for the debt was the price of oil, which shot up during the 1970s. Brazil, with little rail transportation, is dependent on trucks and cars and has few oil wells. So Brazil paid for foreign oil and went deeper into debt. Trying to offset its oil dependency, Brazil turned to alcohol distilled from its own crops. Now Brazilian gasoline, which goes for about $3 a gallon, is 20 percent alcohol. Some vehicles run on pure alcohol. The slowdown in the Brazilian economy in the 1970s was heavily related to the fact that the price of oil increased more than tenfold during this period. As the economy slowed, inflation climbed.

The point here is that the "Brazilian miracle" had feet of clay. The boom of the early 1970s, when it seemed Brazil could soon be one of the world's great powers, gave way to a declining GDP a decade later. From 1980 to 1993 Brazil's GDP grew at an annual average of only 1.5 percent. Per capita GDP (which takes into account population growth) *declined* an average of half a percent a year. Brazilians grew poorer.

The Politics of Debt

The American approach to Brazil's debt—much of it owed to U.S. banks—was vintage Calvin Coolidge: "They hired the money, didn't they?" Brazilians didn't see

"They Got an Awful Lot of Everything in Brazil"

Brazil has economic problems, but these should not overshadow its amazing achievements. In recent decades Brazil has developed rapidly to become the:

- tenth largest economy of the world
- seventh biggest steel producer of the world
- ninth largest producer of cars in the world
- second largest producer of iron ore
- eighth largest producer of aluminum
- second largest soybean and cocoa producer
- fifth biggest arms exporter
- of course, world's biggest coffee producer

With a burgeoning economy that still has great growth potential, one can see why foreign banks put an awful lot of money into Brazil. If Brazil ever deregulates its economy, it could be a growth wonder.

things quite the same way. Most agreed the debt should be paid, but on their terms and at their pace. They argued, first, that much of the debt has been incurred by the previous, military, regime which borrowed and invested foolishly. They pointed out, further, that the floating interest rate attached to many loans had saddled them with payments no one could have anticipated. They also noted that many of the lending banks had more than recovered their investments over the years. Brazil's interest payments alone accounted for nearly a fifth of the profits of Citicorp and Chase Manhattan.

Brazilians emphasized with pride that they were exporting like crazy to meet their obligations, but that debt repayment devoured $2 out of every $5 they earned, stunting Brazil's further growth. And they warned that poverty and unemployment in Brazil was like a bomb that could wreck everything, including the American banking system. The world held its breath to see if Brazil would default on its debts, that is, announce that it couldn't or wouldn't pay. Brazil didn't default, but it came close. Brazil often suspends interest payments. This is leverage on the major international banks to give them some new loans and stretch out payments. Brazil in effect tells its creditors, "Give us a helping hand or you'll lose everything." Meekly, leading U.S. bankers usually acquiesce.

Debt is an important domestic issue in Brazilian politics. No politician likes to be seen as knuckling under to foreign bankers. In general, leftist and populist politicians are more likely to repudiate their country's debts. But even conservative Sarney told Brazil on television, "We are not going to pay the debt with the hunger of the people." Both he and Collor sought compromises with major creditors and debt rescheduling.

A particular target for nationalist ire is the International Monetary Fund, a UN agency that can facilitate loans for developing countries. But the IMF demands drastic austerity before it will come to the financial rescue of an ailing country. IMF officials argue that there is no point in shoveling more money into a rapidly inflating economy like Brazil's; the loans will simply disappear and do no good. If you want a loan, says the IMF, you've got to bring down your rate of inflation by drastic cuts in government spending and wages.

The prescription is painful and perhaps impossible for countries such as Brazil, where people are already in dire economic circumstances. IMF demands raise nationalist anger among Brazilians. They feel they are being pushed around by big

Great Brazilian Wisecracks

"If you owe $100,000, you're in trouble with your banker. If you owe $100 billion, your banker's in trouble."

Headed for Extinction: Brazil's Indians

With Brazil's expansion into the vast Amazon frontier has come the pushing back of its Indians until they may be facing extinction. Brazil's constitution guarantees Indians rights to traditional rain forest lands, but in practice the need of ranchers and miners for ever more territory has made enforcement spotty at best. Of the 270 tribes of Brazilian Indians found at the begining of the twentieth century, 90 have disappeared altogether and others are slipping fast. Particularly vicious have been gold miners, who readily invade Indian reserves and kill them either with guns and dynamite or by poisoning the water with the mercury they use to isolate gold particles. More intent on economic development and jobs, few Brazilians worry much about the plight of the Indians.

capitalist countries. Some politicians vow not to knuckle under, to repudiate their gigantic debts rather than accept the harsh austerity. Brazilians recalled that Getúlio Vargas had declared a unilateral moratorium on Brazil's foreign debt in 1934, forcing foreign creditors to settle for thirty-three cents on the dollar.

Brazil's State Capitalism

While leftists point to foreign dependency as the root of Brazil's problems, many businessmen and economists point to Brazil's very large state sector and red-tape controls on the economy. Brazil, they emphasize, is not really a free-market country relying on private initiative. Some 60 percent of Brazil's industry has been in government hands—including mines, petroleum production, and electric companies. In addition, the majority of loans come from government banks, giving the state the power to determine what gets built and where. Collor de Mello said he would dismantle this statist empire, but he did not.

The technocrats who run the empire say that the projects they undertake are so big and risky no private business people would handle them. Brazilian investors tend to speculate in sure-fire enterprises such as real estate rather than in industrial growth. Consequently, the technocrats say, if Brazil is to expand boldly, much investment must be under state guidance.

Statism—where the government is the number-one capitalist—can both accomplish big projects and make big mistakes. Some projects Brazil has poured money into are prestigious but money losers. For example, the government invested heavily in nuclear power in a country where hydroelectricity has scarcely been tapped. The nuclear program was a foolish waste—although it made Brazil look like an advanced country—and by 1980 it was greatly curtailed.

Government loans were sometimes extended foolishly, too. The interest on these loans was so low, and Brazil's inflation so high, that the credits amounted to free money, which the borrower could immediately loan out at high interest. Why work for a living when you can just shift some paper around? The subsidized loans from the government, however, ultimately come from working Brazilians in the form of inflation. Brazil's cheap government loans are another reason the rich get richer and the poor poorer.

State control produces other distortions in the economy. There are so many laws and regulations that businesses have to employ red-tape specialists called *despachantes* (expediters) to jog the bureaucracy into giving a license or allowing a price change. Many *despachantes* are related to the bureaucrats they deal with; some are former bureaucrats themselves. The Brazilian word for getting around a regulation is *jeito*, literally "knack," meaning having someone who can fix it for you. The whole system feeds corruption.

Another problem area is minimum wages, a holdover from Vargas's populist paternalism. As in other countries, minimum wages dissuade employers from hiring unskilled workers. Many poor people then cannot find entry-level jobs. Minimum wages, aimed at helping the working poor, simply mean more unemployed marginals in the *favelas*.

Even worse, many of Brazil's grandiose projects have been capital-intensive (using lots of machinery) rather than labor-intensive (using lots of workers). Brazil is short of capital but has lots of labor. More labor-intensive projects would kill two birds with one stone, alleviating both the capital shortage and tremendous unemployment. But such projects are not to the taste of Brazil's technocrats, probably because they are less prestigious than mammoth capital investments.

Who's right, the leftists, who point to dependency, or the business people, who point to state strangulation? Actually, the two views complement each other. State control does stunt domestic capital formation, and this makes Brazil chronically dependent on foreign capital. Instead of a vigorous private sector of local businesses, the Brazilian economy is divided between the foreign multinationals and the state. Brazilian entrepreneurs tend to attach themselves to one of the two. The cure for statism is privatization, but many Brazilian politicians still favor the inefficient and overstaffed state sector, precisely because it is a source of patronage jobs.

Growth for Whom?

Another weakness of the Brazilian economy is that its fruits are distributed highly unequally, and the inequitable distribution has only gotten worse. Now the richest

 ### *Great Brazilian Wisecracks*

"Brazil is the country of the future and always will be."

Great Brazilian Wisecracks

Brazil is tottering on the edge of the abyss! Don't worry, Brazil won't fall in. It's too big to fit into the abyss.

1 percent of Brazilians earns as much as the poorest 50 percent. At the bottom of the heap, 32 million Brazilians, more than a fifth of the population, earn less than $120 a year. Per capita income in the Northeast is lower than in Bangladesh. The "Brazilian miracle" overlooked these people.

Critics on the left argue that the "miracle," because it was controlled by U.S. multinationals and Brazilian technocrats, produced semiluxury goods and grandiose projects that benefited the better off. It made cars and swanky apartments rather than public transportation and basic housing. The leftists would redistribute income to the poor.

Those defending the system point out that Brazil contains two economies, a First World economy that is modern and productive and a Third World one that is traditional and unproductive. Actually, most Third World countries have First World sectors within them. In Brazil the contrast is stark. But, argue the defenders, the gap cannot be bridged overnight. Brazil must first build up its modern sector until it gradually takes over the whole country. To simply redistribute income to marginals, who produce little or nothing, would be economic folly. The trick is to keep the economy growing so as to absorb the marginals and turn them into producers and consumers. This is known as the developmentalist solution to Brazilian poverty.

The critic on the left rejoins that Brazilian development, because it is capital-intensive, can't begin to create the 1.3 million new jobs needed every year. What is needed, the leftist argues, is a whole new approach to development, one that stresses human beings instead of percentage growth for its own sake. As even the hard-lining President Médici (1969–74) had to admit: "The economy is going well, the people not so well."

The Population Problem

Whatever viewpoint you adopt, one nasty fact will foul up the best laid plans: Brazil's hefty population increase. The Catholic church, of course, frowns on any artificial method of birth control, and the military regime thought a high birthrate contributed to economic growth. Accordingly, in Brazil, until the 1970s, there was no emphasis on curbing population growth, and Brazil's population is now 150 million. The good news is that Brazil's birthrate has dropped sharply since 1970 under the

For poor urban dwellers, streetcorner or beach hawking may be the only way to eke out a living. Here, a Rio woman and her children sell candles to light in the church behind them. *(Michael Roskin)*

impact of birth control, television, and economic downturn. Brazil's popular TV soaps show small, affluent families with only one or two children, and this has become a national norm.

As usual, it is poor people, especially peasants, who have the most children. The poverty-stricken Northeast, where people have especially large families, is an inexhaustible reservoir of marginal Brazilians. However, as many millions of them pour into the cities of the South, there are millions more still coming. The result is "hyperurbanization," common throughout the Third World, where cities are usually surrounded by huge slum belts created by peasants who can no longer live off the land. Two-thirds of Brazilians live in cities, an absurd situation for a big, empty country. São Paulo with 18 million inhabitants is the second largest city in the world; Rio with 11 million is the eleventh.

The rural immigrants to the cities settle in *favelas*. With no education or job skills, many do not find regular work. Those that do usually must travel hours to and from their jobs. With prices rising, most discover themselves getting poorer. If they cannot feed their numerous children, they are forced to abandon them. Millions of "nobody's children" live on the streets. Most steal to survive, and police occasionally shoot them like vermin.

Crime and Punishment, Brazilian Style

Some of Brazil's urban poor, caught at the bottom of a worsening economic situation, turn to crime. Brazilian citizens and police, fed up with astronomical crime rates, turn to extralegal remedies. Unofficial "death squads" of off-duty policemen execute thousands of criminal suspects a year in the *favelas* without resort to courts or laws. Many *favelados*, themselves living in fear, celebrate the executions of local toughs. Young purse and wallet snatchers have become so bold that middle-class Brazilians now grab them and beat them to death on the street. Police shoot street kids as they sleep on the assumption that they are petty criminals. People treat it as an urban cleanup campaign and no one is charged. Laws are for poor people only.

Extralegal punishment is no solution, for rural poor continue to pour into the cities, where many must turn to crime to survive. Brazil's crime rate is a natural concomitant of a society in which the many poor behold the wealth and luxury of the better-off. In principle, traditionally nonviolent Brazilians deplore the acts of savagery, but since the victims are marginal *favelados* or street urchins, few Brazilians really care.

Will Brazilian Democracy Last?

Brazil was not alone in its return to democracy. Since 1979 the entire continent has returned to democratic, civilian rule. Democracy may be contagious. But would Brazil's democracy—or any of the others—last? The problems of all of Latin America's nations are incredible: severe economic difficulties, giant foreign debts, growing populations, military establishments accustomed to intervening in politics, and a lack of seasoned political institutions such as parties and parliaments. Some Latin American nations probably aren't going to make it. We hold our breath for Brazil.

Vocabulary Building

abertura	disinflation	marginals
amnesty	ESG	mobilization
autogolpe	*Estado Novo*	Old Republic
capital-intensive	*favela*	*personalismo*
corporatism	*favelados*	populism
death squads	*fazendeiros*	Positivism
demagoguery	indexation	praetorianism
demobilization	*jeito*	Second Vatican Council
depoliticization	labor-intensive	state capitalism
dependency	*machismo*	theology of liberation
despachante		

Further Reference

BAAKLINI, ABDO I. *The Brazilian Legislature and Political System.* Westport, CT: Greenwood, 1992.

BAER, WERNER. *The Brazilian Economy: Growth and Development,* 3d ed. Westport, CT: Praeger, 1989.

CASTAÑEDA, JORGE G. *Utopia Unarmed: The Latin American Left After the Cold War.* New York: Knopf, 1993.

COHEN, YOUSSEF. *The Manipulation of Consent: The State and Working-Class Consciousness in Brazil.* Pittsburgh, PA: University of Pittsburgh Press, 1989.

DALAND, ROBERT T. *Exploring Brazilian Bureaucracy: Performance and Pathology.* Lanham, MD: University Press of America, 1980.

DIAMOND, LARRY, JUAN J. LINZ, and SEYMOUR MARTIN LIPSET, eds. *Democracy in Developing Countries: v. 4: Latin America.* Boulder, CO: Lynne Rienner, 1989.

GUIMARÃES, ROBERTO P. *The Ecopolitics of Development in the Third World: Politics and Environment in Brazil.* Boulder, CO: Lynne Rienner, 1991.

HUNTINGTON, SAMUEL P. *Political Order in Changing Societies.* New Haven, CT: Yale University Press, 1968.

KECK, MARGARET E. *The Workers' Party and Democratization in Brazil.* New Haven, CT: Yale University Press, 1992.

LIPSET, SEYMOUR MARTIN, and ALDO SOLARI, eds. *Elites in Latin America.* New York: Oxford University Press, 1967.

MAINWARING, SCOTT, and TIMOTHY B. SCULLY, eds. *Building Democratic Institutions: Party Systems in Latin America.* Stanford, CT: Stanford University Press, 1994.

REVKIN, ANDREW. *The Burning Season: The Murder of Chico Mendes.* Boston: Houghton Mifflin, 1990.

ROETT, RIORDAN. *Brazil: Politics in a Patrimonial Society,* 4th ed. Westport, CT: Praeger, 1992.

SADER, EMIR, and KEN SILVERSTEIN. *Without Fear of Being Happy: Lula, the Workers Party and Brazil.* New York: Verso, 1992.

SCHEPER-HUGHES, NANCY. *Death Without Weeping: The Violence of Everyday Life in Brazil.* Berkeley, CA: University of California Press, 1992.

SCHNEIDER, RONALD M. *"Order and Progress": A Political History of Brazil.* Boulder, CO: Westview, 1991.

SKIDMORE, THOMAS F. *The Politics of Military Rule in Brazil, 1964–1985.* New York: Oxford University Press, 1988.

———. *Politics in Brazil, 1930–1964: An Experiment in Democracy.* New York: Oxford University Press, 1986.

STALLINGS, BARBARA, and ROBERT KAUFMAN, eds. *Debt and Democracy in Latin America.* Boulder, CO: Westview, 1989.

STEPAN, ALFRED, ed. *Democratizing Brazil: Problems of Transition and Consolidation.* New York: Oxford University Press, 1989.

VAN DEN BERGHE, PIERRE L. *Race and Racism: A Comparative Perspective.* New York: Wiley, 1967.

29

South Africa

The Impact of the Past

Whose Land?

Afrikaners—the white South Africans of mostly Dutch descent—like to emphasize that when their ancestors arrived three centuries ago, South Africa was largely empty, and they settled it first. This is not completely true. When the Dutch East India Company sent Jan van Riebeeck with two hundred men to start up a "refreshment station" at the Cape of Good Hope in 1652, they encountered Hottentots, a primitive people whom they enslaved, impregnated, and eventually killed off with smallpox. Needing more slaves, they imported them from the Indies and Madagascar. The resulting mixture—Hottentot, Dutch, Malay, and other—produced the so-called Cape Coloureds, a group that resembles African-Americans in that they are a combination of many strands.

So far, this process is reminiscent of the early settlement of Brazil, which also produced a mixed race. The difference in South Africa was that, fairly soon, the whites developed exclusivist attitudes on race and classified the Coloureds as a different and inferior group.

As the Cape colony expanded, Dutch farmers (*boers*) pushed outward, taking whatever land they wanted. When the soil was exhausted, they moved on. Their constant movement earned them the name *trekboers*, or farmers on the move. Further inland, they encountered the even more primitive Bushmen, whom they shot as thieving pests. Very early, Afrikaners developed the attitude that the land was exclusively theirs and that the natives were to be either enslaved or exterminated.

Although the Dutch didn't pay much attention to it, the Cape colony grew, aided in part by the arrival in 1688 of French Huguenots, who brought the many French names found today among Afrikaners as well as skills in wine-making. As the *trekboers* pushed along the Indian Ocean coast, they encountered, in the late eighteenth century, their first African Negroes, bigger, stronger, much better organized, and more warlike than Hottentots or Bushmen. These Africans were slowly moving south, away from population pressure, tribal wars, and slave raids. In a series of battles over a century, the so-called Kaffir Wars, the Boers subdued the Africans and again took all the land they wanted.

Just as stimulus from Napoleonic France triggered the rise of modern Brazil, France also set in motion the rise of present-day South Africa. When a French revolutionary army occupied the Netherlands, the Dutch in 1795 let the British take over the Cape to keep Table Bay—around which Cape Town is built—out of French hands. The British stayed as welcome guests until 1803 but returned in 1806, this

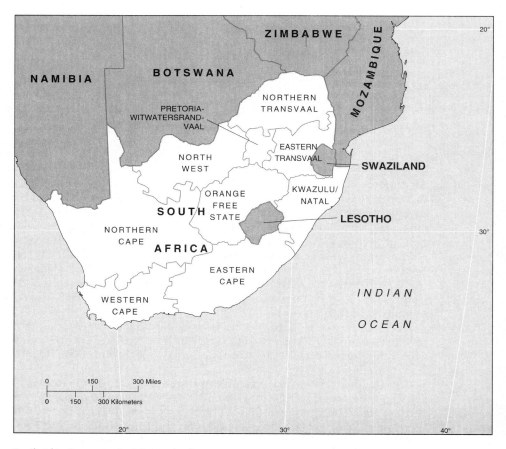

South Africa's new territorial organization.

time for good. In 1814, the Netherlands officially turned over the Cape to Britain, and the English moved to remake it into a British colony.

The Great Trek

Many Boers bristled at British rule. Not only did the British want everybody to speak English, they wanted everybody to be equal before the law. Even Hottentot servants could bear witness against their masters. In 1834, to the outrage of many Boers, slavery was abolished. The Boers became convinced that the English were destroying their language, institutions, way of life, and freedom.

Between 1836 and 1838, an estimated twelve thousand Boer men, women, and children—about a quarter of the Cape's Dutch population—loaded up ox carts and, like American pioneers, moved into the interior seeking land and freedom. The epic is known as the Great Trek and is celebrated by Afrikaners today as a symbol of their toughness, courage, and go-it-alone attitude. At times the *voortrekkers* (pioneers) had to disassemble their wagons to get them over roadless escarpments. Some columns fought battles with Africans, drawing their wagons into a circle called a *laager*. One column disappeared without a trace. Members of another were treacherously slaughtered by Zulus (see box).

The *voortrekkers'* dealings with Africans paralleled the Americans' with Indians. Sometimes by force and sometimes by persuasion, the *voortrekkers* made treaties with chiefs to obtain land. The Africans, who had no concept of *owning* land, thought they were letting the Dutch *use* the land for a while. Disputes were settled by the pioneers crushing the natives.

The rich soil and good rainfall of Natal, fronting the Indian Ocean, was the goal of most *voortrekkers.* But the British also took an interest in this lush province and annexed it in 1843. The British claimed it was to prevent further bloodshed between *voortrekkers* and Africans; the Boers retorted that it was to rob them of their land once again. In disgust, many *voortrekkers* repacked their ox wagons and moved back inland where, they thought, they would be forever free of the hated British.

The *voortrekkers* consolidated their inland settlements into two small republics, the Transvaal (meaning on the far side of the Vaal River) and the Orange Free State. Here the Boers were at home. The language, religion (Dutch Reformed), governmental institutions, and way of life were all theirs. The Boer republics lived in uneasy peace with the British in the Cape and Natal, until diamonds and gold were discovered.

The Boer War

With the discovery of diamonds in 1870 and gold in 1886, English-speaking people poured into the Boer republics, chiefly the Transvaal. There, on the Witwatersrand (literally, "white-water ridge"), gold was mined in such quantities that a new city, Johannesburg, was built atop the waste rock. It soon became South Africa's largest city—and English-speaking.

For the Boers, it looked as if the English were once again pursuing them and destroying their way of life. By 1895, the English-speaking *uitlanders* (outlanders) outnumbered the Boers more than two to one. The Transvaal government under Paul ("Oom Paul" or Uncle Paul) Kruger, worried it would be swamped by *uitlanders*, made

South Africa's Population (in millions)

This sign on a bus in the sprawling black township of Soweto shows what is on white minds: a rapidly growing black population. *(Michael Roskin)*

	1960	1993
Africans	12.0 (70%)	30.7 (76%)
Whites	3.1 (18%)	5.1 (13%)
Coloureds	1.5 (9%)	3.3 (8%)
Asians	.5 (3%)	1.0 (2.5%)

South Africa's white population increases at a modest 1.7 percent a year (high compared to Europe). The nonwhite population, however, increases at Third World rates, 2.5 percent for Africans, 2.2 percent for Coloureds (mixed descent), and 2.1 percent for Asians (chiefly Indians). Every year, whites become a smaller minority. Take these figures with caution; they may have undercounted the Africans.

life difficult for them, denying them the vote and ignoring their petitions. Disenfranchising other groups became an Afrikaner tactic in preserving their dominance.

Meanwhile to the south in the Cape, the British were plotting to add the Transvaal and Orange Free State to the British Empire. Sir Cecil Rhodes, the Cape millionaire who set up the Rhodes scholarships to Oxford, hankered after the mineral wealth of the Boer republics. He had already sent a column around the Boers to the north to found Rhodesia. Said Rhodes: "Expansion is everything." Agreeing with him was the British high commissioner in the Cape, Alfred (later Lord) Milner, who dreamed of a white empire ruled by London. Using the issue of *uitlander* rights in the Transvaal, Rhodes and Milner provoked Kruger into declaring war in 1899.

British propaganda portrayed the conflict as a crusade to liberate Africans from Boer misrule, but that was window dressing. The English treated blacks no better than the Boers did. The English simply wanted to consolidate their rule over the

Dingaan's Kraal: Still Remembered

In 1838 the Zulu king Dingaan invited the *voortrekker* leader Piet Retief and some seventy Boers to a feast at Dingaan's *kraal* (group of huts forming a courtyard). They had been on friendly terms; Retief had recovered some stolen cattle for Dingaan from another tribe, and Dingaan had given the Boers land around present-day Durban. But Dingaan was suspicious of the ultimate intentions of the white man, and with the cry "Kill the wizards!" had them dragged to a hill and beaten to death. Then he killed five hundred settlers—including women and children—in Retief's column.

Later that year, the Boers got their revenge.

Setting up a strong *laager* on a river and letting the Zulus attack, the Boers gunned down three thousand of Dingaan's warriors with no loss of their own. Before the battle, the *voortrekkers* vowed that if God granted them victory they would commemorate the day for evermore. December 16, the anniversary of the Battle of Blood River, is still celebrated as the Day of the Covenant.

On a monument at Dingaan's *kraal*, Afrikaners can read the names of the massacred, most of which can be found in a present-day Pretoria phone book. The all-too-obvious link with the past is one that some Afrikaners treasure.

southern part of Africa, and they found the Boers a nuisance. It was the high point of British imperialism and, some say, the beginning of its decline, for the surprisingly long and cruel war drained Britain militarily and morally.

The Boers fought tenaciously. Good riders and marksmen—and equipped with modern arms from a sympathetic Germany—the Boers at first set the British reeling back and laid siege to British-held cities. Wrote Kipling: "We have had a jolly good lesson, and it serves us jolly well right." Ultimately, Britain's superiority in arms and numbers reduced the Boers to bands of guerrilla fighters. To isolate the Boer commandos from food and supplies, the British resorted to rounding up their women and children and placing them in "concentration camps." Typhoid broke out and some 26,000 died in the camps. Even today, every Afrikaner family has the memory of losing at least one relative in a camp; they never forgave the English and depict themselves as the century's first concentration-camp victims.

Finally, in 1902, the Boers caved in and signed the Treaty of Vereeniging. But the British, guilty over the misery they had inflicted, failed to follow up on their victory. Instead of suppressing the defeated foe, they gave them full political rights, and, over time, the Afrikaners used their legal powers to ultimately take over all South Africa. After half a century, the Boers won.

From Defeat to Victory

The defeated Boer republics were made British crown colonies but were soon given internal self-government. In 1908, a National Convention met in Durban to draw up plans for making the four colonies one country, and in 1910, the Union of South

Africa was proclaimed. Politically, the English and the Afrikaners, as they increasingly called themselves, managed to cooperate and even form parties that included members of both language groups. Some of South Africa's leading statesmen, such as the famed General Jan Christian Smuts, had earlier fought the British. A spirit of good feeling and forgiveness seemed to reign.

A considerable strand of Afrikaner opinion, though, was unhappy with the alliance for two reasons. First, it tied them to British foreign policy, because South Africa was now a British dominion. Fighting for Britain was something most Afrikaners did grudgingly, if at all. When South Africa entered World War I, many Afrikaners rebelled rather than let themselves be used to take over the neighboring German colony of South-West Africa. Again in 1939, when a bare majority of parliament voted to enter World War II, an Afrikaner fascist movement known as the *Ossewa-Brandwag* (ox wagon fire guard) sprang up to oppose South African help for a traditional enemy against a traditional friend.

 ## *Why Did Apartheid End?*

With supreme self-confidence the National party relentlessly built its *apartheid* system. Criticism bounced off. But gradually, starting in the mid-1970s, the Afrikaner regime started loosing its nerve. Some of the key dates:

- 1975—Portugal, after years of fighting, pulls out of its colonies of Angola and Mozambique. Black Communists sympathetic to the ANC take power.

- 1976—Young Africans riot in Soweto and cannot be quickly controlled. Some sneak out to join ANC guerrilla forces.

- 1978—P. W. Botha is elected prime minister and soon promises a "new dispensation." He does little but heighten expectations.

- 1980—White-ruled Rhodesia turns into black-ruled Zimbabwe, and South Africa loses the last buffer zone on its north.

- 1985—Major international banks start doubting South Africa's creditworthiness and refuse new loans. The South African business community is severely jolted.

- 1989—Soviet power collapses, and the Cold War ends. The ANC loses its Soviet support, and the Pretoria regime loses its U.S. support. Both sides realize they no longer have any outside aid.

- 1990—New President F. W. de Klerk frees Mandela, rolls back the *apartheid* system, and negotiates an end to white rule.

The interesting thing about this transition is that it was not forced on the white regime, which suffered no military defeats or serious threats and could have stayed in power years longer. It was chiefly the product of sufficient Nationalist leaders coming to realize that the longer they delayed, the worse would be the revolution. They could clearly see the trend: no more protective belt of white-ruled colonies to their north, no more U.S. interest in stopping communism in Africa, and a black population that grew bigger and angrier every year. The Nats split into liberal and conservative wings, and the liberals won. What we have witnessed is a "negotiated revolution" based on the power of human reason.

Second, and of equal importance, the Afrikaners were economic underdogs to the English, who nearly monopolized industry and commerce. The Afrikaners were largely farmers, and when farm prices collapsed worldwide between the two wars, many Afrikaners were scarcely any better off economically than were Africans. Much like characters from the Depression novel *Grapes of Wrath*, Afrikaners streamed to the cities looking for work. Jobs for poor whites became their rallying cry.

Their path to salvation was "ethnic mobilization," organizing themselves to promote Afrikaners in business and politics. They built cultural associations, insurance companies, schools and universities, and above all the National party. The National party was founded in 1914 as the vehicle for Afrikaner political sentiment, but its moderate leaders believed in cooperation with the English. When the party split in 1934, the militant Daniel F. Malan remade the Nationalists into the party of Afrikaner power. Malan stood not only for white supremacy but for making sure every Afrikaner had a job, a pseudosocialist component that survived for decades.

Slowly the Nationalists built their strength. A well-organized party, the Nationalists indoctrinated Afrikaners with the idea that anyone not supporting the party had broken the *laager* and betrayed his brothers. By 1948, they had sufficiently mobilized Afrikaners—who were and still are a majority of the country's whites—to win the general election. Now at last the country was restored to them. No longer would the British push them around. They proceeded to build precisely the system they wished, the *apartheid* (literally, "apartness") system, which ended only in the early 1990s.

The Key Institutions

System in Flux

Until very recently, South African institutions were designed to keep blacks powerless. Beginning with the release of Nelson Mandela from prison in early 1990, however, breathtaking changes occured that made Mandela president in 1994. In 1993 and 1994, a consultative committee representing all the population groups hammered out an interim constitution that went into effect with the first multiracial elections of 1994.

The new parliament is to complete a permanent constitution by 1999, but many believe it will basically be the same as the 1994 constitution. One interesting point: to modify the constitution takes a two-thirds majority of the new South African parliament, and the largest party, the African National Congress, is just short of that. Accordingly, the ANC must debate and bargain for constitutional changes with other parties, and that's good, for it helps build consensus and a gradual approach to change.

From 1910 to 1984 South Africa had been stuctured along British lines—"the Westminster model"—with a prime minister chosen by an all-white parliament. When South Africa broke away from the British Commonwealth in 1961 (it returned in 1994), it instituted a figurehead president as honorific head of state.

A Quasi-Presidential System

No more. In 1990 South Africa switched from a parliamentary to a quasi-presidential system. We say "quasi" (almost) because South Africa's president is elected not by the population directly but by the National Assembly for a five-year term. The president may also be ousted by a parliamentary vote of no-confidence. This makes South Africa's "president" something like a prime minister. The president, however, still has a lot of power, and this gave reform-minded Presidents P. W. Botha and F. W. de Klerk the ability to institute reforms without being blocked at every turn by a conservative majority in the whites-only House of Assembly. As de Gaulle concluded in France, a presidential system is more effective in instituting changes.

Immediately after the 1994 elections, parliament elected Mandela president. Recall that de Gaulle concluded he did not like being elected indirectly and changed it to direct election. A strong president does not like to be elected by an intermediate body; he wants to be elected directly by the people. De Gaulle made this change in 1962, and we may wonder if a South African president will someday make a similar change. If he does, then South Africa would have a straight presidential system.

South Africa's capital moves twice a year. The parliament buildings are in Cape Town rather than in Pretoria, the administrative capital. When the president comes to Cape Town to officially open a parliamentary session, the capital comes with him. This means that every year hundreds of ministers, bureaucrats, journalists, and diplomats must decamp to Cape Town and then trek back to Pretoria when parliament is over.

Territorially, South Africa, like Britain, is a unitary rather than a federal state. The old colonies—the Cape, Natal, the Transvaal, and the Orange Free State—became the country's four provinces. With the sweeping changes of 1994, these were

SOUTH AFRICAN MIGHT-HAVE-BEEN

 ### *The Black and Coloured Vote*

South Africa had black and Coloured voters before. The Cape colony, under more liberal English rule, permitted them to vote, with modest literacy and property qualifications that discouraged most. Nonetheless, it was a beginning, and one that might have paved the way for the gradual expansion of the franchise. The Cape brought its limited black and Coloured franchise with it into the Union in 1910, but parliament dropped the black vote in 1936 and the Coloured vote in 1956. Blacks and Coloured were to be given separate advisory councils, but these had no power.

One of the keys to democratic stability has historically been the gradual enfranchisement of the population, one slice at a time, to give both the people and the institutions time to adjust. South Africa, in instituting the universal voting franchise in 1994, was paying belated respect to the principle that broadening the electoral suffrage is the basis of democratic stability.

turned into nine provinces, and the "black homelands" were abolished, making South Africa a unified country once again (see map on page 410). Each province has a legislature, cabinet, and premier concerned with local affairs such as education, health services, highways, and fish and game. Because the provinces have little autonomy, South Africa is not a federal system, although some thinkers wish it would become one.

A Bicameral Parliament

One curious feature of South Africa's 1984 reform was its parliament, consisting of three houses: a big one for whites and smaller ones for Coloureds and Indians. White

Nelson Mandela: A President for All South Africans

For a man who spent twenty-seven years in prison for opposing *apartheid*, Nelson Mandela is extremely calm. He shows no sign of the revenge or hatred that some other South Africans do. He simply wants to get on with the job of building a prosperous and just South Africa where no one is penalized because of skin color, origin, or gender. He eschews theories and focuses on pragmatism and consensus-building: talk things out until most agree on a practical solution.

Born into a chiefly clan in a village in the Eastern Cape in 1918, Mandela went to missionary boarding school and then to Fort Hare University, where he studied law (but got suspended for leading a student protest). His chiefly lineage still shows in his calm self-confidence and ability to lead by persuasion.

Mandela rejected an arranged marriage back in his village in favor of the cosmopolitan excitement of Soweto, where he opened his law practice and joined the African National Congress. Mandela is not personally caught up in ethnicity or multiculturalism. "I no longer attach any value to any kind of ethnicity," he said.

With the Afrikaners building their *apartheid* system, Mandela and other young ANC members decided that mere petitions would get them nowhere. They organized a militant ANC Youth League and used it to take over the ANC leadership.

The 1960 Sharpeville massacre, where police gunned down 69 peaceful protesters, persuaded the ANC leadership to turn to armed struggle, and Mandela became founder and commander of a guerrilla group, *Umkhonto we Sizwe* (Spear of the Nation). The whites-only government banned the ANC and arrested all the ANC leaders they could catch. For plotting revolution, Mandela, then 44, was sentenced to life on notorious Robben Island off Cape Town.

As is often the case, prison is a kind of university for revolutionaries. They meet, talk, theorize, and plan. Prison did not break Mandela, and every year he grew more legendary, especially among young black South Africans. By 1986, the white regime knew it had to talk with Mandela, and secret meetings began. Mandela was moved to comfortable quarters on the mainland and treated like a VIP.

Shortly after F. W. de Klerk took office, he ordered Mandela released from prison in February 1990. South Africa went crazy. Here at last was a clear sign that major change was underway. In four laborious years of talks among all population groups, South Africa's first free and fair elections were held. Mandela, at age 75, became president unopposed and by unanimous consent of the National Assembly. Even white conservatives knew there was no other possible choice.

supremacy was effectively preserved. Blacks, three-quarters of the population, got no representation, on the theory that they were represented in their tribal homelands. In general, parliaments with more than two chambers (Yugoslavia had a *five*-chambered legislature from 1963 to 1974) have been short-lived experiments.

The new parliament elected in 1994 was more conventional: two houses, one representing population, the other provinces. The lower house, the National As-

SOUTH AFRICAN MIGHT-HAVE-BEEN

 If Reform Had Come Earlier

Since 1985 the South African government has repealed or liberalized most of the more than 350 *apartheid* laws. Some of these laws went back to 1913, but the Nationalists starting in 1949 introduced far more specific, detailed legislation to keep blacks assigned to separate and inferior lands, housing, jobs, education, buses, beaches, rest rooms, and ultimately countries. The culmination of *apartheid*, in the Bantu Homelands Citizenship Act of 1970, was to make all Africans citizens of their tribal homelands and deprive them of South African citizenship. In all this, black South Africans had not one word of input, and protest was illegal.

The crux of the *apartheid* structure was "influx control," keeping blacks from flocking to the cities. As we considered in Brazil, flight from the poor countryside to better opportunities in the cities is typical of the Third World. The white regime in South Africa tried to fight this by an elaborate system of passbooks that had to be carried by all blacks; these had to be officially "endorsed" to live in an urban area. Only long-term black residents and people with guaranteed jobs were entitled to remain; others could be "endorsed out" to some impoverished homeland with the thump of a police stamp. The single thing blacks hated most were the passbooks, accompanied by the policeman's gruff demand, "Where's your pass, boy?"

P. W. Botha came to power in 1978 and began speaking of a "new dispensation" that would give blacks a better deal and calm their growing anger. Just two years before, Soweto had erupted. "*Apartheid* is dead," proclaimed his government. A

positive, almost joyous feeling began to emerge that major reforms would make South Africa a just and happy land. But the reforms came too little and too late. Fearful of backlash from white voters, Botha hesitated for years.

In 1985, the Immorality and Mixed Marriages Acts, prohibiting contact across the color line, were repealed. In 1986, the pass laws, influx controls, and citizenship laws were reformed to make it easier for blacks to live in cities and obtain citizenship in their own country. Some of the reforms were word games that left the system intact. Influx control became "orderly urbanization"; passbooks became "identity documents"; *apartheid* became "separate development." Blacks, now sensing they had the regime on the defensive, became angrier than ever. Half-hearted reforms can be worse than no reforms.

However, President de Klerk picked up where Botha had chickened out. De Klerk's reforms went much further and were faster than Botha's. For example in 1990 and 1991 de Klerk had parliament repeal the segregationist Separate Amenities Act, Group Areas Act, Land Acts, and Population Registration Act, virtually ending the legal basis of *apartheid*.

The tantalizing question remains: If major reforms had come earlier could the violence have been avoided? If Botha had done what he said he was going to do, would it have headed off revolution? Alas, we can't go back and rerun history. Major reforms would eventually have amounted to a revolution, but it might have been a gradual and unbloody revolution with a better chance of creating just and stable institutions.

sembly, consists of 400 members elected by proportional representation, but on two levels, one national, the other provincial. Two hundred are chosen from nationwide party lists, the other 200 from the nine new provinces with seats proportional to population. The large but arid and sparsely inhabited Northern Cape gets only four seats; the small but industrial and thickly settled Rand (now the Pretoria-Witwatersrand-Vaal province) gets 44 seats. Thus South Africa's new lower house represents both the country as a whole as well as regional perspectives.

The upper house, the Senate, consists of 90 members, ten from each province, elected by provincial legislatures. The Senate has less power than the lower chamber, the norm for all parliaments except the United States. In 1994, voters also cast ballots for their provincial legislatures.

Notice that no population groups are directly represented. That is, Zulus do not automatically get a certain number of seats; instead, Zulus are represented by being able to vote for whomever they wish. In KwaZulu/Natal province, Zulus divide their votes between the Zulu-based Inkatha Freedom party and the African National Congress (ANC), both of whom run Zulu candidates locally. Tswanas, who live mostly in the Northwest province, vote mostly for the ANC whose local candidates tend to be Tswanas. The effort here, a praiseworthy one, is to keep any one population group from identifying too closely with just one party, for that is the path of tribalism and civil conflict that has bedeviled much of Africa.

As expected, Mandela's African National Congress took the lion's share of these seats, 252 out of 400, but short of the two-thirds needed to change the constitution. This means the ANC will have to earn the cooperation of other parties (such as the Nats, who took 82 seats) for such changes. This is probably a good thing, as it tends to inhibit the dictatorial and corrupting tendencies that arise when one party gains complete power. Early drafts of South Africa's electoral law contemplated a German-style 5-percent threshold, but numerous small groups protested, so the threshold was abolished. Theoretically, a party that wins as little as 0.25 percent could get a seat in parliament.

The Cabinet

The new South African cabinet is rather large, with up to twenty-seven ministers. Under the interim constitution, each party that won 5 percent of the popular vote was entitled to a share of cabinet ministers roughly proportional to its vote. Thus in the national-unity government of 1994, the ANC with 63 percent of the vote got twelve ministries; the Nats with 20 percent got six; and Inkatha with 10 percent got three. This "consociational" (see box on page 431) provision was designed to make sure no major population group feels left out. It also changes the meaning of a cabinet from a purely executive body to a partly representative one.

Such representation in the cabinet, which resembles a German grand coalition, raises the question of how a president can govern with ministers of opposing and even hostile viewpoints. Can the black militants work with white conservatives? The inclusionary nature of the cabinet may serve to calm and reassure some groups, but it will likely make it difficult to reach decisions on important matters. Disgruntled ministers, fearing their group's interests are threatened, may simply walk out of the cabinet. On balance, though, considering that ethnic violence is South Africa's greatest danger, the "consociational" cabinet is worth trying.

The Parties

Theoretically, there are no longer "black" parties and "white" parties in South Africa. All citizens over 18 receive common ballots and may, in the secrecy of the voting booth, mark an X by whichever party they wish. Each party is identified on the ballot by name, symbol, and photo of its leader to help illiterates vote. Further, it is highly desirable in a democracy that some voters cross the color line and vote for parties not closely related to their own group. In the main, though, most South African blacks vote for black parties while most nonblacks vote for traditionally white parties.

In 1990 black political parties were legalized in South Africa. They had existed over the decades, either labeled as cultural associations or underground and in exile. The oldest and most important black party is the African National Congress, founded in 1912 by blacks educated in missionary schools. The ANC still likes to call itself "the world's oldest liberation movement." For half a century the ANC practiced nonviolent protest; its leader during the 1950s, the great and gentle Chief Albert Luthuli, won the 1961 Nobel Peace Prize. He was, nonetheless, banished to a remote village. The ANC was banned in 1960 and, as the Nationalist regime relentlessly implemented its *apartheid* structure, came to the conclusion that violence was the only way to communicate its message. In 1964, its leaders were convicted of plotting revolution and sentenced to life imprisonment.

But the ANC did not die. Operating in exile, it gave young blacks weapons training (with Soviet-bloc help) and had them infiltrate the Republic for sabotage and attacks on police stations. Its leader, Nelson Mandela, grew more legendary with every year he spent in prison. When he was released, along with many other black leaders in 1990, mass rejoicing broke out. "He is the symbol of our struggle," said a

A Constitutional Court for South Africa

A first for South Africa (and rare worldwide), the interim constitution sets up a Constitutional Court whose eleven members are appointed by the president for seven-year terms. Theoretically above the political fray like the U.S. and German high courts, South Africa's Constitutional Court interprets the constitution and settles disputes between levels of government. Included in the new constitution are U.S.–style guarantees of freedom of speech and assembly; equality of race and gender; and rights to hold property, to join a union and strike, and to receive a fair trial.

Although it proceeds on the basis of cases brought before it, South Africa has moved away from the Common Law, which is what gives such enormous power to the U.S. Supreme Court. Instead of the great power of precedent, which is the heart of the Common Law, South Africa uses old Dutch-Roman law, based on codes and statutes and paying less attention to precedent. Accordingly, the powers of South Africa's Constitutional Court will likely be less sweeping than those of the U.S. Supreme Court.

black high school student. "To me, he is like Jesus Christ." As expected, the ANC and Nelson Mandela won the 1994 national elections.

The ANC defines itself as a multiracial party, and some of its leaders are white, for example, Joe Slovo, a Communist. Decades ago, the tiny South African Communist party (SACP) threw in with the ANC and came to be well represented in its leadership. In 1994, the SACP did not run a separate slate but stayed under the wing of the ANC. Slovo became minister of housing and welfare. In 1992, five parliamentarians from the liberal white Democratic party moved to the ANC. Whites in the ANC, although few in number, do two things: They help educate ANC members away from revolution and toward liberalism, and they help calm white fears that the ANC will be out for revenge against whites. An estimated 2 percent of South Africa's whites voted for the ANC in 1994.

To the left of the ANC, the smaller Pan-Africanist Congress (PAC) doesn't want white partners. PAC broke away from the ANC in 1958 over the question of building a black society as opposed to a multiracial one. PAC continues on the path of violence the ANC abandoned. PAC's chilling slogan, proudly displayed on T-shirts: "One settler, one bullet." It was PAC militants who slashed to death American Fulbright student Amy Biehl in 1993, not knowing or caring that she was pro-liberation. PAC did poorly in 1994. To the left of PAC the even smaller Azanian People's Organization (AZAPO), did even worse.

Meanwhile to the right of the ANC, the Zulu-based *Inkatha* turned itself from a "cultural movement" founded in 1975 to the Inkatha Freedom party in 1990. The IFP, anti-Communist and pro–self-determination, at times dialogued with right-wing whites of the same views. Well-organized, and with a territorial base (the homeland of KwaZulu), the IFP fought the ANC in virtual civil war. Inkatha leader Mangosuthu Buthelezi, a Zulu chief, almost boycotted the 1994 elections. Afraid of losing his power base, Buthelezi signed Inkatha up for balloting only a week before the elections to win control of Natal/KwaZulu province. Inkatha attracts few non-Zulus, and radical blacks despise Buthelezi as a sellout and Zulu fascist.

The National party dominated South Africa from 1948 to 1994. Originally a purely Afrikaner party, it crafted most of the institutions of *apartheid*. In the early

Beware the Confusion: South Africa's Two "National" Parties

South Africa's two largest parties both have "national" in their names. South Africa's main party, formed to fight for black rights, is the African National Congress (ANC), headed by Nelson Mandela. The National party (the "Nats" for short) was the vehicle for the Afrikaner imposition of *apartheid* but under F. W. de Klerk broadened its base to capture most of the white, Coloured, and Indian vote. Both are nationalist parties, but the ANC used the term to connote the African nation, whereas the Nats used the term to connote the Afrikaner nation. Both parties now welcome votes from all persons regardless of race.

1994: A New Proportional Representation System in Action

While most of Europe moved away from proportional representation, South Africa in its first nonracial elections in May 1994 moved from single-member districts with plurality win (the Anglo-American system) to strict PR:

	Percent of Vote	Lower House Seats
ANC	62.70	252
Nationalists	20.40	82
Inkatha	10.50	43
Freedom Front	2.20	9
Democrats	1.73	7
PAC	1.25	5
Christian Democrats	.45	2

Turnout was around 85 percent of those eligible, a measure of how much previously disenfranchised people treasure the right to vote. (Americans should take a lesson here.) As expected, the ANC won nationwide but did not reach the two-thirds necessary to amend the constitution; the ANC will need help from at least one other party. Two provinces eluded the ANC: the Western Cape, where Coloureds shifted heavily to the Nats, and KwaZulu/Natal, where Zulus went mostly to Inkatha.

Why a PR system? Such a system tends to fragment the parliament into several parties, and that is just what South Africa needs. A single-member system exaggerates the rewards to the largest party, and in South Africa's case would have given parliament almost entirely to the ANC. From there it is but a few easy steps to rebellion by minority groups who feel they've been disenfranchised, and then to dictatorship by the leading party. PR, especially with South Africa's extremely low minimum of 0.25 percent, makes sure all important groups win seats, and this can have a calming effect. The white separatists of the Freedom Front and the Zulu chauvinists of Inkatha, for example, dislike the ANC majority, but they must ask themselves if they get a better deal by being in parliament or by leaving. (Correct answer: stay in.) In this way, the fragmenting tendencies of PR paradoxically help South Africa hang together.

Was the election free and fair? Not completely. There were numerous reports of stuffed ballot boxes and "private" polling stations, especially in KwaZulu/Natal, scene of the murderous ANC-Inkatha competition. Officially, though, the balloting was nowhere contested. Mandela seems to have decided to let Buthelezi have his power base in order to calm things down. Besides, observers say, both the ANC and Inkatha probably cheated and roughly offset each other. Third World elections are rarely free and fair.

1990s, F. W. de Klerk totally transformed the Nats by turning to a program of serious reform and welcoming all voters into National ranks. In short order, most English-speakers, Coloureds, and Indians concluded the Nats were their best ticket to survival. No longer a white party, the Nats in 1994 suddenly became the leading non-black party.

The white opposition Democratic party was formed in 1989 from the old Progressive Federal party. A classic liberal party—free society, free economy—its few votes are in English-speaking cities such as Johannesburg, Cape Town, and Durban. Much earlier than the Nats, the Democrats worked to dismantle *apartheid* and share power with blacks and browns.

In protest at rolling back the *apartheid* system, in 1982 the right wing of the National party walked out to form a new Conservative party that ran well in the farming districts where the Nats used to hold sway. In 1994 most Conservatives joined the Freedom Front under retired General Constand Viljoen. Further right, the Afrikaner

Home for Four Million People?

KwaZulu (meaning the "place of the Zulus") is home to close to half of the 8 million Zulus. Broken into twenty-nine fragments and already overpopulated, there is no way it could survive unless many of its people worked outside the homeland and white industry set up facilities to take advantage of the plentiful, cheap labor.

(Michael Roskin)

Resistance Movement (AWB) waved Nazilike flags and vowed violence to preserve white power, but did not run in 1994.

Farewell to the Homelands

The ultimate aim of *apartheid*, or separate development, was to make Africans citizens only of their homelands and not of South Africa. This policy permitted South Africa to treat blacks as temporary workers in the Republic without voting or residency rights. Originally the homelands were native reserves left after the Kaffir Wars of the last century. (Americans would call them Indian reservations.) Policy was to gradually turn the territorially fragmented reserves into homelands and then into "independent republics," one for each tribe.

These ten homelands, supposedly home to all of South Africa's black population, accounted for only 13 percent of RSA territory. Half of Africans did not live in the homelands but in the cities and on white farms. Many had never seen their homeland and didn't want to. The law let authorities forcibly send Africans to their homeland if they were not needed in an urban area or formed a "black spot" in a farming area designated for whites. Some 3.5 million were thus "resettled" on hopeless, overcrowded, marginal lands.

Four homelands, under pliant, hand-picked leadership, opted for nominal independence: Transkei in 1976, Bophuthatswana in 1977, Venda in 1979, and

Ciskei in 1981. Aside from South Africa, no country granted them diplomatic recognition. Other homeland leaders, following the lead of KwaZulu chief minister Buthelezi rejected independence as a sham designed to deprive Africans of their national birthrights. In 1994, in time for elections, all the homelands were legally merged back into the RSA; in reality, they had never left.

South African Political Attitudes

The Africans

There is some truth to the white view that the Africans are still tribal in outlook. For those born and raised in rural areas who speak only the native language, it is the case. When asked their nationality in a 1994 survey, 63 percent of South African blacks named their tribe; only 16 percent said South African. But for the many millions—about one-third of all Africans—who reside in urban areas to work in mines, factories, homes, or offices, this is changing. Here, under modern economic conditions, Africans from many tribes integrated with Africans from other tribes and see themselves as Africans suffering a common fate rather than as Xhosas, Tswanas, or others. (The Zulus—the largest group of Africans—are an exception here. Zulu workers in the Rand tend to live in single men's hostels, isolated from, and at odds with, members of other tribes. Murderous fighting has broken out between Zulus and members of other tribes.)

Paradoxically, it is the whites whose policies broke down tribalism and integrated Africans into a whole. In the mines, for example, they found that work teams composed of only one tribe were prone to fight teams of other tribes. They integrated the work crews and fighting stopped. The mining companies even invented a synthetic work language so men from different tribes could communicate. Typically, though, urban blacks are fluent in several African languages and generally get along with people from other tribes. Most also speak English, although they are reluctant to learn Afrikaans, "the language of the oppressor."

Are all Africans revolutionaries? Far from it. African political opinion spans the range from mild, even conservative, to violent and radical. Older Africans especially tend to think in terms of specific problems: avoiding violence, the long commute from the black township, decent housing, making ends meet, and so on. Some black South African religions teach submission to authority. A number of young black South Africans, especially in urban areas, are, however, radicalized. They want and expect speedy change. It was, in fact, high school students who led the massive 1976 Soweto riots—triggered by a government edict that made learning Afrikaans in school mandatory—that left some 700 dead. Thousands of young blacks then sneaked out of the country to join the ANC. Decades of school boycotts subsequently left a generation of black youths uneducated.

The Afrikaners

In the last century, the Boers began to think of themselves as Afrikaners rather than Dutch. Their language, *Afrikaans*, had evolved from the original Dutch. No longer citizens of the Netherlands, they felt that Holland had turned its back on them. They had become, to all intents and purposes, Africa's white tribe, *die volk* (the people), as they called themselves.

And Afrikaner attitudes are indeed tribal. They even frown on marriage to English-speakers. Like the black tribes in other African countries, they did not like to share power with other tribes. A dour people, Afrikaners take pride in their stead-fastness, religiosity, strength, and determination. Until recently, most were convinced they were right and were rarely willing to compromise or admit they might be wrong. They are not, however, arrogant or elitist; among themselves they are quite democratic. Toward foreigners they are friendly if somewhat reserved.

Afrikaners treat blacks firmly but (they think) fairly; on a personal level they may esteem individual blacks but are convinced blacks need white supervision. They see blacks as behind whites in civilization, work habits, and level of organization. Because blacks are still largely tribal, thought Afrikaners until recently, they must not be accorded political equality with whites. Blacks are still, the Afrikaner believed, happiest with their own people; that's why the homelands were a plausible solution.

Toward the British, the Afrikaners still feel some hatred; they stubbornly nurse their historical grudge. They recite tales of their subjugation in the Cape colony, the British takeover of Natal, the British-provoked Boer War, the forced involvement in two world wars, and now having to hear Britain preach human rights to them. To their own English-speaking whites they transfer some of their anti-British sentiment in the form of contempt. They consider English liberals hypocrites and cowards who see blacks exactly the way Afrikaners do but lack the guts to say so. They regard the English who have joined them as junior partners who have at last come to their senses.

One important factor eluded outside critics of South Africa: the Afrikaners never saw themselves as oppressors but rather as the aggrieved party, the hurt vic-

From Euphoria to Dysphoria

Great was the outpouring of joy and emotion at the election of South Africa's first African (or, more precisely, nonracial) government in 1994. Africans stood in line hours and even days to cast their first ballot, mostly for the ANC. All things seemed possible. Soon, many believed, Africans would enjoy improved living standards, education, and employment. They were euphoric.

But little improved. Their elected leaders tried to explain that there simply were no funds to fix everything immediately. It would take time and the patient building up of the economy. Some Africans felt they had been betrayed. They felt let

down and lapsed into dysphoria, the opposite of euphoria.

In actuality, South Africans were passing through the standard psychological stages that accompany most revolutions. The ouster of a bad or repressive regime almost always brings euphoria, the exaggerated and naive joy that things will quickly and automatically get better. Soon, sometimes in a matter of weeks, reality settles in. Life, admid scarcities and economic disruption, often gets worse. Now comes dysphoria, the exaggerated and overly pessimistic letdown after the euphoric high.

A Lost Generation of African Youth

From the Soweto riots of 1976 until the ANC electoral victory of 1994, a large portion of urban African youth dropped out of school and sought no employment. Instead, they busied themselves with revolutionary protests. Many wore ANC insignia and tee shirts, gave clenched-fist salutes, and called each other "comrade." They enforced rent-boycott programs and gave suspected police spies (and there were many) a grisly death: a "necklace" of a burning car tire around their head. And many just hung out and did little.

What to do with them now? Observers see them as a lost generation that is increasingly bitter that life has passed them by. Many have neither education nor skills. Nelson Mandela, immediately upon release from prison, urged African youths to return to school. He still urges them to. Unless integrated into the new South Africa, these urban Africans, many of them no longer "youths," are a potential disruptive and destabilizing force that could wreck the new democracy.

tims of historical injustice, namely, at the hands of the British. Afrikaners expected ethnic solidarity from their fellow Afrikaners. An Afrikaner who criticized *apartheid* broke the *laager*, the *voortrekkers'* ring of ox carts, and thus betrayed *die volk*. Actually, Boers and later Afrikaners were never monolithic in their views. Afrikaners such as novelist André Brink, Reverend Beyers Naude, and Afrikaner members of the Democrats were among the regime's severest critics. With de Klerk's takeover of the National party and the country's presidency in 1989, the Nats and many Afrikaners shifted to a reformist position that in five years led to the Mandela presidency. Hardline Afrikaners joined the Conservatives.

The English-Speakers

English-speaking people constitute about 40 percent of South Africa's whites. In terms of ethnic origin, English-speakers can be Greek, Irish, Italian, Jewish, Portuguese, German, or even Dutch. As in Canada, most new immigrants elect to learn English. Sometimes referred to as "the English" for short, they are actually a diverse group who have clustered around the original British colonials of the last century.

As mentioned earlier, the English, after winning the Boer War, walked away from politics, preferring business instead. As a result, they lost most political power but almost completely dominated commerce and industry. The rural Afrikaners discovered capitalism only recently; the urban English were capitalists from the start. This gave them a more liberal outlook: let economics and market forces take care of social problems, rather than imposing numerous controls and regulations as the Nationalists have done. The English never formed an "English party" but were happy to join with Afrikaners in fusion parties, such as the old South Africa and United parties, which were usually Afrikaner-led, as is the current Democratic party.

Do Afrikaners Change?

Not long ago the conventional wisdom was that Afrikaner attitudes were set in concrete, that they had always been white supremacists and always would be. The common supposition that racial superiority was part of the Dutch Reformed faith of Afrikaners erred by taking too narrow a slice in time. A brilliant young Afrikaner historian, Hermann Giliomee, examined the historical record and found that over the centuries Afrikaner thought on race had changed quite a lot to accommodate new situations. Whatever seemed the way for Boers and later Afrikaners to survive soon turned into their religious and social teachings.

Accordingly, Giliomee suggested in the 1970s, Afrikaners were perfectly capable of adapt-

ing to the new situation of black political participation and were already beginning to adapt. Giliomee was absolutely right. Even at the time, one of the foundations of the Afrikaner community, the Dutch Reformed Church ("the National party at prayer," as it was called), was rethinking the church's position on race and finding that inequality among the races was inherently un-Christian. This shift in attitude enabled many Afrikaners to accept and even support the new political system. For example, in 1994, William Verwoerd, the grandson of Hendrik Verwoerd, the chief architect of *apartheid*, campaigned for the ANC, and his wife, Melanie, was elected as an ANC member of Parliament! These people do know how to survive.

The Afrikaners' scorn for English liberals was at least partly justified. Few protested as the Nationalists built the *apartheid* system, and many English-speaking business persons benefited from the cheap, controlled labor supply it produced. English liberals questioned the form but not the substance of *apartheid*. With the Nats' move to reform, many English switched to them.

The English are more likely than the Afrikaners to voice their fears openly. Some wonder if South Africa will be a good place for their children; some ask visitors about jobs in the United States and if they would like to exchange a few dollars. Every year, several thousand quietly emigrate. (Favorite destination: Australia.) Some secretly retain British passports—illegal under South African law—for a possible speedy escape. One question for Americans to consider: How many South Africans should we accept?

The Browns

Perhaps the saddest, most worried South Africans are neither the whites nor the blacks but the "browns," as the Indians and Coloureds are known collectively. They are neither in the economically privileged position of whites nor in the numerical superiority with blacks. The browns are the classic middlemen, squeezed between forces they cannot control. Held to an inferior status by whites, they cannot look forward to being treated any better by blacks.

There is little feeling of solidarity between the Coloureds, most of whom live in the Cape, and the Indians, most of whom live in Natal. The Coloureds, who once

SOUTH AFRICAN MIGHT-HAVE-BEEN

 If the English Had Retained Power

Would it have made a difference in South Africa if the English had retained political power in this century? Afrikaners argue no, that the English spouted liberal rhetoric but were just as concerned about securing their place as the Afrikaners. Some Africans agree. One told me in 1980: "The English say they want to help, but they're pious fakes. The Afrikaners are at least honest. When they call you a bloody *kaffir* to your face, at least you know where they stand."

The British record in other colonial situations where there have been substantial numbers of white settlers is hardly liberal. In Kenya and Rhodesia, English settlers fought for years to prevent the rise of black power. Rhodesia even copied South

African *apartheid* legislation. And Afrikaners gleefully used to point out that some of the country's earliest segregation laws were enacted by the British in Natal in the last century.

Others—especially English-speaking liberals—think continued English power would have made a difference. While many agreed that, basically, English racial attitudes were not much different from Afrikaner attitudes, the English were restrained by a sense of fair play, by rule of law, by a more modern business mentality, and by extensive overseas contacts. They might have been less thorough in attempting to separate the races and more willing to listen to blacks and to compromise.

had the vote in the Cape, became more politically restless and resentful. The Indians, many of whom inched their way up from indentured sugar-cane workers to prosperous merchants, are more inclined to leave national politics alone and settle for self-governance within the Indian community. The Indians brought with them a strong sense of identity and culture from their native country. The Coloureds have severe identity and culture problems: most speak Afrikaans and wanted to be the little brown *baas* (Afrikaans for boss) but were rejected by the *apartheid* system.

What happened in 1994 was both amazing and logical. Many Coloureds and Indians went to the Nats, the party that had made them victims along with the black majority. Not long before, many browns identified with the ANC as the force that would liberate all persons of color. But as the election neared, browns grew worried that black radicals would seize their property; some received threats. Quickly, they perceived their interests were with the party that might give them some protection, the Nats, who flung open their doors to welcome the browns.

Patterns of Interaction

Politics within the ANC

Like the alignments or fronts that overthrew the Communist regimes in Central Europe in 1989 and then went on to win free and fair elections, the African National Congress is a broad "catchall" party (see page 199), including everything from black-power extremists, militant trade-unionists, moderate Africans, black entrepreneurs, conciliatory whites and browns, and Communists. And, like its East European counterparts, the ANC could fracture in the years ahead, its component groups spinning off to form new parties or join existing ones. This would be quite natural; catchall parties by definition cannot be all things to all persons. They may bloom in the initial euphoria of liberation, but if they contain seriously contradictory views, they split apart.

The ANC to a considerable extent is required to be two-faced. To its black voters it must promise jobs, housing, and education rapidly, no matter what the cost to whites and browns. Moderate as it tries to be, the demands of Africans are so urgent that if the ANC delays, it risks loosing much of its black voters to more radical movements, such as Winnie Mandela (estranged second wife of Nelson) and her militant wing of the ANC or PAC.

The other face of the ANC, required under the circumstances, is to calm and reasure whites, especially white capitalists, who are their only hope for making the economy grow rapidly. Many ANC leaders understand the weaknesses of socialism and strengths of capitalism. They interact intensively with white capitalists and are prepared to see a vigorous private sector in South Africa. But if they play an economic-rationality game of free markets and private enterprise, they make white capitalists a little richer and move the ANC away from the needs of black masses. What's good economics is sometimes bad politics.

In sum, the ANC is likely to be riven by tensions over race and economics and could divide into several components. A two-faced strategy of promising different things to different audiences is a common technique of governance, but eventually you have to deliver something. If the ANC is to hold together, the trick will be to deliver economic growth, and for this it needs the cooperation of white capitalists.

The ANC and the Whites

Fortunately, the ANC leadership has plenty of contact with the great economic engines of South Africa, such as the Anglo-American Corporation. The dialogue goes both ways. The capitalists explain investment and growth to the former ANC radicals, and the ANC explains to the capitalists that if they wish to ultimately retain wealth and position in the new South Africa, they will have to quickly deliver new jobs and mass economic improvement. Otherwise, black discontent will turn to radical parties that preach nationalization of private industry and redistribution of wealth. This, of course, would lead to white flight and the impoverishment of South Africa. The ANC must persuade white capitalists to invest like crazy to create rapid economic growth, putting jobs for blacks ahead of immediate profit. This will not be easy, as capitalists are by nature careful investors who aim precisely for profit.

Paradoxically, it is the richer, English-speaking white liberals of the Democratic party that are more likely to understand and accept this argument. As professionals and executives, they have little worry about their economic and social status. It is the white working class, centered in the National party, that will have to pay the price of rapid improvement for Africans. For working-class whites, this means a leveling downward. Their educational and occupational privileges will end, their taxes will rise, and (especially for Afrikaners) their monopoly on government jobs will

WHY DO PLURAL SOCIETIES COHERE?

 ## *"Cross-Cutting Cleavages"*

One of the puzzles of highly pluralistic or multiethnic societies is why they hold together. Why don't they all break down into civil strife? One explanation offered by the German sociologist Georg Simmel early in the twentieth century is that successful pluralistic societies develop "cross-cutting cleavages." They are divided, of course, but they are divided along several axes, not just one. When these divisions, or cleavages, cut across one another, they actually stabilize political life.

In Switzerland, for example, the cleavages of French-speaking or German-speaking, Catholic or Protestant, and working class or middle class give rise to eight possible combinations (for example, German-speaking, Protestant, middle class). But any one of these eight combinations will have at least one attribute in common with the other seven (for example, French-speaking, Protestant, middle class). Therefore, the theory goes, they cannot totally hate each other because they will always have at least one point in common.

Where cleavages do not cross-cut but instead are "cumulative" (reinforce one another), dangerous divisions grow. A horrible case is ex-Yugoslavia, where all Croats are Catholic and all Serbs are Eastern Orthodox. The one cross-cutting cleavage that might have helped hold the country together—working class versus middle class—had been outlawed by the Communists. The several nationalities of Yugoslavia had little in common.

Many of Africa's troubles stem from an absence of cross-cutting cleavages. Tribe counts for everything and differences of religion or social class do no cut across tribal lines. It will take a combination of skill and luck for South Africa to build cleavages that cut across the color line. A few appeared in 1994, such as the Coloured vote that went to the previously all-white National party and the white intellectuals who voted ANC.

erode. Getting everything that these whites lose will be Africans. Thus cooperation between the ANC and Nats will be difficult.

The ANC versus Inkatha

The bloodiest interaction in South Africa was not at all black against white but black against black, namely the turf war between the ANC and the Inkatha Freedom party in its stronghold of KwaZulu/Natal. Inkatha staked out a claim to represent gradual, nonviolent change but engaged in a great deal of violence, mostly against ANC members. In part, the struggle was between Zulus and non-Zulu Africans. In the Rand townships, where Zulus live mostly in single-men's hostels, white authorities had long encouraged them to crush protest movements and break strikes. The authorities played to the Zulus' sense of warrior superiority over other tribes and pointed out that disturbances meant lost wages. Accordingly, in the townships the Zulus became extralegal enforcers of the status quo. Furthermore, the police, practicing the ancient tactic of divide and rule, quietly armed, funded, and sided with Inkatha.

In Natal, the Zulu home area, things are even worse. As noted, Buthelezi built up a power base in the *Inkatha* movement, which was never outlawed. Mem-

WHY DO PLURAL SOCIETIES COHERE?

 "Consociational Democracy"

Another explanation why pluralistic societies hold together focuses less on the social level (see box on "Cross-Cutting Cleavages") and more on the political level. UC San Diego political scientist Arend Lijphart finds that certain deeply divided countries can find stability if the elites of the several groups share executive power. This is quite different from conventional "majoritarian" democracy, where the majority rules. If there is too big a gap between the majority and minorities, civil strife may result. The majority thinks it can get its way, and minorities feel no need to obey.

Clever political leaders may calm such situations by making sure all important groups have a share not only of seats in parliament but of executive power as well. In a consociational democracy, the elites of each major group have struck a bargain to share power and restrain their followers from violence. Every group gets something; no group gets everything.

Lijphart's chief example of consociation is his native Netherlands, but he thinks it also might fit South Africa, where a straight majoritarian system would invite rebellion from the minorities. Notice the consociational element in the 1994 interim constitution: Parties get one ministry in the cabinet for every 5 percent of the vote they have won. The ANC had to share executive power with the Nats (representing whites, Coloureds, and Indians) and with Inkatha (representing Zulus, the largest tribe).

Mandela named the Nats' leader de Klerk second deputy president. (First deputy president was the ANC's top diplomat, Thabo Mbeki, a likely Mandela successor.) Mandela also named his arch-foe Inkatha head Buthelezi as home affairs minister. If this consociational attempt works—and there is no guarantee that it will—each major party will figure it got something, and that something is better than violence, so they go along with the new system. If South Africa survives without major upheaval, will it be due more to cross-cutting cleavages discussed above or to a consociational setup?

bership was to some degree coerced, and rival movements were not tolerated. Not all blacks in Natal are Zulus, however, and not all Zulus wish to join a Zulu nationalist movement. In the 1980s, some joined the United Democratic Front, a front for the ANC. Sensing ANC encroachment on its turf, Inkatha reacted violently, slaughtering any blacks suspected of ANC sympathy. ANC supporters defended themselves, leading to virtual civil war in Natal. From 1990 through 1994, some 15,000 had been slain for political reasons, mostly in Natal, many by clubs and spears. Black-on-black violence, long feared, had become standard.

The real horror here is that violence got worse as the white regime *eased* its controls. The big increase in violence came after Nelson Mandela was released from prison and the ANC was unbanned in 1990. When all black politics were suppressed, there was relative calm, at least on the surface. With the legalization of black political parties in 1990, an immoderate struggle for turf and predominance broke out. Major reforms by themselves do not prevent bloodshed. Chief Buthelezi had no intention of giving up his power to Mandela (who is also of chiefly lineage, as a Xhosa, a tribe which has long fought the Zulus). Is this a political struggle or a tribal struggle? It is both, for in Africa, politics tends to be tribal.

South Africa's Bloodshed: Whose Fault?

Black-on-black violence causes some South African whites to smirk: "You see, we told you liberal foreigners that *apartheid* was the only workable system. Thought it was so easy, did you? Just abolish the old system and everything will be fine, eh? This bloodshed is your fault." This charge should make some critics of old South Africa think things over. To what extent did well-intentioned liberals naively underestimate the difficulty of achieving freedom and democracy?

    The ultimate finding of fault has got to look carefully at the steps—or non-steps—the white government took in preparing black South Africans for political participation. Democracy needs an educated population. Why was black education so inferior? Democracy needs a substantial middle class. Why did *apartheid* all but prohibit black entrepreneurship? Democracy requires "cross-cutting cleavages," whereby members of different groups have some things in common. Why did *apartheid* prohibit contacts across the color line? Yes, there is terrible black-on-black violence, but much of it could have been avoided if the white regime had, starting decades ago, begun preparing its black majority for full citizenship.

An Emerging Party System

South Africa's party system is more complicated than most European party systems. In South Africa, we need not only a left-to-right axis but a black and nonblack one

South Africa's New Party System

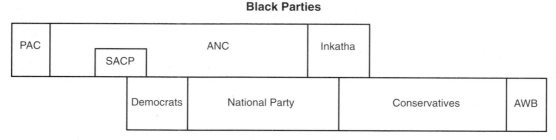

Black Parties

| PAC | | | ANC | | Inkatha | |
| SACP | | | | | | |

| | Democrats | National Party | | Conservatives | AWB |

Left   **Nonblack Parties**   **Right**

New Player: COSATU

In 1985, black South African unionists merged thirty-four black labor unions into an umbrella organization called the Congress of South African Trade Unions, COSATU. With some million members, COSATU works not only for higher wages and better conditions but for an end to all vestiges of South Africa's segregated system. Long a front for the ANC, COSATU ran on a joint ANC-SACP-COSATU alignment in 1994. COSATU head Jay Naidoo is in the top ANC leadership and became a cabinet minister in 1994.

COSATU's biggest component is the National Union of Mineworkers, which claims a membership of a quarter of a million. NUM strikes can close down gold, diamond, and coal mines over issues of wages and mine safety. Every year, hundreds of miners, most of them black, die in mine disasters.

If the European experience is any guide (see Chapter 15), large, unified labor federations can serve to calm anger and channel demands for change into constructive politics that give their members a stake in the system. South Africa, alas, is not Europe, and COSATU finds itself in a Latin American situation of a pampered government-related union speaking for a comparatively well-off black working class, blocking change rather than demanding it. If COSATU keeps wages too high, there will be no new jobs for the millions of black unemployed, and foreign investment will look elsewhere. We may anticipate showdowns between the ANC leadership and COSATU.

as well. In a rough schematic, here is what the emerging South African party system looks like:

The areas where black and nonblack parties touch, say between Inkatha and the Conservatives, means they are able to dialogue although not necessarily agree. Between the Conservatives and PAC, dialogue is impossible. The crucial area is where the the Nats are able to conduct a dialogue with the ANC. The success of this dialogue, now formalized in the Mandela cabinet, is the make or break for South Africa's political stability. If the ANC and Nats together can govern with a stable cabinet, we may yet see a free and democratic South Africa. And if not, we may see white flight and a black dictatorship.

South Africa's emerging party system looks like bad news. First, so far no party links Africans and nonblacks in a serious way. The only party that really cuts across the color line, ironically, are the Nats, with their white, Coloured, and Indian supporters. Second, the black political spectrum is further left than the nonblack spectrum, making a policy consensus difficult. Third, both the ANC and Nats face "bilateral opposition," with forces tugging them both leftward and rightward. The ANC has Inkatha on its right and PAC on its left. The Nats have the Democrats on their left and the Conservatives on their right. Both larger parties could be pulled apart.

This party system could collapse. Three things might save it: (1) the emergence of a large, moderate multiracial party; (2) a decrease in the number of parties; and (3) a weakening of both black and white extremist parties. If this doesn't happen, we may see something like Sartori's "polarized pluralism," discussed on page 159, with all its accompanying problems.

Former President de Klerk meets with new President Nelson Mandela. The two men jointly won the 1993 Nobel Peace Prize. (*South African Consulate General*)

Harvest of Hatred

For over four decades, there was no constructive dialogue between South Africa's blacks and whites. The regime simply governed with coercion and repression. Avenues of legal protest were systematically closed off; black and brown protests were automatically illegal and brutally stopped by the South African police. It was virtually a prescription for violence: plenty of injustice but no way to protest it legally. Riot police used dogs, whips, tear gas, clubs, shotguns, and automatic rifles to disperse crowds of Africans. Secret police and army "hit squads" assassinated dozens of regime opponents.

South Africa made its own contribution to the art of coercion with the "ban," an order from the justice minister prohibiting a suspected troublemaker from normal contacts. A typical banning order might specify that for five years the subject would not be allowed to work in a large group (such as a factory); might not have more than one visitor at a time; would not be quoted by others or by the press; and must be home by 6 P.M. Banning also could include exile to remote villages or round-the-clock surveillance by the security police. Since no court was involved, no banning order could be appealed.

South Africa jailed prodigious numbers each year; those jailed for simple passbook violations could be released after a short time. Political detainees, on the other hand, could be held indefinitely without charges, beaten to death in jail, or shipped off to Robben Island for life. Until recently, life imprisonment in South Africa did indeed mean for life.

When some of the worst police-state restrictions eased in 1990 and black movements became legal, there were still few constructive interactions between blacks and whites. Instead of building bridges between the two groups, the Nationalist government had deliberately, over the decades, destroyed them. Few whites had contact with Africans outside of a master-servant or boss-employee relationship. For decades there had been no church, club, university, sports association, or political party to serve as a meeting ground. Today most whites wish a constructive dialogue with blacks. This is difficult. After decades of abuse, many blacks are angry; some are revolutionary. Their leaders have difficulty keeping them in check. In its dreadful way, the *apartheid* program worked: now black and white South Africans really are apart.

What South Africans Quarrel About

How to Manage a Revolution

Nelson Mandela has an incredibly difficult task cut out for him: how to carry out a virtual revolution without spilling much blood and retaining his government's legitimacy among all population groups. Some might say it's impossible, and the chances of this entire enterprise failing are indeed quite high.

The Mandela government is pulled in several different directions. Many black militants want "socialism," although they have a poor understanding of what that means, whereas whites generally want capitalism. Without paying much attention to theory, the impoverished black masses demand a rapid improvement in their living standards, and they recall Nelson Mandela seeming to promise precisely that.

The gap between black and white is huge and has got to be narrowed. Black household income is roughly one-tenth of whites'. Half of black South Africans live below the official poverty line, which is not set very high. Unemployment runs at least 40 percent among blacks, 4 percent among whites. Whites, 13 percent of the population, own 86 percent of the land and 93 percent of the wealth. Nearly all young whites (along with 92 percent of Indians and 85 percent of Coloureds) graduate high school; only 35 percent of blacks do. Black infant mortality is 57 per 1,000 live births, white is 13.

Campaigning in 1994 was easy for Mandela and the ANC. They simply promised African crowds free medical care and education, jobs for all, pensions for the old, loans for African entrepreneurs, and land for African farmers. "Each and every person will be entitled to decent housing, like the whites have now," Mandela told crowds. He admitted it can't happen overnight; "It is going to take a year, two years, even as much as five years" to lift up Africans to decent levels.

No way. Decades might not solve the problems. If all the wealth of South Africa now in white hands could suddenly be redistributed, it would make blacks only a little better off, and that would be temporary, for the white-run economic machine would shut down and leave all impoverished. Still, the socialist temptation for the ANC government will be strong.

Socialism for South Africa?

For many decades the ANC and its SACP junior partner denounced capitalism and vowed a socialist future for South Africa. For a black South African, the capitalism

From Disinvestment to Reinvestment?

Nelson Mandela has put out the welcome mat for foreign investors. Should you help him with this? A few years ago, it was fashionable on some campuses to support disinvestment in South Africa, to demand that colleges hold no investments whatsoever in South Africa. But disinvestment and trade sanctions have outlived their purpose. You might consider taking the lead on your campus to encourage investment in South Africa. Unless someone turns the switch back on, it will stay off.

One of the things that can help save South Africa is foreign investment. Marxists and other socialists have disliked foreign investment, but it has proven to be one of the most important ingredients in rapid economic growth. The United States itself industrialized with massive European investment in the nineteenth century. Specifically, South Africa must generate 2 million jobs a year for blacks for several years. There is no way to do this without massive foreign investment.

practiced by whites looked an awful lot like brutal exploitation. Actually, South Africa never had a truly free-market economy; too much of it was controlled. When they took power in 1948, many Nats thought the law of supply and demand was strange and dubious. They fixed farm prices, severely restricted black labor mobility, and all but outlawed black entrepreneurship. South Africa's white capitalists, ironically, were the big liberals and progressives. When, in the late 1980s, white business leaders visited the ANC in Zambia to seek assurances against nationalization, they could get none. It looked like the ANC was committed to socialism.

The release of Mandela and legalization of the ANC in 1990, however, came at an interesting time. Communist governments had just collapsed in East Europe, and the Soviet economy was revealed as a failure. Socialism—meaning here state ownership of industry—simply had no success stories. Gradually, the lesson began to penetrate some sections of the ANC. Maybe free markets and private initiative should be given a chance? Especially if blacks can get in on the capitalist deal. Some ANC members, however, motivated by rage and revenge, cling to socialist dogma.

Which way will South Africa go? A government committed to socialism could inflict economic catastrophe on South Africa. White businesses, skills, and capital would flee, leaving chaos behind them. Black unemployment, already terrible, would skyrocket. Highly productive white farms would fold before trained black farmers could take them over. Starvation could break out. Responsible black leaders are increasingly aware of this. As black politics came home from exile and out of the underground, it engaged in less ideological debate and in more pragmatic debate.

Diluting and calming the black tendency for socialistic solutions is one of the more important functions of political alignments across the color line. Mandela's re-appointment of the Nats' white finance minister, Derek Keys, showed that the top ANC people understood the importance of a balanced (or not-too-far-out-of-balanced) budget for noninflationary growth and for attracting foreign loans and investment. Undoubtedly, the finance minister will have to say "no" often and firmly to proposals to increase government spending. The ANC rank-and-file will surely holler for his scalp. Amid growing pressure from below, will Mandela be able to retain Keys as finance minister? One quick test for which way the Mandela government will turn: Is Keys (or someone a lot like him) still finance minister by the time you read this? If Keys has been ousted, it probably means that South African government, like Brazil, is off on a spending spree with money it doesn't have.

The Brazilianization of South Africa?

As in Russia, the temptation to play it the Brazilian way is constant in the new South African regime. You have tremendous, urgent demands that have to be at least partly satisfied. You have yourself whipped up these demands during the election campaign. Now in office, you discover your treasury is nearly empty. What can you do? Simple: print more money, money without limit, to cover your subsidies, projects, and budget deficit. Inflation quickly takes off; currency soon loses value daily. You try to suppress inflation by imposing wage and price controls, but these are unworkable and easily avoided. You dare not turn off the printing presses at the national mint, for that would increase unemployment. You are now on a treadmill you can't get off of, a treadmill that runs faster and faster.

Meanwhile, your employment and housing projects to lift up the African majority run into trouble. By expanding the interface of the state and private sectors, you multiply the opportunities for corruption. Inexperienced ANC bureaucrats, until recently bush fighters, figure the whites have ripped off the system long enough,

Favelas in South Africa?

Another point of resemblance between Brazil and South Africa are the shantytowns that spring up at an increasing rate around South Africa's cities. Much like Brazilians from the impoverished Northeast, poor Africans stream in from the countryside looking for work in the cities. With South Africa's terrible passbook, influx, and residential controls now scrapped, shantytowns grow.

Many critics of *apartheid* never understood that the original purpose of "influx control" was to *prevent* the black shantytowns that started with the rapid industrialization of World War II. The Nats bulldozed these shantytowns and offered "townships" instead: neat, planned, rows of spartan cottages (without plumbing or electricity, so the "temporary workers" shouldn't get too comfortable) set up several miles from the main cities to be easily controlled by police and army. With the townships, the largest of which is Soweto (South West Townships) near Johannesburg, South Africa's white cities could have black labor by day but have them out of town by night.

"Why, without influx control," the Nats used to say with horror, "we'll become like Brazil." Now they have. Their influx controls just stored up people in the impoverished hinterlands; now they rush to the cities in a flood. They delayed the shantytowns so characteristic of the Third World; they did not prevent them. If the new regime is not careful and/or lucky, South Africa will soon look very much like Brazil.

A Separate KwaZulu?

Inkatha chief Buthelezi was always at odds with the ANC and halfhearted about joining the national unity government of Mandela. He consented to run Inkatha in the 1994 elections with only a week to go. What matters for Buthelezi is control of KwaZulu (place of the Zulus), now combined with its surrounding province into KwaZulu/Natal. His cooperation with the Mandela government was purchased at the price of ceding him control of this province. He hates ANC inroads into this area and goes to any lengths to stop them. Most of the bloodshed has been over this.

But if Buthelezi feels control slipping from him, he is likely to bolt from the Pretoria cabinet and demand a federal system or even an independent KwaZulu/Natal. If it comes to that, what should South Africa do? Let the entire province go? Or fight a war to keep it? Neither is a very pretty choice. Either way there would be a great deal of bloodshed, as Zulus in other provinces come under pressure to flee homeward and as non-Inkatha people in KwaZulu/Natal are eradicated. South Africa has the potential of becoming a sort of Yugoslavia.

"Now I'll get mine." Public money gets skimmed off at an accelerating rate. Everywhere in Africa—indeed, in most of the Third World—corruption is gigantic and normal. Do we expect South Africa to be immune?

South Africa's crime rate, always high, skyrockets. The old, white-dominated police, now thoroughly discredited for stirring up trouble and covertly aiding Inkatha against the ANC, is ineffective, but a new, black-led police has not yet been trained. With uncontrolled influx and the availablity of firearms from the struggle, unemployed young men, some fancying themselves revolutionaries, form criminal gangs. In these ways and others, South Africa comes to resemble Brazil.

Bringing Down or Building Up?

As political philosopher Hannah Arendt observed, rage is the indispensable ingredient for revolution, but rage is absolutely worthless in building anything after the revolution. How to shift from a revolutionary mode to a constructive post-revolutionary mode is South Africa's great challenge. One of the biggest challenges is education. Many of South Africa's black young people are enraged, uneducated, and unskilled.

More fundamentally, there must be jobs for all. Black unemployment has been disguised by forcing many of them to live in the homelands. Some estimate that black unemployment is effectively 50 percent. South Africa desperately needs rapid economic growth that creates 2 million new jobs a year. Johannesburg, known colloquially as Jo'burg, had better become Job'urg. White capitalists, who already know that their futures are on the line, must be encouraged to invest and reinvest. For this, they must be firmly assured that they will keep their property; the ANC must drop its remaining socialistic rhetoric.

The payoff will be either a prosperous South Africa with political participation and jobs for all or a chaotic bloodbath of warring tribes and economic collapse.

"Jobs Now or Don's Guns?" Here a black mini-entrepreneur tries to sell avocados on a Durban sidewalk. If the new South African system can't come up with a lot of jobs soon, it will take more guns than Don has to keep order. *(Michael Roskin)*

What we are watching in South Africa now is a great test of humanity. Sufficient numbers of whites concluded that the *apartheid* structure was immoral and unworkable and dismantled it. What will new, black leadership put in its place?

Whose Land?

We end with our beginning question on South Africa: Who owns the land? This was one of the first and most difficult questions on the agenda of the new government. *Apartheid* moved 3.5 million Africans off their land and dumped them in homelands. Most of these people or their descendants now want back their old lands, which are now mostly owned by white farmers. It won't be easy or pretty giving these lands back to their original inhabitants. Many whites will scream that they're being robbed. It will also not necessarily be an economic plus, as a few acres worked for subsistence yield far less than a large farm worked commercially.

But some kind of land deal is a political necessity for the ANC, which must deliver something to its constituents and soon. Another part of the land question: Just before the 1994 election, the de Klerk government, in order to get Inkatha cooperation, turned over large tracts of state-owned land in KwaZulu/Natal to the Zulu king, Goodwill Zwelithini (Buthelezi's cousin). The ANC didn't even know about it and opposes it. Look for major trouble if the Mandela government tries to take back this land.

Vocabulary Building

Afrikaans	disinvestment	laager	*trekboers*
Afrikaner	homelands	PAC	township
ANC	influx control	*platteland*	UDF
apartheid	*Inkatha*	separate	*uitlanders*
Boers	*kaffir*	development	*voortrekkers*
Coloured	*kraal*	Soweto	

Further Reference

BREYTENBACH, BREYTEN. *Return to Paradise.* New York: Harcourt Brace, 1993.

CROCKER, CHESTER A. *High Noon in Southern Africa: Making Peace in a Rough Neighborhood.* New York: W. W. Norton, 1992.

DE VILLIERS, MARQ. *White Tribe Dreaming: Apartheid's Bitter Roots as Witnessed by Eight Generations of an Afrikaner Family.* New York: Viking, 1988.

FOSTER, DON. *Detention and Torture in South Africa: Psychological, Legal, and Historical Studies.* New York: St. Martin's, 1987.

GILIOMEE, HERMANN, and LAWRENCE SCHLEMMER. *From Apartheid to Nation Building.* New York: Oxford University Press, 1990.

GRUNDY, KENNETH W. *South Africa: Domestic Crisis and Global Challenge.* Boulder, CO: Westview, 1991.

HEARD, ANTHONY HAZLITT. *The Cape of Storms: A Personal History of the Crisis in South Africa.* Fayetteville, AK: University of Arkansas Press, 1990.

HOCHSCHILD, ADAM. *The Mirror at Midnight: A South African Journey.* New York: Viking, 1990.

HOLLAND, HEIDI. *The Struggle: A History of the African National Congress.* New York: George Braziller, 1990.

LIJPHART, AREND. *Power-Sharing in South Africa.* Berkeley, CA: Institute of International Studies, University of California, 1985.

MALLABY, SEBASTIAN. *After Apartheid: The Future of South Africa.* New York: Times Books/Random House, 1992.

MARÉ, GERHARD, and GEORGINA HAMILTON. *An Appetite for Power: Buthelezi's Inkatha and South Africa.* Bloomington, IN: Indiana University Press, 1987.

MEER, FATIMA. *Higher Than Hope: The Authorized Biography of Nelson Mandela.* London: Hamish Hamilton, 1989.

MOSTERT, NOEL. *Frontiers: The Epic of South Africa's Creation and the Tragedy of the Xhosa People.* New York: Knopf, 1992.

MUFSON, STEVEN. *Fighting Years: Black Resistance and the Struggle for a New South Africa.* Boston: Beacon Press, 1990.

OTTAWAY, DAVID. *Chained Together: Mandela, de Klerk, and the Struggle to Remake South Africa.* New York: Times Books/Random House, 1993.

ROTBERG, ROBERT I., with MILES F. SHORE. *The Founder: Cecil Rhodes and the Pursuit of Power.* New York: Oxford University Press, 1988.

SPARKS, ALLISTER. *The Mind of South Africa.* New York: Knopf, 1990.

SUZMAN, HELEN. *In No Uncertain Terms: A South African Memoir.* New York: Knopf, 1993.

THOMPSON, LEONARD. *A History of South Africa.* New Haven, CT: Yale University Press, 1990.

VAN DER MERWE, HENDRIK W. *Pursuing Justice and Peace in South Africa.* New York: Routledge, 1989.

WILLIAMS, WALTER E. *South Africa's War Against Capitalism.* Westport, CT: Praeger, 1989.

30
Lessons of Eight Countries

1. The past is alive and well and living in current politics. The past forms a country's political institutions, attitudes, and quarrels. The past is especially lively in the resentments of aggrieved people, for example, among regions and social groups that feel they've been shortchanged.

2. Wars are dangerous to political systems and other living things. War, said Marx, is the midwife of revolution, and that seems to be true. Several of our eight countries have undergone total system change as a result of war. Moral: think twice about going to war; it may mean the end of your entire system.

3. Economic growth is destabilizing, especially rapid growth. Economic growth and change bring new people into politics, some of them bitterly discontent. Don't think economic growth solves political problems; it often makes them worse. Political change must accompany economic change in order to head off revolution.

4. A system that cannot change to meet new challenges may be doomed. The wisest rulers are those who make gradual and incremental changes in order to avoid sudden and radical changes. Rulers who wait until revolution is nigh to reform may actually fan its flames by offering concessions. All regimes tend to petrify; the good ones fight the trend.

5. Revolutions usually start at the top—in disagreement among elites. Conflict among elites brings latent mass discontent to the surface. Most of the revolutions in our book were preceded by the breakup of elite consensus and the efforts by some elites to mobilize the masses to serve elite ends. Only rarely is revolution a strictly mass affair.

6. Watch those middle-class intellectuals; they're the revolutionaries. Most revolutionary movements we can think of are headed by middle-class intellectuals rather than by common folk. Brains and education help make a revolutionary leader, just as they help make any leader.

7. Really want to bring down a regime? Try inflation. At least three of our countries endured revolutions after periods of galloping inflation that destroyed people's means of making a living and their confidence in government. Russia, watch out.

8. Solid, time-tested institutions that people believe in are a bulwark of political stability. No political leader, however clever, has pulled a functioning institution out of a hat. Even revolutionaries have years of experience building their revolutionary parties and armies. A country with good institutions is immune to revolution. In a certain sense, a revolutionary is replacing defective institutions with better ones. How do we know they were defective? Because they lost.

9. Constitutions rarely work the way they're supposed to on paper. Many factors modify the working of constitutional machinery: popular attitudes, usages that change over time, powerful parties and interest groups, and behind-the-scenes deals.

10. Everywhere parliaments are in decline. Some have become little more than window dressing; some are under such tight executive and/or party control that they have lost their autonomy, and only a few are fighting to regain it. As governance becomes more complex and technical, power flows to bureaucrats and experts.

11. Everywhere bureaucracies are in the ascendancy. In some systems, such as Japan, the permanent civil service is already the most powerful institution. Bureaucrats tend to see themselves as indispensible, virtually the saviors of their countries. No country has yet devised a way to control its bureaucracies.

12. Multiparty systems tend to be more unstable than two-party systems. Much depends on other factors, such as the rules for forming a cabinet or choosing the executive. Deft institutional reforms can stabilize multiparty systems so that their behavior is not much different from two-party systems.

13. Electoral system helps determine party system. Single-member districts with a simple plurality required to win tend to produce two-party systems because third parties have difficulty surviving in such systems. Proportional representation tends to produce many parties.

14. There are no longer purely federal or purely unitary systems. Instead, the trend is for federations to grant more and more power to the center, while unitary systems set up regional councils and devolve some powers to them. Eventually, it appears, federal and unitary systems could become similar.

15. Most cabinets consist of about twenty ministers. By American standards, other cabinets are large and their portfolios rather specialized. In the United States, there is a reluctance to add new departments. Elsewhere, ministers are added, deleted, or combined as the prime minister sees fit; the legislature automatically goes along.

16. In some ways, prime ministers in parliamentary systems are more powerful than presidents in presidential systems. A prime minister, with the assured discipline of his or her majority party in parliament, can get just about whatever he or she deems necessary. There is no deadlock between executive and legislative. Prime ministers who have to rely on multiparty coalitions, of course, are weaker.

17. Most people most of the time aren't much interested in politics. As you go down the socioeconomic ladder, you usually find less and less interest in political participation. Radicals deny this when they call for "power to the people," but they are usually middle-class intellectuals, sometimes intent on power for themselves. Mass participation in politics tends to be simple and episodic, such as voting every few years.

18. Democracy arouses little enthusiasm in most countries. Only countries with a history of democratic rule have democratically inclined masses. More typically, masses admire regimes that give them law and order, a feeling of national greatness, and a sense of material progress. More-educated people have stronger commitments to democratic values.

19. Political culture is at least as much a reflection of government performance as it is a determinant of the workings of government. Political culture can be taught—intentionally or inadvertently—by a regime. Countries with a cynical, untrusting political culture have usually earned it with decades of misrule. By the same token, when a democratic regime does a good job over many years, as Germany has, it firms up democratic attitudes.

20. Social class is only one factor in establishing political orientations. Often other factors, such as religion and region, are more important. Usually these three—class, religion, and region—in varying combinations explain a great deal of party identification and voting behavior.

21. There is more regional resentment the farther you go from the national capital. Political scientists call this center-periphery tension. Typically at the periphery of the national territory you find the strongest regionalist or antiregime political movements.

22. Religion is important in politics. In some countries, political parties are based on religion or religiosity (degree of religious feeling). Germany's Christian Democrats were originally based on the Catholic church and South Africa's National party on the Dutch Reformed church. In Catholic countries such as France, the more religious vote for the more conservative parties.

23. Political systems are rarely totally ideological, but neither are they totally pragmatic. Parties and regimes usually have at least some ideological underpinning—to justify themselves to the masses, if for no other reason—but at the top, rulers tend to be rather pragmatic in making decisions. Leaders may talk a certain ideology but find that in actual governance it is not wholly relevant. Using ideology as window dressing is a common political device.

24. Every country has its elites. Elites are the top people with a great deal of influence. Depending on the system, party elites, labor elites, business elites, military elites, even education and communication elites may assume great importance. Elites pay attention to politics, usually battling to preserve and enhance the status of the groups they lead. Elites rather than masses are the true political animals.

25. There are differences between the political culture of the masses and of the elites. Elites pay much more attention to politics and with greater consistency than masses. Elites, especially intellectual elites, create and articulate political ideas (ideologies, reform movements, media commentary), something the masses rarely do. Further, elite attitudes tend to be more democratic than mass attitudes.

26. Education is the nearly universal gateway to elite status. Except in revolutionary regimes, most elites now have university educations or the equivalent. Some elites are selected by virtue of the special colleges they attend. Educational opportunity is never totally equal or fair; the middle class usually benefits the most from it.

27. Much of politics consists of competition and bargaining among elites. Occasionally elites, in order to gain leverage on competing elites, refer matters to the masses in elections or referendums and call it democracy. Of all the political interactions discussed in this book, notice that relatively few of them involve mass participation.

28. Mass politics is easier to study than elite politics. With mass politics— elections, voter alignments, popular attitudes—political scientists can often get accurate, quantified data. But since much of elite politics is out of the public eye, we have to resort to fragmentary anecdotal and journalistic data. This means that some of the most crucial political interactions are hard to discern and even harder to document.

29. Democracy exists when elites open their decisions and deals to public scrutiny and approval. Typically, bargains are struck among elites and then presented to parliament and the public. Much legislative and electoral behavior is in ratifying decisions made earlier among elites. The difference here between authoritarian and democratic governments is one of degree.

30. Politicians tend to be addicted to money. They need it for election campaigns and sometimes to make themselves rich. Countries with very different institutions and political cultures thus tend to have similar fund-raising scandals.

31. Parties are balancing acts. Parties are invariably composed of different groups or factions. To hold the party together, politicians dispense favors, jobs, and promises to faction leaders. This holds for both democratic and Communist parties.

32. Every party has a radical wing. Social-democratic and labor parties have Marxist wings; conservative parties have reactionary wings. Even Communist parties have moderates and radicals, conservatives and liberals. Radical wings tend to be the home of young party militants, especially in leftist parties. How to control their radical-youth wings is one of the hardest tasks facing party chiefs.

33. A party that lets it radical wing dominate is headed for trouble. When radicals push the party to take extreme stands, average voters tend to go the other way. Pragmatic politicians therefore always fight domination by the radical wing, knowing it frightens away voters.

34. In the Third World, radical parties provoke reactionary impulses. In most of Latin America, for example, the coming to power of a radical or leftist party triggers military takeover, welcomed by conservative sectors of the society, which fear for their status and property. Brazil, watch out.

35. Third World reformist politicians tend to move to radicalism. The problems of developing areas are so big and the gap between rich and poor so huge that reformers are often drawn to radical, socialist prescriptions. Sometimes these prescriptions are demagoguery, aimed at arousing the masses without thought of consequences. This then often leads to reactionary military takeover. Perhaps only time and economic growth—leading to a large and moderate middle class—can move Latin American and some other Third World countries out of this pattern.

36. Once the army has taken over a government, chances are it will do so again. Once a country catches praetorianism, it seems never to fully recover from the disease. Democracy and reformism are often short-lived phenomena between periods of military rule. Praetorianism can be seen as an incurable, self-reinfecting illness endemic in the Third World.

37. The Third World is trying to get into the First. One of the big problems of West Europe is the new class of foreign workers—Pakistanis in Britain, Algerians in France, Turks in Germany—that have come seeking jobs and often intend to stay. Likewise, the United States has become a magnet for Latin Americans. Given the differential rates of birth and economic growth, the trend is increasing and becoming a major political issue worldwide.

38. Within Third World countries, people are flocking to the cities. High birthrates and few jobs in the countryside push people to the cities, where they often live in squalor. The Third World already has the globe's biggest cities, and they're growing fast. Some countries, such as China and South Africa, attempted "influx control," but most countries just let the slums grow.

39. Racism can be found nearly everywhere. South Africa isn't the only country mentioned in this book that practices racial discrimination. Most nations would deny it, but discrimination based on skin color, religion, or ethnic group is widespread. When asking if there is racism, look to see what a country does, not what it says. Underdog racial and ethnic groups are locked out of economic and political power.

40. Cutting welfare benefits is extremely difficult; recipients protest too much. Conservatives often come to power with promises to "clean up the welfare mess," but they seldom touch the problem. Once a benefit has been extended, it's almost impossible to withdraw it. The most conservatives can do is restrain expansion of the welfare system.

41. Much of what people and politicians quarrel about is economic. Some economists go so far as to claim that economics is the content of politics. That's going a little too far, since there are important political conflicts that are not directly economic, such as questions of region, religion, and personality. Still, on any given day, people are most likely to be arguing who should get what. Study economics.

42. At almost the same time, countries rediscovered the market economy. Leaders as diverse as America's Reagan, Britain's Thatcher, Russia's Yeltsin, and China's Deng found that statist control retarded growth. Markets are now the intellectual trend.

43. No political system has a sure-fire method of motivating people to work hard. All the countries we've considered in this book are making efforts to stimulate populations to work harder; none is consistently successful. Neither capitalist incentives (as in Britain), Stalinist terror (as in the Soviet Union), Maoist sloganeering (as in China), nor technocratic planning (as in Brazil) has proven effective over the long term.

44. Unemployment is a problem nearly everywhere and one that few governments solve. Worldwide, there is a struggle for jobs, ranging from difficult in Western Europe to desperate in the Third World. The Soviet Union was able to provide jobs, but that's only because Soviet industry and agriculture were grossly inefficient.

45. Many political issues are insoluble. They are the surfacing of long-growing economic and social problems that can't be "fixed" by government policy. Often only time and underlying economic and social change gradually dissolve the problem. Politics has been overrated as a way to cure problems. Often the best politics can do is keep things stable until time can do its work.

46. Things are getting more political, not less. As government gets bigger and takes on more tasks, what were previously private social interactions (such as those of the marketplace) become political interactions with all the fighting that entails. Modernization brings increased politicization. As more areas become political footballs, we can look for more political quarrels. Even trying to cut the role of government is an intensely political act that generates new frictions.

47. No country has ever run out of problems or political controversies. As soon as one problem is solved—and they're rarely solved by politics alone—new ones appear, usually relating to the administration of the problem-solving mechanism. No country is so advanced that it has no more problems. Indeed, the more advanced a country, the more political problems it seems to have because everything becomes political.

48. Political movements, parties, ideologies, and regimes are hard to judge by *a priori* criteria. We never know how something is going to work until we see it in practice for a while. We learn to judge what's good and bad politically by consequences.

49. Whenever you look closely at political phenomena, you find they are more complicated than you first thought. You find exceptions, nuances, and differentiations that you didn't notice at first. You can modify and sometimes refute generalizations—including the ones offered here—by digging into them more deeply.

50. Ultimately, in studying comparative politics we are studying ourselves. One of the lessons that should have emerged from this book is that neither our country nor we as citizens are a great deal different from other countries and peoples. When you compare politics, be sure to include your own system in the comparison.

Glossary

Following are some frequently used words or technical terms from the field of comparative politics. Each is defined here in its *political* sense. The country where the term originated or is most commonly used is given where appropriate, but often the word is now used worldwide.

abertura   (Brazil) Portuguese for "opening," the liberalization of a military regime.

absolutism   tendency of some European monarchs, starting in the sixteenth century, to amass power until they ruled singlehandedly.

affect   individual citizens' feelings of fondness toward their political system.

Afrikaner   (South Africa) formerly ruling white group of South Africa, which speaks the Dutch-derived language *Afrikaans.*

agitprop   (Soviet Union) combination *agitation* and *propaganda;* the mass-mobilization arm of the Soviet Communist Party.

ancien régime   (France) the old regime that preceded the 1789 Revolution.

anticlericalism   movement aimed at curbing influence of Roman Catholic church in politics.

apartheid   (South Africa) system of strict racial segregation.

apolitical   taking no interest in politics.

apparatchik   (Soviet Union) person of the party apparatus, a full-time Communist Party worker.

arable   land that can be cultivated; denotes sufficient water for farming.

authoritarian   political system that concentrates power in hands of a few and is not responsible to the public.

autocracy   one-person rule, as in tsarist Russia.

autonomy   degree of self-government granted to a region.

backbencher   (Britain) a less-important member of Parliament, one who does not sit on the front bench.

Basic Law   Germany's constitution.

bicameral   a legislature that has two houses.

Big Mac Index   quick estimate of purchasing power parity (see below) by comparing world prices of well-known hamburger.

blat   (Soviet Union) Russian for "influence" or "pull."

Boers   (South Africa) name by which Afrikaners were formerly known; Dutch for "farmers."

Bolshevik   (Soviet Union) Russian for "majority"; faction of Russian Social Democratic party that Lenin led to seize power in 1917; became the Soviet Communist Party.

Bourbon   (France) ruling royal family of pre-revolutionary France and currently of Spain.

bourgeoisie   French for "middle class"; connotes procapitalist conservatism; pejorative in Marxist usage.

Boxers   (China) late nineteenth-century Chinese patriotic society that rose up against foreigners in 1900.

Bundesrat   German upper house of legislature that represents *Länder* (states).

Bundestag   German lower house of legislature, more powerful than *Bundesrat*.

bureaucracy   the civil service of a country; connotes rigid, hierarchical administration.

by-election   (Britain) a special election to fill a vacant seat in Parliament.

cabinet   the group of ministers or secretaries who head the executive departments of a government; in Europe, synonymous with *government*.

cadre   (China) originally the French word for "framework," it now denotes the Communist structure for mobilization and leadership.

caesaropapism   the combining of head of state and head of a national church in one office, as was done by the tsar of Russia.

capital   accumulated wealth, either money or goods, that is used to produce more goods.

catchall party   a large, ideologically loose party that aims to enlist as many groups of supporters as possible.

center   politically moderate or middle-of-the-road, neither left nor right.

center-periphery tensions   resentment of outlying regions at rule from nation's capital city.

centralization   the concentration of administrative power in the nation's capital, allowing little or no local autonomy.

chancellor   German equivalent of prime minister.

charismatic leader   one who is capable of moving people through force of words or personality.

chauvinism   extreme and prideful nationalism.

civility   preserving good manners in politics and public life.

class bias   the slanting of jobs, schools, and political power to favor one class at the expense of another.

class struggle   basic tenet of Marxism that social classes, especially the working class and the rich, are of necessity antagonistic toward each other's interests.

class voting   tendency of a given class to vote for a party that claims to represent its interests.

coalition   in a parliamentary system, the combining of two or more parties to form a cabinet.

cohabitation   (France) executive and legislative branches dominated by opposing parties.

Coloured   (South Africa) a person of mixed Hottentot, white, and Malay descent, found chiefly in Cape Province.

Common Law   (Britain) system of laws based heavily on previous court decisions, "judge-made law."

Common Market   officially the European Union, a grouping of West European nations that eliminates tariffs and trade and labor restrictions between its member nations.

Commons   (Britain) the lower, popularly elected and more important house of Parliament.

Communist party   a political party combining Marxist economics with Leninist organization aimed at building a socialist utopia.

conservatism   political mood or movement aimed at preserving older or traditional values, economic systems, and laws.

constituency   the district or population that elects a legislator.

constitution   document structuring the political and sometimes social institutions of a nation.

corporatism   legislative representation based on profession rather than district or party, often a component of fascist systems.

coup d'état   the sudden and extralegal takeover of state power by armed groups, usually the military.

decentralization   the diffusion of administrative power from the nation's capital to regions, localities, or economic units.

deferential   political attitude in which lower classes defer to the rule of their perceived superiors.

deification   the glorification of a leader into an artificial god.

demagoguery   the ambiguous or tricky use of political issues to enable the user to attain power.

demobilization   the tranquilizing or even anesthetizing of mass interest in politics, often attempted by dictators.

democracy   political system in which the power and authority of leaders is accountable to the broad mass of the population.

département   one of ninety-six administrative districts into which France is divided.

dependencia   Spanish for "dependency"; theory that developing countries are economically tied and subordinate to rich capitalist nations.

depoliticization   either a loss of political involvement or the turning of political issues into neutral administrative matters.

de-Stalinization   (Soviet Union) the criticism and downgrading of Stalin that occurred under Khrushchev.

détente   A French term meaning relaxation of political tensions, usually referring specifically to improved relations between the United States and Soviet Union.

devolution   the granting of regional autonomy or home rule by the central authority.

diet   name of Japanese and Finnish parliaments.

dissident   (Soviet Union) person who openly criticizes his or her political system.

Dolchstoss   German for "stab in the back"; myth fostered by German right that Germany had been betrayed during World War I by disloyal domestic elements.

Dreyfus Affair   French trial in late nineteenth century over alleged treason by Jewish artillery officer; badly split France into liberal supporters of Dreyfus and conservative detractors.

Duma   Russian parliament under tsar in early twentieth century; also name for current lower house.

electoral system   laws structuring the manner in which persons are elected to office, such as from single- or multimember districts, and by proportional representation or simple plurality.

electorate   that part of a population entitled to vote.

elites   the top or most influential persons in a society or institution.

Elysée Palace   French equivalent of the White House.

emergency powers   clause in most constitutions permitting chief executive to take on extraordinary powers under certain circumstances.

environmentalism   political movement of the late twentieth century stressing industrial, chemical, and especially nuclear dangers to the environment.

equalitarian   a policy aiming at making persons more equal in income, political power, or life opportunities; a leftist political viewpoint.

Establishment   (Britain) the alleged unofficial club of British elites who work to support the status quo and keep themselves in power.

Estado Novo   (Portuguese for "New State") fascist-appearing system of Brazilian President Vargas from 1937 to 1945.

Estates-General   seldom-convened French parliament before the Revolution.

étatisme   (French "statism") government leading of the economy by means of plans and subsidies.

Eurocommunism   alleged independent movement of West European Communist parties (chiefly the Italian) from Moscow's rule, emphasizing commitment to democratic norms.

Events of May   euphemism for French student and worker strikes of 1968.

Exchequer   (Britain) medieval revenue officer, now chief treasury official.

factious   tending to break up into quarreling factions.

favela   (Brazil) urban shantytown or slum.

federation   political system in which component territories enjoy a high degree of autonomy or home rule.

feudalism   political pattern of medieval Europe in which power was spread among lords rather than concentrated in a king.

Five-Year Plans   (Soviet Union) series of coercive plans initiated by Stalin in 1928 to industrialize country rapidly.

fragmented   condition of political cultures with marked divergence of views among subgroups and little or no consensus.

franchise   right to vote.

Gang of Four   (China) group of alleged ultra-radical conspirators who brought on chaos of Cultural Revolution; arrested after Mao's death in 1976 and later tried.

Gastarbeiter   (German; "guest worker") foreign worker in Federal Republic of Germany, usually from a poor Mediterranean country.

Gaullism   (France) policies of President de Gaulle aimed at making France stable, unified, prosperous, militarily strong, and independent in foreign policy.

General Will   theory of French philosopher Rousseau that holds that underlying the many and conflicting "particular wills" in society is an overarching consensus.

gentry   better-off, educated class in traditional societies.

gerontocracy   rule by the elderly.

gerrymander   the drawing of electoral-district boundaries so as to favor one party.

glasnost   Soviet policy of openness or publicity under Gorbachev.

Gosplan   (Soviet Union) central economic-planning authority.

grand coalition   coalition of two or more large parties who previously opposed each other.

grande école   one of France's elite schools, considered superior to universities, which train the country's leading administrators, engineers, industrialists, and teachers.

Great Leap Forward   (1958–60) a failed Chinese effort at overnight industrialization.

Great Purge   (Soviet Union) Stalin's murder of thousands of Communist Party members from 1936 to 1938 based on faintest suspicion of disloyalty.

Gulag   (Soviet Union) central prisons administration.

Guomindang   (China) Chinese Nationalist party ousted from mainland in 1949; earlier spelled Kuomintang and abbreviated KMT.

Habsburg   royal house of empire that grouped Austria and Spain on Catholic side in sixteenth- and seventeenth-century wars of religion.

head of government   the chief executive of a country's government, either a prime minister or a president, who engages in day-to-day political affairs.

head of state   the symbolic national leader, either a monarch or a president, who normally stands above the political fray.

Holocaust   the destruction of six million European Jews by the Nazis during World War II.

homelands   (South Africa) tribal reserves for black natives.

Hundred Flowers   (China) 1956 campaign to encourage expression of different views; crushed when views grew too critical.

hyperinflation   an extremely high inflation rate that makes currency worthless.

identity   recognition on the part of the people as to their nationality, ethnic group, region, or party.

ideology   interrelated set of ideas for the improvement of society.

immobilism   inability of a government to decide important issues, often due to quarreling of coalition partners.

infant mortality rate   number of infants who die in their first year, usually expressed per thousand.

indicative planning   (France) governmental economic research and suggestions for business expansion; not the same as Soviet-style central economic control.

industrialization   the shifting of a country's economy from agriculture to industry.

inequality   degree of difference in wealth, income, social status, or political power among individuals.

influx control   (South Africa) measures to limit number of black persons in urban areas; major component of *apartheid.*

infrastructure   the network of highways, railroads, electricity, and other basic prerequisites of economic growth.

institution   a web of political relationships lasting over time, an established structure of power; may or may not be mentioned in a constitution or housed in a building.

intelligentsia   Russian (from Italian) for "educated class."

intendants   (France) central administrators sent out to the provinces; started by Cardinal Richelieu.

interior ministry   in most countries, the important ministry that controls police and internal security.

iron triangle   combination of politicians, interest groups, and bureaucrats who aid each other without regard for public interest.

Jacobins   radical clubs in revolutionary France.

jeito   (Brazil) Portuguese for "knack," meaning bureaucratic connections that get things done, sometimes by means of bribes.

Junker   (Germany) Prussian aristocratic class.

Kaiser   (German; "caesar") title of Germany's kings.

karoshi   (Japan) death by overwork.

kolkhoz   (Soviet Union) collective farm.

Komsomol   (Soviet Union) Communist youth organization.

kowtow   (China) to prostrate oneself ritually before emperor.

Kremlin   (Soviet Union) ancient walled fortress in Moscow that serves as center of government.

kulaks   (Soviet Union) class of better-off peasants that Stalin ordered liquidated as part of farm collectivization during first Five-Year Plan.

laager   Afrikaans for "camp"; specifically, a circle of ox wagons drawn up for defense.

Land   German equivalent of U.S. state (plural, *Länder*).

laissez faire   French for "let it be"; doctrine advocating no government interference in a free-market economy.

left   politically more radical; aiming at greater equality.

legitimacy   popular attitude that regime's rule is rightful; not the same as *legal*.

liberalism   in its original late eighteenth- and nineteenth-century sense, an ideology that proposed free economic, social, and political arrangements rather than government supervision, in the belief that such individual freedom would lead to the greatest happiness. In the twentieth-century United States, the favoring of welfare measures and greater equality.

liberation theology   in the Third World Catholic countries, especially Latin America, the view of some clergy that helping the poor through direct political action is proper Christian duty.

Lockean   following thoughts of John Locke, who emphasized natural right to "life, liberty, and property."

Long March   (China; 1934–35) exodus of Chinese Communist Party from southern to northern China to escape *Guomindang*.

Lords   (Britain) upper, aristocratic house of Parliament; minor government body compared to *Commons*.

lycée   French academic high school.

MacArthur Constitution   Japan's current constitution, devised by U.S. occupation staff.

machismo   (Latin America) strutting, exaggerated masculinity.

macroeconomics   the economics of the country as a whole.

Magna Carta   (Britain) agreement nobles obtained in 1215 from the king to preserve their rights.

Mandarin   (China) traditional administrator, schooled in Confucian classics.

Maoism   (China) Communist leader Mao Zedong's Marxist ideological variation that revolution can be based on poor peasantry and must continue indefinitely to prevent bureaucratization.

Marshall Plan   program of U.S. economic aid for Europe after World War II.

Marxism-Leninism   or communism, the ideology combining the economic and historical theories of Marx with the organizational techniques of Lenin.

Meiji   period of Japanese rapid modernization starting in 1868.

Menshevik   Russian for "minority"; the less-radical faction of the Russian Social Democrats whom Lenin repudiated.

mercantilism   economic policy of absolutist monarchs, especially French, favoring state guidance of industry and amassing of gold.

microeconomics   the economics of individual firms.

minister   head of an executive department or ministry and member of cabinet.

Mitbestimmung   (German; "codetermination") worker participation in company policy in present-day Germany.

MITI   Japan's Ministry of International Trade and Industry; it promotes exports.

mobilization   the awakening of political awareness in previously apolitical masses.

monocolor   in parliamentary systems, a cabinet composed of a single party, not a coalition cabinet.

multiparty   party system of three or more competing parties.

Narodniki   Russian student radicals of the 1870s who tried "going to the people" to mobilize peasants.

nationality   belonging to a nation or, in the case of the Soviet Union, to an ethnic group.

nationalization   governmental takeover of private industry.

New Class   term coined by Yugoslav writer Milovan Djilas to describe the new Communist elite of party leaders, bureaucrats, and security officials.

no-confidence   parliamentary motion to oust the current cabinet.

nomenklatura   (Soviet Union) list of sensitive positions reserved for carefully screened Party members.

October Revolution   1917 Bolshevik seizure of power in Russia.

Old Republic   1889–1930 Brazilian regime of limited, conservative democracy.

Opium War   1839–42 British war against China that Britain waged for the right to sell opium to Chinese.

opportunist   calculating person bent only on pursuing his or her own self-interests.

opposition   in parliamentary systems, the parties not in the government or cabinet.

Ostpolitik   policy of West German Chancellor Willy Brandt for improving relations with the Soviet Union and East Europe.

Oxbridge   (Britain) the elite universities of Oxford and Cambridge.

paranoid   unreasonable suspicion toward other persons; not the same as *fearful.*

parliamentary system   political system in which cabinet is responsible to, and can be ousted by, parliament; chief executive is a prime minister who is not elected directly.

parochial   focused on local concerns only; ignorant of national politics.

participation   citizen involvement in politics in such ways as voting, helping a party or candidate, or contacting an official.

party identification   psychological attachment of a voter to a particular political party.

party image   the way the electorate perceives a given party.

party list   in proportional-representation systems, a party's list of candidates for parliament, elected in descending order of priority according to portion of the vote the party obtains.

party system   the number and competitiveness of parties in a given country; five general types: no-party, one-party, two-party, dominant-party, and multiparty systems.

perestroika   policy of restructuring the Soviet economy under Gorbachev.

personalismo   (Latin America) the respect-commanding qualities and governing style of a leader, often connected with *machismo*.

personality cult   adulation and deification of political leaders, such as Stalin and Mao.

plebiscite   a mass vote on an issue, often concerning national status and boundaries.

pluralism   political system that openly acknowledges interplay of many groups—interest, ethnic, regional, and political; also, theory that politics works in this manner.

Politburo   in Communist systems, the highest ruling body of the party, above the Central Committee.

political culture   the psychology of the nation in regard to politics, the pattern of a country's political attitudes.

Popular Front   combination of all leftist parties, especially Communist and Socialist, in France and Spain in the 1930s.

praetorianism   tendency of military to take power.

pragmatic   nonideological politics, adopting whatever policy works.

prefect   (France) centrally appointed supervisor of a *département*.

presidential system   political system in which a powerful president is elected directly and separately from parliament and cannot be ousted by parliament.

prime minister   in parliamentary system, the chief executive officer and head of government, confirmed by and answerable to parliament.

privatization   the selling of state-owned enterprises to private business.

proportional representation   electoral system that assigns parliamentary seats in proportion to party vote.

Protestant ethic   theory of Max Weber that hard work and capitalist reinvestment originally sprung from Protestant Christianity.

public schools   (Britain) private boarding schools; so named because they train boys for public life.

purchasing power parity   way of comparing cross-nationally how well people live based on how much they can buy rather than on how much currency they earn.

Question Time   (Britain) period in Commons reserved for questioning governmental ministers.

Red Guards   (China) radical youths who, at Mao's behest, attacked traditions and authorities during Cultural Revolution.

redistribution   taxation and welfare measures that generally take from the wealthier and give to the poorer.

referendum   a mass vote on an issue rather than on candidates.

Reform Acts   (Britain) nineteenth-century series of reforms broadening the electoral franchise.

reformism   political movement aiming at change and improvement in a moderate and noncoercive way.

regionalism   political movement that emphasizes regional autonomy and distinctiveness.

regierungsfähig   German for "able to participate in a government."

regressive tax   tax that is lighter on rich than on poor.

Reign of Terror   (France) period of mass executions led by Robespierre during the Revolution.

revisionism   changing or rethinking a political ideology or conventional view of history.

right   politically more conservative, favoring preservation of or return to previous status quo.

Roman law   legal system in most of Europe and Latin America based on relatively fixed codes, as opposed to judge-made Common Law.

russification   policy begun under tsars and continued by Stalin of spreading use of Russian language and culture among non-Russian ethnic groups.

safe seat   (Britain) constituency where voting has long favored a given party.

samizdat   (Soviet Union) Russian for "self-published"; manuscripts, often by dissidents, circulated underground.

sarariman   (Japan, "salary man") mid-level employee.

scapegoating   unfairly blaming persons or groups for the ills of a political or economic system.

secular change   long-term, irreversible trends.

secularization   removing church influence from social and political institutions.

Shinto   state religion of Japan, includes worship of nature and ancestors.

single-member district   constituency that elects only one legislator, usually by simple plurality, as in Britain and the United States.

social class   a portion or layer of society, usually determined by wealth or income.

social cleavages   the splitting of society among class, regional, religious, or ethnic lines or over important issues.

socialism   political movement aiming at greater equality by means of welfare measures and/or nationalization of industry.

sovereignty   legal concept that national government is supreme in its territory.

soviet   Russian for "council"; name of 1917 revolutionary bodies and of legislatures in Soviet Union.

sovkhoz   (Soviet Union) a state farm where workers are employees of the state, as opposed to members of a collective farm or *kolkhoz*.

Sozialmarkt   German for "social market"; the economic policy of West German Christian Democratic governments promoting a generally free market with progressive social goals.

sphere of influence   foreign area under the control or influence of a powerful nation.

Stalinism   (Soviet Union) policies and style associated with Stalin, namely, coerced industrialization, personality cult, and brutal control over society and party.

state capitalism   economic system where government is an important investor, as in France and Brazil.

Supreme Soviet   national legislature of Soviet Union.

technocrat   official who governs by technical as opposed to political or human criteria, a pejorative term.

terrorism   use of political murder and fear thereof to win or consolidate power.

Third Estate   (France) the third house of the Estates-General representing commoners, as opposed to the First and Second Estates, representing clergy and nobles.

threshold clause   a numerical minimum required to win seats in parliament, as the 5-percent national vote required of a German party.

Tory   (Britain) nickname for Conservative.

totalitarian   a dictatorial regime that attempts to impose total ideological, economic, and political control over society.

Treaty Ports   (China) series of seaports on China coast in which foreign powers established by treaty their spheres of influence during the nineteenth century.

unicameral   parliament with only one chamber.

unification   process of pulling a nation together out of diverse and sometimes recalcitrant regions.

unimodal   a single-peaked distribution of political attitudes or opinions; a bell-shaped curve.

unitary   a political system governed by the center with little or no autonomy allowed to subunits or regions.

urbanization   the shift of population from countryside to city.

value-added tax   a large, hidden sales tax used throughout West Europe.

Vatican II   short name for Second Vatican Council; meetings in 1962–65 that turned Catholic church toward problems of the poor.

Versailles   palace near Paris, originally that of Louis XIV, where treaty—highly punitive to Germany—was drawn up after World War I.

Vichy   French government during world War II that collaborated with German occupation.

Volk   German for "people"; used by Nazis to connote racial superiority of Germans.

Waldsterben   German for death of a forest from pollution.

warlords   (China) independent regional military rulers who took over in the 1910s and 1920s.

Weimar   democratic republic set up in Germany after World War I and destroyed by Nazis.

welfare   redistributive measures that provide health care, food, housing, and insurance to poorer classes.

Weltanschauung   German for "world view"; the comprehensive ideologies European parties once tried to inculcate into their members.

Westernizers   nineteenth-century Russian intellectuals who favored borrowing from and imitating the West.

Westminster   (Britain) building housing Parliament.

whip   party official in legislature who makes sure party's members are present and voting correctly.

Whitehall   (Britain) chief government executive offices.

xenophobia   fear and hatred of foreigners.

Yalta   town in Soviet Crimea where in early 1945, leaders of the United States, Britain, and Soviet Union decided the post–World War II status of Germany and East Europe.

Index